ASIA-PACIFIC: NEW C

*Editors*
R.F. WATTERS AND T.G. MCGEE

*Assistant Editor*
GINNY SULLIVAN

# Asia-Pacific

## New Geographies of the Pacific Rim

UBC PRESS / VANCOUVER

Printed in Hong Kong

Published in Canada by UBC Press

First published in the United Kingdom by
C. Hurst & Co. (Publishers) Ltd.

ISBN 0-7748-0646-X (hardcover)
ISBN 0-7748-0647-8 (paperback)

---

**Canadian Cataloguing-in-Publication Data**

Main entry under title:
Asia Pacific

Includes bibliographical references and index.
ISBN 0-7748-0646-X (bound) -- ISBN 0-7748-0647-8 (pbk.)

1. Asia -- Economic integration. 2. Asia -- Economic conditions. 3. Pacific area -- Economic integration. I. Watters, R.F. (Raymond Frederick) II. McGee, T.G. (Terence Gary) III.

HC460.5.A742 1997 337.1'5 C97-910545-5

---

UBC Press
University of British Columbia
6344 Memorial Road
Vancouver, BC V6T 1Z2
(604) 822-5959
Fax: 1-800-668-0821
E-mail: orders@ubcpress.ubc.ca

# ACKNOWLEDGEMENTS

On behalf of the Geography Department, Victoria University of Welllington (VUW), we wish to thank the Overseas Development Administration, London, for their generous support of the Department's research in the Western Pacific and for assisting publication of its results. This involved eight Ph.D.-level academics, students and staff, and several Pacific Islanders and ten separate reports. We are also grateful for grants from the Ministry of Foreign Affairs and Trade, Wellington, and Victoria University which have also assisted the publication of this book.

Many people have kindly contributed their skills and time to assist this publication; in most cases they are thanked by the individual authors. The editors are also grateful for the cartographic editing of Robin Mita.

The greatest acknowledgement of all goes to the local villagers, and governments and company officers in the Asia-Pacific regions in which fieldwork was undertaken by the various authors of this book. Without their active cooperation and interest in the research and the issues involved, this work would not have been possible. Needless to say, none of these many people are responsible for any of the contents of this volume.

*Wellington,*
*June 1997*

RAY WATTERS,
TERRY MCGEE
GINNY SULLIVAN


# DEDICATION

For all past and present students of Wellington and the Asia-Pacific: may they also share the joy of learning.

> **"... if geography itself has significance, it is that we are made to lift our eyes from our small provincial selves to the whole complex and magnificent world."**

*Richard Burton, explorer and geographer*

# CONTENTS

# TABLES

# FIGURES

# ABBREVIATIONS

| | |
|---|---|
| ADB | Asian Development Bank |
| AFTA | ASEAN Free Trade Area |
| AHRC | Asian Human Rights Commission |
| AIDAB | Australian International Development Assistance Bureau |
| AIP | autarchic industrial policy |
| ANU | Australian National University |
| APEC | Asia Pacific Economic Cooperation |
| ASEAN | Association of Southeast Asian Nations |
| BIE | Bureau of Industry Economics |
| BKKBN | National Family Planning Coordinating Board (Indonesia) |
| CCP | Chinese Communist Party |
| CEE | creation of an enabling environment |
| CEEC | Central and Eastern European Countries |
| CEPT | Common Effective Preferential Tariffs |
| CER | Closer Economic Relations (between Australia and New Zealand) |
| CIDA | Canadian International Development Agency |
| CIP | competitive industrial policy |
| CUP | Cambridge University Press |
| EAEC | East Asia Economic Caucus |
| EEZ | Exclusive Economic Zone |
| EIE | Electronic and Industrial Enterprises |
| EMR | Extended Metropolitan Region |
| EPA | Economic Planning Agency (Japan) |
| EU | European Union |
| f.o.b. | free on board |
| FAO | Food and Agriculture Organisation |
| FDI | Foreign Direct Investment |
| FEER | Far Eastern Economic Review |
| FSDP | Food Systems Development Project |
| FTAA | Free Trade in the Americas Agreement |
| G5 | Group of Five |
| G7 | Group of Seven |
| GAD | Gender and Development |
| GATT | General Agreement on Tariffs and Trade |
| GDP | Gross Domestic Product |
| GNP | Gross National Product |
| HCI | heavy and chemical industry |
| HIER | Harvard Institute of Economic Research |
| IHI | Ishikawajima-Harima Heavy Industries (Japan) |

| | |
|---|---|
| IMF | International Monetary Fund |
| IMR | Infant Mortality Rate |
| Jabopunjar | Jakarta, Bogor, Puncak and Cianjur (Indonesia) |
| Jabotabek | area around Jakarta: Jakarta, Bogor, Tanggerang, Bekasi (Indonesia) |
| JDB | Japan Development Bank |
| JETRO | Japan External Trade Organisation |
| LDC | less developed countries |
| MERCOSUR | Latin American trade agreement |
| MFN | Most-Favoured Nation |
| MIDA | Malaysian Industrial Development Authority |
| MITI | Ministry of International Trade and Industry (Japan) |
| NACLA | North American Congress on Latin America |
| NAFTA | North America Free Trade Association |
| NAP | National Agricultural Policy (Malaysia) |
| NASTEC | national system of technological and entrepreneurial capacity |
| NCP | National Coalition Partnership (Solomon Islands) |
| NCR | Native Customary Rights (Malaysia) |
| NCR | Native Customary Rights (Sarawak) |
| NEP | New Economic Policy (Sarawak) |
| NET | New economic territory |
| NFDL | National Fisheries Development Limited (Solomon Islands) |
| NGO | Non-governmental organisation |
| NHS | National Health Service (United Kingdom) |
| NIC | Newly Industrialised Countries |
| NIE | Newly Industrialising Economies |
| NSC | Nippon Steel Corporation |
| OCW | Overseas contract workers |
| OECD | Organisation for Economic Cooperation and Development |
| OUP | Oxford University Press |
| PATA | Pacific Travel Association |
| PBEC | Pacific Basin Economic Council |
| PECC | Pacific Economic Cooperation Conference |
| PLA | People's Liberation Army (China) |
| PNG | Papua New Guinea |
| PPP | Purchasing Power Parity |
| PRC | People's Republic of China |
| PSS | Pepper Subsidy Scheme |
| QALYs | Quality After Life Years |
| R & D | Research and Development |
| SEZ | Special Economic Zone |
| SIFIA | Solomon Islands Forestry Industry Association |

| | |
|---|---|
| Sijori | Singapore - Johor - Riau |
| SINURPP | Solomon Island National Unity, Reconciliation and Progressive Pati |
| SLDB | Sarawak Land Development Board |
| STL | Solomon Taiyo Limited |
| TRF | Total Fertility Rate |
| UBC | University of British Columbia |
| UMNO | United Malays National Organisation |
| UNDP | United Nations Development Programme |
| UPV | University of the Philippines in the Visayas |
| UR | Uruguay Round (GATT) |
| VUW | Victoria University of Wellington |
| WBS | Work Breakdown Structure |
| WHO | World Health Organisation |
| WID | Women in Development |
| WTO | World Trade Organisation |

# THE CONTRIBUTORS

WARWICK ARMSTRONG, Professor of Geography at McGill University, taught at Victoria University of Wellington (VUW) from 1965 to 1971. He was director of a regional development project in Ecuador, and of a food systems development project in the Philippines. He has written widely on international development, comparative industrialisation and food systems.

RICHARD AUTY, Senior Lecturer in the Department of Geography, Lancaster University, has special interests in natural resources and economic development. He is a consultant for the World Bank, UNCTAD and KIET. Recent titles are *Patterns of Development: Resources, Policy and Economic Growth* (1995), and *Economic Development and Industrial Policy: Korea, Brazil, Mexico, India and China* (1994).

GERALD CHAN, Senior Lecturer in International Relations, Department of Politics, VUW, is co-editor of *Political Science*, editorial board member of *Global Society*, and advisory board member of *New Zealand Journal of East Asian Studies*. His interests include Chinese international relations, Japanese foreign policy and Taiwanese foreign aid policy.

DAVID W. EDGINGTON is Associate Professor, Department of Geography, University of British Columbia (UBC). His research centres on Japanese urban and regional restructuring, and Japan's trade and investment in the Pacific Rim. He is author of *Japanese Business Downunder* (1990) and co-author of *Planning for Cities and Regions in Japan* (1994).

DEAN FORBES, Professor of Geography, Flinders University of South Australia, has research and consultancy experience on urban and regional development in Asia-Pacific countries. He recently completed *Asian Metropolis: Urbanisation and the Southeast Asian City* (1996). Current research activities include projects on Cambodia and Laos. In 1994 he was elected Fellow of the Academy of Social Sciences in Australia.

HARVEY FRANKLIN is Emeritus Professor of Geography, VUW. His publications include *The European Peasantry: The Final Phase* (1969), and *Trade, Growth and Anxiety: New Zealand Beyond the Welfare State* (1978). Recently he has been investigating issues of income, wealth and consumption in the richer nations of the world. His book, *Inferior Goods: Wealth, Consumption and Social Order,* will appear in 1997.

IAN FRAZER teaches in the Department of Anthropology, University of Otago. He is mainly interested in the history and political economy of the newly independent states of Melanesia, especially the Solomon Islands and Vanuatu.

David S.G. Goodman, Director, Institute for International Studies, University of Technology, Sydney. He author of *Deng Xiaoping and the Chinese Revolution* (1994), and (with Gerald Segal) *China Without Deng* (1995). His most recent publication is (with Richard Robison) *The New Rich in Asia: Mobile-Phones, McDonalds and Middle Class Revolution* (1996).

R.D. Hill was a student in the VUW Department of Geography. Since 1962, he has lived and worked in Asia, since 1973 at the University of Hong Kong where he is now Professor of Geography. His research focus has always been in agriculture, rural land use and development, with books on *Rice in Malaya*, *Agriculture in the Malaysian Region* and *Indigenous Agriculture in Southeast Asia.*

Graeme Hugo is Professor of Geography at the University of Adelaide. His books include *Australia's Changing Population*, *The Demographic Dimension of Indonesian Development* (with T.H. Hull, V.J. Hull and G.W. Jones) and the *Atlas of Australian People Series*. Much of his research has dealt with population issues in Southeast Asia, especially Indonesia. In 1987 he was elected Fellow of the Academy of Social Sciences in Australia.

Yok-shiu F. Lee received his PhD degree from the Massachusetts Institute of Technology. In 1989, he joined the East-West Center as a Fellow in the Program on Environment and has since conducted research on a wide range of urban environmental management issues in the Asia-Pacific region. He was a visiting assistant professor in the Department of Sociology at the Chinese University of Hong Kong in 1995-96.

George C.S. Lin, Assistant Professor, Department of Geography and Geology, The University of Hong Kong, is the author of *Red Capitalism in South China* (forthcoming, UBC Press), and many articles. His research interests include urban and regional development in southern China.

T.G. McGee is Director, Institute of Asian Research, and Professor, Department of Geography, UBC. He has carried out extensive research on urbanisation in Asia over the last 40 years. He is the author of *The Southeast Asian City* (1967), *Third World Urbanization* (1971), and together with Warwick Armstrong *Theatres of Accumulation* (1985). More recently, he has co-edited *The Extended Metropolis in Asia* (1991) and *Mega-Urban Regions in Southeast Asia* (1995).

John McKinnon, a graduate of the Department of Geography at VUW, taught briefly at the University of the South Pacific in Suva, and was research advisor in Thailand. He is now Senior Lecturer in Geography at VUW. Principal publications focus on minority people, *Highlanders of Thailand* with Wanat Bhruksasri (eds) (1986), and *The Hill Tribes Today* with Bernard Vienne (eds) (1989).

PHILIP MORRISON is a former student and now Senior Lecturer in the Deparment of Geography, VUW. A former VSA volunteer in Sarawak in 1966, he conducted field work in the Kemena Basin, Bintulu, during 1990 and 1991 with colleagues from the then Branch Campus of the University Pertanian, Malaysia, under a project on off-farm employment. A return visit was made to Kuching in 1995.

PETER J. RIMMER is Professor of the Department of Human Geography, Research School of Pacific and Asian Studies, Australia National University (ANU), Canberra. He has been engaged in studying Japan and its role in the Asia-Pacific region since 1979.

RON SANDREY is an economist, and is currently working with the Ministry of Foreign Affairs and Trade in Wellington. His academic training was from Lincoln University and Oregon State University. Formerly Ron worked at Treasury and the Ministry of Agriculture and Fisheries in Wellington and as a lecturer at Lincoln University.

CHRISTOPHER TREMEWAN is Director of the New Zealand Asia Institute, University of Auckland, and has specialised in economic development and social regulation in Singapore. His latest book is *The Political Economy of Social Control in Singapore*. Although Singapore's Controller of Undesirable Publications recently banned distribution in Singapore, a second edition is in production. His current research focuses on the intersection of human rights, democracy and development in Asia.

ROBERT WADE is a New Zealander with degrees in economics from Otago and Victoria Universities, and a D.Phil. in social anthropology (Sussex). He has been a fellow of the Institute of Development Studies, Sussex University, since 1972, held visiting professorships at Princeton and MIT, and was a World Bank economist 1984-1988. He is the author of *Governing the Market: Economic Theory and the Role of Government in East Asian Industrialization*, joint winner of the Best Book in Political Economy Award from the American Political Science Association, 1989-1991.

RAY WATTERS was Professor of Geography, VUW, and specialised in development and social change in peasant and tribal societies in Latin America and the South Pacific. He recently worked in Guizhou, southwest China. Among his books are *Poverty and Peasantry in the Peruvian Andes* (1994), *Shifting Cultivation in Latin America* (1971) and *Abemama: Social Change in Kiribati and Tuvalu* (1983).

# 1. INTRODUCTION

*T.G. McGee and R.F. Watters*

Each new era brings with it new geographies and each era struggles to define those geographies. In the late eighteenth and early nineteenth centuries when technological and institutional change was laying the foundations for our current world, it was not described as an industrial revolution. It was only years later that historians began to talk about the industrial revolution in order to impose meaning on time. In a similar manner, intellectual constructs concerning our current era are equally unclear. But two concepts have surfaced to capture the changes of the current era. The first is 'globalisation' which assumes the increasing integration of national economies into global systems of production, distribution and consumption. The second is the concept of 'time-space collapse' which is said to be the consequence of technological innovation in transport, communications and computer technology. The fusion of these two concepts creates the possibilities of new political, economic and social configurations in global society.

The discourses that have emerged concerning these configurations are the subject of this book. But obviously we cannot incorporate all of them. Thus, the discourses concerning the roles of transnationals or diasporic communities are not dealt with specifically. Rather we have focused on the discourse which centres on the construction of new regions of economic, social and political interaction which are developing seemingly as one consequence of globalisation.

We make no apologies for such an approach since we are centrally concerned with the discourse of globalisation as it affects the spatial patterning of the globe and especially the Asia-Pacific region. The components of this concern involve a focus upon integration as opposed to separation, on flows in contrast to places, on international institutions as opposed to national institutions and, perhaps more controversially, convergence rather than diversity. We recognise that this focus leads to an ideology which in its most extreme form becomes a type of rhetoric which sees the promotion of business as the only rationale for the 'idea' of the Pacific Rim. But we have sought to create a book which explores these issues as they affect the idea of the Pacific Rim; as they lead to the construction of a region of shared experiences and goals.

As the essays in this book show, this idea of the Pacific Rim – the world of the Asia-Pacific – is precarious, which suggests that more powerful constructs need to be formulated if we are to understand the forces changing this vast region. In particular, it becomes clear that the construction of the supra-region of the Asia-Pacific glosses over the reality of globalisation. A far more powerful theoretical framework, we would argue, is the concept of the local-global dialectic in which the local forces in a variety of political, regional and cultural forms are always negotiating with the global. A news item from Beijing reporting that the Chinese government is setting up a studio to develop Chinese cartoon characters that will replace those of Disneyworld is an example of such negotiation.

There is, thus, a need to escape from the idea of the global steamroller constructing new regions which reflect this globalisation ideology. We have to reassert the local embedded in 'place' as the reality of local groupings negotiating their control of the local with varying degrees of success. The idea of negotiation enables a major focus to be placed upon the role of local movements engaged in resistance against global elements. Escobar, Slater, Pred and Watts, Sacks and Schuman[1] have produced important contributions to the understanding of this interaction. In this concept, the core elements that make up the roots of place – the environment, local culture, local economies, historical layerings of shared experience, the lived experience of the place – are crucial to explaining the global-local relationship.

This approach avoids the dangers of portraying the local and global as bounded separate entities and also enables flexibility in scale of the local, whether it be a village, nation, region or, in some cases, an ethnic group geographically dispersed within a national unit. It also enables the investigation of the role of collaborating local units (e.g. the Mexican State's adoption of structural adjustment policies and their effect on local regions such as Chiapas) which Corbridge[2] and Peet[3] have urged us not to neglect, particularly as they reflect in class liaisons between different levels of the local and international capitalism.

The contortions of the preceding paragraph indicate the difficulties of applying this concept of the local-global dialectic. It is particularly difficult to analyse the relations between the different levels of the local on 'domains', as they have been called.[4] In the end, the most fruitful approach is to define a 'geographic site' in which the local-global dialectic is being worked out. It is often thought that such sites are contested terrains in which the local and global are duelling for control, but in fact, as Lefebvre[5] has pointed out, the local and global are constantly interacting in the shaping and production of spaces.

The second way to escape from this view of the global steamroller is to attack it on empirical grounds. Clearly, the countries of the globe are very unevenly impacted by these global processes. Perhaps 80% of the world's inhabitants, particularly many of the poor in Asia, Africa and Latin America, still exist in localities where networks remain primarily interpersonal and local; indeed, such local networks may be the crucial element in their battle for survival. The persistence of the informal sector in Africa, Latin America and Asia is ample evidence of this assertion.[6] Part of this emphasis upon the unevenness of global impact derives from the fact that it is a Eurocentric concept, making an assumption that the global forces emanating from the wealthier countries are so powerful that the local will collapse. Global forces do not always impact directly, but are sometimes filtered into the local through collaboration with the national state. The strategy of regional alliances to promote free trade areas is an interesting example of the diverse ways in which global ideologies can be introduced.[7]

Thus, the essays in this book reassert the need to study the dialogue between localism and globalism as they are worked out in the Asia-Pacific region and, despite the disparate disciplinary contributions, return to the heart of geography.

## *Constructing the Asia-Pacific Region*

Despite much reference to the Asia-Pacific region, there is still confusion as to its composition. Geographically it is well-defined, involving all countries that abut the Pacific Basin which include Russia, a group of East Asian countries (Japan, China, the Koreas, Taiwan, Hong Kong), Southeast Asia, Australia, New Zealand, the United States, Canada, Mexico, Columbia, Ecuador, Peru, Chile and the Central American states as well as the numerous Pacific island states such as Fiji, Papua-New Guinea and the mini-states of Melanesia, Micronesia and Polynesia.

Thus, within this region, there is immense geographic and social diversity. Within it lies the world's largest country, China, with a population of over 1.25 billion, and some of the smallest countries such as Nauru (12,000). Within the region are some of the oldest nations such as Korea and some of the most recent such as Vanuatu. There is also immense linguistic and cultural diversity ranging from the Catholicism of the Latin American countries to the Islam of Malaysia or Indonesia.

Another way of looking at the region is to portray it in terms of wealth and population. The region is characterised by a high degree of inequality. Thus the two super economies of the region, Japan and the United States (which have decreased their share of population in the region from 21.5% in 1965 to 17.4% in 1990), have increased their share of gross domestic product (GDP) from 77.1% to 79.2%. Canada, Australia and New Zealand with little more than 2% of the population have declined and the Latin American and Asian components of the region with 80% of the population contribute 13.1% of the region's GDP.

How then has this very diverse, large region come to be viewed as some kind of logical sub-global system? This is where the processes of globalisation come into play involving the construction of a 'mindset' which accepts the legitimacy of this region. The first idea in this mindset is the view that the world's centre of economic gravity is moving from the Atlantic to the Pacific. This is not a new idea. Dean Forbes[8] cites Marx and Engels writing in 1850 as follows:

> Thanks to California gold and the tireless energy of the Yankees, both coasts of the Pacific Ocean will soon be populous, as open to trade and industrialised as the

coast from Boston to New Orleans is now. And then the Pacific Ocean will have the same role as the Atlantic has now and the Mediterranean had in antiquity and the Middle Ages.

A far more acceptable prophecy is more often cited. In 1900, the American Secretary of State, John Hay, wrote that 'the Mediterranean is the ocean of the past, the Atlantic the ocean of the present and the Pacific is the ocean of the future'.

But it is since the 1980s that the idea of the Asia-Pacific region has been vigorously promoted, largely in response to the economic dynamism of the area led by the growth of Japan and the Newly Industrialised Countries (NICs) which experienced fast rates of economic growth in the 1980s and 1990s. The Asian component of the GDP in this system grew by 47.3% between 1983 and 1990, representing an increase from 28.4% of the region's GDP to 38.9%. The latter figure was roughly 28% of the world's GDP in 1990. This 'image' of rapid economic growth is vigorously promoted by authors such as Elegant[9] and Winchester.[10]

A second element in this 'mindset' derives from the growing predominance of America's Pacific trade over its Atlantic trade. The former first exceeded the latter in 1982; from 1978 to 1991 trans-Pacific trade (excluding trade in services until 1994) quadrupled from US$80 billion to $361 billion.[11]

Thirdly, the Pacific Rim has been seen to be evolving as a sub-global system in which the countries are drawing closer together through increased trade, communication, investment and population movement. The establishment of a series of loosely structured organisations such as the Pacific Basin Economic Council (PBEC) (1980s), the Pacific Economic Cooperation Conference (PECC) (1980) and Asia-Pacific Economic Cooperation (APEC) (1989) which consists of 18 nations of the Asia-Pacific region that produce some 50% of the world's GDP, are examples of the way this integration is being facilitated institutionally. The meetings of the Heads of State of these organisations are becoming as important, some would argue, as the 'Group of 7' (G7), and the activities of these groups foster the idea of the Asia-Pacific region as a unified global sub-system.

Since 1994-95 with the promotion of both the pan-Pacific APEC and the more truly Asian East Asian Economic Caucus (EAEC) favoured by Prime Minister Dr Mahathir of Malaysia, some discussion has focused on the proposal that the Association of Southeast Asian Nations (ASEAN) Free Trade Area (AFTA) should be expanded as an economic grouping to link it with Australia and New Zealand's decade-old Closer Economic Relationship (CER) pact. As part of these debates, Prime Ministers of Australia and New Zealand have asserted that both of their countries are 'part of Asia'. Thus in 1993, the Australian Prime Minister at the time, Paul Keating, stated: 'We will see ourselves as a sophisticated trading country in Asia and we've got to do it in a way where everybody's got a part in it'.[12]

This mindset is obviously expedient if it will achieve greater integration with market access to the most economically dynamic areas in the world, but in New Zealand it has been strongly opposed by one or two other politicians who, with different political agendas, prefer more conventional geographic definitions. Thus it has been stated by Winston Peters that New Zealand is not an Asian, Polynesian or European country, it is essentially a South Pacific country. On a visit to New Zealand, Mahathir reminded people that moves against Asian immigration would be seen as inconsistent with New Zealand's efforts to forge closer links with Asia.[13]

## *Concepts and Terms*

Since the creation of the concept of a 'Pacific Rim' implies increased integration between countries or regions around the Pacific Basin, these terms and concepts are used variously throughout the book. Globalisation implies increased integration of national economies in an international system. Global transformation, too, would appear to be occurring, perhaps firstly through an 'international steam roller' effect with growing transnational corporate dominance and power and also by means of cultural convergence and the globalisation of consumption practices. The emergence of a global culture would seem to follow from a breakdown in boundaries, a great 'thickening' in transactions between countries of information, goods, people and capital, of growth in global forces that emphasise increased connectivity of systems and the creation of numerous networks, and even 'network landscapes'. The other important contemporary processes identified by McGee are the increased rate of urbanisation and the emergence of sub-global regions. These trends pose an enormous challenge for the future: that of creating sustainable societies. The challenge must be faced first in the great mega-regions of the world by dealing with the excesses of high energy consumption and resource use.

Integration is another key term in understanding Pacific Rim evolution. One form is 'horizontal integration' which has created an intra-Asian trade and investment network. As each country in East Asia has moved up the ladder of development, it has tended to stimulate the growth of those at the next tier of development. For example, Japanese pre-eminence in shipbuilding and steel manufacturing a generation ago has now passed to South Korea, which is also now increasingly competing with Japan in semiconductors and consumer electronics. Japan has relocated production facilities for automobiles and electronics to Thailand, Malaysia and other ASEAN members, both to create 'global export platforms' and to import products back to Japan. The newly industrialising Tigers have been relocating labour-intensive industries such as textiles, toys, athletic footwear and electronic assembly to China, other ASEAN members and Viet Nam.

Trade and investment figures show that an increasingly powerful core of the Pacific Rim is rapidly developing, for intra-Asian trade now accounts for about 45% of East Asia's total trade.[14] Hong Kong and Taiwan account for more than two-thirds of foreign direct investment (FDI) in China. And since 1990 the four Tigers have carried out more investment in ASEAN countries than either Japan or the United States.

The beneficial regional effects of this process of integration are also clear, for when a region prospers, its good fortune spills over into adjacent territories inside and outside of the political federation of which it is a part. Thus Hong Kong's prosperity means neighbouring Guangdong province benefits from investment, technology and jobs, powering ahead of the rest of China. The per capita gross national product (GNP) in the boom town of Shenzhen is nearly US$6,000, which is about 10 times greater than China's average GNP. 'What is happening is the integration of China's coastal provinces, especially Guangdong and Fujian, into the economies of neighbouring Hong Kong and Taiwan – not the reverse'.[15] Economically at least, the most dynamic regions of China look more like players in a regional trade zone and less like the rest of the mainland.

*Examining Key Ideas*

Scarcely more than a generation ago most of Asia was as poor as any region in the world. Hong Kong was little more than a bare rock overrun by refugees and facing the spectre of poverty and overpopulation. Taiwan was a stagnant outpost of a beleaguered, defeated government. Malaysia and Indonesia, backward peasant economies, were on the brink of war. South Korea, just recovered from a calamitous civil war, had a GNP roughly equal to Haiti, Ethiopia and Yemen, and Thailand was immersed in the problems of communist aggression in its neighbour, Indochina. Singapore, a tiny fledgling nation state, had only just achieved an uneasy independence. In the Asia-Pacific Rim, only Japan looked healthy and successful.

Yet in spite of formidable constraints, the East Asian economies in the last 30 years have grown faster than those of any other region in the world. Between 1965 and 1990, the 23 East Asian countries grew at over 5% GNP per capita annually – which was more than double the rate of the Organisation for Economic Cooperation and Development (OECD) economies, about three times as fast as Latin America and South Asia, and five times as fast as sub-Saharan Africa.[16] Between 1965 and 1985, real income per capita more than quadrupled in Japan and the four 'Tiger' countries (Republic of Korea, Taiwan, Hong Kong and Singapore). In almost every measurable area, such as life expectancy, education, trade, elimination of poverty, meeting basic needs and the like, progress in these five states left all other countries far behind.

There have been a number of studies that have sought to explain the secret of this success and this book in part addresses the same issue. But in achieving economic advance, the countries of East Asia and Southeast Asia have increasingly become part of a globalisation or internationalisation process that has tended to integrate a growing number of countries of the Pacific Basin in several ways.

The paradox of the East Asian miracle is associated with the euphoria and inflated expectations of those who merely marvel at the Asian achievement yet fail to consider the challenge of sustainability. Of course the impressive rate of economic growth is an enormous advantage enabling part of the economic surplus to be used to finance a more appropriate response to the challenge of adopting sustainable practices, for it is clear that many production processes will have to become more environmentally friendly and also deal with (rather than ignore) issues of social justice. It is clear that policies that more adequately meet the demands to deal with inequality, human rights, environmental, welfare and pension needs of ageing Asian societies, together with infrastructural development, would, if they were met, greatly reduce the rate of growth from a miraculous to a more modest level. But the imposition of such modern Western standards on Asian countries would be as historically unfair and inappropriate as to expect them to have been introduced in Dickensian England or Mazzini's Italy. Certainly the East Asian model of industrialisation requires cool analysis, as Forbes suggests (see chapter 2), rather than hyperbole or ahistorical analysis.

Associated with growing recognition that an 'East Asian miracle' has in fact occurred there is a widespread belief that Western nations are losing their traditional advantage as a major diffusion of world technology reaches countries recently regarded as backward. Secondly, it is thought that the world's economic centre of gravity will inevitably shift to the Asian nations of the Pacific Rim.

Recently it has been powerfully argued by Krugman that the Asian economic miracle is, on the contrary, merely a myth.[17] It simply repeats the apparently very successful Soviet industrialisation of the 1930s in which Stalinist planners moved millions of workers from farms to cities, pushed millions of women into the labour force and millions of men into working longer hours, initiated massive programmes of education, and above all ploughed an ever-growing proportion of industrial output back into the construction of new factories. The impressive feature of this Stalinist policy was its ability to mobilise resources and to achieve very high savings and investment ratios. The application of growth accounting techniques shows, however, that the rate of efficiency growth in the use of resources was very low and well below those of Western economies.

In the same way Asian economic growth is seen to be much less miraculous when subjected to growth accounting analysis. Although the Singapore economy grew at the remarkable rate between 1966 and 1990 of 8.5% or three times as fast as the United States, and per capita income at 6.6% roughly doubled every decade, the miracle 'was based on perspiration rather than inspiration':

> Singapore grew through a mobilisation of resources that would have done Stalin proud. The employed share of the population surged from 27 to 51%. The educational standards of that workforce were dramatically upgraded; while in 1966 more

than half the workers had no formal education at all, by 1990 two-thirds had completed secondary education. Above all, the country had made an awesome investment in physical capital: investment as a share of output rose from 11 to more than 40%.[18]

Even without going through the formal exercise of growth accounting, these numbers should make it obvious that Singapore's growth has been based largely on one-time changes in behaviour that cannot be repeated. Over the past generation the percentage of people employed has almost doubled; it cannot double again. A half-educated workforce has been replaced by one in which the bulk of workers has high school diplomas; it is unlikely that a generation from now most Singaporeans will have PhDs. And an investment share of 40% is amazingly high by any standard; a share of 70% would be ridiculous. So one can immediately conclude that Singapore is unlikely to achieve future growth rates comparable to those of the past.

In short, the 'Krugman thesis', based mainly on the work of Lau, Kim and Young, suggests that all of Singapore's growth can be explained by increases in measured inputs and that there is no sign of increased efficiency.

While Singapore's case is admittedly the most extreme, it is also argued that while Japan's economic growth has indeed been miraculous, that era is now well in the past and the gap between its growth rate and other advanced countries is now much smaller. In short there has been a great Japanese growth slow down. It is believed that the growth in efficiency in the East Asian 'Tigers' is no higher than those of many advanced countries. While it is true that China's growth since 1979 has seen dramatic improvements in efficiency as well as rapid growth in inputs, the exponents of the Krugman thesis argue that growth in East Asia overall is running into diminishing returns.

If indeed the idea of an East Asian economic 'miracle' is perhaps an exaggeration and almost a cliché, the attendant ideas of a 'Pacific century' and the emergence of a Pacific 'community' have also, in parallel fashion, acquired an unchallengeable status of their own. In the same way these geopolitical assumptions also require sober, cool analysis. The bold rhetoric of political and numerous business and official leaders on the notion of a burgeoning prosperous community that encompasses both sides of a dynamic Pacific Rim has become such an article of faith that it shows scant regard for intractable Pacific realities.

Although East Asia has become an engine of the world economy and a definitive part of the post-cold war international system, only a brief reflection is necessary to remind us that the cherished notion of a Pacific community – involving shared interests, values, responsibilities and mutual respect, as well as a common psychology of belonging – involves much wishful thinking. Resting as it does on a vision of noble proportions, it may well prove to be a chimera. Today, as new Asia-Pacific regional institutions are being formed, numerous economic, political, military, cultural and psychological trends are testing the durability of the Pacific community idea. Forces from above, such as global economic integration (consistent with the policies of GATT [General Agreement on Tariffs and Trade] and the World Trade Organisation [WTO]), extra-regional political and security mechanisms and democratisation; and from below such as intra-Asian and sub-regional economic and financial networks and local security perceptions are threatening the American-driven Pacific community concept.[19] As Manning and Stern have recently pointed out, the Pacific might 'remain more of a rim than a community', for trade, investment and a Pacific coastline do not necessarily make for a broader sense of belonging together.[20]

It is true that the achievement of European union was a great triumph of regionalisation, overriding cultural and national differences and entrenched parochialisms, but the Pacific Rim involves far greater cultural diversity and less shared history. The glue that tends to bind together its member states has yet to prove its strength and durability. Just as European union began with France and Germany settling their security problems 40 years ago and then working out the Schuman Plan, so the two Asian giants, China and Japan, need to work out the security problems involved in their relationship. Such a settlement would mark a real starting point.

In the meantime the Pacific Rim may be undergoing a revolution in the movement of capital and people involving the creation of many new geographies. But the fact that immigration has become a substantial issue in election campaigns in Australia, New Zealand and the United States in 1996 shows that the politics of xenophobia and of envy can still attract many followers, especially among those for whom internationalisation has meant little but disorientation and loss. Sadly our shared future can still be hampered by blinkered and defeatist populisms. Millions of people, even in well-educated societies, show an inability to comprehend the global economy and its implications for their own country. These comments are not intended to undermine the search for unity, community and economic growth in the Pacific Rim, or to be short-sighted, defeatist or iconoclastic in the name of 'realism'. These essays are intended to inform and sharpen the debate on the emergence of the Pacific Rim.

Yet we must beware of too gloomy a prognosis. For although America's long-term economic power is gradually waning, it remains the only military superpower and the dominant player in Asia-Pacific geopolitics and security issues. Moreover, Asian leaders at the Osaka APEC meeting in October 1995 confounded many sceptics in surmounting many difficult obstacles in committing their countries boldly to courses of rapid trade liberalisation. The Asia-Pacific region is in a state of flux, but resolute, sweeping innovation in regional economic and political integration might just be achievable.

*Structure of the Book*

The book is organised to incorporate essays reflecting these ideas. Part 1 entitled 'Globalisation and the Emergence of Sub-global Regions: The Case of the Asia-Pacific' analyses the macro forces of globalisation and their effects on the creation of a sub-global region in the Asia-Pacific. Four essays deal with this topic. The first by Forbes focuses upon new geographies; McGee deals with the forces of integration in the Pacific Basin; Sandrey with the growing inter-dependence of Asia-Pacific trade and Tremewan with the challenges to social justice and the reactions of non-governmental organisations (NGOs). All these essays focus on region-wide interaction.

Part II is entitled 'Processes of Change in the Asia-Pacific Region'. Franklin's essay on the imperatives of consumption raises a powerful argument concerning the end-product of the dynamic growth of Asia-Pacific economies, a world of abundance in which the next step is never clear. Hill provides a corrective to the generally accepted models of agricultural decline in association with the growth in industry and services in the region; Rimmer discusses Japanese investment in the Pacific Rim; Wade the replicability of East Asian industrial policies in other parts of the East Asian edge; and Yok-shiu Lee analyses the environmental consequences of rapid urbanisation.

In Part III entitled 'National Responses to Globalisation in the Asia-Pacific Region', the analysis focuses at the national level with a series of essays that discuss the reaction of the nation state to the impacts of globalisation. Auty deals succinctly with the issue of industrial policy in the East Asia region, particularly with reference to South Korea. Edgington deals with the 'hollowing out' of Japanese industry and should be read in conjunction with Rimmer's paper in the previous section. Goodman provides a perceptive view of how Chinese modernisation will evolve in a carefully orchestrated negotiation with global agencies and forces. Taiwan's 'southward policy', designed to redirect its investment focus from China towards Southeast Asia, indicates a tendency for sub-regional processes to occur within the sub-global larger region which point to ongoing tensions in the future of the Asia-Pacific region. Hugo deals with the issues of population growth in Indonesia, the third largest country in the Pacific Rim.

Finally in Part IV, 'Sites of Resistance, Negotiation and Capitulation', four essays shift the focus to an even more local level. Lin's paper shows how a fruitful combination of local level initiative and Hong Kong capital has led to the rapid economic transition from agriculture to industry in the county of Dongguan in the Pearl River Delta. Armstrong perceptively reevaluates the meaning of development at the local level as filtered through levels of international, national and local bureaucracy in the fishing villages of the island of Panay in the Visayan island group of the Philippines. McKinnon looks at the issues of ethnicity as a rallying point for negotiation with the global in mainland Southeast Asia, and Morrison discusses the apparent collapse of local negotiation in Sarawak State. Finally, in the Solomon Islands Frazer examines how local control of resources is not parlayed into development benefits; rather, the benefits are consumed by an over-large administrative bureaucracy and political elite.

In conclusion, the editors enumerate the major challenges that the emergence of the Asia-Pacific region pose to global stability and economic growth.

Most of the essays in this book were written in 1994 and 1995. Given the remarkable speed at which the Asia-Pacific region is being transformed, it would be impossible to capture the most recent developments. For example, the incorporation of Hong Kong may have important consequences for the competing mega-urban gateways of the region. But it is impossible to speculate on these developments. The book, thus, represents a slice of change in a period of rapid social, economic and political transition.

### *Genesis of the Book*

This book was conceived in the Department of Geography, Victoria University of Wellington, and represents an extension of its continuing research and focus over the last 35 years on the countries of Asia and the Pacific Basin expressed in the work of Keith Buchanan, Terry McGee, Harvey Franklin, Ray Watters and other staff and students and especially in its journal *Asia Pacific Viewpoint*. From its beginnings, the editors of this journal have attempted to focus on the evolving aspects of the Asia-Pacific region. It is a remarkable coincidence that McGee, the co-author of this book, now chairs the Editorial Board of *Pacific Affairs*, for many years edited by an expatriate New Zealander, William Holland. This book includes chapters by current or former staff members of VUW Geography, Armstrong, Franklin, Hill, McGee, McKinnon, Morrison and Watters, together with other Wellington academics or graduates, Chan, Frazer and Wade. Nine authors are also graduates of this University. The remaining chapters in the book are written by specialists on countries or topics that illustrate the evolving Pacific Rim: Auty on South Korea; Edgington and Rimmer on Japan; Forbes on Pacific Rim trends; Goodman on China; Hugo on Indonesia; Lee on environmental issues; Lin on the Pearl River Delta, South China; Sandrey on APEC and trade; and Tremewan on human rights. Ginny Sullivan works as editor at the Institute of Policy Studies, VUW, and is a graduate of the Universities of Canterbury and Leeds. While this volume primarily represents the work of human and economic geographers, it involves inter-disciplinary approaches, including also economists, political scientists and anthropologists.

NOTES

[1] A. Escobar, 'Imagining a post-development era? Critical thought, development, social movements', *Social Text*, 31-32, 1992a, pp. 20-56; D. Slater, 'Theories of development and

politics of the post-modern – exploring a border zone', *Development and Change*, 23 (3), 1992a, pp. 283-319; A. Pred and M. Watts, *Reworking Modernity: Capitalism and Symbolic Discontent*, New Brunswick: Rutgers University Press; W. Sacks, *The Development Dictionary: A Guide to Knowledge as Power*, London: Zed, 1992; F. Schuman (ed.), *Beyond the Impasse: New Directions in Development Theory*, London: Zed, 1993.

[2] S. Corbridge, 'Marxism, post-Marxism and the geography of development', in R. Peet and N. Thrift (eds), *New Models in Geography*, Winchester, Mass.: Unwin Hyman, 1989, pp. 224-48.

[3] R. Peet, *Global Capitalism: Theories of Societal Development*, London: Routledge, 1990.

[4] T.G. McGee, 'Domains of analysis - perspectives on the study of inequality in Malaysia: a review article', *Pacific Affairs*, 60 (1), 1986-87, pp. 655-64; L. Brown, 'Reflections on third world development: ground level reality, exogenous forces and conventional paradigms', *Economic Geography*, 64, 1988, pp. 255-78.

[5] H. Lefebvre, *The Production of Space*, Oxford: Blackwell, 1991.

[6] T.G. McGee, 'The persistence of the proto-proletariat, occupational structures and planning for the future of the third world cities', in P. Haggart (ed.), *Progress in Geography*, London: Edward Arnold, 1976, pp. 3-38; T.G. McGee, 'Invitation to the ball – formal or informal dress?', in P. Rimmer et al, *Studies of Food, Shelter and Transport in the Third World: Challenging the Unconventional Wisdom*, Canberra: ANU, Department of Human Geography, Monograph, 1978, pp. 121-53.

[7] T.G. McGee, 'Presidential address. Eurocentrism in geography: the case of Asian urbanisation', *The Canadian Geographer*, 35 (4), 1991, pp. 332-442; A. Dirlik, *What's in a Rim? Critical Perspectives on the Pacific Region Idea*, Boulder: Westview, 1993.

[8] Dean Forbes, 'What's in it for us? Images of Pacific Asian development', in C. Dixon and D. Drakakis-Smith (eds), *Economic and Social Development in Pacific Asia*, London: Routledge,1993.

[9] R. Elegant, *Pacific Destiny: The Rise of the East*, London: Headline, 1991.

[10] S. Winchester, *The Pacific*, London: Hutchinson, 1991.

[11] Robert A. Manning and Paula Stern, 'The myth of the Pacific community', *Foreign Affairs*, November/December 1994, p. 82.

[12] *Far Eastern Economic Review (FEER)*, 25 March 1993, p. 16.

[13] *The Dominion*, Wellington, 27 March 1996.

[14] Ibid, p. 83.

[15] 'Rags to Riches', *FEER*, 12 October 1995, p. 47, quoting the Japanese economist, T. Watanabe.

[16] The World Bank, *The East Asia Miracle. Economic Growth and Public Policy*, Oxford: Oxford University Press (OUP), 1993, p. 2.

[17] Paul Krugman, 'The myth of Asia's miracle', *Foreign Affairs*, November/December 1994, pp. 62-78.

[18] Statistics used by Krugman are cited from Alwyn Young, and Kim and Lau. For detailed references, see Krugman, op. cit., 1994.

[19] Manning and Stern, op. cit., 1994, pp. 79-93.

[20] Ibid.

# Part I
# Globalisation and the Emergence of Sub-global Regions: The Case of the Asia-Pacific

## 2. REGIONAL INTEGRATION, INTERNATIONALISATION AND THE NEW GEOGRAPHIES OF THE PACIFIC RIM

*Dean Forbes*

The ascendance of Asia's industrialising nations has ramifications throughout the region as well as globally. Significant levels of interaction between the new industrialising economies (NIEs) and the powerful economies of North America have fanned comment on the growing integration of the Pacific Rim countries.[1] Often this debate has been characterised by hyperbole rather than cool analysis. Whereas two decades ago predictions of Asia's future were predominantly gloomy, now scholars are more likely to encounter frenzied speculation and inflated expectations about the expansion of Asian economies in the context of the fast approaching 'Pacific century'.[2]

The aim of this chapter is to map some of the changing contours of the human and economic geographies of the Pacific Rim. New and important centripetal and centrifugal forces bring visible changes to the spatial structures and linkages which determine the way in which the region is organised. This chapter analyses selected empirical evidence of interaction among Pacific Rim nations, with a particular focus on economic linkages, population movements, communications development and institution-building.

### *The New Geographies of the Pacific Rim*

Scholarly writing on the Pacific Rim has historically been concerned with the integrity of continents as the basis for the construction of regions. The comprehensive regional geographies of Asia written in the first half of the twentieth century typically centred on continental Asia in its entirety, or else on sub-regions of continental Asia. Stamp, for example, defines a region which stretches from Cyprus to Japan, Asiatic Russia to the East Indies (Indonesia).[3] Ginsburg's 'Asian Asia' similarly includes all the territory between the Mediterranean and the Pacific, but without the 'European' parts of Russia.[4] The Pacific has generally meant the island states of the Pacific Ocean. Freeman incorporates Indonesia, Melanesia, Micronesia and

Polynesia (which includes New Zealand), with Australia added in for completeness.[5] Spate's magisterial *The Pacific Since Magellan* similarly emphasises the ocean and its islands, though it goes further than most books of this kind in seeing a unity to the Pacific region as a whole.[6]

Contemporary discussion has perpetuated the separateness of the various entities which make up the Pacific Rim. The global economy is sometimes portrayed as tripolar, consisting of poles of economic activity centred on Europe, North America and East and Southeast Asia.[7] Scholars writing regional geographies still favour constructions of geography, the loci of which are continental regions and the attached outlying islands,[8] or focus on clusters of islands, as is the case in work on the Pacific.[9] Another separation common to writings since the 1960s has been the distinction drawn between 'developed' and 'developing' or 'underdeveloped' countries. By the conventions of such constructions different kinds of sub-groups can be identified, such as the NIEs or the 'low-income economies' favoured by the World Bank. In the recent past a sub-division between the 'socialist' and 'non-socialist' made some sense.

However, a growing number of studies, often with a strong economic theme, are beginning to demonstrate the connections and common experiences of countries across the broader entity of the Pacific Rim.[10] There is a disturbing tendency in the strands of this literature which are oriented to business promotion to exaggerate the changes occurring along the Asian edge of the Pacific Rim, which is often described by tropes such as 'dynamic' and 'miraculous'.[11] Cumings labels this exaggeration 'Rimspeak', and challenges the meaningfulness of the term Pacific Rim, which he labels 'an American construct'.[12] Nevertheless, new geographies of the Pacific Rim[13] are being shaped by the uneven processes of economic growth and accelerated economic integration which characterise the region. This chapter explores three main developments in the way in which the geography of the Pacific Rim is evolving.

First, it is argued that economic development is the principal force orchestrating the main changes occurring throughout the region. The emergence of first, second and third generation NIEs has had a determining impact on labour movements, communications development and the political thrust towards creating a new institutional framework for Pacific Rim cooperation.

The second theme is that national boundaries have become more permeable as new forms of regional interaction and cooperation have evolved. The chapter highlights the importance to the functioning in the Pacific Rim of new and deeper economic, social, infrastructural and institutional links between countries. In some cases this has led to new regional groupings of countries, which transcend national borders, the regions formed being labelled 'new economic territories' (NETs).

Third, an increased level of regional restructuring and integration must be set in a context of the internationalisation of the more robust economies of the region. This trend towards internationalisation means greater porosity, or what is sometimes called 'open regionalism', in the links between Pacific Rim countries. It is argued that this is more important than some boosters of the Pacific Century recognise.

*Economic Development and Interdependence*

In the past, the countries of the Pacific Rim were seldom considered to have constituted a functionally integrated community, nor have they generally been thought to share significant economic complementarities. The great global trading links scattered throughout human history have been centred on China and India, the Mediterranean, and more recently the Atlantic. Most East and Southeast Asian countries were colonised by European powers, so their economic linkages by the end of the 19th century were predominantly in a westwards direction, connecting them to the metropolitan economies of Europe. In the post-World War II period, the expansion of the American economy ensured that Pacific trade grew in importance, but until recently this was dominated by Japan's emerging links with the US.

The extraordinary pace of economic growth in some of the Asian countries of the Pacific Rim is well known. For example, from 1980-92 the per capita GNP of South Korea, Thailand, Hong Kong, Singapore and China grew at faster than 5% per annum.[14] An important characteristic of that growth has been the high levels of economic integration. Okita argues that the critical ingredients of economic integration have been the significance of Asian nations' commitment to open market economies, the opportunities created by an expanding world economy, their parallel interest in fostering comparative advantages, and their commitments to economic efficiency.[15]

In the last decade there has been a growing realisation of the remarkable levels of growth in trade among the key economies of the Pacific Rim. In 1992, for instance, two thirds of all exports from APEC countries were destined for other APEC countries, a proportion unchanged since 1988.[16] Just 17.2% of exports were sent to the European Community (or European Union [EU], as it is now known), and 16.7% of exports went to the rest of the world.[17] In parallel fashion, 67.2% of imports into APEC countries were sourced in other APEC economies, whereas only 14.3% came from the European Community, and 18.5% from all other countries combined.

Brunei, Canada and Taiwan experience the highest levels of dependence in terms of their exports to APEC members. The lowest levels occur, not unexpectedly, in Japan and the USA, and a little surprisingly, Thailand. Shifting to imports, Hong Kong, Malaysia and Canada all acquired over 77% of their imports from APEC member countries. The significance of the Japanese and American economies to the cluster of APEC countries sometimes can distort trade data. If trade with Japan and the USA is excluded from APEC trade patterns, it is possible to distinguish between APEC countries with strong trade connections with Japan and the United States and those that are well connected to the remainder of the APEC economies.

Examining the APEC trade data from this perspective shows that China, Malaysia and Hong Kong have the highest levels of exports to APEC members excluding Japan and the USA. In contrast, Canada, the Philippines and Thailand have the lowest levels. It is notable, but not unexpected, that Canada has the lowest proportion of its trade with APEC countries, if Japan and the US are not included, given the huge impact that the United States has historically had on the Canadian economy.

APEC countries minus the two economic superpowers provide the market for more than 37% of the exports of Japan and the USA as well as supplying each of these two countries with over 40% of their total imports. This forcefully demonstrates that APEC trade integration is not simply a product of superpower trade, but is more diversified than is sometimes thought. The significance of APEC trade to these two very large economies highlights the important levels of economic integration which currently characterise the countries of the Pacific Rim.

While the increasing levels of intra-APEC trade are a striking component of Pacific Rim economic integration, at the same time it is important to recognise trends towards greater internationalisation within the APEC economies. The available statistics make identification of a general trend rather difficult. Between 1988 and 1992 the level of exports from APEC members to other members remained steady at 66%, though imports crept up from 65.7% to 67.2%. It remains to be seen whether these levels of economic integration have reached a plateau. An important unknown is whether the development of new institutions such as APEC and AFTA will ease internal trade barriers and thus encourage greater intra-APEC trade.

In picturing the different trends in the Pacific Rim, it is helpful to divide APEC countries into two groups: those in which exports to other APEC members grew faster than overall exports between 1988 and 1992, and those countries for which the reverse is true. This is a crude indicator of internationalisation, but it generates some identifiable patterns.

On the one hand, China and Australia have experienced a much faster growth of trade with APEC members than with the rest of the world. Canada, Thailand, Taiwan, Malaysia and New Zealand show a similar trend, although the differences are not as marked. The Australian case is best explained by a determined government thrust since the 1980s to increase economic linkages with East and Southeast Asian countries. China's strong level of linkage with APEC economies is a reflection both of the important gateway role that Hong Kong plays, as well as an indicator of the importance of China's links with key APEC economies.

On the other hand, South Korea stands out as the economy in which global trade is increasing at a considerably faster pace than trade with other APEC members. The rapid expansion of the Korean economy has meant exporters have sought significant markets outside the Pacific Rim. Indonesia, Brunei and the USA also increased their exports to non-APEC countries more quickly than to APEC members between 1988 and 1992.

The increased openness of Pacific Rim countries to intra-regional and international trade is paralleled by the flows of FDI. On a broad note, all APEC countries recorded significant increases in inward and outward FDI between 1980 and 1992. In Singapore, Indonesia and Malaysia, the stock of FDI reached the equivalent of 74.8%, 55.7% and 39.2% of GDP respectively.[18] The stock of FDI in Australia, New Zealand and Hong Kong exceeded 20% of GDP in 1992. All APEC members, with the exception of Canada, recorded increases of investment over the decade. In China's case this represented nearly a 15-fold increase and in Indonesia a five-fold increase since 1980. In general the economies of the Pacific Rim experienced a major opening up to foreign investment through the 1980s and early 1990s. Intrinsic to this opening up is a spread of inward and outward investment across the globe. Pacific Rim countries could not be accused of being excessively inward-looking in their investment strategies.

While on a global scale the major source and destination countries for FDI remained the well-established economic powers (the UK, USA, France and Japan), there were some large shifts within the Pacific Rim. First, the NIEs, Taiwan, Hong Kong, Singapore and South Korea have significantly increased their stocks of capital in the developing countries of the region during the past decade. In particular they have established themselves as the major investors in ASEAN.[19] Second, China has emerged as both the world's largest developing country host of FDI and also a major source of capital exports in its own right. China's growth and attractiveness have meant that many source countries for foreign investment have diverted investments away from the NIEs and the ASEAN countries towards China.

The economic growth being experienced by Asian countries is characterised by a high level of economic integration, as is evidenced by the trade and investment data. It has been referred to as a flying geese pattern of development, which contrasts with the experience of Latin American countries where regional economic integration is of a much lower magnitude.[20] At the same time, there is continuing economic interaction beyond the region in both trade and investment, not only by the economic superpowers but also by the NIEs, China and South Korea. As a result, the economic geography of the Pacific Rim is changing under the influence of the accelerated economic growth of Asian countries.

It would be premature to argue that the Pacific Rim has emerged as an identifiable economic entity in itself. However, there are clearly evident increases in economic interaction, and shifts in the structure of the links between the countries in this region. These patterns of economic interaction provide a different perspective on the geography of the region, but are only one dimension of the changes that are occurring.

### *International Population Movements*

High levels of economic integration, together with a trend towards economic internationalisation, are one important characteristic of the region. Long-distance movements of population are another ingredient of the glue which links countries together and accelerates the restructuring of the geography of the Pacific Rim. Population movements take a variety of forms: they can be temporary or permanent; most are driven by the search for higher income jobs; some are motivated by political events; in other cases they reflect a desire to see more of the world. In significant measure, population mobility in the Pacific Rim is economically motivated, in two key senses: either from the search for better jobs, or by the higher discretionary incomes generated by economic development. Yet political tensions continue to simmer, and the ebb and flow of refugees still affects most countries.

Extensive long-distance migration is not new to the Pacific Rim. The migration of Chinese into Southeast Asia and beyond to Australasia and North America is centuries old. The British colonial regime in Malaya brought in workers from India, while the French encouraged Chinese labourers to settle in Indochina. Against a background of this long history of large-scale population movements, there is little doubt that the mobility of people throughout the Pacific Rim has increased since the 1970s. This is attributed by Castles and Miller to 'the opening up of the [Asian] continent to economic and political relationships with the industrialised countries in the post-colonial period'.[21] To be more precise, greater economic integration has facilitated inter- and intra-regional population mobility.

The most significant movement of people has occurred from Asia into the United States following the promulgation of the Immigration Act in 1965. Since 1981 around a quarter of a million Asians have annually moved to the USA, especially from the Philippines, China, South Korea and Viet Nam.[22] Canada and Australia have experienced flows of similar proportions compared to their overall populations, although much smaller in absolute numbers. From 1981-90 settler arrivals in Australia totalled 76,664 from Viet Nam, 47,339 from the Philippines, 35,361 from Hong Kong, 34,853 from Malaysia and 31,275 from China.[23] Asian migrants to New Zealand have been notably fewer in number because of a restrictive regulatory environment until the 1990s.

Japan's experience differs significantly from the other developed countries in the Pacific Rim. Despite severe labour shortages since the mid-1980s, the Japanese government has been strongly opposed to immigration. During the 1980s women from the Philippines, Korea and South Asia were admitted to work in the 'entertainment' industries, and they were followed by men from the same countries who gained work illegally.[24] Japanese employers needing labour have devised various mechanisms to get around restrictions, such as recruiting 'trainees' from poor countries or providing opportunities for workers to register as language students.[25] However, the Japanese government stubbornly refuses to dilute its supposedly ethnically homogeneous population and hence has turned its back on long-term migration to Japan.

A striking example of recent migration has been the outflow of Hong Kong Chinese in the lead-up to the re-incorporation of Hong Kong into China in 1997. Emigration peaked at 62,000 in 1990, in the wake of China's Tiananmen Affair, with estimates suggesting that in total about half a million citizens had moved, primarily to the USA, Canada or Australia. It is estimated that up to 20% may have subsequently returned, and applications for visas have dropped significantly in recent times. Many emigrants departed under the various business migration schemes of the host countries, and have continued to do business in Hong Kong. Commuting between Hong Kong and their new permanent homes has led to the label 'spacemen' (*sic*) or 'astronauts'. Partly due to this process it is estimated that in 1993 there were large numbers of foreign passport holders resident in Hong Kong, including 26,100 from the USA, 20,400 from Canada, and 16,700 from Australia.[26]

This recent wave of emigration has added to the long-standing Chinese diaspora within the Pacific Rim. Spread throughout the so-called overseas Chinese countries of Taiwan, Hong Kong and Singapore, and in concentrations in places such as the USA, Canada, Australia, Indonesia, Thailand, Viet Nam and the Philippines are millions of citizens of Chinese ancestry. This group, it is argued, has been a significant influence in forging economic linkages between various Pacific Rim countries. Their key role in the expanded economic growth in Guangdong province in southern China has been particularly notable, but it is argued that overseas Chinese investment is playing an important role in Thailand and Viet Nam as well.[27]

Viet Nam has been the source of the largest flow of international refugees in the Pacific Rim since 1945. Up to 2 million left Viet Nam in the late 1970s and through the 1980s. Many travelled overland into China, whereas others left by boat, eventually reaching staging camps in Southeast Asia. After 1979, many travelled overland to Thailand, where they were housed in camps along the Thai-Cambodian border.[28] Ultimately they went on to settle in the USA, Canada, Australia, France and China. Between 1975 and the early 1980s there was a strong representation of ethnic Chinese among the Vietnamese leaving the country, but through the 1980s the flow came to be dominated by ethnic Vietnamese. Since the early 1990s the overseas Vietnamese (who are known as the *Viet Kieu*) have been encouraged to return to Viet Nam and invest capital and skills in Vietnamese development. Continued harassment in Viet Nam meant return movements started slowly, but the process is quickly building up momentum, and the Vietnamese government sees these overseas residents providing an important contribution to the economic development of the country.

Apart from the link between refugee movements and economic interaction, there are also several different kinds of international labour migration throughout the Pacific Rim which are gradually displacing migration to the main destination, which has been the Middle East. A handful of countries have promoted the export of labour as a means of improving the domestic balance of payments. Chief among the Pacific Rim countries are the Philippines and Thailand. South Korea was once a significant exporter of labour, but is no longer. Like other NIEs it has a labour shortage. Furthermore it is predicted that Thailand, a second generation NIE, will become a net labour importer during the next few years. Indonesia is increasing its efforts to promote the export of labour, with the result that the *de jure* number of labour migrants has increased significantly through the 1980s. Unofficial labour migration of Indonesians, especially to Malaysia, is significant but difficult to quantify (see Hugo, chapter 15).

Another overlooked dimension is the steadily increasing export of labour, many of whom are skilled and professional, from Western countries to other Pacific Rim economies. The number of New Zealanders (the definition used in the statistics changed in 1987 from locally born to nationals) leaving the country peaked in the second half of the 1970s, then again in the second half of the 1980s. Australia was the predominant destination, never accounting for fewer than 40% of departures, followed by the United Kingdom.[29] This is an indication of the long-standing connections between New Zealand and Australia, but is also a reflection of the integrated labour market which has come about under the policy of CER.

Since 1988-89 the number of Australian-born permanent and long-term departures has increased significantly. This particular stream of emigration is directed towards the United States and Canada, a number of Asian destinations (particularly Hong Kong, Singapore and Malaysia), and New Zealand.[30] In the year 1991-92 the Australian-born comprised a significant component of the total number of emigrants from Australia shifting to Oceania (55.9%), the Middle East (51.1%), North America (50.9%) and Southeast Asia (43.2%).[31] This is indicative of a trend in which younger Australians are attracted in rapidly increasing numbers to jobs overseas, though there are other processes involved including children of immigrants returning to their parents' place of birth.

Finally, rising incomes and improved marketing have resulted in increased tourist travel throughout the region. However, Pacific Rim tourism in general needs to be clearly placed in its global context. In the early 1980s around four-fifths of international tourist movements were between the wealthier core countries of Europe and North America (and Japan). West Germany and the USA were the main generators of tourists, Italy and Spain the principal destinations.[32] Pacific Rim tourism is a sideshow to the main global tourist activity which remains centred on Europe.

Nevertheless the picture is far from static. The growth in Japanese tourism has been most striking. In 1964 the number of Japanese travelling abroad totalled about 100,000. By 1981 this had risen to 4 million, of which 89.9% was to destinations in Asia, North America and Oceania.[33] By 1990 Japanese international tourists numbered in excess of 10 million. Some estimates predict it could grow to 20 million by the year 2000.[34]

The Australian case highlights the growing significance of Pacific Rim tourists in the overall tourism industry. In 1980 the Pacific Rim provided

64% of all incoming short-term visitors to Australia, whereas this had risen to 70% by the end of the decade. More specifically, Asian (including Japanese) tourists to Australia increased from 138,700 in 1980 to 670,500 in 1989, an increase of over 480% in just under a decade.

Population movements, in all their complexity, have subtly contributed to the reshaping of the geographies of the Pacific Rim. Most significantly, the various strands have increased the interaction between countries which in the past experienced very little contact. Australia is a good illustration. The links with Korea brought about by trade connections have been significantly supplemented by tourism. Conceptually this has further blunted the previously sharp distinction between the continental entity of Asia and the conceptual category of the islands of Oceania.

## *Information and Communications*

Technological development is, of course, central to the new geographies of the Pacific Rim. The growth of information services and the expansion of communications infrastructure make societies more porous to a range of external influences.[35] Time and space are compressed, but determining to what extent technology is the cause of change, and to what extent the effect, is a rather more complex question. Two examples of this explosive sector of activity illustrate some of the potential impact of new information and communications systems: the first is telecommunications infrastructure, notably fibre optic cable, and the second is the expansion of regional electronic media, particularly television provided by satellite.

Fibre optic cables provide a crucial backbone to high volume, high speed communications systems.[36] Thousands of times more bits of information can be channelled through light pulses which pass along a fibre optic strand than could be transmitted through a conventional copper wire. The first sea-bed fibre optic cable was laid across the Atlantic Ocean, followed later by the Pacific. The initial trans-Pacific fibre optic cable (called TPC-3) went into service in 1989, linking Japan to the United States via Hawaii. It had the capacity to handle 16,500 calls simultaneously. A second generation connection – TPC-4 – was installed in late 1992, connecting Japan with the US and Canada. A third generation fibre optic cable, labelled TPC-5, was installed in 1995. It circles the Pacific, connecting Japan to Guam, Hawaii and southern California, and Canada directly to Japan to complete the loop. Due to more sophisticated construction of the cable, TPC-5 will have the capacity to handle around 300,000 calls simultaneously.[37] Asian countries such as Hong Kong, Singapore and Korea were the first to be connected to the network through Japan and Guam, while Australia and New Zealand are connected to the Pacific spine via PacRimWest and PacRimEast through Guam and Hawaii respectively.

While this telecommunications infrastructure is developing rapidly, the telephone systems within Asian countries are not always commensurate with the standard of their fibre optic connections to the rest of the world. It is estimated that it will take Indonesia 2.6 years to eliminate the present waiting list for new telephone lines, while China and Malaysia require a little under one year.[38] At the other end of the spectrum, the telecommunications systems in some Pacific Rim countries are equivalent to the best in the world. As an illustration, cellular telephones have been adopted with alacrity in the richer Pacific Rim countries. In Australia in 1994 there were 5 cellular telephones per 100 population, 4.9 in Hong Kong, 4.7 in Singapore and 3.7 in New Zealand. By contrast, the corresponding figures were 0.02 in Indonesia and 0.05 in China.[39]

The improvement of trans-Pacific communications links fulfils a number of functions. It is a significant facilitator of the growing economic links within the region, as the rapid exchange of information is crucial to economic growth. McGee and Lin have argued even more strongly that the time-space convergence which has characterised the Asian NIEs has been vital to economic development.[40] At the same time, emigrant communities have taken advantage of improved telecommunications to intensify contacts with friends and relations in their original communities. Such thinking spurred Australia's Telstra to play a significant role in setting up satellite telecommunications systems in Viet Nam.

An increase in the number of satellites stationed over Asia is opening huge parts of the region to satellite television services. Currently the most significant is Star TV, which was purchased in mid-1993 by Rupert Murdoch's global media empire, News Corp. It broadcasts multiple channels of various language programmes, music, news and sport, from the satellite known as AsiaSat 1, which was launched in 1991 and is owned by Asia Satellite Telecommunications. StarTV has exclusive rights to the transponders on AsiaSat 1, thereby preventing other broadcasters from using that particular satellite. AsiaSat l's footprint incorporates most of India and China, and peninsular Southeast Asia.

Another group of broadcasters leases space on Indonesia's Palapa B2P satellite. These include key American organisations such as the Turner Broadcasting System (the parent of CNN), Viacom, Time Warner and ESPN, a sport channel, as well as Hong Kong's TVB. Being Indonesian-owned, the satellite footprint covers mainly Southeast Asia, a little of southern China, and the east coast of the Indian sub-continent.

The launch of another satellite in mid-1994, Apstar 1, by a consortium representing Chinese government and other regional interests, added significant additional capacity for satellite television broadcasters. Apstar 2 was launched in early 1995 but exploded in flight. Customers who signed up to use the services of these two satellites include many of the American companies currently leasing space on Palapa B2P, as well as Reuters, China Telecommunications Broadcast Satellite Corporation and the Australian Broadcasting Corporation. The footprint of Apstar 1 centres on China and Southeast Asia, whereas Apstar 2 was planned to extend from Europe and the Middle East through to Japan, and reach southwards to incorporate Australia.

Hong Kong's centrality to the populations of East and Southeast Asia, and in particular China, has meant it is the hub of transmission signals 'uplinked' to satellites. StarTV, for example, is based in Hong Kong. However, uncertainties about licences after 1997 have meant that companies such as Turner Broadcasting System and Television New Zealand are increasingly attracted to Singapore, despite that country's censorious approach to the media in general.

Delivering satellite television services to Asia is a relatively new phenomenon, and so the consequences are far from clear. The rapid growth of free to air television, and the increased capacity of households to afford receivers, opens the possibility of unprecedentedly rapid circulation of information through the region. Recognition of the political risks that may stem from a better informed public has led Singapore and Malaysia to ban private ownership of parabolic satellite dishes.[41] Other countries, such as China, have tried to curtail use of satellite dishes, but find it very difficult to have much of an impact.

The greater ease of access to the cultural products of Western countries, particularly America, and local producers of bulk made-for-TV material, notably Hong Kong, will fuel the arguments of the critics of cultural imperialism. Yet others believe that the impact of the Western media to date should not be underestimated. As an example, Segal[42] believes the impact of the media has been to promote cultural pluralism and bring people closer together, with a 'loss of only some individual cultural habits'. In the absence of detailed empirical evidence, such a benign conclusion is heroic. In contrast, there is little dispute about the impact of Western Pacific Rim cultures on North America – it is infinitesimally small.

### *Institution Building in the Pacific Rim*

Pacific Rim governments have played an important part in guiding economic development and facilitating the links that have developed within the private sector. The last decade has seen a step-up in the intensity of efforts by governments to create a broad institutional structure to facilitate further economic development of the countries of the Pacific Rim. An often cited antecedent of an institutional framework is Japan's war-time invention of a Greater East Asian Co-Prosperity Sphere. Not surprisingly, its association with Japan's attempt to conquer the region militarily served to discredit this particular manifestation of regional fraternalism.[43]

In more recent years the idea of a Pacific community has been promoted in a number of forums. Discussions initiated by the Japanese as far back as 1968 proposed a connection between Japan, the US, Canada, Australia and New Zealand.[44] PBEC was formed and the Pacific Trade and Development Conferences commenced in the same year. However the most significant move came with the creation of the forum known as APEC in 1989. APEC's most prominent achievement has been the bringing together of heads of APEC governments in Seattle in late 1993, an event which generated worldwide press and media coverage, and has been repeated annually ever since.

APEC is intended to promote economic growth rather than be a focus of debate about security issues or politics.[45] Nevertheless there is still lack of clarity about the precise role that it might play within the Pacific Rim and beyond. One line of argument proposes a form of 'open regionalism'.[46] This is a mechanism for reducing barriers to trade and investment within the group, particularly through the phased reduction of tariffs and quotas, while at the same time making access to APEC economies easier (and cheaper) for countries outside the community. The intention of 'open regionalism' is to concentrate on trade reforms within APEC that are consistent with the broader GATT and WTO move towards trade liberalisation. APEC's Eminent Persons Group[47] has argued that implementation of the trade liberalisation process should begin in the year 2000 and be completed by 2020. The Bogor Declaration announced by President Suharto after the 1994 APEC leaders' summit commits APEC's industrialised members to free trade by 2010, and the developing economy members to the same goal by 2020.[48]

The 'open regionalism' goal is paralleled by a number of less ambitious, but not necessarily less complex, goals. For example, APEC provides a forum for dialogue on significant matters affecting regional trade and investment. It also provides an opportunity to examine, with the intention of working towards standardisation, the detailed country-specific rules and regulations affecting tradeable goods and services.

The idea of a meaningful economic association spanning the countries of the Pacific Rim is still regarded with scepticism by many. While more liberal access to economies of the region is generally supported as a long-term goal, in reality there are significant tensions between APEC members. Japan and the USA frequently clash on trade issues, and the smaller, poorer economies are generally fearful of the impact of too much openness. Moreover, despite the evidence of close economic links, it is often argued that the sheer size of the Pacific Rim combined with its historical and cultural heterogeneity, are sufficient to preclude any likelihood of an equivalent to the EU being formed. Sometimes this represents wishful thinking by those who feel threatened by the possibility of the world breaking up into large economic blocs. For others it reflects a parochial regionalism that is unnecessary and outdated in a globalising world.

APEC's future is by no means assured. However, it will inevitably mean that Pacific Rim countries are significantly better informed about their respective economic strategies, and it just might form the basis of something considerably more substantial in the way of regional economic integration.

Existing regional organisations operate on a much smaller scale than APEC. The most successful has been ASEAN, with seven member countries by the middle of 1995. Other countries such as Sri Lanka and Australia have often been mentioned as possible future members of ASEAN, but nothing has come of it. ASEAN annual meetings also provide a regular opportunity for broader regional dialogue through meetings with interested neighbour countries.

ASEAN is seeking to expand its economic role through the formation of AFTA,announced in the Singapore Declaration of 1992.[49] However, ASEAN's record on economic issues has been less successful than expected, and so there is considerable scepticism about whether AFTA can bring about greater levels of regional economic integration.

Paralleling the development of ASEAN and APEC has been the emergence of the sub-regional groupings, NETs.[50] The most prominent of these is the Singapore-Johor-Riau (Sijori) Growth Triangle which formalises economic connections between Singapore, the southern region of Malaysia and parts of Indonesia's Riau Province. Motivated, in part, by the success of this grouping of territories, others have been suggested linking together northern Sumatra, the north-west region of peninsular Malaysia and southern Thailand, and another centred on Indonesia, eastern Malaysia and the southern Philippines.[51] The Asian Development Bank (ADB) is channelling infrastructure lending into a multi-country region centred on the Mekong River, out of which may emerge a functional economic zone. At the end of 1994 a Mekong River Commission was set up by Cambodia, Laos, Thailand and Viet Nam, replacing the Interim Mekong Committee.

## *New Geographies*

The nations of the Pacific Rim are more diverse, in almost every significant respect, than the countries of other major regions such as Western Europe, Africa south of the Sahara, or Latin America. Yet the economic development of the region is altering its geographical configuration and creating new multi-stranded economic linkages. Time and space have been compressed by transport improvements, telecommunications and satellite television. National borders are reduced in significance by the urgency of trade. And new groupings of nations are emerging, providing impetus for further change. Together these processes provide a challenge to the way in which scholars write about the Pacific Rim.

Business and government initiatives together have helped forge the new regional geographies coming into existence throughout the region. Economic entrepreneurs have contributed significantly to the high levels of trade and investment flows throughout the Pacific Rim. The overseas Chinese have performed a decisive part in developing many of these economic linkages. International labour movements and the expansion of the communications and media infrastructure, it would seem, have been energised by the efforts of the private sector.

At the same time institutional developments in the Pacific Rim are evolving in parallel with the emerging economic and social geographies. The new economic territories and bilateral arrangements demonstrate the alacrity with which new regional formations are being encouraged by governments. Some believe this goes beyond the mere emergence of new economic geographies, instead arguing it is a pretext for the demise of nations as key territorial institutions. Such claims may be premature. In taking initiatives towards restructuring, national governments are ensuring that regional economic integration remains under their control. Moreover, nationalism remains very strong throughout the Pacific Rim and is strengthened, not diluted, by the emergence of affluent middle classes.

While there is evidence of greater regional integration of the Pacific Rim, there is also a concurrent trend towards internationalisation. Examples of this include the role of the Middle East in attracting labour from the region; the international rather than regional trade orientation of Japan, the US and South Korea; and the thrust in discussions of APEC's role towards 'open regionalism'.

On a global scale the emergence of the EU, the North American Free Trade Agreement (NAFTA)and APEC has fuelled fears of the emergence of exclusionary global trade zones. This pictures the world divided into three essentially hostile trade blocs, which would facilitate linkages within, but erect barriers to economic linkages outside, the bloc. It is precisely this scenario which APEC is designed to counter by incorporating all the Pacific Rim countries within it, not just those which belong to the Asian pole.

The new geographies which are being created, particularly on the Asian edge of the Pacific Rim, demonstrate the need for a rethinking of the approach taken to understanding the dynamics of this region. Increasingly scholars will need to be better attuned to the great complexity of interaction and less fettered by traditional expectations of the significance of national boundaries. Economic growth has sent ripples through the geographies of the Pacific Rim which, though far from finished, already demand new constructions of the geography of the region.

## *Acknowledgements*

Alice Bass and Cecile Cutler assisted with library research and editing at Flinders University. In addition I am grateful to the Centre for Asian Studies at the University of Adelaide for providing an office and general support.

NOTES

[1] A definition of the Pacific Rim typcially centres on those countries bordering the Pacific Ocean, both in the Americas and Asia. It also includes those parts of Southeast Asia, such as Singapore and the land-locked PDR Laos, which we technically excluded because they are not immediately adjacent to the Pacific Ocean, but are generally included because of their obvious functional links with their neighbours.

[2] M. Daly and M. Logan in *The Brittle Rim: Finance, Business and the Pacific Rim*, Melbourne: Penguin, 1989, pp. 214-17, thought that by the mid-1980s the structural weaknesses of Pacific Asian economies had become evident and would slow down long-term growth.

[3] L.D. Stamp, *Asia: A Regional and Economic Geography*, London: Methuen, 8th edition, 1957.

[4] N. Ginsburg (ed.), *The Pattern of Asia*, London: Constable, 1958.

[5] O.W. Freeman (ed.), *Geography of the Pacific*, New York: Wiley, 1951.
[6] O. Spate, *The Pacific Since Magellan*, Canberra: ANU Press, 1979, 1983, 1988, 3 volumes.
[7] See P. Dicken, 'The growth economies of Pacific Asia in their changing global context', in C. Dixon and D. Drakakis-Smith (eds), *Economic and Social Development in Pacific Asia*, London: Routledge, 1993, p. 26.
[8] J. Rigg, *Southeast Asia: A Region in Transition*, London: Unwin Hyman, 1991.
[9] H. Brookfield with D. Hart, *Melanesia: A Geographical Interpretation of an Island World*, London: Methuen, 1971.
[10] An example is B. Bora and C. Findlay, *Regional Integration and the Asia-Pacific*, Melbourne: Oxford University Press (OUP), 1996.
[11] See R. Higgott, 'Competing theoretical approaches to international cooperation: implications for the Asia-Pacific', in R. Higgott, R. Leaver and J. Ravenhill (eds), *Pacific Economic Relations in the 1990s: Cooperation or Conflict?*, Sydney: Allen and Unwin, 1992, pp. 290-311; and D.K. Forbes, 'What's in it for us? Images of Pacific Asian development', in Dixon and Drakakis-Smith (eds), op. cit., 1993, pp. 43-62.
[12] B. Cumings, 'The political economy of the Pacific Rim', in R.A. Palat (ed.), *Pacific-Asia and the Future of the World-System*, Westport: Greenwood Press, 1993, pp. 21-37. One wonders whether reducing the Pacific Rim to 'an American construct' is not an interpretation equally patronising to residents within the region as those he criticises.
[13] The phrase 'reshaping the geography of the world' is used by Daly and Logan, op. cit., 1989, p. 88.
[14] World Bank, *World Development Report 1994*, New York: OUP, 1994, Table 1.
[15] S. Okita, 'Developing the Asia-Pacific region', in K.S. Sandhu, S. Siddique, C. Jeshurun, A. Rajah, J.C.H. Tan and P. Thambipillai, *The ASEAN Reader*, Singapore: Institute of Southeast Asian Studies, 1992, pp. 500-3.
[16] In this paper I will focus my discussion on the APEC countries rather than all the nations of the Pacific Rim. APEC's original 12 members included Australia, Brunei, Canada, Indonesia, Japan, Malaysia, New Zealand, Singapore, South Korea, Thailand, the Philippines and the USA. China, Hong Kong and Taiwan were included in 1991 (having had observer status at the first meeting), Mexico and Papua New Guinea were admitted in 1993, and Chile in 1995.
[17] Trade data is from Department of Foreign Affairs and Trade, *The APEC Region: Trade and Investment*, Canberra: Department of Foreign Affairs and Trade, 1993, Tables 2.1 - 2.17.
[18] Foreign investment data is from B. Bora, 'Foreign direct investment', in Bora and Findlay (eds), op. cit., 1996, pp. 78-98.
[19] ASEAN's membership includes Indonesia, Malaysia, Philippines, Singapore, Thailand, Brunei and Viet Nam, with Laos, Cambodia and Myanmar proposed.
[20] On the contrasting experiences of Asia and Latin America, see R. Jenkins, 'Learning from the gang: are there lessons for Latin America from East Asia?', *Bulletin of Latin American Research*, 10 (1), 1991, pp. 37-54.
[21] S. Castles and M.J. Miller, *The Age of Migration: International Population Movements in the Modern World*, New York: The Guildford Press, 1993, p. 155.
[22] Ibid, p. 156.
[23] G. Hugo, *The Economic Implications of Emigration from Australia*, Canberra: Australian Government Publishing Service, 1994, p. 58.
[24] Castles and Miller, op. cit., 1993, p. 159.
[25] S.A. Spencer, 'Illegal migrant laborers in Japan', *International Migration Review*, XXVI (3), 1992, pp. 754-86.
[26] L. do Rosario, 'Home sweet home', *FEER*, 31 March 1994, p. 28.
[27] N. Tracy and C. Lever-Tracy, 'The dragon and the rising sun: market integration and

economic rivalry in East and Southeast Asia', *Policy Organisation and Society*, 6, Summer 1993, pp. 3-24; N. Tracy, 'The Chinese diaspora and the reshaping of Pacific economic relations', Asia Impact Study, The Australian Centre for American Studies. See also chapters 14 and 16 by Chan and Lin.

[28] National Population Council, *The National Population Council's Refugee Review*, Canberra: Australian Government Publishing Service, 1991, pp. 70-81.

[29] Population Monitoring Group, *On the Move: Migration and Population - Trends and Policies*, Report No. 6, Wellington: New Zealand Planning Council, 1991, pp. 28-31.

[30] Hugo, op. cit., 1994, p. 40.

[31] Ibid, p. 115.

[32] D. Pearce, *Tourism Today: A Geographical Analysis*, London: Longman, 1987, p. 41.

[33] Ibid, p. 57.

[34] Australia-Japan Research Centre, *Japanese Tourism to Australia*, Canberra: Research School of Pacific Studies, ANU, 1992, p. 6.

[35] R. Scalapino, 'The United States and Asia: future prospects', *Foreign Affairs*, 70 (5), 1991-92, p. 25.

[36] See, for instance, J.V. Langdale, 'Telecommunications and international transactions in information services', in S.D. Brunn and T.R. Leinbach (eds), *Collapsing Space and Time: Geographic Aspects of Communications and Information*, New York: HarperCollins, 1991, pp. 193-214.

[37] B. Johnstone, 'The "more for less" solution', *FEER*, 4 June 1992, pp. 46-8.

[38] M. Clifford, 'Pressure for change', *FEER*, 7 April 1994, pp. 36-8.

[39] M. Clifford, 'A question of money', *FEER*, 7 April 1994, pp. 47-8.

[40] T.G. McGee and G.C.S. Lin, 'Footprints in space: spatial restructuring in the East Asian NICs 1950-90', in Dixon and Drakakis-Smith (eds), op. cit., 1993, pp. 128-51.

[41] M. Vatikiotis, 'Outlook: partly cloudy', *FEER*, 12 May 1994, p. 68.

[42] G. Segal, *Rethinking the Pacific*, Oxford: Clarendon Press, 1991, p. 156.

[43] Some maliciously argue that Malaysia's advocacy of an East Asian Economic Caucus provides a modern day parallel to the Co-Prosperity Sphere, with its emphasis on an 'Asian' bloc separate from the 'non-Asian' countries of the Pacific Rim.

[44] E.G. Whitlam, *A Pacific Community*, Cambridge: Harvard University Press, 1981, p. 43.

[45] M. Rudner, 'APEC: the challenges of Asia Pacific economic cooperation', *Modern Asian Studies*, 29 (2), 1995, pp. 403-7.

[46] A. Elek, 'Pacific economic co-operation: policy choices for the 1990s', *Asian-Pacific Economic Literature*, 6 (1), 1992, pp. 1-15; A. Elek, 'Trade policy options for the Asia-Pacific region in the 1990s: the potential of open regionalism', *American Economic Review*, 82 (2), 1992, pp. 74-8.

[47] Eminent Persons Group, *Achieving the APEC Vision: Free and Open Trade in the Asia Pacific*, Singapore: Asia-Pacific Economic Cooperation, 1994.

[48] J. McBeth and V.G. Kulkarni, 'Charting the future', *FEER*, 24 November 1994, pp. 14-15.

[49] P. Imada, and S. Naya (eds), *AFTA: The Way Ahead*, Singapore: Institute of Southeast Asian Studies, 1992; S. Kumar, 'Assessing AFTA', in Sandhu et al, op. cit., 1992, pp. 516-18.

[50] Scalapino, op. cit., 1991-92, p. 21.

[51] Further illustrations of this kind of development include the Shenzhen region, which provides an economic bridge connecting China and Hong Kong, and the CER strategy linking Australia and New Zealand.

# 3. GLOBALISATION, URBANISATION AND THE EMERGENCE OF SUB-GLOBAL REGIONS: A CASE STUDY OF THE ASIA-PACIFIC REGION

*T.G. McGee*

This chapter is about three processes occurring in contemporary international relations which reflect growing concerns with 'global sustainability'.[1] These developments are as follows: first, the increasing integration of national economies into a single global economic system which is labelled *globalisation*; secondly, the inevitable increase in *urbanisation* and emergence of global and sub-global systems of highly linked cities; and thirdly, the processes of sub-global integration which are reflected in the emergence of *sub-global regions* such as the European Union and NAFTA.[2] It can be argued that the processes are supported by the 'neo-liberal' policies of free trade and privatisation which dominate the agendas of many states and international agencies today.

It is extraordinarily difficult to disentangle the interaction between these processes. The solution put forward here is to discuss the three processes separately and then to conclude with an assessment of the challenges posed by these developments.

## *The Globalisation Process*

Globalisation has been the subject of increasing interest particularly with respect to technology and economics. It is well understood that globalisation, in its economic manifestation, involving the increasing integration of national economies into a global system of production, consumption and trade, is not a recent phenomenon as world systems theorists have convincingly argued.[3]

However, many researchers suggest that the current phase of globalisation (post-1947) is qualitatively different for two reasons. First, economic activity is now being functionally integrated at a global level,[4] often owned and directed by large transnational enterprises which are assuming such economic power that the nation state is losing its formerly pre-eminent position. As Barnett and Cavanagh write in their somewhat breathless manner:

> ... relatively few companies with worldwide connections dominate the four intersecting webs of global commercial activity on which the new world economy largely rests: the Global Cultural Bazaar; the Global Shopping Mall; the Global Workplace; and the Global Financial Network ... The driving force behind each of

> them can be traced in a large measure to the same few hundred corporate giants with headquarters in the United States, Japan, Germany, France, Switzerland, the Netherlands and the United Kingdom. The combined assets of the top 300 firms now make up roughly a quarter of the productive assets in the world.[5]

Secondly, this worldwide network is made more functional because developments in new micro-electronic-based computers enable 'large amounts of data to be transported cheaply over long distances' and thus 'have radically changed the worldwide organisation of finance, of competition, of supply, and of demand. Other technological developments, like wide-bodied aircraft and container ships which have facilitated the rapid movement of large volumes of people and freight'[6] are also important.

These developments spawn concepts such as 'global cities', 'global consumption' and the 'global village' which suggest that global transformation is a one-way process. Thus the major forces shaping development at the state or local level become less important. This idea is best summarised by Castells:

> The new international economy creates a variable geometry of production and consumption, labor and capital management and information - a geometry that denies the specific meaning of place outside its position in a network whose shape changes relentlessly in response to messages of unseen signals and unknown codes.[7]

This view of globalism as some form of 'international steamroller'[8] is even further reinforced by views of cultural convergence, globalisation of consumption practices and ideas of time-space compression.[9] Some writers see these processes as destroying local cultures and reconstructing them in globally understood terms. The pervasive flow of international media images reinforces this view of the 'mac-isation' of the world.[10] In many ways, it is a continuation of the modernisation project in which the world will ultimately end up as a developed version of the United States. Other writers have even gone so far to see new 'network landscapes' in this cultural formation. Thus, Appadurai writes of ethnoscapes (flows of people, immigrants, refugees, tourists, etc.); technoscapes (machinery, technology and information); finanscapes (capital); mediascapes (flows of images in television, film, magazines, etc.); and ideoscapes (ideologies and world views).[11]

Some writers have seen the emergence of global 'cyborg cultures' in which the boundaries between people and machines break down.[12] Others[13] present the emergence of global culture in terms of constant mobility through networks that facilitate the movement of individuals through an increasingly boundaryless world.

Such ideas of globalisation lead to a view of the world where an increasing thickening of transactions of information, goods, people and capital has important implications for the relationship of the nation state. These global forces which are emphasising increased connectivity of the systems of exchange are seen by some writers as posing potential conflicts with the state. Thus at one level the state, especially in developing countries, is concerned with emphasising historical continuities in what Benedict Anderson has called 'the reinvention of tradition',[14] which invents the idea of 'bounded culture' identical with the perceived boundaries of the state. On the other level the forces of globalisation are emphasising a 'public culture' which is in a sense boundaryless, manifest in its most extreme in the cyberspace of the Internet. Despite the fact that globalisation is said to de-emphasise place, it is clear that the forces of globalisation are most apparent in the largest mega-urban regions of the world. Thus the major challenges of creating sustainable societies have to be tackled in *places* such as the mega-urban regions. Since these global forces generally promote the development mode of high-energy consumption-urban based development, their relationship to the overall global growth of urbanisation is crucial. This aspect is discussed next.

### *The Global Urbanisation Process*

It is currently expected that during the first years of the twenty-first century, for the first time in human history more than half of the world's population will live in urban areas and that by 2025 that proportion will be nearing 58%. Consequently, the world seems to be on a path leading to inevitable urbanisation. However, this overall trend masks substantial differences between the major world regions, particularly between more and less developed regions.[15] By 1990 the world's population stood at an estimated 5.2 billion persons, with 4.1 billion living in developing countries and 1.2 billion in developed countries. Approximately 45% of the total population of the world (2.4 billion) lived in urban places, with 1.5 billion in developing countries and 0.9 billion in developed countries. Although the proportion of urban dwellers in developing countries was only 37%, their total urban population surpassed by a considerable margin that of developed countries where the level of urbanisation stood at 73%. By 2025, the level of urbanisation in the developing world is likely to rise to 61%, suggesting that 4.4 billion people will live in the urban centres of developing countries, accounting for about 88% of the total urban population in the world at the time.[16]

Thus, underlying the discussion of current world urbanisation trends is the massive volume of population that already resides and is expected to reside in the urban areas of the developing world. The numbers involved pose major challenges for the achievement of sustainable urbanisation in developing countries, meaning the ability to manage cities so that they do not impose an undue burden on existing resources and so that they provide an adequate quality of life to their residents. The challenges ahead are even more daunting given that increasing urbanisation levels are occurring even as existing urban systems remain characterised by the concentration of the population in one or a few urban centres. If such a pattern of urban concentration prevails, the developing world will experience the emergence of mega-urban regions as major components of the urban system.

Whereas in the countries that are currently identified as developed the levels of urbanisation began to increase rapidly almost 200 years ago so that most saw their urban population reach the 50% level during the last decade of the nineteenth or the early twentieth century, most of today's developing countries will reach similar levels of urbanisation only during the first decades of the twenty-first century. Between 1990 and 2005, the population living in the urban areas of the developing world is expected to increase by over a billion people. It is important to understand the historical differences between developed and developing countries that underlie this situation.

Most historical evidence indicates that population growth rates of the developed countries were much lower than those being experienced today by developing countries. Thus, between 1776 and 1871 the population of developed countries grew at approximately half the rate of that of developing countries today. In addition, the migration of Europeans to colonies or former colonies greatly relieved population pressures in Europe and in the urban areas of the continent since many of these emigrants would have migrated to European cities if overseas migration had not been an option.[17]

Although there were structural blockages in employment and city growth related to the rates of economic growth, the urban transition in the developed countries generally involved the growth of cities populated mostly with wage-earners, engaged in factory and service occupations. The existence of large segments of the urban population engaged in informal activities, characterised by low income and low productivity, was not a dominant feature of this pattern of urbanisation except for relatively small periods of time (London between 1830 and 1870) and in the more slowly evolving economies of the European south. The urban transition therefore gave rise to growing urban domestic markets for the products of the industrial revolution.[18]

The current phase of the urban transition in the developing countries has very different historical roots. The urbanisation process has been deeply associated with their incorporation into the global economy, which is variously described as colonisation or imperialism. While there are substantial variations in the way this process has affected urbanisation in individual countries and broader regions, which are partly related to the pre-existing experience of urbanisation and the cultural resilience of certain societies,[19] the overall impact of the incorporation was broadly similar during the period extending from 1500 onwards.

One of the major consequences of the process of incorporation was the creation of large primate cities dominating the urban hierarchies of the countries in which they were located. Thus, the literature about the history of urbanisation in the developing countries is very much focused on cities such as Rio de Janeiro, Mexico City, Jakarta, Ibadan and Nairobi, because they are administrative centres and conduits for the flow of raw materials to the developed world.

The process of incorporation also created dualistic societies in which much of the rural population lived in poverty, characterised by low productivity and a lower status, while the urban population consisted of a comparatively small elite of colonialists, foreign entrepreneurs and indigenous oligarchy. The rest of the population in cities worked largely in the informal sector, being engaged in low-paid service and cottage-industry occupations.

There was, however, considerable differentiation in how the process of incorporation occurred through time and in space. The process of political decolonisation, which began in Latin America in the nineteenth century but was not completed until the 1970s, resulted in different patterns of urbanisation at the regional level, especially with respect to the major regions including Latin America, the Asia-Pacific region and Africa.[20]

Table 3.1 shows the sharp difference in the levels of urbanisation between the different developing regions in 1990. Latin America has attained levels of urbanisation similar to those of the developed countries. Asia and Africa, in contrast, are just entering the 'accelerated' phase of the urban transition. Because Latin America has already largely experienced the urban transition, the major problems it faces relate to managing the growth of the urban population rather than the absorption of population moving from rural to urban areas.[21]

Attempts to explain the reasons for the different urbanisation experiences of the developing regions include the fusion of theoretical explanation drawn from neo-classical theory, world system theory and convergence theory.[22] In the current phase of accelerated urbanisation in Africa and Asia, the latter will experience the largest urban growth in terms of the number of people involved, and therefore it is important to highlight its experience.

In the contemporary world, sharp variations in population size underlie the differences in the urbanisation process experienced by Africa, Asia and Latin America. Thus, the prospects for Asia, with 3.1 billion people in 1990, differ from those of Africa, with 642 million, and Latin America, with only 448 million in 1990 (Table 3.1). Asia's demographic profiles tend to be dominated by China and India whose combined population stood at nearly 2 billion in 1990. In fact, in 1990 six countries accounted for 83% of the population in Asia, namely, Bangladesh, China, India, Indonesia, Japan and Pakistan.[23] Among those countries, only Japan has accomplished a successful urban transition and the remaining five present the major challenge regarding urbanisation in developing Asia.

Much of this large volume of population will move to the largest mega-urban regions which are exhibiting the processes of city expansion and the location of industrial activity on the fringes of existing cities. This has

Table 3.1. TOTAL URBAN AND RURAL POPULATION AND PERCENTAGE OF THE POPULATION LIVING IN URBAN AREAS BY MAJOR REGION, 1950-1990

| *Region* | | *1950* | *1960* | *1970* | *1980* | *1990* |
|---|---|---|---|---|---|---|
| | | | | *Population (millions)* | | |
| World Total | Total | 2,516 | 3,020 | 3,698 | 4,448 | 5,292 |
| | Urban | 734 | 1,032 | 1,352 | 1,757 | 2,390 |
| | Rural | 1,783 | 1,98 | 2,345 | 2,691 | 2,902 |
| More developed regions | Total | 832 | 945 | 1,049 | 1,137 | 1,207 |
| | Urban | 448 | 572 | 699 | 799 | 875 |
| | Rural | 384 | 373 | 350 | 338 | 331 |
| Less developed regi‹ ns | Total | 1,684 | 2,075 | 2,649 | 3,312 | 4,086 |
| | Urban | 286 | 460 | 654 | 959 | 1,515 |
| | Rural | 1,398 | 1,615 | 1,995 | 2,353 | 2,571 |
| Europe | Total | 393 | 425 | 460 | 484 | 498 |
| | Urban | 222 | 260 | 307 | 341 | 366 |
| | Rural | 171 | 166 | 153 | 143 | 133 |
| North America | Total | 166 | 199 | 226 | 252 | 276 |
| | Urban | 106 | 139 | 167 | 186 | 207 |
| | Rural | 60 | 60 | 59 | 66 | 68 |
| Oceania | Total | 13 | 16 | 19 | 23 | 26 |
| | Urban | 8 | 10 | 14 | 16 | 19 |
| | Rural | 5 | 5 | 6 | 7 | 8 |
| USSR (former) | Total | 180 | 214 | 243 | 266 | 289 |
| | Urban | 71 | 105 | 138 | 167 | 190 |
| | Rural | 109 | 110 | 105 | 98 | 99 |
| Africa | Total | 222 | 279 | 362 | 477 | 642 |
| | Urban | 32 | 51 | 83 | 133 | 217 |
| | Rural | 190 | 228 | 279 | 345 | 425 |
| Asia | Total | 1,377 | 1,668 | 2,102 | 2,583 | 3,113 |
| | Urban | 226 | 359 | 481 | 678 | 1,070 |
| | Rural | 1,151 | 1,309 | 1,621 | 1,905 | 2,042 |
| Latin America | Total | 166 | 218 | 286 | 363 | 448 |
| | Urban | 69 | 107 | 164 | 236 | 320 |
| | Rural | 97 | 111 | 122 | 127 | 128 |

Table 3.1 continued

| | *Percentage urban* | | | | |
|---|---|---|---|---|---|
| World Total | 29.2 | 34.2 | 36.6 | 39.5 | 45.2 |
| More developed regions | 53.8 | 60.5 | 66.6 | 70.3 | 72.6 |
| Less developed regions | 17.0 | 22.1 | 24.7 | 28.9 | 37.1 |
| Europe | 56.5 | 61.1 | 66.7 | 70.4 | 73.4 |
| North America | 63.9 | 69.9 | 73.8 | 73.9 | 75.2 |
| Oceania | 61.3 | 66.3 | 70.7 | 71.2 | 70.6 |
| USSR (former) | 39.9 | 48.8 | 56.7 | 63.0 | 65.8 |
| Africa | 14.5 | 18.3 | 22.9 | 27.8 | 33.9 |
| Asia | 16.4 | 21.5 | 22.9 | 26.3 | 34.4 |
| Latin America | 41.5 | 49.3 | 57.3 | 65.0 | 71.5 |

Source: United Nations, *World Urbanization Prospects 1991*, 1991.

certainly been the assumption of Berry, Richardson, and Champion.[24]

These large mega-urban regions have been labelled *extended metropolitan regions.* Cities such as Jakarta, Shanghai, Hong Kong, Bangkok and Tokyo are all extending their influence into the surrounding rural areas, sometimes located up to 100 kilometres from the urban core. The main difference between their urban configurations and the megalopolis typical of North America is the high population density in both the urban cores and the rural areas surrounding them.[25]

An example of an extended metropolitan region is Singapore and its surrounding area, which includes the Malaysian state of Johor and the Indonesian Archipelago of Riau. In this region, market interchanges have been growing and links with areas once considered rural are gaining strength. It is characterised by high levels of economic diversity and interaction, a high percentage of non-farm employment (over 50%), and a deep penetration of global market forces into the countryside.[26] The expansion of Singapore's sphere of influence has resulted in greater population concentration and a change in the economic activities over the area.

The major conclusion to be drawn from this analysis is that the macro-trends do not necessarily signal a deconcentration of urban settlement or counterurbanisation. It can be argued that deconcentration is actually occurring in a zone of agglomeration much larger than those defined by the UN. The processes of residential outward movement (suburbanisation), industrial decentralisation into new industrial estates (as described for Dongguan in chapter 16), the creation of transportation networks, the consumption needs of the elite and middle classes and the deterioration and changing land use of the inner cores of many of these regions all precipitate the creation of Extended Metropolitan Regions (EMRs).

The EMRs are extremely important locations for the generation of national income. In Latin America, up to 80% of the GDP is generated in urban areas.[27] In Asia, up to 40% of the GDP of some countries is produced in the large EMRs.[28] Some writers have argued that the reasons for this growth of large mega-urban regions result from some aspects of the political economy of globalisation.

In a recently published article, De Mattos[29] has argued that the major effect of globalisation has been to erode the entrenched Keynesian theories that argued it was possible to correct the problems of economic growth by rational state intervention. De Mattos suggests that one of the main goals of state policies from 1950 to 1970 was to achieve a more balanced spatial distribution of productive activities, employment and population influenced by such researchers as Hirschmann, Myrdal, Nurske, Robinson and Rosenstein-Rodan. He says:

> ... three basic principles constituted the core of national development strategies adopted during that period: (a) the promotion of inward-oriented economic growth, so that internal markets would become the main support of productive activities, (b) the promotion of industrialisation for import substitution, and (c) the establishment of a new mode of regulation which embodied the new theory of development planning ...[30]

De Mattos argues that these policies were successful in many parts of Latin America and Asia between 1950 and the mid-1970s. Industrial growth rates in Latin America and Asia averaged 6% per annum and were responsible for accelerating the penetration of rural areas by the capitalist mode of production and increased migration and urbanisation.

At the same time in the capitalist or mixed economies of the majority of states in the less developed world, these structural policies encouraged the focus of private capital in existing urban centres, thus 'sustaining the process of concentration and the uneven territorial distribution of both capital and people'.[31]

By the late 1970s, the grave structural crisis, which began to manifest itself in both developed and developing countries, led to falls in productivity, increased political instability and a development crisis in Latin America and Africa. The response was to adopt 'structural adjustment policies' designed to reduce the welfare role of the state, give priority to market forces, and foster an open economy with strong linkages to the global economy and the international division of labour. This structural adjustment has exhibited significant differences in the developing world.

In the economically dynamic countries of Asia, some writers have argued that these policies were already effectively implemented in countries such as Korea, Taiwan, Hong Kong and Singapore in the 1970s and have continued in the 1980s. In all these countries the rural population has fallen dramatically and urbanisation levels have increased rapidly. On the other hand, in Latin America the crisis had a different and much more dangerous impact. Already highly urbanised (64% in 1980), city growth began to slow as the GNP actually declined. Governments which had previously been able to finance the provision of some essential services were faced with a debt crisis and could no longer afford to provide comprehensive services. Inflation was rampant, unemployment increased and the proportion of urban poor and numbers living in squatter settlements grew rapidly. Gilbert citing Iglesia reports that 'based on conservative estimates, the percentage of poor people rose from 41% in 1980 to 44% in 1989 – that is 183 million inhabitants', with an estimated 104 million living in urban centres. While this development crisis particularly affected urban areas, rural poverty remained high at 61%.[32] Gilbert sees some basis for optimism for some countries in the 1990s as growth rates have begun to increase with greater integration into the world economy, but the entrenched problems of highly unequal income, sizeable urban poverty and ineffective government management still remain.

This analysis of urbanisation in developing countries indicates the unevenness of development. But what is striking in this analysis is the fact that the concentration of economic activity is still highly focused upon the mega-urban regions. This supports De Mattos' view that the collaboration between the national state and capitalists and international capital strengthens the emergence of these mega-urban regions.

Finally, there is a great deal of evidence that an evolving system of urban linkages between these mega-urban regions is emerging. This is a reflection of growing interaction as measured by flows of international finance, international transportation and trade-oriented manufacturing. Hardly surprisingly this is most marked in the most economically dynamic of the sub-global regions of the developing world – the East Asian edge of the Pacific Basin. One writer suggests that, 'As a rough approximation, we can say that fewer than a dozen urban centres in Asia (representing perhaps 4% of the total population) are the locus of 90% of international finance, of international transportation, of trade oriented manufacturing and of international information networks'.[33]

Thus the states of the developing world are openly embracing these forces of globalisation which emphasise the concentration of population and economic activity in large mega-urban regions. Both global and national investment find these areas ideal 'investment sinks' in which to locate manufacturing of consumption goods, invest in the built environment and create the landscape of global consumption. Since much of this development is currently focused in the Asia-Pacific region, we will explore its effects in the next section.

## *Sub-Global Regions: The Case of the Asia-Pacific*

The emergence of sub-global regions involves the setting-up of regional blocs of states within the global system. These regional blocs involve very definite commitments involving consultative arrangements to facilitate interaction within a region such as PECC and the APEC. On the face of it the development of these sub-global regions may appear to be at odds with the integration of economic activity at a global level; certainly they are sometimes portrayed in this manner. But I would argue that they are in fact largely arrangements which facilitate the globalisation processes already outlined. There are several dimensions to the construction of these new sub-global regions. The ideological rationale has been discussed in the introduction but the structure of the system must also be analysed.

*The components of the Asia-Pacific system.* There are considerable problems in measuring the emergence of the Asia-Pacific system. There is the question of measuring the degree of interaction within the system. One might also argue whether the sub-components of the system are in fact more important that the total system itself. Certainly this would be a strong argument in the case of the super economies which dominate the system.[34]

There are two main features of the system: first, the components of the system concerned with production and population; and secondly, the transactive components of the system which involve the various transactions carried out in the region.

*Components of the system: production and population.* It is clear from Table 3.2 showing the distribution of GDP that the super economies remain dominant, producing almost 80% of the GDP. In terms of the distribution of the GDP within the system, it has been remarkably stable during the three decades since 1965. Despite the much heralded rise of the NICs, the largest shifts in GDP and the value of industry and manufacturing have been in Japan's share of the Asia-Pacific output at the expense of the USA. Essentially the system has witnessed a relative shift in contribution to regional GDP within the super economies and this has led to growing friction between them. Despite the fanfare of economic growth in the NICs, which does reflect their rapid economic transformation and growth, they still represent a small proportion of total GDP output. The disparity between the very large proportion of population in the less developed parts of the region and the small proportion in the super economies and white settler states is an important component of the system. The fact that 80% of the population produces only 20% of the GDP is reflected in low levels of living and poverty in many of the developing countries. This simply reinforces the view that while the system is economically dynamic it is also highly unequal.

*The transactive components of the system.* A number of researchers have begun to chart the transactional components[35] of the Asia-Pacific system,[36] and the general conclusion is that the technological revolutions in communications, travel and transport including the growth of bulk carriers, containerisation and wide-bodied jets have accelerated the movement of capital, goods and people in the region.

One can indicate just a few of the dimensions of this transactional revolution. In the last 20 years there has been a significant shift in the distribution of scheduled air traffic routes in favour of the Asia-Pacific. Today air

Table 3.2. PERCENTAGE GDP AND POPULATION OF PACIFIC RIM COUNTRIES, 1965-1990

| | *1965* GDP (Population) % | | *1979* GDP (Population) % | | *1983* GDP (Population) % | | *1990* GDP (Population) % | |
|---|---|---|---|---|---|---|---|---|
| 1. Supereconomies | | | | | | | | |
| USA | 68.7 | (14.3) | 52.6 | (12.3) | 56.8 | (12.2) | 49.9 | (11.6) |
| Japan | 9.1 | (7.2) | 21.8 | (6.3) | 18.4 | (6.2) | 29.3 | (5.7) |
| | 77.8 | (21.5) | 74.4 | (18.6) | 75.2 | (18.4) | 79.2 | (17.3) |
| 2. White Settler | | | | | | | | |
| Canada | 5.2 | (1.4) | 5.1 | (1.2) | 5.6 | (1.2) | 4.4 | (1.2) |
| Australia | 2.3 | (0.8) | 2.9 | (0.7) | 2.9 | (0.8) | 2.5 | (0.8) |
| New Zealand | 0.6 | (0.1) | 0.4 | (0.1) | 0.4 | (0.1) | 0.1 | (0.1) |
| | 8.1 | (2.3) | 8.4 | (2.0) | 8.9 | (2.1) | 7.0 | (2.1) |
| 3. NICs[1] | 0.9 | (3.3) | 2.6 | (3.4) | 2.8 | (3.4) | 3.6 | (3.4) |
| 4. Other Asian[2] | 8.2 | (64.8) | 8.5 | (67.0) | 7.2 | (67.7) | 6.0 | (68.1) |
| 5. Latin American[3] | 5.1 | (7.6) | 6.2 | (8.5) | 5.9 | (7.9) | 3.5 | (8.8) |
| *TOTALS* | *100.1* | *(99.5)* | *100.1* | *(99.5)* | *100.0* | *(99.5)* | *99.3* | *(99.7)* |

[1] NICs: Korea, Hong Kong, Taiwan, Singapore.
[2] Other Asian countries: People's Republic of China, ASEAN (except Singapore).
[3] Latin American: Mexico, Columbia, Peru, Chile, Argentina.
Source: United Nations, *World Urbanisation Prospects, 1990*, New York: United Nations, 1991; World Bank,*World Development Report, 1992*, New York: OUP, 1992.

traffic is double that of the European and American markets. By 2010 there will be a fourfold increase in the number of air passengers to 375 million. At this point the Asia-Pacific will generate 51% of the world's scheduled passenger traffic. Business travel will increasingly be replaced by tourism. Between 1980 and 1992 the Asia-Pacific region's share of global tourism revenues grew from 3 to 16% and the number of tourist arrivals grew dramatically. Figure 3.1 shows the growing importance of the East Asia Pacific Rim.

The movement of freight via cargo air and landbridges in the region has also grown rapidly, focusing upon the development of a few major points of intermodal transportation. Information flows through various forms of telecommunication have increased massively along with the investment in telecommunications infrastructure. These are the 'netscapes' of Appadurai. The combination of this dynamic economic growth and increased transactive capacity will accelerate the growth of urbanisation in the region which will in turn accelerate the emergence of major urban nodes which are the connectivity points in these intense transactive networks (see Figure 3.2). Often they will be parts of corridors of linked transactions which are shown in Figure 3.2. Clearly corridors such as Tokyo-Osaka which is the focus of the Tokkaido metropolis or the Taipei-Koashung corridor are now well developed. But others such as the Southeast Asian corridor are only just beginning. These urban corridors are the major loci of economic growth concentrating on the coastal corridor regions of their countries. Figure 3.3 separates out the GDP for some of these countries emphasising the importance of these coastal corridors' contribution to the GDP of their nations. Such corridor regions will also contain a significant proportion of their countries' population as urbanisation increases.

## *Thoughts for the Future*

The principal conclusion of this paper is simple. The processes of globalisation, urbanisation and sub-global regionalism are combining to produce a form of mega-urban regionalism which appears to be economically dynamic but produces many problems of urban environmental deterioration, urban management and the creation of sustainable societies. While it is clear that policy solutions that can alleviate these problems are being developed, it is not clear that this 'trilateral mode of development' carried out within a 'neo-liberal' global system of imperatives will be adaptable enough. The issue of creating sustainable societies will ultimately depend upon the ability of local societies to negotiate solutions for the places in which they live. And while some writers such as Amin and Thrift[37] see the use of NGOs and associations as an optimistic possibility for local control, there is little evidence that this has proceeded far in Asia, the pivotal region for global sustainability. Perhaps the EMRs of Asia in which agriculture, industry and suburbs coexist may offer an environment in which the local communities can utilise low-cost solutions to the high energy

Figure 3.1. ASIA-PACIFIC TOURISM, 1990, SHOWING AVERAGE ANNUAL RATE OF INCREASE, 1980-1992

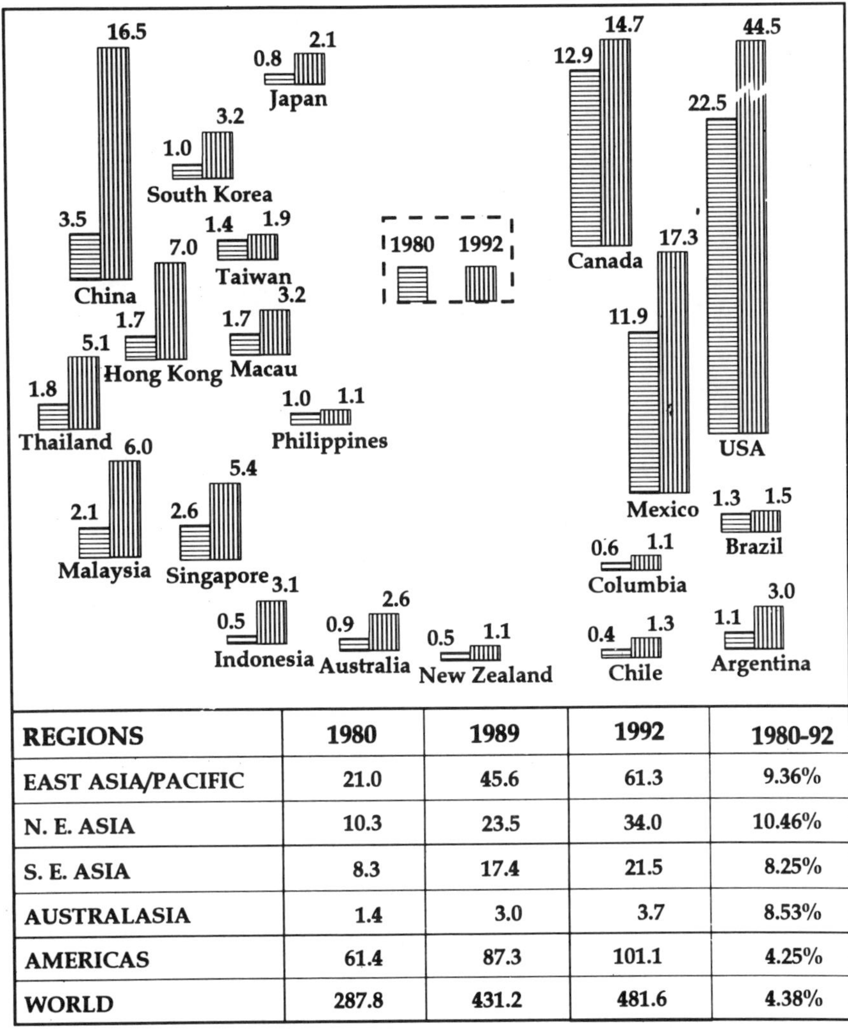


| REGIONS | 1980 | 1989 | 1992 | 1980-92 |
|---|---|---|---|---|
| EAST ASIA/PACIFIC | 21.0 | 45.6 | 61.3 | 9.36% |
| N. E. ASIA | 10.3 | 23.5 | 34.0 | 10.46% |
| S. E. ASIA | 8.3 | 17.4 | 21.5 | 8.25% |
| AUSTRALASIA | 1.4 | 3.0 | 3.7 | 8.53% |
| AMERICAS | 61.4 | 87.3 | 101.1 | 4.25% |
| WORLD | 287.8 | 431.2 | 481.6 | 4.38% |

Source: *Yearbook of Tourism Statistics 1994*, Madrid: World Tourism Organization.

Figure 3.2. ASIA-PACIFIC RIM (Major extended metropolitan regions with population in excess of 2m., 2000 A.D.)

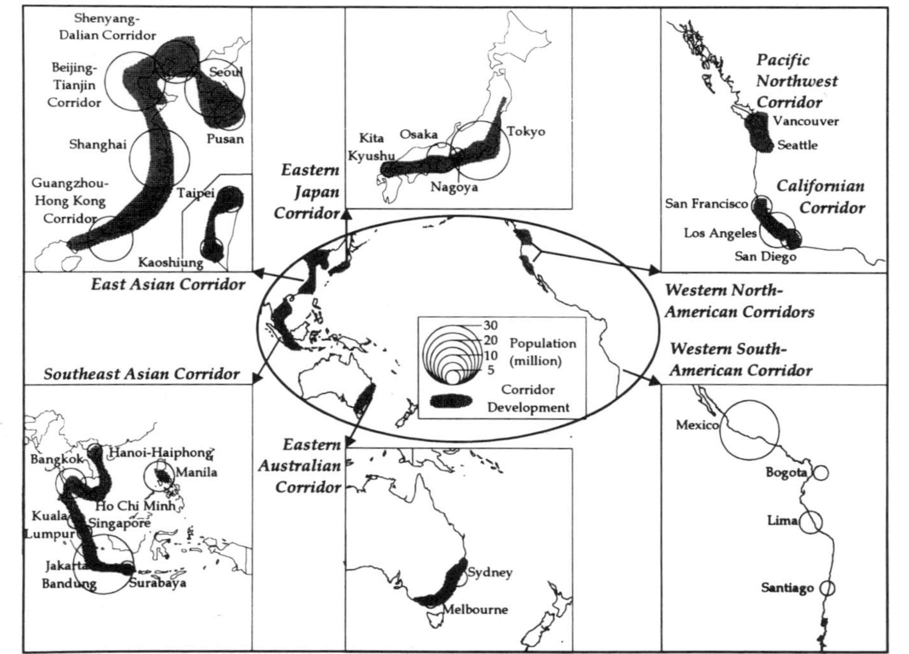


Source: United Nations, 1991 (after Peter J. Rimmer, 'International transport and communications interactions between Pacific Asia's emerging world cities', in Fu-chen Lo and Yue-man Yeung (eds), *Emerging World Cities in Pacific Asia*, Tokyo: UN University Press, 1996, pp. 48-97).

Figure 3.3. ASIA-PACIFIC RIM (Cartogram to show distribution of GDP emphasising coastal regions of China, USA and Canada)

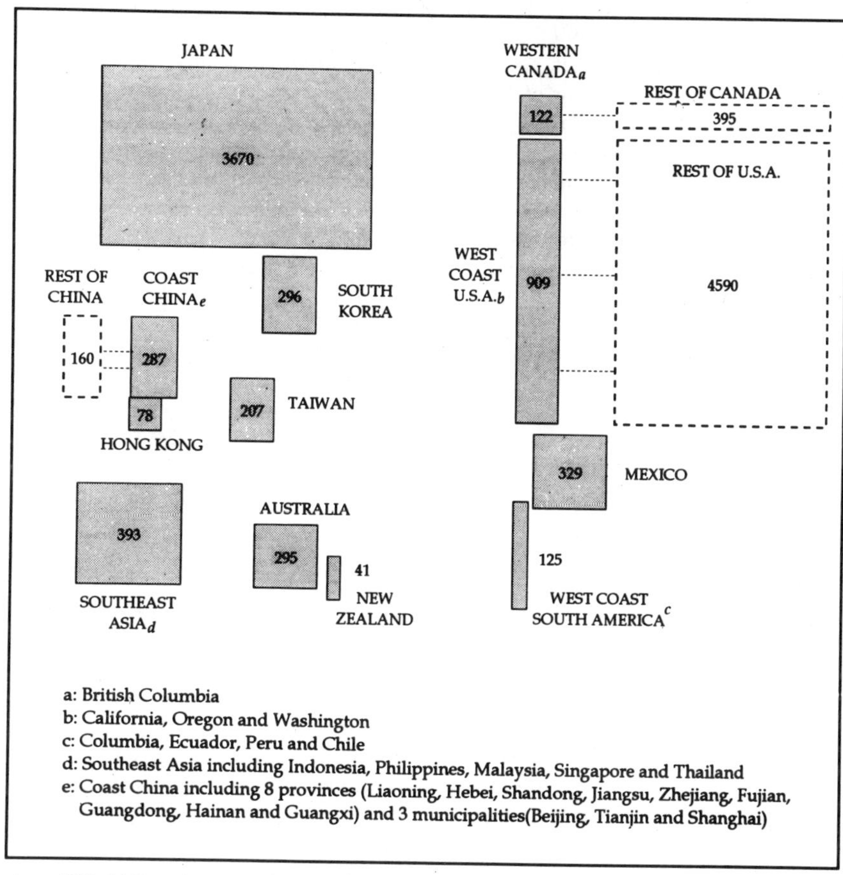


Sources: 'World Development Report 1994', OUP, pp. 166-7.
Data for Canada from *Canadian Economic Observer*, April 1995, p. 58.
Data for USA from *Statistical Abstract of the United States 1994*, p. 449.
Data for China from *Statistical Yearbook of China 1994*, p. 32 and 36.
Data for Taiwan from *Economic Statistics Annual Taiwan Area, the Republic of China 1993.*

option. But this may be altogether too optimistic; the globalisation process has imperatives which challenge sustainability. For the present these imperatives are in the ascendancy.

## *Acknowledgements*

This paper is drawn from research carried out over the last decade funded by the Social Sciences and Humanities Research Council of Canada and the International Development Research Council of Canada. I should like to thank Catherine Griffiths for working on the graphics and editorial aspects of this paper. Mark Wang has produced the majority of the figures.

## NOTES

[1] 'Sustainability' is a concept which receives much currency these days. In this paper I have used it to mean a form of 'development that meets the needs of the present without compromising the ability of the future generations to meet their own needs' (World Commission on Environment and Development, *Our Common Future*, OUP, 1987, p. 443). Implicit in my interpretation of sustainable development is the assumption that the highly unequal use of resources (heavily concentrated in the developed countries) and the limited but expanding demand for resources to satisfy the basic needs of the developing countries will lead to 'unsustainable development'. I prefer to identify the problem of creating 'sustainable development' as resting in the realm of the political economy , for if states had the desire to implement comprehensive plans for sustainable development, there is no doubt they could be carried out. However, the result would rest upon the acceptance of these policies by political elites, capitalist managers and the middle classes who support many of these governments. There is as yet little evidence of a global or indeed national will to implement policies of 'sustainable development'.

[2] See the excellent discussion of these issues in Ash Amin and N. Thrift, 'Institutional issues for the European regions: from markets and plans to socioeconomics and powers of association', *Economy and Society*, 24 (1), 1995, pp. 41-65.

[3] I. Wallerstein, *The Modern World-System*, New York: Academic Press, 1974.

[4] P. Dicken, *Global Shift: The Internationalization of Economic Activity*, London: Paul Chapman, 1992.

[5] Richard J. Barnett and John Cavanagh, *Global Dreams. Imperial Corporations and the New World Order*, New York: Simon and Schuster, 1994, p. 15.

[6] G.J.R. Linge and D.J. Walmsley, *Global Transformation and Social Development. An Australian Perspective*, Occasional Paper Series 2/1995, Canberra: Academy of Social Sciences, 1995, pp. 1-2.

[7] M. Castells, *The Informational City*, Oxford: Blackwell, 1989, p. 348.

[8] Linge and Walmsley, op. cit., 1995, p. 3.

[9] See F. Fukuyama, *The End of History and the Last Man*, New York: Free Press, 1992; W. Armstrong and T.G. McGee, *Theatres of Accumulation: Studies in Asian and Latin American Urbanization,* New York: Methuen, 1985; and D. Harvey , *The Condition of Postmodernity: An Enquiry into the Origins of Cultural Change,* Oxford: Blackwell, 1989.

[10] B.W. Barber, 'Jihad vs. Macworld', *Atlantic Monthly*, March 1992, pp. 58-63.

[11] A. Appadurai, 'Disjuncture and dif ference in the global cultural economy', *Public Culture*, 2 (2), 1992, pp. 1-24.

[12] D.J. Haraway, *Simians, Cyborgs, and Women. The Reinvention of Natur e*, London: Free Association Books, 1991.

[13] See N. Thrift, 'Inhuman geographies - landscapes of speed, light and power ', in P. Cloke et al, *Writing the Rural: Five Cultural Geographies* , London: Paul Chapman, 1994.

[14] Benedict Anderson, *Imagined Communities: Reflections on the Origins and Spr ead of Nationalism*, London: Verso, 1993.

[15] While the emergence of NICs and oil exporting countries has created a class of semi-developed countries, this is not included here. Thus the division between developed and developing follows the usual division between the OECD countries and the more developed socialist countries and the rest of the world.

[16] United Nations, *World Urbanization Prospects 1991,* Department of International Economic and Social Affairs, ST/ESA/SER.A/121, 1991.

[17] P. Bairoch, *Cities and Economic Development Fr om the Dawn of Histor y to the Present,* Chicago University Press, 1988.

[18] Armstrong and McGee, op. cit., 1985.

[19] As, for instance, in Thailand, Japan, and China (T.G. McGee, *The Southeast Asian City*, New York; Praeger, 1967; and 'The emergence of Desakota regions in Asia: expanding a hypothesis', in N. Ginsburg et al, *The Extended Metropolis: Settlement Transition in Asia*, Honolulu: University of Hawaii Press, 1991, pp. 3-25).

[20] This paper does not attempt to deal with the Islamic countries of North Africa and the Middle East. In broad terms the historical patterns of their incorporation into the global system are not very different from that of Africa or some parts of Asia-Pacific. There are excellent accounts of the different historical experience of Africa and Latin America in R. Stren, 'Urban policy in Africa: a political analysis', *African Studies Review (Cambridge)*, 15 (3), 1972, pp. 489-516; and B. Roberts, *Cities of Peasants*, London: Edward Arnold, 1978.

[21] B. Roberts, 'Urbanisation, migration and development', *Sociology Forum* (Austin), 4, 1989, pp. 665-91.

[22] Armstrong and McGee, op. cit., 1985.

[23] United Nations, op. cit., 1991.

[24] Brian J.L. Berry, *Urbanisation and Counter-urbanisation*, Vol. 11, Urban Affairs Annual Reviews, Beverly Hills: Sage Publications, 1976; H.W. Richardson, 'The big, bad city: megacity myth', paper presented at the meeting of the American Association for the Advancement of Science, San Francisco, 1988; A.G. Champion (ed.), *Counterurbanisation: The Changing Pace and Nature of Population Deconcentration*, London: Edward Arnold, 1989.

[25] Ginsburg et al, op. cit., 1991.

[26] Scott Macleod and T.G. McGee, 'Emerging extended metropolitan regions in the Asia-Pacific urban system: a case study of the Singapore-Johor-Riau growth triangle', in Yue-man Yeung and Fu-chen Lo (eds), *The Asia-Pacific System: Towards the 21st Century*, Tokyo: UN University Press, forthcoming.

[27] Alan Gilbert, *The Latin American City*, London: Latin American Bureau, 1994.

[28] T.G. McGee and I.M. Robinson, *The Mega-Urban Regions of Southeast Asia*, Vancouver: UBC Press, forthcoming.

[29] Carlos Antonio De Mattos, 'The moderate efficiency of population distribution policies in developing countries', in *Population Distribution and Migration. Proceedings of the UN Expert Meeting on Population Distribution and Migration*, UN Population Division, 1994, pp. 220-40.

[30] Ibid, p. 221.

[31] Ibid, p. 223.

[32] Gilbert, op. cit., 1994, p. 169.

[33] Thomas P. Rohlen, *A Mediterranean Model for Asian Regionalism. Cosmopolitan Cities and Nation States in Asia*, Asia Pacific Research Center, Stanford University, 1995, p. 2.

[34] This sub-division of the system was first used in a paper presented by the author in 1986; see T.G. McGee, 'The changing Pacific economy: challenges to the post-industrial economy', in R. Hayter, and P.D. Wilde (eds), *Industrial Transformation and Challenge in Australia and Canada*, Ottawa: Carleton University Press, 1990, for more detail on the historical justification of this sub-division.

[35] For this paper I have not attempted to produce a comprehensive set of statistics on the transactions within the region. See Rohlen, op. cit., 1995.

[36] See in particular P.W. Rimmer, 'Transport and communications in the Pacific economic zone during the early 21st century', in Yue-man Yeung, *Pacific Asia in the 21st Century: Geographical and Development Perspectives*, Hong Kong: The Chinese University Press, 1993, pp. 195-232; Howard Dick and P.J. Rimmer, 'The trans-Pacific economy. A network approach to spatial structure', *Asian Geographer*, 12 (1 & 2), 1993, pp. 5-18; Rohlen, op. cit., 1995.

[37] Amin and Thrift, op. cit., 1995, pp. 41-67.

# 4. PACIFIC RIM TRADE AND APEC LIBERALISATION

*Ron Sandrey*

Growing interdependence in world trade and the increasingly important role played in it by the Asia-Pacific region have characterised the world economy since the 1970s. The rapid growth of Japan in the 1950s and 1960s was duplicated by the NIEs of the region during the 1970s and 80s, and followed by the middle-income ASEAN countries during the 1980s and early 90s. China has continued this trend in the late 1980s and 90s. Completing the Pacific Rim power base are the still dominant economies of North America, the developed and latterly growing economies of Australasia, and the 're-emerging' economies of the Americas a decade after their debt crises.

Most of the core economies surrounding the Pacific Rim are now members of APEC. From its beginnings in 1989, APEC moved very quickly to the November 1994 Bogor Declaration of Common Resolve, which announced the commitment to achieve the goal of free and open trade and investment in the Asia-Pacific region for the industrialised countries by 2010 and the others no later than the year 2020. A primary motivation for APEC was the belief among members that this dynamic business-led growth was bringing economic interdependence and sustained economic growth to the region; it was contended that the liberal multilateral trade regime should be preserved and strengthened.

The objective of this paper is to examine the future of the Asia-Pacific region, and in particular the implications of APEC's Declaration of Common Resolve. The examination is set against the background of current economic and trading patterns, the current regional groupings of CER, AFTA and NAFTA, and the GATT Uruguay Round (UR). Attention is also given to the likely place of China in the early part of the next century and the implications for APEC. The region has changed dramatically over the last quarter of a century. This change is continuing and by the early part of next century when APEC liberalisation is scheduled it will be different again. The chapter concentrates on the major economies within the region, and addresses neither the issue of regional income distribution within economies nor the role of some of the lesser economies.

### *Background*

APEC contains some 40% of the world's population. The members truly reflect the tapestry of the region, from the US, with nearly half of the region's economic output and wealth, to Papua New Guinea and Brunei which are tiny, to China, the re-emerging giant. APEC members are detailed in Table

4.1 along with their economic profiles as measured by GDP, and, as a comparison, the per capita estimates of both the GNP and the Purchasing Power Parity (PPP) estimates of that GNP. PPP adjusts GNP for factors such as exchange rates and relative prices, and is considered by many to be the best indicator of the real wealth of a country. It is expressed as a relative ranking, using US per capita purchasing power as the index. The PPP analysis shows the dramatically increased economic importance of China, ASEAN, Mexico and Chile.

Table 4.1. MEMBER ECONOMIES OF APEC

| *Economy* | *GDP 1993, US$bn.* | *% World GDP* | *Population 1993 m.* | *GNP 1993, per capita US$* | *PPP estimate of US$ per capita* |
|---|---|---|---|---|---|
| USA | 6,260 | 27.1 | 258 | 24,740 | 24,740 |
| Japan | 4,214 | 18.2 | 125 | 31,490 | 20,850 |
| China | 426 | 1.8 | 1,178 | 490 | 2,330 |
| Canada | 477 | 2.1 | 29 | 19,970 | 20,230 |
| Korea | 331 | 1.4 | 44 | 7,660 | 9,630 |
| Mexico | 343 | 1.5 | 90 | 3,610 | 6,810 |
| Australia | 289 | 1.3 | 18 | 17,500 | 17,910 |
| Taiwan | 190 | 1.0 | 21 | 10,566 | na |
| Indonesia | 145 | 0.63 | 187 | 740 | 3,150 |
| Thailand | 125 | 0.54 | 58 | 2,110 | 6,260 |
| Hong Kong | 90 | 0.37 | 6 | 18,060 | 21,560 |
| Malaysia | 64 | 0.28 | 19 | 3,140 | 7,930 |
| Philippines | 54 | 0.23 | 65 | 850 | 2,670 |
| Singapore | 55 | 0.24 | 2.8 | 19,970 | 19,510 |
| New Zealand | 44 | 0.19 | 3.5 | 12,600 | 16,040 |
| Chile | 44 | 0.19 | 14 | 3,170 | 8,400 |
| PNG | 5 | 0.02 | 4 | 1,130 | 2,350 |
| Brunei | 4 | 0.02 | 0.3 | 1,605 | na |
| *APEC* | *13,160* | *57.11* | *2,122.6* | | |

Source: APEC for Taiwan; World Bank, *World Development Report, 1995*, New York: OUP, 1995, elsewhere.

The assumption is made that APEC membership will remain as it was during 1995. However, several nations, most of them with close ties to the Asia-Pacific Rim, are actively interested in APEC membership. A fuller Pacific Rim membership might include Russia, India, Viet Nam and several of the Central and South American countries, for example, which would further contribute to the dynamics and diversity of the APEC organisation.

Accepting the World Bank's rather controversial forecasts (discussed later), within a generation China may overtake the US as the world's largest economy and APEC will have 7 of the 10 largest world economies: China, the US, Japan, Indonesia, Korea, Thailand and Taiwan. Currently, it only has four: the US, Japan, China and Canada. This demonstrates the rise of Asian economies as the power bases of the world and the changing role of the so-called currently developed countries, and sets the likely scene for 2020 when APEC liberalisation is scheduled

However, a note of caution must be added. While recognising impressive Asian growth, recent evidence suggests it has been largely built on an extraordinary mobilisation of resources with associated high savings and investment rates.[1] To obtain the extrapolated growth figures above, these economies will need to improve their technological efficiency, efficiencies which still lag behind the Western industrial nations and Japan.

### *Trade Flows*

Associated with this growth, and to a large extent driving it, is the expansion of trade in the region. APEC was the source of 46% of world exports in 1994, or 64% if trade which does not cross the wider European Union-12 border is excluded. From 1988 to 1993, trade among APEC members grew at an average annual rate of about 9.0%. In contrast, world trade growth averaged 6.0% over the same period. Intra-regional trade is important to APEC, accounting for 70% in 1993. This figure grew rapidly (from 53.4% in 1980) over the 1980s, but has since stabilised.

World merchandise trade increased by 9% during 1994, the largest increase since 1976. This expansion was attributed to the recovery in Europe, and continued expansion in Asia, North America and Latin America. A reflection of the internationalisation of the world's economies can be shown when trade growth is compared with the lesser 3.5% increase in global merchandise output.

Within the region, ASEAN and China's share of trade have increased in recent years, while the region's exports to the United States and Japan have decreased in percentage terms. The EU remains the most important counterpart to APEC, and has run a trade deficit with the region in recent years. In short, the region's dynamic growth has resulted from the enhanced competitiveness of ASEAN and China in particular, with this change boosting their exports which in turn allows them to increase imports. This encouraged the dynamic Asian members of APEC to act as an engine for the region to boost overall growth during a period when the two largest parties, Japan and the US, were going through a consolidation phase.

Table 4.2 summarises the world and APEC major trade flows for 1993. Intra-EU trade is about one quarter of total world trade, with intra-APEC trade somewhat more. NAFTA trade is about 8% of world and 25% of APEC trade. US trade with East Asia highlights an imbalance of almost 2 to 1. The other major flows are as listed, with US/Japan the major flow outside of NAFTA.

Table 4.2. WORLD TRADE FLOWS, 1993 (US$bn.)

| | | | |
|---|---|---|---|
| World | World | 3,645 | |
| West Europe | West Europe | 903 | |
| APEC | APEC | 1,188 | |
| NAFTA | NAFTA | 301 | |
| *(A)* | *(B)* | *from (A) to (B)* | *to (B) from (A)* |
| APEC | EU | 160 | 230 |
| US | East Asia | 125 | 238 |
| Hong Kong | China | 44 | 22 |
| Japan | Korea | 19 | 12 |
| Japan | China | 17 | 16 |
| Japan | Taiwan | 23 | 9 |
| US | Japan | 48 | 106 |
| US | Korea | 15 | 18 |
| US | China | 9 | 17 |
| US | Hong Kong | 10 | 31 |
| US | Taiwan | 17 | 23 |

Source: GATT, *International Trade: Trends and Statistics*, Geneva, 1994; and United Nations, *International Trade Statistics Yearbook*, New York: UN, 1995.

Table 4.3 details trade flows in East Asia. Intra-East Asia trade accounts for just over one third of Japanese trade flows (the lowest) to highs above 50% for Indonesia and Malaysia. These flows are now greater than the trade with NAFTA (excluding the Philippines), a change that took place during the 1980s. The EU is the other main trading partner. Japan dominates all trading relationships within the region except the Singapore-Malaysia and Hong Kong-China flows.

The share of agricultural products in world merchandise trade over the period 1970 to 1994 declined from 15% to 9.3%. Data for 1994 is summarised in Table 4.4.

The principal flows are

- Intra-Asia
- North America to Asia (mostly Japan)
- Intra-North America
- Latin America to firstly Europe and secondly North America
- North America to Europe
- Both Europe and Asia to North America.

Service trade flows are difficult to quantify, partly because there is no agreement on the statistical definition of traded services, but mostly because of the difficulty of identification. There is, however, agreement that available data significantly underestimate these flows. Official data show

Table 4.3. ASIAN TRADE FLOWS, 1994 (US$bn. and %)

| *Origin* | *Destination* | | | | | | | | | | | | | | |
|---|---|---|---|---|---|---|---|---|---|---|---|---|---|---|---|
| | *Japan* | *Taiwan* | *Korea* | *China* | *Hong Kong* | *Singapore* | *Thailand* | *India* | *Philippines* | *Malaysia* | *Asia* | | *NAFTA* | | *EU* |
| | | | | | | | | | | | *$bn.* | *%* | *$bn.* | *%* | *%* |
| Japan | | 24 | 24 | 19 | 26 | 20 | 15 | 8 | 6 | 12 | 153 | 38 | 130 | 32 | 14 |
| Taiwan | 10 | | 2 | 13 | 13 | 4 | 2 | 1 | 1 | 3 | 47 | 50 | 28 | 29 | 13 |
| Korea | 14 | 3 | | 6 | 8 | 4 | 2 | 3 | 1 | 2 | 42 | 43 | 23 | 24 | 10 |
| Hong Kong | 8 | 4 | 2 | 50 | | 4 | 1 | 1 | 2 | 1 | 74 | 49 | 38 | 25 | 14 |
| China | 22 | 2 | 4 | | 32 | 3 | 1 | 1 | 1 | 1 | 67 | 56 | 23 | 19 | 13 |
| Singapore | 7 | 4 | 3 | 2 | 8 | | 5 | na | 2 | 19 | 50 | 52 | 19 | 19 | 13 |
| Thailand | 8 | 1 | 1 | 1 | 2 | 4 | | .3 | .2 | 1 | 18 | 43 | 10 | 25 | 17 |
| India | 12 | 2 | 3 | 1 | 1 | 3 | .4 | | .4 | 1 | 21 | 53 | 7 | 17 | 15 |
| Philippines | 2 | .5 | .3 | .2 | 1 | 1 | .2 | .1 | | .2 | 5 | 38 | 5 | 41 | 15 |
| Malaysia | 7 | 2 | 2 | 2 | 3 | 12 | 2 | 1 | 1 | | 31 | 53 | 13 | 23 | 13 |

Source: IMF Direction of World Trade Statistics (Taiwan is derived).

Table 4.4. REGIONAL FLOWS OF FOOD EXPORTS, 1994

| | *US$ billion* | *% Share* |
|---|---|---|
| Intra-West Europe | 160 | 32.9 |
| Intra-Asia | 59 | 12.0 |
| North America to Asia | 36 | 7.5 |
| Intra-North America | 24 | 5.0 |
| Latin America to West Europe | 18 | 3.7 |
| North America to West Europe | 16 | 3.2 |
| Latin America to North America | 13 | 2.6 |
| Asia to West Europe | 14 | 2.8 |
| West Europe to CEEC[a] | 11 | 2.2 |
| West Europe to Asia | 12 | 2.1 |
| Total Above | 363 | 74.0 |
| *World* | *487* | *100* |

Note: [a] Central and Eastern European Countries
Source: GATT.

a gradual increase in world service trade as a percentage of merchandise trade, increasing from 21% in 1980 to 26% in 1994. Table 4.5 outlines the major service flows for APEC.

Among the APEC economies, the US and Japan are the largest exporters, followed by Hong Kong and Singapore. Japan and the US are again

Table 4.5. WORLD SERVICE TRADE, 1994 DATA

| | *Exports* | | *Imports* | | *Balance* |
|---|---|---|---|---|---|
| *Exporter* | *Value US$ bn.* | *Share % World* | *Value US$ bn.* | *Share % World* | *US$bn.* |
| US | 178.2 | 16.2 | 120.7 | 11.4 | 57.5 |
| Canada | 17.6 | 1.6 | 25.5 | 2.4 | -7.9 |
| Mexico | 14.4 | 1.3 | 12.1 | 1.1 | 2.3 |
| Japan | 57.2 | 5.2 | 109.2 | 10.3 | -52 |
| Taiwan | 13.5 | 1.2 | 21.1 | 2.0 | -7.6 |
| Korea | 18.8 | 1.7 | 20.3 | 1.9 | -1.5 |
| Hong Kong | 32.5 | 3.0 | 18.6 | 1.8 | 13.9 |
| Canada | 12.5 | 1.1 | 13.1 | 1.2 | -0.6 |
| APEC | 414.7 | 37.7 | 414 | 39.1 | 1 |
| EU(12) | 420.3 | 38.2 | 412 | 38.9 | 8.3 |
| *World* | *1,099* | *100* | *1,060* | *100* | *39* |

Source: GATT.

the largest importers, followed by Canada and Taiwan. Highlighted is the large US service trade surplus and the Japanese deficit. In both cases these offset their respective deficits and surpluses in merchandise trade by 40%. Hong Kong and Singapore recorded large surpluses, while Canada and Taiwan recorded equally large deficits.

The issue of services liberalisation is gaining international momentum, and therefore the APEC examination and declaration are timely. The developed countries are moving into high-tech, value-added activities, with the developing world seeking to exploit its comparative advantage in low-cost labour. To date, the services liberalisation agenda has been dominated by access arguments amongst the major developed economies, and the developed economies have strengthened their high tech advantage in the developing world. The converse, the access of the low-labour-cost developing world to richer markets, remains protected through the movement-of-persons criterion. Thus, one issue will be the shape of any final deal to be reached between developed and developing countries on the access to be granted for the supply of services through investment and that for the supply of services by the movement of persons.

### *The GATT UR Outcome*

On 15 December 1993, the world's longest and most complex series of trade negotiations came to an end. Agriculture was brought more firmly into the General Agreement on Tariffs and Trade, agreement was reached to free up distorted multi-fibre textile markets, services came under the GATT umbrella, and a future work programme for the new WTO in the 'new' areas such as trade and the environment was signalled.

When the GATT was formed, average industrial tariffs were around 40% in the developed countries. By the start of the UR, this average had reduced to 4.7%; it will further reduce in five equal annual instalments to just under 3%. The outcome also includes the elimination of tariffs in major industrial markets for 14 sectors, an increase in market access security through higher levels of tariff bindings (levels of tariffs to which countries commit themselves not to exceed without compensation), and greater security for industrial products entering developed and transition economies. It includes an agreement to phase out restrictions on textile trade over a 10-year period, and an agreement to strengthen the rules associated with disputes settlements, anti-dumping cases, subsidies, safeguards and rules of origin. Intellectual property rights have been strengthened and investment rules have been clarified.

For agriculture, non-tariff barriers such as the EU variable levy on dairy products have been 'tariffied' or converted to an equivalent tariff value. These will be reduced in industrial countries by an average of 36%, and agricultural export subsidies and domestic support must also decline. Finally, (a) there is the continuation clause which requires signatories to resume negotiations in the fifth year of implementation and assess the result, and (b) there are guarantees that tariffs will not increase without compensation.

On the basis of the outcome, some preliminary estimates of the changes to resource-based trade flows in the APEC region may be made. Given the degree of protection in selected markets, and given the likely cut of perhaps one sixth in these levels, the following commodity/country changes are likely:

- Dairy: enhanced production and exports from Australia and New Zealand, with these flows going to the EU, Japan, the US and possibly ASEAN.
- Meat products: a similar scenario to dairy, but with greater imports into Korea from the US and Australasia, with ASEAN's becoming less relevant.
- Rice: increased flows from Thailand, the US and Australia into Japan and Korea.
- Grains: increased flows from Australia and possibly Canada and the US to Japan, Korea and China.
- Horticultural products: increased imports into most of the Asian destinations.

APEC liberalisation must use the UR outcome as the basis for further gains. In the final analysis, a picture emerges from the GATT Round outcome of agriculture falling short of what it could and should have been. However, the counterfactual position is what the world's trading system may have looked like in the absence of an agreement, with a possible trade war between major participants. From this perspective, and considering the dynamic benefits from even the reduced benefits of the Round, the agreement makes a major contribution to the region's prosperity.

In addition to the GATT outcome, there are two regional trading agreements within APEC that, at least by 2010, will be approaching the openness and completeness of the current CER Agreement between Australia and New Zealand. These are the NAFTA between the US, Canada and Mexico, and the AFTA between the ASEAN economies. Further extensions to both are likely within the time frame under examination. These developments, along with unilateral liberalisation from APEC members, can be thought of as analogous to the fitting together of sub-sets of a jigsaw puzzle; the more small pieces that are connected, the easier to complete the picture.

## *The CER Agreement and Further Liberalisation*

The Australia New Zealand Closer Economic Relations Trade Agreement came into force on 1 January 1983. It replaced an earlier trade agreement, and was negotiated against a backdrop of dissatisfaction with its managed and incremental approach and with a view that greater liberalisation of mutual trade would benefit both economies and hasten desired structural adjustment. The agreement is one of the most comprehensive of its type in the world and, given the external tariff reduction policies of the two countries, one of the most open. As such, CER is a useful case study for wider APEC liberalisation.[2]

The first stage, stripping away all restrictions on the trading of goods, is complete. The 1988 review accelerated this by five years, and on 1 July 1990 all remaining tariffs, quantitative restrictions and export incentives on merchandise trade were removed. The review also widened the agreement to cover services and deepened it by extending into areas such as business law and industry assistance. Trans-Tasman anti-dumping provisions were removed, with both countries relying upon their domestic competition laws to impose disciplines.

The Trade in Services Protocol came into force on 1 January 1989, providing free trade in services based on the concept of national treatment with exceptions on 'negative lists' inscribed by each government. Exceptions include some aspects of telecommunications, broadcasting, maritime transport, civil aviation, postal services and insurance services. A review in December 1990 highlighted New Zealand's faster approach to and greater flexibility in pursuing liberalisation. Agreement was reached that, where possible, the exempted services would be brought under CER. In a separate agreement on aviation, plans were finalised for the phasing in of a single aviation market by 1 November 1994, although this was subsequently delayed by the Australians.

In March 1991, Australia announced a continuation of its external tariff reforms, with the general rate being phased down from the 10-15% level that would have applied in 1992 to 5% in 1996. Protection for textiles, clothing, footwear and automobiles has been reduced, but not by as much.

In 1994, New Zealand announced a further series of external tariff reductions from 1996 through to 2000. This continues the major reductions in tariffs and other import barriers which have taken place since the mid-1980s. Tariffs will be reduced to four levels by 2000, with only motor vehicles and their components, carpets, apparel, some textiles and footwear being above the base 5% level.

These reductions will position both countries well for the final stages of APEC liberalisation, with Australia requiring slightly more adjustment than New Zealand. Although the CER agreement is not a Common Market with an agreed level of external tariffs, comparisons between the two levels of tariff protection are valid. The interest lies in the margins of preference which are afforded under the agreement to exporters from one partner into the market of the other and to a lesser but not negligible extent, the differences in the tariff regime as an indicator of the remaining adjustments to meet the APEC Declaration objectives. There is a danger in trade agreements that trade diversion, the consequence of buying from a market with lower tariffs and not the cheapest source of supply, will be a real cost.

However, as the external tariffs of the partners reduce, so does the potential for these trade diversion costs.

CER represents an important process in the internationalisation of the New Zealand economy. Whereas a quarter of a century ago Australia exported three times the value of goods to New Zealand that it imported, today the balance is about even. Granted, this is a mercantilistic approach, but the growth in recent years has been in manufactured exports to Australia. This provided a (closing) window of opportunity for the New Zealand sector to adjust to full international competition.

Equally importantly, it provided a major spur to changing the attitudes towards trade liberalisation in both countries, but particularly so in New Zealand. The 1980s were a tumultuous time for New Zealanders involving radical economic change, and the CER window of opportunity greatly assisted in changing the emphasis from inward-looking domestic policies based on import substitution to recognising the greater benefits of an internationally competitive economy. Rather than concerning itself with lobbying for political support, the private sector in New Zealand began to think about managing international business. CER is a step towards APEC liberalisation, and one, along with the internationalisation process from the mid-1980s, which will make the acceptance of the APEC Declaration a smooth transition for both New Zealand and Australia. Many of their hard economic adjustments have been done.

### *ASEAN Free Trade Area*

The countries of ASEAN – Singapore, Malaysia, Thailand, Indonesia, the Philippines, Brunei and Viet Nam – account for nearly 2% of world output, 5.6% of world trade, and slightly over 6% of the world's population. While including developing members, it also includes Singapore, a small but wealthy duty-free port with limited tariff or border protection. It therefore has many of the ingredients of a 'mini APEC', though weighted towards developing economies.

For the first 20 years, ASEAN concentrated on political and diplomatic cooperation, but from 1987 increased attention has been placed upon economic matters. The ASEAN Summit meeting of 1992 emphasised this by approving the AFTA initiative. The desire for an AFTA reflected the success of the outward-looking, market-oriented policies of Indonesia, Malaysia and Thailand; increasing economic links between the ASEAN countries; a defensive response to developments in Europe and North America; concerns about the challenges posed to ASEAN economies by the rapid development of other Asian countries, and in particular China; and an (unstated) desire to give ASEAN a new raison d'être as the politically important Cambodia issue receded. The objectives include growth through stronger economic linkages and increasing the attractiveness of ASEAN countries for FDI.

The mechanism used is a Common Effective Preferential Tariffs (CEPT) Scheme, introduced on 1 January 1993. CEPT covers *all* manufactured products, including capital goods and processed agricultural products, with at least 40% ASEAN content. Unprocessed agricultural products, together with services, will be included at a later date. The original plan has been accelerated, with the realisation date now 1 January 2003 when the CEPT will be between 0 and 5%. A fast track provision applies to some goods, and, conversely, provision is made for the temporary exclusion of selected goods in the short term. The agreement also contains a commitment to removing non-tariff barriers hindering intra-ASEAN trade.

The dynamics of economic growth in ASEAN and the degree of complementarity which exists between CER semi-processed resources and ASEAN labour-intensive light manufacturing make ASEAN and CER natural trading partners. Any linkages between CER and AFTA which can be formulated in advance of the APEC liberalisation may well provide a mutually beneficial adjustment opportunity.

An indication of the barriers to trade can be found in Table 4.6, which reports on the weighted average, and bilateral tariffs levied by the importing country on all merchandise trade from the respective exporting country. The data is from country data filed with the GATT and pre-dates AFTA. Intra-ASEAN tariff rates were high, indicating that large trade flow changes may result from AFTA.

The timing of AFTA fits well with the APEC plan. At the completion of the 10-year AFTA period, there are still 17 years under the current time-

Table 4.6. AVERAGE BILATERAL TARIFF RATES FOR AFTA

| | | | *Importer* | | |
|---|---|---|---|---|---|
| *Exporter* | *Indonesia* | *Malaysia* | *Philippines* | *Singapore* | *Thailand* |
| Indonesia | | 9.1 | 23.6 | 0.6 | 34.2 |
| Malaysia | 12.3 | | 22.6 | 1.2 | 38.7 |
| Philippines | 10.8 | 10.6 | | 0.3 | 41.6 |
| Singapore | 11.0 | 8.1 | 22.1 | | 27.5 |
| Thailand | 9.7 | 12.9 | 24.7 | 0.4 | |

Source: T. Hertel et al, *Liberalising Manufacturing Trade in a Changing World Economy*, Paper presented to the Uruguay Round and the Developing Economies Conference, Washington D.C.: World Bank, 26-27 January 1995.

table before the AFTA economies will finally fully implement the APEC declaration objectives. This will enable them to build upon the history of success of free trading amongst themselves before the final adjustments are called for. In many ways the success or otherwise of AFTA will provide a useful barometer to APEC prospects, with an accelerated programme for AFTA the best possible outcome for APEC liberalisation progress.

### *The North American Free Trade Agreement*

The NAFTA agreement, between Canada, the United States and Mexico, came into force on 1 January 1994 and is dedicated, *inter alia*, to the progressive elimination of all tariffs on goods qualifying under the rules of origin definition. For most goods and all practical purposes, the tariffs will be phased out over a 5- or 10-year period, with some sensitive agricultural and manufactured goods such as the motor vehicle, clothing and apparel sectors adjusting over a 15-year period. Agricultural trade flows are large within NAFTA, and in the final outcome the political sensitivity of the agricultural sector prevailed. Canada's sensitive supply control industries of dairy, poultry and eggs remain as exclusions to the agreement, although by 2008 all other sectors of agricultural trade will be free.

Major differences between CER and NAFTA include these exemptions, the continuation of anti-dumping within NAFTA, the formalised disputes settlement provisions under NAFTA and the more restricting rules of origin criteria under NAFTA.

Given the differences in the economies of the NAFTA participants and the degree of protection afforded to some parts of these economies, one would expect trade diversion to occur over the implementation period and beyond. The CER agreement has been characterised by the lowering of external barriers to trade in both economies in this way. Such a lowering reduces trade diversion costs, with the implication that NAFTA will face more of an adjustment as part of the APEC process. However, the APEC adjustment will have been foreshadowed and anticipated by the NAFTA process itself.

### *NAFTA Extensions and the Free Trade in the Americas Agreement (FTAA)*

The recent FTAA provides for the convergence of the free trade agreements which already operate in the Americas, and the timetable for this has been set ahead of the APEC objective. This may provide preferential access for the Latin economies into North American markets ahead of that same access being sought by the developing Asian economies, providing an impetus to APEC members.

How well are the Central and South American economies placed to converge into NAFTA? Economic liberalisation gained momentum in the late 1980s in the region, and most of the economies have undergone major structural reforms. Table 4.7 shows the openness and trends of most of the economies concerned, along with their export trade flows for 1994 to indicate their relative importance.

Excluding Mexico, Brazil and Argentina dominate the region economically. Both, along with Uruguay and Paraguay, are members of the MERCOSUR trade agreement. To put MERCOSUR in perspective, its GDP is greater than that of CER, its share of world trade is almost the same,

Table 4.7. TRADE RESTRICTIONS IN SELECTED LATIN AMERICAN ECONOMIES

| | *Average Tariffs* | | *1994 Exports* |
|---|---|---|---|
| *Country* | *1985* | *1991-92* | *US$bn.* |
| Argentina | 28 | 15 | 15.7 |
| Bolivia | 20 | 8 | 0.9 |
| Brazil | 80 | 21.1 | 43.6 |
| Chile | 36 | 11 | 11.6 |
| Colombia | 83 | 6.7 | 8.9 |
| Guatemala | 50 | 19 | 1.7 |
| Mexico | 34 | 4 | 60.8 |
| Peru | 64 | 15 | 4.5 |
| Uruguay | 32 | 12 | 1.9 |
| Venezuela | 30 | 17 | 15.7 |

Source: IMF and GATT.

while its population base is almost ten times as large. Mexico, with exports greater than MERCOSUR but population and total GDP less, is already in NAFTA, and Chile is likely to join. Clearly the economic reforms which these countries have undertaken place them well for free trade in the Western hemisphere.

## *The Importance of China in APEC Liberalisation*

Since 1978, the beginning of its reform process, China's output has quadrupled. Using conventional measurements, the country's GDP is a mere 1.8% of the world's and the Chinese are still among the world's poorest people. However, this conventional measurement is misleading, as indicated by PPP analysis in Table 4.1, although several uncertainties are in turn associated with these controversial estimates. While the recent growth rates can be estimated with some degree of certainty, the actual level of the value of Chinese output is much harder to calculate. Lardy[3] provides an excellent assessment of the issues and problems involved. In the final analysis, by 2020 (or more likely a decade or two later) China may be the world's largest economy. This conclusion results from accepting some of the elevated base levels of national wealth, an extrapolation of recent growth rates, the sheer size of the country and some noble assumptions about the removal of major impediments to future growth. Such a prediction is less fanciful when viewed against the achievements of firstly Japan, secondly the NIEs of Asia, thirdly ASEAN, and finally and most importantly the progress of China to date, notwithstanding the measurement difficulties and reflecting the way in which her economic progress follows that of the earlier Asian growth economies. Although based mainly on factor mobilisation, there is evidence that recent spectacular economic growth also involves some enskilling and productivity growth, a view supported also by Lin (see chapter 16). What are the implications of this potential change for APEC?

There are several questions involved. One is China's likely economic development route and the structure of China's trade over the first two decades of the next century, two factors inextricably linked. This leads to the crucial issues of the relationship with fellow East Asian economies and, possibly the most important issue of all, the relationship with the United States. For under the terms of the Bogor declaration, the US market will be free and open to China 10 years before China is obliged to reciprocate fully. Since 1975, China's share of North American imports has risen from negligible to 0.8% in 1983 and 4.9% in 1993.

Making the reasonable assumption that most of Hong Kong's re-export trade is associated with China places China in fourth position with a world trade share of around 7%. Since the reforms began, exports and imports have expanded at annual rates of 16 and 15% respectively. International confidence in the Chinese economy has grown to the extent that China now attracts a large share of international FDI, with some US$90bn. being invested in the last decade. Foreign firms now account for over one quarter of China's exports. China is being integrated into the world's economy.

As Garnaut reports,[4] the structure of China's trade has shifted. Before the reforms, her exports were dominated by agricultural-intensive products. Both these shares and the share of mineral products have fallen rapidly, to be replaced by labour-intensive manufactured goods. This clearly reflects China's comparative advantage, and the current 15% of world exports in these categories have been at the expense of Japan and the NIEs. Textiles and clothing accounted for 40% of total exports in 1992, and the GATT and APEC liberalisation will ensure that these exports remain important.

An examination of the growth elsewhere in East Asia shows that this growth was built upon an outward export-oriented trade policy, education to improve human capital, labour market flexibility, high savings rates, and sound macroeconomic policies and institutional building. These patterns are being exhibited by China, albeit with some reservations. Over the past three decades the 'developed' world has largely integrated Japan into its trading system, and wrestled with the integration of the NIEs and ASEAN. The integration into the APEC community of a rapidly growing economy containing almost one quarter of the world's population, and with a tremendous comparative advantage in labour-intensive production under liberalised free trade over a generation or less, is a future prospect.

China is actively seeking entry to the WTO, and considerable pressure is being brought to bear to open her markets and economy further as a condition of that entry. The GATT Uruguay Round outcome presents opportunities for China notwithstanding that China is not a member of the WTO and therefore does not automatically benefit from provisions negotiated between WTO members. Particular opportunities are in agriculture and other sectors such as textiles as new markets open up and existing ones expand. However, it must be acknowledged that the dynamics of openness of the economic policy in China are likely to have a greater effect upon the continuation of the country's impressive growth. But there is a symbiotic relationship associated with these two factors: in pursuing the new market opportunities and making the domestic adjustment necessary to capitalise fully upon them China is, in effect, continuing with the thrust of that economic reform process.

The chapter has endeavoured to show the rich tapestry of the APEC economies, their increasing role in world trade, and how the dynamic Asian economies of the region in general and APEC in particular are now becoming a major driving force of the world's economy in their own right. Given the Bogor Declaration of Common Resolve to achieve free and open trade in Asia-Pacific by 2010 for the industrialised countries and the others no later than 2020, it is useful to examine this goal and its implications.

Even by early next century, when the realities of adjusting to the Bogor Declaration are being addressed in hindsight, the Asia-Pacific region will look different than it does today. Growth rates several percentage points above the OECD average are likely to continue in the non-Japanese Asian economies, altering their relative importance and trade flow patterns. These changes must be set against the implications of further trade liberalisation and growth resulting from the Uruguay Round outcome of the GATT and the group effects of the three free trade arrangements of CER, NAFTA and AFTA which operate within APEC.

CER is already well-established, and with the further planned reductions of tariffs in both Australia and New Zealand will operate to reduce the margins of preference which both countries enjoy as a result of the agreement whilst simultaneously positioning the economies well for the final steps for APEC liberalisation. Final adjustment for CER will be less arduous than similar adjustments during the late 1980s and early 1990s. AFTA provides a sub-set of the APEC region, and the progress towards its goals of free trade between its current six members will give a useful barometer on the success of the APEC proposal. The NAFTA agreement, with its most recent addition of Mexico still to be digested followed by the likely prospect of southwards extensions into Latin America, sets up both a challenge and a complement to APEC.

There is a considerable debate as to whether preferential trading arrangements are supportive of wider trade liberalisation or not.[5] The key issues evolve around the degree of openness of the agreement and the extent to which the partners are lowering their barriers to the rest of the world. Certainly the dynamic gains resulting from an agreement are important, and the ability to harness these dynamics to achieve international competitiveness is crucial.

Finally, China emerges as a key figure in the APEC process. Its recent stunning economic performance is likely to continue in the medium term, although several uncertainties exist. Should this growth continue, the result will be the future restoration of China as perhaps the largest economy in the world when that assessment is based on purchasing power parity. Given that the GDP per capita will still be low, the implications of the effects of such a competitive advantage in labour intensive manufacturing with free access to the major markets of the world pose perhaps the greatest challenge to APEC.

There can be no doubt that Asian economies will continue to exhibit growth in the medium-term future, although extrapolation of that growth too far into the future is fraught with dangers. The economies of the Pacific Rim will be different in the year 2020 from what they look now with or without an achievement of the APEC goal. This APEC goal has an announced and defined end point of free trade among members, as distinct from the incremental approach of the GATT process. As such, APEC is likely to overtake the GATT as the major institution influencing trade liberalisation in the region. The potential for APEC liberalisation to change the trading relationships in the region makes the end point of free trade a worthwhile goal to strive for, albeit recognising the challenges which lie ahead in attaining that goal.

NOTES

[1] P. Krugman, 'The myth of Asia's miracle', *Foreign Affairs*, November/December 1994, pp. 62-78.

[2] For a wider discussion of CER, see Bureau of Industry Economics (BIE), *Impact of the CER Trade Agreement: Lessons for Regional Economic Cooperation*, Report 95/17, Canberra, 1995.

[3] N.R. Lardy, *China in the World Economy*, Washington D.C.: Institute for International Economics, 1994.

[4] R. Garnaut and P. Drysdale (eds), *Asia Pacific Regionalism: Readings in International Economic Relations*, Pymble, NSW: Harper Educational, 1994.

[5] A. De la Torre and M.R. Kelly, *Regional Trading Arrangement*, Washington D.C.: International Monetary Fund (IMF), Occasional Paper 93, 1992.

# 5. ASIA-PACIFIC REGIONAL INTEGRATION AND HUMAN RIGHTS

*Christopher Tremewan*

The APEC summit on 15 November 1994 in Bogor, Indonesia, saw the intersection of two major aspects of contemporary international relations in the Asia-Pacific region. The first was the trend to regional economic integration[1] which gained further momentum from the commitment at Bogor to target dates for trade and investment liberalisation. This initiative to institutionalise the penetration of developing countries by foreign capital on terms largely favourable to the latter and to local elites arises during a period of unprecedented economic growth in East and Southeast Asia. The second was highlighted by the 29 East Timorese who entered the US Embassy in Jakarta on 12 November and remained there throughout the APEC forum.[2]

Amidst the East Asian economic boom, questions of human rights continue to surface and disrupt the mannered order of international diplomacy. In Asia, human rights have acquired a new salience in international relations after the cold war.

But, by the time the Bogor summit began, a lot of diplomatic homework had already been done to blunt the negative international consequences of using state violence or administrative coercion to crush dissent. From early in the decade, several Asian governments (especially China, Indonesia, Malaysia, Myanmar, Pakistan, Singapore and Viet Nam[3]) made a concerted attempt to counter the use by the West and Japan of the international human rights debate as a means of political leverage against third world states. From the beginning, the principle of national sovereignty elaborated as non-interference by any state in the domestic affairs of another was invoked, and this was extended by implication to non-intervention in the region by any non-Asian government in the area of human rights.[4]

The United Nations World Conference on Human Rights held in Vienna in June 1993 and the earlier Asian regional preparatory meeting held in Bangkok in March and April of the same year provided a formal process for Asian governments to develop and air their perspectives on human rights. Their declaration in Bangkok appeared to endorse the universality of human rights while rendering it conditional with such circumscriptions as universality 'in the context of a dynamic and evolving process of international norm-setting, bearing in mind the significance of national and regional particularities and various historical, cultural and religious backgrounds'.[5] This relativist approach cut little ice with the 110 Asian non-government human rights and development organisations which were present at the meeting.[6]

However, Asian governments' collective counter to the universality of human rights norms achieved considerable success in that it forced the adoption of the diplomatic device of a contrived ideological separation between such 'political' matters as human rights (including self-determination) and economic issues by the time that Bogor was held. Its success was also partly due to the active, at times aggressive, diplomacy in the human rights debate in preceding years.

When it is remembered that the Indonesian summit followed such widely-publicised events as the Burmese junta's brutal suppression of the democracy movement in September 1988 and the house arrest of Nobel laureate and opposition leader Aung San Suu Kyi, the Chinese government's attack on students in Tiananmen Square on 4 June 1989, and the 12 November 1991 massacre of unarmed East Timorese demonstrators at Dili's Santa Cruz cemetery, such regional political management must be regarded as producing significant dividends. Perhaps the clinching event was the Clinton administration's de-linking of human rights and economic relations when it agreed to the continuance of Most-Favoured-Nation (MFN) status for China in May 1994, five months before the Indonesian summit.[7] This MFN status has also been extended by President Clinton in 1995 and 1996.

Thus, at Bogor, the political leaders of the APEC countries met as the 'economic' leaders of economies. As a collective body, though not bilaterally, governments were able to avoid encountering each other too directly on 'political' questions such as human rights (including self-determination) or the relationship between China and Taiwan. This would appear to be the agreed diplomatic strategy for advancing the development of regional economic integration and recognising that mutual interests outweigh areas of competition or conflict.

But will it work over the longer term as APEC becomes more institutionalised? Will it be possible to isolate the leverage that human rights offers governments in their bilateral relations and in multilateral contexts (such as the United Nations) from 'purely economic' relationships within the APEC region?

Such questions require attention to the underlying assumptions and dynamics of the human rights discourse in Asia at an international level among governments and among non-government organisations. To understand the new significance of human rights in the Asia-Pacific region, it is also helpful to distinguish the theoretical bases of the main approaches to human rights.

I have argued in detail elsewhere[8] that these are characterised by two broad underlying analyses of the post-cold war order which I have termed the post-colonial approach and the neo-colonial approach. They are simplifications and therefore should not be understood as the definitive positions of particular writers. Nevertheless, elements of the post-colonial approach tend to prevail in international relations theory and in Western human rights rhetoric. The neo-colonial approach is more typical of political economy and the Asian human rights discourse. But many writers owe theoretical debts to both tendencies. Here I offer only a summary of these approaches in order to provide a theoretical context for the second part of this chapter: an examination of the present state of the human rights discourse in the region.

### *The Post-Colonial Approach*

The post-colonial approach has interpreted the post-World War II process of decolonisation as a qualitative change in international relations and now sees another fundamental transformation of what it describes as 'the international system'.

Many writers therefore claim a global victory for liberal democracy and a vindication of Western human rights values and of the market economy. Not all writers who could be placed within the post-colonial approach would go so far, preferring the more modest claim that there is a new era, if not yet quite a new order, in which major powers co-operate and international organisations and international law have a greater role.[9]

There are five main elements of the post-colonial approach:

- First, the post-colonial approach claims there is a qualitatively New World Order emerging or already in existence.
- Secondly, the unit of analysis is either the state or the collectivity of states and international organisations termed 'international society'. The latter refers primarily to Western states, the others being on their way to becoming Western or simply peripheral.
- Thirdly, the focus is on the relationship between Western capitalist states and European socialist states as the determinant of the whole world system. The collapse of the Soviet state and its allies is seen as a victory for liberal democracy and human rights not only in Europe but everywhere.
- Fourthly, the difference between first and third world states is noted as a peripheral issue and placed in a post-colonial framework which implies that political equality has arisen from the new status of political independence.
- Finally, the post-colonial approach presents itself as purely descriptive. But the reason that its ideas appear reasonable, uncontroversial and non-ideological to Western analysts might be ascribed to the fact that they are deeply lodged in a Western ideological tradition.

Much of the current debate on human rights is conducted within the ideological parameters of the post-colonial approach. Since the framing of the UN Charter and the subsequent Covenants on Civil and Political Rights and on Economic, Social and Cultural Rights, an ideological division has arisen between those states which put most emphasis on one or other of these sets of rights. Western industrialised countries have seen themselves as champions of the civil and political rights derived from their tradition of 'natural law' and their constitutional development. Socialist states and third world countries have been seen as placing priority on economic, social and cultural rights, claiming the protection of international principles of sovereignty and non-intervention in defence of their failure to grant civil and political rights. This antithesis cannot be sustained once the covenants are examined in depth: both sets of rights have collective and individual application. As noted above, this distinction has a new elaboration in the APEC process where economic discussions are regarded as non-political and, by implication, all human rights are somehow assigned to a removed political sphere.

The post-colonial approach has also begun to work itself out in terms of heavy pressure on strategically important remnants of state socialism (China, Cuba and North Korea) and the targeting of third world states as the primary violators of human rights.

Thus, in the field of human rights, the post-colonial approach, which is the basis of the strong consensus among industrialised nations on a core of international human rights values and laws, has raised the prospect of the conflation of human rights, the doctrine of 'basic needs'[10] and the self-evident need for emergency humanitarian relief to provide an internationally acceptable basis for intervention in third world countries.[11] This humanitarian intervention is seen by many Asian governments as a fig leaf for the pursuit of the major powers' foreign policy interests and as a potential threat to their national sovereignty. The humanitarian aspects of a situation are perceived as addressed only when and to the degree that other interests are served by doing so and thus Western intervention is perceived as self-interested and inconsistent or selective. Situations ranging from the Gulf War and the former Yugoslavia to the increasing debt burden on least-developed countries and the huge profits of Western arms traders have entrenched this cynicism.

Underlying the post-colonial approach is the conviction that history is moving into a new and more positive stage. Political development towards liberal democracy and human rights is a means of ensuring that third world states are pressured into liberal democratic practices. 'Some kind of pluralist democracy ... would seem to be a precondition for the establishment and safeguarding of human rights'.[12] Not only is the basis for universal human rights seen as already laid out in UN documents but, now, the UN itself is seen as having the potential of acting as a truly global institution provided some necessary reforms are carried out and criteria for humanitarian intervention agreed upon. Admittedly, the conservative lurch of the Republican-dominated US Congress and the Bosnian situation have rendered this position more conditional, the latter providing an opportunity for third world governments to launch a stinging critique of the European human rights position.[13]

### *The Neo-Colonial Approach*

In contrast, the neo-colonial approach sees a fundamental continuity from the colonial era to the present. It sees the transition to political independence of third world states and the recent development of a post-cold war order as important changes in the form but not in the substance of political relationships – changes which are to be viewed as stages of imperialism.

For many Western writers, imperialism ended with colonialism. The very use of the term is considered unfashionable. Deterministic formulations echoing the polemics of political debate have played their part in contributing to this negative view. However, there is a new insistence by both governments and NGOs in Asia on the accuracy of the term for describing the relationship between the industrialised countries and the developing countries. This is not to say that the general use of the term 'imperialism' goes beyond the rhetorical especially in the case of governments. Rather, governments derive legitimacy from reviving the revolutionary spirit and ideology of past anti-colonial struggles in the present context of a capitalist revolution. But this appropriation must be distinguished from the substantive analytical tradition which provides important insights into the current situation, insights which are assumed and regarded as unexceptional by many Asian intellectuals and NGOs.

While there are many formulations, the stages of imperialism have been succinctly described by Rob Steven, a specialist in Japan's relations with other Asian countries.[14] He characterises the first stage of imperialism as the classical system of a major power holding state power in a colony. The nationalist struggles against colonisation eventually forced imperialist powers to give up state power in the colonies. However, because these powers wanted continuing access for their corporations to their former colonies, most intervened militarily in these independence struggles to ensure that a local upper class was fostered to take over state power. In this way an alliance was formed between capitalist classes in imperialist countries and the emergent upper classes in neo-colonies. The United States was preeminent in such intervention and in providing the subsequent military guarantee for local regimes and thus for the accumulation strategy. This second phase covered the period from the end of World War II to the mid-1980s.

This neo-colonial arrangement meant that no one imperialist power had exclusive access to any third world country. Because a local upper class held state power, the corporations of all industrialised countries might obtain access. Imperialist powers shared neo-colonies. They remained economic rivals but not military ones. They did not need to fight wars against each other. But, as in the earlier period, the main political relationship was still the economic exploitation of the resources of underdeveloped countries by the major powers.

Thus the main economic rivals, the US, Japan and Europe, competed economically during this period but they could all benefit under the overall military control of the US. The Soviet Union's support of some of the peoples of underdeveloped countries threatened this world order and thus engendered the long-lasting tendency to war among the two superpowers.

The third stage of imperialism, according to Steven, came with the rise of the political and economic power of Japan and Europe. Other important developments of this period were the military exhaustion of the US and the collapse of a Soviet Union already increasingly reluctant to support political movements in the neo-colonies. This phase has seen a new degree of technical and economic co-operation among the big powers paralleled by intensifying military co-operation: groups of major powers working through a legitimating institution like the United Nations.[15]

In the neo-colonies, the upper classes and the lower classes do not have opposing superpowers championing them any more. Those political movements which challenge an alliance between a local ruling class and that of a major power cannot count on a rival major power to support them. However, the many military or military-backed regimes in Asia can now count not just on one major power supporting them against domestic or other threats to exploitative economic strategies but blocs of them. Hence, this post-cold war order is coming to be termed ultra-imperialism or simply the new imperialism.

Unlike the post-colonial approach, the neo-colonial analysis does not see a fundamentally new order. It identifies the exploitation of the underdeveloped countries by industrialised countries as the basic problem which is brought to a new level of intensity after the mid-1980s. The end of the cold war is the end of superpower rivalry and of an unsound, unsustainable attempt at state socialism but that is all. The alliances between ruling classes in industrialised countries and third world countries continue to function in their mutual interest and to the detriment of third world people.

The collapse of such an analysis of imperialism into the determinism typical of some neo-Marxian dependency theory, focusing as it does on the state and international trade within a world system, brings it close to the post-colonial approach in terms of the unit of analysis and the focus on international commodity exchange, though not in terms of causation.

The more theoretically creative emphasis of the neo-colonial approach focuses on the relations not simply between states but also between different parts of each society and their connections, alliances and conflicts with parts of other societies. The stages of imperialism can therefore be understood as shifting pressures exerted by the differing power of social relationships forged internationally. Of primary significance, however, are the relations within each society. Conflicts or tensions owing to inequalities, discrimination or historical injustices which are configured around the fault lines of class, race, religion, gender or caste (often affected by the legacy of colonialism and unresolved issues of political self-determination) reflect underlying social relations which exert their own pressures towards rejecting or concluding international relationships and influence the terms on which such relationships can be developed. These conflicts often surface as human rights issues (e.g. East Timor, Aceh, Sri Lanka, Kashmir, Tibet, the rights of women and indigenous peoples).

Imperialism can therefore be understood in terms of the capacity of capitalist businesses to relocate their problems abroad, a trend often expressed in terms of the availability of raw materials, cheaper or more obedient labour or profitable markets.[16] This ability to shift one's problems on to people elsewhere relies on several factors. First it requires constantly increasing power which, today, comes from the integration of major banks, and large, technically-advanced industrial companies and trading companies. Secondly, it relies on access to other social formations through a class alliance between ruling elites. As noted above, the terms on which such alliances may be concluded (if at all) are affected by the social relations and conflicts within each society. This theoretical approach therefore gives primacy to each country's social and political context.

While acknowledging new forms of cooperation or resistance (often reflected in the patterns of human rights violations), this approach would not anticipate any fundamental change in the social power of the relationships sustaining imperialism, and therefore no substantive break in the pattern of increasing inequality within and between countries is expected.

The current human rights discourse in the Asian region draws heavily on the neo-colonial approach but in contradictory ways which need clear differentiation. Three key entry points to the debate are the use of political metaphor as a disguise for real social relations, the claims for an Asian perspective on human rights and the disorientation and obstacles faced by Asian non-government organisations.

## *Metaphor: The Disguise of Partnership*

The continuing economic inequalities between industrialised and developing countries provide the moral underpinning for the appropriation of the North-South metaphor by some Asian states. It is now a truism to note, as indicated by the neo-colonial approach, that the end of the cold war has laid bare the long-standing conflict between North and South and the exploitative nature of many economic relationships. But the use of the language of anti-imperialism by Asian governments needs careful scrutiny. Unlike their antecedent nationalist anti-colonial movements, all these governments (including China and Viet Nam) now embrace the market and favour export-oriented industrialisation strategies of economic growth. Even in their rhetorical use of the language of anti-imperialism, there is little suggestion that these governments seek any alternative economic strategy. This is the reason that the impression of a fundamental division is misleading and largely rhetorical.

The most fundamental political reality is that of underlying co-operation between the governments and capitalist classes of Asian developing countries and the major industrialised countries – not conflict. This partnership is expressed mainly in the form of enormous flows of foreign investment and trade, indicating a high degree of co-operation. These inter-government, intra-class relationships facilitate the revolutionary force of economic development in Asia which is changing social life at great speed, subverting local cultures and traditions, marginalising huge numbers of people whose livelihoods it is destroying and often proceeding with high levels of coercion in order to induct millions of people into the routine of an industrial life-style, giving them the same aspirations and the same means of achieving them.

Asian governments welcome the legitimacy that economic growth lends to their governance but wish to distance themselves politically from their collaboration with Western capital and from the social effects of this collaboration. The rhetoric of anti-imperialism is an effective disguise for this purpose on the domestic and regional level.

On the international level, an anti-imperialist stance as part of a lobby of developing countries is also a response to the evaporation of the superpower rivalry which formerly helped developing countries to extract better terms in their dealings with foreign capital and the governments of the industrialised countries. The development of an Asian perspective on human rights is part of this response. Elaborated as a critique against the remaining superpower, the United States, and the major industrialised countries, it has provided some diplomatic leverage.

This analysis brings into focus the differing characteristics of the ruling classes in the North and the South. In broad terms, the capitalist classes of the major industrialised countries with their centuries of accumulation, technological leadership and class rule have acquired enormous social power. They have been able to secure their positions and even accommodate victories of their working classes in areas of political participation, labour conditions and human rights. This social power, as noted in Steven's formulation of the stages of imperialism above, enables them to overcome problems at home by displacing them abroad, an ability reflected in the relocation of production, the seeking of the cheapest raw materials, the most disciplined labour and the best markets.

In contrast, the ruling classes of the South are much less secure. By collaborating with foreign capital to strengthen themselves, they also confront the destabilising effects of the massive social transformation that integration into the world market economy brings. In order to ensure the success of the economic strategy that their partnership with Western and Japanese capital necessitates and which serves their overall political interests, they use forms of state violence and social control to maintain political loyalty and social discipline that violate international human rights norms. In this sense, higher levels of coercion indicate greater weakness in terms of ruling elites' domestic political bases. To put it another way, governments of developing countries in Asia have varying degrees of autonomy in relation to their own capitalist classes and to foreign capital and these relations influence the process of industrialisation and the nature of state repression in each situation.

The highlighting of North-South inequalities by Asian governments is therefore often aimed at striving for greater leverage in unequal political and economic relationships, at trying to strike a better deal in the terms of these relationships (e.g. the conditions on which foreign investment enters the country) or at trying to blunt strong pressure from the industrialised countries to integrate Asian economies on terms most favourable to foreign capital. Malaysia's promotion of its EAEC proposal and prime minister Mahathir Mohamad's frequent anti-Western pronouncements are examples of this.

Malaysia held out against institutionalisation of APEC and against a timetable for free trade amongst all APEC countries. It proposed the EAEC as a counter organisation of an inner circle of Asian countries with ASEAN at its core and excluding Western countries (the United States, Canada, Australia and New Zealand). Paradoxically, Malaysia's new confidence on the international stage derived at least partially from the enormous flows of direct foreign investment it has received in the past few years which have enabled it to reach a new level of intermediate industrialisation.[17] This inflow of investment and technology has greatly strengthened the Malaysian ruling elite, making the United Malays National Organisation (UMNO) and its partners in the *Barisan*, the governing coalition, almost unassailable in the parliamentary political process for the time being. This strength is reflected in the government's ability to displace its domestic communalist politics into the international arena by taking an anti-Western stance, a racist tinge which played well with the communally-minded domestic electorate.[18] Through populist, diversionary rhetoric, the negative social effects of industrialisation (a process with which the Malaysian government is fully co-operating) can be blamed solely on the decadent West.

It should be noted that at the same time that Malaysia was leading the charge against Western hegemony, its prime minister was building much closer ties with the United States. In May 1994 Mahathir became the first Malaysian premier to visit the White House on official business and described his meeting with Clinton as very positive.[19] This was consummate diplomacy but it also showed that Malaysia was careful never to put its fundamental interests at risk.

The North-South metaphor does describe the concrete reality of economic and social injustice which constitutes a profound violation of human rights. But its use by some Asian governments often misrepresents that reality, obscuring the fact that Asian ruling classes are in partnership with the ruling classes of the industrialised countries, relationships which are frequently not concluded in the interests of the majority of their citizens. In this regard we need an historical recall of the role of national elites of the post-1945 generation in mobilising anti-colonial mass struggles only to take state power for their own class. While Asian governments have a legitimate role in mobilising domestic public opinion to demand greater economic justice from industrialised countries, it must be remembered that the population at large which is stirred to nationalist fervour rarely shares on an equitable basis any benefits such pressure might produce. Thus the North-South divide is not simply a geographic or ethnic divide but is a fault line which runs primarily between alliances of ruling elites and those they rule. The elimination of the notion of class from the metaphor is a prerequisite for its appropriation by governments.

## *Asian Perspectives on Human Rights*

Arguments for an Asian perspective of human rights have been advanced by ASEAN governments and, with less sophistication, by other Asian states. They have been articulated in consonance with the North-South metaphor. This 'politicisation of the discourse of human rights along the North-South divide'[20] has been part of a more general initiative to deny the major industrialised countries absolute control of the international agenda on such major issues as the environment, media and information technology, labour conditions and security issues as well as human rights.

Undoubtedly many of the points raised by Asian governments have validity: the major powers' historic disregard of the economic and social rights of developing countries, the undeclared national interests which result in a high degree of selectivity in Western reactions to violations of human rights and international law, the targeting of third world states as the main perpetrators of abuses when they are often implementing policies which sustain the profitability of foreign investment, continuing insensitivity to the legacy of centuries of colonialism and racism, the cultural imperialism mediated through the transnationalised Western media, and the domination of the UN Security Council by the governments of the industrialised countries. It must indeed rankle when human rights is seized as a convenient diplomatic lever by major powers which have rarely concerned themselves with the enormities of their own interventions in the third world either now or in the past, interventions which in scale and degree of human suffering remain a blot on human history. ASEAN governments have not been slow in rehearsing this litany as a counter to criticism of their own record of serious human rights violations.[21]

But the constant focus on the state and the fora in which it can be held accountable for human rights violations (especially the United Nations) has monopolised public perceptions of the development of an Asian perspective on human rights and blurred the distinctions between several dimensions of the Asian human rights debate. There are at least three distinctions to be made: the contest between states, the competition for dominance between cultural norms and the struggle between the rulers and the ruled.[22]

In the contest between states, Asian governments have elaborated varying perspectives on human rights but have established a general consensus which gives primacy to political stability and economic development over individual rights. This is argued for on the basis of the particularity of

Asian values, culture and religion and the alleged differing nature of the relationship between the individual and the state in Asian culture. Thus the imperatives of the state are dressed up in the discourse of cultural relativism.

It has already been established that this is at least partly a cynical tactic in that the same Asian governments which advance such perspectives are those which are also collaborating with the economic forces which are undermining traditional cultures and producing the disjunctions railed against. It may also be a product of the resentment that Asian governments feel at their unequal power in such relationships, that their partnership with the North opens them to social and legal norms of the industrialised countries which represent the political achievements of their middle and working classes in obtaining human rights and democratic participation. The major powers are seen as attempting to impose these achievements within a different social formation in which they have no political legitimacy even while they are actively undermining them at home. The triumphalist post-colonial view of the victory of the freemarket, free enterprise and human rights is a misrepresentation of social reality in both the North and the South.

However, it is important to note that the appearance of there being a uniform Asian perspective on human rights as represented by the consensus among Asian governments is misleading:

> What conveys an apparent picture of a uniform Asian perspective on human rights is that it is the perspective of a particular group, that of the ruling elites, which gets international attention. What unites these elites is their notion of governance and the expediency of their rule. For the most part the political systems they represent are not open or democratic, and their publicly expressed views on human rights are an emanation of these systems, of the need to justify authoritarianism and occasional repression. It is their views which are given wide publicity domestically and internationally.[23]

The diplomatic value of such a consensus is nevertheless considerable. The resonances of Asian nationalism can be tapped in a way which makes it very difficult for Asian governments which have made more genuine attempts at nationalist economic policies and have had more integrity in their approach to human rights (at least formally) – such as India – to decline to stand in solidarity.

The second dimension of the Asian human rights debate, the competition for dominance between cultural norms, has been characterised by the extended debate on cultural relativism.[24] Originally developed as a counter to imperialist ideological hegemony and cultural domination by demonstrating the commonplace of anthropology that differing societies have differing social norms, cultural relativism has been co-opted by Asian governments as a defence for their authoritarianism and as a disguise for their collaboration in facilitating such hegemony. The critique of Western cultural domination needs to be made and questions of cultural and intellectual incorporation need to be addressed. The examination of the Western cultural origins of the concept of human rights is a necessary part of the process of rethinking the cultural implications of human rights and developing norms which protect human rights in particular Asian contexts. But the leading public role of ASEAN governments in advancing this critique raises a number of issues.

These governments hold that they assent to the international consensus on fundamental human rights[25] and seek only to ensure their application in culturally appropriate ways in their own countries. However, neither Singapore nor Malaysia have signed any of the major international human rights treaties and Indonesia has signed but not ratified only the Convention Against Torture.[26] Even the minimal international accountability to treaty bodies regarding their adherence to the international consensus is therefore avoided.

Asia is so diverse in culture, religion, economic and political systems and social structure that a single understanding of human rights cannot be expected except, as indicated above, at the level of the state if governments find such an outcome expedient. However, with the increasing economic power of the region and the increasing salience of the relationship between religion and state, the possibility is emerging of a pan-Asian 'neo-Asianism' as a counter to the cultural domination which has accompanied foreign capital's penetration of the region.[27] This tendency has been presaged by a simplistic debate in conservative circles in the West initiated by Samuel Huntington's 'Clash of Civilisations' thesis.[28] The cultural debate in both North and South, East and West, again covers up the reality of inequality and class relations.

The third dimension is the struggle between rulers and the ruled. That is, the struggle to establish human rights norms and laws and the degree of their implementation reflect the state of underlying social conflicts:

> The body of declarations, conventions, agreements, resolutions, and statements related to human rights and accumulated in history are not fully a product of the West, nor can they be reduced to the Western notion of individual freedom ... [They are] primarily products of decades and decades of struggles for human dignity, conducted by both people in the East as well as in the West, individually and collectively, and that the very concept of human rights, especially in the post war period, has been signally enriched through people's struggles.[29]

This places the role of NGOs in the current Asian debate in a critical position. They often articulate the voice of those who are voiceless, who have no political power. The NGO strength in the Vienna World Conference and in the Bangkok preparatory conference may have been unsettling for Asian governments. It can be expected that their ability to build international partnerships within Asia and with NGOs in the North will be watched carefully and may be impeded. Already it is impossible for human rights NGOs to exist in a number of countries (e.g. Singapore, China) and very difficult in others. As a response to the increasing diplomatic weight of NGOs, some governments have sought to neutralise the activism of local NGOs by painting them as puppets of Western interests or by forcing them to be co-operative with government management of the human rights discourse. In addition, Asian governments' championing of the cause against Western cultural domination has drawn some NGOs, which perhaps have not comprehended the political consequences of the conflation of the state and cultural dimensions of the Asian human rights debate, into appearing to support government strategies.[30]

There is a problem of definition when referring to NGOs. Often the term is understood as applying to organised special interest groups focusing on some aspect of human rights. These are often viewed from outside as being rather weak in terms of their influence on the state. However, they ought to be viewed in relation to the broad range of social movements with which they connect: labour movements, opposition parties, grassroots environmental movements, loosely organised coalitions of women's groups or even unorganised resistance to various state measures. It might be possible, for example, to say that the human rights movement in Korea or the Philippines was comparatively weak in the 1980s (although I would dispute this) but quite untenable to state that the broad citizens' movements (or, in local parlance, people's movements) were ineffective in political developments.

In the current context, an initiative by an NGO may encapsulate a working consensus of the network of NGOs which has emerged across the region. The consensus itself may have a powerful influence rather than the individual NGO. Such an example is an initiative in 1995 by the Asian Human Rights Commission (AHRC), a regional NGO in Hong Kong, to draw up an Asian Charter of Human Rights. The Charter reflects more general moves by NGOs to overcome government co-option of the human rights discourse, and to provide the policy framework to maintain NGO unity and the basis for strengthening links with grassroots constituencies. It draws on the NGO declaration from the Bangkok preparatory conference for Vienna as a resource document.

The difference between the government-articulated human rights discourse based on cultural relativism and such NGO documents can best be illustrated by the AHRC charter's sub-title, 'Our Common Humanity'. The charter arises from the concrete historical experiences of Asian peoples and seeks resonances with peoples in all regions rather than defining an Asian exclusivity.

One value of an NGO-formulated Asian perspective on human rights is that it may act as a critique of the relativist position of governments. Such a document can claim the universality and indivisibility of human rights arising from common experience. It can claim the value of cultural pluralism while condemning cultural practices which derogate from human rights. It can recommend international co-operation in the promotion of human rights and refute arguments on the encroachment on national sovereignty. It can reject economic injustice but connect it with both foreign domination and domestic oppression and recommend alternatives to the market-led system of economic growth. Thus such a document can be a statement for social justice by Asian peoples pressing for equitable distribution of resources and the empowerment of women and the advancement of the rights of disadvantaged communities[31] without giving ground to relativist special pleading. It can indeed act as a unifying force within Asia and between Asia and other regions.

The implications of the above analysis for current processes of regional economic integration are sobering.

It is unlikely that governments will be able convincingly to continue the fiction of separating political and economic issues even within the limited confines of 'economic' discussions. This is because such questions as labour standards and their conformity to international standards such as those proposed in the context of the WTO-based multilateral trade negotiations, the social provisions of NAFTA and the Social Charter of the European Union, have already been politicised as examples of imposing Western standards for the purposes of protecting Western competitiveness.

Undoubtedly, NGOs, citizens' groups and opposition political movements will raise questions of gender justice in relation to employment as well as labour conditions in general and will create political pressure nationally and internationally. As APEC member states prepared for their summit in Osaka in November 1995, NGOs in the Asia-Pacific region were also preparing for their meeting in the same city with labour relations at the top of their agenda.

The economic integration of the region into the global economy is exacerbating many social and political conflicts by bringing rapid social transformation, building up volcanic tensions beneath the surface of many societies. The inequality that is represented by the global figure of more than a billion people in absolute poverty and the income of the richest 20% of the world's population being 150 times that of the poorest 20%[32] will need to be addressed if economic growth is to be sustainable.

In the event that such inequality is regarded as marginal or its solution as a natural outcome of present patterns of economic growth, it can be expected that there will be a political convergence, not in the post-colonial direction of liberal democracy which, in the UK and elsewhere, is already becoming less democratic and less respectful of human rights,[33] but convergence with the authoritarianism of Singapore with its regime of social regulation.[34]

NOTES

[1] Martin Rudner, 'The challenges of Asia Pacific economic cooperation', *Modern Asian Studies*, 29 (2), 1995, pp. 403-37. See also Stuart Harris, 'Policy networks and economic cooperation: policy coordination in the Asia-Pacific region', *The Pacific Review*, 7 (4), 1994, pp. 381-95.

[2] *Asia 1995 Yearbook*, Hong Kong: FEER, 1994, p. 136.

[3] Christina M. Cerna, 'Universality of human rights and cultural diversity: implementation of human rights in different socio-cultural contexts', *Human Rights Quarterly*, 16, 1994, p. 740.

[4] See Statement by Liu Huaqiu, Head of Chinese Delegation, UN World Conference on Human Rights, Vienna, 17 June 1993.

[5] Declaration adopted by ministers and representatives of Asian states in Bangkok, 2 April 1993, at UN regional preparatory meeting for the World Conference on Human Rights. (Japan and Cyprus recorded reservations.) See also 'Vienna Showdown', *FEER*, 17 June 1993, p. 17.

[6] See 'An NGO response to the Asia-Pacific governments', Final Draft Declaration, Bangkok, 2 April 1993.

[7] For an earlier examination of the MFN debate in the US, see Robert F. Drinan S.J. and Teresa T. Kuo, 'The 1991 battle for human rights in China', *Human Rights Quarterly*, 14, 1992, pp. 21-42.

[8] Christopher Tremewan, 'Human rights in Asia', *The Pacific Review*, 6 (1), 1993, pp. 17-29.

[9] Adam Roberts, 'A new era in international relations', Paper delivered at the Institute of International Relations, Peking University, Beijing, 17-19 June 1991, p. 2.

[10] R. J. Vincent, *Human Rights and International Relations*, CUP, 1986, pp. 86-7.

[11] For an overview of the issues and political dilemmas surrounding the debate on humanitarian intervention, see Kelly Kate Pease and David P. Forsythe, 'Human rights, humanitarian intervention, and world politics', *Human Rights Quarterly*, 15, 1993, pp. 290-314.

[12] John Girling, *Human Rights in the Asia-Pacific Region,* Canberra: ANU, 1991, p. 3.

[13] For example, see statement by Datuk Abdullah Haji Ahmad Badawi, Minister of Foreign Affairs, Malaysia, UN World Conference on Human Rights, Vienna, 18 June 1993.

[14] Rob Steven, 'Imperialism strengthened', in David Small (ed.), *Third World War*, Hongkong: CCA-IA, 1991, p. 8.

[15] Ibid, p. 9.

[16] Rob Steven, *Japan and the New World Order – Global Investments, Trade and Finance*, London: Macmillan, 1996, pp. 1-40.

[17] James V. Jesudason, 'Malaysia: a year full of sound and fury, signifying ... something?', *Southeast Asian Affairs 1995*, Singapore: Institute of Southeast Asia Studies, p. 208.

[18] Ibid, p. 218.

[19] *Asia Yearbook*, Hong Kong: FEER, 1994, p. 168.

[20] Yash Ghai, 'Human rights and governance: the Asia debate', Faculty of Law, University of Hong Kong, 1994, p. 6.

[21] A. Acharya, 'Human rights and regional order: ASEAN and human rights management in post-cold war Southeast Asia', in James T. H. Tang (ed.), *Human Rights and International Relations in the Asia Pacific*, London/New York: Pinter, 1995, pp. 169-70.

[22] Ichiyo has similarly identified three human rights discourses: of the state, of civilisational transformation and of people's struggles and social movements. See Muto Ichiyo, 'Debates on human rights must remain free of state discourse - a letter to Chandra Muzaffar', *AMPO Japan-Asia Quarterly*, 26 (2), 1995, pp. 48-51.

[23] Ghai, op. cit., 1994, p. 10.
[24] See Jack Donnelly, 'Cultural relativism and universal human rights', *Human Rights Quarterly*, 6 (4), 1984, pp. 400-19; Alison Dundes Renteln, *International Human Rights Universalism Versus Relativism*, Newbury Park: Sage, 1990; Tremewan, op. cit., 1993, pp. 22-4; Rhoda E. Howard, 'Cultural absolutism and the nostalgia for community', *Human Rights Quarterly*, 15, 1993, pp. 315-338.
[25] See statement by Singapore's Permanent Representative, Kishore Mahbubani, to the Coordinator of the World Conference of Human Rights, quoted in Cerna, op. cit., 1994, p. 745. See also Statement by Ali Alatas, Minister for Foreign Affairs of the Republic of Indonesia, to the UN World Conference in Vienna, 14 June 1993, in which he denies advocating 'an alternative concept of human rights, based on some nebulous concept of "cultural relativism"' and then proceeds to do so.
[26] James Tang, 'Towards an alternative approach to human rights protection in the Asia-Pacific region', in Tang (ed.), op. cit., 1995, p. 188.
[27] Ichiyo, op. cit., 1995, p. 51; Richard Higgott, 'Ideas, identity and policy coordination in the Asia-Pacific', *The Pacific Review*, 7 (4), 1994, p. 368.
[28] Samuel Huntington et al, *The Clash of Civilisations? A Debate – A Foreign Affairs Reader*, New York Council on Foreign Relations, 1993.
[29] Ichiyo, op. cit., 1995, p. 49.
[30] The International Conference on Rethinking Human Rights, held in Kuala Lumpur 6-7 December 1994, was organised by Dr Chandra Muzaffar, a respected NGO leader of the Just World Trust. But his invitation to the Malaysian Prime Minister and his deputy to speak at the opening and closing of the conference, respectively, has been a matter of considerable debate throughout the region. See Ichiyo, op. cit., 1995; and Douglas Lummis, 'Rethinking human rights', *AMPO Japan-Asia Quarterly Review*, 26 (2), 1995, pp. 52-7.
[31] Ghai, op. cit., 1994, pp. 21-2.
[32] *Human Development Report 1993*, UNDP, OUP, 1993, p. 1.
[33] Conor Foley, *Human Rights, Human Wrongs: The Alternative Report to the United Nations Human Rights Committee*, London: Rivers Oram Press, 1995.
[34] Christopher Tremewan, *The Political Economy of Social Control in Singapore*, London: Macmillan, 1994.

# Part II
# Processes of Change in the Asia-Pacific Region

## 6. IMITATING THE RICH: THE IMPERATIVES OF CONSUMPTION

*Harvey Franklin*

'Consumption is the sole end and purpose of production' (Adam Smith). This epigram comes at such a late stage in *The Wealth of Nations*, it leaves one undecided as to whether it should be treated as a conclusion or an afterthought. Certainly the economists have given it short shrift, preferring to study production rather than consumption. The geographers have largely followed suit. To investigate consumption requires one to take a number of adventurous steps, adventurous that is for anyone brought up within this framework of the economics of production; which is just about all of us. A number of these steps are encompassed in one quite unremarkable scene in the early part of the *Forsyte Saga*.

### *Technology and Shifting Consumer Preferences*

The Forsytes are at dinner, and Galsworthy draws to the reader's attention the fact that they are about to eat something of a speciality – Canterbury lamb. For many interwar British consumers, their first image of New Zealand was of the Canterbury Plains, for they were widely displayed in the windows of Dewhursts, a national chain of butcher shops, intent on purveying this delicacy. By the 1930s, rising living standards had brought the Sunday roast within the purchasing power of the working classes; whereas at the end of the 19th century only the well-to-do had sufficient discretionary income to afford what was then something of a rarity. Rising incomes had permitted significant shifts in consumer preferences to occur in the first 30 years of the 20th century, shifts that have continued to the very end; so that as Britain's consumers approach the millennium, very different schedules of consumer preferences have emerged to those prevailing when the Forsytes were the dominant class.

In the period 1957-85, spending on food declined from 34% of total household expenditure to 20%; though, of course, total spending on food has increased, with a shift away from the rougher diets of the earlier period. The era of the inferior goods has long since passed. British tastes now prefer New Zealand Chardonnay and kiwi fruit. By the end of the century it is estimated that the significant increases of spending will be for household and garden products, medical and school fees, insurance and pensions. Ready to grasp the new opportunities, Marks and Spencers at the beginning of 1995 opened 50 outlets retailing pensions on a non-commission basis.

Evident at the Forsytes' dinner table were two powerful factors responsible for the continuous industrial restructuring experienced by all the rich economies throughout the twentieth century: technology and discretionary income.[1] Industrial restructuring will occur so long as there is the discretionary income available to allow consumers to exercise their preferences for whatever novelties the entrepreneurs and technology bring to market. The effect import penetration has upon industrial restructuring is but a special case of this persistent tendency. Changes in consumer preferences will always produce loss of jobs in some industries, whilst creating jobs in others. Old style butchers have gone out of business, just as the old style music halls went out of business, but in their case it was because the consumers stayed home for their entertainment as televisions and videos became popular, whereas in the case of the butchers it is because eating out has become more popular. Shifting consumer preferences are by no means a feature of this age alone. Shifts have always occurred, but in the past the concentration of income and wealth has meant that these shifts have been largely the provenance of the rich. A study of consumption that concentrates on the affairs of the ordinary consumer alone leads the investigator into an ideological and semiotic cul de sac.

Technology, discretionary income and shifting preferences are currently having a profound effect on the distribution of income and wealth. The disparity between the incomes of the better educated and the less educated in the labour force is widening. The demand for manual labour is declining: an effect of technology. Changing consumer demand is creating jobs for people who can provide those medical, educational, insurance and pensions goods and services that are now in such demand.[2]

Trends similar to the ones that have occurred in Britain have been evident in parts of Asia for quite some time. With the acceleration of development throughout Asia, these trends are now catching the attention of newspaper correspondents, so that within the last year or so headlines like the following have appeared: 'Ice-cream retail war hots up in China'; and 'Asia's big spenders put luxury back into shopping'. But these trends have features peculiar to this age, which makes it notably different to the era of the Forsytes. As the Asian consumer market expands, the latest consumer technology appears in quite remote places: Thai hill tribe people have access to video libraries; the *Economist* writes of India's entrance into the washing-machine age. The issue of Asia's new elites is taken up in the weeklies. To become active consumers, a minimum annual income equivalent to US$5,000 is required. By the end of this century, one estimate forecasts a consumer market of 200 million for China. Jakarta, where most of Indonesia's spending power is concentrated, is thought to contain more high-spending consumers than are to be found in the whole of Portugal.[3]

For theoretical purposes the economists have been prepared to treat goods simply as utilities; and this has proved to be a useful convention. But no one in the real world acts as if goods and services are a collection of homogeneous utilities. Nobody would argue that a Lada is the equivalent of a Lamborghini. Certainly not Mr Putra, the youngest son of President Suharto, whose company Megatech has paid US$40m. for the full control of Lamborghini's famous marque.[4] It is quite clear what sort of people, and what sort of discretionary incomes, he will be catering for. Incidents like this make it clear also that studies of wealth and income distributions, of shifting consumer preferences and the analysis of the rich are as pertinent to the study of the developing nations as they are to the study of the developed.

### *Positional, Popular and Other Goods*

No economist has ever devised a classification of goods that goes much beyond the twofold distinction of necessities and luxuries; a distinction that never holds water for long because of the persistent seepage that allows so many luxuries to become, with the passage of time, necessities. In the classification adopted for this analysis there are, to begin with, two sorts of goods: Popular goods and Positional goods. The first is defined by a supply function that is elastic. In the developed world, most of us end up with a car, a TV, a video, a fridge, food to put in it, the electricity to run it, the insurance to cover the loss of it; and a pair of jogging shoes. And in the developing world many aspire to owning these goods in the not too distant future. These are the products of mass production, mass marketing and mass consumption now manufactured in a global competitive market in which industrial restructuring is the rule. At our high standard of living, greater consumer choice appears alongside greater structural unemployment. Exercising today one's freedom to consume is as likely as not to put a fellow citizen out of work tomorrow, especially if one happens to choose the imported and probably cheaper article.

Positional goods, in stark contrast to Popular goods, display most inelastic supply functions; and they constitute the fortunes of the rich of this world who make their money, one should note immediately, by providing the goods and services consumed by the mass market. Whenever someone consumes a Mars Bar, or applies Vicks Vapour Rub, or turns on CNN news – or purchases a packet of Rothmans in China, or a Walls icecream in Bangkok – they contribute their mite to the fortunes of the rich; which, in turn, they preserve against the depredations of time, taxation and inflation by acquiring Positional goods.

Between 1945 and 1992 in America, farmland, art, commercial and residential property, gold and most equities and bonds returned an annual rate of return above the rate of inflation. Only the top decile of wealth holders in developed countries include these items in their portfolios. Prince Charles is a good example. He owns 130,000 acres of farmland, heavily subsidised by the EU. He has a residential and property portfolio. Jointly, farmland and property gave him £9m. gross in 1993. He has, in addition, a £40m. investment portfolio, invested in environmentally sound companies. All this and Camilla Parker-Bowles too. For most people in the West, their wealth, if they have any, consists of their home, their pension rights and what money they have in the bank.

## *Public Goods*

There is a third and peculiar category of goods, here termed Public goods, whose supply curve can best be described as tax elastic. To' stay in power, governments have promised their electorates an endless and ever growing supply of Public goods. That is until, as occurred in New Zealand, the fiscal basis of the state was undermined. And what a barny ensued when the government tried to reduce the supply of Public goods. The electorate believed they had a right to these goods, and that for some reason these goods being provided by the public sector are fundamentally different to all other goods. Some people would like them to be considered as sacrosanct; which is simply not the case.

Our age has been the age of Public goods. They were supplied to counter the injustices of capitalism and to promote social justice and harmony. And they have not. What they have produced is contention. Just as there is no such thing as a transport good, only cars of different marques, there is no such thing as a health or an educational or a cultural good. Like Popular goods, Public goods are subject to the shift in consumer preferences that accompanies rising living standards.

The diphtheria hospital to which I was committed when I was three has gone the way of the Birmingham music hall and family butcher. As one astute British doctor put it: when the NHS was founded in Britain, the assumption was that there was a fixed pool of illness to be treated, not an expanding lake of medical need to be serviced. Into this lake, the stone of Quality After Life Years (QALYs) has been pitched, with all the inevitable ripples, ripples that will be slow to disappear. QALYs represent an attempt to assess the cost effectiveness of different sorts of modern surgical treatments. Simply to report that by this measure breast cancer screening is approximately five times more costly than a hip replacement indicates how contentious health goods can be.[5]

Because of rising living standards, consumers now require a quite different combination of Public goods and services to what was previously required; and who is best suited to providing them is strongly influenced by the changing nature of the goods and services themselves.

## *Transactional Costs*

The greater range of goods included in this study requires one to move beyond the scope, vocabulary and ideologies of those who write about consumerism and the issues of mass consumption and mass cultures and their inauthenticities, real or imagined. The acquisition of all goods involves the consumer in meeting the inevitable transactional costs, whether they be large or small. The assumption regarding Public goods is that the transactional costs involved in obtaining them, for rich and poor alike, should be both minimal and equal. Both the school and the health centre ought to be available, just around the corner. This is not always the case, and the divergence of the real transactional costs from the supposed is a cause of much political heartburn. Nevertheless, in principle, the transactional costs of acquiring Public goods ought to be low because of the promise of universal provision.

In contrast, the acquisition of Positional goods, by their nature, involves high transactional costs. This is clearly demonstrated in Peter Watson's account of the auction of Van Gogh's Portrait of Doctor Gachet.[6] The auction price was US$75m. and the total transactional cost of the sale amounted to US$9.75m., a small fortune in itself. The question comes to mind immediately: what were the purchasers paying for? In the case of the vendor's family, they paid for a clause in the sale contract to protect their investment. The auctioneers also guaranteed the picture's provenance, undertook care of the insurance and security during the period of the auction, provided the estimate price for the sale and were prepared to meet legal costs should a dispute over ownership arise. These are all normal services which have to be provided, in addition to the costs associated with the catalogue and the arrangements of the auction itself, plus the house knowledge of likely purchasers and their credit ratings – a vitally important matter. Only when all these matters were covered could the painting be brought to market.

Doctor Gachet's portrait demonstrates that Positional goods are information goods, or insider goods, par excellence. They are valuable because they embody information that is so rare, so difficult and so time consuming to acquire. Their acquisition requires an unusual degree of expert appraisal in order to find them, in order to guarantee their worth and complete the deal. Consequently one may go television shopping for Popular goods; never for Positional goods. Even to consider entering the market for Positional goods, one has to be exceedingly rich.

Take the case of those Positional goods, heiresses and heirs. There is a market for them today as there was in the time of Sir Thomas Grosvenor who, in 1677, paid £5,000 for the hand in marriage of Mary Davies to his 10-year old son. Mary's inheritance was the meadows we now know as Belgravia. When Aristotle Onassis asked for the hand of Jacqueline Kennedy, the Kennedys asked for a marriage settlement of US$22m.; Onassis offered US$3m. (These prices preceded the inflation subsequent to the first and second oil shocks.) In the end Mrs Kennedy-Onassis did rather better than that. That is not the point. The important question to answer is: what was Onassis buying? He was buying, investing in, access to that vast network of information and influence which the Kennedy family commanded.

Heiresses and heirs are still to be found amongst the rich and influential. Unless they are extraordinarily egalitarian in their taste – and some do prefer truck drivers – the costs of acquiring one are beyond the resources of most ordinary people. Sceptics will soon be disabused by the costs of seeking the hand of, say, Lady Charlotte Morrison, with £48m. in land and property; or Donatelle Moores, with a fortune worth £235m. derived from retailing and football pools; a Popular good, if ever there was one! Suitors not only have to deal with the heiress herself, but also in all probability with a father, who, even in these libertarian times, may have plans of his own for his daughter. This seems to have been the case with one of the richest men in Asia, Y.K. Pao, who divided his businesses amongst his four daughters in 1986. Anna, the eldest daughter, was married to the Austrian national Helmut Sohmen and jointly they control Pao's shipping interests. Bessie married Peter Woo Kwongching, who was born in Ningbo, China, as was Pao, and they control the family conglomerates Wharf and Wheelock, on whose board sit two of Pao's other sons-in-law, and a younger brother of a third son-in-law. Cissie married Shinichiro Watari, a Japanese national, and they look after Pao's Japanese business interests. The youngest daughter, Doreen, with her husband controls the family's financial holdings; and he, Edgar Cheng Wai-kin, comes from a Singapore-based family whose forbears also hail from Ningbo.[7]

There are transactional costs involved in the acquisition of all goods and services. Consumers are aware of them, in terms of frustration and irritation, even though to quantify them may not be easy. The process of acquisition can be very time consuming and disappointing; and it is something, one would suppose, most people would seek if possible to avoid. Presumably as a rule, satisfaction exceeds dissatisfaction and utility exceeds disutility by an appreciable margin. Otherwise consumers would abandon their search or seek alternatives. It seems, therefore, that to suggest, as some writers concerned with mass consumption do, that there is something irrational about the behaviour of the masses in all of this is a viewpoint that cannot, in the main, be sustained. True, one can argue, people might be better off if, rather than going shopping, for example, they chose to spend their time acquiring consumption skills which would enable them to appreciate the finer things in life and lift their vision a little above the mundane.[8] But as anyone knows who has gone in search of some suitable uplifting university course, that choice is not without its own transactional costs and disappointments.

## *Providential Goods*

A long-standing assumption has been that when, of a morning, one stepped outside one's door, the air would be clean and fresh, the sunlight unimpeded and undamaging to one's health; that having got to the beach the sea water would be clear and inviting; or, having got to the national park, one could enter at will and enjoy the wilderness – but increasingly for many people those assumptions do not hold any longer.

Providential goods have long been a part of everyone's schedule of consumer preferences (perhaps without their realising it). This is particularly true of the rich who, indeed, have been wealthy enough to invest in the creation of their own preferred environments – Sir James Goldsmith's hideaway in Mexico, for example – or to employ people like Capability Brown to do the job for them. What was once assumed to be available at no cost is now impinging on the household budgets of most families. The trouble is that we have not as yet been able to decide how the costs of polluting the environment will be borne, and by whom. But more and more consumers demand a clean environment. This significant shift in consumer preferences is heavy with portent. The successful containment of environmental problems will require the enforcement of social control to a degree few people appreciate. The guardians of America's National Parks hesitate to institute a peak-season reservation system to the parks themselves, not just the camping grounds. But with a forecast of 500 million visitors by the year 2010, they may have no alternative.[9]

Singapore's unhesitant approach to its traffic problems may become the style of the future. Certainly the world's elites have recognised the importance of influencing, if not of controlling, the environmental issues as a recent example makes clear. Disney's plan to develop a theme park (a Popular good) within 12 miles of Washington and near historic battlefields of the Civil War raised a storm of criticism. The actor and farmland owner, Robert Duvall, fearful of the loss of rural tranquillity and the destruction of the nation's heritage that would ensue, appeared on the TV screen proclaiming, NIMBY! ('Not in my backyard'). In the end, the protests of the well-off forced Disney to abandon its plan.

### *A Conservative Force*

The convergence with the consumer behaviour of the West displayed by the more affluent strata of the developing world is matched by a demographic convergence in the case of Japan, Taiwan and Singapore. These countries are beginning to grapple with the problems of an ageing population and the fiscal burden of providing for their pension needs, problems that have beset the governments of the other OECD countries. In its usual trenchant manner, Singapore has dealt with these same issues via the now long-established Central Provident Fund and the regime's firm insistence that the care of the old is the responsibility of the family and not the state, this despite the fact that divorce rates have doubled in the past 10 years, and amongst the affluent and educated classes birth rates have fallen. These trends run counter to the requirements needed for a successful implementation of the Maintenance of Parents Bill. In Taiwan the extended multi-generational family living under one roof has given way to the nuclear family, leaving greater numbers of the elderly to fend for themselves. It is estimated that one third of those 65 and over now live alone, twice the proportion that prevailed in the mid-1970s.

Most OECD countries are now set upon a course that will enlarge the proportion of the electorate responsible for their own pension provisions. Susan St John[10] arrives at an estimate of savings to the value of NZ$250,000 needed by ordinary citizens for pension purposes in New Zealand. A British estimate is £150,000. No matter what the final amount may be, it is substantial. And these savings will typically have to be made between the ages of 25 and 60. Like the rich, many citizens will turn to acquiring Positional goods: bonds, equities, real estate, art and treasure. Unlike the rich, however, their small investments will be lumped together with those of many others and placed in the care of professional investors in charge of a whole variety of investment schemes, a matter that can only create anxiety for many, given the recent crop of pension scandals in Britain.

The British Railways Pension Fund fared variously with their art investments. In real terms they received an annual rate of 11.9% on Impressionist and modern art; 7.5% for English silver; 7.1% for Chinese porcelain; 4.6% for English paintings; and they lost on Tribal art (is there a warning there?). The art market is not dead, but if one chooses it as an investment, one should get some very good advice and pay the transactional costs; as did the Japanese dealer who bought the Van Gogh. Otherwise a person, or a fund, could end up buying one of the 8,000 paintings of Camille Corot acquired by US art lovers. A remarkable figure, given that the total of authenticated works by him is said to be around 3,000.[11]

The realisation for most people that they will have to provide for their own retirement needs must act as one of the great conservative forces of the next decades, especially as equities bulk large in all pension funds. The growth equities of the future will be found in parts of Asia, even Latin America. Their worth will be sustained only if the demand for Popular goods continues to rise in its past spectacular fashion; only if the age of consumerism continues to spread amongst the populations of the developing world, as it shows every sign of doing at present. Next century the future of New Zealanders and many people in other parts of the Western world will be tied to the future of Asia in a way few can now envisage. Already investment analysts even in this remote corner of the globe are hawking the investment attractions of the Asia-Pacific region. Forecasts for the coming decade indicate a real return of 6.3% on sterling bonds and a fractionally higher real return of 6.4% for UK equities, with only the Pacific Rim equities outstripping these figures with a real return of 10.7%, albeit with high risks.[12]

Land and real estate are sound investments; especially the sort of real estate owned by the British BP Pension Fund: property near Harrods worth £278 million, where the land alone is valued at £9m. an acre; and more in Mayfair, where the price of land rises to £23m. an acre. Most pension fund investors cannot hope for such sound investments as these. People will have to be wary of fund managers who invest in the commercial centres of some large cities. They may become graveyards for skyscrapers as the electronically based move to work at home. The choice of cities and city blocks will require great care and considerable knowledge. Russian (and Serb!) property buyers have given a lead to other new entrants to the world of capitalism. In the past two years, more than 70 purchases have been made by Russians in London, for cash, with prices ranging between a quarter and two million pounds. Anarchy, it appears, is not a zero sum game.

The Russians are after another Positional good as well – education at private schools – at a cost £7,335 per annum, for example, for each of the 18 Russian pupils taken on by one school located near Cirencester. Education may be a Public good for the masses. In Britain, however, the 6% of the school population attending independent schools win 50% of the places at Oxford and Cambridge and 25% of the places at Redbrick and beyond. When it is realised that at 16, the age at which most British youth until very recently have left school, 23% of the remaining school population are attending fee-paying schools, these university figures become more comprehensible. Forty-five percent of the fee-paying parents, it should be added, themselves attended the state system. They recognise that education materially affects a person's chances in the job market, the income level they are likely to achieve and their prospects of rising in the corporate and public bureaucracies – the rank they are likely to reach. Consequently they are prepared to pay for what they consider to be a superior form of education. And in this belief they are supported by the rankings attained by the fee-paying schools in the educational stakes.

### *Rank and Status*

There is one Positional good remaining to be dealt with: Rank. Rank is status conferred. Status is a feature of animal societies; the term, pecking order, acknowledges this. The difference is, as the economist Robert Frank has demonstrated, we are prepared to pay for our status – it is a good.[13] And so, too, are some of us prepared to pay for Rank. During Margaret Thatcher's reign, over 40 knighthoods were awarded to private sector industrialists. In the year of their award, their donations to the Conservative Party had been never less than £10,000, and as much as £71,500.[14] Rank being status conferred requires some body to confer it. Like all Positional goods, its function is to fix the social order, to avoid faction. Our egalitarian society is shot through with rank and status, a fact the politically correct are reluctant to accept. Recently the *Financial Times* reported an airline with 54 job titles, including four ranks of tea lady; a bank with more than 30 tiers, with nearly a dozen known as manager; and a hotel chain with more than 40 job titles. So much for flat management structures.[15]

Why do these ranks persist in self-declared egalitarian societies? Because we are human, and our overriding preoccupation is to fix the social order.

## *Entirely Without Adaptive Significance*

Positional goods, unlike Popular and Public goods, have a long history, even an archaeology. In his study of the civilisation of the Cyclades, Colin Renfrew notes the first appearance of Positional goods, towards the end of the neolithic. He writes 'the development of new classes of goods, offering new and tempting scope for the acquisition of wealth, was instrumental in the transformation of a self sufficient peasantry ... to the acquisitive proto-urban and later urban citizens of civilisation'.[16] Renfrew then continues with this remark: by giving social and symbolic significance to goods, by developing new classes of goods, and by acquiring wealth, a whole set of individual and collective aspirations, ambitions and needs are satisfied 'which are at first sight entirely without adaptive significance in facilitating the continued existence of the individual or the species'.

The adaptive significance of Positional goods lies in their ability to counter the anarchic tendency that is our special human inheritance; and one that makes economics the secondary aspect and politics the primary aspect of human existence. The human species is the only species on earth which has the will and the capacity to change or to destroy an existing social order, to create anarchy, and for some individuals and factions to profit from these acts. *Vide*, the Serbs taking up residence in London. The proper name for the human race is not Homo Sapiens, but Homo Anarchensis. To put it more boldly, the human species is the only species whose social order is not genetically determined, the only species capable of envisaging a social order different to the one it has already created.

To speak of the adaptive significance of Positional goods is, of course, to use a sort of shorthand: it is the individual, not the species, that adapts. It is the individual not the society that displays anarchic tendencies. The function of rank – status conferred – is to bond the individual with the society, with the institutions of society of which the individual becomes a representative; to encompass the individual within the boundaries established by society. Who shall compete for what is determined by society, which rewards the successful individuals with goods, status and rank? The superabundance of goods has allowed the creation of a vast array of reference groups within industrial society; groups within which all sorts of people establish their relative status in a host of ways. At the same time there is competition for absolute rank, and the individual's pursuit of rank and wealth turns out to be a very successful adaptive strategy. The higher ranked individual not only has a better chance of survival but also enhances that of his or her offspring too. The wealthier are healthier; the healthier are wealthier; and the wealthier have more offspring.[17]

## *A Better Society*

When people are offered a vision of an alternative social order, they judge it not on the basis of sentiment, but what goods and services are provided.

When Daniel Miller envisages a socialist society, he writes: 'The better part of the present vast array of goods will be preserved, the consumer will be allowed a measure of choice, but the state will regulate the social implications of these goods. Mass consumption will, therefore, work in exactly the opposite tendency to the way it works in capitalist society'. It will create 'an inalienable world in which objects are so firmly integrated into the development of particular social relations and group identity as to be as clearly generative of society'.[18] In short, by redefining goods, a new social order will be created.

The Caring Society which the Labour Party promised the New Zealand electorate in 1984 was a society whose sentiment was vastly different to the one that now prevails in the country. But judgement of these promises is not a matter of sentiment alone. The electorate judges whether or not those promises have been kept by noting the arrangement of goods and services, especially Public goods and services, actually provided. And in the opinion of that significant proportion of the electorate now supporting the Alliance Party, that particular array of goods is visibly absent. A society very different to the one promised has emerged. And the electorate knows this because of the different sorts of goods and the arrangement of goods that prevails. In particular, they have witnessed the enormous shift of Positional goods that has occurred in favour of the classes who manufactured the restructuring that has affected the lives of so many citizens. 'Market freedom', wrote David Calleo, 'is all too often a euphemism for a radical devaluation of one kind of power at the expense of another'.[19]

A part of communism's failure was its inability to turn the additional wealth produced into higher living standards for the consumer. The assumption of a uniformity of needs meant that the discretionary income that ought to have become available could find few suitable outlets, for the good reason that discretionary income is the vehicle for expressing greater freedom of choice which the dictates of the Soviet system could never allow. A return of communism is most improbable. Victory has gone to the free market system. Social engineering has been vanquished. But this does not spell the End of History. The ideological debate will be transferred from a debate about how wealth ought to be produced (and who ought to produce it), to one about how wealth should be consumed and who should consume it. In future, within all societies, Eastern and Western, different factions will hotly contest the provision of Public goods, the protection of Providential goods, and the cultural inanities associated with an even greater availability of Popular goods. The issue of Consumption will heat up the debate, already underway, between the different civilisations that compose the global economy. A spat between Dr Mahathir and Rupert Murdoch's Star TV over the anti-establishment overtones of the Simpsons cartoon series is illustrative of this wider trend. A rejection of the Western way in Asia and the Islamic countries is being fuelled by the grosser aspects of Western consumerism. The politics of Consumption are replacing the politics of Production. But, amidst all of this turmoil, the demand for and value of Positional goods and the influence of those who own them can only be enhanced. Currently in London 39% of residential property is bought by foreigners; those from the Far East, alone, accounting for 12%. One Oxford senior tutor has already been quoted as saying, 'if in 10 years, 25% of our intake is from the Continent, the British parent who has paid large public school fees in the hope of buying an easier route to Oxbridge may begin to squeal'.[20]

A high proportion of fortunes is inherited. About 55% of America's fortunes belong to members of rich families rather than rich individuals. Families control one third of *Fortune's* Top 500 Firms. The family that stays together is obviously the family with the Positional goods; a few infidelities apart, that is. One of the remarkable facts to emerge from the present confusion of the House of Windsor is Camilla Parker-Bowles' ancestry. She is a great-granddaugther of Alice Keppel; which makes her a descendant of Joost van Keppel, a favourite who accompanied William III when he ascended to the English throne in 1688. She is a member of one of England's many elite reference groups whose status and power have been maintained by the possession and manipulation of Positional goods. Lundberg, a tireless investigator of America's rich, summed up both the economic and adaptive significance of the family when in 1937 he wrote, the family 'is a private entity which in the strictest legality may resist public scrutiny, it lends itself admirably to alliances of a formal character and serves as an instrument of confidential financial transactions. The family alone provides a safe retreat from democratic processes, not outside the law, but, for all practical purposes, above the law'.[21] It was not surprising to learn, therefore, that like many wealthy Asians Mr Robert Kuok shuns the media. A Malaysian Chinese, he first made his money in commodities: sugar, oil, rubber, palm oil, tin; and then moved on to hotels (23 luxury hotels around the world), shopping complexes, beach resorts; and more latterly, a 33% share of TVB Hong Kong, followed by the acquisition of the *South China Morning Post*. His business is still, fundamentally, a family business, whose dealings are informal and secretive. He is close to the leadership in Malaysia, Indonesia, the Philippines and China, where he has invested in six hotels, an oil refinery, a port and numerous building projects. His only Hong Kong listed company, Shangri-La Asia, has Mainland minority shareholders.[22]

Mr Li Kashing, the Hong Kong property tycoon, in his negotiations with the communist elite, has forged close relations with Deng Zhifang and Wu Jianchang, the son and son-in-law of Deng Xiaoping; with Chen Weili, the daughter of Chen Yun, Deng's ideological rival; and with Zhou Guanwu, a Deng protege. According to one analyst, 'the fact is that Deng's children are all important people. They know other important people and their power will survive the death of their father'.[23] A reasonable assumption, one would argue; for, as Trotsky wrote, the bureaucracy 'must inevitably in future stages seek to support itself in property relations. One may argue that the big bureaucrat cares little what are the prevailing forms of property, provided only they guarantee him the necessary income. This argument ignores ... the question of his descendants. ... Privileges have only half their worth, if they cannot be transmitted to one's children'.[24]

It is striking that the era marked by the decline of the nuclear Western family is also the one in which the families of the positionals, all over the world, conspicuously retain their historic strengths and functions. Towards the end of his *Treatise on the Family*, Gary Becker writes:

Uncles and aunts, nieces and nephews, cousins, and other kin meet often to transfer gifts, plan family strategy, teach younger members, and inspect and monitor one another's performance and behaviour. Indeed, families can be considered to be small specialised schools that train graduates for particular occupations, land or firm, and accept responsibility for certifying the qualifications of their graduates when qualifications are not readily ascertained.[25]

When he wrote this, he believed he was describing the traditional family; the family that has been replaced by the modern version, which has largely been the case. But as this snippet makes clear, amongst the well-to-do, in the West as well as in the East, the traditional family lives on:

He comes from a wealthy family whose fortunes stem from the Schweppes' patented process, and his father was the second most powerful man at Cazenove. Though all Cazenove partners have a right to introduce one son or daughter into the firm, Mr Kemp-Welch's father would not bring him aboard until he had proved he could survive elsewhere. So in 1954, at the age of 18, he became a messenger, working for the most aggressive stockbroker of the time. He joined Cazenove in 1959. Cazenove's senior partners are educated at just two schools, Eton and Winchester, and come from a handful of Families.[26]

Cazenove, it should be noted, claim they have more than 40 of the FT-SE 100 companies among its clients. This is but one example of the reconsiderations of currently received opinions that are forced upon one by adopting Consumption, rather than Production, as the focus of one's investigations. Goods embody inequalities. Goods are used to mark social boundaries and they are the instruments of social discrimination, helping as they do with the identification of reference groups. Goods fix the inchoate flux of events. They help to establish order for a species that is desperate to establish order. The worldwide drive to produce an ever-increasing supply of goods and services – Popular goods especially – facilitates the proliferation of reference groups and the establishment of interest groups that now stretch across both national and cultural boundaries. At the same time these goods act as a focus for the antagonisms and rivalries of different classes, different nations and different civilisations.

The electorate's unceasing demand for an ever greater supply of Public goods, ever more sophisticated and costly to provide, threatens the state's capacity to fulfil these demands without, in the process, endangering its financial stability; a requirement the EU has made a basic condition for any member state seeking further economic and political integration. The emergence of new elites in the rapidly growing economies of the developing world increases the competition for Positional goods, whilst the threat to the world's Providential goods raises profound political issues whose solutions may require stricter degrees of social control in societies whose professed aim is to allow every citizen the exercise of greater freedom of choice.

For Fukuyama, history ends in consumption and status. 'As standards of living increase, as populations become more cosmopolitan and better educated ... people begin to demand not simply more wealth but recognition of their status ... [They] demand democratic governments that treat them like adults ... recognising their autonomy as free individuals'.[27] Fukuyama belongs to that long line of visionaries who have imagined societies in which abundance leads to status and autonomy, by means of either democracy and the market economy in his case, or democracy and the planned economy in the case of an earlier writer, Eric Fromm. Both men were invoking what Duby described as 'the immemorial image of utopia ... the image of a society no longer riven by class distinctions, and yet still ordered. The dream...'.[28] It is true, an abundance of Popular goods allows many people to seek status, but within relatively narrow limits. Where rank is concerned, the aspirations of the majority cannot be fulfilled. Life remains a competition for a good whose supply must remain inelastic, if that good is to retain any value. Abundance, pace Fukuyama and Fromm, does not put an end to competition, unless abundance puts an end to power. And that is most unlikely given the present state of affairs within the world. For as J.S. Mill recognised long ago, when he, too, was contemplating the consequences of abundance – a condition in which minds 'ceased to be engrossed by the art of getting on'; even in these circumstances, he noted, 'For the safety of national independence it is essential that a country should not fall much behind its neighbours in the mere increase of production and accumulation'.[29] And not only the safety of the nation is involved. So is the security of all those investments that have been made, that will be made in the years to come, for the provision of consumption in the future.

NOTES

1 United Nations, *Economic Survey of Europe in 1980*, Geneva: UN, 1981, chapter 4, section 2.

2 Dianne Summers, 'Survey predicts 17% increase in UK consumer spending', and 'Mintel sees "self reliant" consumer', *Financial Times*, 1 February 1994 and 11 May 1994; and Frank Levy and Richard Murname, 'US earnings levels and earnings inequality: a review of recent trends and proposed explanations', *Journal of Economic Literature*, September 1992, pp. 1333-81.

[3] Guy de Jonquires, 'Temptations along the eastern aisle', *Financial Times*, 6 April 1994.
[4] Kieran Cooke, 'Suharto family a driving force at Lamborghini', *Financial Times*, 11 February 1994.
[5] Alan Maynard, 'Developing the health market', *The Economic Journal*, 101 (408), 1991, pp. 1277-86.
[6] Peter Watson, *From Manet to Manhattan: The Rise of the Modern Art Market*, London: Vintage, 1993, pp. 3-26.
[7] *Euro money*, 'Asia's most powerful families', October 1994, p. 96.
[8] Tibor Scitovsky, *The Joyless Economy: an Inquiry into Human Satisfaction and Consumer Dissatisfaction*, New York: OUP, 1976.
[9] *National Geographic*, 'Our National Parks', 186 (4), October 1994, p. 96.
[10] Susan St John and Toni Ashton, *Private Pensions in New Zealand*, Wellington: Institute of Policy Studies, 1993.
[11] Sotheby's, Christies and other London art dealers and auction houses are tapping the Asian market. Hong Kong is the base for all the main sales of Chinese works of art; there are keen collectors in Mainland China for Chinese paintings, stamps, jade and ceramics. The Singapore government is trying to build the country into a thriving art entrepot, and in the past decade sales have risen from nothing to more than £20m. a year (Anthony Thorncroft, 'London dealers follow where markets lead', *Financial Times*, 7 and 8 October 1995).
[12] Barry Riley, 'How pension funds can rebalance without tears', *Financial Times*, 15 February 1995.
[13] Robert H. Frank, *Choosing the Right Pond: Human Behavior and the Quest for Status*, New York: OUP, 1985.
[14] John Walker, *The Queen Has Been Pleased: The British Honours System*, London: Secker and Warburg, 1986.
[15] *Financial Times*, 14 May 1993.
[16] Colin Renfrew, *The Emergence of Civilisation. The Cyclades and the Aegean*, London: Methuen, 1972, pp. 496-97.
[17] M.G. Marmot et al, 'Health inequalities among British civil servants: the Whitehall II study', *The Lancet*, 337, 8 June 1991, pp. 1387-93; Susan M. Essock-Vitale, 'The reproductive success of wealthy Americans', *Ethology and Sociobiology*, 5, 1984, pp. 45-9.
[18] Daniel Miller, *Material Culture and Mass Consumption*, OUP, 1987, p. 200.
[19] David P. Calleo, *The Imperious Economy*, Cambridge, Mass.: Harvard University Press, 1982, p. 189.
[20] *Financial Times* , 1 January 1995 and 27 August 1994.
[21] Ferdinand Lundberg, *America's Sixty Families*, New York: Vanguard, 1937, p. 9.
[22] Simon Davies and Kieran Cooke, 'Secret life of the rich and well connected', *Financial Times*, 13 September 1993.
[23] Simon Holbertson, 'HK's superman finds warmer winds from China', *Financial Times*, 22 June 1993.
[24] Leon Trotsky, 'The rise of soviet bureaucracy', in C. Wright Mills, *The Marxists*, New York: Penguin, 1962, p. 332.
[25] Gary Becker, *A Treatise on the Family*, Cambridge, Mass.: Harvard University Press, 1981.
[26] *Financial Times*, 15 January 1994.
[27] Francis Fukuyama, *The End of History and the Last Man*, New York: Free Press, 1992, pp. xiv-ix.
[28] Georges Duby, *The Three Orders: Feudal Society Imagined*, University of Chicago Press, 1980, p. 356.
[29] J.S. Mill, *Principals of Political Economy*, London: John W. Parker, 1848, book IV, chapter VI, section 2.

# 7. AN AGRICULTURAL TRANSITION ON THE PACIFIC RIM: EXPLORATIONS TOWARDS A MODEL

*R.D. Hill*

The notion that the Asian countries of the Pacific Rim have seen, since the Second World War, a substantial movement of labour out of agriculture and into the manufacturing and service sectors is remarkably pervasive. Owen,[1] for example, suggests, in respect of Southeast Asia, that the shifting composition of the GDP was due in part to the movement of labour out of agriculture, which had employed an average of 70-80% of the workforce before the War and in the immediate postwar period. Other examples could be given but the simple facts are that the proportionate decline of which Owen speaks is not the same as an absolute decline, and that for 'a movement of labour out of agriculture' to have occurred it would be necessary to show an absolute decline in the numbers of workers in agriculture. This chapter examines and compares the structural changes of Asia-Pacific countries in the period 1960-92 and considers some of the broad implications. I make no apology for presenting a process-oriented study, for processes underlie all spatial patterns.

## *Farmers and Agriculture, 1960-92*

The simple and striking fact is that in every country in Asia there are now more farmers than in 1960; Japan, South Korea, Taiwan and, of course, the city-states of Hong Kong and Singapore, are the only exceptions. Obviously there have also been changes in the degree to which farmers are really farmers though official statistics rarely document this.

It is not just in Japan, where less than a quarter of all farmers are now full-time workers in agriculture, that farmers participate to some degree in the non-agricultural sectors. The growing literature on circular migration from the country (and small towns) to the city clearly indicates strengthening rural-urban economic linkages as countryfolk undertake temporary urban employment, and as 'detached' family members remit funds back to their rural kin.[2] But, at least in gross terms, the fact remains that in most Asian countries there are now more farmers, broadly defined, than in 1960 though in every one of them, the proportion of the total workforce in agriculture has fallen (see Table 7.1).

The growth in the numbers of farmers over the 32-year period is very substantial. Taking only the countries of East and Southeast Asia enumerated here, the number of farmers rose from some 306 million in 1960, to some 558 million by 1992. If China be omitted by reason of its overpower-

Table 7.1. NUMBER AND PROPORTION OF WORKFORCE IN AGRICULTURE – SELECTED ASIAN COUNTRIES, 1960, 1992

| | *1960* | | *1992* | | *Growth in Agricultural Workforce* |
|---|---|---|---|---|---|
| | *No. (000s)* | *Proportion (%)* | *No. (000s)* | *Proportion (%)* | *1960-1992 (%)* |
| *East Asia* | | | | | |
| Japan | 14,529 | 32.9 | 3,663 | 5.8 | -74.8 |
| South Korea | 5,433 | 66.4 | 4,496 | 22.6 | -17.2 |
| China | 227,445 | 75.2 | 462,079 | 66.0 | 103.2 |
| cf. India | 137,568 | 74.1 | 220,799 | 65.8 | 60.5 |
| *Southeast Asia* | | | | | |
| Indonesia (1961) | 23,516 | 71.9 | 35,077 | 48.5 | 49.2 |
| Laos | 1,064 | 83.2 | 1,399 | 71.6 | 31.5 |
| Malaysia | 1,724 | 63.0 | 2,255 | 32.1 | 30.8 |
| Philippines | 4,094 | 67.9 | 10,956 | 45.9 | 167.6 |
| Thailand | 11,342 | 83.8 | 18,782 | 64.3 | 65.6 |
| Viet Nam | 16,478 | 80.2 | 19,506 | 60.6 | 18.4 |

Note: No data for Taiwan. Inadequate date for Cambodia.
Source: *FAO Production Yearbooks.*[3]

ing influence upon the figures (and also because of an unexplained 'jump' of 120 million farmers between 1970 and 1975), the totals are still fairly impressive: 78 million in 1960 to 96 million in 1992, the equivalent of 18 million farm workers, roughly the number in present-day Viet Nam.

While specifically rural or farm population growth rates are not available in an extended time-series, broad quinquennial growth-rate data serve to underline the demographic basis for the very substantial growth in the agricultural population (see Table 7.2). What are particularly striking are the rates of increase for China (though, as noted already, there was an unexplained growth in the numbers between 1970 and 1975, possibly as a result of incorporating women in the agricultural workforce statistics), and especially in the Philippines where no such enumerative accident occurred. In the latter country, the effects of high population growth rates coupled with rather slow rates of economic growth, especially in the 1980s and 90s, and of slow structural change away from agriculture, resulted in a piling up of poor workers in agriculture. (In 1960 agriculture contributed about 34% of the production of total industries in the Philippines, compared with 24% in 1992.) Their productivity in 1960 was about half that of workers in other sectors – as measured by the ratio of the proportion of

Table 7.2. QUINQUENNIAL ESTIMATES OF ANNUAL POPULATION GROWTH RATES, 1960-1990 (%)

| | *1960-65* | *1965-70* | *1970-75* | *1975-80* | *1980-85* | *1985-90* |
|---|---|---|---|---|---|---|
| *Americas* | | | | | | |
| Canada | 1.88 | 1.61 | 1.27 | 1.15 | 0.90 | 1.13 |
| USA | 1.45 | 1.08 | 1.04 | 1.06 | 0.92 | 0.94 |
| Mexico | 3.20 | 3.21 | 3.14 | 2.60 | 2.40 | 2.22 |
| Ecuador | 3.14 | 3.17 | 3.01 | 2.88 | 2.72 | 2.50 |
| Peru | 2.88 | 2.80 | 2.78 | 2.63 | 2.31 | 2.08 |
| Chile | 2.39 | 2.05 | 1.71 | 1.48 | 1.68 | 1.66 |
| *East Asia* | | | | | | |
| China | 2.07 | 2.61 | 2.20 | 1.43 | 1.44 | 1.49 |
| (cf. India) | 2.26 | 2.28 | 2.24 | 2.08 | 2.14 | 1.97 |
| S. Korea | 2.64 | 2.25 | 2.00 | 1.55 | 1.36 | 1.22 |
| Japan | 0.99 | 1.07 | 1.33 | 0.93 | 0.68 | 0.44 |
| *Southeast Asia* | | | | | | |
| Viet Nam | 1.97 | 2.17 | 2.34 | 2.24 | 2.18 | 2.15 |
| Laos | 2.22 | 2.18 | 2.18 | 1.16 | 2.29 | 3.12 |
| Thailand | 2.99 | 3.08 | 2.92 | 2.44 | 1.83 | 1.32 |
| Malaysia | 3.09 | 2.66 | 2.44 | 2.32 | 2.60 | 2.64 |
| Philippines | 3.01 | 3.17 | 2.72 | 2.48 | 2.58 | 2.39 |
| Indonesia | 2.14 | 2.33 | 2.41 | 2.14 | 2.06 | 1.93 |
| *Southwest Pacific* | | | | | | |
| Australia | 1.98 | 1.95 | 1.64 | 1.51 | 1.40 | 1.62 |
| New Zealand | 2.05 | 1.41 | 1.79 | 0.19 | 0.84 | 0.87 |

Source: *World Population Prospects, The 1992 Revision*, Table A2.

total production contributed by agriculture to the proportion of the total workforce in agriculture. And that ratio had not changed between 1960 and 1992, reflecting the relative stagnation of the economy at the time (see Table 7.3).

China's structural change has also been slow and the data appear to show a piling up of farm-based poor, though matters are complicated by the existence of a 'floating population' totalling 100-110 million, much of which is nominally 'agricultural'. From a 40% contribution of agriculture to total production in 1970 – no earlier data are available – the contribution fell to 35% by 1992. (Data are not exactly comparable with capitalist countries because of differences in the way in which the system of national accounts is constructed. They are, however, consistent through time.) India, the other Asian giant, has, by comparison, seen a much smaller build-up in the number

Table 7.3. PRODUCTIVITY INDEX FOR AGRICULTURE (AND FORESTRY), 1960-1980

| | *1960* | *1965* | *1970* | *1975* | *1980* | *1985* | *1990* |
|---|---|---|---|---|---|---|---|
| *Americas* | | | | | | | |
| Canada | 0.53 | 0.66 | 0.66 | 0.75 | 0.95 | 0.90 | 1.10 |
| USA | 0.59 | 0.77 | 0.78 | 0.82 | 0.83 | 0.85 | n.a. |
| Mexico | 0.34 | 0.35 | 0.27 | 0.25 | 0.25 | 0.29 | 0.28 |
| Ecuador | 0.65 | 0.57 | 0.55 | 0.41 | 0.39 | 0.43 | 0.57 |
| Peru | n.a. | n.a. | 0.43 | 0.33 | 0.33 | 0.36 | 0.47 |
| Chile | 0.42 | 0.37 | 0.38 | 0.56 | 0.55 | 0.77 | 0.73 |
| *East Asia* | | | | | | | |
| China | n.a. | n.a. | 0.61 | 0.55 | 0.48 | 0.50 | 0.51 |
| (cf. India) | 0.66 | 0.67 | 0.70 | 0.60 | 0.57 | 0.51 | 0.51 |
| South Korea | 0.59 | 0.72 | 0.68 | 0.58 | 0.45 | 0.47 | 0.35 |
| Japan | 0.48 | 0.39 | 0.32 | 0.34 | 0.33 | 0.40 | 0.45 |
| *Southeast Asia* | | | | | | | |
| Thailand | 0.45 | 0.44 | 0.37 | 0.42 | 0.31 | 0.31 | 0.23 |
| Malaysia | 0.60 | 0.61 | 0.61 | 0.61 | 0.63 | 0.65 | 0.64 |
| Philippines | 0.50 | 0.59 | 0.55 | 0.56 | 0.51 | 0.52 | 0.51 |
| Indonesia | 0.73 | 0.84 | 0.73 | 0.64 | 0.60 | 0.46 | 0.43 |
| *Southwest Pacific* | | | | | | | |
| Australia | 1.13 | 1.02 | 0.79 | 0.88 | 0.59 | 0.78 | 0.90 |
| New Zealand | n.a. | n.a. | n.a. | 1.03 | 0.84 | 0.94 | 1.12 |

Note: The Productivity Index = *Agriculture & Forestry as Proportion of Total Output (%)*
Workforce in Agriculture & Forestry (%).

The Index is sensitive to prices and inter-sectoral terms of trade. It may be interpreted as follows: 1.0, agriculture (and forestry) are as productive in labour-force terms, as other sectors; > 1.0, agriculture (and forestry) are more productive than other sectors; < 1.0, agriculture (and forestry) are less productive than other sectors, e.g. 0.67, one-third, 0.50, one-half, 0.25, one-quarter.

of farmers, despite slightly higher population growth rates than China. Its rate of structural change – agriculture accounted for 47% of production in 1970 and 34% in 1992 – has been more rapid though the productivity of its farmers is, like China's, about half that of other sectors.

By contrast, Thailand, Malaysia and Indonesia have seen quite rapid structural change in their economies. In Thailand and Malaysia the swing away from agriculture, in terms of production, was already well under way by 1960 when only 37-38% of production came from that source. By 1992 Thai agricultural production, lacking the substantial tree-crop sector of Malaysia, had fallen to contribute only 15% of the total compared with

21% in Malaysia. Thailand had proportionately fewer workers in agriculture compared with Malaysia, for their productivity was only one-fifth that of those in other economic sectors. By contrast, in Malaysia by 1992 the productivity of agricultural workers was about two-thirds of those in other sectors.

Indonesia's economy in 1960 was much more like that of China or India, with 53% of the total production being derived from agriculture. By 1992 the corresponding figure had fallen to 21%, the same as Malaysia, though agricultural-worker productivity was only around two-fifths that of other sectors.

Amongst the former socialist countries of Southeast Asia, Viet Nam and Laos contrast markedly with their neighbours in showing rather small gains in the agricultural workforce between 1960 and 1992. Whether this is a 'statistical accident' resulting from changes in enumeration is unclear, especially as population growth rates have been and, in the case of Laos, remain at fairly high levels. Laos, however, remains a virtual demographic terra incognita, though substantial international out-migration, especially in the 1970s, is indicated. For Viet Nam, growth in the number of farmers by only 3 million in 32 years, a rise of only 18%, is, to put it mildly, surprising. Such a small increase could be accounted for only by a massive drop in the proportion of production contributed by agriculture and a corresponding take-up of labour in the secondary and tertiary sectors. Yet such a drop has clearly not occurred. War, though causing substantial losses, probably does not account wholly for these somewhat anomalous patterns which may be due to enumerative changes.

Japan, South Korea, and were data available, Taiwan, show patterns that are quite the reverse of those discussed so far. While they share with other countries a substantial fall in both the proportion of the workforce in agriculture and the proportion of production derived from that sector, there was also a substantial fall in the numbers of workers in agriculture. However, like the other countries of the region, the productivity of their agricultural workers has remained low compared with that of other economic sectors.

### *A Pattern of Change*

Despite some inconsistencies in the data, a broad pattern of change is readily discernible. Since 1960 the agricultural workforce has grown in numbers, except in Japan, South Korea, the city-states and, it can be assumed, Taiwan (Table 7.1). The driving force behind that growth is basically demographic with annual growth rates mostly over 2% at least until the mid-70s (Table 7.2). Some countries, notably Malaysia and the Philippines, show rates over 3% annually. At varying points in time those rates have tended to fall, except in Viet Nam and Laos, so that by the 1985-90 quinquennium in most countries growth rates were below 2.5% and in many, notably China and Thailand, below 1.5. Had there been no change in the structure of the

Table 7.4. NUMBER (MILLIONS) AND PROPORTION (%) OF WORKFORCE IN AGRICULTURE, 1960-1992

| | *1960* | | *1965* | | *1970* | | *1975* | | *1980* | | *1985* | | *1990* | | *1992* | |
|---|---|---|---|---|---|---|---|---|---|---|---|---|---|---|---|---|
| | *No.* | *%* | *No.* | *%* | *No.* | *%* | *No.* | *%* | *No.* | *%* | *No.* | *%* | *No.* | *%* | *No.* | *%* |
| *Americas* | | | | | | | | | | | | | | | | |
| Canada | 0.85 | *13.1* | 0.79 | *10.7* | 0.67 | *8.1* | 0.64 | *6.5* | 0.62 | *5.3* | 0.53 | *4.2* | 0.44 | *3.3* | 0.4 | *3.0* |
| USA | 4.68 | *6.6* | 4.05 | *5.1* | 3.22 | *3.9* | 3.20 | *3.4* | 3.80 | *3.5* | 3.33 | *2.8* | 2.87 | *2.3* | 2.68 | *2.1* |
| Mexico | 5.96 | *55.1* | 6.29 | *50.3* | 6.61 | *45.9* | 6.98 | *40.4* | 7.91 | *36.6* | 8.37 | *33.2* | 8.80 | *30.0* | 8.92 | *28.7* |
| Ecuador | 0.84 | *56.5* | 0.83 | *52.1* | 0.82 | *52.0* | 0.95 | *44.5* | 0.94 | *38.6* | 0.98 | *34.3* | 1.00 | *30.3* | 1.00 | *28.8* |
| Peru | 1.56 | *49.8* | 1.68 | *48.7* | 1.73 | *44.8* | 1.98 | *43.5* | 2.15 | *40.0* | 2.31 | *37.3* | 2.44 | *34.7* | 2.50 | *33.7* |
| Chile | 0.65 | *27.5* | 0.72 | *26.9* | 0.69 | *23.8* | 0.64 | *19.7* | 0.60 | *16.4* | 0.60 | *14.3* | 0.59 | *12.5* | 0.58 | *11.9* |
| *East Asia* | | | | | | | | | | | | | | | | |
| China | 227.45 | *75.2* | 240.72 | *71.3* | 242.26 | *67.2* | 367.52 | *76.3* | 406.13 | *74.2* | 438.54 | *71.0* | 458.43 | *67.5* | 462.08 | *66.0* |
| (cf. India) | 137.57 | *74.1* | 142.94 | *71.7* | 148.84 | *68.5* | 166.09 | *68.7* | 185.02 | *69.7* | 199.77 | *68.1* | 214.66 | *66.5* | 220.80 | *65.8* |
| South Korea | 5.43 | *66.4* | 5.61 | *58.5* | 5.51 | *51.0* | 5.63 | *43.8* | 5.36 | *36.4* | 5.09 | *30.1* | 4.70 | *24.6* | 4.50 | *22.6* |
| Japan | 14.53 | *32.9* | 12.92 | *26.4* | 10.49 | *19.7* | 8.50 | *15.1* | 6.37 | *11.2* | 5.09 | *8.5* | 4.01 | *6.4* | 3.66 | *5.8* |
| *Southeast Asia* | | | | | | | | | | | | | | | | |
| Viet Nam | 16.48 | *80.2* | 14.02 | *78.9* | 14.35 | *76.4* | 15.53 | *72.8* | 16.54 | *67.5* | 17.99 | *64.1* | 19.51 | *60.6* | 20.11 | *59.2* |
| Laos | 1.06 | *83.2* | 1.13 | *80.9* | 1.18 | *78.8* | 1.23 | *76.9* | 1.23 | *75.7* | 1.30 | *73.7* | 1.40 | *71.6* | 1.44 | *70.7* |
| Thailand | 11.34 | *83.8* | 12.13 | *81.8* | 13.45 | *78.2* | 14.92 | *76.6* | 16.72 | *70.9* | 18.04 | *67.7* | 18.78 | *64.3* | 18.98 | *63.0* |
| Malaysia | 1.72 | *63.0* | 1.79 | *59.4* | 2.03 | *56.5* | 2.13 | *47.7* | 2.22 | *41.6* | 2.25 | *36.7* | 2.26 | *32.1* | 2.25 | *30.3* |
| Philippines | 4.09 | *67.9* | 6.11 | *59.0* | 7.32 | *53.2* | 8.43 | *53.3* | 9.25 | *51.9* | 10.00 | *49.4* | 10.71 | *46.9* | 10.96 | *45.9* |
| Indonesia | 23.52 | *71.9* | 26.38 | *70.4* | 30.97 | *66.3* | 31.20 | *61.8* | 32.18 | *57.2* | 33.73 | *52.8* | 35.08 | *48.5* | 35.49 | *46.7* |

Table 7.4 continued

| | *1960* | | *1965* | | *1970* | | *1975* | | *1980* | | *1985* | | *1990* | | *1992* | |
|---|---|---|---|---|---|---|---|---|---|---|---|---|---|---|---|---|
| | *No.* | *%* | *No.* | *%* | *No.* | *%* | *No.* | *%* | *No.* | *%* | *No.* | *%* | *No.* | *%* | *No.* | *%* |
| *Southwest Pacific* | | | | | | | | | | | | | | | | |
| Australia | 0.47 | *11.4* | 0.46 | *10.0* | 0.43 | *8.1* | 0.46 | *7.4* | 0.47 | *6.9* | 0.43 | *5.8* | 0.41 | *5.0* | 0.40 | *4.7* |
| New Zealand | 0.13 | *14.7* | 0.13 | *13.0* | 0.13 | *11.9* | 0.14 | *11.5* | 0.15 | *11.2* | 0.14 | *10.1* | 0.14 | *9.2* | 0.13 | *8.8* |

Notes: Compiled from *FAO Production Yearbooks*. Where two figures have been given for any year in the sources, the average has been taken. The large rise in numbers in China between 1970 and 1975 is unexplained in the source. The 1960 figure for Malaysia was derived from its later component parts. Figures for Peru and Indonesia are for 1961. All figures are official but may ignore significant numbers which may be illegal migrants (e.g. Malaysia), or not actually engaged in agriculture (e.g. China).

whole economy and of the workforce, by 1990 there would have been the prospect of slower growth in the number of farmers and their dependants entirely for demographic reasons.

In reality, of course, there was a substantial structural change of both workforce and economy (Table 7.3, 7.4 and 7.5). This accounts for the fact that there are far fewer farmers than there would have been in the absence of such change. It is noteworthy that the Asian countries with rather slow structural change, as measured by the contribution of agriculture (and forestry) to total production, are precisely those with substantial growth in the number of farmers, i.e. China and the Philippines, both of which have experienced more than a doubling of the numbers in agriculture. By comparison with other sectors, the farmers were also notably inefficient as producers (Table 7.3), though this phenomenon is by no means confined to those countries in which structural change has been slow.

Of the exceptional countries, first Japan and then South Korea entered a phase of low population growth coupled with substantial and sustained structural change away from agriculture which resulted in falls in both the proportion and number of farmers in the workforce. In 1960, Japan had 14.5 million farmers, representing 33% of the workforce. Fifteen years later the number had decreased to 8.5 million agriculturalists, 15% of the total workers, and by 1992 there were only 3.7 million farmers, just under 6% of the workforce. Over the whole period productivity remained at just under half that of other sectors, with a dip to a third in the 70s and 80s. By contrast, South Korea's agricultural workforce fluctuated around 5.5 million in the 60s and 70s, falling steadily in the 80s to reach about 4.5 million by 1992. In percentage terms, the change was from 66% in agriculture in 1960, to roughly 44% in 1975 and 23% by 1992, the sharpest fall on an annual basis occurring between 1990 and 1992. Unlike Japan, in South Korea productivity fell sharply.

Having thus briefly sketched the broad changes in the number and proportion of workers in Asian agriculture and their productivity, several large questions arise. Can the picture be pushed back beyond 1960 if reasonably comprehensive statistics are available? Can the pattern observed be extended to other countries of the Pacific region? Or, to put the second question in a different way, do the data show fragments of a long-continued process in which, with the structural changes that accompany economic growth, countries move from a situation in which agriculture is overwhelmingly dominant to one in which it employs few farmers and contributes only a small proportion of production (see Figure 7.1)?

The answer to the first question is 'yes' but only if qualitative rather than quantitative data are accepted. The reply to the second question is also 'yes' for, as Figure 7.2 clearly shows, after making due allowance for varying rates of change in the numbers and proportion of agriculturalists in the workforce, the general trends are clear. They conform to the model. In addition, the provision of quantitative data allows conclusions to be drawn

Table 7.5. QUINQUENNIAL ESTIMATES OF AGRICULTURE (AND FORESTRY) AS A PROPORTION OF TOTAL VALUE OF OUTPUT, 1960-1990

| | *1960* | *1965* | *1970* | *1975* | *1980* | *1985* | *1990* |
|---|---|---|---|---|---|---|---|
| *Americas* | | | | | | | |
| Canada | 6.9 | 7.0 | 5.3 | 4.9 | 5.0 | 3.8 | 3.6 |
| USA | 3.9 | 3.9 | 3.1 | 3.2 | 2.9 | 2.4 | n.a. |
| Mexico | 18.8 | 17.9 | 12.7 | 10.0 | 9.0 | 9.7 | 8.4 |
| | | | | | | | |
| Ecuador | 36.8 | 29.9 | 28.6 | 18.4 | 14.6 | 14.7 | 17.4 |
| Peru | n.a. | n.a. | 19.1 | 14.5 | 13.2 | 13.4 | 15.2 |
| Chile | 11.6 | 10.0 | 9.1 | 11.0 | 9.1 | 11.0 | 9.1 |
| | | | | | | | |
| *East Asia* | | | | | | | |
| China | n.a. | n.a. | 40.4 | 39.4 | 36.0 | 35.5 | 34.7 |
| (cf. India) | 48.6 | 48.7 | 47.2 | 42.1 | 40.0 | 35.0 | 33.7 |
| S. Korea | 39.3 | 41.9 | 34.5 | 25.0 | 16.3 | 14.2 | 8.5 |
| Japan | 15.6 | 10.3 | 6.3 | 5.3 | 3.7 | 3.4 | 3.7 |
| | | | | | | | |
| *Southeast Asia* | | | | | | | |
| Thailand | 37.4 | 35.6 | 28.3 | 31.6 | 21.7 | 21.1 | 14.9 |
| Malaysia | 37.9 | 36.3 | 34.3 | 28.4 | 26.4 | 23.9 | 20.7 |
| Philippines | 33.9 | 35.1 | 29.5 | 30.3 | 26.5 | 25.9 | 23.8 |
| Indonesia | 52.8 | 59.0 | 48.4 | 39.8 | 34.4 | 24.5 | 21.0 |
| | | | | | | | |
| *Southwest Pacific* | | | | | | | |
| Australia | 12.9 | 10.2 | 6.4 | 6.5 | 4.1 | 4.5 | 4.5 |
| New Zealand | n.a. | n.a. | n.a. | 11.9 | 9.4 | 9.5 | 10.3 |

Notes: Compiled from *UK Yearbooks of National Accounts Statistics*. Data for China are for PRC only and are compiled on the MPS basis. Total Value of Output is at current prices for each year and excludes 'Producers of government services' and 'Other producers'. Unlike workforce estimates, these are price-sensitive. No data for Viet Nam and Laos.

about relative rates of change and variations in the timing of major transitions such as the fall in the proportion of agricultural workers that invariably precedes the fall in their absolute numbers.

## *A Model of Agricultural Transition*

Figure 7.1 sets out, in a simple schematic or stage form, the trajectory of basically agricultural economies to modernity, the final stage of which is characterised by both low numbers and proportions of agriculturalists. It uses simple direct measures, both available in recent times. In Figure 7.1 the upper curve represents the number of agriculturalists. The lower curve represents the proportion of agriculturalists in the workforce, shown not directly, but inversely by the distance between it and the upper line. Thus

Figure 7.1. AGRICULTURAL ECONOMIES: THE MOVE TO MODERNITY

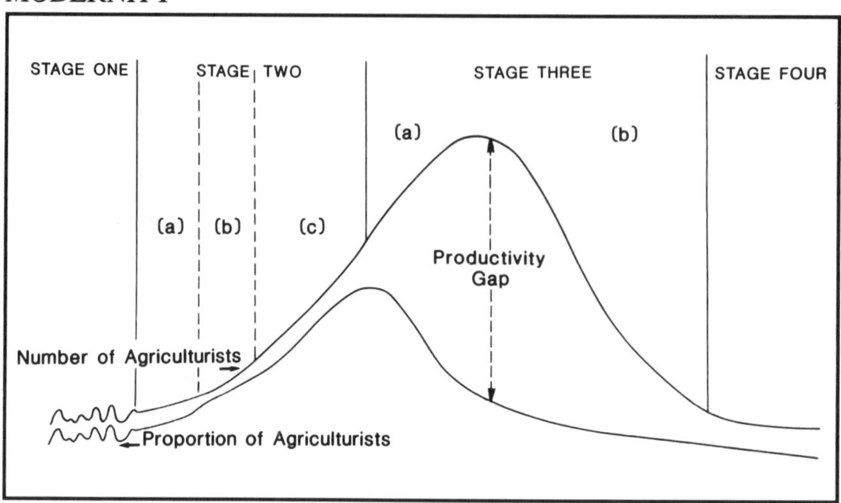


at Stage One the number of agriculturalists is low but the proportion is high. At Stage Two (b), the proportion, as a result of agrarianisation, rises even higher. At Stage Three (a), the number of farmers is still increasing but their proportion in the workforce is falling. In the next Stage (3b), the number is falling but the proportion is levelling out and the curves are converging so that by Stage Four numbers and proportion, both low, are again parallel.

The model is basically descriptive and heuristic. (The possibility that it may be made predictive is left to others to explore.) It is thus of a piece with other stage models such as Rostow's 'stages of economic' growth[4] – which, however, has an explicit political agenda – and Zelinsky's model of the 'mobility transition'.[5] Its relationship to the familiar Notestein-Thompson model of the demographic transition and to its kin, the epidemiological transition, is obvious, for growth in the number of agriculturalists is demographically driven.[6]

At Stage One, the agricultural workforce, like the population as a whole, is fairly small and its numbers fluctuate in step with the general population, reflecting the classical Malthusian controls which lead to fairly high birth and death rates. The agricultural oecumene is slow growing and may show short-term fluctuations because of epidemic disease, other natural disasters and warfare, especially, as in Asia, that accompanied by wholesale transfers of people. Agriculture is fairly extensive because of little pressure upon land except, perhaps, that placed by the needs of personal and group security. The proportion of agriculturalists in the workforce is high, probably at least four-fifths rising to 99% in remoter regions of shifting cultivation. (The Chin Hills of the India/Burma border are an example.) Where political and environmental stability prevail, trade and craft industry may expand with possibly a lower proportion of agriculturalists. Where instability prevails, trade (and craft industry) decline with periods of 'subsistence regression'. Agriculture is about as productive as other sectors so that the Productivity Ratio is close to unity. (This Ratio is calculated by dividing the proportionate contribution of agriculture to production by the proportionate contribution of agriculturalists to the workforce.)

Stage Two comprises three sub-stages, the second of which may be suppressed. At Stage Two, in much of Asia a sustained but fairly slow rise in population began prior to significant imperialist penetration and the economic restructuring that accompanied it.[7] Trade in imported manufactures initiates a decline in some kinds of craft industry, notably hand-spinning and hand-weaving, together with iron-smelting and the craft-manufacture of some kinds of metal goods, especially utensils. This displacement tends to result in some degree of agrarianisation of the workforce. But this may be partly offset by increasing involvement in trade. In Asia agricultural intensification begins as the agricultural frontiers start to close to further settlement, as, for example, in the lowlands of Guangdong and in Tonkin.

Stage Two (b) sees the expansion of imperialist control to territory rather than merely to trade which was characteristic of Stage Two (a). This expansion results in, first, enhanced rural investment and trade in basic commodities. In Southeast Asia, rice is particularly important in this context. Consequently there is a large and rapid expansion of the agricultural oecumene as in Java, Lower Burma, Siam and Cochinchina. The agricultural workforce begins to grow, partly by migration, but the development of long-distance trade in staples requires the expansion of infrastructure, including export-oriented *points d'appuy*. This results in economic diversification and a small fall in the proportion, but not the number, of agriculturalists which continues to expand. Agriculture becomes more intensive and more specialised with, in Southeast Asia, a rice monoculture becoming characteristic in environmentally-suitable areas.

In the second place, the expansion of imperialist territorial control results in the rapid spread of non-staple crops (sugar, tobacco, abaca); and on the hills of well-watered equatorial regions, rubber, coconuts and later oil-palm. These enterprises are organised both as small holdings and as large-scale plantations. Foreign agricultural labour imports expand – Javanese to north-central Sumatra; Indians to Lower Burma and to western Malaya; and Chinese to Malaya, Siam and the British territories in northern Borneo. The proportion and number of agriculturalists continues to rise and in terms of specific activities is increasingly specialised. Foreign labour in partly agriculturally-related secondary and tertiary sectors tends to displace indigenous participants in these sectors leading to ethnically-based agrarianisation.[8] Labour productivity in agriculture is moderate but tends to fall in areas of over-population – 'agricultural involution', to use Geertz's term,[9] in some wet-rice areas. Area productivity is about the same as it was in earlier stages, but it tends to rise as 'scientific' agriculture begins to take hold and as production infrastructure, especially irrigation, is improved.

Stage Two (c) continues trends begun in the previous substage but in much of Asia is post-colonial. Population growth accelerates with improved water supply, sanitation and health care spreading to rural areas. Production intensifies with improved irrigation, fertilizer application and the spread of high-yielding varieties of major crops. Agricultural colonisation slows with the closing of the rice frontier, followed by partial closing off of lands for other crops such as rubber and coconuts. The contribution of agriculture to production begins to fall as the effects of investment directed to other sectors begins to be felt. Towards the end of the Stage the proportion of workers in agriculture begins to fall though the numbers increase. Productivity of agriculture in relation to other sectors begins to fall and a 'productivity gap' begins to open.

Stage Three sees a dramatic widening of the productivity gap, with productivity in agriculture generally falling to between one quarter and one-third that of other sectors. In substage (a) there is a piling up of relatively poor workers in the rural areas, some of whom begin to be drawn partly or wholly into the urban-industrial economy. At a point of inflection marking the fall in the numbers of agricultural workers, sub-stage (b) begins and the curves for numbers and proportion increasingly tend to converge, becoming close to parallel in Stage Four. Late in Stage Three, part-time urban-based farmers begin to appear, in contrast to rural-based part-time off-farm workers characteristic earlier. In addition, land consolidation begins, at first operationally through renting, and later tenurially by sales and purchases of land. The contribution of agriculture to production continues to fall but tends to stabilise as the following stage is reached. Population growth rates are falling.

Stage Four sees a situation in which both the number and proportion of agriculturalists in the workforce is small, as is the contribution of agriculture to total production. The productivity index tends to rise towards 1, meaning that agriculture, in terms of labour, is as efficient as other sectors, reflecting a high level of capital intensity. However, subsidies and protectionism may delay this. They may also lead to a situation in which agriculture is characterised by a dualistic structure in which small 'uneconomic' family farms survive for social welfare reasons and co-exist with larger fully-commercial units. (Size, in this context, refers to scale, not area.) At this Stage, population growth is slow. Any upward movement in the agricultural workforce derives from the introduction of high-value labour-intensive crops, but the long-term trend is for stability. Major structural realignments have thus taken place, though early in Stage Four there may be continued land consolidation, both operationally and tenurially.

### *Testing the Model*

Does reality fit the model, bearing in mind that quantitative data are available for a reasonable range of countries only from 1960? (It is for this reason that Stage One and Two have been telescoped in a temporal sense in Figure 7.1.) The evidence for Stage One need not long detain us. While it is true that in early times there were, as there are now, rural communities which were not substantially based upon agriculture, this writer has been unable to find a single country other than city-states and late out-growths of colonialism in which agriculture did not at some time employ the bulk of the population. Obviously, however, lands of recent colonisation, such as Australia and New Zealand, were not participants in this Stage.

Much of the evidence for Stage Two is generally known and does not require detailed documentation. The question of agrarianisation of the workforce in (b), however, does require support, much of which comes from outside the Pacific Rim countries, for in them the issue has been little addressed. In nineteenth-century Madras, for example, an official reported that as a consequence of competition with machine-made clothes, 'many weavers had emigrated or taken to agriculture'.[10] In early nineteenth-century Bihar, 18.6% of the workforce, mainly women, was industrially employed, mostly in handcrafts, but by 1901 the equivalent proportion was only 8.5%.[11] For the Malay Peninsula in the late nineteenth and early twentieth centuries, Hill[12] has documented some degree of agrarianisation and it seems reasonable to suppose that this was one response to competition from imported manufactures such as bar-iron in competition with indigenous iron-smelting, imported machine-made cloth in competition with handloom weavers. In passing, it may be noted that Southeast Asian weavers seem to have suffered doubly, first by competition with Indian handloom weavers and then from machine-made cloths.

Evidence supporting the transition from Stage Two (c) to Stage Three begins to be available in the FAO data summarised in Table 7.2.[13] Unfortunately these data do not go back quite far enough to distinguish clearly the point of inflection at which the proportion of workers in agriculture begins to fall from its earlier high levels. (Outside the region even the data for such a strongly agricultural country as the Central African Republic, with 94.1% of the workforce in agriculture in 1960, do not show a point of inflection.) The timing of this important transition cannot, therefore, be precisely established, but happen it clearly did, thus initiating Stage Three.

Stage Three is characterised by a declining proportion of the workforce in agriculture. The rate of this decline, which occurred in every country around the Pacific Rim, is quite variable from country to country, rather rapid in the case of South Korea, averaging 1.4% a year, rather slow in China (and India) at 0.3% a year. As Figure 7.2 shows, the rate of decline was mostly quite even in the period 1960-1992. By contrast, the curves for absolute numbers mostly show an initial steady rise followed by much sharper rises in the late 60s and early 70s, reflecting increasingly effective 'death-control'. These patterns mostly continue to 1990, though for Malaysia the curve shows the beginning of flattening by the early 70s and in a gentle inflection spread over 22 years shows an actual decline in the agri-

Figure 7.2. CHANGES IN NUMBER (CROSSES) AND PROPORTION (DOTS) OF AGRICULTURAL WORKERS IN THE WORKFORCE, 1960-1992

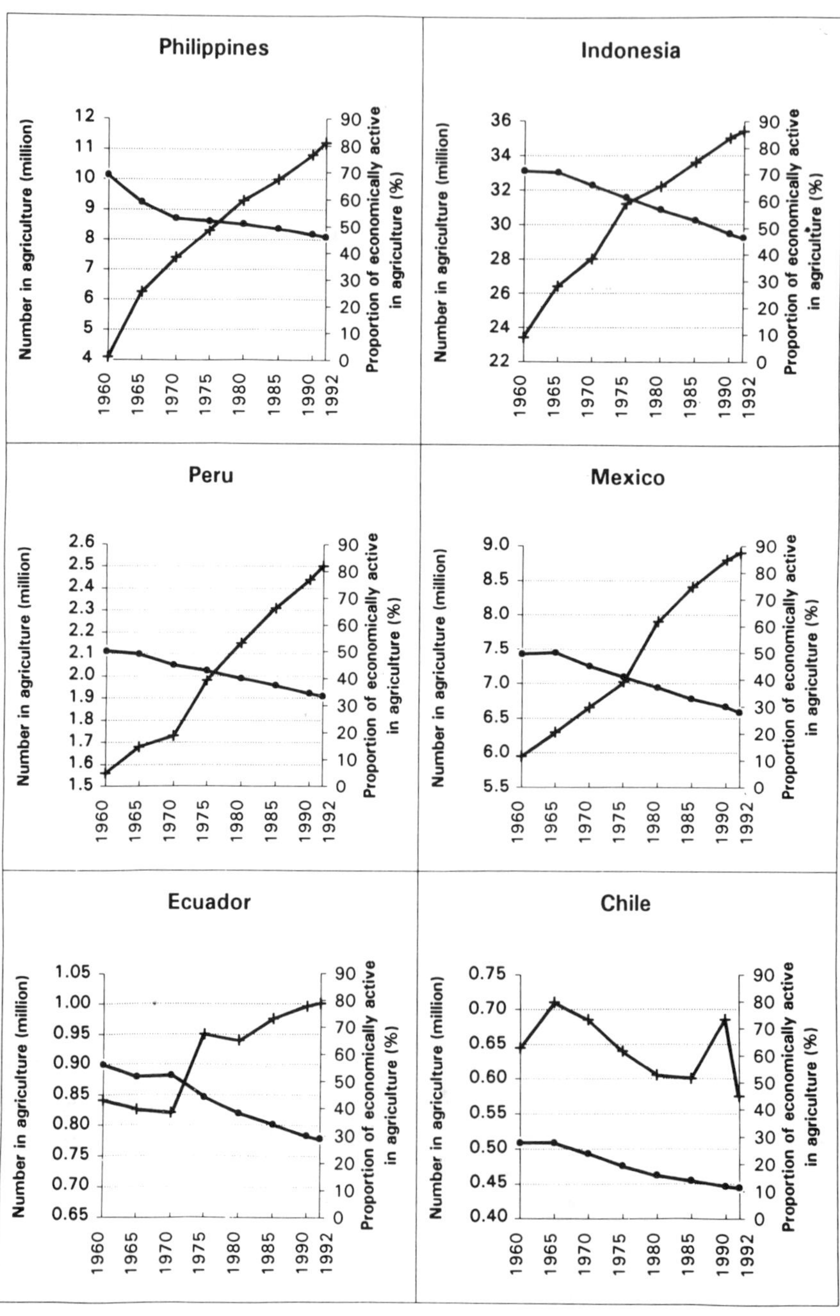


Figure continued overleaf

Figure 7.2 continued

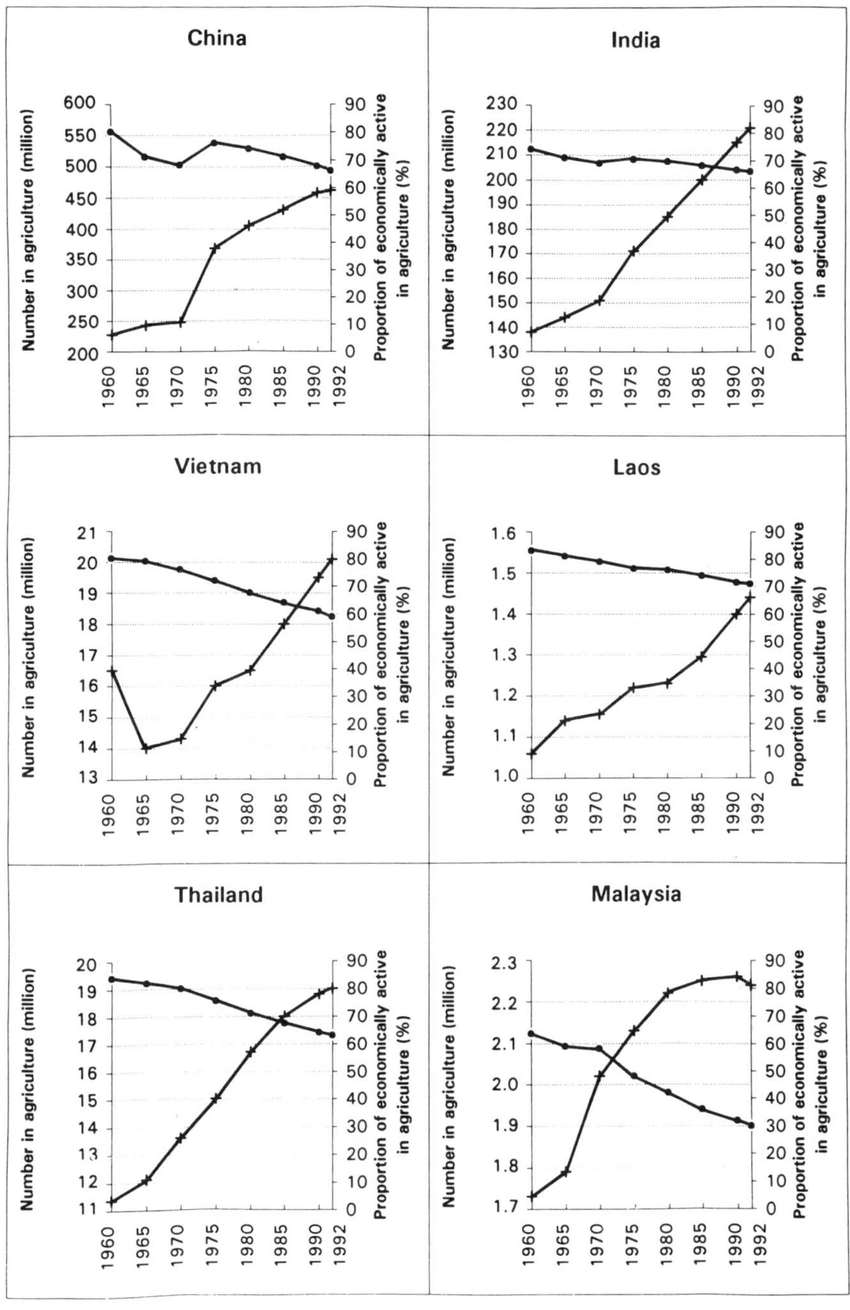


Figure continued overleaf

Figure 7.2 continued

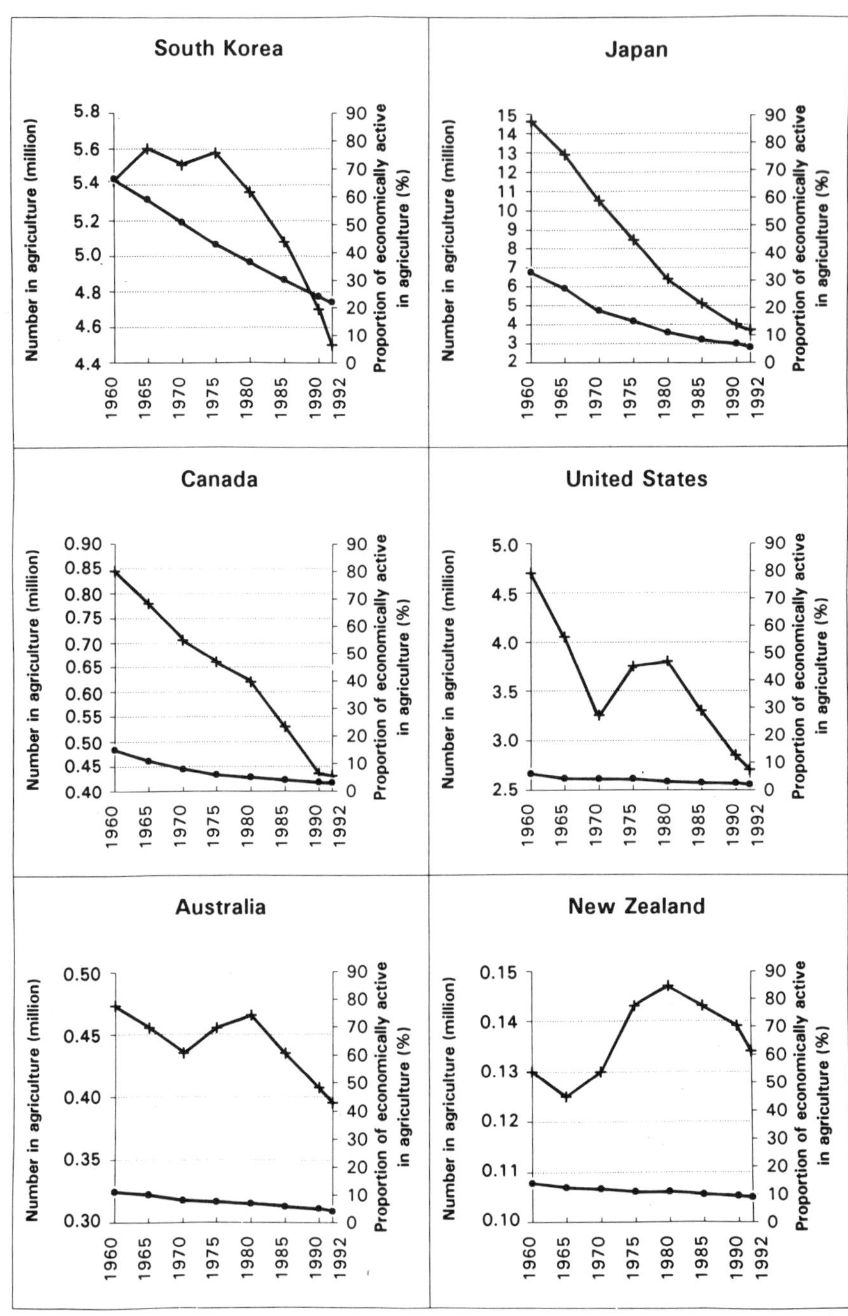


Source: FAO Production Yearbooks.

cultural workforce thus entering Stage Three (b). (Unfortunately this case is a chimera, for the official statistics seem to ignore the presence of some half-million illegal migrant workers, mainly in agriculture. But the point remains.) China and Thailand show what may be the beginnings of an inflection in the curves for their agricultural workforces and thus may be entering Stage Three (b). In the case of China it seems probable that this is definitely so since official statistics appear to count as 'agricultural' some 100-110 million 'rural surplus labourers' who have effectively withdrawn from the agricultural workforce and are now part of an urban 'transient' population.[14] By contrast, the curve for India shows no such flattening and nor do those of most Southeast Asian countries. The Philippines actually shows a steepening of the curve suggesting that it is still early in Stage Three (a), the category into which the other countries of that region also fall.

The Latin American countries of the Pacific Rim considered here, Mexico, Ecuador, Peru and Chile, begin the period from 1960 with a substantially lower proportion of the workforce in agriculture than the countries of East and Southeast Asia, except that Chile had a lower fraction in that sector even than Japan. The rates at which the proportion has declined have been similar to that of Japan, about 0.8% per year, in the cases of Mexico and Ecuador, but rates were substantially slower than in most Southeast Asian countries though much faster than those for China and India where structural transformation, as reflected in the workforce data, has been notably slow. The substantially lower proportion of the workforces in agriculture in the Latin American countries suggests a rather slow transformation of their economies in the longer term, as well as the urban nature of the Hispanic colonisation and the earlier importance of the latifundia system of large estates in rural areas of Latin America. But Chile, except for a small upwards 'blip' in the total number of workers in 1965, shows a clear decline in the number as well as the proportion of agricultural workers. It thus falls into Stage Four. The remaining Latin American countries, like the Asian countries (other than Japan and South Korea and, probably, Taiwan) show continued growth in the number of agriculturalists, though Ecuador may just be starting to show the beginnings of a levelling off. Mexico, Ecuador and Peru are thus firmly in Stage Three (a) with Ecuador possibly being nearest to entering Stage Three (b).

Stage Three (b) is characterised by continued declines in the proportion of farm workers in the workforce, accompanied by a fall in the total numbers as well. Around the Pacific Rim, three countries clearly fall into this category, Japan, South Korea and Chile, the two latter showing clear evidence of passing from Stage Three (a) to (b) in the mid-60s (Figure 7.2). The speeds of the transition have been rather different, however, with the proportion in agriculture in Chile falling at an average rate of just under 0.5% annually over the period. By contrast the average rate for South Korea was just under 1.4% a year. The numbers involved, too, are strikingly different. Chile shed less than 100,000 workers from an initial agricultural workforce of some 650,000, whereas South Korea shed about 900,000 from 5.4 million and Japan almost 10.9 million from 14.5 million in 1960. Japan in thus likely to be about to move into Stage Four.

At Stage Four the proportion and number of agricultural workers approach and reach stability. Early in the stage the number falls and the proportion may also decline slowly, but, given current demographic patterns and in the absence of large-scale innovations of highly-profitable labour-intensive forms of agricultural production, both the numbers and proportion may be expected to stabilise eventually though at the moment the data for the countries in this category, Canada, USA, Australia and New Zealand, still show overall slow declines. However, all, except Canada, show some small fluctuation in numbers, though whether this is a response to agricultural innovations, to price trends or to government incentives is difficult to say.

## *A Predictive Model?*

An important question is whether this model, which is essentially descriptive of the direction of change – but nonetheless useful as an heuristic device – may be made predictive. What is clear is that the fragments of data represented by Figure 7.2 and the statistical tables do fit the model. (Lest it be thought that analysis of the data preceded the model, let the reader be assured that the model is the product of an evening of cerebration in a military guest-house in Hanoi.)

What is also clear is that all countries have passed through Stage One. Most have also passed through Stage Two, though were data available, it is possible that some African countries and, possibly, Afghanistan and Bhutan in Asia, remain at Stage Two (c) with the proportion of agriculturalists in the workforce yet to fall. Similarly, most Asian countries and the Pacific Rim Latin American countries analysed here, except Chile, fall into Stage Three (a), with China, Malaysia and Ecuador about to move into the later phase of that Stage, though in the two former countries the future is clouded by the failure of the statistics to reflect the objective situation. But on present trends, given continued structural change, change that only major catastrophies would reverse, these countries seem set to move into the next phase as numbers in agriculture fall. The speed at which the transitions will occur will obviously vary from country to country but reversal seems unlikely.

Much, of course, will depend upon rates of population increase and of economic growth. But it is also clear that high population growth does not necessarily lead to 'stagnation' at Stage Three (a) as the case of Malaysia demonstrates. The examples of Japan and South Korea would suggest that the combination of low population growth and high economic growth may result in rapid transitions. Certainly, it seems likely that Japan and Chile will, in the next decade or so, move into Stage Four to join 'Anglo' North

America, Australia and New Zealand. South Korea, given the rapid rate of decline in the number of its agricultural workers (1.2% annually from 1975 to 1992), will probably not be far behind. However, as in Japan, for political and social welfare reasons the fall in numbers will not be as rapid as it might be in a wholly 'free-market' situation. These considerations, however, are very far from being predictive in any rigorous sense and the question of prediction of timing or magnitude of change will require rather more sophisticated analysis than that presented here.

Little mention of productivity has been made in the foregoing discussion since it is a derivative measure. However, it has the advantage of quantifying the degree to which low-earning workers may 'pile up' in rural areas, creating a 'labour bank' on which development processes draw. Productivity, as measured by the Productivity Index (Table 7.3), at Stage One is probably close to unity, given that economies are overwhelmingly agricultural. In Stage Two, especially in (c), as the importance of agriculture in the economy begins to decline, productivity may fall relatively as the more developed capitalist sector penetrates the 'traditional' economy. At Stage Three, and this can now be documented (Table 7.3), the traditional agricultural sector may be left behind, for a longer or shorter time.

Consider first those countries in which in 1960 agricultural production was already low but by 1990 had gone much lower. This group includes China (and India), South Korea, Thailand, Indonesia and Mexico, all of which have little large-scale commercial agriculture as well as a large peasant group and fiscal and investment policies which favour the secondary and tertiary sectors. Each has major problems related to increasing rural-urban and interregional income disparities, some, as in Mexico, of very long standing. Other countries (Malaysia, Philippines, Japan, Ecuador) have more or less maintained productivity in agriculture though it is lower, and in the case of Japan and the Philippines, much lower than that of the other sectors. The existence of strong 'commercial' or plantation-type agriculture, or in the case of Japan, deliberate policies, may explain this pattern. By contrast, those countries in or approaching Stage Four show a rising trend of productivity or fluctuation around unity, reflecting high levels of technical efficiency and capital intensity and resulting in relatively insignificant regional and social class differences in income.

Ultimately the countries of the region will all fall into Stage Four, some sooner than others as has been suggested already. The question of when 'ultimately' may be is not a matter that can be forecast accurately, especially for countries still at Stage Three (a). But with increasingly long time-series data and with greater understanding of the factors responsible for the patterns observed, in a word, with further explorations, there seems little reason why the model itself should not be further refined and its capacity to forecast improved, for its regularities are too compelling to dismiss.

## NOTES

[1] N.G. Owen, 'Economic and social change', in N. Tarling (ed.) *The Cambridge History of Southeast Asia*, vol. 2, CUP, 1992, p. 493.
[2] See R.D. Hill, 'The impact of urbanisation and rural-urban linkages in Thailand and Malaysia,' *Asian Geographer*, 14 (1), 1995, pp. 28-44, for example.
[3] United Nations, *FAO Production Yearbooks*, Rome, various issues.
[4] W.W. Rostow, *The Stages of Economic Growth, A Non-Communist Manifesto*, CUP, 1967.
[5] W Zelinsky, 'The hypothesis of the mobility transition', *Geographical Review*, 61, pp. 219-49.
[6] See W.S. Thompson, 'Population', *American Journal of Sociology*, 34, 1929, pp. 959-75; F.W. Notestein, 'Economics of population and food supplies. Economic problems of population change', *Proceedings of the 8th International Conference of Agricultural Economists*, London, pp. 13-31; H. Jones, *Population Geography*, London: Paul Chapman, 1990; A.R. Omran, 'Epidemiological transition: theory', *International Encyclopedia of Population*, New York: Free Press, vol. 1, 1982, pp. 172-4; and, for a brief summary of both the demographic and mobility transitions, R. Skeldon, *Population Mobility in Developing Countries*, London and New York: Bellhaven Press, 1990, 25 ff.
[7] N.G. Owen (ed.), *Death and Disease in Southeast Asia*, Singapore: OUP, 1987.
[8] R.D. Hill, *Rice in Malaya: A Study in Historical Geography*, Kuala Lumpur: OUP, 1977, p. 190.
[9] C. Geertz, *Agricultural Innovation in Indonesia*, Berkeley: University of California, 1963.
[10] D. Kumar, 'South India', in his *Cambridge History of India*, CUP, vol. 2, 1983, p. 370.
[11] N. Charlesworth, *British Rule and the Indian Economy 1800-1914*, London: Macmillan, 1982, p. 34.
[12] Hill, op. cit., 1977, pp. 68-9, 190-1.
[13] UN, FAO, op. cit.
[14] *China Daily*, 9 June 1995, p. 3.

# 8. JAPAN'S FOREIGN DIRECT INVESTMENT IN THE PACIFIC RIM, 1985-1993[1]

*Peter J. Rimmer*

Since the mid-1980s, the Pacific Rim has become the world's most dynamic sub-global region. Earlier its development was shaped largely by outside funds but since then there has been accelerating investment from within the region, notably from Japan and the NIEs of Hong Kong, Singapore, South Korea and Taiwan. This has given substance to 'the flying geese' pattern of economic development.[2] Japan is the 'model' lead goose, followed by the NIEs, and a group of ASEAN countries comprising Thailand, Malaysia, Brunei, Indonesia, the Philippines and Viet Nam.

Before the Pacific War, Japan's FDI was directed to its colonies of Formosa (Taiwan), Korea and Manchukuo (Manchuria), and afterwards it increased slowly until a marked upsurge during the early 1980s. The real turning point, however, was the Plaza Accord in September 1985 which led directly to an appreciation of the yen and heralded Japan's emergence as an economic superpower.

These developments raise a series of issues. How can these post-war changes in Japanese FDI within the Pacific Rim be interpreted? More specifically, how have trends in Japan's FDI changed since the Plaza Accord? To what extent are the differences in investment between the region's nation states attributable to sectoral changes in manufacturing, resource development, and commerce and services? What are their likely political implications?

This chapter provides an historical context for Japan's FDI and examines it in detail from 1985-93.[3] Its emphasis on macroeconomic changes is complemented by analysis of the Electronics and Industrial Enterprises (EIE) Group[4] whose varying fortunes are illustrative of the microeconomic issues involving the strategies, activities and behaviour of corporate investors, and underline the way in which FDI has complemented changes in Japanese foreign trade (i.e. through investments in manufacturing subsidiaries, marketing networks and tourism).[5]

## *Japan's FDI, 1951-1984*

Between 1951 and 1984 the Ministry of Finance's *Approval/Notification of Overseas Direct Investment* and the Bank of Japan's direct investment of the balance of payment statistics recorded 34,314 cases of FDI valued at US$71,432 million.[6] The cases included: (a) the purchase of an existing enterprise (or productive facilities); (b) the establishment and management of a new enterprise; and (c) participation in the management of an enterprise (all in a foreign country).[7] Thus, FDI differed from portfolio investment which involved earning a return on an investment without being involved in management.

In practice, however, it is difficult to distinguish between direct and portfolio investment (i.e. whether the intention of the investment is to control or participate in the enterprise's management). Consequently, this examination of regional trends in Japan's FDI covers any Japanese investment in a foreign company in which 10% or more of a company is acquired. Although FDI statistics are notorious for their lack of precision, Japanese statistics rank second after the United States for their consistency.

Japan's FDI statistics would not have recorded the existence of the EIE which was established in 1948 by Mrs Yuriko Go to distribute recording tape.[8] The company was rescued from bankruptcy by Yoshiharu Takahashi in June 1975 who added magnetic and adhesive tapes to its list of products. In 1976 he became Chairman and Owner of the Company as Mrs Go had no heir. In 1977 Yoshiharu's son, Harunori Takahashi, joined the debt-ridden company and founded a subsidiary, EIE Development Co. Ltd. In 1978 Harunori became its Vice-President and in May 1983 its President. When Yoshimaru Takahashi died in 1985 his son took effective control of the EIE Group. There were no signs that EIE – with its headquarters in a backstreet in Tokyo's Ginza – would be at the forefront of Japanese FDI after 1985.

The most conspicuous feature of the period 1951-84 was the overall decline in mining and manufacturing, and increase in non-manufacturing activities, such as commerce, finance and insurance, transport and real estate (see Figure 8.1). Four different periods, however, can be recognised in the pattern of Japan's FDI reflecting marked volatility in the investment climate.[9]

(1) *Infancy (1951-66)* when FDI was concentrated on a narrow range of products (notably mining and manufacturing) and developing countries especially in Asia (e.g. copper ore in Malaysia and the Philippines; iron ore in India, Malaysia and the Philippines; oil in Indonesia; and natural gas in Brunei) and loan repayments were through the long-term delivery of specific products.

(2) *Remarkable increase of FDI in manufacturing enterprises (1967-73)* bolstered by special tax provisions for labour-intensive medium and small enterprises in developing countries and low-interest loans supplied by the Japan Export-Import Bank for oil and resource-related projects.

(3) *Oil shock's aftermath (1973-80)* when investment was primarily in resource development, export marketing and labour-intensive manufacturing (e.g. textiles and electrical/electronics) within the NIEs and ASEAN.

(4) *Bid to counter growing protectionism (1980-85)* in Europe and North America by accelerating mainstream investment in the iron and steel and chemicals industries and electric/electronic and transport equipment fields as lenders sought to overcome domestic restrictions and take advantage of the progressive liberalisation and internationalisation of Japan's financial sector.

Reflecting a shift from developing countries to advanced capitalist countries, the new trends between 1981 and 1985 presaged more fundamental changes in Japan's FDI after 1985 – a move from trade-related FDI to financial and insurance activities, real estate and services, and a pronounced shift to Europe and North America at the expense of Asia and the Middle East (see Table 8.1).

Table 8.1. JAPAN'S FDI BY INDUSTRY, 1951-1985

| *Industry* | *1951-60* % | *1961-70* % | *1971-75* % | *1976-80* % | *1981-85* % |
|---|---|---|---|---|---|
| Agriculture, Forestry & Fisheries | 2.5 | 2.7 | 2.0 | 2.7 | 0.7 |
| Mining | 30.4 | 31.8 | 25.1 | 15.4 | 9.9 |
| Manufacturing | 44.9 | 24.7 | 33.3 | 36.7 | 25.1 |
| Commerce | 11.3 | 10.7 | 14.8 | 15.8 | 15.4 |
| Finance & Insurance | 3.9 | 9.4 | 8.0 | 5.5 | 17.9 |
| Transport | 0 | 0 | 0 | 0 | 12.5 |
| Real Estate | 0 | 0 | 0.1 | 1.7 | 5.4 |
| Other | 7.0 | 20.7 | 16.7 | 22.2 | 13.1 |
| | 100.0 | 100.0 | 100.0 | 100.0 | 100.0 |

Source: Komiya Ryutaro and Wakasugi Ryuhei, 'Japan's foreign direct investment', *Discussion Paper 90-DF-11,* Discussion Paper Series, Research Institute of International Trade and Industry, Tokyo: Ministry of Trade and Industry, 1990, p. 23.

## *Japan's FDI, 1985-1993*

An analysis of trends in Japan's FDI between 1985 and 1993 underlines the differences from the preceding period (see Table 8.2). The acquisition of securities had superseded cash loans as the leading sector by 1993 – the establishment or expansion of branches still remained minor. The more significant feature was the unprecedented growth in the number of cases and value of FDI until 1989 – the most remarkable development in the world economy's recent history. After 1989 there was a progressive decline in the number of cases until 1993 and in value until 1992.

(1) *Unprecedented growth in FDI between 1985 and 1989* associated with the 'bubble economy'during which manufacturing improved its

Figure 8.1. JAPAN'S FOREIGN DIRECT INVESTMENT, 1960-1985

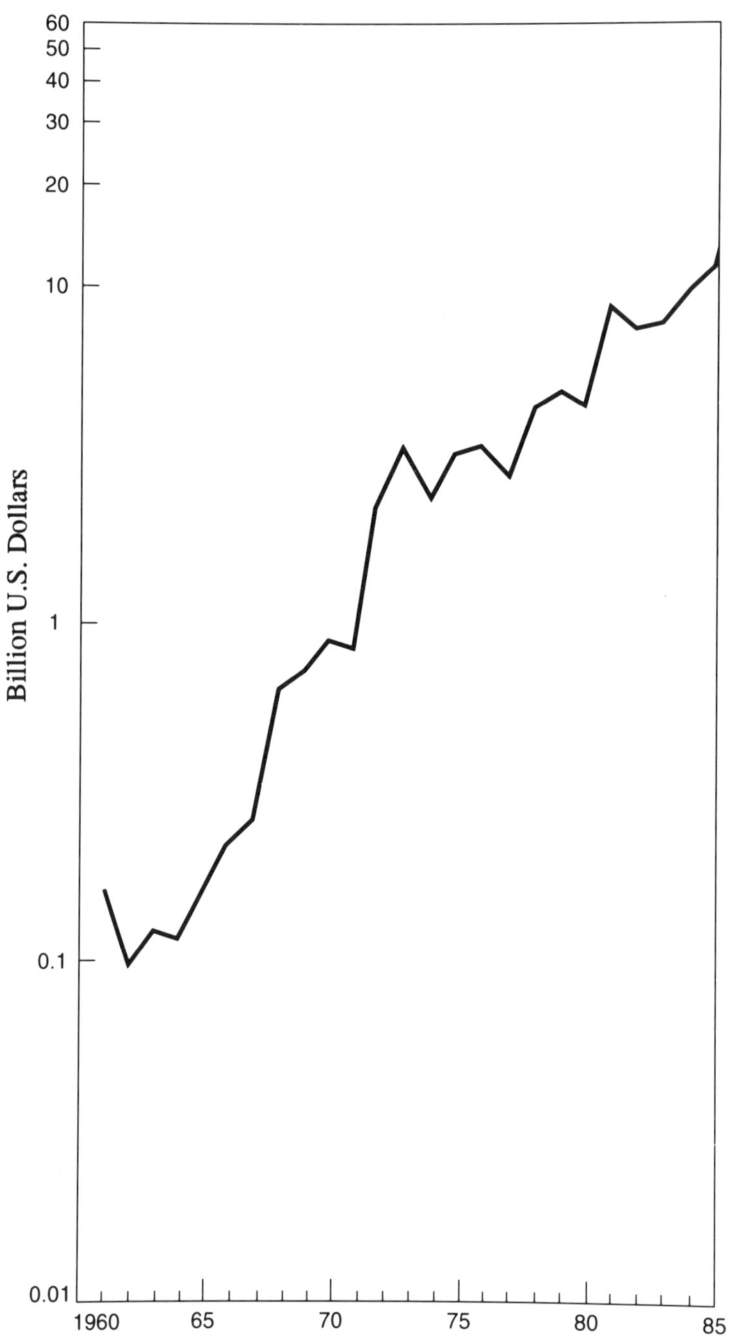


Source: Komiya and Wakasugi, op. cit., 1990, p. 21.

position against non-manufacturing (though the latter was still responsible for three-quarters of Japan's FDI). The improved position of manufacturing stemmed from growth in the manufacture of electrical/electronics equipment (e.g. semi-conductors and high-definition TV sets) and chemicals (e.g. pharmaceuticals), whereas the marked increase in investment in real estate and services did not match the relative decline in finance and insurance, commerce and transport services.

(2) *A decline in FDI between 1989 and 1993* related to the bursting of the 'bubble economy' which led to another increase in manufacturing's share at the expense of the non-manufacturing sector (though the latter still accounted for two-thirds of Japan's FDI). The key manufacturing increases were made by chemicals and electrical/electronics equipment, and the key non-manufacturing increase by commerce which was offset by a marked decline in investment in finance and insurance, services and real estate.

Table 8.2. JAPAN'S FDI BY REGION, 1951-1985

| *Region* | *1951-60* % | *1961-70* % | *1971-75* % | *1976-80* % | *1981-85* % |
|---|---|---|---|---|---|
| Asia | 17.3 | 21.3 | 28.1 | 27.3 | 20.4 |
| (NIEs) | (4.6) | (5.0) | (10.2) | (10.2) | (8.7) |
| (ASEAN) | (9.2) | (13.1) | (17.6) | (16.8) | (10.8) |
| North American | 31.1 | 25.0 | 24.3 | 28.6 | 36.4 |
| (USA) | (30.7) | (18.6) | (22.0) | (26.6) | (34.8) |
| Oceania | 0.7 | 7.6 | 5.3 | 7.8 | 3.6 |
| *Subtotal* | 49.1 | 53.9 | 57.7 | 63.7 | 60.4 |
| Europe | 7.1 | 19.3 | 15.2 | 9.5 | 13.9 |
| Middle East | 13.8 | 8.4 | 5.2 | 6.2 | 1.5 |
| Other | 30.0 | 18.4 | 21.9 | 20.6 | 24.2 |
| *Total* | 100.0 | 100.0 | 100.0 | 100.0 | 100.0 |

Note: Rounding errors.
Source: Komiya and Wakasugi, op. cit., 1990, p. 22.

Rather than concentrate on changes by industry, however, it is more revealing to use shift-share analysis to highlight variations in the spatial distribution of Japan's FDI during these two critical sub-periods.

## *The Bubble Economy, 1985-1989*

When the yen nearly doubled in value between 1985 and 1989, the behaviour of Japanese firms was epitomised by the EIE Group. When stock prices soared and interest rates plummeted, EIE financed its property expansion by using its highly valued Tokyo real estate as collateral with the Long-Term Credit Bank of Japan and four other banks. From its base in electronics and industrial holdings, EIE expanded under the presidency of Harunori Takahashi into financial services (including Kyowa Saving & Loan, and Anzen Saving & Loan), eight golf courses, transport and communications, and real estate. The Group also moved offshore and sought to broaden its leisure activities into the Pacific Rim with Japan and Australia as the twin poles of its operations. Properties were also acquired in Europe and North America. At its peak the Group owned 17 overseas hotels, 5 golf courses, travel agencies, cruise ships, marinas, helijets, shares in hotel management, holdings in 3 regional airlines and 5 office buildings. These assets were reputedly worth US$7 billion and brought with them the power to influence Pacific Rim governments and politicians, and to excite the interest of local developers. The EIE Group also invested in Bond University and the proposed Darwin-Alice Springs Railway.

EIE's acquisitions were part of Japan's increased FDI from US$12.2 billion in 1985 to US$67.6 billion in 1989. Japan became the world's largest investor with the number of cases of FDI rising from 2,613 to 6,589. In searching for the key to Japan's successful performance, a series of theories has been advanced. Rather than examining these theories and the implied economic threat from Japan, attention is focused on the changing distribution of the country's FDI during the unprecedented boom by considering regional trends.

There were few signs of a new Greater East Asian Co-Prosperity Sphere between 1985 and 1989.[10] Japan's economy was too interdependent globally. Most of the growth in investment occurred within North America and Europe – a sharp contrast to earlier years when most of Japan's FDI went to developing countries (see Table 8.3). Collectively, these two regions accounted for more than two-thirds of Japan's FDI. (The United Kingdom alone attracted over 200 Japanese firms.) Other areas to record growth were Oceania and, to a much lesser extent, Asia. Conversely, Latin America's share plummeted sharply, and the Middle East and Africa also recorded reduced shares. Rather than showing these differences in percentage terms, a shift-share analysis was undertaken to express the changes in value terms.[11] Attention in interpreting these changes is switched from the regional to the national level.

Strong positive showings – matching those of the United States and Canada – were recorded by Australia, Hong Kong and Thailand (see Figure 8.2). Panama, Mexico and Peru, together with Indonesia, were primarily responsible for the 'losses'. How are these major 'gains' and 'losses' to be interpreted?

No single factor was responsible. Influences included the yen appreciation, trade barriers, direct investment in the real estate industry, the im-

Table 8.3. COMPOSITION OF JAPAN'S FOREIGN DIRECT INVESTMENT, 1985-1993 (US$ millions)

| *Year* | *Acquisition of securities* | | *Cash loans* | | *Branches (established or expanded)* | | *Total* | | *Annual change* |
|---|---|---|---|---|---|---|---|---|---|
| | *Cases* | *Value* | *Cases* | *Value* | *Cases* | *Value* | *Cases* | *Value* | *%* |
| 1952-84 | 15,180 | 28.010 | 13,061 | 30,905 | 1,036 | 1,768 | 31,815 | 61,277 | |
| 1984 | 828 | 4,595 | 1,636 | 5,340 | 35 | 221 | 2,499 | 10,155 | +20.3 |
| 1985 | 1,023 | 5,963 | 1,552 | 5,924 | 38 | 329 | 2,613 | 12,217 | +82.7 |
| 1986 | 1,419 | 12,546 | 1,728 | 9,208 | 49 | 566 | 3,196 | 22,320 | +49.5 |
| 1987 | 2,126 | 19,941 | 2,387 | 12,971 | 71 | 452 | 4,582 | 33,364 | +40.9 |
| 1988 | 2,725 | 28,638 | 3,263 | 17,801 | 89 | 584 | 6,077 | 47,022 | +43.6 |
| 1989 | 2,602 | 43,169 | 3,910 | 23,632 | 77 | 739 | 6,589 | 67,540 | -15.7 |
| 1990 | 2,249 | 38,507 | 3,565 | 17,598 | 49 | 808 | 5,863 | 56,911 | -26.9 |
| 1991 | 1,556 | 27,129 | 2,983 | 13,991 | 25 | 464 | 4,564 | 41,584 | -17.9 |
| 1992 | 1,397 | 21,667 | 2,318 | 12,110 | 26 | 360 | 3,741 | 34,138 | +5.5 |
| 1993 | 1,530 | 23,947 | 1,925 | 11,812 | 33 | 266 | 3,488 | 36,025 | |
| | 32,635 | 254,115 | 38,328 | 161,292 | 1,528 | 6,555 | 75,029 | 422,555 | |
| 1994 | 1,203 | 28,476 | 1,236 | 12,184 | 39 | 391 | 2,478 | 41,051 | |

Note: The method of calculating cases changed in 1994.
Source: Ministry of Finance, 1994.

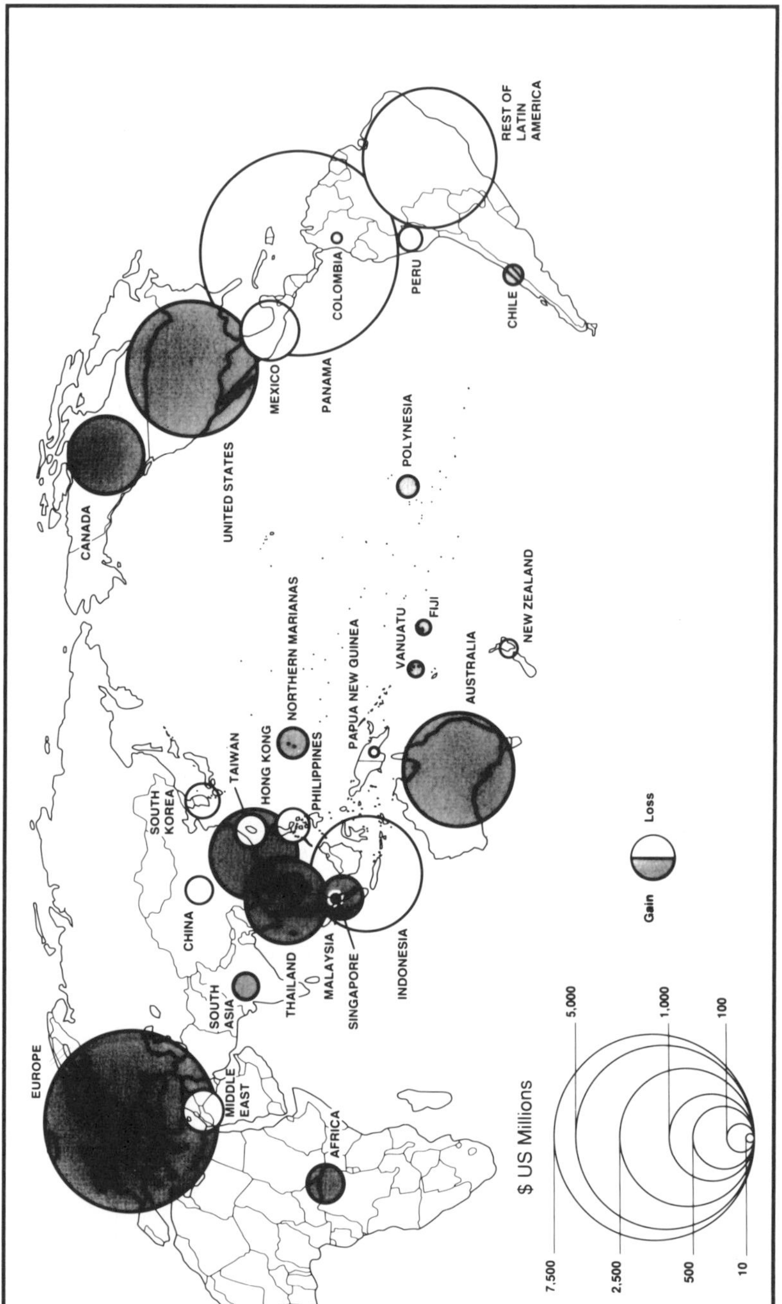

Figure 8.2. SHIFT-SHARE ANALYSIS OF JAPAN'S FDI BY MAJOR REGION AND HOST COUNTRY IN THE PACIFIC RIM, 1985-1989

proved managerial ability of Japanese enterprises, direct investment in the financial and insurance sectors, and government policies.[12] Their relative importance varied between countries. The key factors contributing to sharp increases in direct investment in the United States, for example, were the marked increase in the yen's value since 1985, measures to cope with trade friction and protectionist moves, the increased competitiveness of Japanese companies in international markets, and globalisation of management.[13]

The yen appreciation accounted for the 'gains' recorded by the United States and specific countries in East and Southeast Asia (e.g. Hong Kong, Malaysia and Thailand). Between 1985 and 1989 the yen rose by 90% against the dollar and reduced the cost of initial investment in these countries compared with Japan. As wages, salaries and land costs were higher in Japan, many enterprises established production activities in overseas locations, especially in labour-intensive activities.

Trade barriers increased the positive showings of Western Europe, North America and specific East and Southeast Asia countries (e.g. Hong Kong, Malaysia and Thailand). Japanese enterprises located production plants in these areas to circumvent import restrictions, anti-dumping duties, and new, threatened or anticipated requests for voluntary restraints against Japanese exports. They attracted Japanese enterprises into the local production of colour televisions, video tape recorders, passenger cars, machine tools and photocopying machines because there were no restraints on exports. In particular, Japanese companies were eager to gain a foothold in the European Community as market insiders before 1992, England and the Netherlands being the main destinations for Japanese firms.[14] In the United Kingdom, for example, Nissan established its car manufacturing operations in Sunderland (1984), Honda in Swindon (1985) and Toyota in Derbyshire (1989).[15] Conversely, the gains by Thailand and Malaysia stemmed from Japanese investment in labour-intensive manufactures (e.g. electrical/electronics industry). These were bolstered by investments in commerce, services and finance as Japanese firms spread from their traditional bases in Hong Kong and Singapore. Hong Kong's marked gain stemmed from its use as a base for penetrating China.

Direct investment in the real estate industry by life insurance companies for asset management was also reflected in the 'gains' made by Western Europe, the United States, Australia, Hong Kong, Singapore and a host of Pacific Island groups. Large Japanese construction companies and real estate companies also sought to expand their overseas sales in these locations.[16] Most of the investment by Japanese companies and individuals in foreign real estate was designed to earn rents and capital gains on investments rather than to seek profits from controlling or managing property (e.g. hotels were turned over to management agencies). In other words, it was indirect foreign investment driven by investors rather than direct foreign investment as part of a planned company strategy.[17]

As illustrated by the EIE Group, the upsurge in real estate investment stemmed from Japan's large current account surplus, the stock market boom and the marked increase in domestic land prices between 1986 and 1989.[18] The rise in land prices was pronounced in central Tokyo where advanced information technology and the internationalisation of financial business led to the further concentration of business activities. These higher land prices reduced the yields of real estate companies and institutional investors based in Tokyo. Consequently, they used their appreciating assets – stocks and bonds, and land holdings – as collateral to borrow money from Japan's deregulated banking industry and from overseas lenders to invest in off-shore office, hotel, resort and residential properties. Low-cost finance was readily available during Japan's asset bubble in both stocks and land because of the country's loose monetary policy, favourable exchange rates and the lax borrowing rules applied by financial institutions.[19]

Large corporations, especially in the manufacturing sector, however, borrowed more from the capital market and less from banks and financial institutions. Not all of the borrowing by large corporations was for investment in plant and equipment. A large proportion was used for financial engineering (called *zai*-tech) involving the purchase of financial assets giving high yields. The banks faced difficulties in finding borrowers among large corporations and their targets shifted to smaller companies and the real estate industry.[20] Japanese financial institutions not only recycled Japan's current account surpluses but also functioned as financial intermediaries by converting short-term funds procured from overseas and reinvesting them abroad. If the Japanese Government had channelled the surplus into bonds for public works, the massive increase in funds to the real estate industry would not have occurred.

Speculative investment in cheap overseas real estate led to 'gains' in Western Europe, the United States, Asia and Australia. Japanese firms invested in offices and hotels in 'world cities' such as London, Los Angeles, New York, Hong Kong, Singapore and Sydney. They also targeted leisure resort centres such as Australia's Gold Coast, Hawaii, Guam, Saipan and other Pacific Islands to cater for the upsurge in Japanese tourists taking advantage of the appreciation of the yen.[21] A major outcome of this investment activity was the internationalisation of and close relationship between the Japanese construction, hotel, investment, real estate and resort industries. A large number of the overseas projects were financed with cheap loans and built for Japanese consumption. This practice mitigated the relative inexperience of Japanese investors in overseas markets. Initially, Japanese investors had sought local partners but as investment became increasingly speculative, they initiated projects on their own account. This practice led to increased hostility to their 'trophy' central city investments in the United States, and resorts in Australia and Hawaii where there was strong resistance to golf course construction.[22]

The improved managerial ability and technical skills of Japanese manufacturing enterprises acquired during the 1980s were a powerful factor behind the strong 'gains' recorded in Europe and the United States.[23] Japanese investment in the United States concentrated on establishing production and sales bases. Some diversification and deepening occurred as Japanese corporations sought to strengthen R&D bases, establish information networks, locate regional bases for speedy decision-making and bolster sales capabilities.

The advance of Japanese companies into the United States has often been accompanied by investment friction stemming from conflicts between companies and local communities, management and labour, and cross cultural differences in employee attitudes and employer expectations. The location of Japanese financial institutions in world cities, however, has attracted attention to their financial activities. These included mergers and takeovers, loans to third countries, overseas ventures in retail banking, services to Japanese manufacturing and commercial subsidiaries in advanced capitalist countries, and financial subsidiaries in offshore tax havens (e.g. Bahamas, Bermuda and Cayman Islands).

In hindsight, it is easy to rationalise the reason for the gains and losses during the boom between 1985 and 1989. Because FDI expanded so vigorously once the yen appreciation had occurred, it was difficult to imagine when it would stop. Inevitably, the rate of increase was bound to moderate as it could not continue at such a pace forever. By 1990 investment was more sluggish than anticipated. The speculative domestic asset bubble had burst! Economic observers began to raise doubts about the quality of Japanese management and contemplate the threat to the country's economy of a medium- or long-term structural decline. Others saw an end to Tokyo's new youth subcultures created by the bubble's prosperity.[24]

### *After the Bubble, 1989-1993*

Symptomatic of the end of the bubble economy was the demise of the EIE Group.[25] Unable to meet its payments on loans, the Group sought assistance from its lead banker, the Long-Term Credit Bank of Japan. The Bank's initial response represented the traditional willingness of Japanese financial institutions to assist troubled clients both financially, by arranging a rescue package with other banks, and by despatching senior management to oversee restructuring. A loan was provided to the Group which turned from buying to selling properties. After EIE's rescue package collapsed, the Long-Term Credit Bank of Japan and four other key creditors froze its loans and seized its properties.[26] Apparently EIE survived by drawing loans from two small credit associations – Anzen and Tokyo Kyowa. EIE's President was Tokyo Kyowa's Chairman and effectively controlled Anzen. Kyowa lent EIE more than seven times its equity. By Japanese banking law it should not have exceeded 20% of its capital.[27]

EIE's misfortunes stemmed from the government's decision to burst the bubble economy in a way that reduced land price without triggering a collapse of the entire credit system. From 1990 the Bank of Japan progressively tightened domestic credit to overcome the threat of a financial implosion. Specific restrictions on lending to the real estate sector were imposed by the Ministry of Finance. Between 1989 and 1993 FDI from Japan declined from US$67.5 billion to US$36 billion – the number of cases also fell from 6,589 to 3,488.[28] Reflecting slower economic growth, this decline was triggered by falls in stocks and land prices in Japan, and a loss in corporate investor confidence.

The regional changes reignited the idea of the East Asian Co-Prosperity Sphere led by Japan because marked growth in Asia was the key feature between 1989 and 1993 – a reflection of the sluggish recovery in the global economy and renewed trade friction with the United States and Europe (Table 8.4). Latin America also experienced modest growth and, to a lesser extent, so did the Middle East and Africa. Europe barely held its own but both North America and, to a lesser degree, Oceania experienced reduced shares. Again, these differences in percentages are translated into values using a shift-share analysis.[29] As before, attention is switched from the regional to the national level to interpret these changes.

Clearly, there was less volatility between 1989 and 1993 (see Figure 8.3). The most conspicuous feature was the 'loss' made by the United States. Other losses were recorded by Singapore, Australia and Canada. Conversely, the strongest positive showing was recorded by China. Malaysia, Indonesia and Hong Kong recorded 'gains' as did the Philippines, South Asia, Taiwan and Panama. This pattern was almost the mirror reverse of the preceding period though on a much reduced scale.

Interpreting these changes is more complex. The simple pattern of capital being transferred from principal to subsidiary firm has been supplanted by diversified capital procurement schemes reflecting the globalisation of industry. Attention here is focused on country-specific factors to explain the major 'losses', particularly those incurred in Japan's FDI to the United States; and the major 'gains', especially those in China, Thailand and Malaysia.

The United States, and, to a lesser degree, Singapore, Canada and Australia, were more adversely affected by the decrease in FDI after 1989. Initially, this trend was attributed to the ending of the massive investment in the United States, the global recession centred on the United States and Europe, and tight credit supply arising from a global capital shortage.[30] Later reflections saw the continuing trend being due to the decline in the willingness to invest following decreases in the profits and assets of Japanese enterprises, the excessive number of production plants stemming from the rapid direct investment of the late 1980s, and the anticipation of slower growth in American and European markets.[31]

In particular, the losses in the United States, Canada and Australia were attributed to the downturn in Japanese and overseas property values, triggered by tighter credit in Japan and restrictions on real estate lending. As Japanese investors had little appreciation of the cyclical nature of real es-

Table 8.4. JAPANESE DIRECT INVESTMENT BY INDUSTRY, 1985 AND 1989 ($US millions )

| | *1985* *Amount* | *%* | *1989* *Amount* | *%* |
|---|---|---|---|---|
| *Manufacturing* | | | | |
| Foodstuffs | 90 | 0.7 | 1,300 | 1.9 |
| Textiles | 28 | .02 | 533 | 0.8 |
| Lumber & pulp | 15 | 0.1 | 555 | 0.8 |
| Chemicals | 133 | 1.1 | 2,109 | 3.1 |
| Iron & steel/ non-ferrous metals | 385 | 3.2 | 1,591 | 2.4 |
| Machinery | 352 | 2.9 | 1,762 | 2.6 |
| Electrical/Electronic | 514 | 4.2 | 4,480 | 6.6 |
| Transport equipment | 627 | 5.1 | 2,053 | 3.0 |
| Others | 208 | 1.7 | 1,901 | 2.8 |
| Sub-total | 2,352 | 19.2 | 16,284 | 24.0 |
| *Non-manufacturing* | | | | |
| Agriculture & Forestry | 12 | 0.1 | 151 | 0.2 |
| Forestry | 42 | 0.3 | 47 | 0.1 |
| Mining | 598 | 4.9 | 1,262 | 1.9 |
| Construction | 94 | 0.8 | 646 | 1.0 |
| Commerce | 1,550 | 12.7 | 5,148 | 7.6 |
| Finance/Insurance | 3,805 | 31.1 | 15,395 | 22.8 |
| Services | 665 | 5.4 | 10,616 | 15.7 |
| Transportation | 1,240 | 10.1 | 2,927 | 4.3 |
| Real estate | 1,207 | 9.9 | 14,143 | 20.9 |
| Others | 322 | 2.9 | 180 | 0.3 |
| Sub-total | 9,535 | 78.2 | 50,517 | 74.8 |
| Branches | 329 | 2.7 | 739 | 1.1 |
| Total | 12,216 | 100.0 | 67,540 | 100.0 |

Note: Rounding errors.
Source: Ministry of Finance, 1994.

tate investment, they continued to invest after the cycle had peaked. When they sought belatedly to liquidate their overseas holdings, they did so without conspicuous success. Many Japanese investors had made acquisitions at inflated prices which were difficult to justify after the asset bubble in stocks and land had burst. Some of their large office and resort projects commenced during the late 1980s had not been completed. Japanese construction companies which had retained offices, hotels or real estate for capital sale also suffered losses.[32] Supported by Japanese financial institutions following the downturn in lending to major corporations, speculative real estate companies had incurred debts that outstripped their capacity to

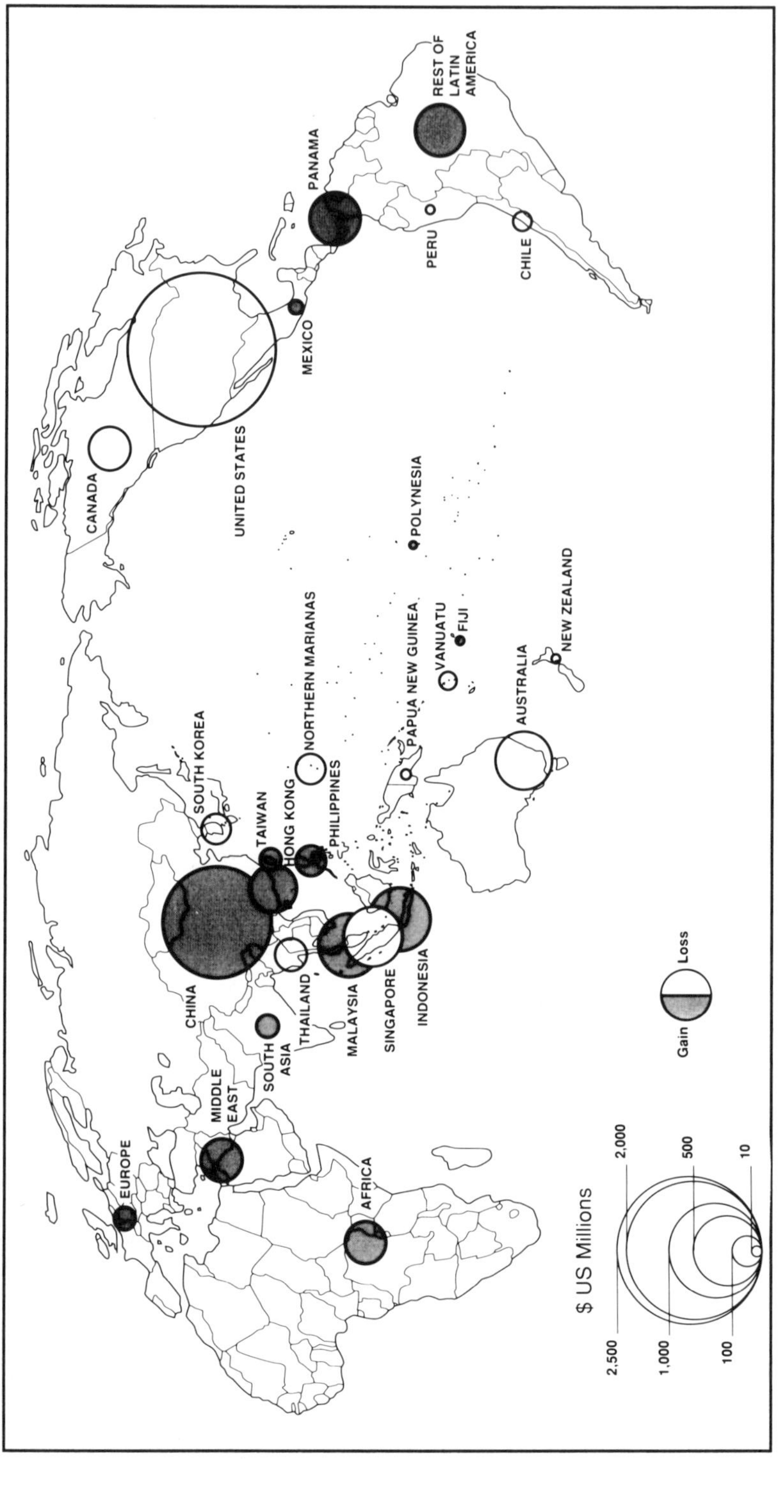

Figure 8.3. SHIFT-SHARE ANALYSIS OF JAPAN'S FDI BY MAJOR HOST COUNTRY IN THE PACIFIC RIM, 1989-1993

service these loans. Further financing to cover debts from the chastened banking sector was not forthcoming.

In these circumstances China's marked gain was remarkable. Initially, Japanese investors – especially large firms – were reluctant to invest there.[33] Since 1992, however, Japanese FDI has soared, concentrated mostly in Liaoning Province, Beijing and Shanghai. Initially, the emphasis was on manufacturing but there is now active investment in services.

Although Japanese enterprises were investing in China, few had reduced their production in Malaysia and Indonesia. This was not necessarily reflected in Japan's FDI statistics because corporate investors used their own funds or borrowed locally. The Pacific Rim's low cost of labour was the prime attraction for export-oriented enterprises. Opportunities in the region's rapidly growing domestic market were an additional bonus.[34]

Surveys in China, Malaysia and Indonesia underline their attractiveness for Japans' FDI.[35] The affiliates of Japanese manufacturing enterprises in these areas have a distinctive set of management characteristics compared with their Japanese counterparts in other parts of the world. These include the dependence on labour-intensive production, the large number of joint ventures, the local funding of capital investment, the expansion of local procurement of component parts, and the large percentage of exports destined for Japanese buyers.

While investment in China, Malaysia and Indonesia has been buoyant, Japanese investors have experienced problems stemming from high labour turnover; inadequate infrastructure; and difficulties in the implementation of systems, laws and regulations (especially in China and Viet Nam and, to a lesser extent, in Indonesia and the Philippines). Conversely, the recipients of Japanese FDI want the leading edge of technology to be transferred to them rather than being sealed in a factory which exports advanced components for assembly.

## *Looking Ahead*

The political and financial fall-out from the post-bubble adjustment phase is still being cleared away, as instanced by developments involving the EIE Group.

Its overseas investments were brought to an end by the indictment of its President, Harunori Takahashi, on 18 July 1995.[36] Also implicated in unsecured and irrecoverable loans for golf course development and dummy sales of art works were the President of the Anzen Credit Bank; Diet members including an ex-Labour Minister, Toshio Yamaguchi; senior bureaucrats; and bank executives. The Kyowa and Anzen companies had been taken over by the Tokyo Kyodo Bank which was created as part of a much criticised rescue plan drawn up by the Bank of Japan, the Finance Ministry and other organisations.

The process of correcting the after-effects of the bubble economy has given Japan the opportunity to tackle its medium- to long-term structural problems and avoid sliding into decline.[37] A prime aim of the Japanese Government is to double the proportion of its manufacturing in other countries. Consequently, FDI in the United States will further bolster manufacturing activities, such as car components and electronics, but there will be no investment in real estate. There will also be strong investment in Europe's manufacturing sector rather than its financial sector, the United Kingdom being the prime target for its firms rather than France and Germany. Prospects for Japanese investment in South American manufacturing are also more promising.

Japan's main investment thrust, however, will be on expanding its local presence in Asia because it offers higher profits.[38] Inevitably, this will lead to Japan deepening its economic and trading interdependence with other Asian countries.

Particular attention will be focused on China's rich potential, though the absence of a well-developed legal framework will be a barrier to strong and broad-based Japanese investment. Consideration will be given to investment in Viet Nam and Myanmar, especially the former because of its industrial linkages. Japanese interest will be rekindled in the stable investment climate in the Philippines. This country has been forced to take up the rear in the ASEAN's 'flying geese' formation but the Philippines now has a comparative advantage in wage levels. South Asia, especially India, will attract the attention of Japanese investors although their interest has been partly quelled by a state government reneging on a contract held by the Enron Corporation.

For a rounded picture of Japan's FDI in the Pacific Rim, more attention will have to be focused on microeconomic factors by highlighting the new objectives of Japanese firms investing abroad. These are reflected in strategic alliances and new cross-border collaboration. Small and large Japanese firms are creating regional sources of competitive advantage through Asian partnerships to strengthen their position both internationally and domestically.[39] Further examination of the subsequent development and consolidation of the regional production networks of Japanese firms is warranted. Clearly, how to be part of Asia is the most pressing economic issue for Japan.

Reflecting Japan's 'new Asianisation', the number of Japanese firms in Asia increased from 58,000 to 120,000 between 1985 and 1994; those stationed in North America declined from a peak of 291,000 in 1991 to 277,000 in 1994.[40] There have also been changes in Japanese preferences for imported fashion, cuisine and pop music. Japan's contribution to Asian development has been marked in financial terms but it has not yet triggered protectionism or threats to free trade.

Forecasting is made difficult by variations in exchange rates, balance of payment factors, interest rates and untoward events such as the Hanshin Awaji earthquake in January 1995. For instance, the yen's appreciation against the US dollar reached ¥80 in April 1995. At this 'superyen' level, Japanese companies were uncompetitive and lost market share to their East Asian rivals. There was, therefore, a 'big push' for sustained outward investment in East Asia to avoid increasing wage costs (i.e. creating the fear the Japanese economy was being 'hollowed-out'). An agreement among the G7 in April 1995 was reached to underpin the dollar and push down the value of the yen. If the yen continues to lose ground and the sharemarket is stronger, the Japanese Government's task of artificially sustaining corporate profits from funds from domestic savings will be eased. Japan's major financial institutions have been left with large stockholdings held as collateral against loans and bad debts since the collapse of the 'bubble economy' of the late 1980s. Debts of the banks alone exceeded US$900 billion.[41] A further US$165 billion in debt has been incurred by bankrupt housing co-operatives (*jusen*), and reconstruction plans involve the expenditure of public money to ease the bailout.[42] Any downward trend in stocks below the Nikkei index level of 16,000 means that major financial institutions cannot meet their capital adequacy requirements.

The drawback to the weakening of the yen's strength is that marginal investors will have a choice of continuing overseas moves or reassessing the situation. As with the Plaza Accord of 1985, the agreement of April 1995 means that the Japanese Government has been able to resist further opening of the economy to full-scale competition and – like the Government of the United States – avoid tackling fundamental structural problems.

If firms abandon the restructuring of Japan's overexpanded export manufacturing sector, the country will experience a long-term setback in economic efficiency and expansion. Old practices have to be jettisoned. These include corporate management based on hidden assets in stocks and land, the reliance on maximising sales above all else, and the use of the convoy system in financial regulation which forces the entire sector to adjust its pace to the lowest performer.[43]

Structural transformation after the mid-1990s will require greater openness and transparency by purging the exclusiveness of the country's giant corporate groups (*keiretsu*) and their bid-rigging practices (*dango*), and less government involvement in the market place by increasing economic deregulation. Slavish copying of specific features of 'Japan as a model' are increasingly unfashionable. The strategy of government regulation and private cartelisation is not good for all times and places.

These developments are unlikely to lead to a modern Greater East Asian Co-Prosperity Sphere. A reluctant Japan may form an Asia-Pacific economic bloc under its leadership if trading relations with the United States deteriorate.[44] Despite the economic recession of the early 1990s, Japan's economy is still twice the size of the rest of Asia. As its economic involvement in Asia has deepened, there are raised expectations of Japan playing a greater role in the region.

## *Acknowledgements*

The assistance of Roger Farrell (Australia-Japan Centre, ANU) in locating some of the literature is appreciated. Elanna Lowes (Department of Human Geography, Research School of Pacific Studies, ANU) undertook the calculations for the shift-share analyses. The study has benefited from discussions with Masahiko Agata, Director General, Research, The Export-Import Bank of Japan. The opinions expressed in the paper, however, are the responsibility of the author.

NOTES

[1] Japan's FDI statistics are given for financial years. They cover only outflows of investment capital. No account is taken of the reinvestment of profits earned at a local site though these generally increase over time. Although the volume of investment flows may decline, assets of local affiliates can increase through reinvestment (Satake Takanori, 'Trends in Japanese foreign direct investment in FY 1989', *EXIM Review*, 11 (1), 1991, pp. 85-110). However, this is not recorded in the statistics.

[2] The 'flying geese pattern of industrial development' was originally applied to industries in Japan developing one after another through three stages: import, production and export (Akamatsu Kaname, 'Wagakuni sangyo hatten no ganko keitai - Kikaikigu kogyo ni tsuite' [The flying geese pattern of Japanese industrial development: machinery and appliances], *Hitosubashi Ronso* [The Hitosubashi Review], 36 (5), 1956, pp. 68-80).

[3] The causes, consequences and resolution of the low levels of Japan's inward FDI are not discussed here (see Wakasugi Ryuhei, 'On the causes of low levels of FDI in Japan', and M. Mason, 'Japan's low levels of inward direct investment: causes, consequences and remedies', in E.K. Chen and P. Drysdale (eds), *Corporate Links and Foreign Direct Investment in Asia and the Pacific*, Sydney: Harper Educational, 1995). No consideration is given to the large influx of unskilled labour into Japan.

[4] P.J. Rimmer, 'Japan's "bubble economy" and the Pacific: the case of the EIE Group', *Pacific Viewpoint*, 34 (1), 1993, pp. 25-44.

[5] See Chen and Drysdale, op. cit., 1995.

[6] Information on the activities of Japanese subsidiaries in foreign countries is published by the MITI in its 'Survey of trends in Japanese enterprises' overseas business activities'. The Japan External Trade Organization (JETRO) and Toyo Keizai Inc. also publish reports on the subject (see TKS, *Kaigai Shinshutsu Kigyo Soran*, Tokyo: Toyo Keizai Shinposha, 1994). Mapping Japanese subsidiaries in foreign countries would give undue weight to the number rather than the size of firms and would favour Asia at the expense of North America.

[7] See Komiya Ryutaro and Wakasugi Ryuhei, 'Japan's foreign direct investment', *Discussion Paper 90-DF-11*, Discussion Paper Series, Research Institute of International Trade and Industry, Tokyo: Ministry of Trade and Industry, 1990.

[8] Rimmer, op. cit., 1993.

[9] Ikeda Masahito, 'Japan's direct investment for Asia – with emphasis on investment in manufacturing industries', *EXIM Review*, 6 (2), pp. 56-96, 1985a; Ikeda Masahito, 'Trends of Japan's direct investment for Europe – with emphasis on investment in manufacturing industries', *EXIM Review*, 6 (2), pp. 97-137, 1985b.

[10] Lee Poh-ping, 'Japan and the Asia-Pacific region: a Southeast Asian perspective', in C. Garby and M.B. Bullock (eds), *Japan: A New Kind of Superpower*, Washington, D.C.: Woodrow Wilson Center, 1994, pp. 121-39.

[11] Initially, Japan's FDI in 1989 is divided by 1985 percentages to derive an estimated value. This figure is subtracted from the actual 1989 value to determine relative 'gains' or

'losses'. For example, Asia would have recorded a value of US$7,902 million dollars if it had maintained its 11.7% share of the 1985 total. Asia's actual FDI from Japan, however, was US$8,238 million. Compared with the estimated figure this represented a net gain of US$336 million.

[12] Komiya and Wakasugi, op. cit., 1990; Takaoka Hirobumi and Satake Takanori, *Trends in Japan's Direct Investment Abroad in FY 1988: The Results of a Survey on Global Management and Overseas Direct Investment*, Tokyo: Research Institute of Foreign Investment, The Export-Import Bank of Japan, 1989; Satake Takanori, 'Trends in direct investment abroad in FY1988', Tokyo: Research Institute of Foreign Investment, The Export-Import Bank of Japan, 1989.

[13] Takaoka Hirobumi, 'Present status and impact of Japan's investment of manufacturing industries in the United States', *EXIM Review*, 11 (1), 1991, pp. 57-83.

[14] Watanabe Soitsu, 'Trends in Japan's direct investment in Europe – mainly investment in manufacturing into EC', *EXIM Review*, 6 (2), 1988, pp. 43-97.

[15] TKS, op. cit., 1994.

[16] P.J. Rimmer, 'The internationalization of the Japanese construction industry: The rise and rise of Kumagai Gumi', *Environment and Planning A*, 22, 1990, pp. 346-68.

[17] The acquisitions of hotels by airlines and travel/leisure companies to offer integrated tourism packages, however, was more like direct than indirect investment. See R. Farrell, 'Japanese direct investment in overseas property: overview and assessment', unpublished paper prepared for the Japanese Direct Investment Workshop, ANU, December 1992.

[18] In 1986, the Nikkei average of 225 issues on the Tokyo Stock Exchange was 16,401 (annual average). By the closing session of 1989, the Nikkei average hit 38,915 (see Y. Noguchi, 'The "bubble economy" and its aftermath', in *The Japanese Economy in the 1990s: Problems and Prognosis*, Tokyo: Foreign Press Center/Japan, 1993, p. 33).

[19] C. Wood, *The Bubble Economy: The Japanese Economic Collapse*, London: Sidgwick and Jackson, 1992.

[20] Noguchi, op. cit., 1993.

[21] 'World cities' came into prominence during the 1960s and 1970s following the development of office space to accommodate the internationalisation of producer services (especially finance, insurance and real estate).

[22] P.J. Rimmer, 'Japanese investment in golf course development: Australia-Japan links', *International Journal of Urban and Regional Research*, 18 (2), 1994, pp. 234-55.

[23] Takaoka, op. cit., 1991.

[24] K.T. Greenfield, *Speed Tribes: Children of the Japanese Bubble*, London: Boxtree, 1995.

[25] Rimmer, op. cit., 1993.

[26] *Nikkei Weekly*, 19 July 1993.

[27] *Financial Times*, 16 February 1995.

[28] One shortcoming in comparing the first and last year of a period is evident in Japan's FDI statistics. The combined total for the period between 1989 and 1993 was US$236 billion compared with US$182.4 billion between 1985 and 1989.

[29] In this instance Japan's FDI in 1993 is divided by 1989 percentages to derive an estimated value. This figure is subtracted from the actual 1993 value to determine 'gains' and 'losses'. Thus, Asia would have recorded a value of US$4,395 million dollars if it had maintained its 12.2% share of the 1989 total. Asia's actual FDI from Japan, however, was US$6,637 million. Compared with the estimated figure, this represented a net gain of US$2,242 million.

[30] Takaoka Hirobumi and Satake Takanori, 'Report on results of FY 1990 foreign direct investment survey', *EXIM Review*, 11 (1), 1991, pp. 2-25.

[31] MITI, 'Activities of Japanese corporations in East Asia', *White Paper on International Trade*, Tokyo: MITI, 1994.

[32] Rimmer, op. cit., 1990.

[33] Kinoshita Toshihiko, 'Japan's economic development and lessons for China', mimeo 10 July 1995 (Kinoshita is Executive Director and Head of Research Institute for International Investment and Development, The Export-Import Bank of Japan).

[34] MITI, op. cit., 1994.

[35] Ibid.

[36] *Mainichi Daily News*, 25 August 1995.

[37] EPA, *Economic Survey of Japan (1993-1994) – A Challenge to New Frontiers Beyond the Severe Adjustment Process – (Summary) July 26 1994*, Tokyo: EPA, Government of Japan, 1994; EPA, *Economic Survey of Japan (1994-1995) – Toward the Revival of a Dynamic Economy in Japan – (Summary) July 25 1995*, Tokyo: EPA, Government of Japan, 1995.

[38] KTKH, 'Japan's outward foreign direct investment during fiscal 1994 – expansion continues to focus on Asia', *Kaigai-toshi-kenkyusho-ho* [Journal Bulletin of the Research Institute for International Investment and Development], 21 (7), 1995, pp. 1-19.

[39] D.F. Simon and Jun Yongwook, 'Technological change, foreign investment and the new strategic thrust of Japanese firms in the Asia Pacific', in Chen and Drysdale (eds), op. cit., 1995.

[40] *Nikkei Weekly*, 3 July 1995, 14 August 1995.

[41] *Australian Financial Review*, 17 August 1995.

[42] *The Australian*, 5 March 1996

[43] Saito Seichiro, 'The transition to a new stage of development', in *The Japanese Economy in the 1990s: Problems and Prognosis*, Tokyo: Foreign Press Center/Japan, 1993, pp. 55-80.

[44] Lee, op. cit., 1994.

# 9. EFFECTIVENESS AND REPLICABILITY OF EAST ASIAN INDUSTRIAL POLICIES

## *Robert Wade*

The World Bank study of East Asia's growth, *The East Asian Miracle,*[1] draws two main conclusions about sector-specific industrial policies.

- 'Promotion of specific industries generally did not work and therefore holds little promise for other developing countries' (p. 312).
- Even had they worked in northeast Asia, they could not be recommended for other developing countries because other developing countries have a lower level of institutional capacity.

Three comments on these conclusions follow.

### *The effectiveness of selective sector-specific industrial policies in Japan, Taiwan and South Korea remains an open question.*

The methodology and evidence behind the Miracle study's conclusion that 'promotion of specific industries generally did not work' has been criticised. There are three main methodological and philosophical problems.

One is that the East Asian industrial policy has always had three parts: the growth-promoting part, the easing-of-decline part, and the national security part. The easing-of-decline part involves a lot of social expenditure to ease the pain of exit and rationalisation, and it may be accompanied by a lot of rhetoric to give the *impression* that the help is growth-promoting when it is not (rhetoric which people with only book knowledge of the situation may take at face value).[3] Conflate all three parts, and of course there is no positive correlation between cost to the state and measures of sector performance. Yet many studies of the effectiveness of industrial policy do conflate all three parts, and then conclude that East Asian industrial policy picked losers.[4]

A second problem comes from 'externalities'. Assistance given to one industry may spill over from one industry to another, in a way that escapes the 'outcome' measures. The Japanese government subsidised upstream infrastructural industries like steel and oil-refining as a way of facilitating the growth of downstream consumer products. But slower growth of more subsidised infrastructural industries, and faster growth of less (directly) subsidised consumer products, hardly attests to the 'failure' of the targeted measures. It is extraordinary how little evidence seems to be available on where externalities fall (on *how big* is the impact of support for petrochemicals on plant engineering, for example); which presumably reflects the falling-out-of-fashion of input-output analysis, the key technique for tracing such connections. The industrial policy debate can never be resolved without better knowledge of externalities.

A third more philosophical problem is the built-in bias towards non-intervention (of the selective kind). The bias is seen in the neglect of the risks, the costs and the dangers of non-intervention. The non-intervention scenario is treated as unproblematic, reflecting the underlying assumption that 'development' is fairly easy and fairly automatic, if only government does not mess it up.[5]

Having said this, it should be noted that industrial policy advocates have done no better at providing evidence about the *outcomes* of East Asian industrial policy. My own evidence is mostly indirect, and supports a modest conclusion: that the way remains open for a reasonable person to believe that industrial policy in East Asia has been too important to ignore.[6] Not a conclusion to set the world on fire, to be sure, but the fact is that the great majority of economists interpreting East Asia's economic success, guided by faith in largely free markets, *have* either ignored it or emphasised only the *costs* of interventions.

### *Sector-specific industrial policies should not be equated with 'picking winners'; and 'market failure' should not be used as a necessary condition of intervention.*

'Picking winners' is the phrase normally used to describe sector-specific industrial policies, but it is a caricature of what is involved. The debate should be about whether it is worthwhile for a government to formulate a comprehensive 'vision of the future', and put in place a coherent set of measures to facilitate the realisation of this vision. If so, what measures in which markets? The standard answer is that intervention is only justified, even potentially, where there is an identifiable market failure; the debate then centres on the prevalence and significance of market failure. But this is wrong: the trouble with markets is often not that they fail but that they work well with terrible results (as in 'the operation was a success but the patient died').

Think of British financial markets. By standard measures they are much more competitive than German or Japanese ones. But they discourage investment in R & D and encourage dividend payments. Hence the difference in the ratio of R & D spending to dividends for the countries' biggest firms: Japan 8.57, Germany 8.54, Britain 0.74. (The US figure is 1.87.)[7] Hence also the dramatic fall in Britain's OECD rank in terms of US patents per million population, and Japan's even more dramatic rise: Britain from fifth to tenth between 1963-68 and 1986-90, Japan from twelfth to third. (Germany remained in fourth place in both periods.)[8]

Of course, results of this kind are not due just to the differences in financial markets. They follow from differences in at least six national 'systems': (1) the financial system; (2) the education and training system; (3) the corporate management system; (4) public administration; (5) the political system; and finally, (6) industrial policies.

The debate about the role of government has focused too much on the last of these six, industrial policies, and not enough on the other elements of what might be called the 'national system of technological and entrepreneurial capacity' (NASTEC).

Among the OECD countries, the countries of English-settlement (Britain, US, Ireland, Canada, Australia, New Zealand) have strong and not accidental similarities in their NASTECs. In particular, their institutional arrangements reflect a basic principle of 'keep options open', 'minimise commitment', so that resources can be quickly and smoothly shifted to more efficient uses. The spot market is the ideal (or as *Le Monde* once put it, 'cette attitude très Anglo-Saxon – le wait-and-see', wait and see if an opportunity for quicker profits turns up). In the past decade or more, they have all been intensifying the application of this principle throughout their societies. Yet they also have worse economic performance than more 'rigid', higher 'commitment' northwest European and East Asian societies – higher consumption, lower savings, higher trade deficits, higher budget deficits, higher inflation.

The relevance for developing countries is this: the World Bank is heavily influenced by the kind of economics developed in the institutional milieu of the countries of English settlement. Think what would have happened if it had sent missions to a variety of OECD countries over the past 10 to 20 years, and if the missions had examined only economic institutions (such as product and factor markets), not economic performance. Britain would have got an A- (the minus for labour market rigidities), Germany a B- (interlocking rigidities in relations between banks, insurance companies and industrial firms; defective market for corporate control; rigidities in labour market in the form of collective bargaining; excessive safety nets leading to high levels of unemployment), Japan a C- or worse (financial system a nightmare, distribution system and big firms' employment systems even worse).

The World Bank, that is, has been committed to a notion of markets and associated institutions that is most fully reflected on the ground in those OECD economies with *below average performance*. But the problem of those economies is not mainly 'market failure'. Even when working well, their markets are structured in ways that yield inferior economic performance.

Industrial policy (or better, 'industrial strategy', because 'industrial policy' lends itself to an ad hoc assemblage of measures to correct particular market failures) needs to consider not just the design of policies to affect resource allocation decisions directly, but also the design of policies to work directly on components of the NASTEC so as indirectly to promote productive activity, and some activities more than others. Much of this involves measures that are not normally called industrial policy – measures to restructure incentives in economic bureaucracies (think of Japan's Ministry of Finance/Ministry of International Trade and Industry, compared to Britain's Treasury, for example) or to change the rules of firms' relations with banks.

NASTEC-strengthening measures are not substitutes for sector-specific support. Why sector-specific support, when World Bank economics is so much against it?

(1) Costs of production for firms in low-wage countries trying to sell manufactures in Western markets are often higher than those of established competitors in those markets. (In the 1960s, Korean cotton spinners and weavers had higher production costs than Japanese ones, despite much lower wages.)[9] Some help, be it protection or subsidy, may be a necessary condition for them to enter those markets. Given limits on the state's ability to raise revenue, this help may have to be concentrated on particular activities in order for it to be big enough to make a difference. Devaluation, as an alternative, has political, as well as economic limits;[10] and anyway, so much hot money is prowling the world for speculative gains from exchange rate changes that many governments have lost control of the exchange rate.

(2) Across-the-board measures to improve information and generic management skills are important but not enough. Horses taken to water will not necessarily drink: information services may not be used, skills created may not be demanded (as the Irish know but as much current policy prescription ignores). What is also needed is something to work directly on stimulating entrepreneurial initiative, investment and risk-taking. And this must, because of its costliness in cash and elite official attention, be sector-specific.

(3) The cumulative, 'path-dependent' nature of technological and entrepreneurial learning also enjoins a targeted approach. In particular, the issue of whether a country develops a capital goods industry, and of what kind, should not be left to free market forces, because the social costs of not developing a capital goods industry are not captured in free market prices used to choose between domestic and imported capital goods. Free market prices do not include either the costs of the chronic trade deficits of medium- and large-sized countries that lack capital goods industries or the costs of the lack of capacity to innovate or adapt technologies associated with capital goods industries. This is all the more so now that the development of microelectronics and capital goods has become so closely intertwined. Industrial strategy has a still bigger role to push domestic producers into the new microelectronics technology than was true of the older electromechanical technology;

for entry barriers are typically much bigger (as in numerically-controlled machine tools compared to conventional machine tools, for example.)[11]

Of course, there are real dangers in giving any state discretion of this kind. The dangers can be checked by beginning small, with measures that do not entail much state spending. (The industrial policy debate assumes, wrongly, that industrial policy must be done big or not at all.) The support should always be conditional, given against a *quid pro quo*; and with more emphasis on 'backing winners' than on creating them. The dangers of proceeding in this direction must be weighed against the dangers of not trying: the dangers of 'lock in' to a low growth, low skills, low wage, widening income distribution trajectory, following the British model. The weighing must also allow for a learning effect in bureaucracy; a bureaucracy that does not attempt to formulate a comprehensive vision and take steps to facilitate it will not learn how to do so.

All this may be contrasted with the way the World Bank presents the issue. It distinguishes three approaches to the question of industrial policy: total absence of any measures to strengthen industry, reliance on market forces with selective intervention in clear cases of market failures, and comprehensive industrial planning and central allocation. No prizes for guessing which the Bank favours. It is a familiar technique for rhetoric to identify two extreme positions and then claim the 'sensible', 'pragmatic' middle ground, the convincingness of which derives from the foolishness of that which it is not. Having claimed the sensible middle ground, the Bank then asserts that clear market failures are rare in the real world. *Hence it refuses to provide its clients with assistance in the design of industrial policies of a selective type (such as providing them with information about the nuts and bolts of such policies in other countries).*[12] Instead, it provides them with advice about establishing markets – financial markets, for example – that implicitly takes the institutions of the English-settlement countries as the model (rather than say, Germany, Sweden or Japan, about which the Bank knows remarkably little).

### *Beware the 'unreplicability' argument.*

As externalities are the last refuge of industrial policy champions, so 'unreplicability' is the last refuge of its enemies. Even if industrial strategy worked in East Asia, the argument goes, it cannot work in other developing countries because those other countries lack the requisite 'institutional capacity'. The beauty of this argument is that, institutional capacity being left undefined, it can never be disproved. But did the Meiji reformers in late nineteenth century Japan say: our institutions are obviously very different from those of the West, therefore we cannot learn much from them? Of course not. While recognising that Western institutions were, as a set, 'unreplicable' in Japan, they paid the closest attention to the design of specific organisations in specific countries, those they took to represent best real-world practice (Britain's navy and post office, France's police and internal ministerial organisation, Germany's state). Then they imitated them, with amendments – producing a set of public organisations very different from those of any other country.[13] Developing countries today should take heart from the Japanese example, and study closely best practice elsewhere in specific organisational domains. Today, the models may lie as much in the East as in the West.

But those who talk about unreplicability usually refer to the idea of a strong state in East Asia and a weak state elsewhere. Again, this has to be unpackaged. As Stephan Haggard[14] and others[15] have emphasised, the two key supply-side characteristics of the East Asian state are (1) concentrated executive authority, and (2) delegation to relatively insulated technocratically-oriented industrial policy agencies. These can be achieved by a democratic regime as well as by an authoritarian regime. And they can be achieved even in a generally miasmic bureaucratic environment, such as Taiwan in the 1950s and 1960s or Thailand today.[16]

Much the same applies to social values or culture. Those who stress unreplicability often have in mind characteristics of Confucian culture that were in some unspecified way necessary conditions for East Asian policies to work. The outlook for learning from East Asia then seems hopeless, because culture cannot be changed. But when culture is broken down into measurable components, we find that (1) components do change over decadal time, (2) some components are causally relevant to economic development, and (3) these components can be changed by politics. In particular, attitudes to 'thrift' seem to matter causally, and are a function of how children are socialised – a matter within the influence of the state. The density of a society's associational network – and especially in developing countries, unions, political parties and professional associations – also seems to matter causally, and can also be made the object of policies.[17]

In short, those who claim that East Asian experience is somehow 'unreplicable' have not done their homework. Their statement is best understood in terms of the art of paradigm maintenance – maintenance of the paradigm of the countries of English settlement, as theorised in neoclassical economics and refined by World Bank economics, which for unsurprising reasons is implicitly taken *not* to suffer from the replicability problems of East Asian models.[18]

## NOTES

[1] World Bank, *The East Asian Miracle: Economic Growth and Public Policy*, OUP, 1993.

[2] See Albert Fishlow, Catherine Gwin, Stephan Haggard, Dani Rodrik, Robert Wade, *Miracle or Design: Lessons from the East Asian Experience*, Washington, D.C.: Overseas Development Council, 1994, p. 354.

[3] Ronald Dore, *Flexible Rigidities: Industrial Policy and Structural Adjustment in the Japanese Economy 1970-1980*, Stanford University Press, 1986, chapter on industrial policy. I am indebted to him for discussions of the same issue.

[4] See 'Picking losers in Japan', *The Economist*, 26 February 1994, p. 69, summarising Richard Beason and David Weinstein, 'Growth, economies of scale, and targeting in Japan (1955-1990)', Harvard Institute of Economic Research, Discussion paper 1644.
[5] See, for example, the essays by Helen Hughes and James Reidel in Helen Hughes (ed.), *Achieving Industrialisation in East Asia*, CUP, 1988, reviewed in Robert Wade, 'East Asia's economic success: conflicting perspectives, partial insights, shaky evidence', *World Politics*, 44, January 1992, pp. 270-320.
[6] Robert Wade, *Governing the Market*, Princeton University Press, 1990, chapter 10, esp. p. 343.
[7] 'Technology: R & D scoreboard', *Financial Times*, 17 June 1994, p. 14. The figures refer to the firms from each country that are listed in the world's 200 biggest firms, 1993.
[8] Pari Patel and Keith Pavitt, 'National innovation systems: why they are important and how they might be measured and compared', mimeo, Science Research Unit, Sussex University, 1994, table 2.
[9] See Alice Amsden, *Asia's Next Giant: South Korea and Late Industrialisation*, OUP, 1989, p. 68 and appendix 3.1.
[10] See Wade, op. cit., 1990, pp. 358-9.
[11] Ibid, pp. 350-8.
[12] A milestone was the Bank management's attempt to prevent publication of a report by the Bank's Operations Evaluation Department (OED) on industrial policies in NICs. The report recommended that 'the Bank [should] help governments design appropriate industrial policies by collecting, analysing and disseminating *information* ... Where selective policies are found, on the basis of strict eligibility criteria, to be economically desirable, the Bank should consider these as an integral part of a package of policies to promote industrial development' ('OECD study of Bank support of industrialisation in newly industrialising countries', World Bank, 1991, p. 54). The report was for the Bank's Executive Directors (representatives of member countries), and hence could not be directly suppressed by management, which appealed to the Executive Directors not to release it: 'Even if the causes of government failure could be identified and minimised, the report calls for the impossible: fine-tuning an array of trade and industrial interventions to deal with real or perceived market failures is generally not feasible'. Due partly to the insistence of Japan's Executive Director, the OED report was published unrevised. But the Bank's refusal to follow the quite mild recommendations of the report continues.
[13] D. Eleanor Westney, *Imitation and Innovation: The Transfer of Western Organisational Patterns to Meiji Japan*, Cambridge: Harvard University Press, 1987.
[14] See 'Politics and institutions in the World Bank's East Asia', in Fishlow et al, op. cit., 1994; also his *Pathways from the Periphery: The Politics of Growth in the Newly Industrialising Countries*, Ithaca: Cornell University Press, 1990.
[15] For example, Chalmers Johnson, *MITI and the Japanese Miracle: The Growth of Industrial Policy 1925-1975*, Stanford University Press, 1982.
[16] See A. Cole, 'Political roles of Taiwanese enterprisers', *Asian Survey*, 7, 1967, pp. 645-54, and Wade, op. cit., 1990, pp. 286-9. I emphasise that these are important features on the 'supply' side. But note that several Latin American countries have also met these conditions, more or less, especially during the periods of military rule. What enabled these conditions in East Asia to be 'effective' has also to do with differences in basic demand patterns, in particular a lower income elasticity of demand for sophisticated (and 'Western') consumer durables. For the difference in development 'styles', see Wade, op. cit., 1990, figures 2.2 and 2.3.
[17] Ronald Inglehart, 'The impact of culture on economic development: theory, hypotheses and some empirical tests', mimeo, University of Michigan, 1994.
[18] See further Robert Wade, 'The World Bank and the art of paradigm maintenance: the East Asia Miracle report as a response to Japan's challenge to development theory', mimeo, Institute of Development Studies, Sussex University, 1994.

# 10. FACING THE URBAN ENVIRONMENTAL CHALLENGE

*Yok-shiu F. Lee*

Managing environmental resources in the midst of a rapid urban transition taking place in Asia and the Pacific poses one of the greatest challenges to governments in this vast region. A significant proportion of the world's total population resides in the Asia-Pacific region. In 1990 Asia contained 3.1 billion people and accounted for 59% of the global total.[1] Whereas in 1990 the world was 45% urbanised, the level of urbanisation in Asia was recorded much lower at 33%.[2] However, the pace of urbanisation, which refers to the average annual growth rate of urban population, has remained uniformly high through the 1970-1990 period in the region, particularly in the lower-income countries.

The region also contains some of the world's fastest growing economies, such as those of ASEAN. With an average of 7% growth rate over the 1990-1995 period, compared to just 1.7% for the entire world, ASEAN as a group has become the world's most dynamic economic region.[3]

The combination of rapid urban population and industrial growth in the Asia-Pacific region has resulted in an increasing rate of pollution and accelerated deterioration of the natural and living environment. Cities in the developing countries in particular have been besieged by heightening environmental risks, both modern and traditional,[4] for several decades. The most critical and immediate environmental concerns faced by governments in the lower-income countries in the region include the provision of safe and adequate water supply, sanitation, drainage, and solid waste management as well as the control of the emission of air pollutants.

Dubbed the 'brown agenda', all of these issues have adverse impacts primarily on the urban poor in terms of higher rates of morbidity and mortality, leading to reduced earnings and an overall decline in their quality of life.[5] To meet the challenges posed by the brown agenda, all types of resources at the household, community, city, national and international levels need to be mobilised in a process of making basic environmental infrastructure and services affordable by and accessible to the urban poor as well as radically reducing pollution and environmental degradation.

This chapter focuses on the most critical aspects of the enormous urban environmental challenge in the region:

(1) the improvement of the provision of basic environmental infrastructure and services in developing country cities; and

(2) the control and reduction of air pollution.

A review of the scope and the nature of that challenge will help provide a proper perspective to assess and evaluate the role of various stakeholders – governments, non-governmental organisations, private enterprises, communities and citizens – in addressing the twin problems of poverty and environmental deterioration.

### *Inadequate Infrastructure and Services*

'The gap between those being served and the unserved is widening more today than in 1977. ... [The concept of] some for all versus more for some is not working ... investment is going to supply rich and middle classes [with water and sanitation systems]. And the low-income groups are paying the price'.[6] This is the testimony presented to the June 1990 Asia-Pacific Regional Consultation on Water Supply and Sanitation in Manila by Saul Arlosoroff of the United Nations Development Programme/World Bank. Then, in September 1990, the Global Consultation on Safe Water and Sanitation held in New Delhi concluded that the priority areas of concern are urban sanitation and water supply in Asia and the Pacific because this region makes up the bulk of the unserved projected for the year 2000 (see Table 10.1). Moreover, low-income communities make up by far the largest part of the unserved in urban areas.[7]

No official statistics or estimates are available on urban drainage in Asia.[8] Nevertheless, studies show that many low-income communities in developing country cities consider drainage to be their most urgent need because they usually occupy land sites such as river banks subject to flooding or steep hillsides subject to erosion and landslides.[9] Moreover, without proper drainage systems to prevent flooding and ensure ground stability, the other sanitation measures are practically impossible or ineffective. Without adequate solid waste management, the urban drainage systems will not work. Accumulated domestic waste, however, is the most common cause of blockage of urban drainage channels in Asian cities.

This is not surprising, given that the overall coverage of solid waste collection service, particularly among the urban poor, is low in many Asian cities – on average, only about 60 to 70% of the refuse is collected (see Table 10.2). In some cities, such as Karachi, Hanoi and Dhaka, less than half of the waste is collected, and uncontrolled dumping is common. In Jakarta, for instance, about 55% of urban households are served by some form of garbage collection. However, there is a serious geographic inequality in the distribution of local needs and resources: whereas 70% of Jakarta's wealthy households receive garbage collection services, only 19% of the city's poor have access to similar services.[10]

Thus, while it is true that, in terms of the scope of shortfall, the overall level of urban infrastructure and service provision is extremely inadequate in many developing country cities, *unequal access* to such services by different social groups is nonetheless a prominent issue that stands out and characterises one important facet of the fundamental nature of the prob-

Table 10.1. URBAN WATER SUPPLY AND SANITATION COVERAGE BY REGION, 1980-1990, AND COVERAGE FOR 2000 AT CURRENT RATE OF PROGRESS, FOR DEVELOPING COUNTRIES

| | *Coverage (%)* | | | *Number unserved (population in millions)* | | |
|---|---|---|---|---|---|---|
| | *1980* | *1990* | *2000* | *1980* | *1990* | *2000* |
| *Africa* | | | | | | |
| Water supply | 83 | 87 | 76 | 20.36 | 26.33 | 79.48 |
| Sanitation | 65 | 79 | 73 | 41.92 | 42.53 | 90.32 |
| *Latin American and the Caribbean* | | | | | | |
| Water supply | 82 | 87 | 89 | 42.61 | 42.13 | 47.00 |
| Sanitation | 78 | 79 | 79 | 52.08 | 68.06 | 89.39 |
| *Asia and the Pacific* | | | | | | |
| Water supply | 73 | 77 | 71 | 148.35 | 175.07 | 314.43 |
| Sanitation | 65 | 65 | 58 | 192.30 | 266.41 | 453.16 |
| *Western Asia* | | | | | | |
| Water supply | 95 | 100 | 100 | 1.38 | 0.17 | 0.00 |
| Sanitation | 79 | 100 | 100 | 5.78 | 0.00 | 0.00 |
| *Global totals* | | | | | | |
| Water supply | 77 | 82 | 77 | 212.70 | 243.70 | 445.83 |
| Sanitation | 69 | 72 | 67 | 292.08 | 377.00 | 633.05 |

Source: J. Christmas and C. de Rooy, 'The decade and beyond: at a glance,' *Water International,* 16 (3), pp. 127-34.

lem.[11] If we are concerned with achieving major social goals such as improving environmental living conditions in developing country cities, particularly in low-income settlements, then it is necessary first to examine and delineate the *nature* of the lack of urban environmental infrastructure and services before we determine what policy options are the most appropriate to tackle the problem.

## *Fundamental nature of the problem*

There are two important issues that constitute two principal facets of the nature of the deficiency of urban environmental infrastructure and services in developing country cities; namely, (a) the urban poor have limited access to land, and (b) local authorities lack autonomy.

Many governments have narrowly viewed the problem of providing clean water and basic sanitation services to the urban poor as infrastructure questions rather than as land or locational ones. In the cities of almost all developing countries in the region, one of the major problems underlying the crowding of the urban poor into unsanitary conditions is limited access to land. Urban land markets, which have been created in most Asian countries through legalisation of rights to private property and the commodification of land over the past century, are vastly more competitive and much more subject to speculative investments than in the rural areas, and are invariably too expensive for most low-income households to enter.[12] The formation of slums and squatter settlements and the environmental problems found in them are not due to the low income levels of the urban poor alone. They are also closely linked to the lack of access to suitable land as well as the lack of incentives to invest in community infrastructure due to the insecurity of land tenure.

First, the urban poor usually occupy land that is unsuitable to settle: on steep hillsides, in flood-prone areas, near factories and garbage dumps. The lack of access to an adequate supply of land often limits the scale of provision of infrastructure. The components in a good physical environment require physical space for their installation: neither piped-water systems nor latrines can be provided without land being made available. The cleaning of drains and the collection of garbage is greatly facilitated if pathways have been built.[13]

Second, because much of the land occupied by the urban poor is deemed by governments to be illegally captured, such settlements are characterised by high levels of insecurity of tenure. The lack of secure tenure in turn has led to low levels of investment by the community in neighbourhood infrastructure outside of the household itself. Illegality also leads to the denial of infrastructure and other basic services needed to improve the living conditions. Governments are often reluctant to provide these services lest such assistance should be taken as *de facto* legitimisation of squatter areas.

Resources for urban local bodies such as municipalities and corporations in most developing countries in the region have not expanded at rates that would permit them to make any major capital investments in cities. This is the direct consequence of several factors: central-local fiscal relations, which heavily favour the central coffers, have not changed much over decades; local governments' abilities and capacities to generate local revenue are very limited; and pricing policies are exclusively the domain of the central governments.[14] In most developing countries in Asia, therefore, local government budgets are highly dependent on central government transfers and thus are always at the discretion of central government ministries.[15]

The lack of financial autonomy on the part of municipal governments has led to the decline in resource base of municipal authorities, which, in turn, has seriously hindered their ability to invest in new projects or provide essential services satisfactorily. For example, in 1960-1961, the tax revenues of municipal authorities constituted roughly 8% of the total revenues raised in India. In 1986-1987, this figure was estimated to have de-

Table 10.2. CHARACTERISTICS AND RATE OF COLLECTION OF SOLID WASTE IN SELECTED CITIES IN ASIA AND THE PACIFIC

| *City* | *Total weight (tons/day)* | *Generation rate (kg./person/day)* | *Bulk density (tonne/m³)* | *Rate of collection (%)* |
|---|---|---|---|---|
| *East Asia* | | | | |
| Beijing | - | 1.59 | 0.48 | - |
| Shanghai | - | 0.87 | 0.50 | - |
| Wuhan[a] | 4294 | 1.20 | - | - |
| Seoul | - | 1.59 | 0.30 | - |
| Tokyo | - | 1.48 | 0.19 | - |
| *Southeast Asia* | | | | |
| Bangkok | 8000[b] | 0.90 | 0.25 | 75 |
| Chiang Mai[c] | 250 | - | - | - |
| Hat Yai[c] | 230 | - | - | - |
| Nakorn Ratchasima[a] | 45-53 | 0.64 | 0.32 | - |
| Songkhla[a] | 70 | - | - | - |
| Hanoi | - | 0.89 | 0.42 | 46 |
| Kuala Lumpur | - | 1.29 | 0.27 | - |
| Penang[d] 1984 | 282 | - | - | - |
| 1986 | 370 | - | - | - |
| 1988 | 348 | - | - | - |
| Bandung[e] | - | - | - | 80 |
| Jakarta | 5000[f] | 0.75 | 0.25 | 70 |
| Surabaya[e] | - | - | - | 80 |
| Manila[g] | 4250-5000 | 0.50 | 0.33 | 68-80 |
| Singapore | 5600[h] | 0.98 | 0.21 | 100 |
| Vientiane | - | 0.65 | - | - |
| *South Asia* | | | | |
| Bombay | 5800[i] | 0.50-0.60 | 0.33 | 86[i] |
| Calcutta[i] | 3500 | - | - | 90 |
| Delhi[i] | 3880 | - | - | 62 |
| Madras[i] | 2675 | - | - | 80 |
| Pune[i] | 540 | 0.30 | - | - |

Table 10.2 continued

| | | | | |
|---|---|---|---|---|
| Chittagong[k] | 600 | 0.60 | - | 50 |
| Dhaka | 3000[a] | 0.50[a] | - | <50[l] |
| Islamabad[a] | 300 | - | 0.35-0.50 | - |
| Karachi | 4500[m] | 0.55a | - | 33[n] |
| Colombo | 700-800[n] | 0.75 | 0.35 | 90[o] |
| Kathmandu[p] | - | 0.30-0.50 | - | - |
| *Pacific* | | | | |
| Honiara | - | 0.38 | 0.27 | - |
| Pohnpei | - | 0.38 | 0.12 | - |

Notes:
– Not available
Regional Network of Local Authorities for the Management of Human Settlements (CITYNET), *Proceedings of the ESCAP/CITYNET Regional Seminar-cum-Study Visit on Final Disposal of Solid Wastes,* New York: UN, 1993. [b] *The Sunday Post*, Bangkok, 22 January 1995. [c] *The Sunday Post*, Bangkok, 9 October 1994. [d] Asian Productivity Organization (APO), *Emerging Trends in Management of Urban Services, French Experiences,* Tokyo: APO, 1990. [e] E. Indrayana and John Silas, 'Waste management in Surabaya: a partnership approach', *Regional Development Dialogue*, 14 (3), 1993, pp. 54. [f] J. Walker, Jerry VanSant, Gene Brantly and Ronald Johnson, 'Private sector participation in Indonesia: water supply, wastewater, and solid waste', Staff Working Paper, Research Triangle Park, North Carolina: Center for International Development, 1992. [g] Salvador P. Passe, 'Metropolitan Manila: issues and future prospects of solid waste disposal', *Regional Development Dialogue,* 14 (3), 1993, p. 180. [h] Preparatory Committee, 'Singapore's national report', Prepared for the 1992 United Nations Conference on Environment and Development, 1992. [i] *India Today*, 'Can we clean up the mess?', XIX, 1994, pp. 40-1. [j] D.V. Deshpande, 'Waste management: a case study of Pune City', in United Nations Center for Human Settlements (HABITAT), *Urban Management in Asia: Issues and Opportunities,* New Delhi: National Institute of Urban Affairs, 1989. [k] United Nations Economic and Social Commission for Asia and the Pacific (UNESCAP), *Innovative Approaches to Municipal Environmental Management,* New York: UN, 1992. [l] Iqbal Ali and Syed Mansoor Ali, 'Solid waste recycling through informal sector in developing countries', *Journal of Resource Management and Technology,* 21 (2), 1993, p. 83. [m] *Bangladesh Observer,* 12 September 1991, taken from UNESCAP, *Human Settlements News Briefing: A Selection from the Region's Press,* Bangkok, 1991. [n] J.E. Hardoy, Diana Mitlin and David Satterthwaite, *Environmental Problems in Third World Cities,* London: Earthscan Publications Ltd, 1992. [o] Ministry of Environment and Parliamentary Affairs, 'Sri Lanka national report', Prepared for the United Nations Conference on Environment and Development, 1991. [p] Ministry of Housing and Physical Planning, 'Background paper on municipal infrastructure services in Nepal', prepared for Regional Seminar on Partnership in Municipal Infrastructure Services, New Delhi, January 1994.

Source: All numbers unless otherwise noted are from: H. Ogawa, 'Generation and nature of waste', Regional Workshop on Solid Waste Management in the Pacific Countries, Suva, 18-22 May 1992.

clined to about 3.4%. Consequently, municipal authorities in India were only able to spend Rs143 per capita per year in 1986-1987 on the operation and maintenance of various services and facilities, as against the national norm of Rs239. The level of expenditure was particularly low in water supply and sanitation services, where Rs47 per capita per year were disbursed. As a result, the rate of coverage of water supply and sanitation facilities is extremely low in India's cities, where a quarter of the population does not have access to safe drinking water supply and nearly 80% of the population have inadequate sanitation facilities.[16]

The weak financial base of local governments is further aggravated by the chronic deficits suffered by many municipal services, which is again a result of the lack of local authority to determine and collect an adequate level of user fees. In Bangkok, for example, the Public Health Act of 1941 placed the garbage disposal responsibilities with the local authorities. The rate structure for urban solid waste disposal fees was established by Thailand's central government, however. Local governments can charge users only up to the maximum rate established in this nation-wide rate structure, but not more, regardless of actual costs. Thus, while an average Bangkok household earns Baht 50,000 a year and produces 1.46 tons of garbage per year, which costs the city Baht 248 to dispose of, the Bangkok Metropolitan Authority is legally allowed to collect only Baht 150.[17] In Chiang Mai, Thailand's second largest city, the solid waste disposal services cost the city Baht 50-80 million a year, but the municipal government was only able to collect about Baht 3 million to cover such expenses.[18]

Chronic deficits are also found in the urban water supply and sanitation sector in many Asian countries. The most recent data from the WHO indicate that with the exception of Singapore and the Philippines, the average water tariffs in countries in the region do not cover the average operating costs of water production. In most developing countries, the conventional wisdom is that the poverty of the vast majority of the citizens may make cost recovery very difficult.[19] In Bombay, for example, the provision of water was still viewed as a social service and water was distributed free to nearly all categories of users until January 1986, when water fees were introduced at the insistence of the World Bank for relatively affluent domestic consumers. As a result, out of nearly 150,000 households with water connections, only about 35,000 (23%) have started to pay water fees.[20]

Combined with the highly competitive urban land market that denies the poor access to suitable and serviced land, the fact that only limited power and resources are made available to municipal authorities by central ministries seems to suggest that the roots to the problem of deficient urban infrastructure and services lie beyond the domain of most local authorities in many Asian countries. This tracing of the roots of the problem, however, should not be construed as an argument to absolve the municipal bodies from several critical problem areas that arise from their 'inefficiency' and 'mismanagement' of urban environmental infrastructure and services.

### *Air Pollution*

Most outdoor air pollution in urban areas is generated from the combustion of fossil fuels during industrial processes, heating and electricity generation and by motor vehicles. The use of fossil fuels in the above activities tends to expand with economic growth and thus causes increased air pollution unless measures are taken to promote efficient fuel use. The most common air pollutants threatening human health in urban environments include suspended particulate matter, lead, carbon monoxide, sulphur dioxide, ozone, nitrogen oxides and toxic substances.

Since the Asia-Pacific region contains some of the world's fastest growing industrial economies, it is not surprising that many cities in this region have recorded alarming levels of air and industrial pollution. In 1988, the Population Crisis Committee collected data on a wide range of socio-economic and physical indicators from a survey of local authorities and environmental experts in the world's hundred largest cities. Of the seven cities that received the worst ranking for air pollution, five were found in Asia: Calcutta, Jakarta, Delhi-New Delhi, Beijing and Shenyang.[21]

Globally, Asia is a relatively minor source of air pollution from vehicular emissions. Although 59% of the world's population live in Asia, it has only 11% of the world's cars and 28% of its trucks and buses, and they generate less than 20% of the common types of vehicular emissions, including carbon monoxide, hydrocarbons and nitrogen oxide, and only about 10.5% of carbon dioxide. Within Asia, however, motor vehicles account for a substantial amount of air pollution in most urban areas (75-90% of carbon dioxide emissions, 55-59% of carbon monoxide, 30-70% of nitrogen oxide, 90% of lead, up to 60% of particulate matter, and considerable ozone).[22]

Vehicular emissions could pollute water and food and lead to increased environmental health risks. A study of environmental risks in Bangkok reported that vehicular emissions may be the main source of two of the three most serious environmental threats in Bangkok, suspended particulate matter and lead, and of one of the two 'medium' risk factors, carbon monoxide. The concentrations of suspended particulate matter in Bangkok's ambient air were found to exceed substantially both Thai and US health standards, and the levels of concentrations were worsening in recent years. The major impacts of suspended particulate matter were estimated to include 9 to 51 million days per year of restricted activity because of respiratory illnesses and up to 1,400 deaths per year among Bangkok residents. Lead was also found at dangerous levels in air, drinking water and food, and in the blood, body tissue, hair and urine of the city's residents. The health impacts from lead pollution include an estimated 200,000 to 500,000 cases of hypertension, 300-900 cases of heart attack and stroke, and 200-400 deaths per year among adult males. Lead pollution also caused the loss of three to five IQ points for each child in Bangkok through age seven.[23]

There are two major characteristics of vehicles in Asia that contribute particular harmful effects to urban air quality. First, the proportionate number of motorcycles is higher in Asia than in other parts of the world. In some cities, they actually outnumber four-wheel vehicles. A large number of these motorcycles are two-stroke engines of old design which emit as much as ten times more hydrocarbons and smoke than four-stroke motorcycles or even automobiles. Second, the proportionate number of diesel-powered vehicles in Asia also exceeds that of the world. These heavily polluting vehicles are concentrated in Asia's many large cities and they produce huge amounts of toxic emissions. The fuels consumed in many Asian cities are among the dirtiest in the world.[24]

In some highly industrialised cities, industries, rather than vehicles, produce most of the ambient air pollution such as sulphur dioxide, nitrogen oxide and suspended particulate matter. Delhi is a good example of such cities. In Delhi, 75% of the city's total suspended particulate matter was discharged by industries. The industrial sector is also responsible for 40% of the total carbon monoxide emission, 31% of sulphur dioxide emission and 21% of nitrogen oxide.[25]

In many cities, open fires or inefficient solid fuel stoves are also major sources of outdoor air pollution. In Seoul, heavy oil burned in domestic heating units and power stations and anthracite briquettes used for domestic heating and cooking contribute to high levels of air pollution.[26] Ambient lead is attributed to motor vehicles burning leaded gasoline (except in Bangkok which has a number of lead smelters). In Jakarta, motor vehicles emitted 4,300 kg. of lead each day in 1987. The comparable figure for Delhi is 600 kg. per day.[27] Apart from these common air pollutants, toxic substances like benzene, ethylene, formaldehyde (associated with gasoline and diesel fuels), and occasionally substances like ethyl isocynate which was released from the Union Carbide plant in Bhopal, India, are also present.

The magnitude of air pollutants and the air pollution monitoring capacity in selected Asian cities is illustrated in Table 10.3. Suspended particulate matter, which can have especially toxic effects if it carries heavy metals or hydrocarbons, is a serious issue in all the cities. Sulphur dioxide remains a serious problem in Beijing and Seoul, while it has become less serious in other cities. Except for ozone which is identified as a serious air pollutant, Tokyo has been able to minimise the emission of the other major air pollutants. Ozone may probably turn out to be a serious problem in other Asian cities as well. However, most cities in the region do not have the capability to monitor this harmful air pollutant. Most cities in the region also have limited or no capability to monitor the emission of carbon monoxide, nitrogen dioxide and lead. There is therefore a strong possibility that the levels of ambient air pollution in Asia's cities are under-estimated.

Indoor air pollution occurs in both the home and the workplace. Since people spend most of their time indoors, indoor air pollution (which includes tobacco smoke) poses a greater threat to human health than outdoor air pollution in both developed and developing countries. Women and children of low-income households who are regularly exposed to high concentrations of pollutants from cooking and heating sources in poorly ventilated houses are at a significant health risk from this type of pollution.

In Ahmedabad, India, the mean measurements of suspended particulate concentrations during cooking in coal-burning households were as high as 25,000 micrograms per cubic meter. In cases where wood and dung are used for cooking, the mean particulate concentrations of 15,000-20,000 micrograms per cubic meter have been calculated. The mean benzo(alpha)pyrene (BaP) levels are as high as 9,000 nanograms per cubic meter during cooking. In comparison, US standard, not to be exceeded even once per year, is 150 micrograms per cubic meter for particulates, and proposed standards for occupational (8-hour) exposure to BaP are 150-200 micrograms per cubic meter. In Chinese cities, high levels of particulates, sulphur dioxide, carbon monoxide and benzopyrenes were recorded in households with coal stoves for heating and/or cooking. In Shenyang, the lung cancer risk is thought to be 50 to 70% higher among those who spend most of their lives inside the home.[28]

Air pollutants in workplaces include toxic chemicals and heavy concentrations of dust. In Bombay, workers in asbestos factories are exposed to asbestos fumes which are very harmful; and cotton dust is inhaled in large quantities by workers in textile mills. A 10-16% incidence of byssinosis was reported for the textile workers. In Bangkok, workers in pesticide plants

Table 10.3. STATUS OF AIR POLLUTANTS IN SELECTED CITIES, 1992

| *City* | $SO_2$ | *SPM* | *Pb* | *CO* | $NO_2$ | $O_3$ |
|---|---|---|---|---|---|---|
| Bangkok | • | ••• | •• | • | • | • |
| Beijing | ••• | ••• | • | - | • | •• |
| Bombay | • | ••• | • | • | • | - |
| Calcutta | • | ••• | • | - | • | - |
| Delhi | • | ••• | • | • | • | - |
| Jakarta | • | ••• | •• | •• | • | •• |
| Karachi | • | ••• | ••• | • | • | • |
| Manila | • | ••• | •• | - | - | - |
| Seoul | ••• | ••• | • | • | • | • |
| Shanghai | •• | ••• | - | - | - | - |
| Tokyo | • | • | - | • | • | ••• |

Key: ••• Serious problem, WHO guidelines exceeded by more than a factor of two.
•• Moderate to heavy pollution, WHO guidelines exceeded by up to a factor of two (short-term guidelines exceeded on a regular basis).
• Low pollution, WHO guidelines normally met (short-term guidelines are exceeded occasionally).
- No data available or insufficient data for assessment.

Source: The World Resources Institute, *World Resources, 1994-95*, New York: OUP, 1994.

are exposed to organphosphorus chemicals; workers in dry cell and lead-cell battery factories are exposed to high levels of manganese and lead. Between 1978-1987, Thailand experienced a tenfold increase in occupational diseases attributable to toxic substance exposure. In addition, an enormous number of cases of ill heath, disablement and death to which workplace exposure has contributed go unreported, especially for long-term illnesses.[29]

A study done on indoor air pollution in three cities (Bangkok, Pune and Beijing) revealed that 'household fuel switching from lower to higher quality fuels, i.e., movement up the "energy ladder", generally leads to substantially lower emissions of health-damaging pollutants'. The study showed that 'household choice seems to have the most impact on air pollution exposures at the lowest level of development (Pune), intermediate at middle stages even with the use of coal (Beijing), and least in the more economically advanced developing country, where fuel choice seems to have little or no impact (Bangkok)'.[30]

Considered together, ambient and indoor air pollution have caused much human suffering, especially in low-income Asian cities. For instance, lung cancer mortality is from four to seven times higher in Chinese cities than in the nation as a whole. Sixty percent of people who live in Calcutta and 30% of those living in Delhi suffer from serious respiratory diseases, as compared to the national average of 2.5%.[31]

## *What Can be Done?*

Meeting the challenge posed by the 'brown agenda' requires every source of planning and management (including national governments, local authorities, the private sector, non-governmental organisations and communities) to be engaged in a process of interaction and cooperation to identify the most viable and effective strategies to address the fundamental concerns. Some general policy recommendations on how to improve the provision of infrastructure and services and to control air pollution, as well as the appropriate role of each of the stakeholders, are discussed below.

### *Strategies to address infrastructure shortfall*

Focusing our attention on the urban water supply and sanitation sector in the ensuing discussion, four major approaches to address a number of crucial managerial and institutional issues can be identified.[32]

*Concentrate on cost-effective operation and maintenance.* One major lesson from the experience of numerous projects and programmes implemented during the International Water Supply and Sanitation Decade is that far too much emphasis was given to the construction of new facilities by national and international agencies at the expense of developing appropriate provisions for the proper operation and maintenance of existing and new installations.[33]

An excellent example of the serious consequences of inadequate operation and maintenance is the large volume of unaccounted-for-water in many developing country cities. In many cities in Asia, between 20-50% of the water that is treated and distributed at public expense is not accounted for by sales (see Table 10.4). Implementing a formal control policy to reduce both physical losses (through leakage detection and repair) and non-physical losses (through improved management practices) typically costs US$5-10 per capita. Studies have shown that savings and increased revenue will repay this cost within one or two years.[34] Investment to improve the performance of existing assets is thus highly cost-effective. Despite the ready availability of commonsense and well-intentioned measures to reduce high levels of unaccounted-for-water, however, little progress has been made in this area.[35]

*Adopt appropriate technology and standards.* The availability and quality of urban water supply and sanitation services depend to a great extent on the standards of physical infrastructure systems such as water piping and sewer networks. In many developing countries, there is a tendency to insist on standards higher than necessary, sometimes doubling the cost of service delivery. The result is poor access to water supply and sanitation services.[36] Per capita unit costs of providing services have continued to increase despite the development of less expensive technologies.

With few exceptions the technologies currently in use in many developing countries are the same as those employed in the developed countries: piped water, full internal plumbing and conventional water-borne sewerage.[37] Estimates indicate that the current distribution of sector investments in developing countries to high-cost and low-cost technology is in the order of 80% and 20% respectively.[38] This essentially means that 70 to 80% of funds are being spent to serve 20 to 30% of the population, mostly the higher income groups. Experience gathered from the International Water Decade programmes, however, informs us that only a drastic revision of design standards to reduce construction costs sharply is likely to offer hope of providing even minimal levels of public water services to extensive low-income urban neighbourhoods.

*Emphasise and accept inputs from the users' community.* The first half of the International Water Decade was marked by the development of new, low-cost, technologies appropriate to the needs of the developing countries. Yet both the urban and rural landscapes of the developing world are littered with inoperative pumps that may have been well conceived at the office of a donor agency and a country ministry but have fallen into disrepair because of the lack of commitment and participation of the local populations who were purportedly the beneficiaries of such projects.[39]

The success of introducing appropriate technologies, therefore, requires a thorough understanding of the perceived needs of the user communities. In particular, the participation of women, who are the major system users,

Table 10.4. WATER SUPPLY CHARACTERISTICS IN SELECTED CITIES IN THE ASIA-PACIFIC REGION

| *City* | *Institutional status of water utility* | *Unaccounted-for water (%)* | *Service coverage (%)* | *Water availability (hrs./day)* | *Per capita consumption (l/c/d)* | *Staff per 1,000 connections* | *Operating ratio* |
|---|---|---|---|---|---|---|---|
| *East Asia* | | | | | | | |
| Seoul | Govt. Department | 42 | 100 | 24 | 180 | 2.3 | 0.98 |
| Beijing | Govt. Department | 28 | 95 | 24 | 149 | 17.0 | 1.47 |
| Hong Kong | Govt. Entity | 26 | 100 | 24 | 111 | 2.7 | 1.15 |
| Shanghai | Govt. Department | 25 | 100 | 24 | 193 | 5.3 | 1.92 |
| Taipei | Govt. Enterprise | 24 | 100 | 24 | 281 | 1.2 | 0.38 |
| *Southeast Asia* | | | | | | | |
| Yangon | Govt. Department | 60 | 50 | 8 | 120 | 5.3 | 0.34 |
| Metro Manila | Govt. Corporation | 58 | 71 | 16 | 133 | 12.8 | 0.37 |
| Jakarta | Govt. Corporation | 57 | 25 | 19 | 148 | 10.2 | 0.42 |
| Hanoi | Govt. Enterprise | 53 | 69 | 12 | 157 | 28.8 | 0.79 |
| Bandung | Govt. Enterprise | 42 | 39 | 6 | 96 | 12.0 | 0.43 |
| Ho Chi Minh City | Govt. Enterprise | 41 | 65 | 24 | 131 | 4.6 | 0.59 |
| Chiang Mai | Govt. Corporation | 39 | 65 | 24 | 172 | 4.0 | 0.74 |
| Cebu | Govt. Corporation | 38 | 26 | 18 | 139 | 12.6 | 0.63 |
| Kuala Lumpur | Govt. Department | 37 | 100 | 24 | 222 | 1.8 | 0.13 |
| Medan | Govt. Enterprise | 34 | 39 | 24 | 153 | 6.9 | 1.02 |
| Mandalay | Govt. Department | 33 | 30 | 24 | 153 | 12.2 | 0.39 |
| Vientiane | Govt. Enterprise | 33 | 33 | 24 | 140 | 19.2 | 0.92 |
| Bangkok | Govt. Enterprise | 31 | 79 | 24 | 217 | 5.5 | 0.43 |
| Penang | Statutory Body | 22 | 100 | 24 | 203 | 5.4 | 0.54 |
| Singapore | Govt. Authority | 8 | 100 | 24 | 168 | 2.4 | 0.43 |

Table 10.4. continued

| | | | | | | | |
|---|---|---|---|---|---|---|---|
| *South Asia* | | | | | | | |
| Dhaka | Govt. Corporation | 62 | 64 | 6 | 44 | 21.3 | 0.75 |
| Colombo | Govt. Corporation | 51 | 51 | 12 | 168 | 9.2 | 0.26 |
| Kathmandu | Govt. Corporation | 45 | 100 | 6 | 97 | 18.6 | 1.60 |
| Calcutta | Govt. Corporation | 36 | 64 | 10 | 213 | 16.2 | 1.11 |
| Delhi | Govt. Corporation | 30 | 69 | 7 | 257 | 8.9 | 0.81 |
| Karachi | Semi-Auton. Body | 30 | 83 | 5 | 172 | 11.7 | 1.08 |
| Bombay | Semi-Govt. Entity | 24 | - | 5 | - | 61.0 | 0.66 |
| *Pacific* | | | | | | | |
| Port Vila | Govt. Department | 42 | - | 24 | - | 5.8 | 0.43 |
| Honiara | Govt. Department | 55 | 100 | 22 | 184 | 12.8 | 1.54 |
| Suva | Govt. Department | 36 | 100 | 24 | 203 | 4.8 | 1.84 |
| Rarotonga | Govt. Department | 27 | 100 | 24 | 464 | 12.6 | - |
| Nuku'alofa | Statutory Body | 25 | 98 | 20 | 81 | 14.8 | 0.86 |
| Apia | Govt. Department | 15 | 100 | 24 | 475 | 32.6 | 8.74 |

- Not available

Source: Compiled from data in Asian Development Bank, *Water Utilities Data Book,* Manila: Asian Development Bank, 1993.

in the design, construction, and sustained effective use and management of projects has been increasingly recognised as critical to the success of sector initiatives.[40] Reorienting project design and implementation methods to incorporate meaningful users' participation is not an easy task, however. Most important of all, it requires substantial structural and attitudinal changes within the implementing agencies at the local and regional level.

*Design and implement innovative cost recovery programmes.* Although given little attention previously, by the late 1980s many external support agencies and governments in developing countries were looking seriously at ways to implement cost recovery programmes.[41] By now the question is no longer whether to charge but how much and to whom. A related debate is over whether water supply tariffs should cover only operation and maintenance costs or whether they should also generate resources for future investment.

Even though the 1980s saw a widespread commitment to adopting more cost-recovery programmes, a 1990 United Nations report on progress on water management issues in the Asia-Pacific revealed that only nine of 26 countries surveyed had been able to achieve full cost recovery in water supply operations.[42] Earlier data from the WHO[43] indicated that with the exception of Singapore and the Philippines, the average water tariffs in countries in the region did not cover the average operating costs of water production.

In most developing countries, the conventional wisdom is that the poverty of the vast majority of the citizens may make cost recovery very difficult. Yet the widespread practice of water vending in poor communities indicates a higher level of affordability and willingness to pay than is often assumed. Evidence also shows that service from water vendors costs substantially more than the per unit water costs borne by households served by piped water systems in the same area. The poor may pay as much as 30% of their income for water whereas the well-to-do pay less than 2%.[44] Supplying free or almost free piped water therefore often produces very inequitable results, with only better-off consumers with house connections reaping the benefits. Cross-subsidising water delivery to lower income groups through higher charges on more affluent users is a policy option, but care must be taken to assure that the poor actually pay the lower charges rather than being charged more by unofficial tariffs on, for example, access to standpipes.

Another major barrier to securing financial involvement of low-income groups lies not with their absolute inability to contribute but with the lack of appropriate or credible cost recovery programmes.[45] There is an understandable reluctance of many low-income people in developing countries to pay money to a government department which they suspect of corruption or in which they have little or no confidence. There is thus a need to focus on how revenues are to be collected and managed.[46]

### *Strategies to control air pollution*

Strategies to address air pollution problems must be multi-faceted to cover various sources and differential impacts on the rich and poor. In the region's developing country cities, for example, many forms of transportation available to the poor are subject to high levels of ambient air pollution, primarily from vehicular exhausts. While overall urban pollution levels may be within safe levels, specific areas in the city could experience very high concentrations of air pollution. People who must work or travel daily along or next to heavily-used roadways experience dangerously high exposure to lead and other emissions from fossil-fuel powered vehicles. Directly reducing vehicular emissions will therefore have a positive effect on those who through their work along roadways and reliance on open air bus transportation are more likely to be exposed to the worst impacts.

Any automobile emissions reduction policy must be set within the framework of a knowledge of both air quality and the sources of emissions so that targets can be set and progress monitored. The most significant improvements in automobile emissions can be made through developing alternative, less polluting, modes of urban transportation; regulations and incentives for more fuel efficient automobile engines to meet higher emissions standards; and reduction of traffic congestion and the engine idling times created by it.[47]

For instance, Singapore has introduced a comprehensive motor vehicle control programme which aims at improving the emission control devices on vehicles and fuel quality to reduce emissions. Emission standards for both petrol and diesel vehicles have been set at levels comparable to those in the US and Europe. Moreover, all vehicles are required to undergo periodic inspections to ensure exhaust emissions at idle mode remain within the set standards.[48]

Since many poorer households are located in undesirable areas near polluting industries, special attention should be paid to industries around low-income neighborhoods that practise uncontrolled burning of organic and non-organic materials at the shop and household level, which can be a significant source of localised air pollution. Extra attention is also needed to improve the quality of the environment in urban work places. Some of the worst forms of indoor pollution and poor environments are found in shops and factories that employ low-wage, unskilled labour, including children. Enforcement of regulations to limit the harmful effects of working in urban industries that use toxic chemicals and other health-threatening processes, including unsafe work processes, needs to be greatly improved.

The only long-term solution to indoor air pollution is to move to cleaner fuels. As there are millions of urban households which will not be able to move up the energy ladder for many decades due to relative costs and availability of the fossil fuels required, the promising interim measures include improved stoves and improved housing design with better ventilation.[49]

In the 1980s many programmes to improve cook stoves were introduced in developing countries. For instance, China's National Improved Biomass Stove Programme and India's National Programme on Improved Chullahs constituted two of the world's largest programmes on the production and dissemination of improved stoves. In China, more than 129 million households (in both urban and rural areas) switched to improved cook stoves during the 1983-1991 period.[50] In the same period, about 8 million improved stoves were disseminated in India.[51] Because the programmes on improved stoves were concentrated on those who were most likely to benefit from and would consequently adopt the improved stoves, they were targeted at purchasers of biomass fuels as well as at those who were spending a substantial portion of their limited cash income on cooking fuels. This means that although many households were reached, the beneficiaries were not the poorest groups in society.

Meeting the urban environmental challenge in the Asia-Pacific region requires responsibilities to be shared and actions to be taken by a host of stakeholders including national governments, local governments, NGOs, communities, the private sector and international agencies.

Overall, national governments can play a crucial role in enhancing urban environmental conditions by formulating appropriate urban environmental health policies to protect public health, formulating appropriate economic policies to create an effective implementation incentive system with a judicious mix of regulatory and economic instruments, and strengthening local government's legal and institutional structures and enhancing their capacities to generate local-level revenue sources.

Most of the actions, however, need to be implemented at the city level and assumed by municipal governments. For instance, with regard to controlling outdoor air pollution, national governments are generally responsible for establishing environmental policies, regulations and standards and for providing technical and financial assistance to local authorities for policy and programme implementation. Thus, with regard to the respective role of national and local governments in the design and implementation of key control strategies relating to automobile emissions, setting emissions standards for vehicles, designing mandatory vehicle inspection programmes, and the introduction of economic instruments are primarily the responsibilities of national governments, whereas the implementation of vehicle inspection programmes and the enforcement of traffic management strategies lie mostly within the domain of local metropolitan authorities.

Moving the action agenda down the spatial scale from the city level to the community level, community-based organisations can play an important role in mobilising resources within and outside the communities to address the shortfall of environmental infrastructure and services, particularly in low-income settlements. Recognising the limits of the conventional model of direct state-delivery systems, an increasing number of Asian countries in the past several years have begun to adopt an alternative, community-based approach to provide basic infrastructure and services in low-income settlements.[52] Reorienting the conventional method of state-delivered infrastructure and services to an alternative, community-based approach, however, requires the development of a ready availability of funding and technical and legal assistance to individuals, households and communities. This implies the need for intermediary institutions such as non-governmental organisations which can provide on a continuing basis funding and technical support to community-level initiatives.[53] It also implies the need for city governments to establish local institutions to provide financial and technical support for innovative community infrastructure and services improvement projects initiated by both non-governmental and community-based organisations.

Since the late 1980s, some governments in the region have also turned to privatisation as a way of grappling with the shortfall of infrastructure and services. Limited evidence from selected Asian cities lends support to two propositions: (1) private-sector operators are able to provide certain urban services more efficiently than public agencies, and (2) contracting out selected urban services to private firms can result in cost savings to the government.[54] However, it is imperative that governments do not lose sight of an important point that is sometimes forgotten in the midst of enthusiasm for privatisation: it is not a totally cost-free and risk-free undertaking and it comes with a litany of potential disadvantages.[55]

In conclusion, as an increasing number of Asians make cities their home, the challenge to provide them with adequate infrastructure and services and a liveable environment requires innovations and cooperation between established and new actors including national governments, local authorities, non-governmental organisations, communities and the private sector. Recognising and accepting that each of them equally possesses a set of strengths and weaknesses is one of the first steps toward identifying mutually enhancing and reinforcing strategies in meeting the urban environmental challenge in this rapidly changing region.


## *Acknowledgements*

Miroo Desai Brewer provided invaluable research assistance in the preparation of this manuscript. Mike Douglass, Kem Lowry, Kirk Smith and James Nickum have been a source of intellectual stimulation at various stages of my research on urban environmental management issues in Asia.


## NOTES

[1] United Nations, *World Urbanisation Prospects: The 1992 Revision*, New York, 1993.

[2] There is considerable subregional heterogeneity in the urbanisation pattern in Asia. Whereas developed countries such as Japan, Republic of Korea, New Zealand, Australia, Hong Kong and Singapore have arrived at levels of urbanisation of more than 70%, the less developed countries including China, all of the South Asian countries, most of the Pacific Island

countries, Indonesia, Thailand and the other Southeast Asian countries have registered levels of urbanisation of below 35%.

[3] *South China Morning Post*, 16 December 1995.

[4] Traditional sources of health risks, highly associated with poverty, include infectious and parasitic diseases, whereas modern health risks are linked with cancer and heart diseases. See Kirk Smith and Yok-shiu F. Lee, 'Urbanisation and the environmental risk transition', in John Kasarda and Allan M. Parnell (eds), *Third World Cities: Problems, Policies and Prospects*, Newbury Park: Sage, 1993, pp. 161-179.

[5] C. Bartone, J. Bernstein, J. Lietmann and J. Eigen, *Toward Environmental Strategies for Cities*, Washington, D.C.: The World Bank, 1994.

[6] Asian Development Bank, 'Water supply and sanitation – beyond the decade', *Proceedings of the Asia and Pacific Regional Consultation*, 1990.

[7] Secretariat for the Global Consultation, 'Global consultation on safe water and sanitation for the 1990s, Background paper', 1990.

[8] Yok-shiu F. Lee, 'Urban planning and vector control in Southeast Asian cities', *Kaohsiung Journal of Medical Sciences*, 10,1994a, pp. S39-S51.

[9] J.E. Hardoy, Diana Mitlin and David Satterthwaite, *Environmental Problems in Third World Cities*, London: Earthscan Publications Ltd, 1992.

[10] Jane Walker, Jerry VanSant, Gene Brantly and Ronald Johnson, 'Private sector participation in Indonesia: water supply, waste water and solid waste', Staff Working Paper, Research Triangle Park, North Carolina: Center for International Development, 1992, p. 16.

[11] Yok-shiu F. Lee, 'Myths of environmental management and the urban poor', in Roland Fuchs, Ellen Brennan, Joseph Chamie, Fu-Chen Lo and Juha I. Uitto (eds), *Mega-City Growth and the Future*, Tokyo: UN University Press, 1994b, pp. 390-411.

[12] M. Douglass, 'Urban poverty and policy alternatives in Asia', prepared for the Division of Industry, Human Settlements & Environment, United Nations Economic and Social Commission for Asia and the Pacific, 1992.

[13] For example, in Manila, it was found that 'the slums and squatter settlements are not usually served by the municipal collection services because of narrow access streets and fewer recyclable components of waste' (J. Passe and T. Salvador, Jr., 'Metropolitan Manila: issues and future prospects of solid waste disposal', *Regional Development Dialogue*, 14 [3], 1993, p. 181).

[14] For instance, in Pakistan, '90 percent of the total revenues in 1981-1982 accrued to the Federal government, only 7 percent to the four provincial governments and about 3 percent to the multitude of local bodies in the country' (O.P. Mathur, 'The financing of urban development', in *Urban policy Issues*, Manila: ADB, 1987, p. 122).

[15] Ibid.

[16] M. Mehta and D. Mehta, 'Privatization of municipal services', *Urban India*, 12 (2), 1992, p. 6.

[17] K. Suwarnarat and Watana Luanratana, 'Waste management and the need for public participation in Bangkok', *Regional Development Dialogue*, 14 (3), 1993, pp. 68-9.

[18] *Bangkok Sunday Post*, 9 October 1994.

[19] The available evidence clearly shows that service from water vendors (widely patronised by the poor) costs substantially more than is paid by customers served by piped water system in the same area (World Resources Institute, *World Resources 1990-1991*, New York: OUP, 1990, p. 77). See also D.A. Okun, 'The value of water supply and sanitation in development: an assessment', *American Journal of Public Health*, 78 (11), 1988, pp. 1463-7.

[20] S.K. Bhattacharya, 'Problems of water supply in congested city areas - Calcutta, a case study', in John Pickford (ed.), *Developing World Water*, Hong Kong: Grosvenor Press International, 1988.

[21] Population Crisis Committee, *Chart on Quality of Life in One Hundred Cities*, 1988.
[22] G.T. Kingsley, B. Ferguson, B. Bower, with S. Dice, *Managing Urban Environmental Quality in Asia.*, World Bank Technical Paper Number 220, Asia Technical Department Series, Washington, D.C.: The World Bank, 1994.
[23] Ibid.
[24] Ibid.
[25] Ibid.
[26] Hardoy et al, op. cit., 1992.
[27] Yok-shiu F. Lee and James Nickum, 'Urban environment', prepared for the Division of Industry, Human Settlements & Environment, United Nations Economic and Social Commission for Asia and the Pacific, 1992.
[28] Ibid.
[29] Ibid.
[30] K. Smith and Youcheng Liu, 'Indoor air pollution in developing countries', in J.M. Samet (ed.), *Epidemiology of Lung Cancer*, Lung Biology in Health and Disease Series, v. 74, 1994.
[31] Kingsley et al, op. cit., 1994.
[32] See also Yok-shiu F. Lee, 'Rethinking urban water supply and sanitation strategy in developing countries: lessons from the international decade', in Michael Bonell, Maynard M. Hufschmidt and John S. Gladwell (eds), *Hydrology and Water Management in the Humid Tropics*, CUP, 1993, pp. 547-55.
[33] D.B. Warner and L. Laugeri, 'Health for all: the legacy of the water decade', *Water International,* 16 (3), 1991, pp. 135-41.
[34] J. Richardson, 'Non-revenue water – a lost cause?', *The Proceedings of the 14th WECD Conference,* 1988.
[35] Lee, op. cit., 1993.
[36] M.A. Ridgley, 'Evaluation of water-supply and sanitation options in Third World cities: an example from Cali, Colombia', *Geo Journal,* 18 (2), 1989, pp. 199-211; R. Gakenheimer and C.H.J. Brando, 'Infrastructure standards', in L. Rodwin (ed.), *Shelter, Settlements, and Development*, Boston: Allen and Unwin, 1987.
[37] Ridgley, op. cit., 1989.
[38] J. Christmas and C. de Rooy, 'The decade and beyond: at a glance', *Water International* 16 (3), 1991, pp. 127-134; J.M. Kalbermatten, 'Become reality or remain a dream?', *Water International,* 16 (3), 1991, pp. 121-26.
[39] Okun, op. cit., 1988.
[40] P. Najlis and A. Edwards, 'The international drinking water supply and sanitation decade in retrospect and implications for the future', *Natural Resources Forum,* 15 (2), 1991, pp. 110-17.
[41] T.S. Katko, 'Cost recovery in water supply in developing countries', *Journal of Water Resources Development,* 6 (2), 1990, pp. 86-94.
[42] T. Lee, 'Water management since the adoption of the Mar del Plata Action Plan', *Natural Resources Forum*, August 1992.
[43] WHO, *The International Drinking Water Supply and Sanitation Decade, 1981-1990*, Geneva, 1987.
[44] Okun, op. cit., 1988.
[45] Najlis and Edwards, op. cit., 1991.
[46] M.G. McGarry, 'Matching water supply technology to the needs and resources of developing countries', *Natural Resources Forum*, 11 (2), 1987, pp. 141-51.
[47] Priorities for automotive emissions control strategies include: introducing an effective vehicle inspection and maintenance programme; devising transportation planning and traffic

management strategies to improve traffic flow and reduce car usage; introducing cleaner vehicles (e.g., with exhaust catalysts) and cleaner fuels needed for their optimal operation (e.g., unleaded gasoline); introducing economic instruments such as vehicle tax, fuel tax and road user charges; accelerating the efforts to diversify modes of transport as alternatives to automobiles, particularly mass rapid transit systems; and linking transportation with land-use and spatial planning to make cities more compact, reduce commuting and increase transportation efficiency. A more detailed discussion of these strategies can be found in M. Douglass and Y.F. Lee, 'Urban priorities for action', *World Resources: A Guide to the Global Environment, 1996-97,* Washington, D.C.: World Resources Institute, UNDP, UNEP and World Bank, 1996, chapter 5, pp. 103-24.

[48] World Resources Institute, *World Resources, 1994-95*, New York: OUP, 1994.

[49] Smith and Liu, op. cit., 1994.

[50] K. Smith et al, 'One hundred million improved cookstoves in China: how was it done?', *World Development*, 21 (6), 1993, pp. 941-61.

[51] D. Barnes et al, 'The design and diffusion of improved cooking stoves', *The World Bank Research Observer*, 8 (2), 1993, pp. 119-41.

[52] *Asian Journal of Environmental Management*, Special Issue on Community-Based Urban Environmental Management in Asia, 2 (1), May 1994.

[53] Yok-shiu F. Lee, 'Intermediary institutions, community organizations, and urban environmental management: the case of three Bangkok slums', *East-West Center Working Papers: Environment Series*, No. 41, 1995a; Yok-shiu F. Lee, 'Community-based urban environmental management: local NGOs as catalysts,' *Regional Development Dialogue*, 15 (2), Autumn 1994c, pp. 158-76.

[54] Yok-shiu F. Lee, 'Privatization of urban environmental infrastructure and services in Asia', *East-West Center Working Papers: Environment Series*, No. 46, 1995b.

[55] The potential disadvantages associated with privatisation include: higher unemployment among public employees, increased prices of public services, greater opportunities for corruption, lower wages and decreased employment security, reduction and elimination of unprofitable but necessary services, particularly those that address the needs of the urban poor who cannot afford to pay market prices, reduced public control over services, and increased possibility of converting public monopolies into private monopolies (Mehta and Mehta, op. cit., 1992).

# Part III
# National Responses to Globalisation in the Asia-Pacific Region

## 11. THE EAST ASIAN GROWTH MODEL: SOUTH KOREAN EXPERIENCE

*R.M. Auty*

This chapter examines the postwar economic development of South Korea in the context of the East Asian development model which is characterised by high investment, outward-oriented trade, a small public sector, a competitive labour market and prudent state intervention.[1] It focuses on the controversy over the role which South Korea's distinctive industrial policy played in its rapid economic growth after the 1950s.

The chapter is structured as follows. The East Asian development model is summarised and the debate over the importance of the industrial strategy is briefly reviewed. The evolution of South Korea's industrial policy is then analysed through each of three critical stages of the East Asian model. The final section of the paper qualifies the conclusions that can be drawn from the South Korean experience.

### *The East Asian Model and the Industrial Policy Controversy*

A four-stage East Asian development model can be recognised, based largely upon the experience of South Korea and Taiwan, in which the industrial policy changes systematically as per capita income rises. Briefly, in stage one the emphasis is upon primary import substitution but switches to export-oriented, labour-intensive manufacturing in stage two. Capital-intensive and also skill-intensive manufacturing are targeted in stage three (the drive into heavy and chemical industry [HCI]), while research-intensive sectors are encouraged in stage four as the economy is liberalised. With the exception of the initial stage, such a development sequence carefully tracks the country's evolving comparative advantage. The government seeks to anticipate these changes and to facilitate them through appropriate macroeconomic and microeconomic policies.

The optimum degree of state intervention is hotly disputed by orthodox economists and institutional economists. There is general agreement on both sides of the debate as to the desirability of the switch into stage two and also of the need for state intervention in doing so.[2] Such intervention is required to offset any biases against export-oriented activity which may have arisen from institutional and market failures, including the legacy of the earlier primary import substitution policy.[3] However, the merits of intensifying the intervention in stages three and four, through the targeting of incentives at specific sub-sectors of manufacturing and even at specific firms,[4] is controversial.

It is useful to recognise three variants of industrial policy in reviewing the controversy. They are, ranked in order of decreasing market-suppression: autarchic (AIP); competitive (CIP), after Ohno and Imoaka;[5] and the creation of an enabling environment (CEE). Their major characteristics and likely outcomes are summarised in Table 11.1. Research into the relationship between the different forms of intervention and economic performance has yielded three robust conclusions:

- AIP stresses the build-up of physical production over efficiency and has been strongly favoured by the larger countries of Latin America and Asia (notably India and China). It overrides markets (and runs the

Table 11.1. THREE DEVELOPMENT STRATEGIES

| | *Enabling Environment* | *Competitive Industrial Policy* | *Autarchic Industrial Policy* |
|---|---|---|---|
| *Macro Policy* | | | |
| Basic stance | Orthodox | Orthodox | Structuralist |
| Fiscal stance | No/Low deficit | No/Low deficit | Lax & seignorage |
| Exchange rate | Floating | Competitive depreciation | Over-valuation |
| *Sectoral Intervention* | | | |
| Market impact | Failure correction | Broad market-conforming | Market-suppressing |
| Sectoral targeting | None | Emerging comparative advantage | Wide 'infant' support |
| Incentives | None | Tightly targeted & tapered | Widespread & renewed |
| Trade orientation | Open | Moving protected swathe | Widespread strong protection |
| Effective production | Neutral | High for target range | High, wide & variable |
| Export subsidies | None | Compensatory only | Substantial |
| *Likely Policy Outcomes* | | | |
| GDP growth | Modest | Rapid | Erratic, but slowing |
| Incremental capital Output rates | Low | Low, but rising | High, but rising |
| Inflation | Low <5 | 5-15% | >-20% |
| Foreign debt | Modest | Modest | High |
| Debt source ratio | <20% | <25% | >30% |
| Trade/GDP ratio | >30% | >30% | <15% |
| Income rich 1/5:Poor 1/5 | 10-15 | <10 | >15 |
| Sectoral maturation (years) | <3 | 3-10 | >20 |

risk of policy capture by those receiving the state incentives) on a scale likely to depress the economy-wide efficiency of capital usage and to result in erratic economic growth.[6]

- CIP overrides markets less by intervening with a tapered package of incentives to encourage new entrants into areas of emerging comparative advantage. The institutionalists make a plausible case that CIP can be successfully pursued by efficient states.[7] But the evidence is not definitive: the impact of CIP on economic growth may be only neutral, at best.[8]
- CEE calls for a commitment to prudent macroeconomic policy and the correction of market failures through the public provision of infrastructure, skills and environmental protection. CEE, according to the World Bank,[9] is the strategy that is likely to be both the least risky and the most efficient user of scarce resources.

More specifically, an AIP stresses a level of self-sufficiency which pushes the ratio of exports to GDP down towards 5% compared with a ratio in excess of 30% in the successful East Asian NICs. The policy confers rents (returns in excess of those required by an efficient producer) on 'infant' manufacturing firms and fosters policy capture so that the incentives for new entrants are not withdrawn. Under this system the effective rates of protection are often in excess of 100% of value added and provide little incentive to mature.

Infant industry maturation rates under AIP frequently exceed 30 years, well above the five to eight years considered by orthodox economists to be the maximum that can be allowed if the discounted costs of the initial protection are to be recouped by the stream of benefits from the matured sector. Consequently, as the size of the slow-maturing manufacturing sector within GDP rises, the demands for foreign exchange and subsidies from the shrinking non-manufacturing tradeable sector become overly burdensome. But the rent recipients in the protected industries block reform so that governments frequently resort to forcing economic growth through populist booms which are inflationary and counter-productive, leading to erratic growth and/or growth collapses.[10]

CIP is more selective in its targeting than AIP and anticipates the country's evolving comparative advantage. Like AIP, it lowers the risk for new entrants with a package of incentives (higher tariffs, tax holidays, low-interest loans and assistance with technology acquisition and marketing). But unlike AIP, the infant incentives are quickly phased out and made conditional on the rapid maturation of the assisted enterprise.[11] Orthodox economists, however, dispute the merits of even such market-conforming intervention. Rather they attribute East Asian success to sound macroeconomic policy (notably, fiscal prudence and an open trade policy) and the correction of market failure.[12] These characteristics describe CEE (see Table 11.1), and are certainly *essential*, although many non-Asian countries failed to achieve them. Attention now turns to South Korea's passage through the three key stages of the East Asian model (see Table 11.2).

Table 11.2 SOUTH KOREA AND THE EAST ASIAN DEVELOPMENT MODEL, 1963-1993

| *Stage* | *Two Export-Led* | *Three HCI Big Push* | *Four Liberalisation* | |
|---|---|---|---|---|
| | *1963-73* | *1974-82* | *1983-88* | *1989-93* |
| *Absorption (% GDP)* | | | | |
| Private consumption | 76.8 | 64.3 | 56.6 | 53.7 |
| Government consumption | 9.2 | 10.4 | 10.5 | 10.4 |
| Investment | 22.5 | 32.5 | 29.7 | 36.1 |
| *Capital Efficiency* | | | | |
| GDP growth (%/Yr) | 10.5 | 8.1 | 10.4 | 7.2 |
| Incremental capital output ratio | 2.1 | 4.0 | 2.9 | 5.0 |
| *Foreign Debt* | | | | |
| Current account (% GDP) | -6.5[a] | -5.5 | 2.5 | -0.5 |
| Foreign debt (% GDP) | 36.6[b] | 41.1 | 40.8 | 14.2 |
| Debt service (% Exports) | 19.2[b] | 15.3 | 23.9 | 9.3 |
| *Economic Structure (% GDP)* | | | | |
| Agriculture | 31.5 | 19.5 | 11.7 | 8.1 |
| Manufacturing | 17.0 | 27.7 | 30.6 | 29.1 |

Notes: a 1965-73 only; b 1971-73 only.
Source: World Bank (1995).

## *South Korea's Labour-Intensive Export-led Phase, 1963-73*

The prospects for South Korean economic success did not appear propitious in the 1950s. At that time, US aid propped up an inefficient economy in which manufacturing accounted for only 6% of GDP and mainly comprised inefficient import substituting industry. The government stressed political unity in the recovery from the civil war. It persisted with land redistribution and the provision of universal primary education, measures which subsequent research[13] has identified as two pre-requisites for the elimination of poverty because they expand the effective participation of the populace in economic activity. A third condition for poverty alleviation, the rapid growth of labour-intensive employment, was achieved by pursuing stage two of the East Asian model.

From 1963 a new government adopted a different development strategy which emulated Taiwan whose similarly deficient natural resource endowment (0.1 hectares of cropland per capita in the mid-1950s) had underlined the need to find an alternative source of foreign exchange to agricultural exports.[14] The new government targeted competitive light manufactured exports. Its planners set a GDP growth target and a rate of capital efficiency from which they deduced the capital investment required. They then targeted incentives at exporters which were designed to offset any discrimination against them arising from the use of high-cost domestic inputs. The Export Promotion Conference provided intelligence on export markets and coordinated the activity of the state and private firms.

During the second stage of the East Asian development model in South Korea, the economy expanded at more than 10% per annum (see Table 11.2) and per capita GNP grew with a 12-year doubling rate. The incremental capital output ratio averaged 2.5, indicating a highly efficient use of capital. Meanwhile, import substitution proceeded alongside export promotion as backward linkage pushed domestic demand towards the minimum viable size thresholds for the production of intermediate goods like steel and petrochemicals. By the early 1970s, the rapid expansion of light industry had absorbed much surplus labour and pushed the labour market towards its turning point where rising labour costs require increased worker productivity. The wage pressure speeded up the shift into more skill-intensive and capital intensive HCI, a move that was reinforced by a desire to be industrially more self-sufficient as the US withdrew from Viet Nam.

### *The HCI Big Push, 1974-79*

The South Korean decision to diversify into HCI as a Big Push was viewed as risky by the more cautious Taiwanese planners. It required the simultaneous expansion of both basic industry, like steel and petrochemicals, and also downstream users, like auto assembly and shipbuilding, in order to maximise the external and internal economies of scale.[15] But the Big Push not only targeted specific industrial sectors, it also favoured large domestic conglomerates (the *chaebol*) which seemed better-suited than small firms to the task of acquiring the new technology from multinational partners. Finally, many of the new plants were located in the southeast of the country within 130 kilometres of Pusan, for both strategic and regional policy considerations.

State enterprises were occasionally used to enter new sectors, notably integrated steel production. Posco built a 9 million tonne plant in four stages during 1970-81 and then constructed a second plant of similar size during 1984-91. The addition of each successive stage enhanced the overall scale economies and achieved greater efficiency as the firm moved along the learning curve. Average investment costs were two-thirds those of OECD producers and one-half to one-quarter those of the Latin American NICs and India.[16] The steel sector matured in 8 years within the orthodox efficiency threshold, but the financial return was low, while the returns made by the downstream steel users were similar or worse.

For example, although the shipbuilding sector matured within two years and quickly established one-third of global capacity, a shipbuilding slump led to heavy losses (a situation not helped by the huge expansion in South

Korean capacity). Low financial returns encouraged the *chaebol* to diversify into construction and engineering, including auto assembly. But the country's entry into auto assembly in the mid-1970s was premature because domestic demand was well below the threshold for a producer of minimum viable size, let alone for the three producers which were licensed. Nevertheless, by 1985 Hyundai had captured a share of the US car market which suggested the sector had matured. But the profit margins were reported to be only $50 per car and needed to be offset by the state permitting the sale of high-margin imported cars in the captive Korean market. Worse, Hyundai lost US market share due to poor quality control. Elsewhere, the skill-intensive heavy engineering plant at Chongwon experienced heavy losses and its maturation rate exceeded 15 years.

In addition to the initially disappointing financial returns and mixed results on sectoral maturation, the HCI Big Push adversely affected macroeconomic performance. It led to the accumulation of foreign debt on a scale which, relative to the size of the economy, resembled that of Latin America.[17] The Big Push boosted the share of investment in GDP from 18% to 30% during the late 1970s (Table 11.2) and outstripped domestic project implementation capacity. It triggered the typical three-stage sequence of an HCI Big Push: a construction boom (the economy expanded at 10% per anum 1974-79) ignited inflation and an exchange rate appreciation that needed deflationary stabilisation policies. The resulting economic slow-down of 1979-82 depressed demand just as the HCI plants came into operation: the economy-wide ICOR doubled to 5.5. The third stage of the Big Push sequence, an HCI rebound following successful stabilisation, did not occur until the mid-1980s. Consequently, the economic slow-down of the early-1980s prompted fierce criticism of South Korea's industrial policy.[18] This, in turn, accelerated the reduction in state intervention which an increasingly complex economy requires.

### *The Post-1982 Liberalisation Phase*

After economic stabilisation was secured, the South Korean government retreated from sectoral and corporate targeting and concentrated on improving the efficiency of price signals and financial markets. It raised real interest rates in order to boost domestic saving and lower the country's dependence on foreign capital. The pro-HCI bias on loan capital was eliminated and the government, mindful of the fact that the HCI Big Push had concentrated wealth on the *chaebol* and widened income inequality,[19] attempted to encourage small- and medium-sized firms. It also sought to restrict the activities of the *chaebol* to three core sectors in order to reduce the risk of excess capacity. From the late-1980s the reduction of import tariffs and non-tariff barriers was accelerated as the country prepared itself for OECD status.

Meanwhile, the economy recovered strongly from the stabilisation measures and grew in excess of 10% per annum through the mid-1980s. The orthodox critics of CIP attributed this to the effects of liberalisation. Corbo and Nam[20] ascribe two-thirds of the improvement to a real depreciation in the exchange rate which allowed the maturing HCI to export and expand to design capacity. Operation at full capacity generated the cash flow required to retire the HCI debt and to undertake low-cost capacity expansion. By the mid-1980s, manufactured goods accounted for 91% of total exports and more than half were HCI in the form of ships, steel and autos, while textile exports declined in relative importance.

The dynamic export expansion helped with debt service so that the country's sizeable foreign debt fell absolutely, in sharp contrast to the outcome in Latin America under AIP. As the South Korean economy continued to grow robustly into the 1990s and to close the gap on Taiwan, the more cautious Taiwanese industrial policy no longer appeared the sounder policy of the two, as had been the case in the immediate aftermath of the South Korean HCI Big Push.

### *Some Qualifications Regarding the South Korean Strategy*

The factors responsible for South Korean economic success are difficult to untangle in the absence of some counter-factual scenario. The country was undoubtedly helped by important pre-conditions which include the Japanese colonial legacy of industrial infrastructure and of experience with industry. As noted earlier, substantive land reform and the early attention accorded to primary education helped redistribute resources, so that when the second stage of the East Asian model commenced, effective participation in the economy was widespread. This helped to reduce poverty and to retain an equitable income distribution which, in turn, gave political legitimacy to the state and maintained policy continuity.[21]

In addition, the espousal of orthodox economic policies with their twin commitment to prudent fiscal policy and an outward-oriented trade policy was an essential ingredient of South Korean success. The institutionalists have also made a convincing case that Korean macro efficiency was complemented by pragmatic and *effective* state intervention which raised the rate of investment, anticipated emerging comparative advantage and lowered the social risks of entry into new sectors by giving incentives. Critically, the incentives carried obligations in terms of targets for export growth or import substitution and were tapered to foster rapid maturation and to avoid the creation of the powerful pressure groups of the kind which prolonged industrial maturation under AIP in Latin America and elsewhere, at the expense of efficient resource use. But there remain doubts about the institutionalist case and also about the lessons of South Korean experience for other late-industrialisers.

Firm evidence that the targeted sectors had higher total factor productivity growth is lacking in studies of, for example, South Korea,[22] Taiwan[23] or Japan, where Beason and Weinstein[24] argue that most intervention went in favour of *sunset* industry. By the 1990s, even Krugman[25] had reduced his earlier support for sectoral targeting because the benefits appear to be small compared with the potential costs of incurring reprisals from aggrieved trading partners. An exception is made for sectors with strong external economies like auto assembly where Krugman speculates the gains from state intervention in their promotion may be up to 2-3% of GDP.

But even this restated view ignores three counter-arguments: the macroeconomic costs imposed when a Big Push over-strains domestic implementation capacity, as in South Korea 1974-79; the costs of policy capture which have hitherto been neglected in the East Asian countries;[26] and the evidence that comparative advantage in many industries is shifting to the developing countries, as their domestic markets grow.[27]

Finally, there is new evidence that the impact of the East Asian countries' natural resource endowment on their economic performance may have been under-estimated.[28] In particular, resource-deficient countries soon become aware of the fact that they cannot support a slow-maturing manufacturing sector for as long as a resource-rich country like Brazil. Also, in contrast to large, resource-deficient countries like China, the limited initial domestic demand of the small, resource-deficient country dictates early access to world markets in order to secure the scale economies. Lal[29] concludes that the resource-deficient countries have an easier transition from rent-driven growth to skill-driven (i.e., manufacturing-led) growth than resource-rich countries do.

The resource-rich countries must make the industrial transition with higher labour costs than resource-deficient countries and, more importantly, with labour costs that are also high relative to labour productivity. In effect, the resource-rich countries leap-frog the second labour-intensive growth stage of the East Asian development model so that their industrialisation creates fewer jobs per unit of investment and requires greater public expenditure on skill acquisition. This in turn tempts the governments of resource-rich countries to force the pace of growth with over-ambitious interventions that lead to growth collapses. The spartan East Asian resource endowment provided less scope for policy discretion, less tolerance of policy error and, in the end, an easier route to industrialisation so that lessons for resource-rich developing countries must be qualified.

The case for South Korean levels of intervention was stronger in the 1960s and 1970s when the OECD grip on industrial production seemed unassailable and the strategic imperatives linked to the cold war rendered the costs associated with industrial self-sufficiency worth incurring. But in their efforts to establish the universality of their case, the protagonists in the industrial policy debate risk forgetting that both the specific time context and differences in the resource endowment affect the outcome.

NOTES

[1] P.W. Kuznets, 'An East Asian model of economic development: Japan, Taiwan and South Korea,' *Economic Development and Cultural Change*, 36 , 1980, pp. 11-43.

[2] S. Cho, 'Government and market in economic development,' *Asian Development Review*,

12, 1994, pp. 144-65.
[3] H. Hughes, 'Why have East Asian countries led economic development?', *The Economic Record*, 71, 1995, pp. 88-104.
[4] K-H. Mihn, 'Industrial policy for industrialisation of Korea,' *KIET Occasional Papers 8803*, Seoul: KIET, 1988.
[5] K. Ohno and H. Imoaka, 'The experience of dual industrial growth: Korea and Taiwan,' *The Developing Economies*, 35, 1987, pp. 310-24.
[6] R.M. Auty, *Economic Development and Industrial Policy*, London: Mansell, 1994.
[7] Alice Amsden, *Asia's Next Giant: South Korea and Late Industrialisation,* New York: OUP, 1989; Robert Wade, *Governing the Market*, Princeton University Press, 1990.
[8] J.J. Stern et al, *Industrialisation and the State: The Korean Heavy and Chemical Industry Drive*, Cambridge, Mass.: Harvard Institute for International Development, 1995.
[9] World Bank, *The East Asian Miracle*, New York: OUP, 1993.
[10] D. Lal, 'Why growth rates differ. The political economy of social capability in 21 developing countries', in B.H. Koo and D.H. Perkins (eds), *Social Capability and Long-term Economic Growth,* Basingstoke: MacMillan, 1995, pp. 299-309.
[11] Amsden, op. cit., 1990.
[12] Hughes, op. cit., 1995.
[13] L. Squire, 'Fighting poverty', *American Economic Association: Papers and Proceedings*, 1993, pp. 377-82.
[14] K. Liang and C.H. Liang, 'Development policy formulation and future priorities in the Republic of China,' *Economic Development and Cultural Change*, 36, 1988, pp. 67-101; S.C. Tsiang, 'Taiwan's economic miracle: Lessons in economic development', in A.C. Harberger (ed.), *World Economic Growth*, San Francisco: ICS Press, 1984, pp. 301-31.
[15] K.M. Murphy, A. Shleifer and R.W. Vishny, 'Industrialisation and the Big Push', *Journal of Political Economy,* 97, 1989, pp. 1003-26.
[16] Auty, op. cit., 1994.
[17] Y.C. Park, 'Foreign debt, balance of payments and growth prospects: The case of the republic of Korea 1965-88', *World Development*, 14, 1986, pp. 1019-58.
[18] World Bank, *Korea: Managing the Industrial Transition, Vol. 1, Conduct of Industrial Policy*, Washington, D.C.: World Bank, 1987; S.Y. Kwack, 'The economic development of the Republic of Korea, 1965-1981', in L.J. Lau (ed.), *Models of Development*, San Francisco: ICS Press, 1990, pp. 65-125; J.J. Yoo, 'The industrial policy of the 1970s and the evolution of the manufacturing sector in Korea', *KDI Working Paper 9017*, Seoul: KDI, 1990.
[19] S.M. Suh and H.C. Yeon, 'Social welfare during the period of structural adjustment', in V. Corbo, and S.M. Suh (eds.), *Structural Adjustment in a Newly Industrialized Country: The Korean Experience*, Baltimore: Johns Hopkins University Press, 1992, pp. 281-304.
[20] V. Corbo and S.W. Nam, 'Korea's macroeconomic prospects and policy issues for the next decade', *World Development*, 16, 1988, pp. 35-45.
[21] A. Leftwich, 'Bringing politics back in: Towards a model of the developmental state', *Journal of Development Studies*, 31, 1995, pp. 400-27.
[22] Stern et al, op. cit., 1995.
[23] H. Pack, 'New perspectives on industrial growth in Taiwan', in G. Ranis (ed.), *Taiwan: From Developing to Mature Economy*, Boulder: Westview Press, 1992, pp. 73-120.
[24] R. Beason and D.E. Weinstein, 'Growth, economies of scale and targeting in Japan (1955-1990),' *HIER Discussion Paper* 1644, Harvard Institute of Economic Research (HIER), Cambridge, Mass., 1994.
[25] P. Krugman, 'The narrow band and the broad arguments for free trade', *American Economics Association: Papers and Proceedings*, May 1993, pp. 362-66; and *Strategic Trade Theory and the New International Economics*, Cambridge, Mass.: MIT, 1986.
[26] R.M. Auty, 'Industrial policy capture in Taiwan and South Korea', *Development Policy Review*, 13, 1995, pp. 195-217.
[27] Auty, op. cit., 1994.
[28] J.D. Sachs and A.M. Warner, 'Natural resources and economic growth', Mimeo, *HIID*, Cambridge, Mass., 1995.
[29] Lal, op. cit., 1995.

# 12. THE RISE OF THE YEN, 'HOLLOWING OUT' AND JAPAN'S TROUBLED INDUSTRIES

*David W. Edgington*

This chapter addresses the issue of how Japan is managing the transition from a production to an information and service sector economy. It is based on a literature review of government assistance to its 'troubled industries' (such as steel and shipbuilding), as well as interviews with Japanese government officials and business executives during 1992 and 1994. The study covers the period following the Plaza Accord in 1985 and the sharp revaluation of the yen.[1] At the time of writing (late 1994) the yen had broken through the sensitive 100 yen to the US dollar level, whereas in mid-1993 it stood at 120 yen to the US dollar, and at 250 yen to the US dollar in early 1985.[2]

The yen's persistent appreciation against major foreign currencies over the last ten years (known as *endaka*) dramatically changed Japan's competitive position vis-à-vis other Pacific Rim countries, both in terms of comparative production costs as well as the price gap between domestic and imported goods. For example, Japanese labour was roughly 30% less expensive than that in the USA before 1985, yet it finished up marginally more expensive than US labour during the early 1990s. As a result, manufacturers found their exports from Japan more expensive and harder to sell, while imports increased and found new markets.[3]

More recently, 1991 saw the bursting of Japan's 'bubble economy' and the commencement of the worst economic downturn since the end of the war.[4] In the 'post-bubble' period, an intensification of Japanese offshore production has occurred mainly involving other Asia-Pacific countries, especially China, due to their combined advantages of lower labour costs and market growth (see Figure 12.1). Investment in Asia's manufacturing sector has climbed especially rapidly, reaching US$3.6 billion in fiscal 1993 when it accounted for about one-third of Japanese manufacturers' total overseas investment.[5] This process accelerated during 1994 and, according to a survey conducted by the Japan Development Bank (JDB), major manufacturers planned to increase their capital investments abroad in the 1994 fiscal year by 18.1%.[6]

The strong yen and the transfer of Japanese factories overseas has brought unemployment through a process known as the 'hollowing out' (or decline in competitiveness) of domestic industry vis-à-vis more low-cost locations. Observers of this trend in Japan point to similar trends in the United Kingdom during the 1970s and the United States in the 1980s leading to deindustrialisation of these economies and an adverse impact on their industrial communities.[7]

Figure 12.1. JAPANESE DIRECT FOREIGN INVESTMENT IN SELECTED ASIAN COUNTRIES, 1983-1993

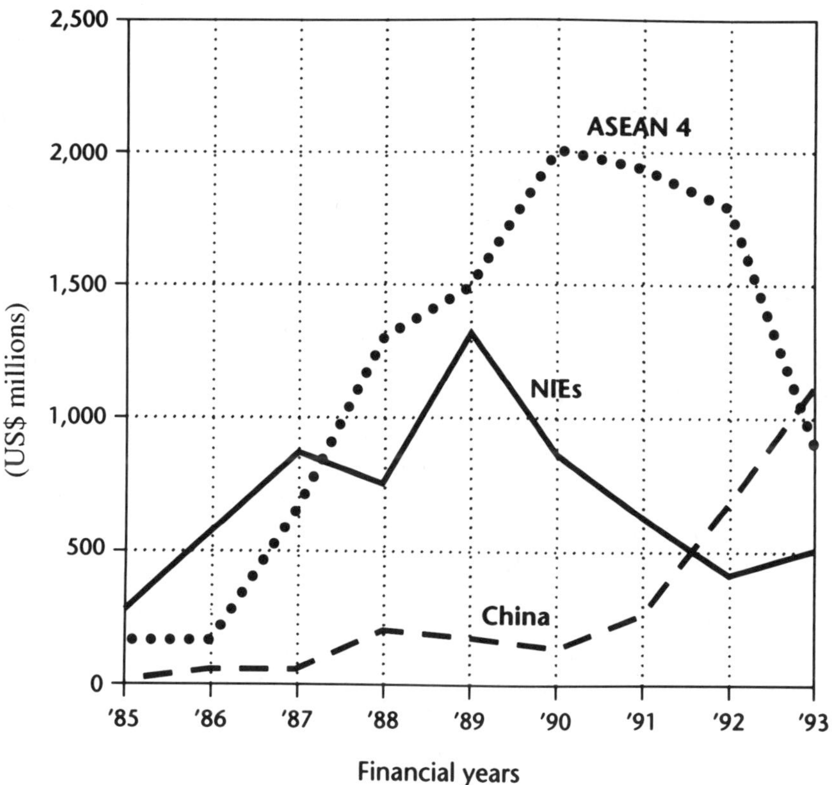


Source: Bank of Japan, unpublished statistics.

With this background, the chapter examines some of the policies and programmes which have assisted industrial adjustments in Japan between 1985 and 1994, a period which saw the adaptation of the economy from largely smokestack and assembly industries to high technology, from export-led manufacturing towards a more balanced economic base favouring the domestic economy, and from production to services. While there has been much research into Japanese industrial policy at a national level,[8] very little has been covered at a regional level.[9] This is surprising considering that much of Japanese industry has been rooted in traditional industrial communities of small firms.[10] Accordingly, special attention will be paid to interpreting the geographic outcomes of Japanese corporate strategies towards *endaka* and their implications for labour markets. A related issue concerns the role of Japanese government policy in moving Japan's comparative advantage to a more advanced industrial structure. The research for this chapter draws mainly from existing studies of government restructuring programmes designed to address the challenges posed by 'hollowing out', and provides four examples of how corporate responses and government policies have intersected to produce different regional outcomes. It concludes by evaluating this material and reflecting on the challenges Japan will experience through further 'hollowing out' in the future.

## *Government Policies to Assist Industrial Restructuring*

The rise of the yen and its impact on domestic industrial competitiveness opened up a great debate about the future of the Japanese economy, its major institutions and the implications for Japan's traditional social cohesion. Well aware of the potential frictions, the Japanese national government took a number of actions to assist the smooth transformation of the country's industrial structure. Its overall stance toward overseas manufacturing investment and the problem of troubled, older domestic industries was set down in the Maekawa Report of 1986. This called for Japan to be more active in overseas investment in order to promote closer economic interdependence with other Pacific Rim countries through a horizontal division of labour.[11] Since then, the attitude of the government and its main bureaucratic agencies has not changed. The Ministry for International Trade and Industry, for instance, while acknowledging that a continued growth of direct overseas investment places pressure on domestic manufacturing jobs, feels that these problems can be overcome. It places emphasis on achieving economic growth centred on the development of new industrial frontiers and exploiting opportunities created by the shift toward a service-oriented industrial structure as Japan advances towards the 'information society'.[12]

It has been shown elsewhere that this industrial transformation has had uneven sectoral and spatial outcomes within Japan, generally leading to more sophisticated production and service industries and a renewed geographic concentration of economic activity.[13] In the growing high technology manufacturing sector the most prominent geographical concentration of new investments has occurred in the core region surrounding metropolitan Tokyo. This is confirmed by a spatial analysis of factories in selected technology-intensive sectors, taken from the most recent Census of Manufacturing at the time of writing (see Figure 12.2). The main reasons for this pattern include the presence of existing major research and development laboratories in the belt running from Tsukuba Science City in Ibaraki prefecture through Tokyo down to Yokohama, together with numerous subsidiary and independent companies dealing in software and hardware. In total, this complex of high technology is much stronger than those contained in the regions focused on Osaka and Nagoya.[14] Apart from sophisticated production facilities, the increasing dominance of the wider Tokyo region over information services and other white collar industries has been striking since the mid-1980s. In particular, large corporate head office functions expanded there more than in Osaka, Japan's second commercial city.[15]

Nonetheless, faced with a deterioration of the general labour market

Figure 12.2. HIGH TECHNOLOGY FACTORIES, JAPAN, 1992

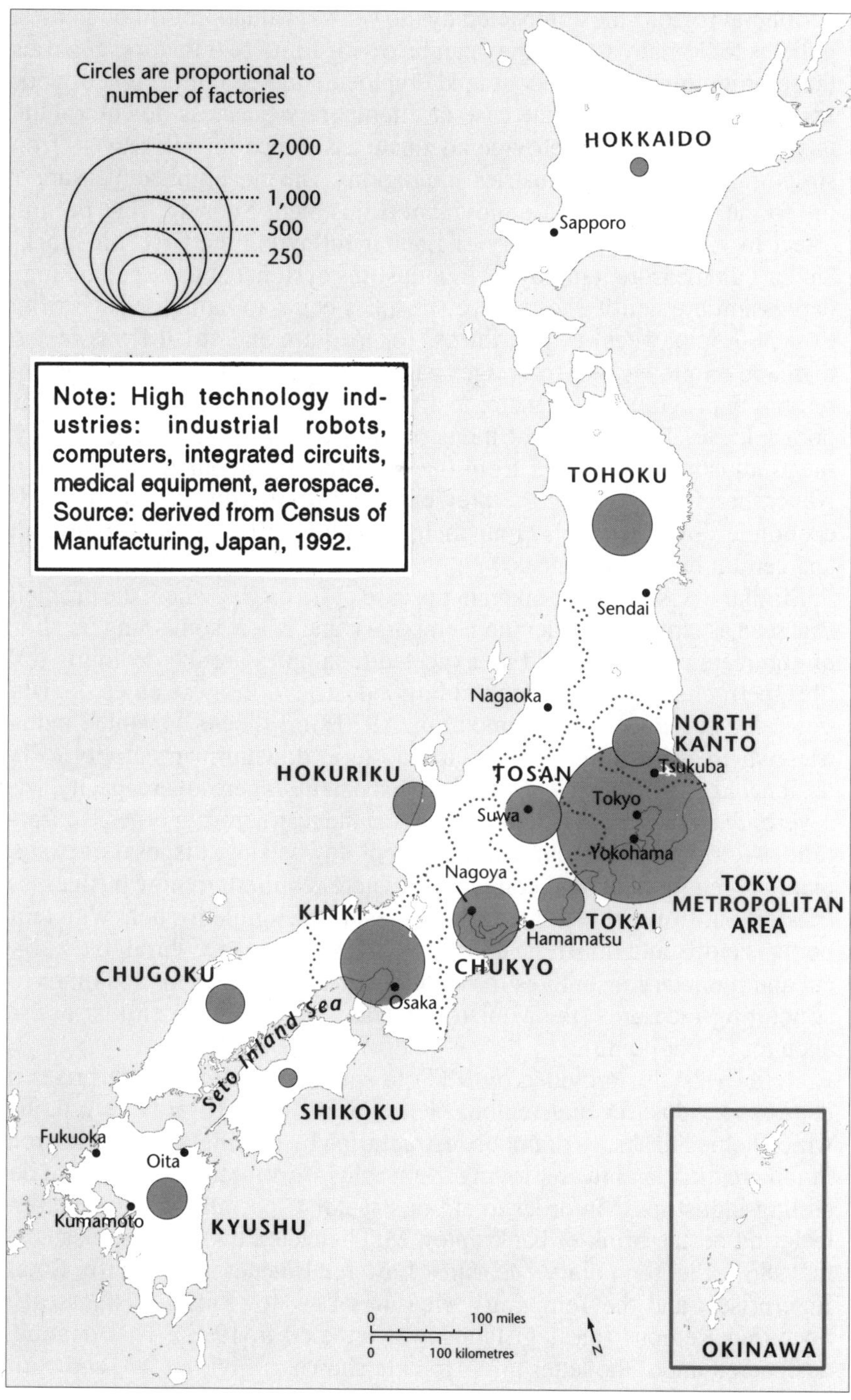

situation after 1986, the Japanese government developed specific measures to support employment adjustment, particularly for industries and peripheral regions most impacted by the yen's revaluation. Although these policies took many forms, they can be divided into two major categories: those programmes that encouraged employers to keep unoccupied workers within their firms in the case of a temporary business downturn, and those that attempted to provide adequate assistance for job leavers from structurally depressed industries and regions. The most typical measure of the former type was the Employment Adjustment Subsidy, first put into effect in 1975 by the Ministry of Labour following the first 'oil shock'. Under this measure, employers in industries designated as experiencing a depression are entitled to receive subsidies equal to half (for large firms over 300 employees) or two-thirds (for medium and small firms of less than 300 employees) of the wages paid to idle workers who participate in retraining programmes, transfer to affiliated companies or are put on temporary leave. The number of industries qualifying for receiving employment adjustment subsidies from the Ministry of Labour reached 315 in November 1993, topping the previous peak of 165 during Japan's 1986 economic slowdown. This group included automobiles, computer software and certain home appliances.[16]

Similar measures were taken in the case of industries where the problem was seen as structural rather than temporary, and where something far short of complete recovery could be expected (examples are the declining textiles, petrochemicals and shipbuilding industries). In these cases, legislation (also introduced at the time of the 1970s 'oil shocks') enabled industries which were suffering from a long-term downturn in activity to be designated as 'depressed industries', especially where overcapacity was severe. These cases were targeted to assist the restructuring of large corporations to promote smooth and permanent downsizing, disposal of excess plant and equipment, and conversion, where required, to new businesses. In addition, firms in designated industries were eligible for help with temporary layoffs and transfers, as well as MITI's assistance through tax, fiscal and monetary incentives for technological improvement and other restructuring measures (the Ministry of Transport has given similar assistance for shipbuilding).[17]

Relief was also provided by MITI to small and medium enterprises in depressed industries and regions. These were found to provide a buffer which helped to absorb dramatic restructuring by playing an important role in job creation, and in employing the surplus workforce released from declining industries.[18] In order to aid this sector, especially small exporters teetering on the brink of bankruptcy, MITI enacted two special measures in 1986 – the Temporary Measures Law for Business in Specific Small Enterprises, and the Temporary Measures Law for Small Businesses in Specified Regions (the legislation was updated in 1992). The locations designated under the latter provision are shown in Figure 12.3, and com-

Figure 12.3. INDUSTRIAL REGIONS DESIGNATED UNDER THE TEMPORARY MEASURES LAW FOR SMALL BUSINESSES

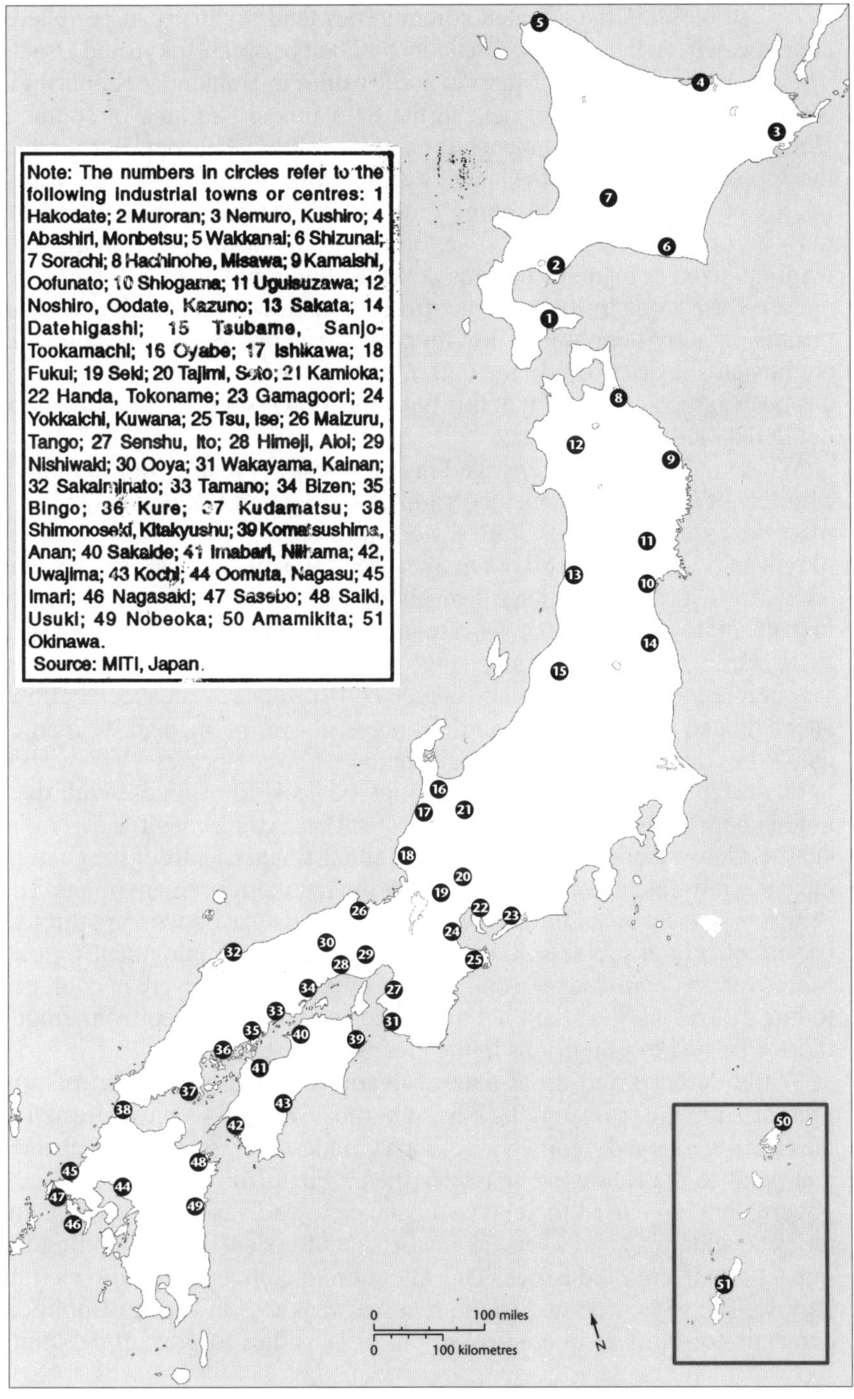

prise local communities where designated depressed industries (such as steel and shipbuilding) contributed 40% of the total value of production or the total unemployment in the district.

As can be seen, the affected communities tend to cluster in peripheral areas away from the main Pacific industrial belt between Tokyo and Osaka. They include the cities of Muroran and Kushiro in Hokkaido, Kamaishi in Northern Tohoku, Shimonoseki in the Seto Inland Sea area of southern Honshu, and Hakata (Kitakyushu) and Nagasaki in Kyushu. Rather than the approach adopted for the large firms in capital-intensive sectors, which mainly concentrated on planning industry-wide capacity reductions, the purpose of these programmes was to assist labour-intensive small- and medium-sized companies provide continued employment for their workers. This was done by encouraging firms to upgrade and switch into more promising activities through low-interest financing and exemption from credit status restrictions. In the current post-bubble recession, however, it has been agreed generally that this type of action resulted in far fewer jobs being retained than in the past.[19]

Where industries were engaged in the process of restructuring, Japan's Ministry of Labour implemented parallel legislation in an attempt to minimise the extent of the resulting dislocation. Thus the 1987 Law for Employment Security for Workers in Specified Industries and Areas provides for various subsidies for large firms in designated industries and areas of high unemployment. It promotes retraining, or employment adjustment such as *shukko*,[20] as well as the exchange or movements of workers to more favourable locations. A second category of subsidy covers special allowances related to early retirement. As noted above, permanent discharges tend to be concentrated among older employees, so companies which wished to downsize through retiring their senior staff had to negotiate with their unions both a regular retirement bonus and an extra bonus for early discharge. Consequently, the Ministry of Labour financed part of the costs of the early retirement bonus, although not the regular retirement bonus. The Ministry also set up additional services to help displaced workers through special efforts of job search and training by public employment offices. Moreover, in depressed areas public works programmes were encouraged to hire at least 40% of the total number of workers required from among those who had lost their jobs in the process of restructuring.[21]

While detailed and up-to-date evaluations of these government programmes are unfortunately lacking, a number of reviews have attested to the effectiveness and significance of Japan's industrial restructuring schemes and point to the following characteristics.[22] First, MITI and the Japanese government have tried to achieve a balance towards tacitly allowing currency revaluations and overseas investments to occur yet cushioning the impact on affected industries. This attention to compensating the victims may well have contributed to the relative weakness in Japan of political demands for tariff or quota protection, or subsidies to prevent declining industries from downsizing. Second, a distinctive feature of the programmes reviewed above is that employment support payments have been made to firms, not directly to workers. The effect of this style of Japanese government support generates a bias towards labour hoarding by large firms, and smooths out the process of inter-firm mobility. This reflects the sentiment that large firms in Japan should bear responsibility for providing permanent employment until retirement age; and so the declining industries, rather than the government, have carried most of the burdens of financing and administering the adjustment process. By contrast, governments in the United States and many countries of Western Europe have tended to take exclusive responsibility for unemployment compensation programmes as well as training and relocation schemes. Third, special government support was available to assist companies and workers affected by restructuring, but only on condition that industries reduced surplus capacity and attempted to shift into more productive areas, as well as workers agreeing to participate in retraining and placement programmes. This results-oriented approach has given the government a certain influence over corporate resources and the labour force, allowing it to direct firms and workers into more competitive sectors of the economy. Fourth, the government's adjustment policy has certainly not been neglectful of small firm and regional interests. It realised that there was a close relationship between fundamentally ailing industries and geographical areas with particular employment problems.

In this regard, mention must also be made of the ongoing programmes of the national government to revitalise local areas and achieve greater regional balance in Japan. The Fourth National Comprehensive Land Development Plan (*Yonzenso*), for instance, has as its goal the breaking down of Tokyo's dominance and achieving decentralised development through a multipolar spatial structure.[23] This is to be implemented through a number of nationally-sponsored programmes and infrastructure projects, such as the new Kansai International Airport and Kansai Science City, located near Osaka in western Japan. In addition, there are many locally-based programmes conducted jointly by local government and the central ministries (e.g. technopolis, new media community and teletopia), designed to promote small- and medium-scale technology-based enterprises in regions outside of the major metropolitan areas.[24]

Despite these comprehensive measures, perhaps the best contribution the Japanese government has made to the process of structural adjustment and in the labour field throughout the period under review has been its overall management of the economy. Thus, following the fall in manufacturing production and investment and the rise in unemployment after 1986, the government adopted forceful macroeconomic policy intervention to stimulate domestic demand, such as cuts in bank interest rates and an increase in public works.[25] These policies invigorated the home consumer and investment markets and helped generate new and alternative product lines to those shifted overseas. In turn, they helped Japanese companies maintain profits in the face of the high yen and so softened the impact on domestic employment. In April 1993, the government adopted a package of economic measures totalling ¥13.2 trillion, the largest in Japan's history, with the aim of revitalising the depressed economy.[26]

Beyond mere fiscal and monetary stimulation, the government was also active in promoting more technologically-focused development. While most R & D was carried out in private industry, MITI's Industry, Science and Technology Agency supported basic science and technology and made positive contributions to private R & D efforts.[27] Government bureaucracies played the important role of mediators between industry and public research institutions, including universities, to promote cooperation in research. The government also tried to improve data, statistics and standards concerning science and technology, and promote basic research and development in specific areas such as advanced electronics, new materials, biotechnology, space and marine development. MITI also developed programmes to help the promotion of new service sectors such as leisure and resort developments.[28]

### *Impacts on Labour and Community: Four Case Studies*

The four case studies described below exemplify the broad-scale review presented above, and show the interplay between government, business and local employment outcomes.

*Steel.* Japan's steel industry, which was its leading industry since the beginning of the century, has been in decline since the oil crises of the 1970s. Nonetheless, *endaka* left its own particular mark. In the two years following 1985, the yen's appreciation diminished the industry's international competitiveness, and the profitability of steel exports continued to deteriorate while imports of foreign steel products soared.[29] The rationalisation plans of Japan's largest and most spatially scattered steel maker – Nippon Steel Corporation (NSC) – may be used to represent corporate strategies in this sector.

In 1986, NSC was already experiencing difficulties resulting from the oil shocks, and had nine steel plants, six of which were losing money and just three of which were breaking even. In early 1987 the company instituted its Medium and Long-term Plan through which it intended to scale down production capacity by 30% by 1990 while promoting new business in electronics, biochemistry and information services.[30] As part of these measures, NSC planned a complete restructuring and downsizing of its workforce by 20,000 employees – a full 30% of the total, and the closing down of three blast furnaces. Two of those to be closed comprised its earliest and therefore least productive facilities; these were located in peripheral towns (Muroran in Hokkaido and Kamaishi in Iwate prefecture) where in 1985 they accounted for about half of the local economy. The other terminated facility was at Sakae, part of metropolitan Osaka. In addition, pig iron production was cut back at another of its original production centres, the Yawata plant at Kitakyushu. By comparison, the newer more efficient plants at Kimitsu (near Tokyo), Nagoya and Oita (in Kyushu) gained employment following *endaka.*[31]

In the case of Kamaishi – located in the Tohoku region, about 600 kms north of Tokyo – the wire rod mill remaining in the town after the steel plant closure needed only around 800 workers, leaving 1,500 of the 1985 workforce in NSC's Kamaishi steel operations to be dealt with by transfer to Kimitsu and Nagoya, natural attrition, retirement, *shukko* or the creation of jobs in new business fields. While Nippon Steel took great pains to look after its own workers who were made redundant, the 'knock-on' effect among local subcontractors and suppliers made several thousand local people register for unemployment benefits. NSC later established some of its new diversified industries at Kamaishi and Muroran, but so far they have been very small. Philips Electronics of Holland was invited to Kamaishi in the early 1990s to engage in a joint venture; NSC transferred some of its own land to them in return for Philips taking a certain number of NSC's workers. Other NSC-sponsored projects included a grain warehouse, a marine research centre (sponsored by a local semi-government or 'third sector' agency), and a precision machinery company. The prospects of creating substantial new jobs in Kamaishi to make up for the losses in the traditional steel sector appear far from promising, due mainly to its remote location and shortage of industrial sites. Consequently it is likely that the population of Kamaishi will continue to fall in the years ahead.[32]

At Muroran, in Hokkaido, NSC was poised to close its remaining blast furnace during 1990, but after realising the negative impact on the community it changed its mind. Moreover, in 1992 it arranged for Mitsubishi Speciality Steel Company to come to Muroran from Tokyo, to engage in a joint venture and share both staff and steel-making facilities with NSC. In a further attempt to reallocate its full-time staff, NSC set up in Muroran what has become the third largest software company in Hokkaido. Besides these corporate moves, the Hokkaido Development Agency (a national government agency) directed substantial resources into Muroran (population roughly 60,000 persons) in the form of public works schemes such as a harbour bridge, waterside redevelopment and downtown revitalisation.[33] At Kitakyushu, in the southern part of Japan, NSC similarly felt it had an obligation and responsibility to continue its involvement in the local community and so kept one blast furnace. In addition, it opened a Space World theme park on part of its former Yawata plant, hoping that this would form the core of Kitakyushu's regional development plans to transform the steel city into one more focused on service sector growth. It is likely that both of NSC's facilities at Muroran and Kitakyushu are loss making, yet upper management appears to be resigned to this.[34] Kitakyushu, as with Muroran, has received substantial national government funding from both the Ministry of Construction and MITI to assist its revitalisation strategies based around jobs in convention halls and hotels.[35]

*Shipbuilding.* Shipbuilding in Japan has been faced with a general overcapacity problem since the collapse of the world tanker market in the 1970s. Nevertheless, as most contracts were drawn up in US dollars, the revaluation of the yen brought increased competition from South Korea in the mid-to-late 1980s. Faced with a long-term fall in the number of new orders, and the realisation that a reduction in the number of docks was urgently required, Japan's Ministry of Transport took concrete measures to reduce shipbuilding capacity in 1978, following the first oil crisis, by setting up a production cartel.[36] After *endaka*, the Ministry of Transport introduced similar legislation in 1987 with the intention of again reducing excess plant and encouraging business regroupings. Production facility disposal plans were drawn up collectively by the government and the industry, and implemented – as in the 1970s – through the joint cooperation of the major shipbuilders concerned, with the government giving financial support and loan guarantees for the acquisition of scrapped plant and equipment. The new law mandated that shipbuilding capacity be reduced by 20% by 1988. In the event, around 24% of shipbuilding facilities were disposed of – thereby reducing the nation's total dockyard capacity from 6.0 million to 4.6 gross tons – and at the same time 44 major shipbuilders in 21 business groups were amalgamated into 26 firms in eight groups.[37]

As the number of docks and new production decreased, so the workforce fell sharply, by 40% to 55,000 employees over the 1985-1988 period. Major companies such as Ishikawajima-Harima Heavy Industries (IHI) cut back around 7,000 employees, mainly through early retirements and transfers to other subsidiaries. In addition, many small firms went bankrupt. Consequently, the total number of workers engaged in Japan's shipbuilding, including subcontractors and associated industries, declined to roughly 121,000 at the end of 1988, almost one-third of the peak activity recorded in 1974.[38] During the 1980s, displaced staff had several options open to them including retirement, moving to a different dockyard within the same industrial group or shifting into a different industry within the same corporate group (e.g. engineering). Yet only the large shipbuilding companies had the capacity to send their employees to other affiliated firms or to their non-shipbuilding activities. Many of the displaced workers were reported to have left Japan to find technical or engineering jobs in the growing shipyards of the Republic of Korea; others found work in the auto industry as well as industries linked to new public works contracts (e.g. the Seto Inland Sea bridge construction project completed in 1988).[39]

Employment decline in the shipbuilding industry caused particular problems for certain communities during 1987-88. Thus IHI shut its shipyards in Chita in Aichi prefecture, and at Aioi in Hyogo prefecture (which was the birthplace of the Harima Shipyard and the world's largest in terms of launchings from 1962 through 1964). Mitsubishi shut its yards in Shimoneseki and Hiroshima in Honshu, and Hitachi shut its yard in Enoshima in Shikoku. At a regional level, the most affected areas during the 1980s were the Seto Nankai region, especially the northern coastline (the Chugoku region), although the period since 1989 has seen employment gains in this area and in Kyushu (see Table 12.1). At a lower scale of spatial aggregation, the round of shipyard closings since *endaka* caused particularly serious problems in certain outlying company towns, such as Hakkodate in Hokkaido and Sasebo in Kyushu, as many of these communities were without other industries, and the effects of their contraction on employment were reflected in increased bankruptcies of local service firms

Table 12.1. MANUFACTURING EMPLOYMENT CHANGES BY SECTOR, 1985-1992

| *Sector* | *1992 Employment Levels ('000)* | *1985-92 Change* |
|---|---|---|
| Food | 1,017.3 | +9.9 |
| Drink/Tobacco | 127.3 | -8.9 |
| Textiles | 465.7 | -18.7 |
| Clothes | 567.1 | +5.1 |
| Wooden products | 236.7 | -14.4 |
| Furniture | 220.7 | -0.5 |
| Pulp and paper | 281.2 | +5.7 |
| Publishing/Printing | 566.2 | +9.9 |
| Chemicals | 415.1 | +4.9 |
| Coal products | 34.2 | -9.3 |
| Plastics | 447.4 | +17.1 |
| Rubber | 171.2 | +3.6 |
| Leather | 77.1 | +0.8 |
| Glass/Clay | 454.2 | -2.4 |
| Steel/Iron | 330.5 | -14.9 |
| Non-ferrous metals | 170.1 | +4.1 |
| Metal products | 850.4 | +8.1 |
| General machinery | 1,197.5 | +6.5 |
| Electrical equipment | 1,926.5 | +5.5 |
| Shipbuilding* | 78.7 | -33.3 |
| Other transport* | 894.9 | +6.1 |
| Precision instruments | 236.4 | -9.7 |
| Weapons | 9.7 | +75.2 |
| N.E.C. | 251.2 | -3.0 |
| *Total* | *11,157.5* | *+2.5* |

Note: excludes establishments with less than 4 employees.
* = 3 digit codes.
Source: derived from Census of Manufacturing, Japan, 1985 and 1992.

and population decline. These towns are now trying to generate new industries to overcome their difficulties, often with the assistance of government programmes. Aioi City, for example, has developed a major resort zone.[40]

The government's production cartel was lifted in 1992 as orders finally began to rise.[41] Yet with the shipbuilding business competing with South Korea and in the midst of another downturn, many shipbuilding firms have turned their attention recently to industrial diversification. Thus for Hitachi Zosen Corporation, construction of ships, once the firm's mainstay, made up only a quarter of sales in 1994. Corporate personnel, facilities and capital have been targeted toward businesses that showed good prospects for future growth such as waste disposal and garbage incinerator technology, hoping to obtain 15% of all revenue from these new businesses by fiscal 1996.[42]

*Automobiles.* The announcement in 1993 by Nissan Motor Company that it would halt production of passenger cars at its highly automated Zama Plant near Tokyo while increasing production overseas, revealed the severity of the post-1991 recession and the problems facing the automobile industry.[43] The yen's upward shift dealt a particularly harsh blow to auto manufacturers, which still have relatively high export rations. However, in this industry too, there are mediating geographic factors at work. In contrast to the relatively dispersed investment strategy of Nissan, its major rival – Toyota Motor Corporation – had long adopted a concentrated network of production facilities and associated suppliers in Chukyo, a region centred on Aichi prefecture.[44]

The development of a strong regional auto production system, and the tight integration of subcontractor operations with just-in-time assembly, gave Toyota a decisive lead over Nissan during the postwar period. By the late 1980s, however, the Chukyo region was also under threat from 'hollowing out'. This was both due to *endaka*, which cut into export competitiveness, as well as the rapid speed of overseas investment brought on by auto trade conflict with the United States and Europe.[45] Yet any substantial hollowing out was deferred by the domestic economic boom of the late 1980s. This period was characterised by high production runs, the introduction of Toyota's prestigious 'Lexus' model in 1990 and a severe labour shortage in Aichi prefecture.[46]

By the end of the study period, however, the industry confronted another threat in the form of the bursting of Japan's 'bubble economy' in 1991 and the slowdown in both domestic and export markets. Toyota responded to this, together with the latest round of yen appreciation, by rigorously cutting costs and by expanding its production overseas both at its plants in North America and at new ones planned in China and Southeast Asia. In the past, such production shifts did not cause cuts in its Japanese production because domestic sales remained strong. But the current recession in Japan has impacted significantly on domestic sales, forcing Toyota to reduce its employees by around 2,350 through attrition in the year up to mid-1994. Toyota also won the compliance of regional auto-parts suppliers in changing specifications and materials to reduce production costs. This cost-cutting strategy led to cuts in new recruitment by both Toyota and its suppliers due to a perceived surplus of its existing assembly workers.[47]

Clearly, the Chukyo region cannot rely upon the exports of automobiles for its continued growth, and must now define other domains of competition. Yet in contrast with the steel and shipbuilding sectors, automobile producers such as Toyota have been rather reluctant to move significantly into new businesses. Still, the new pressures have brought about a change in attitude. Toyota, normally a very conservative company, began plans in the early 1990s to develop aluminium motor-boats with Mitsui Engineering. Toyota also acquired interests in the machine tools, aerospace and telecommunications sectors, as well as finance. Significantly, Toyota has made plans to locate certain of these new lines of business close to major markets (such as Tokyo) or in production bases where there were related and existing technologies and facilities (e.g. motor boat production in Nagasaki) – in other words, not all are likely to replace production losses in Aichi Prefecture. Moreover, despite these new ventures, it is unlikely that Toyota's new business sectors would account for more than 5% of total sales in the foreseeable future, due mainly to the present dominance of auto production.[48]

The response of Chukyo's public officials to the hollowing out threat has been to strive for regional rejuvenation based on new industries such as aerospace, new ceramics, textile designs and bio-technology.[49] Governments in Chukyo are also absorbed in providing new forms of regional economic infrastructure with an emphasis on 'mega' transport projects to reinforce the centrality of their location within Japan. These include the second Shinkansen express rail line (the proposed Tokaido 'maglev' linear rail line) and the second Tomei national expressway.[50] No doubt these and other new infrastructure will benefit local industry; for example, newly proposed research institutes have been planned to address the negative blue-collar 'image' of the region and attract new private investment. One problem, however, is that this strategy may not address the needs of local small-scale supply firms, many of which will have less work from Toyota in the future as it expands outside Chukyo and into the Pacific Rim.[51]

*Jiba Sangyo.* Finally, apart from large industries, community-based industries (e.g. textiles, ceramics and various metal products) comprised mainly of small entrepreneurs (*jiba sangyo*) have also faced pressure to restructure. Due to the rise in the yen, they have been challenged by South Korea, Taiwan, Hong Kong and Singapore, which have become formidable competitors vying for both foreign and domestic markets. Over the late

1980s and early 1990s these industries have also been confronted with other problems such as labour shortages and the difficulty in finding successors to the present owner-managers. However, because of their strong commitment to the regional economy in which they are located, there has been a strong desire to reorganise and overcome these problems. As noted above, MITI has long recognised that community-based industries have strong linkage effects in regional economies and so help prevent the economic and social collapse of local municipalities.[52] Accordingly, to assist their restructuring MITI set up special legislation – the Temporary Measures for Business Conversion by Specified Medium- and Small-Sized Enterprises – in 1986 and 1992. The intention of this programme has been not to encourage small- and medium-sized companies to export, but rather to help them move into lines of production for which domestic demand in strong.[53]

The case of the city of Tsubame cutlery industry in Niigata Prefecture is fairly representative of the *jiba sangyo* sector, and provides an illustration of its adaptability and resilience to date. Due to the onset of *endaka* in 1985, exports from this industrial region declined substantially. In particular, the export sales ratio of traditional 'flatware' (knives and other cutlery) declined from 73% in 1975 to just 60% in 1983. One successful adjustment strategy was to move production away from cutlery, which faced severe competition from cheaper locations in South Korea and Taiwan, into higher value-added stainless steel cooking pots and thermos flasks and, increasingly, non-cutlery related items. Yet another strategy was to produce novel cutlery designs for the high quality domestic market and sell directly to department stores. These entrepreneurial initiatives were assisted by MITI's designation of Tsubame for small- and medium-firm assistance (see Figure 12.3) as well as by programmes of the Tsubame Development Association, set up in 1985 to provide research and development facilities to help firms experiment in new uses for stainless steel.[54]

Several themes have shaped this chapter: the debate over the rapidly appreciating yen, the shift of production overseas and industrial 'hollowing out', corporate investment and disinvestment strategies, the relative geographical dimensions of *endaka* and public policy responses. The principal findings may be summarised as follows.

First, the government appears to have so far been able to manage the conflicts associated with rapid restructuring. This has been achieved through a comprehensive array of measures to promote rationalisation or adjustment in declining sectors and judicious promotion of new technologies. Despite another round of production moving overseas since 1993, the unemployment rate in Japan has stayed remarkably low compared with other industrialised countries. In part this is due to the role played by large firms where – in contrast to Western Europe and the United States – they augment government programmes to assist declining industries. To preserve their corporate image they play a leading role in absorbing the costs of keeping employees in times of economic downturn and relocating workers, as well as in phasing out excess capacity where necessary. Nonetheless, it is often the smaller firms which take the full brunt of this pressure by being forced to release labour to reduce costs, shift into new business lines or go bankrupt. Accordingly, government assistance has been directed mainly towards smaller firms, depressed regions and displaced workers.

Second, the effect of hollowing out has been mediated by sectoral and regional differences. Heavy industry and smaller companies, ill-equipped to shift production abroad, have been particularly vulnerable. Consequently, persistent unemployment has occurred in shipyard regions as well as other small industrial towns and steel cities, such as Muroran. These appear likely to lose population steadily. In the current recession even large metropolitan areas have been hard hit. The bottom line, however, is that Japan's 'developmental state'[55] has a strong regional dimension through committing resources to peripheral areas and harmonising regional policy more closely with industrial adjustment strategies. By contrast, mainstream approaches to manufacturing in most Western countries typically encourage workers and community residents to bid down the costs of industry in their area under the rubric of 'creating a good business climate'. National governments have largely supported this position and have been generally unwilling to intervene further.[56]

A further important issue – and one not directly answerable here – involves the continuing evolution of the Japanese economy. Because of the persisting strength of Japanese exports, companies have to make plans to cope with a strong yen at least through the rest of this decade, and the current apprehension over the high yen-induced recession (*endaka fukyo*) gives a taste of the difficulties that the Japanese economy will face as it goes into the next century. Certainly, as Japan becomes more and more intertwined with the Asia-Pacific countries through trade and investment, its own manufacturing will become less important in job creation, and indeed this has been the case for some time. More and more jobs will be in industrial goods production and services such as R & D, distribution, management services and computer software.[57] But to pay for employment generation in the more unproductive domestic service sector (e.g. transport, distribution and commerce), Japan has no option but to reduce its regulatory role to make both manufacturing and service businesses more competitive, and to generate added value production and technologies. However, if Japanese industry retreats to export-dependent economic expansion, with a likely resulting increase in its trade surplus, then the yen will once more begin its ascent. Consequently, it is presently far more important than before for Japan to attain substantial growth fuelled by domestic demand.

A related problem centres around the likely increase in employment 'mismatches' as Japan shifts further to an 'information-based' society. Thus, where once a shipbuilder could be readily retrained to make cars and a carmaker to make aircraft, it is now harder to retrain a steelmaker, for example, to write a software programme. Yet a recent government labour white paper sounded confident that the economy could cope smoothly with a forecast need to transfer about 2 million jobs from manufacturing to services by the end of this century.[58] It will be a challenge, and as indicated, there is a geography attached to this challenge. The jobs of middle-aged generalist white-collar workers and skilled blue-collar workers in the Pacific sea-coast heavy industries are likely to disappear and even the jobs of mainstream mass production electronics factories in peripheral regions such as Tohoku and Kyushu will be under threat. By contrast, the jobs for young specialists in new technologies and information service industries will likely cluster in the big cities such as Tokyo, Osaka and Nagoya, as well as certain provincial centers. Even though Japan has been more enthusiastic than most industrial countries when it comes to retraining, it will not be easy to bridge that sort of spatial gap. There may be an uncomfortable 15-year transitional period ahead. The vital task for public policy over that time will be to care for Japan's technologically obsolete middle-aged workers – just the sort of people who created 'Japan Inc.' in the high-growth years of the 1960s and 1970s. They are likely to become big consumers of social welfare and leisure, which will probably mean that there will be political pressures in Japan for a higher priority to be given to the issues of consumption than has been the case in the past.

NOTES

[1] In September 1985, agreement was made by the finance ministers and central bank governors of the so-called G5 (group of five) countries to modify the US dollar's appreciation (the so-called 'Plaza Accord'). This decision had the effect of raising the value of the yen from about 265 to the US$ in summer 1985 to roughly ¥125 to the US$ by mid-1988 (see B. Balassa and M. Noland, *Japan in the World Economy*, Washington DC: Institute for International Economics, 1988; B.G. James, *Trojan Horse: The Ultimate Challenge to Western Industry*, London: Mercury, 1990).

[2] Bank of Japan, unpublished data.

[3] Economic Planning Agency (EPA), *Survey of Japan, 1991-1992*, Tokyo: EPA, 1992; D.J. Daly, 'Exchange rates and trade flows: recent Japanese experience', *Business and the Contemporary World*, IV (2), 1992, pp. 86-100.

[4] C. Wood, *The Bubble Economy: The Japanese Economy Collapse*, London: Sidgwick and Jackson, 1992.

[5] C.H. Kwan,'Flying geese aiding Asia's economic growth', *Mainichi Daily News*, 30 September 1994, p. S4.

[6] *Nikkei Weekly*, 3 October 1994.

[7] H. Takayoshi, 'The distressing hollowing out of industry', *Journal of Japanese Trade and Industry*, 14 (1), 1995, pp. 36-7.

[8] See, for example, R. Komiya, M. Okuno and K. Suzumura (eds), *Industrial Policy of Japan*, Tokyo: Academic Press, 1988; G.W. Nobel, 'The Japanese industrial policy debate', in S. Haggard and Chung-in Moon (eds), *Pacific Dynamics*, Colorado: Westview Press,

1989, pp. 53-95; D.I. Okimoto, *Between MITI and the Market: Japanese Industrial Policy for High Technology*, Stanford University Press, 1989; J. Vestal, *Planning for Change: Industrial Policy and Japanese Economic Development, 1945-1990*, OUP, 1993.
[9] For exceptions, see R.C. Hill, 'Industrial restructuring, state intervention, and uneven development in the United States and Japan', in J.R. Logan and T. Swantrom (eds), *Beyond the City Limits: Urban Policy and the Economic Restructuring in Comparative Perspective*, Philadelphia: Temple University Press, 1990, pp. 60-85; R. Wiltshire, 'Inter-regional personnel transfers and structural change: the case of the Kamaishi Steelworks', *Transactions of the Institute of British Geographers*, 17, 1992, pp. 65-79; K. Fujita and R.C. Hill (eds), *Japanese Cities in the World Economy*, Philadelphia: Temple University Press, 1993.
[10] M. Yamazaki, *Japan's Community-Based Industries: A Case Study of Small Industry*, Tokyo: Asia Productivity Organisation, 1980.
[11] EPA, *Survey of Japan, 1986-1987*, Tokyo: EPA, 1987, p. 231.
[12] Interview with M. Ogawa, Deputy Director, Industrial Structure Division, Ministry of International Trade and Industry, Tokyo, July 1992.
[13] For details of the sectoral and spatial impacts of the yen's revaluation, see D.W. Edgington, 'The geography of *endaka*: industrial transformation and regional employment changes in Japan, 1986-1991', *Regional Studies*, 28, 1994a, pp. 521-35.
[14] T. Toda, 'The location of high-technology industry and the technolopolis plan in Japan', in J.F. Brotchie et al (eds), *The Spatial Impact of Technological Change*, London: Croom Helm, 1987, pp. 271-83; H. Nishioka and A. Takeuchi, 'The development of high technology industry in Japan', in M.J. Brehney and R. McQuaid (eds), *The Development of High Technology Industries: An International Survey*, London: Croom Helm, 1989, pp. 262-95; M. Castells and P. Hall, *Technopoles of the World: The Making of Twenty-First Century Industrial Complexes*, London: Routledge, 1994.
[15] D.W. Edgington, 'Managing industrial restructuring in the Kansai region of Japan', *Geoforum*, 21, 1990, pp. 1-22; R. Cybriwsky, *Tokyo: The Changing Profile of an Urban Giant*, London: Pinter, 1991.
[16] K. Ikeya, 'Harsh edges in labor market moderate', *Nikkei Weekly*, 10 October 1994, p. 3.
[17] For details of these programmes, see A. Seike, 'The employment adjustment in Japanese manufacturing industries in the 1970s', *Keio Business Review*, 22, 1985, pp. 1-23; M. Uekusa and H. Ide, 'Industrial policy in Japan', in H. Mutoh et al (eds), *Industrial Policies for Pacific Economic Growth*, Sydney: Allen and Unwin, 1986, pp. 147-71; M.J. Peck, R.C. Levin and A. Goto, 'Picking losers: public policy towards declining industries in Japan', *Journal of Japanese Studies*, 13 (1), 1987, pp. 79-123.
[18] MITI, *White Paper On Small and Medium Enterprises In Japan, 1987*, Background Information BI-65, Tokyo: MITI, 1987.
[19] Interview with T. Konno, Small and Medium Enterprise Agency, MITI, Tokyo, July 1992.
[20] *Shukko* refers to the transfer and loaning of workers from companies in slow growing industries (e.g. steel or shipbuilding) to affiliated companies in rapidly growing sectors (e.g. electronics). See K. Sugeno, 'Shukko (transfers to related firms): an aspect of the changing labour market in Japan', *Japan Labor Bulletin*, April 1989, pp. 3-8.
[21] Personal comment from Y. Tagata, International Department, The Japan Institute of Labour, October 1994.
[22] See R. Dore, *Flexible Rigidities: Industrial Policy and Structural Adjustment in the Japanese Economy: 1970-1980*, London: Athlone Press, 1986; Peck et al, op. cit., 1987; S. Sekiguchi and T. Horiguchi, 'Trade and adjustment assistance', in Komiya et al (eds), op. cit., 1988, pp. 369-93.
[23] National Land Agency, *The Fourth Comprehensive National Development Plan*, Tokyo: National Land Agency, 1987.

[24] See D.W. Edgington, 'Planning for technology development and information systems in Japanese cities and regions', in P. Shapira, I. Masser, and D.W. Edgington (eds), *Planning for Cities and Regions in Japan,* Liverpool University Press, 1994b, pp. 126-55.
[25] A. Okumura, 'Japan's changing economic structure', *Journal of Japanese Trade and Industry*, 6 (5), 1987, pp. 10-13.
[26] Y. Makino, 'Stimulus plan breaks new ground', *Nikkei Weekly*, 12 April 1993, p. 1.
[27] Interview with Ogawa, op. cit.
[28] See H. Patrick and L. Meissner, *Japan's High Technology Industries*, Seattle: University of Washington Press, 1986; J. Howells and I. Neary, 'Science and technology policy in Japan: the pharmaceuticals industry and new technology', in S. Wilks and M. Wright (eds), *The Promotion and Regulation of Industry in Japan*, London: MacMillan, 1991, pp. 81-109; P.J. Rimmer, 'Japan's "resort archipelago": creating regions of fun, pleasure, relaxation, and recreation', *Environment and Planning A,* 24, 1992, pp. 1599-625.
[29] A. Kishine, 'Making the best of restructuring: steel', *Journal of Japanese Trade and Industry*, 6 (5), 1987, p. 14.
[30] Nippon Steel, *Nippon Steel Report, 1986-87*, Tokyo: Nippon Steel, 1987.
[31] Interview with T. Yamamoto, Senior Manager, Corporate and Economic Research Division, Nippon Steel Corporation, Tokyo, July 1992.
[32] Interview with Yamamoto, op. cit.; R. Wiltshire, 'A new future for a company town: diversification and employment in Kamaishi City', *Science Reports of the Tohoku University, 7th Series (Geography)*, 41 (1), 1991, pp. 1-22; Wiltshire, op. cit., 1992.
[33] T. Shingo, 'Collapse of a steel town', *Japan Echo*, XIV (2), 1987, pp. 22-7; D.W. Edgington, *Restructuring Japan's Rust Belt: the Case of Muroran, Hokkaido*, paper presented to the American Association of Geographers Meeting, San Francisco, March 1994c (mimeo).
[34] Interview with Yamamoto, op. cit.
[35] P. Shapira, 'Steel town to space world: restructuring and adjustment in Kitakyushu City', in Fujita and Hill (eds), op. cit., 1993, pp. 224-56; P. Shapira, 'Industrial restructuring and economic development strategies in a Japanese steel town: the case of Kitakyushu', in Shapira, Masser and Edgington (eds), op. cit., 1994, pp. 155-83.
[36] E. Vogel, *Comeback, Case by Case: The Resurgence of American Business*, Tokyo: Tuttle, 1985.
[37] Maritime Technology and Safety Bureau, Ministry of Transport, *Shipbuilding in Japan, 1989-90*, Tokyo: Japan Ship Exporters Association of Japan, 1990.
[38] Ibid.
[39] Interview with K. Matsui, Manager, Operations Department, Japan Ship Exporters Association, Tokyo, June 1992.
[40] T. Imanishi, 'Shipbuilding', *Journal of Japanese Trade and Industry*, 6 (5), 1987, p. 16.
[41] Maritime Technology and Safety Bureau, Ministry of Transport, 1993.
[42] *Nikkei Weekly,* 19 September 1994.
[43] H. Kato, 'Automakers see profits disappear in high yen, recession whipsaw', in Nihon Keizai Shimbun (ed.), *Japan Economic Almanac, 1994,* Tokyo: Nikkei Weekly, 1994, pp. 92-6.
[44] M.A. Cusumano, *The Japanese Automobile Industry: Technology and Management at Nissan and Toyota,* Cambridge, Mass.: Council on East Asian Studies, Harvard University, 1985; Hill, op. cit., 1990, pp. 60-85.
[45] K. Fujita and R.C. Hill, 'Global production and regional "hollowing out" in Japan', in M. Smith (ed.), *Pacific Rim Cities in the World Economy*, Comparative Urban and Community Research, vol. 2, New Brunswick, New Jersey: Transaction, 1989, pp. 200-31.
[46] D.W. Edgington, *Planning for Industrial Restructuring in Japan: The Case of the Chukyo Region,* Vancouver: Centre for Human Settlements, UBC, 1992a; D.W. Edgington, *Flexibility*

*and Corporate Change in Chukyo, Japan: A Study of Five Industries*, CAPRI Special Series No. 1, Vancouver: Institute of Asian Research, UBC, 1994d.
[47] *Nikkei Weekly,* 12 September 1994.
[48] Edgington, op. cit., 1994d.
[49] Edgington, op. cit., 1992a.
[50] D.W. Edgington, 'Industrial restructuring and new transportation infrastructure in Chukyo, Japan', *Geography*, 77, 1992b, pp. 268-70.
[51] Edgington, op. cit., 1992a.
[52] Yamazaki, op. cit.
[53] Interview with Konno, op. cit.
[54] J. Patchell and R. Hayter, 'Dynamics of adjustment and the social division of labour in the Tsubame cutlery industry', *Growth and Change,* 23, 1992, pp. 199-216; T. Kiyonari, 'Restructuring urban-industrial links in Greater Tokyo: small producers' responses to changing world markets', in Fujita and Hill (eds), op. cit., 1993, pp. 141-56.
[55] C. Johnson, *MITI and the Japanese Miracle: the Growth of Industrial Policy, 1925-1975*, Stanford University Press, 1982.
[56] P. Clavel and N. Kleniewski, 'Space for progressive local policy: examples from the United States and the United Kingdom', in Logan and Swanstrom (eds), op. cit., 1990, pp. 199-236.
[57] One particular vision of Japan's industrial and business future emerged in 1994 from a subcommittee of the Industrial Structure Council, a consultative agency of Japan's MITI. This committee responded to an inquiry on how Japan's business and industrial future should be improved in the long range looking toward the 21st century. The recommendations focused on a dozen areas of growth based on building up a wide variety of domestic sectors, rather than a small number of export-oriented ones. The 12 new areas were: housing, medical care, social welfare, life style services such as education and personal services, urban environmental improvement, new energy systems, information and communications, distribution services, contract employment services, international services, business support services and new production technology. Coupled with these new growth services, the report called for the steady trimming and downsizing of four traditional industries. Specifically these were electronic machinery, and transportation equipment including automobiles, steel and non-ferrous materials (*Japan Economic Review*, 15 June 1994).
[58] Ministry of Labour, *White Paper on Labour, 1994*, Tokyo: Japan Institute of Labour, 1994.

# 13. CHINA IN THE YEAR 2000: PROSPECTS FOR THE LATE REFORM ERA

*David S.G. Goodman*

The most imponderable factor affecting the future shape of the Pacific Rim, including its economic, political and cultural character – and indeed the social stability of the region as a whole – is the future of China. China in the year 2000 is dramatically different to the China that faced Deng Xiaoping and the reformers within the leadership of the Chinese Communist Party (CCP) when they embarked upon their reform programme in 1978. Twenty years of reform have transformed the society and politics of the People's Republic of China (PRC) as well as its economy, in ways that were frankly inconceivable in the early 1980s. At that time as China embarked on its 'New Long March', targets were set that were greeted with widespread scepticism by analysts outside China and not a few even within the PRC. The most derided was the aim of doubling and then redoubling output by the year 2000 – in the event it was achieved easily by 1995.[1]

China's economic transformation has been the most obvious feature of the past 20 years of reform. Poor economic performance has been replaced by fast and sustained economic growth so that it now seems likely that sometime in the second decade of the twenty-first century, China will be the world's largest aggregate economy. Though the command economy still exists and still remains at the heart of China's economic system, its role is substantially diminished, not least because economic management has moved from a system of direct intervention to one based on the introduction of market forces and the exercise of macro-economic controls.[2] Most dramatically in aggregate terms, the state sector of the economy now produces about 27% of industrial output value and is responsible for less than a fifth of GDP. [3]

Reform has effected social and political change no less significantly, not least because of the introduction of the market and the development of a consumer society, as well as the redefinition of politics that has accompanied change. The essential principle of reform has been that the party-state is prepared to surrender absolute control in return for economic growth and the continuation of its own political leadership, in the belief that it can still guide through moral suasion where once it commanded. The results have included considerably less centralisation, greater foreign involvement and influences in China, and increased social mobility, as well as significant social dislocation.

China is now altogether more socially complex, economically developed and politically open than was the case in the late 1970s, though the consequences of reform remain uncertain. These dramatic changes invite comparison with similar processes experienced elsewhere and at other times. There are elements of the experience of imploding communism (and the subsequent political disintegration) in the Soviet Union and Eastern Europe, of the emergence of capitalism and liberal democracy in Western Europe during the nineteenth century, and of the transformation of authoritarianism in East Asia (notably in South Korea, Taiwan and even Japan) since the 1970s to be found in China's reform era.

Social and political change in China since 1978 has indeed been massively dislocating on many levels of its political economy. At the same time, comparison with other historical experiences must also acknowledge China's specific characteristics and particular problems. Geopolitics, geoeconomics and ideology all reinforce the essential unity of the Chinese state rather than suggesting disintegration. The party-state both institutionally and associationally remains at the heart of economic development in the reform era, and indeed central to the emerging political economy. Moreover, China's size is likely to make a qualitative and not just a quantitative difference to the development of its political economy as an East Asian power, so that a more accurate perspective might be to see the PRC as a series of South Koreas or Taiwans rather than in direct comparison.[4]

## *Transformations in the Chinese State*

China's reform era resulted from the crisis facing the CCP leadership in the post-Mao period. When the CCP came to power in 1949, it was with the promise of economic modernisation and political stability, in contrast to the mass starvations, instability and lack of political unity that had characterised the first half of the century. By the late 1970s, the CCP's record on both was considerably tarnished. The economy had stagnated for some 20 years, there had been repeated economic crises leading to famine and starvation and there had been no rise in most people's wages.[5] The poor economic performance was partly a function of political instability. Every four or five years after 1949 there was a major change in the direction of the PRC's development strategy, the organisational forms of the state and the personnel responsible for the implementation of policy.[6] At the same time, from the 1960s on elsewhere in East Asia, economies with many less obvious advantages were transforming themselves into 'tiger economies'.

By late 1978, the CCP had to start to deliver on its promises if it wanted to stay in power. It faced a crisis of confidence which threatened to undermine its position, and the policies that followed were designed to ensure economic growth and political stability, and to restore its legitimacy. It is common to regard China's reform era as one that delivered economic reform and growth, but one in which substantial political change was neither permitted nor attained. It is certainly the case that Deng Xiaoping agreed with Lee Kuan Yew that it would be most desirable to obtain economic modernisation without political change.[7]

Nonetheless, in addition to significant political reforms, the reform era also saw the start of substantial transformations in the Chinese state. Politics has been redefined yielding political space for private activities, and not only in the exercise of economic entrepreneurship. The changing structure of China's economy, and in particular the growth of new corporate entities, has influenced its political economy and the basis of state power. The growth of an intense regionalism has presented a challenge not for the most part to the unity of the state but certainly to the relationship between central government and the provinces.

The growth of the private sector of the economy has generated much interest, both inside and outside China, not least because of the contrast with the recent past. However, it has not led to the development of an independent capitalist class who might challenge for state power. The private sector of the economy has for the most part remained small-scale and low-technology. Large parts of the retail sector and many commercial activities have become dominated by private entrepreneurs, but the private sector's share of industrialisation remains small. When private enterprise wants to grow, the tendency is for it to cease activity in the private sector and to restructure itself as a collective sector enterprise.[8]

The collective sector represents not only the most dynamic sector of the industrial economy, but also the growth of China's new corporate sector.[9] Before the reform era, the collective sector was that part of the public economy not governed by the state plan – collective sector enterprises received no automatic or subsidised allocations. It was essentially a second and poorer state sector. One ideological justification for this difference was that whilst state enterprises belonged to all the people, collective enterprises belonged to the responsible collective: either a locality or the workers in the enterprise themselves.

With reform, the collective sector has been more able to respond to market pressures and structural reforms. State enterprises have larger overheads, including guaranteed labour costs that collective enterprises do not face. Enterprise reform started mainly in the countryside with town and village collectives being encouraged to take advantage of the new economic environment. Underutilised resources were turned to more productive ends – agricultural machinery repair workshops in the suburban villages became light industrial factories manufacturing for export, car pools became taxi services, lorry teams freight delivery services. By the mid-1990s there were many suburban villages in south and east China that had become growing industrial conglomerates with little or no relationship to agricultural production.

Increasingly too after 1984, as the processes of economic reform were also brought to urban China, the same principles of enterprise reform were applied. However, in this case many state sector enterprises, or even social organisations with some economic capacity – such as schools or trade unions – were able to redirect their underutilised resources in the establishment of collective sector enterprises. A steel factory with a glass products workshop might establish a glass bottle and jamjar factory as a collective enterprise; a machining workshop might become an electronic timer factory. Often where the new collectives came out of state enterprises, the latter would establish a holding company. Almost always local government would be involved in the new collective enterprise, through the provision of some equity (usually land and buildings) and administrative regulation. The new collective sector has some claim to be regarded as a local government economy because of the extent of these relationships.

The strength of the local government economy helps explain the third way in which the collective sector has grown. Private entrepreneurs wanting to grow and become more technologically advanced or capital intensive usually turn their enterprise into a collective in cooperation with local government. The latter provides not only some equity and political protection, but also a better economic environment. Collective enterprises can more easily obtain loans for development and at lower rates of interest than for the private sector. They also pay less in taxes and fees and are subject to less administrative regulation.

The growth of the collective sector is likely gradually to alter the political economy of CCP rule, and indeed at the local level has already done so. Local government, business people, local entrepreneurs and enterprise managers still come together under the aegis of the CCP, but with new agendas. Party meetings are more like a cross between a club for local notables and the Rotary or Lions associations.

At the more rarefied end of the political hierarchy, regionalism is also having an important impact on the exercise of politics. China has rarely been as centralised or conformist as the totalitarian image would suggest. Since the late 1930s the CCP has adopted an administrative policy of 'Doing the best according to local conditions' in which the centre laid down broad guidelines with detailed policies on implementation to be a matter for local determination. Even during the height of a Soviet-style political economy in China during the early 1950s, there was considerably more decentralisation permitted in economic management than was the case in the Soviet Union.

Nonetheless, the reform era through its policies of decentralisation in economic management, the introduction of market forces and of increased external economic relations ('the open door') has markedly shifted the balance of power between central and provincial governments. Not least because the 'state idea' of China as a whole predominates the intense regionalism and is unlikely to lead to the break-up in any sense of the Chinese polity. However, there is every indication of the ability for regions and provinces to be more autonomous. Such considerations must be tempered by a recognition that disputes between central government and any specific province remain within a single ruling group at the apex of the CCP, and not between the CCP and the population at large of that province.

However, provincial authorities clearly have more say over their own destinies than ever before since the establishment of the PRC.[10]

### *Political Difficulties*

In general the experience of modernisation would suggest that social dislocation and political change are necessary consequences. The key questions are not whether there will be problems but of what kind and with what consequences. In China's case the rapid pace of change and high economic growth rates since 1978 have probably magnified many of the problems that have resulted. In particular, the transition from a command to a market economy, and the movement of large numbers of economic migrants within the country, both within a relatively short period of time, have created additional strains. At the same time and by the same token, China's experience of problems in the present and immediate future does not of itself indicate an end to political stability or the disintegration of an ordered society.

Political change during the reform era may well have been more fundamental and far-reaching than either the CCP or conventional wisdom would care to admit. Nonetheless it has not occurred without its problems and paradoxes. Perhaps the most startling is the extent to which China remains a pre-modern political system. Indeed, a major paradox of the reform era centred around Deng Xiaoping's personal role in the reform process.

One of the key political reforms was the attempt to institutionalise politics – to remove the personalist characteristics that exemplified the Mao-dominated era of China's politics. To that end reform stressed not the role of individuals, but of collective leadership, 'party life' and the importance of regulation. To that end Deng Xiaoping himself refused the offer of appointment as Chairman of the CCP in the early 1980s.[11] On the other hand, much of the reform momentum, particularly after the mid-1980s, would not have been maintained without Deng's personal intervention. Throughout this time he intervened in politics consistently to check political liberalisation and to ensure the maintenance of relatively fast economic reform. The most spectacular example of the latter was Deng's 'Inspection Tour of the South' which virtually single-handedly reignited national-level enthusiasm for a policy of fast export-oriented growth after the government-induced recession during the second half of 1989.[12]

One reason that Deng Xiaoping may have felt it necessary to intervene personally even after he had withdrawn from the 'front line' of administration in the mid-1980s was because there were genuine political disagreements within the leadership. In the early stages of reform, the leadership could unite relatively easily on what it did not want (the Cultural Revolution) and how to proceed (gradually with the rural areas as the base). However, differences began to appear in the leadership with the introduction of reform to urban China in late 1984. By the National Party Conference of September 1985, these had become quite obvious and well-articulated. This was not a dispute about whether there should be reform, but a series of differences of opinion about the speed and general direction of reform.

In part, disagreement within the leadership of the CCP was a function of the process of China's modernisation. It is easy to equate China's post-1978 economic growth with the modernisation of Taiwan, Hong Kong, Singapore and South Korea in and after the 1960s. Whilst there are many points of similarity, there are also significant differences including in particular that China's post-1978 growth and development has been a second-stage modernisation. From 1952 to 1978, China had already started to modernise, and a modern bureaucracy and education system were established from the early 1950s. The period since 1978 has seen economic restructuring rather than first-stage modernisation. One important political consequence is that China now possesses two modernising elites which may often conflict: those from before 1978 and the era of Mao-dominated politics, and those closely associated with the reform agenda.

In addition, disagreement within the leadership was also simply a function of the greater diversity accompanying modernisation. This is shown most clearly in the context of the changing relations between the centre and the provinces. Decentralisation, the redefinition of politics and the introduction of market forces into the economy have generally strengthened the hand of the provinces vis-à-vis central government. However, that trend has not necessarily meant that every province has aspired to less central involvement; or even that each has favoured faster reform in national debates about that topic.

Some provinces – Guangdong is the obvious example – clearly have sought greater autonomy, less to do with the centre and a fairly rapid sustained reform process.[13] At the same time, there is a wide variety of attitudes to be found on the speed of reform ranging from the cautious to the enthusiastic. There are even provinces which, whilst favouring reform, have preferred to lobby for greater central investment and involvement, sometimes even quite aggressively. Xinjiang, for example, made this point forcefully when it engaged in protectionist measures during 1989 and 1990 because, in its own view, if it was not to receive central assistance then it had to look after its own activities.[14]

Considerations of the elite apart, the problem for the CCP in initiating reform of any kind, but particularly political reform, has always been that it has almost no room for manoeuvre and runs the risk of creating a revolution of rising expectations which it cannot meet. The CCP wants to reform the system it has created but still retain control: to give in to external demands but still to control the extent to which it meets those demands and their results. Nowhere is this problem clearer than in the CCP's appeal to democracy, not least because its meaning has been variable, and remains so for different sections of the population.

As the 1990s move on, it would not be surprising to find the emergence of yet new voices from within the political and economic structures being created by the reform process claiming a slice of the political action. Sometimes, as in the case of the development of the collective sector of the economy to date, those new voices may have very close connections to the established party-state. However, it is the CCP's ability to assimilate interests and maintain its own equilibrium that may well be the key to its future.

The CCP's response to its self-induced problems of social control has been an appeal to 'Chineseness' as a unifying and mobilisatory political myth, rather than to the class conflict that characterised the Mao-dominated years of China's politics. This pre-modern form of nationalism is more of a vague cultural nationalism than one allied to a specific state or government. Though the CCP attempts to portray itself as the guardian of this 'Chineseness', it is almost as if it also subconsciously realises that the political system is in transition. Even within the CCP there is a recognition that the definition of 'Chineseness' may lie outside its control: hence its importance as a current political issue.

## *Economic Development*

The consequences and problems of rapid economic development in China since the late 1970s have been so obvious and so potentially threatening that it is often difficult to imagine that growth can be sustained. The most obvious problems are the lack of an adequate economic infrastructure, both physical and financial, and their consequences, which include inflation and massive dislocation. Whilst these, and other problems, cannot be dismissed, yet more serious difficulties may be found with the inadequacies of the workforce and the scale of environmental degradation.

China's transport difficulties are one set of infrastructural problems that pre-date even the reform era. North-south transportation of people and freight has been historically difficult and was but little improved after 1949. The main river systems – the Yangtze and the Yellow River – flow west-east, with relatively few railroads (for the population and distances covered), and until the 1980s almost no long-distance roads or road-haulage, and a similarly under-developed domestic air-system. China has one of the world's largest coalfields in the Ordos Basin of North China, but because of domestic transport problems South China imports coal from the rest of the world.

The development of the economy's physical infrastructure was distorted not a little by the planned economic geography of the Mao-dominated years. During the 1960s and early 1970s, the overwhelming proportion of capital investment in China was directed to the development of the relatively isolated central-west and southwest of China in line with Mao's belief that the country should be able to defend itself in depth in case of attack. The result was that the more economically advanced areas were starved of resources which were directed to other areas at an even higher unit cost where communications and supplies were weak and markets non-existent.[15]

Dismantling the command economy that enabled such a developmental strategy to be implemented has certainly redressed some of the imbalances. However, at the same time it has caused other social and economic problems. The inequity within the command economy between urban and rural prices was a major and increasing source of tension throughout the 1980s and into the 1990s. Removing that inequity – which effectively meant that rural areas heavily subsidised the towns and cities – has had an inflationary impact and caused social dislocation. The run on banks and saving accounts in urban areas during the middle of 1988 has had shock effects which continue to be felt, and is remembered by both government and population at large.

A major problem is that though the CCP has been committed to the replacement of administrative controls with macro-economic instruments, the latter have long been stymied at the design stage. Central government has done a relatively good job of controlling inflation. Each time it threatens to run away, the situation has been stabilised. However, on each occasion the mechanism used has been crude administrative fiat, rather than any more sophisticated controls of money supply or interest rates.

Beyond the establishment of the central People's Bank of China, few macroeconomic controls have been introduced. This is symptomatic of the lack of an adequate national financial infrastructure which in turn presents limits to the growth of an integrated domestic market. From the available evidence it seems that inter-provincial trade has barely increased during the reform era, and growth has come in exports and imports.[16]

One particularly important area in which infrastructural development has failed to keep pace with rising demand has been in the provision of education and training. Expenditure on education has barely risen during the reform era. There have been considerable increases in the provision of educational services at the most advanced end of the university system. However, there have been few if any improvements at the levels of skilled and semi-skilled labour. This must necessarily act as a brake on economic development as there is a limit to the growth that can be predicated on unskilled migrant (from poorer parts of the country) labour working shift-work on low-technology assembly lines – very much the norm up to now.[17]

Another set of economic problems concerns the impact of modernisation on the environment. Every North China city is thick with coal dust, particularly during winter. Rivers and waterways have similarly become repositories for industrial effluent and waste. These are serious problems and limits to economic growth but still not as immediate as the overuse of natural resources, particularly water, in some areas. Parts of North China have increasingly had severe water shortages for the last few years because of poor environmental controls and husbandry.

Drought is fairly common in North China, and this combined with no environmental protection has reduced or poisoned water tables in many places. In some cities, it is common to find productive enterprises on three-day weeks, even in the state sector and even in strategic industries. There is environmental protection legislation in some of the provinces; and some provincial leaders have made policy stands on the need for environmental protection, sustainable development and 'green' policies. However, the major problem facing all such activities is that there is no generalised acceptance of such regulation, and probably not much recognition of regulation as a whole.[18]

### *Social Outlook*

The social impact of reform has clearly been both great and problematical, though not always in the ways articulated by the leaders of the CCP. They realised at an early stage that whilst reform may have been needed because of a crisis in its popular support, as reform progressed it would also be likely to create new crises of confidence. The response, as already noted, was an appeal to a kind of pre-modern nationalism: an undefined 'Chineseness'. Whilst the CCP has concentrated its attention on the potential for value change – in order to arrest such development – problems of urbanisation, migrant populations and social welfare provision have also become apparent.

It is hardly surprising that 'moral decay', corruption and value change should be important items on the agenda of the CCP during the era of reform. Even a reforming communist party is certain to have problems with its loss of a moral monopoly as it allows and even encourages society to become more complex and diverse. At the same time and almost regardless of CCP predispositions, there remain behaviour and activity that are generally regarded as corrupt.

Though the CCP argues that corruption results from a moral failure, it may also be structurally determined. The lack of both any rule of law or general acceptance of regulation not only makes the definition of corruption very difficult, it basically explains the transitory nature of such concerns. Corruption occurs because in part individuals are being encouraged to take initiatives but the regulatory frameworks within which they operate are weak or non-existent. The CCP in consequence has to try to instil some wider responsibility by stressing the importance of moral decay.

The lack of regulative frameworks in general creates social problems in a number of ways. The impact on environmental conservation has already been noted. In addition, social welfare provision in the new enterprises created by the reform process has until very recently been virtually non-existent and remains extremely poor. One of the reasons for the growth of the collective sector has been its lack of labour regulation, lower labour costs and greater flexibility. New entrepreneurs in the faster growing areas can and do recruit young teenagers from the poorer parts of the country to come and work for relatively low wages by the standard of the faster growing areas, but high earnings by their own home-town standards. There is usually little if any provision for workers' insurance or pension schemes, though most employers provide accommodation.

Those who travel for guaranteed employment in the factories and enterprises of the faster growing areas face and may cause considerable social problems, including those associated with acceptance by their host communities. However, such problems pale into insignificance by comparison with those associated with the estimated 50-100 million 'drifters' who move, largely from economic necessity, looking for work.[19] These migrants are to be found all over China and not only in the faster growing parts of the country. The easing of restrictions on movement, the introduction of market forces into the economy, and the emphasis on individual effort have led many to look for work elsewhere. Many have drifted to Guangdong, Shanghai and the eastern seaboard. However, there has also been significant migration of this kind – involving pedlars, small business people, shopkeepers and the like – into other parts of China. For the most part, whilst such migration undoubtedly causes problems, it is unlikely to have any longer-term adverse significance for social harmony. Tibet is an obvious exception, where Han Chinese migration may threaten local culture.

Almost a defining feature of reform has been a change in the urban landscape. In addition to the development and transformation of central business districts, most cities and towns have expanded their areas of economic activity – even if official government boundaries have not yet been adjusted to take account of such growth. Suburban villages were the first areas to be allowed to experiment with new industrial enterprises and other economic activities, and they have for the most part maintained their development.

The suburban villages have been at the heart of economic growth, particularly in the collective sector. As they have grown they have merged into the urban conurbation – including the ownership, control or management of land within the towns and cities – in a number of ways, whilst still retaining their official 'rural' registration, which provides a more flexible economic environment for enterprise development. Urbanisation of this kind is no problem in itself. However, the existence of two or more regulative frameworks for otherwise identical activities or environments may be a source of tension and dysfunctionality.

Population control is one area in which the reform era has been relatively successful, but which paradoxically has the potential to cause problems for the future. Particularly in urban China, the 'one child' policy has led to radically different expectations for coming generations than those held earlier by their parents. Already it is clear that there is a significant generation gap between those who grew to maturity before 1976 (and the death of Mao Zedong) and later generations. Despite the widespread unpopularity of the politics and policies of the Cultural Revolution, earlier generations seem generally more altruistically-minded. New entrepreneurs from those generations are more likely to engage in acts of public philanthropy, endowing a school or building with a ceremonial arch, than their generational successors. The impact of a generation of single children may cause not simply generational conflict but also a paradigm shift in urban China's world-view.

### *Longer-term Prospects*

The experience of the Soviet Union and Eastern Europe appears to present severe challenges to China's political future. However, it is far from clear that the parallels between China and the former Soviet Union are exact enough to justify predictions of either the implosion of communist rule or the disintegration of the unified state. Although the political structures of the PRC were established by and along the line of the Soviet Union during the early 1950s, there the parallels end. The population of the USSR was more urbanised, intellectualised and more used to mass politics. Unlike its Soviet counterpart, the CCP came to power through a protracted process of war and civil war, based on mass mobilisation. Whilst that contrast does not guarantee the CCP wide popular support, it does provide the opportunity, particularly in North China where its roots run deep.

Moreover, China's contemporary political culture differs in two important respects from that which characterised the former communist party states of Europe and the Soviet Union. The first is that the CCP has presided over a rapidly growing economy. There has been a rising standard of living, not just since 1978, but over the whole period of the People's Republic of China. The second is that, with only two or three exceptions, there are few regional challenges within China to the 'state-idea' of China as a whole. Unlike in the USSR or Yugoslavia, the unity of the state has a long history. Its provinces have been determined by the circulation of people, goods and ideas in each locality over some 2000 years, and not by some twentieth century notion of nationalism and administrative fiat.[20] The exceptions – Tibet, Xinjiang and Inner Mongolia – are precisely those non-Han areas with their own independent traditions which do not share China's 'state-idea'.

China's political economy changed dramatically during 1979-1982. In those years through sheer political will, the leaders of the CCP forced through the major reform that later defeated their communist counterparts in Europe and the Soviet Union. They removed the stranglehold of heavy industry on the economy by diverting sufficient investment into light and consumer industry. The amount was not fantastically large – it is estimated at only some 3-4% of GNP – but it has significantly influenced elite-level politics; altered the trajectory of national economic planning; and resulted in the development of a consumer society, with all the attendant political as well as social and economic implications.[21]

China's future is more likely to be that of an authoritarian and modernising regime, similar in many respects to those that developed in Japan, Taiwan and South Korea. The state's dominance of society and its leading position in the economy is likely to remain a central characteristic of its political economy. Its political institutions are likely to be dominated by the nexus of relationships described by business, bureaucracy and politicians, and their access to wealth, power and status. In those terms it hardly matters how many political parties compete electorally. The formal political system would thus remain dominated either by the CCP or some successor institution which provides the essential framework for the exercise of economic as well as political power.

At the same time China's emerging politics are likely to display an unprecedently high degree of regionalism. Economic growth since 1978 has been regional rather than national with regions having considerable autonomy particularly with respect to their own economic development, and the ability to utilise any comparative advantage in the international marketplace. Continued growth seems certain to be highly regionalised with new areas of growth within China being economically integrated with different East Asian economies, as has already occurred with Taiwan, Hong Kong, South Korea, Singapore and, to a lesser extent, Japan.

China's unity will be affected but not necessarily adversely. Increased economic interaction and a domestic division of labour may strengthen economic integration and political unity. An effective federalism in practice – though not in name or legally, not least because of the absence of a tradition of a rule of law – is also a distinct possibility. Chinese culture has long been polycentric; it was only the rigid conformism of the late Qing Empire and of the state under Mao Zedong that emphasised its centralist aspects.[22]

The future of the CCP is less certain. There can be little doubt that the CCP is currently undergoing considerable change. The new economic elites who have been recruited in the era of reform have radically different perspectives on life as well as politics to their predecessors. Though they may be only too willing to reach accommodations with the current party-state, they are also part of a process which is changing it from within. At the local level this means that the party is much less an organisation for ideological activity and more concerned with economic development and providing opportunities for networking.

## *Agents of Change*

The CCP is not particularly popular, and may even be actively unpopular among certain sectors of the vocal and educated. However, the strongest argument for its continued hold on power is the lack of an organised alternative. Within China at the moment, most ideas for political reform, let alone those advocating radical change, remain muted – understandably since June 1989. Nonetheless they exist, though paradoxically as much if not more within the CCP and the establishment as in society at large.

Stability depends – as it has ever since the Third Plenum of December 1978 – on the CCP's capacity to keep its nerve and to mediate economic and political problems and social conflict. For the most part the evidence of the 1980s and 1990s would seem to suggest such exercise of its power is not wildly impossible. The events of mid-1989, when the leadership of the CCP did appear more than a little bewildered and to have at least temporarily lost its nerve, were clearly an exception. However, an understanding and interpretation of those events are now integral parts of the environment in which the leadership must operate and they limit its room for manoeuvre. Civilian and military reaction to the events of 1989 both contemporaneously and since probably makes it difficult for the CCP leadership to repeat its actions. At the same time, the events of May-June 1989 provide instructive lessons so that preemptive action might be taken to avoid such conflicts and crises in future.

Those who populate the party-state system remain the key organised agents of political change. Without exaggerating their abilities, they both see the need to accommodate China's new social forces and to learn from the lessons of the collapse of communist rule in the former Soviet Union and Eastern Europe. The communist officials in Eastern Europe who placed themselves at the head of movements for radical change were third or fourth generation revolutionaries, facing major economic problems and surrounded by the apparent attractions of democracy. The current CCP leadership in contrast is dominated by the first post-revolutionary generation buoyed by economic success and surrounded by a political discourse in East and Southeast Asia that stresses the synergy between economic growth and authoritarianism.

As elsewhere in East and Southeast Asia, the military may come to play a crucial role in the transformation of China's politics. However, here too there is uncertainty. It might be imagined that with the reform era and the depoliticisation of other aspects of state activity, the People's Liberation Army (PLA) would follow suit, concentrate on becoming a more professionalised, standing army and withdraw from civilian affairs, yet remain as the final arbiter and guarantor of state power.

It is certainly the case that the PLA has lobbied hard for its increased professionalisation since the mid-1970s and a concomitant modernisation of its weaponry. However, it is far from clear that the PLA has completely withdrawn from civilian affairs, though its involvement has changed.[23] Charged with existing in a market-oriented economy the PLA, or rather its various constituent units, has established a large number of enterprises, many of which have only a very tenuous relationship to military activities. PLA unit budgets are now drafted on the assumption that a certain percentage of funds and resources will be generated by commercial and economic activities.[24]

The extent to which the PLA's economic activities may jeopardise or otherwise influence its role as a major organisational support of the party-state is far from clear. The possibility exists that the PLA will still not be able to stand outside any possible civilian conflict or dispute and may on the contrary be forced to intervene either partially or in its own interests. Thus, for example, it would appear that military units have been mobilised to almost purely economic ends during the various 'commodity wars' that have developed since the mid-1980s.[25] Economic competition with other non-military enterprises has already led PLA units in Guangdong – where roughly half of all the PLA's non-military economic enterprises are physically located – into more direct forms of confrontation.[26]

Outside the formal party-state system – which includes the PLA – there is opposition to the CCP and its policies, but accommodation is an inherent part of political life not just for business people but even for those who seek more radical political change. On the whole, both those seeking radical reform and the CCP share to a remarkable extent a fear of social disorder. There is a common recognition that too rapid political change might jeopardise the gains in the standard of living made during the reform era.

The events of 1989 alienated intellectuals and drove many into exile where they remain. Those who were involved in the movement for reform at the time saw themselves as within the system rather than opposed to it root and branch, and that position remains an unreconciled matter of some debate amongst those now in exile. It is possible that the opposition in exile may develop new ideas and even the organisation to represent a significant threat to the CCP at some point in the future. However, at present they face enormous structural problems. They are divided, physically separate and disparate. They are fundamentally a movement of intellectuals, and whilst that leads to a certain influence, there remains a check on their development as a mass movement. Also, they are outside China and thus somewhat tainted in terms of their need to appeal to reactive nationalism.

Chinese intellectuals have flirted with Western ideas of democracy since the end of the nineteenth century, but it could not be said that notions of democracy or even civil society have developed strong foundations. For the most part when democracy was spoken of in the PRC before 1989, the meaning was either that of 'socialist democracy' – perfecting state socialism – or the 'small democracies' – freedom of choice in work, home and marriage. Despite such symbolism as the 'Goddess of Democracy' modelled on the Statue of Liberty which appeared in Tiananmen Square in May, the demonstrations of 1989 did little directly or contemporaneously to develop a new discourse or build towards civil society. However, the 1989 movement could now develop its own mythology which may well play a role in China's political future. There is a foundation for consciousness of democracy that did not exist before and which may develop, particularly with increased exposure to the rest of the world.

Given the role of the party-state in the genesis of new patterns of economic development, it would be remarkable to find the new entrepreneurs generated by China's growth since the late 1970s articulating any demand for regime change of any kind, let alone a Western-style democracy, and there is no evidence to suggest that is the case. On the contrary at this stage, as one might expect with a continually rising market, most of the energy of the new entrepreneurs is concentrated elsewhere.[27] Moreover, the attraction of Western ideas, even of capitalism, must be kept in perspective. Throughout the twentieth century, those seeking change in China have articulated a desire for a fundamentally Chinese modernisation, and for many the CCP still represents the best hope of achieving that nationalist goal.

## NOTES

[1] Scepticism may be found, for example, in C. Howe and K.R. Walker (eds), 'The readjustment in the Chinese economy', *The China Quarterly*, 100, December 1984. Similarly within the PRC it is worth remembering that the failure of Shenzhen and the other Special Economic Zones (SEZ) was heralded on many occasions before the late 1980s with serious consideration given to their closure.

[2] D. J. Solinger, *China's Transition from Socialism: Statist Legacies and Market Reforms 1980-1990*, New York: M.E. Sharpe, 1993, presents a far-reaching analysis of the processes and consequences of these economic changes.

[3] PRC estimates for the year 2000 in *Wen Wei Po*, 13 July 1992, p. 5.

[4] For an analysis of China's political economy in comparative perspective, see David S.G. Goodman, 'Transformations in the Chinese state: historical perspectives on reform', *Journal of the Oriental Society of Australia*, 23-24, 1994, p. 52.

[5] See, for example, R.M. Field, 'Slow growth of labour productivity in Chinese industry', *The China Quarterly*, 96, December 1983, p. 641.

[6] For an overview of the near constant political instability, see, for example, J. Domes, *The Internal Politics of China, 1949-1972*, London: C. Hurst, 1973; and *China after the Cultural Revolution*, London: C. Hurst, 1976.

[7] Deng Xiaoping's favourable comments on Singapore were made in 1992 and may be found in 'Excerpts from talks given in Wuchang, Shenzhen, Zhuhai and Shanghai', 18 January-21 February 1992, IV, in *Selected Works of Deng Xiaoping*, vol. 3, 1982-1992, Beijing: Foreign Languages Press, 1994, p. 366.

[8] S. Young, 'Policy, practice and the private sector in China', *Australian Journal of Chinese Affairs*, 21, 1989; and 'Wealth but not security: attitudes towards private business in China in the 1980s', *Australian Journal of Chinese Affairs*, 25, 1991.

[9] V. Nee, 'Organisational dynamics of market transition: hybrid forms, property rights, and mixed economy in China', *Administrative Science Quarterly*, 37 (1), 1992; and David S.G. Goodman, 'Collectives and connectives, capitalism and corporatism: structural change in China's economy', *The Journal of Communist Studies and Transition Politics*, 11 (1), March 1995, p. 12, both examine changes in the collective sector.

[10] China's new evolving regionalism is discussed in David S.G. Goodman and G. Segal (eds), *China Deconstructs: Politics, Trade and Regionalism*, London: Routledge, 1994.

[11] David S.G. Goodman, *Deng Xiaoping and the Chinese Revolution*, London: Routledge, 1994, p. 97.

[12] See, for example, R. Baum, *Burying Mao: Chinese Politics in the Age of Deng Xiaoping*, Princeton University Press, 1994, especially p. 341 ff.

[13] Feng Chongyi and David S.G. Goodman, 'Guangdong: Greater Hong Kong and the new regionalist future', in Goodman and Segal (eds), op. cit., 1994, p. 177.

[14] Chao Chien-min, 'T'iao-t'iao vs k'uai-k'uai: a perennial dispute between the central and local governments in Mainland China', *Issues and Studies*, August 1991, p. 40; David S.G. Goodman, 'Provinces confronting the state?', in Kuan Hsin-chi and M. Brosseau (eds), *China Review 1992*, Hong Kong: Chinese University Press, 1992.

[15] B. Naughton, 'The third front: defence industrialisation in the Chinese interior', *The China Quarterly*, 115, September 1988, p. 351.

[16] A. Kumar, 'Economic reform and the internal division of labour in China: production, trade and marketing', in Goodman and Segal (eds), op. cit., 1994, p. 99.

[17] See, for example, C. Herrmann-Pillath Marktwirtschaft, in *China: Geschichte-Strukturen Transformation*, Opladen: Leske & Budrich, 1995, especially p. 168 ff.

[18] See, for example, C.W. Lo, 'Law and administration in Deng's China: legalization of the administration of environmental protection', *Review of Central and East European Law*, 5, 1992.

[19] D. J. Solinger, *China's Transients and the State: A Form of Civil Society?* Hong Kong: Institute of Asia-Pacific Studies, The Chinese University of Hong Kong, 1991.

[20] J.B.R. Whitney, *China: Area, Administration and Nation-Building*, Department of Geography Research Paper no. 123, University of Chicago, 1970.

[21] D.J. Solinger, *From Lathes to Looms: China's Industrial Policy, 1979-1982*, Stanford University Press, 1991.

[22] See, for example, S. Naquin and E. Rawski (eds), *Chinese Society in the Eighteenth Century*, Yale University Press, 1987.

[23] See, for example, E. Joffe, *The Chinese Army after Mao*, London: Weidenfeld and Nicolson, 1987; and R.H. Yang, J.C. Hu, P.K.H. Yu and A.N.D. Yang (eds), *Chinese Regionalism: The Security Dimension*, Boulder: Westview Press, 1994.

[24] Tai-Ming Cheung, 'Profits over professionalism: the PLA's economic activities and the impact on military unity', in Yang et al, op. cit., 1994, p. 85.

[25] Chao Chien-min, op. cit., August 1991, p. 40; and David S.G. Goodman, 'The PLA and regionalism: Guangdong Province', *The Pacific Review*, 7 (1), 1994, p. 70.

[26] David S G. Goodman, 'The PLA in Guangdong Province: warlordism and localism', in Yang et al, op. cit., 1994, p. 207.

[27] 'The People's Republic of China: the party-state, capitalist revolution and new entrepreneurs', in David S.G. Goodman and R. Robison (eds), *The New Rich in Asia: Mobile-phones, McDonalds and Middle Class Revolution*, London: Routledge, 1996.

# 14. TAIWAN'S ECONOMIC GROWTH AND ITS SOUTHWARD POLICY IN ASIA

*Gerald Chan*

Taiwan's status in international affairs is rather unique: it is economically strong but politically weak. Measured by most economic yardsticks, it has a robust economy, but diplomatically it is very isolated. It maintained diplomatic relations with only 31 countries as of January 1996,[1] most of which are small, developing states in Africa and Central America. The fact that Taiwan is attracting increasing attention around the world is due mainly to its phenomenal economic growth and the commercial opportunities that it offers. In the post-cold war era in which economic prowess has assumed greater importance relative to strategic-political considerations, Taiwan's international standing is rising steadily. How can Taiwan maintain and make use of its economic vitality and strength to enhance its national interests? With the dynamic growth of the Asia-Pacific economies and the tendency of the world to move towards regionalism, Taiwan is trying to adjust its trade and investment policy towards the Pacific Rim countries.

Arguably the most important policy adjustment in recent years is the adoption of the so-called Southward Policy directed towards its neighbouring countries in Southeast Asia. Basically this policy arises out of a perceived need to adjust Taiwan's political-economic relations with China. Government leaders in Taiwan are worried about the rapid growth in trade and investments between China and Taiwan. In 1993 China absorbed 66.5% of Taiwan's total foreign investments.[2] Because of the increasing economic linkage, any major political or economic upheaval in China will inevitably affect Taiwan's economic stability. By its sheer economic and geographic size, China can, if it chooses, use its trade and investment links with Taiwan to put pressure on the Taiwan government through Taiwanese traders and investors. Also, because of the lack of proper legal protection, Taiwanese investments in China are exposed to great risk.[3] Hence Taiwanese leaders find it necessary to moderate Taiwan's economic integration with China, to coordinate its overall investment resources, and to have a comprehensive strategy for foreign investments. Southeast Asia and Indochina have become attractive alternatives. In a major way the China factor is instrumental in the official adoption of Southward Policy.

This chapter concentrates on an analysis of this policy by addressing the following questions: What is Southward Policy? Why adopt such a policy? What are the economic, political and strategic considerations in the pursuit of this policy? Which countries are its specific targets? How do they respond to it? The chapter focuses on the issues of trade and investment, as commerce is the immediate concern of the policy. It discusses briefly the issue of Taiwanese aid as it impinges on the policy, and concludes by making some observations on the problems and prospects of such a policy adjustment.

## *What is Southward Policy?*

Southward Policy (or *nanjin zhengce* or *südpolitik*)[4] was formulated by the Taiwan government to help channel Taiwanese investments to Southeast Asia as a way to reduce its economic reliance on China. The justifications for adopting the policy are detailed in a report entitled *Nanjin zhengce* read by Chiang Pin-kung, the Minister of Economic Affairs, before the Legislative Yuan, Taiwan's Parliament, on 27 December 1993. The policy directs that Taiwan should improve its relations with its neighbours to the south, in particular Viet Nam and the ASEAN countries. Although this is primarily an economic policy, the political and strategic implications for Taiwan in the Asia-Pacific region are significant.

Because of Taiwan's pariah international status, moves taken to improve its relations with other countries have often been shunned for fear of offending the People's Republic of China. To be effective Taiwan's moves have to be built on strong economic incentives so as to attract potential sympathisers. Hence its diplomacy, including Southward Policy, is driven by economic and commercial considerations. Officials from the Ministry of Economic Affairs and Taiwan's central bank play a crucial role in projecting Taiwan's image abroad, a role that often eclipses the one played by officials from the Ministry of Foreign Affairs. An example is the participation of Vincent Siew and Chiang Pin-kung in the APEC meetings in Seattle in 1993 and in Bogor, Indonesia, in 1994. (At that time Siew was the chairperson of the Economic Planning and Development Council of the Executive Yuan, and Chiang was the Minister of Economic Affairs.) They had the rare opportunity of meeting personally the heads of governments of member-states of the grouping, an opportunity not yet available to Taiwan's president, prime minister or foreign minister.

In fact the official pronouncement of Southward Policy affirms a well-established commercial practice that can be traced back to the 1980s when Taiwanese merchants began to trade with Southeast Asian countries, following Taiwan's rapid economic growth in the seventies. During that time Taiwan had amassed sizeable trade surpluses, but any contact with mainland China, commercial or otherwise, was banned. Accumulated wealth had to seek an outlet for investment and recycling. In the mid-1980s land prices in Taiwan soared, the New Taiwan dollar appreciated, cheap labour became scarce and global trade protectionism was looming.[5] Against such a background Southeast Asia began to attract Taiwan's accumulated funds, for reasons of geographic proximity as well as economic complementarity. In 1986 the Taiwan government started to turn its attention to some newly developing countries, including Southeast Asia, as a way to diversify its economic interests. After Chiang's visit to Singapore and Viet Nam in late

July 1993, the government expressed publicly that it intended to affirm this practice under the name of *nanjin zhengce*, a name first popularised by the media.[6]

Subsequently, in February 1994, in order to implement *nanjin zhengce*, the Economic Planning and Development Council decided:[7]

(1) to set up an insurance scheme to protect Taiwan's overseas investments;
(2) to set up schools to cater for the children of Taiwanese traders in their host countries;
(3) to encourage Taiwanese financial institutions to set up foreign operations in Southeast Asia so as to facilitate the financing of investment projects; and
(4) to forge agreements with the foreign governments concerned to protect mutual investments and to lower various kinds of taxes.

### *Why Adopt Southward Policy?*

According to Chiang Pin-kung, Southward Policy has five objectives:[8]

(1) to help local industries to move their production base to Southeast Asia where the cost of labour is lower;
(2) to make use of some Southeast Asian countries as a replacement for Hong Kong as an 'intermediary stop' for trade with China after 1997;
(3) to combine Taiwan's development expertise and the resources of Southeast Asia to expand bilateral trade and to strengthen Taiwan's local industries;
(4) to maintain Taiwan's economic growth by building production bases in Southeast Asia in preparation for Viet Nam's entry to ASEAN and the development of the ASEAN Free Trade Area; and
(5) to improve substantive commercial relations with the ASEAN five and Viet Nam so as to enhance Taiwan's position in the region's security system.

Of these five objectives the second one is largely subject to changes in China-Taiwan relations and the fifth is indicative of Taiwan's political-strategic aim in the region.

In broad terms the adoption of Southward Policy has been influenced by global and regional developments, apart from China-Taiwan relations which serve as the main stimulant. Within the Asia-Pacific region, there is a recent increase in consultation and cooperation in political-economic as well as political-strategic affairs brought about by the activities of APEC and the ASEAN Regional Forum respectively. Taiwanese leaders acknowledge that the world is moving towards some kind of regional integration, and since Taiwan is a country strategically located in the Asia-Pacific region, it is necessary for Taiwan to maintain and increase its interactions with countries in the region, economically as well as politically.

*Economic considerations.* Since the 1950s the Taiwan government has devoted a lot of attention to the development of Taiwan's economic links with the United States, Japan and Europe, and has largely ignored Southeast Asia. Until very recently it has prohibited official contacts, economic or otherwise, with China. Now that ASEAN, Japan and China are becoming the three major economic forces in the Asia-Pacific region, it has had to revise its long-held economic priorities.

According to the estimates of Asian Development Bank and others, the Asian economy as a whole is expected to have grown at rate of 7-8% per annum throughout 1994, 1995 and 1996. Investments in Southeast Asia from around the world have been increasing substantially, surpassing the US$100 billion mark in 1992.[9] In view of the economic slow-down around the world and a global tendency towards regional protectionism, Taiwan feels the need to adjust its traditional trading pattern. In this light Southeast Asia offers good opportunities for Taiwan to maintain its economic vitality, especially when the ASEAN countries are moving towards the formation of a free trade zone within 10 to 15 years starting from 1994. Hence countries to the south of Taiwan, including the more affluent ones in Southeast Asia and the less affluent ones in Indochina, have become attractive markets for Taiwan's trade and investment.

An interesting theme of the Southward Policy is that by 1997, when Hong Kong is to return to Chinese rule, its position as a transit point for Taiwanese trade and investment in mainland China is likely to be taken over by Singapore, which has established itself as a financial and transportation hub in the Asia-Pacific region.[10] This projection is based on two assumptions: first, that after 1997 Hong Kong will pose a logistical problem for Taiwan's transportation to and from China, despite China's promise to keep Hong Kong's economic and social systems intact for 50 years; and secondly, that the Taiwan government still maintains its policy of no direct contact with China. Whether these two assumptions will stand will be severely tested in the coming years, especially in view of the approval in early 1995 by the Taiwan government to allow trans-shipment to China from designated ports in Taiwan and the Chinese missile tests in the Taiwan Strait in 1995 and 1996. The present situation of Hong Kong is that, despite the often shaky relationship between China and Britain over the territory, the political and economic confidence of local residents as well as foreign investors seems to be holding. However, from the point of view of spreading Taiwan's investment risks, reducing its heavy dependence on trade with China and investing in a fast growing Southeast Asian economy, Southward Policy has its many merits.

As of September 1994, over 3,000 Taiwanese enterprises had invested a total of $20 billion in Southeast Asia (see Table 14.1). This sum would have reached $60 billion by the end of 1995 if Taiwanese investments in China and Hong Kong were included, assuming $30 billion to China and $10 billion to Hong Kong.[11] In the first 10 months of 1993 the two-way trade between Taiwan and the ASEAN countries and Viet Nam amounted to $13.5 billion,[12] accounting for about 10% of Taiwan's total trade. Taiwan exported $7.82 billion worth of goods to ASEAN and Viet Nam, accounting for 11% of Taiwan's total export. These countries formed the third largest export market for Taiwan after the United States and Hong Kong. Imports from ASEAN and Viet Nam to Taiwan stood at $5.72 billion in the same period, accounting for 8.8% of Taiwan's total imports. These countries formed the third largest group of importers to Taiwan after Japan and the United States. Taiwan enjoyed a trade surplus of $2.1 billion with ASEAN and Viet Nam.

Table 14.1. TAIWANESE INVESTMENTS IN SOUTHEAST ASIA, 1949-SEPTEMBER 1994

| *Country* | *Amount (US$ million)* | *Ranking among investor-countries* |
|---|---|---|
| Malaysia | 6,897 | 2 * |
| Thailand | 4,836 | 4 ** |
| Indonesia | 6,803 | 6 |
| Philippines | 449 | 5 |
| Singapore | 90 | 13 |
| Viet Nam | 1,790 | 1 |
| *Total* | *20,865* | |

Notes:
* After Japan.
** After Japan, Hong Kong, and United States.
1. Dollar figures have been rounded to the nearest million.
2. See *Nanjin Zhengce Baogao* for yearly breakdowns from 1986 to 1993.

Sources: 1. *Nanjin Zhengce Baogao* (*Report on Southward Policy*), A report tabled at the Economics Committee of the Legislative Yuan by Minister of Economic Affairs Chiang Pin-kung on 27 December 1993, p. 12.
2. Ministry of Economic Affairs, Republic of China, quoted in Parris H. Chang, 'Foreign security cooperation in Asia-Pacific region: a Taiwan perspective', *The Journal of East Asian Affairs*, 9 (2), Summer/Fall 1995, p. 397.

Three factors account for the rapid rise in the bilateral trade.[13] First, the ASEAN countries and Viet Nam are experiencing fast economic growth and Taiwanese products suit their consumer markets well. Secondly, the region is one of the traditional suppliers of raw materials to Taiwan's industries, including minerals and forestry products. Thirdly, since 1985 Southeast Asia has become an important region for Taiwanese investments, resulting in the demand for capital and semi-manufactured goods from Taiwan.[14]

Despite the absence of diplomatic relations between Taiwan and the ASEAN countries, the Taiwan government has secured a number of bilateral agreements to protect Taiwanese investments with Singapore, Indonesia, the Philippines, Malaysia and Viet Nam. A similar accord is expected to be signed with Thailand shortly. To ensure the protection of Taiwanese investors, Taiwan's Ministry of Finance is working hard to secure double-taxation agreements with these countries. Also, Taiwanese banks are trying to set up offices in these countries to help facilitate finance and credits to Taiwanese investors.[15] Apart from working to establish Taiwan as Asia's financial centre, which is part of Taiwan's Six Years Development Plan, and to set itself up as a regional operations centre, the bank is financing the construction of an international finance complex in Taipei, aiming to continue to ease foreign exchange controls.[16]

Of course, China is too big a market to be ignored, especially from the point of view of private traders and investors. Already Taiwan is the second largest investor in China after Hong Kong. Its investments there grew by about 25% per annum from 1990 to 1993.[17] As of October 1993 Taiwan had over 15,000 investment projects in China.[18] This figure mushroomed to 25,849 by September 1994 with contracted investments standing at $22.6 billion and actual investments at $8.2 billion.[19] In Pudong, a newly developed free industrial zone near Shanghai, nearly half of the 1,000 projects are funded by either Hong Kong or Taiwanese investors.[20] Indirect trade with China, mostly through Hong Kong, was eventually recognised and sanctioned by the Taiwan government in 1987. From 1979, when China adopted its Open Door policy, to the end of 1992, the total volume of trade between the two sides was worth $29 billion, with an average increase of 42.1% per annum. Two-way trade in 1992 was worth $7.4 billion, over $10 billion in 1993,[21] $15 billion in 1994 ,[22] and $20 billion in 1995.[23]

*Political considerations.* As Taiwan has no diplomatic relations with any country in Asia, it is keen to improve all forms of links with countries in the region. From experience Taiwan has learned that this can be done only through gradual steps, starting with less contentious issues such as economic and cultural ones and then moving on to the political sphere. The signing of many trade and investment agreements with Southeast Asian countries, which are based on inter-governmental understanding, is a step in that direction. For the past few years Taiwan has worked hard to become a dialogue member of the ASEAN post-ministerial meetings. So far, only Singapore has openly expressed support for Taiwan to be included as a dialogue member.[24] Other ASEAN members are cautious of China's objection. However, Taiwan has become too important an economic entity to be ignored, and alternative ways to accommodate Taiwan are being sought so that consultation and dialogue can take place.

In the pursuit of Southward Policy two visits made by top Taiwanese leaders represent a significant step forward. In January 1994 Premier Lien

Chan made a private visit to Malaysia and Singapore. (His visit was kept secret until the last minute in order to minimise interference from China – such is the inhibition on Taiwan's diplomatic behaviour.) Billed as *dujia waijiao* (vacation diplomacy) by the Taiwanese media,[25] Lien was the highest-ranking Taiwanese to visit Malaysia. (President Lee Teng-hui previously visited Singapore in 1989.) One interesting result of Lien's visit to Singapore was the exploration of a joint venture by both countries to invest in Hainan province of China. Singapore is in a privileged position to do so because it has maintained friendly relations with both China and Taiwan and has secured investment guarantees from both.[26]

President Lee Teng-hui's nine-day 'vacation' to the Philippines, Indonesia and Thailand in February 1994 is the strongest indication yet of Taiwan's practice of Southward Policy. Lee was accompanied by an entourage of some 40 government ministers, officials and businessmen. Despite China's repeated warnings and protests, Lee managed to meet President Fidel Ramos of the Philippines, President Suharto of Indonesia and King Bhumibol of Thailand.

Southeast Asian leaders welcomed Lee's private visit because they want to attract Taiwanese investments. Taiwan, together with Japan and South Korea, became a major investor in Southeast Asia in the late 1980s. However, in the early 1990s these three countries diverted a large part of their investment flows from ASEAN to China. In the case of Taiwan, its actual investments in the ASEAN countries rose yearly from $282 million in 1989 to top $702 million in 1991, but then dropped in subsequent years to reach $275 million in 1993. Specifically, Taiwanese contracted investments in Indonesia dropped from $1 billion in 1991 to $0.5 billion in 1992 and then to only $0.1 billion in 1993.[27] In comparison Taiwan's direct and indirect investments in China rose from $174 million in 1991 to a staggering $3,168 million in 1993.[28] According to Senior Minister Lee Kuan Yew of Singapore, China was sucking away investments from Southeast Asia. In 1993 investments in Indonesia went down by 30%, and those in Malaysia and Thailand went down by 25%.[29] Realising the importance of Taiwan's capital injection, Southeast Asian leaders were trying to find ways to receive important officials from Taiwan.

As a result of these two visits, Taiwan has achieved high-level contacts with the five ASEAN states, and Taiwanese leaders hope that they may have paved the way for visits to other countries, especially to Japan and the United States and the countries of Europe. Whether or not 'vacation diplomacy' can become a model for Taiwan depends very much on the assessments made by these countries of the relative political and economic gains from Taiwan over China. So far the results have been mixed.

In the absence of diplomatic relations with countries in Southeast Asia, the Taiwan government has established a network of commercial and semi-governmental offices to promote its political and economic interests, and Taiwanese businessmen have set up a network of trade associations.[30] These offices and associations help to strengthen the linkages amongst Taiwanese merchants, to obtain investment privileges, to spread investment risks, and to increase their collective bargaining power in relation to their host governments.

*Strategic considerations.* In a message to the Asia Forum held in Kyoto in 1992 and an interview with CNN in 1993, Lee Teng-hui called for the formation of a collective security system in the Asia-Pacific region. His suggestion was made in line with similar ones proposed by a number of Asian leaders such as the former prime minister of Japan, Miyazawa Kiichi. Most of these suggestions were made in response to the power vacuum created as a result of the collapse of the Soviet Union and the phased withdrawal of American troops from the region. They aimed at building mutual trust and confidence among nations in the region and at resolving some of the region's potential conflicts, such as the territorial disputes in the South China Sea, the military arms build-up and North Korea's nuclear programme. Lee even suggested the creation of a security protection fund to finance the working of such a security system.[31]

The ASEAN Regional Forum met for the first time to discuss these regional security issues in Bangkok in July 1994. Seventeen countries in the Asia-Pacific region were represented, with the exception of Taiwan. Taiwanese leaders felt frustrated that their country had not been consulted or invited. For practical purposes the Forum had to include China, otherwise China would feel that the Forum was aimed against it. Moreover, without the participation and cooperation of China, the Forum is unlikely to go very far. China will certainly object to any attempt to include Taiwan in any future regional security talks, and since all the ASEAN member countries recognise the People's Republic as the sole legitimate government of all China, Taiwan will have to be left out inevitably.[32]

Of the three aspects (political, economic, and strategic) discussed above, the economic one is most important in the pursuit of Southward Policy, at least in the short term, because the success or failure of Taiwan's diplomacy is heavily dependent on its economic power.[33] Ultimately, however, it is political recognition that Taiwan is seeking. Once proper political recognition is secured, Taiwan's economic and strategic interests can be further enhanced through the normal diplomatic channels and practice. To achieve that Taiwan has to work extremely hard at the economic front in order to increase its bargaining power where political recognition is at stake.

### *Asia-Pacific Regional Operations Centre*

While Southward Policy is aimed at protecting Taiwan's trade and investment from possible China sabotage, the plan to develop Taiwan into an Asia-Pacific regional operations centre has wider objectives. In general the plan aims at upgrading Taiwan's industrial capability, internationalising its business operations, and maintaining its competitive advantage and economic growth, especially in face of the dynamism of the region and the change in the global economic environment. In brief Taiwan is trying to lay the groundwork for generating a 'second wave of economic miracle' well into the twenty-first century, and to become the hub of business activities in the Asia-Pacific region.

The idea was first floated in the government and the business community in 1993, and a concrete plan was drafted by the Council for Economic Planning and Development of the Executive Yuan in 1994 and was approved by the government in early 1995. It involves macroeconomic adjustments and the constructions of six operation centres: a manufacturing centre, a sea transportation centre, an air transportation centre, a financial centre, a telecommunication centre and a media centre.

The timetable for implementation is divided into three phases: in the short term from 1995 to 1997, the main emphasis is placed on macroeconomic adjustment programmes, including the liberation of trade and investment and the establishment of the necessary legal framework and environment to allow the free flow of personnel, capital and information; in the medium term from 1997 to 2000, the emphasis will be put on the construction of a manufacturing centre to upgrade its industrial base and to develop hi-tech industries. At the same time work will be started to modernise Taiwan's sea transportation, telecommunications and the media. In the long term from 2000 to 2005 and beyond, attention will be paid to the further strengthening of Taiwan's position as a regional operations centre after economic liberalisation is realised and major construction projects are completed. The implementation plan shows that most of the projects will be carried out in tandem, with a lot of overlap and coordination.[34]

In trying to achieve its goals Taiwan is facing competition from Singapore and Hong Kong, and to a lesser extent, Bangkok. Apart from such competition, some of which might prove to be healthy in the long run in building Asia-Pacific cooperation and growth as a whole, Taiwan's degree of success in achieving its objectives also depends on the political-economic relations between China and Taiwan. Obviously the planned operations centre will work best if the political climate across the Taiwan Strait improves. In any case the whole project will only serve to enhance Taiwan's overall economic development; it will not contradict its Southward Policy which can be regarded as an insurance policy bearing its own fruits.

### *Three Specific Targets*

Three places have been targeted in the pursuit of Southward Policy, for they offer good business opportunities for Taiwan to make use of its industrial experience in running small- and medium-sized enterprises. They are Subic Bay in the Philippines, Batam in Indonesia, and Viet Nam.

Subic Bay, a former American military base, has the infrastructural facilities conducive to the building of an industrial base. The Filipino government plans to turn the area into a free-trade industrial zone. At present

Taiwan is the biggest investor in Subic Bay,[35] but Japan remains the top investor in the whole country and South Korea and Malaysia are significant players. The Subic Bay project is part of the Filipino government's effort to reform the national economy. The growth rate of the Filipino economy in 1994 reached 4.3%, double that in 1993;[36] and the gross national product was projected to expand by 6.5% in 1995.[37] As a way to attract investments from Taiwan amongst other countries, the Filipino government sent its Minister for Industry and Commerce to Taipei to attend the second annual economic meeting between the two countries on 6 August 1993, despite China's protests.[38] On the same day the two countries signed an agreement of cooperation to develop Subic Bay. The total two-way trade between them rose from $1 billion in 1991 to over $1.5 billion in 1994.[39] Taiwan is now the third largest trading partner for the Philippines.[40]

In Indonesia, Taiwan became the top foreign investor in 1991, having injected $1,056.5 million into the country's economy, representing 12% of the total foreign investments in the country in that year. As of February 1994, Taiwan has invested a total of $4 billion, just behind Japan and Hong Kong.[41] Two-way trade rose from $2.4 billion in 1991 to over $3.2 billion in 1994.[42]

The Indonesian government is keen to turn Batam into an industrial zone. Situated just 20 km. from Singapore, Batam has the advantage of being close to the latter's industrial facilities. Also, it occupies a strategic position in the Strait of Malacca – an important passageway for East-West trade. Together with Singapore and the southern Malaysian state of Johor, the region has come to be known as a growth triangle.[43] In order to attract Taiwanese investments, the chief executive of the Batam SEZ visited Taipei in May 1993 to officiate the opening of a trade office there.[44] As a result of the visit by Chiang Pin-kung to Batam in November 1993, the Indonesian government promised to establish a Taiwan desk within its Investments Ministry to help Taiwanese to do business with Indonesians.[45] In a continued effort to attract Taiwanese investments, the Indonesian Investment Minister and Minister of Research and Technology visited Taipei in January and June 1994 respectively.[46]

Of these three places, Viet Nam is the principal target. Foreign investments in the country in the first half of 1993 doubled that in the same period a year before.[47] At present Taiwan is the biggest foreign investor in the country (see Table 14.2). Bilateral trade rose from $232 million in 1991 to over $870 million in 1994,[48] and to $1.3 billion in 1995 with a $700 million surplus in Taiwan's favour.[49]

Compared with the other two places, Viet Nam offers some attractive conditions.[50] First, the country is regarded by most Taiwanese investors as a piece of 'virgin' land for foreign investment, unlike the other two where more cumbersome government regulations are already in place. Secondly, Viet Nam and Taiwan share a relatively similar Confucian heritage, compared with Indonesia's Islamic faith and the Philippines' Christian back-

Table 14.2. VIET NAM'S TOP FIFTEEN INVESTORS: DIRECT INVESTMENTS, 1988-1994

| *Country/Area* | *Number of projects* | *Total amount (US$ million)* |
|---|---|---|
| 1. Taiwan | 164 | 1,901.2 |
| 2. Hong Kong | 164 | 1,551.0 |
| 3. Singapore | 74 | 1,054.9 |
| 4. South Korea | 92 | 860.3 |
| 5. Japan | 68 | 690.1 |
| 6. Australia | 44 | 683.6 |
| 7. Malaysia | 32 | 581.9 |
| 8. France | 59 | 545.6 |
| 9. Switzerland | 12 | 461.3 |
| 10. Virgin Islands | 10 | 355.5 |
| 11. Netherlands | 16 | 350.4 |
| 12. Britain | 14 | 344.6 |
| 13. Thailand | 42 | 226.6 |
| 14. United States | 26 | 223.3 |
| 15. Bermuda | 5 | 170.4 |
| 16. Others | 158 | 932.8 |
| *Total* | *980* | *10,933.5* |

Note: Taiwan more than doubled its investment in Viet Nam in 1995 to $1.2 billion, up 132% from 1994 (*FEER*, 15 February 1996, p. 55).

Source: Modified from information supplied by the State Committee for Cooperation and Investment, Viet Nam; quoted in *The Japan Times*, 14 April 1995, p. 14.

ground. Thirdly, the workforce in Viet Nam is more disciplined and its cost comparatively low, and their work ethics are similar.[51] Fourthly, the Taiwan government estimates that the lifting of the American trade embargo on Viet Nam and the improvement in bilateral relations will lead to a trade boom between Viet Nam and the US. By investing in Viet Nam in good time, Taiwan can expect to reap handsome profits in the near future.

Chiang Pin-kung's visits to Viet Nam in August 1993 and March 1994 paved the way for a surge of investments in the country. Now Viet Nam, together with mainland China and the United States, has become an important trading partner for Taiwan. To strengthen links with Viet Nam, Taiwan established in November 1992 a semi-governmental office in Hanoi and a trade office in Ho Chi Minh City.[52] Many Taiwanese banks and financial institutions are trying to set up branches in Viet Nam in order to facilitate investment financing. The Cathay Investments and Trust Company Limited was the first to open a branch in Hanoi in November 1993, after many years of negotiations with the Vietnamese government.[53] Other banks are trying to follow suit.[54] Furthermore, Taiwanese industrialists have purchased a large piece of industrial estate in Ho Chi Minh City for developing into factory floors for resale or rental to overseas investors.[55]

While Taiwan is concentrating on investments and trade with Viet Nam, it is also looking for business opportunities in neighbouring Cambodia and Myanmar. In late 1994 Taiwan and Singapore decided to join efforts to explore the Myanmar market.[56] In its drive to develop new markets in Indochina, Taiwan faces strong competition from France, the United States and other Western countries, in addition to Asian competitors like Hong Kong, South Korea and Japan.

### *The Coordination of Taiwanese Aid*

Southward Policy calls for the coordination of the policies of several government agencies, including the Ministries of Economic Affairs, Foreign Affairs, Finance and the central bank. Most of these agencies are also responsible for making Taiwan's aid policy.

The Taiwan government has admitted that aid is to be extended in coordination with its trading interest in Southeast Asia. The report on *nanjin zhengce* shows that loans have been extended through the International Economic Cooperation and Development Fund (set up by the government in 1988 to coordinate its aid programme) to Viet Nam, Indonesia and the Philippines. In December 1993 Taiwan decided to extend a loan amounting to $10 million to Viet Nam to help Taiwanese industrialists to set up factories in Hanoi, under a newly-established 'Recycle Fund for the Development of Industrial Zones'.[57] This loan was made in addition to another one worth $15 million approved earlier to help the central bank of Viet Nam to refinance the development of small- and medium-sized enterprises.[58] Another loan of $30 million was pledged in May 1993 to provide financial support to Taiwanese businessmen to help them develop the Hanoi industrial zone and to make improvements to the 97 km. highway linking Hanoi and the coastal city of Haiphong.[59]

Taiwan has also pledged to extend a loan worth $10 million to the Indonesian government to help finance the development of small- and medium-sized enterprises in Batam.[60] It has agreed to extend a loan of $23.57 million to the Philippines to develop an industrial park for Taiwanese merchants to set up their factories at Subic Bay. This is the first of three instalments that Taiwan is contributing towards the economic development of the Philippines. The eventual amount is estimated to reach $100 million. Similar loans extended to the Philippines are aimed at helping the country to develop its small- and medium-sized enterprises.[61]

Together the three countries received about 40% of the total amount of loans extended by Taiwan's International Economic Cooperation and Development Fund from 1988 to 1994.[62]

At this stage it is too early to assess the significance of Taiwan's aid to Southeast Asia because Taiwan began to extend loans to developing countries in 1990 and the extension of loans to Southeast Asia is even more recent. However, at least two policy shifts seem to be apparent. First, the above aid projects to some Southeast Asian countries indicate that Taiwan is beginning to use aid as a means to further its economic interests, apart from serving its political aims. The adoption of Southward Policy represents a shift towards giving more weight to economic considerations in Taiwan's aid policy. In this way Taiwan is acting in a way not dissimilar to most donor countries. Japan, for example, has been using its aid effectively to build a close relationship between government and industry to help its industrialists to gain access to overseas markets. Secondly, Taiwan's aid diplomacy has shifted from its traditional focus on Central America to a new one which includes Southeast Asia as well. Taiwan's relations with Central American countries are primarily guided by political objectives. It wants to maintain diplomatic relations with them and to win their support in its bid to re-enter the United Nations. Taiwan's relations with Southeast Asia, however, have an additional economic dimension because of the increasing economic linkages between Taiwan and countries in this region, apart from political-strategic considerations.

The amount of Taiwan's aid to Southeast Asia is, however, small compared with some major donor countries. In the case of Viet Nam, Taiwan's aid quantity ranks behind that of Japan, France, South Korea and others.

Several observations can be made from the above analysis. First, Taiwan's trade and aid are beginning to intertwine, with aid serving as a means to boost Taiwan's trade and commercial interests. The official adoption of Southward Policy marks the beginning of a new stage in this development.

Secondly, Taiwan's diplomacy is, to a large extent, economically or commercially led. The fact that the report on *nanjin zhengce* grew as a brainchild of the Ministry of Economic Affairs is a clear indication that the government attaches great importance to the use of its economic power to extend its diplomatic reach. Taiwan's economic strength and the political sensitivities of other countries towards it ensure that officials of the Ministry of Economic Affairs and the central bank of the country have greater access to international forums than their colleagues in the Ministry of Foreign Affairs. Once the economic returns from Taiwan are seen to be irresistibly large, some countries which have diplomatic relations with China will be tempted to find appropriate ways to deal with Taiwan in a semi-official capacity.

Thirdly, Taiwan has scored some successes in its effort to improve relations with Southeast Asian countries because the essence for success is there: the ASEAN countries welcome Taiwan's capital injection and in turn Taiwan needs their political recognition. Whether or not Southward Policy will succeed in the long run in diverting investments from China is difficult to predict. It will take several years before a clearer investment pattern emerges. Initial results show that this southward push is bearing some fruits: according to the Ministry of Economic Affairs, Taiwan's investments in Southeast Asia in the first half of 1994 reached $3.03 billion, which was 6.8 times the amount in the same period a year earlier. The cumulated amount of investments in the region had reached over $20 billion (see also Table 14.1).[63] The total two-way trade between Taiwan and the ASEAN countries plus Viet Nam increased from $12.5 billion in 1991 to over $18.3 billion in 1994.[64]

One important variable is the future developments across the Taiwan Strait. Any significant improvement in bilateral relations between China and Taiwan is likely to increase the confidence of Taiwanese investors in China and boost bilateral trade. Any deterioration in relations will have the opposite effect. Southward Policy would not lose its attractiveness, however, as it is prudent not to put too many eggs in one basket (in this case, China). Chiang Pin-kung pointed out that businessmen in Taiwan were free to conduct their businesses; what the government had been trying to do was to open up new opportunities and to identify ways to enhance and protect the interests of the country as a whole.[65]

The rapid increase in Taiwan's trade and investments in China is largely prompted by the private sector. Private businessmen are attracted to China by the prospects of potential profits as a result of the opening up of the market there. On the whole, market forces are at work, with the private business sector in Taiwan exerting pressure on the Taiwan government to relax its control over commercial activities with the mainland. Southward Policy, however, is a deliberate attempt by the government to diversify Taiwan's trade and investments so as to reduce its dependence on China. The recent rise in Taiwanese trade and investments in Southeast Asia is mainly generated by government or party controlled enterprises, as opposed to the initiatives taken by private enterprises driven mainly by market forces in the case of China trade. The strategic move by the Taiwan government represents a good example of the marriage between the government and the private sector in promoting Taiwan's economic interests.

China has criticised Southward Policy, especially its political aspect, as a move to strengthen Taiwan's substantive relations with Southeast Asia and to create a 'two-Chinas' situation. Within Taiwan itself there is a growing recognition, both within and outside of the government, that the pursuit of the policy should not harm Taiwan's economic interests with China and that Taiwan's southward push should serve to complement its 'westward policy' (towards China). A balance between the two is seen to be in the best interests of Taiwan.

Finally, Taiwan has reached a new stage in its economic development. It has to make overseas investments in order to shift abroad some of its own labour-intensive productions and to secure a supply of raw materials as well as a market for its industrial goods. Furthermore Taiwan has to look towards the Asian region for increased trade and investments so as to fend off potential trade protectionism in Europe and North America. The plan to develop Taiwan as an Asia-Pacific regional operations centre can be seen against this context.

Overall Southward Policy has helped to diversify Taiwan's trading relationships and to strengthen its political linkages with the outside world. In the post-cold war era where economic competition has gained relative prominence over military and strategic considerations, Taiwan needs to go beyond its traditional trading reliance on the United States, Japan, Europe and most recently China. As a policy move, Southward Policy represents yet another novel step in Taiwan's comprehensive and pragmatic diplomacy.

## NOTES

For the sake of standardisation, the pinyin transliteration has been adopted throughout this chapter except for names of people living in Taiwan where the Wade-Giles system is used.

[1] Senegal in West Africa was the latest country to establish diplomatic relations with the Republic of China on 3 January 1996 (*FEER*, 18 January 1996, p. 13).

[2] F. Ching, 'Taiwan faces new challenge', *FEER*, 24 March 1994, p. 32.

[3] The Standing Committee of the National People's Congress passed a piece of legislation in January 1994 to protect Taiwanese investments in China (*Beijing Review*, 28 March-3 April 1994, p. 7; *China Daily*, Beijing, 1 April 1994, p. 4). The effectiveness of this law has yet to be tested.

[4] The official English translation of the term *nanjin zhengce* is southward policy. See the advertising section in *Foreign Affairs* 73 (5), September/October 1994. However, southbound policy, go-south policy, and *südpolitik* have been used by English newspapers in Taipei to refer to this policy (*The China Post*, Taipei, 2 November 1993, p. 9).

[5] Pin-kung Chiang, *Nanjin Zhengce Baogao* (*A Report on Southward Policy*), report, Minister of Economic Affairs, Economics Committee of the Legislative Yuan, 27 December 1993a, p. 1.

[6] Interview with Dr Chen Hurng-yu, research fellow at the Institute of International Relations, National Chengchi University, Taipei, 29 December 1993. See also *Lifayuan Gongbao (Legislative Gazette)*, Taipei: Legislative Yuan, 1994, pp. 412, 419, and 420.

[7] *Lian He Bao* (United Daily News), Taiwan, 18 February 1994, p. 1.

[8] *Lifayuan Gongbao*, 83 (4), 1994, p. 410.

[9] *Jingji Ribao* (*Economic Daily News*), Taipei, 1 November 1993, p. 1. All currencies quoted in this chapter are in US dollars.

[10] *Ziyou Shibao* (*Liberty Times*), Taipei, 10 November 1993, p. 19.

[11] *Lian He Bao*, 1 January 1994, p. 19; *Time*, 12 February 1996, p. 26.

[12] The trade statistics quoted in the rest of this paragraph are taken from Chiang, op. cit., 1993a, p. 2. The total two-way trade in the whole of 1993 reached $16.7 billion (*Lian He Bao*, 15 February 1994, p. 3).

[13] Chiang, op. cit., 1993a, p. 2.

[14] Taiwan's economic push towards Southeast Asia is reminiscent of Japan's similar push towards the region since 1965. The years 1975 and 1986 represented two waves of Japanese investments in the region. However, Japan encounters more difficulties in such a move than Taiwan, partly because of the lingering memories of Japanese atrocities during the Second World War and partly because Taiwanese merchants benefit from a network of overseas Chinese traders in the region. Some Japanese companies are trying to cooperate with

Taiwanese merchants in expanding their market share in the region. Both countries can benefit from such cooperation and division of labour: Taiwan can benefit from Japan's business experiences, technologies, and capital injection, avoid falling into business traps, and ease over possible political problems; while Japan can benefit by tapping into Taiwanese business networks and industrial bases in the region. The only impediment is perhaps their mutual suspicion and mistrust of each other (*Jingji Ribao*, 6 December 1993, p. 6). According to Chiang Pin-kung, cases of cooperation between Japan and Taiwan in developing the Southeast Asian market are rare and fewer than those in the China market (*Lifayuan Gongbao*, 1994, p. 430).

[15] *The China Post*, 2 November 1993, p. 9.

[16] *Lian He Bao*, 1 January 1994, p. 19.

[17] 'Asia Now', New Zealand Television One, 20 November 1993.

[18] *Beijing Review*, 20-26 June 1994, p. 26.

[19] *Beijing Review*, 13-19 March 1995, p. 16.

[20] 'Asia Now', op. cit., 20 November 1993.

[21] *Zhongyang Ribao (Central Daily News)*, Taipei, 23 December 1993, p. 7.

[22] *Beijing Review*, 13-19 March 1995, p. 16.

[23] The reasons for such a big increase in trade and investment across the Taiwan Strait are interesting. Most of the Taiwanese traders have family ties in China and networks of friendships and associations. The people on both sides share a common traditional culture and use basically the same language. Added to these are the geographic proximity, economic complementarity and political will on both sides. Above all the cost of labour in China is very low compared with Southeast Asia. Allowing for regional differences, the present rate in China is about the same as in Viet Nam, $38 per month, compared with Malaysia ($160), Thailand ($100), Indonesia ($50), the Philippines ($154) and Singapore ($1,025) (Chiang, op. cit., 1993a, p. 10; and *Lian He Bao*, 8 August 1993, p. 3). See also *Time*, 12 February 1996, p. 26

[24] *Zhongshi Wanbao* (*China Times Evening Post*), Taipei, 15 February 1994, p. 3.

[25] *Huashi* (CTS) evening news, 27 December 1993.

[26] *Jiushi Niandai* (*The Nineties*), Hong Kong, February 1994, pp. 52-5.

[27] *Lifayuan Gongbao*, 1994, p. 424.

[28] *Lian He Bao*, 18 February 1994.

[29] *Time*, 18 April 1994, p. 21.

[30] The roles and functions of these associations are interesting. So far Western literature on international organisations has given little attention to their significance in the international system – a gap which can only be filled by further research.

[31] Tuan Y. Cheng, 'The ROC's changing role in the Asia-Pacific in the 1990s', in Gary Klintworth (ed.), *Taiwan in the Asia-Pacific in the 1990s*, St Leonards, NSW: Allen & Unwin, 1993, p. 69.

[32] *Zhangyang Ribao*, 18 February 1994, p. 2.

[33] Kay Moller, 'A new role for the ROC on Taiwan in the post-cold war era', *Issues & Studies*, 31 (2), February 1995, pp. 67-86.

[34] *Taiwan: An Asia-Pacific Regional Operations Center*, Taipei: Government Information Office, 1995, p. 17.

[35] *The China Post*, 12 February 1994, p. 1.

[36] *FEER* 27 April 1995, p. 22.

[37] *Asiaweek*, 2 February 1994, p. 20.

[38] *Lian He Bao*, 8 August 1993, p. 3.

[39] Ministry of Economic Affairs, Republic of China, quoted in Parris H. Chang, 'Foreign security cooperation in Asia-Pacific region: a Taiwan perspective', *Journal of East Asian*

*Affairs*, 9 (2), Summer/Fall 1995, p. 399.
[40] *Jingji Ribao*, 7 August 1993, p. 9.
[41] *Xingdao Ribao (Xingdao Daily)*, Hong Kong, 14 February 1994, p. A2.
[42] Chang, op. cit., 1995, p. 399.
[43] For some discussion on Singapore's economic strategy towards this growth triangle, see Garry Rodan, 'Reconstructing divisions of labour: Singapore's new regional emphasis', in R. Higgott et al (eds), *Pacific Economic Relations in the 1990s: Cooperation or Conflict?*, St Leonards, NSW: Allen & Unwin, 1993, pp. 223-49. Other growth triangles in Asia include the South China triangle which groups together Hong Kong, Taiwan and the Chinese provinces of Guangdong and Fujian; the Tumen River triangle in northeast Asia, and others (*Time*, 17 January 1994, pp. 18-20).
[44] *Qingnian Ribao (Youth Daily)*, Taipei, 6 May 1993, p. 6.
[45] *Economic Reporter*, 22 November 1993, p. 41.
[46] *The Republic of China Yearbook 1995*, p. 177.
[47] 'Asia Now', op. cit., 30 January 1994.
[48] Chang, op. cit., 1995, p. 399.
[49] *FEER*, 15 February 1996, p. 55.
[50] *Jingji Ribao*, 1 November 1993, p. 6.
[51] It is interesting to note that because of the large amount of construction work occurring in Taiwan, notably the building of the underground rapid system and the second highway linking Keelung and Kaohsiung, and the relatively high cost of local labour, thousands of foreign workers are brought into the country on contract terms to work for two to three years. Most of these are from Thailand, not from the Philippines, because Thai workers are regarded as more disciplined and hard-working than Filipino workers. Also Filipino workers are more inclined to take industrial action than their Thai counterparts (my field work in Taipei in December 1993). As of early 1994, some 30,000 Thais were employed officially in Taiwan and another 30,000 were working illegally (*China News*, 15 February 1994, p. 1).
[52] *Lian He Bao*, 8 August 1993, p. 3.
[53] *Ziyou Shibao*, 10 November 1993, p. 19.
[54] As of December 1993 only seven overseas banks had branches operating in Viet Nam (*Lifayuan Gongbao*, 1994, p. 425), *Jingji Ribao*, 8 November 1993, p. 6 and 6 December 1993, p. 6.
[55] *FEER*, 22 September 1994, p. 80.
[56] *Zhongyang Ribao*, 16 November 1994, p. 1.
[57] *Jingji Ribao*, 15 December 1993, p. 2, and *The China Post*, 9 October 1993, p. 9.
[58] Pin-kung Chiang, *Jingjibu Yuanwai Zhengce Ji Zhixing Chengxiao Baogao* (*A Report on the Ministry of Economic Affairs' Foreign Assistance Policy and Operations*), tabled at the Legislative Yuan, 27 December 1993b, p. 9.
[59] *Jingji Ribao*, 13 December 1993, p. 6.
[60] *Jingji Ribao*, 23 November 1993, p. 2.
[61] Chiang, op. cit., 1993a, pp. 3-5.
[62] My estimation based on information obtained from various issues of the Fund's newsletters.
[63] *Zhongyang Ribao*, international ed., 30 July 1994, p. 7.
[64] Chang, op. cit., 1995, p. 399.
[65] *Huashi* (CTS) evening news, 27 December 1993.

# 15. POPULATION CHANGE AND DEVELOPMENT IN INDONESIA

*Graeme Hugo*

Six out of ten of the world's inhabitants in mid-1994 lived in the Asia-Pacific region, and most major political, economic and social debates in the Pacific Rim must address the issue of population. The population of the region has undergone profound change in the last quarter century as both a cause and a consequence of the massive economic, social and political changes which have swept across the region.

By 1990, the United Nations[1] reported that only eight Asia-Pacific nations[2] had not entered the transition to low fertility. Across the region the Total Fertility Rate (TFR)[3] fell from 5.06 in the early 1970s to 3.48 in the late 1980s, while Life Expectancy at Birth[4] increased from 55.6 years to 62.7 years.[5] Population mobility has reached unprecedented levels so that the spatial distribution of population is changing rapidly. The proportion of Asians living in urban areas has increased from 23.4% in 1970 to 34.6% in 1995, while the numbers of urban residents more than doubled from 503 to 1,198 million.[6]

Migration between nations in the region and out of the region has reached unprecedented levels initiating flows of remittances which are impinging upon economic and social change. While the huge diversity in the Asia-Pacific Rim nations ensures that it is not possible to generalise for the entire region, it is instructive to examine in some detail the change which has occurred in one country in the region. Accordingly, the present chapter focuses on Indonesia which, with an estimated population of 198 million residents in mid-1995, is the world's fourth most populous nation. Moreover, Indonesia has experienced substantial social and economic change since the early 1970s.[7]

The chapter begins by analysing the trends and components of population change during the Suharto era, focusing especially upon fertility and mortality trends. Indonesia's population problem has often been depicted as one of 'unbalanced' distribution rather than of excessive growth. Accordingly, the next section of the chapter addresses the issue of the changing distribution of the population paying special attention to the balance between regions, urban and rural areas and on changing levels and trends in population mobility.

Indonesia's age structure has a broad base, typifying the situation in most Less Developed Countries (LDCs). Hence the implications of this for education and labour force planning are traced. It is also noted that Indonesia, like many Asian nations, is poised for substantial growth in its elderly population. Finally, few countries have placed a greater emphasis on policy interventions to influence patterns of population growth, structure and distribution than Indonesia has, and the chapter assesses the impact of these interventions.

## *Population Growth and Development*

The trajectory of Indonesia's population growth is depicted in Figure 15.1. In the early years of independence, relatively low rates of population growth occurred due to the disruption caused by economic depression, Japanese occupation and the War of Independence with the Dutch. Hence the population grew by only 1.5% per annum over that period. With improvements in mortality in the 1960s and 1970s, the annual growth rate accelerated to 2.1% and 2.4% respectively. However, the decline in fertility which began in the 1970s saw the annual population growth rate decline to 2.2% in the early 1980s and 1.8% in the latter half of that decade. That decline has continued such that the current annual rate of growth is estimated to be 1.6% per annum and over the Sixth Five Year Plan (Repelita VI 1993-98), the population is anticipated to increase at 1.5% per annum so that by 1998 the population will number 204.4 million.[8]

Figure 15.1. INDONESIA: POPULATION GROWTH, 1600-1993

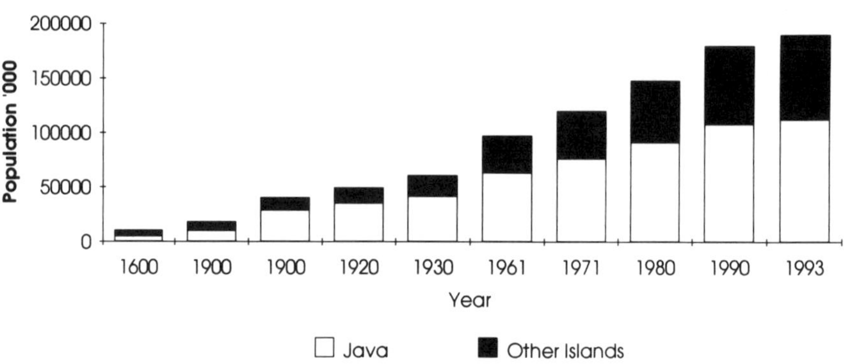


Source: G.J. Hugo et al, *The Demographic Dimension in Indonesia Development*, Singapore, OUP, 1987, p. 31; Biro Pusat Statistik (BPS), *Tren Fertilitas, Mortalitas dan Migrasi*, Jakarta: BPS, 1994; World Bank, *World Development Report 1994 – Infrastructure for Development*, New York: OUP, 1994.

The debate over population growth and economic and social development has raged since Malthus' controversial work of two centuries ago. In the contemporary situation, there is little argument that the demographic transition tends to be strongly associated with improvement in the average economic and social situation of individuals in any given country. In other words, the transition occurs where there is movement from a situation where population growth rates are low because, while fertility and mortality rates are high, mortality levels are much lower than fertility, to a situation of 'low equilibrium' and slow population growth with low levels of both fertility and mortality.

There is debate, however, over the nature and even the direction of the causal relationships involved in this association. In the early post-war decades, there was a view that fertility decline was a necessary precondition to economic development. In the 1960s and 1970s in reaction to this, many argued that economic development was the necessary cause of reductions in population growth and fertility – a view encapsulated in the ubiquitous slogan emerging from the 1970s equivalent of the 1994 Cairo International Conference on Population and Development held in Bucharest, that *'Development is the Best Contraceptive'*. However, over the last two decades, there has been a shift in this view and a consensus that the relationship is much more complex and that rapid economic development was not a necessary condition for the fertility transition, although it could certainly assist and accelerate it. This view was bolstered by the fact that countries like Indonesia and China achieved substantial fertility declines with only minor improvements in the economic well-being of their populations and certainly not the massive industrialisation and urbanisation previously thought to be necessary for the fertility transition.

In the Indonesian context, Figure 15.2 shows that economic growth has considerably outpaced population growth over the last three decades. In-

Figure 15.2. INDONESIA: GDP AND POPULATION GROWTH RATES, 1965-1994

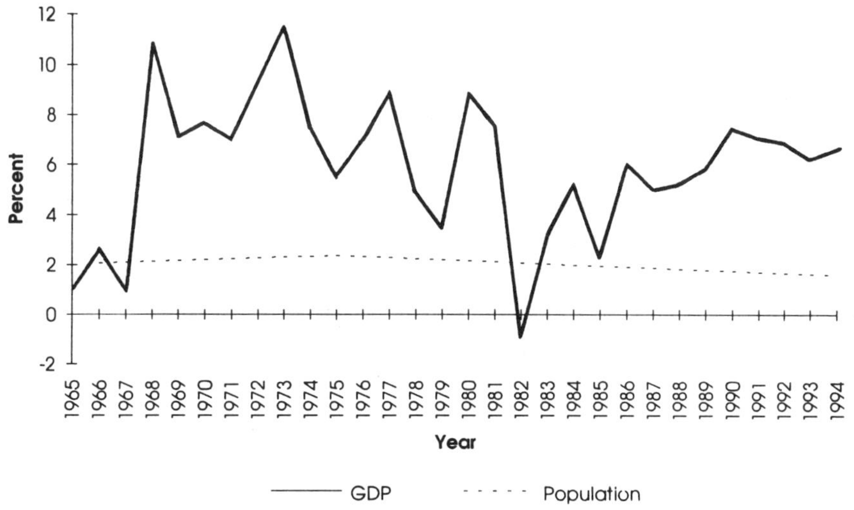


Source: H. Hill, *Indonesia's New Order: The Dynamics of Socioeconomic Transformation*, Sydney: Allen and Unwin, 1994; Indonesian Censuses of 1961, 1971, 1980, 1990.

deed, the average rate of growth in GDP over the 1969-94 First Twenty-Five Year Plan period was 6.8% per annum.[9] This is three times the average rate of population growth over the same period. Indonesia's rapid economic growth in the 1970s and early 1980s was fuelled largely by global increases in oil prices. However, with the decline in oil prices and realignment of international currencies in the mid-1980s, the Indonesian government transformed its economic strategy and adopted a strongly market-oriented approach. Accordingly, strong economic growth has been maintained although this has been largely on the basis of growth of non-oil exports, especially from the rapidly expanding manufacturing sector. In the 1990s there appeared to be something of a divergence in rates of growth of population and the economy so that in 1994 the economy was expanding at a rate of 6.6% per annum, four times the growth rate of the population (1.6%).

The Malthusian argument was based primarily on population growth rates being substantially faster than the growth in the means of subsistence. Accordingly, it is interesting to examine changes in the production of food in Indonesia. Figure 15.3 shows the growth of national production of the staple food of most of Indonesia, rice, over the last quarter century. The output of rice over the 1968-92 period almost trebled from 17.156 million tons to 47.293 million tons while the population increased by less than three quarters. This was largely achieved through an increase in productiv-

Figure 15.3. INDONESIA: RICE-AREA HARVESTED, PRODUCTION AND YIELD, 1974-1992

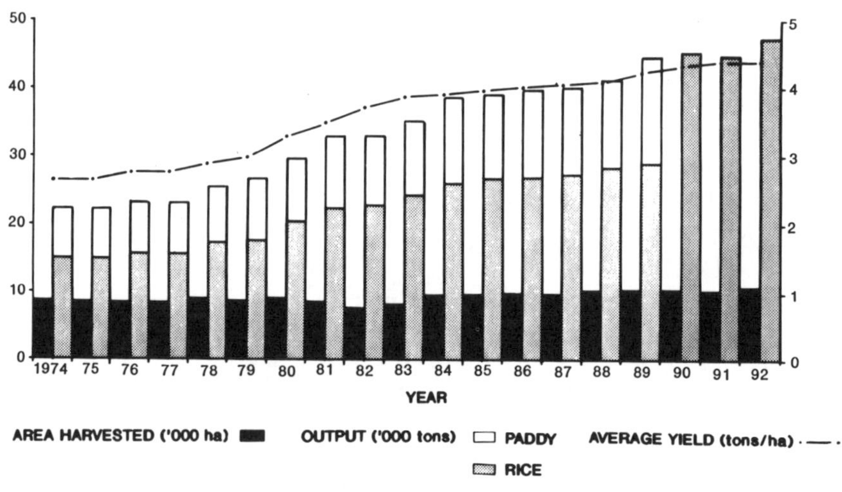


Source: World Bank, op. cit., 1991, p. 194; Indonesia, *Indonesia: A Quarter Century of Progress (1969-1993)*, Jakarta, 1993, p. 75.

ity since the area under rice increased by only 35.5% over that period while the output per hectare rose from 2.13 tons per hectare to 4.35.[10] Hence availability of rice produced in Indonesia has increased more than three times faster than population over the last quarter century. Nevertheless, some would question the sustainability of such a rapid increase in food production given its reliance upon substantial inputs of fertilizers and pesticides and the evidence of increasing environmental degradation.

Much of the expansion in rice production has been achieved through increasing inputs other than labour, although cumulative growth in real agricultural labour productivity was only 10% in the 1980s.[11] The last decade has seen agriculture's share of Indonesia's workforce fall below half for the first time while its share of GDP has fallen below one fifth. It is anticipated that Indonesia's agricultural workforce will begin to decline in numbers in the late 1990s.[12] The 1970s saw a number of modernising and commercialising changes in agricultural technology and practice in Indonesia[13] which led to some displacement of workers from agriculture. However, Naylor[14] has pointed to a number of further such developments which are likely to displace more agricultural labour in the 1990s, especially women.

Despite Indonesia's rapid economic growth in the last quarter century, it is still squarely within the ranks of the world's LDCs. In 1992 it was estimated that GNP per capita was only US$670 – the lowest of the ASEAN nations.[15] Government's official estimates of Indonesians living below the poverty line indicate that the number fell from 54.2 million in 1976 to 27.2 million in 1990.[16] There is considerable debate about the level of poverty in Indonesia although not about the fact that its incidence has declined over the last three decades. Substantial variations exist between different parts of Indonesia in the incidence of poverty.

Figure15. 4 shows that in one set of estimates, the proportion of people living in poverty in 1990 varied between 1.3% in the capital, Jakarta, to 45.6% in East Nusa Tenggara.[17] The highest incidence of poverty tends to be in Southern Sumatra, Central and East Java, Nusa Tenggara, West Kalimantan, Sulawesi and Maluku.

### *Fertility and Mortality*

In examining population growth trends, it is important to examine the components of that growth separately. Of all the waves of social, economic and demographic change which have transformed Indonesia over the last quarter century, none has been so striking or far reaching as the decline in fertility. Women in Indonesia are now having only half as many children as their counterparts in the 1960s. The TFR has declined steadily since the late 1960s when it stood at around 5.6 children per woman to 5.2 in the early 1970s and 4.68 in the late 1970s. At the 1990 census the TFR for the 1985-90 period was 3.326, and at the 1994 Indonesian Demographic and Health Survey a level of 2.856 was recorded for the previous two years.

Figure 15.4. INDONESIA: PERCENTAGE LIVING IN POVERTY BY PROVINCE, 1990

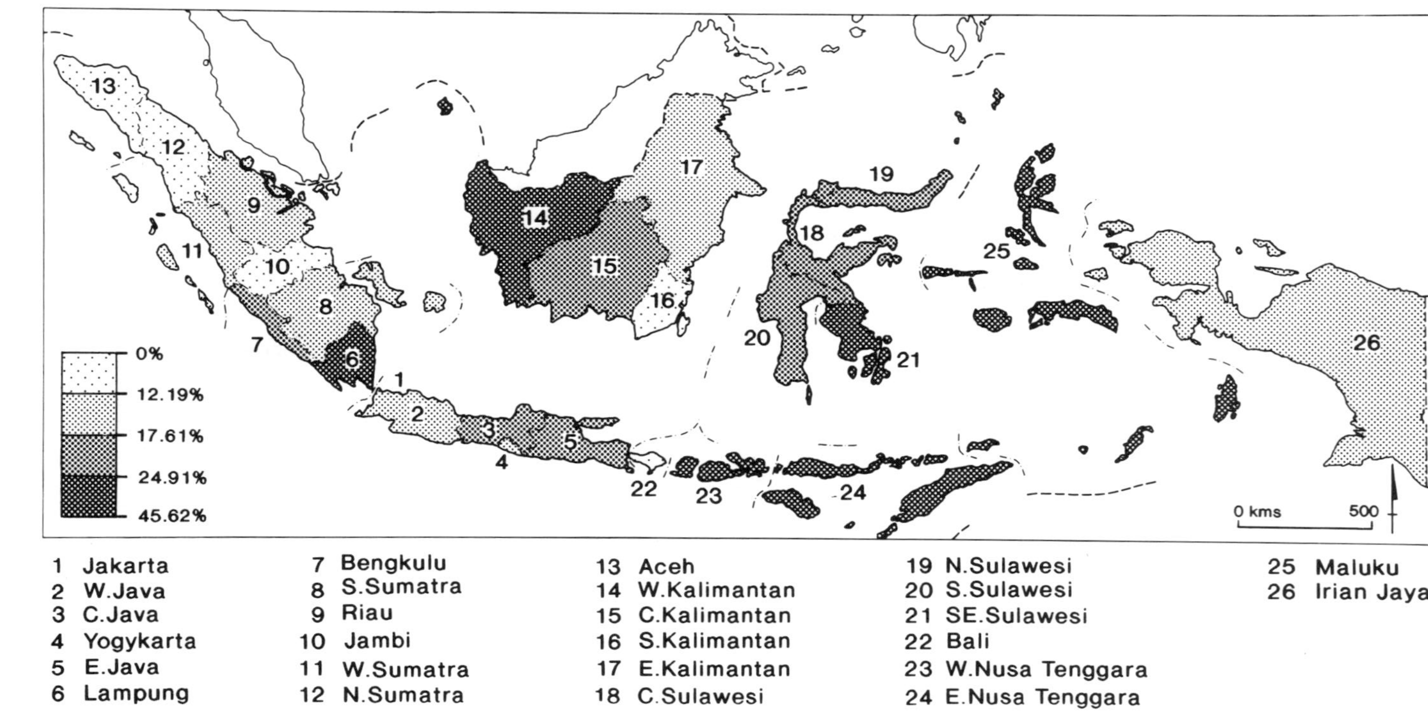


Source: B. Bidani and M. Ravallion, 'A regional poverty profile for Indonesia', *Bulletin of Indonesian Economic Studies,* 29 (3), 1993, p. 53.

While fertility has declined among most groups in Indonesia, Figure 15.5 shows that there still remain significant differences between different regions of Indonesia. Fertility is considerably lower in Inner Indonesia than it is in the Outer Islands.

In 1994, the TFR in Java-Bali was 2.6 compared with 3.26 in the larger Outer Island provinces (Aceh, North Sumatra, West Sumatra, South Sumatra, Lampung, West Kalimantan, South Kalimantan, North Sulawesi, South Sulawesi, West Nusa Tenggara) and 3.3 in the other provinces. This is one of the major reasons why population growth in the Outer Islands outpaces that in Java-Bali. For example, over the 1980-90 decade, Java's population grew at only 1.64% per annum while that of Sumatra grew at 2.47%.

However, there are considerable variations within these broad regions. In 1994, fertility was at or below replacement in Yogyakarta (1.79), Jakarta (1.9) and in the large province of East Java (2.22). The island of Bali too has experienced a remarkable fertility decline to reach a TFR of 2.143 in 1994. Central Java lagged a little with a TFR of 2.77 but the largest province, West Java, had above-national average levels with a TFR of 3.17.

The processes shaping the decline in fertility are complex but are definitely associated with significant changes in the role and status of women and in the structure and functioning of the family. This involves a move away from extended families to nuclear families and involves changes in intergenerational relationships, selection of marriage partners, relationships between marriage partners, etc. These social changes are associated with the introduction of universal education, the penetration of mass media, and the reduction of the significance of the family as a unit of production. The national family planning programme has undoubtedly played a significant role. In 1972, only 400,000 couples were practising some form of family planning, whereas in 1993 there were 21.3 million. In 1994, 96.3% of currently married women interviewed in the National Demographic and Health Survey indicated that they had knowledge of at least one method of family planning.

Despite considerable improvements in recent decades, Indonesia's current life expectancy at birth (58 years for males, 62 for females) is below that of its ASEAN neighbours of Brunei (71), Malaysia (71), Philippines (64), Singapore (74) and Thailand (69). It is estimated that around the time of the 1971 census, male and female life expectancy at birth was around 45 and 48 respectively. Hence the last two decades have seen an improvement of almost 30%. Much of this has been associated with a substantial decline in the Infant Mortality Rate (IMR),[18] estimated to be 145 in 1971, 109 in 1980 and 71 in 1990.[19] Infant mortality is considerably higher among males (79 in 1990) than for females (64). Moreover, as Figure 15.6 shows, there are substantial inter-regional variations in the IMR.

This rate is a sensitive indicator of well-being and it is those provinces which are economically better off and have good access to health facilities

Figure 15.5. INDONESIA: TOTAL FERTILITY RATE BY PROVINCE, 1994

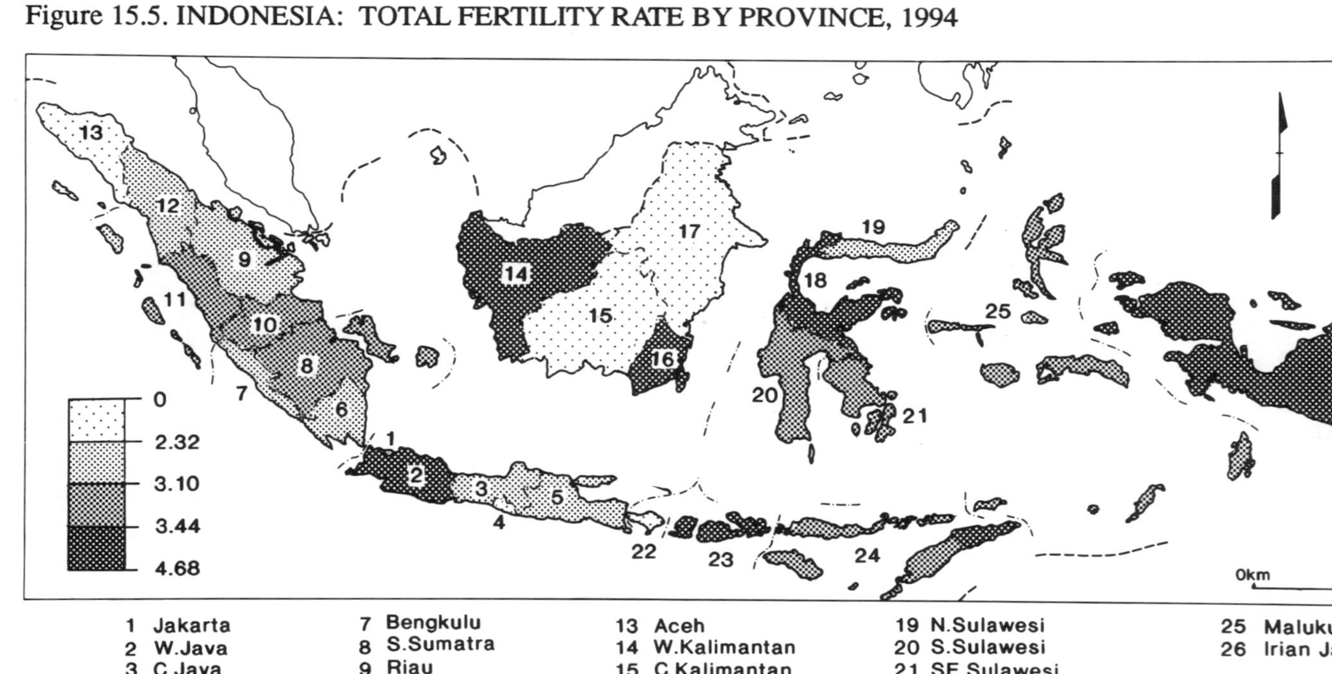


Source: Demographic and Health Survey (DHS), *Indonesia Demographic and Health Survey 1991*, Jakarta: Central Bureau of Statistics, National Family Planning Coordinating Board and Ministry of Health, 1994.

that have the lowest levels of infant mortality. These include Jakarta (40) and Yogyakarta (42). On the other hand, the highest levels of infant mortality tend to occur in the poorer and more isolated provinces, especially in eastern Indonesia (Figure 15.6). Several factors have been associated with the improvements in mortality including the overall improvement in availability and access to food and safe water, education, immunisation and better health services. Nevertheless, infectious diseases remain major causes of death in Indonesia and much remains to be done in the public health, nutrition and sanitation areas as well as in improving real access to basic but high quality health services.

## *Population Distribution and Internal Migration*

Former President Soekarno frequently articulated Indonesia's population problem as being one of 'unbalanced' distribution rather than excessive growth. Figure 15.7 shows that there is a marked difference in population density between 'Inner Indonesia' (Java, Bali and Madura) which in 1990 supported 61.5% of Indonesia's population on 6.9% of the nation's land area, and Outer Indonesia. However, this contrast to a large degree accurately reflects variations in resource endowments and ecological situations between that nation's provinces. Moreover, perceptions of Outer Indonesia as being 'empty' are far from accurate – if Sumatra were a separate nation, its 37 million inhabitants would make it the world's 28th largest nation. While there are parts of the Outer Islands which have potential for development, policies which seek to solve the population growth problem by 'evening out' the distribution of Indonesia's population through massive migration programmes are not feasible either in terms of the potential of the destination areas to absorb them or in terms of the logistic costs of transferring millions of people out of Java and settling them elsewhere. Indonesia has had a transmigration programme to transfer people from Inner to Outer Indonesia since the first decade of this century, although its goals are now predominantly articulated in terms of regional development in the Outer Islands rather than demographic redistribution. Nevertheless, the uneven distribution of population in Indonesia depicted in Figure 15.7 is one of the most salient features of the nation's demography.

For most of this century, Java's population has been growing more slowly than that of Outer Indonesia, with the proportion of Indonesians living in Java declining from around two-thirds at the time of Independence to 60% at the 1990 census. This was given particular impetus in the late 1970s and early 1980s when some 1.29 million families (around 5 million people) were moved under the auspices of the transmigration programme. However, the shift in government policy in the late 1980s to facilitate investment and industrialisation is tending to favour growth in Java. Between 1985 and 1990, the number of people moving into Java (773,789) was almost as great as the number moving in the opposite direction (973,340).

It is not possible to establish the level of population mobility in Indone-

Figure 15.6. INDONESIA: INFANT MORTALITY RATE BY PROVINCE, 1990

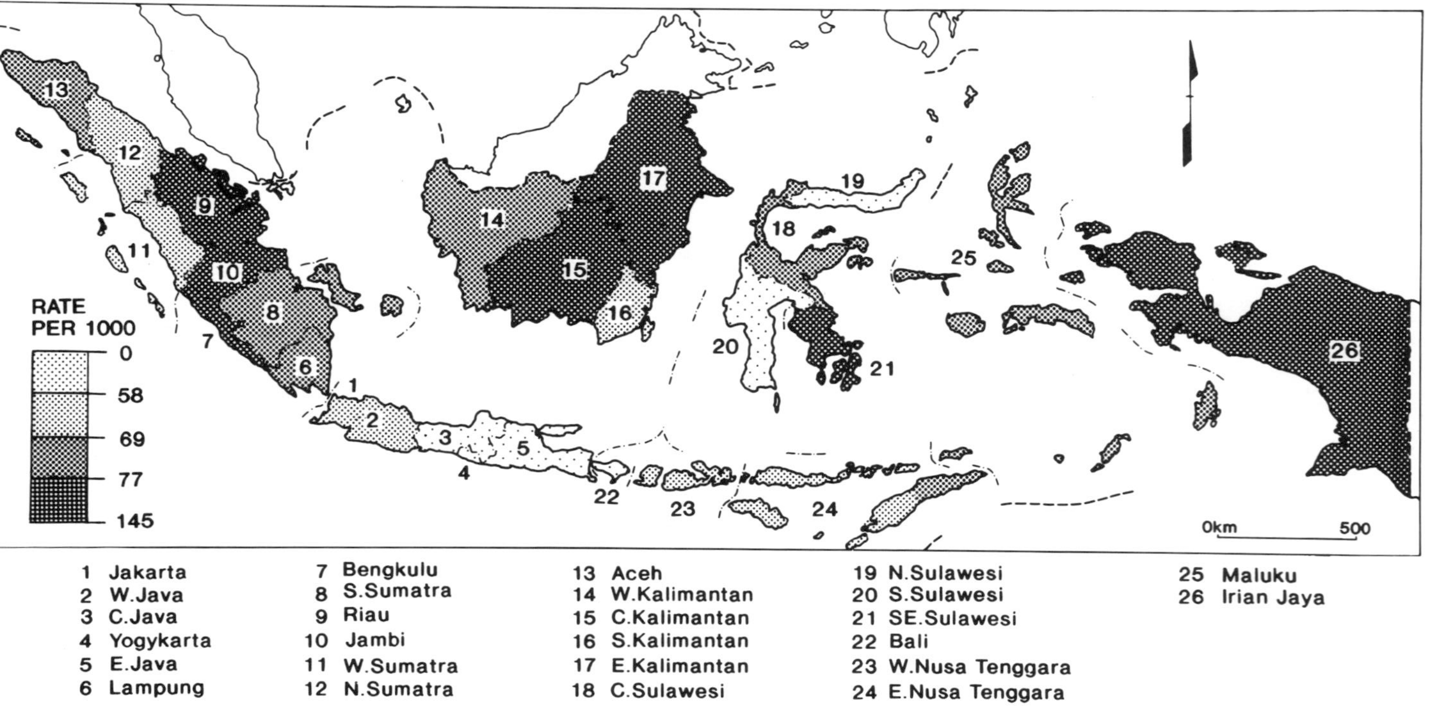


Source: BPS, op. cit., 1994, p. 68.

Figure 15.7. INDONESIA: POPULATION DENSITY, 1990 (persons per square km.)

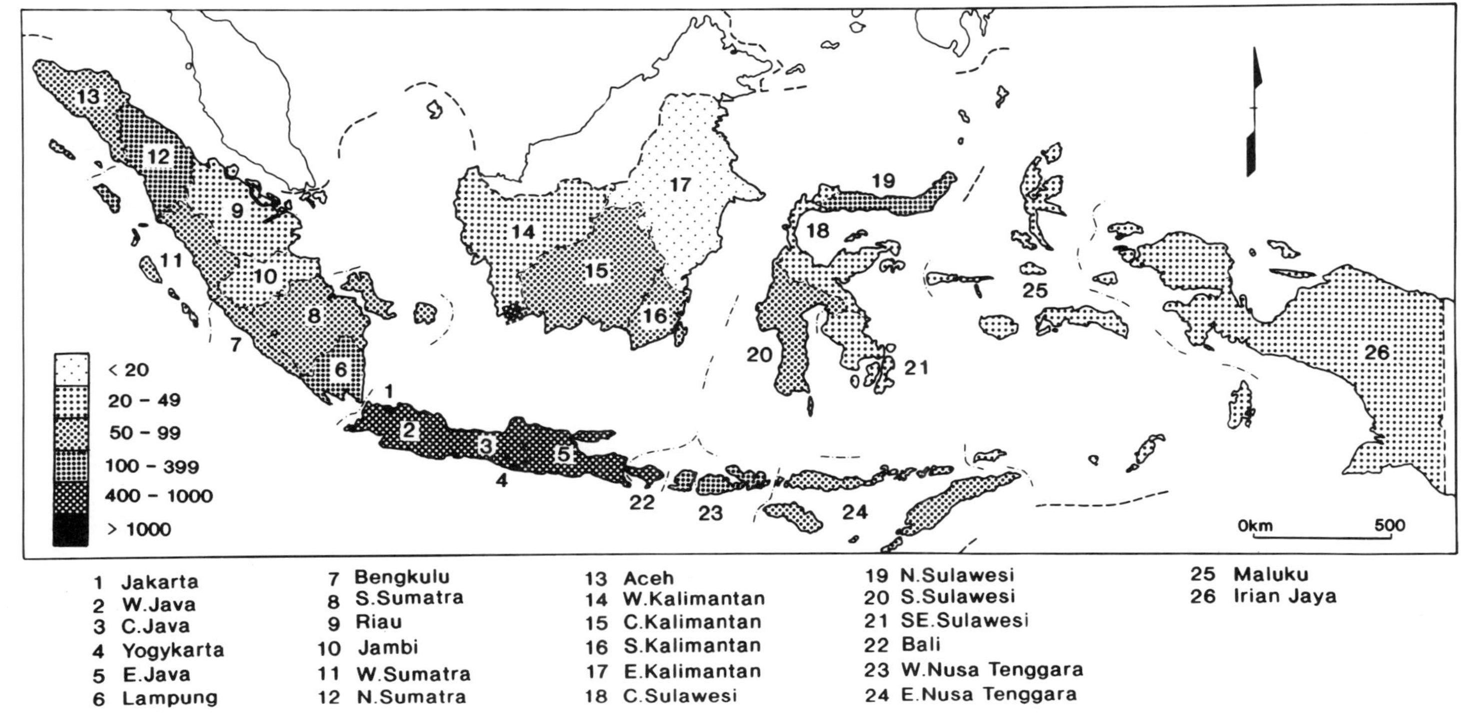


Source: Census of Indonesia, 1990.

sia because the census question detects only a small sub-set of significant movements.[20] At the 1990 census, some 10.62% of males and 9.03% of females had lived in a different province to the one in which they were enumerated. Census data capture only more or less permanent movement between provinces, and it is apparent that intra-provincial movement is substantially greater than that between provinces.

Nevertheless, Table 15.1 shows that there has been a substantial increase in inter-provincial migration rates between 1971 and 1990 and this is undoubtedly indicative of an overall increase in mobility.

Inter-provincial migration, together with the variations in fertility and

Table 15.1. INDONESIA: POPULATION WHO EVER LIVED IN ANOTHER PROVINCE, %

| | *Males* | *Females* |
|---|---|---|
| 1971 | 6.29 | 5.06 |
| 1985 | 8.37 | 7.29 |
| 1990 | 10.62 | 9.03 |
| 1985 Intra-provincial* | 7.04 | 6.75 |
| Five-year migrants | | |
| Inter-provincial 1985 | 2.07 | 1.85 |
| Intra-provincial 1985 | 1.97 | 1.89 |
| Inter-provincial 1990 | 3.48 | 3.05 |

* Moved between regencies (kabupaten), within provinces.

Source: Indonesian Censuses of 1971 and 1990; Intercensal Survey of 1985.

mortality mentioned earlier, has led to significant major regional differences in population growth as is depicted in Figure 15.8.

- *Java's* population grew at low rates during the 1980s – 1.8% per annum in the early 1980s (compared with 2.2% for Indonesia as a whole) and 1.5% in the late 1980s (compared with 1.8%). This was partly a function of the lower fertility in Java than elsewhere but also due to net outmigration from Java to the Outer Islands.
    - *Jakarta* recorded a very low rate of population growth in the late 1980s
        - 0.9%, compared with rates of around 4% per annum over the previous half century. It is clear, however, that this understates the true rate of growth of Jakarta because:
        - Jakarta's residential development has overspilled into the adjoining West Java *Kabupaten* of Bogor, Tanggerang and Bekasi. It is estimated[21] by Jakarta's government that half a million

workers each day commute into Jakarta from adjoining areas. A great deal of Jakarta's new manufacturing employment has also been established in these 'overspill' areas. There has been significant suburbanisation created by Jakarta residents moving out to the adjoining areas of West Java.

- Many residents of Jakarta have recently migrated to the capital but have not registered locally and will have indicated in the census that their home area was their usual place of residence.
- In addition, many people engage in circular migration whereby they work much of the year in Jakarta but keep their family and their stated place of usual residence in their home village. Hence, while they are part of Jakarta's labour force, they are not counted as Jakarta residents at the time of the census.[22]

- *West Java*, on the other hand, grew at well above the national average in the late 1980s (2.8%) and more than twice the rate of other Java provinces. This was partly due to its higher fertility levels but also due to the 'overspill' from Jakarta. West Java was the only Java province to increase its rate of growth between the early 1980s and late 1980s.
- *Elsewhere in Java*, growth rates were very low. In particular, Yogyakarta's population actually recorded a decline between 1985 and 1990. These low growth rates were a function of both low fertility and outmigration to the Outer Islands and to the Jakarta-West Java urban complex.
- In *Sumatra*, a diversity of patterns of growth is in evidence. Especially striking here is the fact that *Lampung's* population barely grew at all between 1985 and 1990 after several decades of growth rates in excess of 5% per annum. This dramatic change was partly due to the government's decision in the early 1980s to stop transmigration from Java to Lampung. Indeed, Lampung now is similar in many ways to the areas in Java which the transmigrants originally left. Other reasons for its lack of growth include the opening of a new road to neighbouring Bengkulu which has facilitated outmigration and resulted in *Bengkulu* having one of the fastest rates of growth in the nation in the 1980s (4.6% per annum in the late 1980s, second only to Riau). Another element in Lampung's population stability is that, like rural Java, Lampung is losing migrants to large urban areas, especially in nearby Jakarta-West Java. Hence Lampung has gone from being the nation's most consistently fast-growing province for the first 85 years of this century to having the second slowest growth rate in the nation in the late 1980s.
- Rapid rates of population growth were recorded in *Riau* where oil-related employment is increasingly being supplemented by the industrial developments in Batam and Bintan. The latter are associated with the *Growth Triangle* concept which sees the development of urban Singapore overspilling into adjoining areas of Malaysia (Johore Baru) and Indonesia. Other provinces in Sumatra to record high rates of growth included the provinces where substantial natural resource exploitation occurs – Jambi,

Figure 15.8. INDONESIA: AVERAGE ANNUAL GROWTH RATE BY PROVINCE, 1980-1990

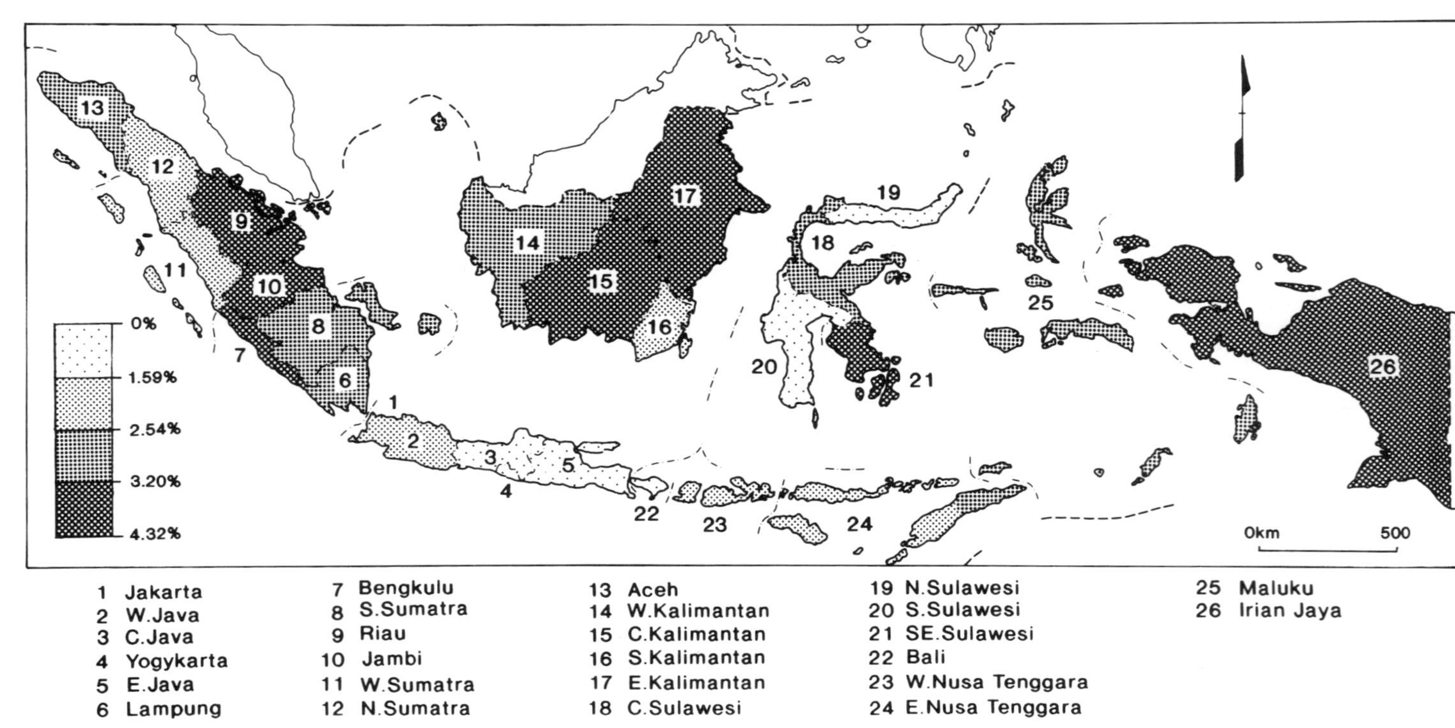


Source: Calculated from Indonesian Censuses of 1980 and 1990.

South Sumatra and Aceh. West and North Sumatra continue to be major areas of outmigration and their populations grew at rates below the national average.

- *Sumatra's* overall rate of growth in the late 1980s was 26% lower than in the early 1980s, and 32% lower than in the 1970s. Its growth was slower than at any time in the independence period, and while it is still growing at above the national average, it would seem that lower fertility and perhaps reduced immigration from elsewhere in Indonesia (especially that associated with land settlement) are bringing about a new era of reduced population expansion in Sumatra.
- In *Kalimantan*, the picture is quite different with population growth being higher than all of the other islands of Indonesia and being almost double the national average in the late 1980s. It was especially high in Central (4.5% per annum) and East (4.4%) Kalimantan. This is associated with continued and expanded exploitation of natural resources as well as increased focusing of transmigration on Kalimantan.
- *Sulawesi's* population, on the other hand, grew only slightly faster than that of Java in the late 1980s. This was mainly because the provinces of South and North Sulawesi, traditionally areas of significant outmigration, grew at well below the national average. Moreover, North Sulawesi has experienced very substantial fertility decline. On the other hand, the frontier provinces of Central and Southeast Sulawesi grew quite rapidly with the expansion of land settlement and, to a lesser extent, resource exploitation activities.
- *Bali's* low fertility is reflected in one of the slowest rates of population growth in Indonesia in the late 1980s (1% per annum).
- In the other islands of Indonesia, *West Nusa Tenggara* has grown at slightly above the national average, while *East Nusa Tenggara's* rate is just below that figure. *Maluku* has maintained a high growth rate while *Irian Jaya* and *East Timor* have grown considerably faster than the nation as a whole. In the latter two areas especially, there have been substantial inmigrations from elsewhere in the nation, especially Java and South Sulawesi and in the case of East Timor and East Nusa Tenggara.

With respect to the long-standing concern with the 'balance' of population between Inner and Outer Indonesia, it is clear that the last decade has seen a slowing down in the *net* redistribution of people out of Java and into the Outer Islands. The government's Transmigration Scheme was given great impetus in the late 1970s and the first half of the 1980s by large infusions of funds generated by taxes on oil and from the World Bank. Hence, as Table 15.2 shows, the large numbers of families who were moved from Java-Bali to the Outer Islands in Repelita III and IV differed greatly from those moved in the previous seven decades of the programme.

However, it will be noted in Table 15.2 that an increasing proportion of the transmigration families were spontaneous (*swarkasa*) as the decade

Table 15.2. TRANSMIGRATION IN INDONESIA'S FIVE-YEAR PLANS

| *Plan* | *Years* | *Target* | | *Achievement* | | |
|---|---|---|---|---|---|---|
| | | | | *Total* | *Sponsored* | *Spontaneous* |
| - | 1951-68 | - | | 95,276 | 95,276 | - |
| I | 1969-74 | 40,000 | Families | 40,193 | 27,309 | 12,884 |
| II | 1974-79 | 250,000 | Families | 82,959 | 82,959 | - |
| III | 1979-84 | 500,000 | Families | 535,474 | 365,977 | 169,497 |
| IV | 1984-89 | 750,000 | Families | 750,150 | 228,422 | 521,728 |
| V* | 1989-93 | 550,000 | Families | 277,808 | 104,247 | 173,561 |

* First four years of programme only

Source: *Indonesia Times XI*, May 1984, p. 21; Directorate General of Transmigration, Jakarta; P. Tjiptoherijanto, 'Settlement and adaptation of regional immigrants (transmigrants) in Indonesia', paper presented at the International Conference on Migration, National University of Singapore, 7-9 February 1991, p. 3; G.J. Hugo, 'Circular migration in Indonesia', *Population and Development Review* , 8 (1), 1982; H.W. Arndt, *Transmigration in Indonesia,* Population and Labour Policies Programme, W orld Employment Programme Research Working Paper No. 146, Geneva: ILO, 1984, p. 30; J.M. Hardjono, 'T ransmigration: looking to the future', *Bulletin of Indonesian Economic Studies,* 22 (2), 1986, p. 29.

proceeded. They received little or no assistance from the government in their movement so that it is probably more realistic to confine attention to the sponsored migrants. Even so, almost 600,000 families were resettled from Java and Bali to the Outer Islands in the 1980s – more than twice the total achievement of the previous 70 years of the programme. With the economic crunch of the mid-1980s, funding of Transmigration was cut back so that numbers of families moved in Repelita V will not approach the ambitious target of 550,000. Indeed, sponsored families numbered around a fifth of that target. Nevertheless, there are some indications of a possible upswing in transmigration in Repelita VI (1993-98).

Transmigration is only one element (and not the largest one) in a substantial migration from Java to the other islands. Table 15.3 shows that the number of people living in the Outer Islands but who had migrated there from Java increased by 73% between 1971 and 1980 while the number who had moved in the opposite direction increased by only 15%.

Hence, there was a net migration loss to Java overall of 2.4 million people. However, during the 1980s there has been a distinct change. There was a net increase of migrants from Java residing in the Outer Islands in the 1980s (1,576,910), a similar magnitude to that recorded in the 1970s (1,510,354), although the percentage increase of 44.1% was lower than that recorded in the 1970s. Hence, although there was a quite significant increase in outmigration from Java in the 1980s, it was somewhat lower

Table 15.3. MIGRATION INTO AND OUT OF JAVA, 1971, 1980 AND 1990

| | | | | *Change (%)* | |
|---|---|---|---|---|---|
| *Java* | *1971* | *1980* | *1990* | *1971-80* | *1980-90* |
| Total outmigrants | 2,062,206 | 3,572,560 | 5,149,470 | +73 | +44.1 |
| Total inmigrants | 1,067,777 | 1,225,560 | 2,434,719 | +15 | +98.7 |
| Net migration | -994,429 | -2,347,000 | -2,714,751 | +136 | +15.7 |

Note: Based upon 'most recent' migration data using census question on province of previous residence.
Source: Censuses of Indonesia, 1971, 1980 and 1990.

than some projections had anticipated on the basis of the experience of the1970s. The most striking change, however, in Table 15.3 is in the number of migrants from the Outer Islands residing in Java – this doubled between 1980 and 1990. As a result there was only a comparatively small (15.7%) increase in overall net migration loss from Java, from 2.35 million in 1980 to 2.71 million in 1990.

It is interesting to pursue this change a little more by examining the extent to which migrants between Java and the Outer Islands settled in urban and rural destinations. Table 15.4 shows that two thirds (65.7%) of migrants from the Outer Islands who have settled in Java lived in urban areas.

Indeed, when only urban-destined migrants between Java and the other islands are considered, Java records a net gain. On the other hand, more than three quarters (76%) of Java people living in the other islands in 1990 resided in rural areas. Hence, while urban destined migrants from Java to

Table 15.4. MIGRATION INTO AND OUT OF JAVA BY URBAN-RURAL DESTINATION, 1990

| | *All Migrants* | | *Migrants Aged 5+ Arriving 1985-90* | | |
|---|---|---|---|---|---|
| | *Urban* | *Rural* | *Urban* | *Rural* | *Total* |
| Total outmigrants | 1,233,874 | 3,915,596 | 361,857 | 601,483 | 963,340 |
| Total inmigrants | 1,600,333 | 834,386 | 464,739 | 309,050 | 773,789 |
| Net migration | +366,459 | -3,081,210 | +102,882 | -292,433 | -189,551 |

Note: Based upon 'most recent' migration data using census question on province of previous residence.
Source: Census of Indonesia, 1990.

the Outer Islands are by no means insignificant in number (1.2 million), they are outnumbered 3 to 1 by rural destined movers, and the net rural flow is heavily in favour of the Outer Islands. It is interesting also to examine only migrants who moved in the five years before the census (1985-90). Table 15.4 shows that the net migration loss to Java over the 1985-90 period was quite small – 189,551 – especially in relation to the gross volume of movement.

One element of population movement which is not reflected in the census-based migration data is non-permanent circulation. It is clear from field-based studies, however, that long-distance commuting and circular migration have increased greatly in scale and significance over the last two decades, especially in Java.[23]

## *Urbanisation*

Indonesia has long been characterised as one of Asia's least urbanised nations, but the stereotype of Indonesians as predominantly rural dwellers is becoming less valid. Whereas at the time of independence less than one in ten Indonesians lived in urban areas, currently a third are urban dwellers, and within two decades more than half of the nation's population will be classified as urban. This represents an important transformation in the Indonesian space economy and in the way in which Indonesians live and work.

The pattern of change in urban growth and urbanisation in Indonesia over the last 70 years is shown in Table 15.5. The top line of the table gives some idea of the rate of *urban growth* in Indonesia. It can be seen that in each of the intercensal periods, the rate of urban growth far outstripped that of the rural population. It is especially notable, however, that in the 1980s, not only was the rate of urban growth more than six times greater than that of the rural population, but also the absolute growth of the urban population (almost 23 million) was twice that of the rural population (9 million).

Although a substantial part of the urban growth is due to reclassification of areas from rural in 1980 to urban in 1990, there has been a substantial increase in the tempo of urban growth in the 1980s in Indonesia. The urban population has increased almost twentyfold since 1920, while the rural population has less than trebled.

If we examine *urbanisation*, however, the gains have been more modest than those in urban growth over the last seven decades. The third line of Table 15.5 shows that the percentage of Indonesians living in urban areas increased fivefold from 5.8% in 1920 to 30.9% in 1990. The table indicates that the rate of increase in urbanisation has exceeded the overall rate of population growth over the last two intercensal periods. Indeed, while substantial urbanisation has occurred throughout the post-independence period in Indonesia, the 1980s represented a period of rapid urbanisation unparalleled in Indonesia's history.

Table 15.5. INDONESIA: URBAN GROWTH AND TRENDS IN URBANISATION

| *Characteristic* | *Census Year* | | | | | | *Annual Growth (%)*[a] | | | | |
|---|---|---|---|---|---|---|---|---|---|---|---|
| | *1920*[b] | *1930* | *1961* | *1971* | *1980* | *1990* | *1920-1930* | *1930-1961* | *1961-1971* | *1971-1980* | *1980-1990* |
| Urban population | 2,881,576 | 4,034,149 | 14,358,372 | 20,465,377 | 32,846,000 | 55,433,790 | +3.42 | +4.18 | +3.61 | +5.40 | +5.37 |
| Rural population | 46,418,424 | 56,693,084 | 82,660,457 | 98,874,687 | 114,089,000 | 123,813,993 | +2.02 | +1.22 | +1.79 | +1.63 | +0.82 |
| Urban (percentage) | 5.8 | 6.7 | 14.8 | 17.2 | 22.4 | 30.9 | +1.45 | +2.59 | +1.51 | +2.98 | +3.27 |
| Rural (percentage) | 94.2 | 93.4 | 85.2 | 82.8 | 77.6 | 69.1 | -0.09 | -0.30 | -0.29 | -0.72 | -1.15 |
| Total population | 49,300,000 | 60,727,333 | 97,018,829 | 119,140,064 | 146,935,000 | 179,247,783 | +2.11 | +1.52 | +2.08 | +2.36 | +2.01 |
| Urban/rural ratio | 0.062 | 0.081 | 0.174 | 0.207 | 0.287 | 0.448 | +2.71 | +2.50 | +1.75 | +3.70 | +4.55 |

Note: The definitions of urban used in this table are those used in each census referred to. In the 1980 and 1990 censuses this is based upon a combined measure including population density, proportion of the population working in non-agricultural occupations and presence of designated urban facilities (see G.J. Hugo, 'Levels, trends and patterns of urbanisation,' in ESCAP, *Migration, Urbanisation and Development in Indonesia,* New York: UN, 1981; and 'International labour migration', in C. Manning and R. Harjono (eds), *Indonesia Assessment 1993. Labour: Sharing in the Benefits of Growth?,* Canberra: ANU, Department of Political and Social Change, Research School of Pacific Studies, 1993d).

[a] All percentage growth rates per annum are compound interest rates.

[b] Source of 1920 statistics: P.D. Milone, *Urban Areas in Indonesia,* Berkeley: University of Calfornia, 1966. An inaccuracy coefficient of 5% has been suggested for analysis of these figures.

Source: Hugo et al, op. cit.,1987, p. 89; Census of Indonesia, 1990.

The increase in urbanisation between 1980 and 1990 in Indonesia could have occurred through any or all of the following:

- Villages (*desa*) classified as rural in 1980 were reclassified as urban in 1990.
- Fertility of urban-based women was higher than their rural-based counterparts.
- Mortality of urban-based people was lower than their rural-based counterparts.
- There was a net redistribution of people from rural to urban areas.

The second and third elements can be discounted. Urban mortality in Indonesia is indeed lower than that in rural areas, but its urbanising impact is counterbalanced by the fact that urban fertility is lower than that in rural areas. Hence the overwhelming bulk of the difference in growth between the urban and rural populations is due to reclassification of areas and rural-to-urban migration. It has been reported[24] that the number of *desa* classified as urban almost doubled between 1980 and 1990 from around 3,500 to approximately 6,700. Hence a substantial part of the urbanisation recorded was due to reclassification associated with a huge increase in the lateral extent of Indonesia's major urban areas. This extension has tended to occur in corridors, along major transport routes radiating out from (and linking) major urban areas.[25] This phenomenon, together with the rapid increase in rural to urban circular migration mentioned earlier, is producing a new form of diffuse urbanisation in Indonesia, especially in densely settled Java. This overlapping of urban and rural populations and areas is producing a blurring of the distinctions between them and can be seen most intensely around Jakarta (Jabotabek),[26] in the area around Surabaya,[27] and along the transport corridors linking major cities (especially Jakarta-Bandung,[28] Jakarta-Cirebon, Surabaya-Malang, Yogyakarta-Semarang). There may also be a situation emerging whereby such a pattern of diffuse urbanisation surrounding a major metropolitan centre is overlapping national boundaries with the development of Sijori. This involves an overspilling of Singapore's industrial development into the adjoining Malaysian state of Johore and Indonesian province of Riau. In the latter case, the rapid urban growth on the island of Batam is very much an extension of Singapore.[29]

Official projections for the 1993-98 Sixth Five Year Plan are shown in Table 15.6 and indicate that all of the nation's net growth over that period is predicted to occur in the urban sector with a small decline in the rural population being anticipated.

In Java alone, it is projected that there will be an absolute decline in the rural population of 0.96 million people and a gain of 7.88 million in urban areas. Some 4.5 million of these will be added to the Jakarta metropolitan area which will see it increase to a city of more than 20 million inhabitants

Table 15.6. POPULATION PROJECTIONS, 1993-1998 (millions)

| | *1993* | *1998* | *Growth (% p.a.)* |
|---|---|---|---|
| Java | 111.9 | 118.9 | 1.2 |
| Sumatra | 39.4 | 43.8 | 2.1 |
| Kalimantan | 10.0 | 11.4 | 2.7 |
| Sulawesi | 13.3 | 14.6 | 1.7 |
| Bali/Nusa Tenggara | 9.9 | 10.5 | 1.3 |
| Other[a] | 4.6 | 5.3 | 2.6 |
| Total | 189.1 | 204.4 | 1.6 |
| Urban | 64.3 | 80.3 | 4.5 |
| Jakarta | 15.5 | 20.0 | 5.2 |
| Surabaya | 4.0 | 5.0 | 4.6 |
| Bandung | 3.8 | 4.7 | 4.2 |
| Medan | 2.6 | 3.1 | 4.2 |
| Rural | 124.8 | 124.1 | -0.1 |

[a] Maluku, East Timor and Irian Jaya.

Source: A. Booth, 'Repelita VI and the second Long-T erm Development Plan', *Bulletin of Indonesian Economic Studies,* 30 (3), 1994, p. 19.

Table 15.7. FOUR-CITY PRIMACY INDEX[1] FOR INDONESIA, 1890-1990

| *Year* | *Index* | *Year* | *Index* |
|---|---|---|---|
| 1890 | 0.39 | 1971 | 1.16 |
| 1905 | 0.59 | 1980 | 1.25 |
| 1920 | 0.69 | 1990[2] | 1.09 |
| 1930 | 0.73 | 1990[3] | 1.49 |
| 1955 | 0.87 | 1993[4] | 1.49 |
| 1961 | 1.17 | 1998 (Projected)[4] | 1.56 |

1 The four-city primacy index represents the population of the lar gest city (Jakarta), divided by the combined population of the three next lar gest centres (Surabaya, Semarang and Bandung up to 1961, thereafter Semarang was replaced by Medan as the fourth largest centre).

2 Index based upon official municipality and provincial boundaries, i.e. Jakarta 8.2 million, Surabaya 2,410,417, Bandung 2,025,159 and Medan 1,685,272.

3 Index based upon contiguous urban area including overspill areas, i.e. Jakarta 13.1 million, Surabaya 3,217,704, Bandung 3,317,704 and Medan 2,282,205.

4 Calculated from Booth, op. cit., 1994.

by the end of the century. This urbanisation is a function both of rural to urban migration and the swallowing up of former rural areas in the lateral expansion of large cities.

The emergence of Jakarta as a giant urbanised region extending far beyond the official provincial boundaries of the Capital City District is becoming an increasingly important part of Indonesia's urban system.

Table 15.7 shows that Jakarta's primacy within the Indonesian hierarchy has been increasing in recent years and this primacy is anticipated to increase in the second half of the 1990s. This is due to the fact that the economic strategy based upon expanding foreign and local investment in export industries, especially manufacturing, is focusing expansion of job opportunities more in the West Java-Jakarta region.

## *Indonesia's Changing Age Structure*

All of the nations of the Pacific Rim are experiencing demographic ageing.[30] Nevertheless, most still have relatively young populations, the product of high fertility-high mortality situations up until the recent past. Indonesia's age structure depicted in Figure 15.9 is typical of those countries which have experienced reductions in fertility and improvements in mortality. The decline in fertility is apparent in the undercutting at the base of the pyramid. Nevertheless, it will be noted that the relatively high fertility of the 1960s and 1970s is reflected in continued rapid growth of the workforce entry age groups in the 1980s and this is also the case in the 1990s.

It will also be noted in Figure 15.9 that Indonesia, like many countries in the Asian region, is poised for substantial growth of its elderly population. At present Indonesia has some 11.5 million people aged 60 years and

Figure 15.9. INDONESIA: POPULATION BY AGE AND SEX, 1980 AND 1990

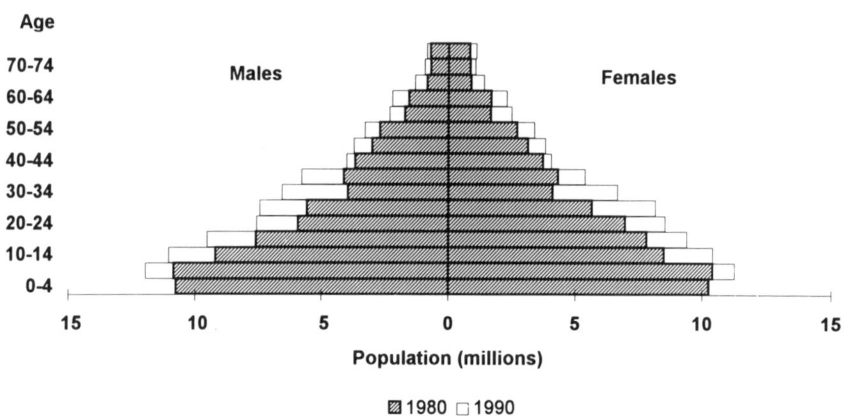


Source: Population Censuses of Indonesia, 1980 and 1990.

over but this will increase to 16 million by 2000 and 29 million in 2020. Over this period, they will increase from 6.4% of the total population to 11.4% in 2020. This represents a considerable challenge to policy-makers since the present availability of support for the dependent elderly is almost totally from family sources, and contemporary changes in the Indonesian family may mean that this source will not be so readily available in the future.[31]

## *Population Policy and Planning in Indonesia*

Few countries of Asia have such a history of government interventions to influence population change as Indonesia.[32] These interventions extend back to the colonial period when under the so-called 'ethical policy' of the early twentieth century a number of initiatives were taken in an attempt to improve conditions of people living in Java; several of these involved attempts to redistribute population and improve health. However, since the New Order government assumed power in 1966, population planning has had an important role in the national development planning process. Each of the six subsequent Five Year Plans has had important population components. Strategies and targets for transmigration, family planning, international labour migration, health and workforce are included in each Five Year Plan and there are government structures to initiate those plans.[33]

As indicated earlier, Indonesia's transmigration programme has sought to redistribute population away from Java-Bali to the less densely populated Outer Islands. For much of its long history beginning in the first decade of the century, the transmigration programme was characterised by overly ambitious and unachieved targets, poorly planned settlements, clashes with local populations in transmigration areas, logistics problems and settlement in unsuitable areas.[34] In the late 1970s and early 1980s, however, huge investments of World Bank loan funds and national oil export earnings into transmigration saw a turnaround in both the scale and success of the programme. The programme, however, continued to be criticised for displacing local groups and causing ecological damage.[35]

There can be no doubt that the high level of acceptance and use of contraception in Indonesia has been due in part to the success of the nation's Family Planning Program. With the installation of the New Order government, there was a government commitment to bring down rates of population growth for the first time, and by 1969, the National Family Planning Coordinating Board (BKKBN) had been formed and the National Family Planning Program initiated as part of Repelita I. The BKKBN has among its responsibilities the planning and co-ordination of the budget, personnel, service delivery and monitoring of family planning. It employs over 25,000 fieldworkers to recruit acceptors, distribute pills and condoms through village-based volunteers and involve key village leaders in achieving local support for the programme. This has led to the programme gaining a great deal of acceptance and support at the grass roots level. It has focused not just on reduction of family size but also on improving the quality of life of families. Another key to its success has been the highly developed logistics system which has generally ensured timely delivery of supplies in difficult geographical circumstances.

While Indonesia's Family Planning Program has been successful, it still faces many challenges in achieving the national goal of reducing fertility levels to replacement level by the year 2005. The Indonesia Demographic and Health Survey of 1991[36] found that there was still substantial unmet need for family planning in Indonesia, and estimated that if all currently unwanted births could be prevented by using contraception the TFR would decline from around 3 to 2.5. Unmet need is highest in East Timor, Irian Jaya, Aceh, West Nusa Tenggara, North Sumatra and Southwest Sulawesi – generally the most remote and peripheral provinces. It is higher in rural than urban areas and among low socio-economic status women than higher status groups. Accordingly, despite Indonesia's success in achieving substantial levels of fertility decline and use of modern forms of contraception, there is no room for complacency.

During the colonial period, there was a range of forced and contract labour programmes which deployed workers both within the Netherlands East Indies and to other nations.[37] Indonesia was a relative latecomer among the Asian nations exporting labour to the Middle East and labour-short Asian countries, but is now a major supplier of international contract workers.[38] A particular feature of the contemporary movement of contract labour out of Indonesia is the migration of workers to East and West Malaysia, although the bulk of this is illegal.[39]

Among the Overseas Contract Workers (OCW) going through official channels who numbered around 150,000 per annum in the first half of the 1990s,[40] the Middle East is the main destination, although Hong Kong, Singapore and Malaysia have increased in significance in recent years. An important feature of the 'official' OCW movement is the dominance of females (predominantly domestic workers). This is an issue of some controversy in Indonesia since these women are vulnerable to exploitation, but the Indonesian government continues to support this movement.[41] The illegal migration to Malaysia, however, is predominantly male. The scale of the migration to Malaysia is not known but it is considered that there may be up to a million Indonesian workers there. This issue remains an important one in relations between the two ASEAN partner countries.[42]

International labour migration is built in to the development planning strategy of the Indonesian Department of Manpower. In the Seven Policy Priorities of the Department for Repelita VI,[43] one is the development of labour exports and the shifting of the current emphasis on unskilled workers to more skilled workers. The targets for the Sixth Five Year Plan are to export through official channels 1.5 million workers (compared with around half a million in the Fifth Five Year Plan). Similarly it is planned to treble the nation's gain of remittances to US$3 billion in Repelita VI.

There have been several attempts within Indonesia to influence patterns of migration, especially that from rural to urban areas. There have been a number of unsuccessful attempts to 'close' individual cities to migrants, most notably in Jakarta in the early 1970s.[44] Several commentators over the last decade have argued that regional development, decentralisation of investment and the reduction of inter-regional inequalities are essential for the improvement of the well-being of all Indonesians.[45] While there are elements of decentralisation evident in contemporary Indonesia, it is doubtful if strong regional development can be achieved without some significant devolution of the power to raise revenue and to make key decisions about regional issues. A recent review of decentralisation in Indonesia concluded that 'a country as large and diversified as Indonesia will inevitably have to move in the direction of more real decentralisation as overall growth continues and the economy becomes more complex and specialised'.[46]

As with a number of nations in Asia, Indonesia's population growth remains one of the greatest challenges facing its policy-makers and planners. Few countries have been more active in seeking to influence their population growth and distribution, and in the case of family planning, few have been more successful. Nevertheless, the demographic momentum built in to the Indonesian age pyramid will ensure that substantial population growth will continue well into the next century, even if fertility continues to decline. It appears that the national population will increase to 210 million by the year 2000, 235 million in 2010 and 254 million in 2020. To provide jobs, education and other services for all these people while improving the quality of living of the total population and preserving the national endowment of resources through using them in sustainable ways presents a huge challenge to the nation.

## NOTES

[1] UN, *World Population Monitoring 1991*, Department of International Economic and Social Affairs, New York: UN, 1992, p. 10.

[2] Afghanistan, Bangladesh, Bhutan, Laos, Mongolia, Nepal, Pakistan and Papua New Guinea.

[3] The TFR is the average number of children women would bear if they went through their childbearing years conforming to the age-specific fertility patterns of the given year (in this case 1991). Hence it indicates approximately the average total number of children women are having at a particular point in time.

[4] Life Expectancy at Birth refers to the average number of years a person might expect to live if the age-specific death rates of the given period continued throughout his or her lifetime.

[5] UN, *World Urbanization Prospects: The 1992 Revision*, New York: UN, 1993.

[6] UN, *World Urbanization Prospects: The 1994 Revision Annex Tables*, New York: UN, 1994.

[7] H. Hill, 'The economy', in H. Hill (ed.), *Indonesia's New Order: The Dynamics of Socio-economic Transformation*, Sydney: Allen and Unwin, 1994.

[8] A. Booth, 'Repelita VI and the second Long-Term Development Plan', *Bulletin of Indonesian Economic Studies*, 30 (3), 1994, p. 19.
[9] Ibid, p. 4.
[10] Indonesia, *Indonesia: A Quarter Century of Progress (1969-1993)*, Jakarta, 1993.
[11] T.P. Tomich, 'Survey of recent developments', *Bulletin of Indonesia Economic Studies*, 28 (3), 1992, p. 8.
[12] G.J. Hugo, *Manpower and Employment Situation in Indonesia 1993*, Jakarta: Indonesian Department of Labour, 1993a, p. 75.
[13] B. White, 'Political aspects of poverty, income distribution and their measurement: some examples from rural Java', *Development and Change*, 10, 1979, pp. 91-114.
[14] R. Naylor, 'Labour saving technologies in the Javanese rice economy: recent developments and a look into the 1990s', *Bulletin of Indonesian Economic Studies*, 28 (3), 1992.
[15] World Bank, *World Development Report 1994 - Infrastructure for Development*, New York: OUP, 1994, p. 162.
[16] Indonesia, op. cit., 1993, p. 1.
[17] B. Bidani and M. Ravallion, 'A regional poverty profile for Indonesia', *Bulletin of Indonesian Economic Studies*, 29 (3), 1993, p. 53.
[18] The Infant Mortality Rate (IMR) is the number of deaths of children under 1 year of age per 1,000 live births.
[19] Biro Pusat Statistik (BPS), *Tren Fertilitas, Mortalitas dan Migrasi*, Jakarta: BPS, 1994, p. 68.
[20] G.J. Hugo, 'Population distribution and redistribution in Indonesia', *Majalah Demografi Indonesia*, VII (13), 1980a, pp. 10-100.
[21] M. Vatikiotis, 'Neglected renewal brings anxiety', *FEER*, 18, April 1991, p. 35.
[22] G.J. Hugo, 'Circular migration in Indonesia', *Population and Development Review*, 8 (1), 1982, pp. 59-83.
[23] Ibid, 1982; G.J. Hugo, 'Recent developments in Indonesian migration', in *Proceedings of International Conference on Migration in Asia, University of Singapore, January, 1991*, 1995.
[24] P. Gardiner and M. Oey-Gardiner, 'Pertumbatian dan perluasan kota di Indonesia' (Growth of lateral expansion of cities in Indonesia), *Kompas*, 7 May 1991.
[25] T.G. McGee, 'The emergence of Desakota Regions in Asia: expanding a hypothesis', in N. Ginsburg, B. Koppel and T.G. McGee (eds), *The Extended Metropolis: Settlement Transition in Asia*, Honolulu: University of Hawaii Press, 1991; T. Firman, 'Pembangunan kota-kota baru di wilayah metropolitan Jabotabek' (Development of new cities in the Jabotabek Metropolitan Region), *Prisma*, 18 (6), 1989, pp. 49-60; T. Firman, 'Penataan koridor antar kota' (Managing inter-city corridors), *Kompas*, 11 January 1991; T. Firman, 'The spatial pattern of urban population growth in Java, 1980-1990', *Bulletin of Indonesian Economic Studies*, 28 (2), 1992, pp. 95-109.
[26] An acronym made up of Jakarta and the three adjoining West Java *kabupaten* of Bogor, Tanggerang and Bekasi.
[27] This incorporates not only Surabaya but also the adjoining *kabupaten* of Gresik, Bangkalan, Mojokerto and Sidoarjo.
[28] This corridor has already been given the acronym of Jabopunjar – Jakarta, Bogor, Puncak and Cianjur.
[29] Hugo, op. cit., 1995.
[30] UN, op. cit., 1992.
[31] G.J. Hugo, 'Ageing in Indonesia and Australia: similarities and differences', in G. Hugo (ed.), *Future Directions in Aged Care in Indonesia,* Proceedings of Joint Indonesia-Australia Seminar, July 1994, Hilton International Hotel, Jakarta, Adelaide: Centreprint, 1994.

[32] G.J. Hugo, T.H. Hull, V.J. Hull and G.W. Jones, *The Demographic Dimension in Indonesian Development*, Singapore: OUP, 1987, p. 298.
[33] For a discussion of the population planning process in Indonesia, see Hugo et al, op. cit.,1987, chapter 9.
[34] J.M. Hardjono, *Transmigration in Indonesia*, Kuala Lumpur: OUP, 1977.
[35] C. Budiardjo, 'The politics of transmigration', *The Ecologist*, 16 (213), 1986, pp. 111-16; M. Colchester, 'Banking on disaster: international support for transmigration', *The Ecologist*, 16 (213), 1986a, pp. 61-70; M. Colchester, 'Unity and diversity: Indonesia's policy towards tribal peoples', *The Ecologist*, 16 (213), 1986b, pp. 89-98; M. Colchester, 'The struggle for land: tribal peoples in the face of the transmigration programme', *The Ecologist*, 16 (213), 1986c, pp. 99-110; M. Otten, '"Transmigrasi": from poverty to bare subsistence', *The Ecologist*, 16 (2/3), 1986, pp. 71-6; C. Secrett, 'The environmental impact of transmigration', *The Ecologist*, 16 (2/3), 1986, pp. 77-86.
[36] Demographic and Health Survey (DHS), *Indonesia Demographic and Health Survey 1991*, Jakarta: Central Bureau of Statistics, National Family Planning Coordinating Board and Ministry of Health, 1992.
[37] G.J. Hugo, 'Population movements in Indonesia during the colonial period', in J.J. Fox, R.G. Garnaut, P. T. McCawley and J.A.C. Mackie (eds), *Indonesia: Australian Perspectives*, Canberra: ANU, Research School of Pacific Studies, 1980b, pp. 95-135.
[38] G.J. Hugo, 'International labour migration', in C. Manning and R. Hardjono (eds), *Indonesia Assessment 1993 Labour: Sharing in the Benefits of Growth?*, Canberra: ANU, Department of Political and Social Change, Research School of Pacific Studies, 1993b.
[39] G.J. Hugo, 'Indonesian labour migration to Malaysia: trends and policy implications', *Southeast Asian Journal of Social Science*, 21 (1), 1993c, pp. 36-70.
[40] G.J. Hugo, 'Labour migration in Asia: Indonesia', *ASEAN Economic Bulletin,* forthcoming.
[41] G.J. Hugo, 'Women on the move: changing patterns of population movement of women in Indonesia', in S. Chant (ed.), *Gender and Migration in Developing Countries*, London: Pinter, 1992.
[42] Hugo, op. cit., 1993c, pp. 36-70.
[43] A. Latief, *Sapta Karyatama Pelita VI Depnaker Seven Policy Priorities of the Department of Manpower*, Jakarta: Department of Manpower, Republic of Indonesia, 1993.
[44] Hugo et al, op. cit., 1987, p. 355.
[45] H. Hill (ed.), *Unity and Diversity: Regional Economic Development in Indonesia Since 1970*, Singapore: OUP, 1989.
[46] G. Ranis and F. Stewart, 'Decentralisation in Indonesia', *Bulletin of Indonesian Economic Studies*, 30 (3), 1994, pp. 41-72.

# Part IV
# Sites of Resistance, Negotiation and Capitulation

## 16. INTRUSION OF GLOBAL FORCES AND TRANSFORMATION OF A LOCAL CHINESE ECONOMY: THE EXPERIENCE OF DONGGUAN

*George Chu-sheng Lin*

The process of economic integration in the Asia-Pacific Rim and its spatial consequences have received much scholarly attention. It has been well documented that many Asian countries have undergone significant structural changes in their economies in response to intensified global competition;[1] that a new integrated Asia-Pacific economy is quickly taking shape to counterbalance the formation of continental trade blocs in Europe and North America,[2] and that the restructuring and integration of the Asia-Pacific economy have significantly facilitated the functional and territorial reorganisation of human activity at various national and regional levels.[3] While the dynamism of Asian-Pacific regional integration has been well researched, the bulk of documentation thus far has tended to be based on either the entire region or individual countries. With few exceptions,[4] the mechanism of regional integration and its spatial consequence at a subregional level remain poorly understood.

One significant example illustrative of the structural and spatial changes taking place at a subregional level as a result of global restructuring is the rapid transformation of the space economy of the Pearl River Delta in China. As a Chinese southern frontier with geographic proximity to Hong Kong, the Pearl River Delta has since 1979 been allowed by the Chinese central authority to move 'one step ahead' of the socialist nation to attract foreign capital investment, acquire Western advanced technology and develop a free market economy. Its great openness to the outside world and its extensive pre-existing socioeconomic ties with Hong Kong make it a typical case for the assessment of how a socialist economy is transformed after the intrusion of global capitalism.

This chapter assesses the impacts of global market forces on the growth and restructuring of a local Chinese economy in the Pearl River Delta.[5] It focuses on the experience of Dongguan which is located in the heart of the Delta, a county-level economy illustrative of the structural and spatial effects of the intrusion of global market forces. Because the impact of global forces is not confined to the economic sphere, social and cultural aspects of the interaction between local and global forces are also investigated.

## *Geographic and Historical Context*

As implied by its name, Dongguan (a town of bushes in the east) is located in the eastern wing of the Pearl River Delta with a close proximity to Hong Kong (Figure 16.1). It had a total population of about 1.5 million in 1994 and covers a land area of 2,465 square kilometres. Although Dongguan lies next to Baoan and Shenzhen, it has fared better than either in developing

Figure 16.1. THE LOCATION OF DONGGUAN IN THE PEARL RIVER DELTA

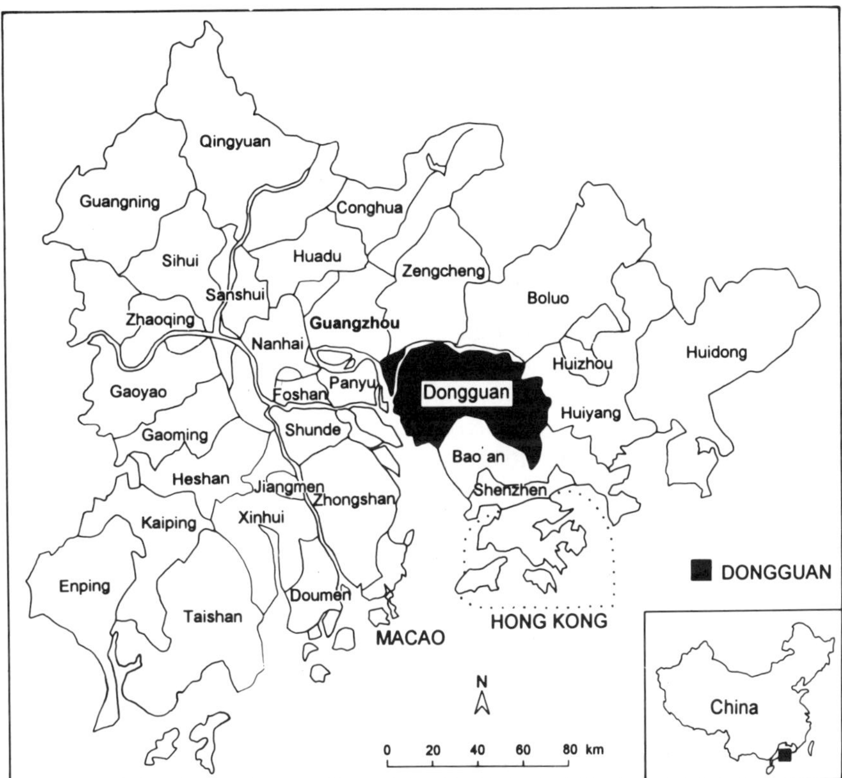


kinship ties with Hong Kong, primarily due to its higher population density and its well-established historical tradition. It was estimated that Dongguan residents had at least 650,000 relatives in Hong Kong and Macao, a number significantly higher than those of Baoan and Shenzhen.[6] The middle position of Dongguan in the Guangzhou-Hong Kong corridor means that it can easily access both the export outlet of Hong Kong and the traditional urban centre of Guangzhou. Such a geographical location has also enabled Dongguan to develop an export processing industry by merging capital, technology and industrial components from Hong Kong in the south with interior cheap labour transferred mainly from Guangzhou in the northwest.

The favourable geographic features of Dongguan, however, brought no benefit to its development in the Maoist era when traditional connections between Hong Kong and the mainland were artificially cut off. Under the prevailing radical ideology of anti-capitalism, the closeness of Dongguan to the capitalist enclave of Hong Kong was considered unfavourable since it was vulnerable, not only to the 'contamination' of decaying capitalism, but also to possible naval attacks from counter-revolutionary enemies overseas including those of Taiwan and the US. This perceived vulnerability to capitalist attack explains the fact that for decades Dongguan never became the focus of infrastructure development funded either by the central or provincial government.[7]

There were few alternatives for the people of Dongguan to make a living except by working in the rice fields and 'learning from Dazhai' in building a self-reliant agrarian economy. On the eve of economic reform in 1978, a total of 390,000 people or 72% of the total labour force were engaged in agricultural production. Annual income on a per capita basis was a mere 193 yuan (US$64). In some places, such as the southern border township of Chang'an, annual per capita income was recorded as low as 83 yuan.[8] Tens of thousands of young people attempted to escape to Hong Kong because there was no hope of their having a reasonable future in their hometown.[9] It was reported that about 20% of the young people in Dongguan had managed to get across the border into Hong Kong in the pre-reform years

The implementation of the open door policy since 1979 has led Dongguan to enter a new era of development. The opening up of Guangdong and Fujian provinces, the establishment of Special Economic Zones, and designation of the Pearl River Delta as an Open Economic Region have renewed and strengthened the economic ties between Hong Kong and the Delta.

### *Development of Export Processing Industry*

Once the cadres of Dongguan realised the fact that their advantageous connections with Hong Kong could be utilised to create jobs and raise income, they began to seek every possible opportunity to promote investment from Hong Kong and overseas. Special policies, including taxation concessions and preferential treatment regarding the import of necessary equipment and the handling of foreign currency, were announced. A special office was set up in Dongguan by the county government to serve Hong Kong investors with efficient personnel and simplified bureaucratic procedures. Economic co-operation between Dongguan and Hong Kong was arranged creatively and flexibly in a variety of forms including export processing *(lailiao jiagong)*, compensation trade (*buchang maoyi*), joint ventures (*hezi jingying*) and co-operative ventures (*hezuo jingying*). It was reported that by the end of 1993, a total of 15,936 contracts had been signed between Dongguan and manufacturers from Hong Kong and overseas, of which 11,588 were already in operation.[10]

Since 1979 such ventures have varied in form and in size, but the most popular one has been the processing of imported materials *(lailiao jiagong)* or assembling product components provided by Hong Kong manufacturers (*laijien chuanpei*). Known as 'three supplies one compensation' (*sanlai yibu*), the arrangement requires the Hong Kong side to supply raw materials, components and models for what is to be processed, while the Chinese side provides labour, land, buildings, electricity and other local utilities necessary for production. The Hong Kong participant of the contract does not hire or pay workers directly. Instead, a lump-sum payment is usually made available to the Dongguan participant for the contracted goods, usually in US or Hong Kong dollars. The contracted Dongguan participant hires workers and pays them in Chinese dollars on a piece-work basis. Needless to say, local governments and cadres of Dongguan, who serve as middlemen in this process, are able to make sizeable profits, either by paying low salaries, or by exchanging US and Hong Kong dollars into Chinese yuan at a high rate on the 'black market'.

Arrangements are also made on a compensational basis, in which the Dongguan side does the processing or assembling jobs for a specialised period of time (for example, five years), and at the end of this period assumes ownership of the machinery or equipment provided by the Hong Kong firm as compensation.

Cooperation in the form of 'three supplies one compensation' has become popular, not only in Dongguan, but also in other parts of the Delta region because it benefits substantially both the Hong Kong and Chinese participants in the contract. With designing and marketing handled in Hong Kong and labour-intensive work done cheaply in Dongguan, small Hong Kong manufacturers are able to compete effectively in the international market. As for the Chinese side, export processing has created jobs and income for local cadres and the general population.

By the end of 1987, some 2,500 processing firms on the basis of 'three supplies one compensation' had been set up in Dongguan, creating up to 171,000 employment opportunities and receiving US$107 million mostly from Hong Kong, which accounted for about 40% of what was received by the whole Guangdong Province.[11] By the end of 1993, the number of export processing firms established in Dongguan had reached 6,963. They hired more than 488,800 factory workers and generated US$401.38 million processing fees for the local economy.[12]

A survey conducted by the Federation of Hong Kong Manufacturers in July 1991 identified Dongguan as the second most-favoured location, next only to Shenzhen, for Hong Kong investment.[13] The considerable success of Dongguan in attracting foreign investment and developing export manufacturing and growth enabled it to be promoted from a county to an officially designated city at the county level in 1985. Further to this, it was promoted to a higher level city directly subordinate to the provincial government in 1988.

### *Reasons for Developing an Export Processing Industry*

Why has Dongguan, formerly a frontier agrarian county, proved so attractive to Hong Kong manufacturers? What are the forces that have helped Dongguan to attract investment and processing activities from Hong Kong and overseas? In answering these questions, local officials of Dongguan frequently quote the words of a well-known ancient Chinese scholar and strategist, Zhuge Kongming, that 'timing, location, and public relations' (*tianshi, dili, renhe*) are three essential factors in seeking any success. Implied in this explanation is the importance of the implementation of the open door policy (timing), the geographic proximity of Dongguan to Hong Kong (location), and the creation of good personal relations with Hong Kong investors (public relations). While the case of Dongguan appears to fit fairly well into the general model of success provided by the ancient Chinese strategist, three specific factors should be highlighted in order to understand the rapid expansion of export processing activities in Dongguan.

First, good personal connections existing between Dongguan and Hong Kong have provided easy and reliable links between investors and their manufacturing partners. With over 650,000 relatives *(gang'ao tongbao)* in Hong Kong and another 180,000 (*huaqiao*) in other foreign countries, mostly in North America, the people of Dongguan have less difficulty than those in other parts of the nation in seeking investors or partners from Hong Kong and overseas. It was estimated by cadres in Dongguan that about half of the contracts they had signed were with their countrymen in Hong Kong.[14] Interestingly, many personal contacts are with former Dongguan residents who escaped from their hometown to Hong Kong during the pre-reform period. Ironically, local cadres who used to be responsible for preventing escapes and apprehending those who dared to try are now in charge of contacting and persuading their former escapees in Hong Kong to invest in their native county.

A second critical contributing factor is the creation of a transportation infrastructure as a necessary means to attract foreign investment. In this regard, the local government of Dongguan has played a leading role in the development process. It was reported that in the eight years of 1980-87 a total of 1.034 billion yuan (US$216 million) was raised by the government of Dongguan through various channels for infrastructure development.[15] Such a huge amount of capital was obtained primarily from local resources such as bank loans (33%), collective enterprises (31%), stocks and bonds (14%) and foreign capital (11%). Budgetary allocation from the central and provincial governments accounted for only 11% of all construction expense.[16]

Heavy investment in the infrastructure has resulted in significant improvements. The existing road system has been substantially extended with the mileage of paved roads increasing from a mere 1 kilometre in 1978 to 860 kilometres in 1987. By the end of the 1980s, Dongguan had more miles of paved roads per square kilometre than any other county in the nation. Dongguan was also one of the first Chinese counties to establish a computerised telephone system which connects it directly with 17 countries and regions in the world. A total of 13,231 telephones have been installed to cover all townships and villages in Dongguan, of which 8,756 phones, or 20% of all installations in China, can dial direct to other countries.[17] The transport capacity of ports and harbours and the generation of electric power have also been increased substantially during the 1980s. The creation of such a good infrastructure has significantly reduced transactional costs for investors and, therefore, underpinned the rapid inflow of overseas investment.

Finally, the availability of cheap labour and land is another important factor that has helped to attract Hong Kong manufacturing to move into Dongguan. In the early 1980s, Dongguan was a county where labour and land could be obtained easily and cheaply. A worker employed by an export processing firm was usually paid a monthly wage of 150-200 yuan which was about one-fifth or even one-sixth of what a Hong Kong worker could make.[18] Although Chinese workers may not be as skilled as their Hong Kong counterparts in certain aspects of industrial production, the low wage rate remains attractive to Hong Kong manufacturers, especially to those who are engaged in highly labour-intensive industries such as toys and electronics.

### *Characteristics of Export Processing Industry*

As the export processing industry continues to grow, it is becoming one of the most dynamic economic sectors in transforming the regional economy of Dongguan. By the end 1990, more than 70% of Dongguan's industrial labour force was engaged in export processing.[19] To understand the dynamics of these structural and spatial changes, it is necessary to analyse the nature and spatial characteristics of the flourishing export processing activities.

The industries that have been developed in Dongguan are simple, unsophisticated, small-scale and labour-intensive. In the main, export processing in Dongguan has centred around four sectors: textile, apparel, toys and electronics. The type of production varies considerably from the processing of toys, assembling of simple radios, sewing of shirts or blouses, to the making of plastic bags, incense, firecrackers, candles, candy, chocolate and other food products. The procedures of production are invariably simple and repetitive, needing a considerable amount of time and labour but little skill. The development of these simple labour-intensive industries has significant implications for changes in employment structure and migration as it opens up opportunities for surplus rural labourers who are eager to enter factories but have little experience or skill in manufacturing.

As processing activities are technologically unsophisticated, many factories that have been set up in Dongguan are relatively small in size. Most of them do not require heavy machinery. Some were converted from the dining halls of former communes or brigades. As production expands, buildings of two or three storeys are constructed containing several large rooms which accommodate fifty to a hundred desks, one for each worker. Thus a typical factory may employ several dozen to a hundred workers which is considered small by Chinese standards. A 1991 survey sampling 2,931 joint ventures and compensational trade enterprises in Dongguan revealed that the average number of workers in each factory was 147 for joint ventures and 105 for the processing of imported materials or compensation trade factories.[20] Some workshops in the countryside were so small that they had only a dozen workers on their payrolls. The fact that the export processing industry in Dongguan is composed of numerous small workshops without a single major plant has been vividly described by the local people as 'a spread of numerous stars in the sky without a large shining moon in the centre' (*mantian xingdou queshao yilun mingyue*).

Another feature of Dongguan's export processing industry is that the concentration of factories is not in a few large urban centres but is widely scattered throughout the countryside. Since the scale of production is small and the processing procedure is simple, factories in Dongguan do not necessarily have to be located in the large urban centres where technical experts or other high ranking social services are easily accessible. This distinct feature is evident from an official survey conducted at the end of 1987: among the 2,500 factories established for the processing of imported materials or compensation trade, 1,591 were found in rural villages and townships. They accounted for 63.64% of the total number of export processing firms, 72.52% of all processing fees received from Hong Kong and overseas, and 87.91% of the total construction area of all factories set up for the processing industry.[21]

### *Consequences of Export Industrial Development*

The most significant outcome of the flourishing of labour-intensive export processing activities in Dongguan has been a disproportionate increase in employment and production in the manufacturing sector and the subsequent restructuring of the local economy. When Dongguan was first opened up to foreign investment in the late 1970s, its economy was predominantly agricultural, with two-thirds of its population working in the fields at a subsistence level. The rapid expansion of the export processing industry since 1978 has greatly increased the pace of manufacturing development. Between the years of 1978 and 1994, an estimated 656,860 jobs were created by the export processing industry and absorbed both local rural labourers, who were released from agricultural production, and immigrants, who moved in from other less developed areas.[22] The labour force in the secondary sector, primarily manufacturing, has expanded at 10.45% per annum since 1978 with its share of the total labour force increasing from 16.85% in 1978 to 40.64% in 1990. At the same time, those who were engaged in agricultural production and other primary activities were reduced in number and their share of the total labour force dropped substantially from 71.57% in 1978 to 36.15% in 1990. Production in the local economy exhibited a pattern of restructuring similar to that of the labour force. The contribution of manufacturing to total output rose from 42.06% in 1978 to 66.20% in 1990 while the share of the agricultural sector declined from 39.40% to only 19% in the same period.[23]

In addition to economic restructuring, the development of the export processing industry has contributed to an accelerated growth of the local economy and helped to raise personal income for the general population. During the years 1980-90, the production of industrial and agricultural output, of which the export processing industry was a main part, recorded a growth rate of 23% per annum, which was significantly higher than the regional average of the Pearl River Delta.[24] The export-processing fees received by Dongguan increased from US$2.34 million in 1979 to US$ 163 million in 1990, which represented an annual growth rate of 53.5%.[25] Per capita income rose substantially from 193 yuan to 1,359 yuan for peasants and from 547 to 3,552 yuan for salaried workers in the 12 years between 1978 and 1990.[26] This extraordinary process of economic structural change and accelerated growth since the late 1970s has been unprecedented in Dongguan's history and was clearly fuelled by the inflow of investment and manufacturing facilities from Hong Kong and overseas.

An interesting phenomenon that has been especially evident in Dongguan as a result of export industrial development is the increasing participation of women in manufacturing. Since export production in Dongguan is predominantly labour-intensive in nature, its rapid expansion has created employment for women who are generally considered by manufacturers to be adept at assembling, particularly in such jobs as making toys, sewing apparel or processing electronic products. A growing number of women have, therefore, joined this army of factory workers and are playing a major role in the process of industrialisation. It was reported in 1989 that among the 166,000 workers employed by export processing firms, 130,000 were women, accounting for 78% of the total workforce.[27] In many workshops, most workers are female with only a few men being responsible for repairing machinery, factory security, loading/unloading of finished products or imported materials, and managerial work. Most female workers are young with an average age of under 25. Some of them have begun to earn incomes equivalent to men's.

Women's participation in manufacturing production has undoubtedly raised their economic and social status, but it has also placed them in a confined environment in which they are asked to work repetitively on the same single piece at a desk for long hours in order to get pay on a piecework basis. For those who are already married, factory work and household affairs have combined to form an almost unbearable burden. For those who are young, entering the factory at an early age means that there will be little chance for them to receive necessary education and, therefore, few alternatives for making career choices or finding advancement. The intrusion of global market forces from Hong Kong has thus pushed Chinese women who might have been housewives or college students to take part in the process of the new international division of labour.

Another distinct demographic feature that characterised the recent development of Dongguan is the rapid growth of immigration. By the mid-1980s, rapid expansion of the labour-intensive processing industry in Dongguan had exhausted the local supply of labour and created a large demand for outside workers. With the relaxation of government control on migration, which took effect in 1984, labour began to flow in from other less-developed counties of Guangdong and interior provinces. Since the mid-1980s, immigration of outside labour has grown substantially at 43% per annum. By the end of 1990, the number of 'outside labour' *(wailai laogong)* had reached 655,902 which almost equalled the local labour force.[28] Considering that outside labourers have an employment rate of 98.39% which is higher than that of local labourers (76.02%), it can be argued that almost half of Dongguan's economy has been run by hardworking outsiders.

By far the vast majority of migrants to Dongguan were engaged in manufacturing production, particularly in export processing. Statistical data have shown that about 80% of the total outside labour force, or 518,971 out of 655,902, were found in the manufacturing sector.[29] A survey conducted in 1988 revealed that 61.12% of all outside labour in Dongguan was in export processing plants.[30] Of all factory jobs created by the export processing industry during the years of 1979-90, 85% was taken by migrants from outside.[31]

Many migrants to Dongguan are young women aged between 18 and 25 who are frequently referred to by the local people as 'working girls' (*da gong mei*) or 'girls from outside' (*wai lai mei*). They usually live in a dormitory room shared by eight to twelve persons near the factory where they work and they pay rent or a 'managerial fee' (*guanli fei*) to local cadres who are responsible for the construction and maintenance of both the factory and dormitory buildings. The money they save is sent back via banks or postal offices to their relatives in poor interior areas. As a result, those townships that have a large number of outside workers tend to have a disproportionately large number of banks and post offices. In Chang'an *zhen* where I did my fieldwork, for instance, the main street of the town, a couple hundred metres long, has 14 banks which are open from 8 a.m. to 9 p.m. to serve outsiders who want to deposit or mail their savings to their hometowns. Some of these outsiders work in Dongguan for several years until they earn enough money to go home. Others stay for a prolonged period of time. A few have married local residents or set up their own businesses in Dongguan.

The experience of working and living in an environment surrounded by strangers is not, however, always pleasant. Outsiders frequently find themselves faced with discrimination as the best jobs with higher pay always go first to locals. Speaking in a language completely different from the local dialect, they can barely communicate with the local residents and loneliness is something they have to get used to, not to mention being cheated when they go shopping. Some of the 'working girls' even have to bear what Westerners would call harassment or assaults from local factory managers or Hong Kong bosses who simply want to take advantage of them or, in the words of the local people, 'treat the girls like a piece of pliable beancurd' *(chi ruan doufu)*. The issue of 'working girls' from outside has become such a national concern that a number of movies and TV programmes have been produced to show the unhappiness and bitterness of these newcomers. The most popular TV movie, which won the top national award in 1992, was named 'The Working Girls'. The penetration of global market forces through Hong Kong into Dongguan has thus not only promoted the participation of local peasants and women in manufacturing production but it has also effectively drawn the young and cheap labour from the interior of China into the theatre of mass production and global capitalism.[32]

The rapid growth of export production and its subsequent economic and demographic changes have found their manifestations over the entire area. Much farmland has been turned over for the construction and expansion of factories. Data obtained from the Agricultural Department of Dongguan reveal that in the years of 1978-1988, a total of 18,585 mu or 3,061 acres of farmland was transformed into industrial land use, mostly for the building of export factories, workshops and industrial districts.[33] Consequently, per capita cultivated land dropped substantially from 1.06 mu in 1978 to 0.67 mu in 1990.

Many small workshops and factories developed in the early 1980s were scattered over the townships and villages of Dongguan. As production expanded, local officials began to realise that such a spatial arrangement made it difficult to provide electricity, water and sewage disposal facilities. A new type of industrial land use has since gradually emerged, covering a sizeable scale of land area and located at the outskirts of towns or villages along trunk roads. By the end 1987, a total of 119 such industrial zones had emerged in Dongguan. In Chang'an *zhen*, I visited an industrial zone which covers an area of 198 mu or 32.6 acres. Developed jointly by Chang'an *zhen* and several Hong Kong companies, this zone absorbed a total investment of HK$236.50 million or US$30.32 million and accommodated over a thousand employees working on the spinning, weaving and dying of textile materials for Hong Kong manufacturers.

The newly-emerged industrial zones are usually built on a piece of farmland and are typically composed of a group of identical factory buildings of two or three storeys. Each factory building belongs to a certain processing firm and the name of that firm in large red Hong Kong-style Chinese characters can be seen at the top of the building. At the entrance to each factory stands a security guard who dresses in a uniform which resembles that of a Hong Kong policeman. All factory buildings in the zone are arranged in straight rows and facing the same direction. Infrastructure facilities for these factories are generally well-established and are utilised more efficiently than those of individual factories that are built separately.

Most of these export processing factories, either built separately or in groups, are located in the vicinity of the headquarters of former communes and brigades. Their development and continuous expansion have greatly fostered the industrialisation of land in the countryside and created a distinct type of land use characterised by a mixture of farmland, factories and housing for peasants.

Such a process of industrialisation did not, however, force those farmers who lost their land to move into the city. Instead, by creating factory jobs in the countryside, the growth of the processing industry has allowed peasants to 'enter the factory but not the city' or 'leave the soil but not the village'. Between 1978 and 1987, for instance, an estimated 154,000 people, most of them surplus rural labourers, joined the industrial labour force of Dongguan. Among them, only 34,000 or 22% went into factories in towns. The other 120,000 new workers or 78% entered factories and workshops in the countryside.[34] Clearly, most of those farmers who were released from traditional agricultural production have acquired factory jobs near their villages without moving into cities and towns.

### *Social Influence of Hong Kong*

The influence of Hong Kong has gone beyond the economic sphere and provoked significant social changes within villages and townships of the Pearl River Delta. Changes in the lifestyle of people in Guangdong and particularly in the Pearl River Delta as a result of the influence of Hong Kong have been vividly described by Gregory Guldin in his excellent study.[35] In this section, I provide only a local example.

With its frontier location and excellent connections with Hong Kong, Dongguan is one of the first among the cities and counties of the delta that has felt the strong 'south wind'which brings the air of capitalism into socialist territory. In the processing plants subcontracted from Hong Kong manufacturers, there is no promise of job security, rewards are tied to the amount of work finished, time requirements are rigid and pressure on workers to keep a quick working pace is high. For those who were used to the socialist production system under which job security or 'iron bowl' is guaranteed and by which equity is achieved at the cost of efficiency, to work in such a Hong Kong subcontract factory or joint venture means fundamental changes in job attitude, value judgement and working behaviour. Doing a factory job is no longer considered as fulfilling the glorious socialist obligation of 'serving the people' but as a way of earning a living for personal gain. As there is nothing that can be counted on, people have become more independent, efficient and sensitive to changes in their living environment. In the meantime, loneliness, frustration and depression over not being able to keep up with the working pace or to realise personal ambition have become increasingly noticeable in the local community.

Visitors from Hong Kong going to Dongguan to do business or to see relatives have often brought with them ideas, information and different lifestyles. Since its opening up in 1979, Dongguan has been visited more frequently than ever before by relatives from Hong Kong. In 1990, for instance, there were 262,586 visitors from Hong Kong either for business or family affairs.[36] These visitors always brought information and materials allowing their countrymen to share the Hong Kong consumerist vision of modernity. In the early 1980s, when modern consumer goods such as TVs, VCRs and freezers were still rarely seen elsewhere in the nation, people in Dongguan had already started to receive a variety of gifts from Hong Kong kinfolk. A survey conducted by Guangdong officials in 1990 revealed that town residents in Dongguan owned 112 colour TV sets, 102 stereo tape decks and 94 washing machines per hundred households, which were all higher than the rates among surveyed households in other cities in Guangdong including Guangzhou, Foshan, Shenzhen and Zhuhai.[37] As well, the ownership rates of colour TVs, motorcycles, freezers and stereo tape decks for the peasant households of Dongguan in 1990 were also significantly higher than the provincial average. Needless to say, these consumer goods have formed a material basis for the imitation of the Hong Kong lifestyle in Dongguan. Modern electronic receivers such as TVs, radios and VCRs are also important conduits for the penetration of Hong Kong culture into the towns and villages of Dongguan.

The most effective means that has transplanted the Hong Kong model of living on to the local people is probably the modern mass communication network which links Hong Kong to almost all local households. The computerised telephone system allows Dongguan's residents to dial direct to their relatives in Hong Kong and overseas for information about the outside world. Electronic conduits such as TV and radio have brought almost all programmes broadcast from Hong Kong stations into nearly all local households. For the first time since the founding of the People's Republic, Dongguan's residents are able to receive sounds and images about the life of their relatives on the other side of the border, a lifestyle which is in sharp contrast to what they have been used to for over 30 years.

When the fieldwork for this study was started in 1984, local households with TV sets were almost all watching the Hong Kong programme, 'Foon Luk Gum Siu' ('Enjoy Yourself Tonight'), which is an imitation of the American 'Latenight Show'. Few of Dongguan's population any longer had an interest in tuning into the Central Broadcasting Station of Beijing for communist propaganda or government-controlled news.

When follow-up research was conducted in 1992, many peasants in rural villages were found watching all sorts of American TV programmes broadcast from the Hong Kong stations, including 'CBS Evening News', '60 Minutes', '20/20', 'Wall Street Journal', 'Dallas', 'Murphy Brown' and 'America's Funniest People', as well as many American movies in bilingual (English/Cantonese) form.

The invasion of Western culture, ideas and information has begun to alter the existing landscape and change the lifestyle of the local people. Visitors to Dongguan who travel around the countryside find a distinct landscape characterised by numerous large antennas, erected on the top of farmhouses to capture coveted television signals from Hong Kong. Within a village or town, the central location is usually occupied by a 'cultural centre' (*wenhua zhongxin*) which was originally set up by the former commune or brigade officials to popularise Marxism, Leninism and Mao Zedong Thoughts or to disseminate directive documents from Beijing.

Ironically, these socialist 'cultural centres' have surrendered to the invasion of Hong Kong influence and become the loci for popularising recreational activities in the Hong Kong style. Instead of studying the quotations of Chairman Mao or reading the editorial comment of the *People's Daily,* people come to the cultural centre to play video games, sing Hong Kong pop songs with Karaoke and see video movies smuggled in from Hong Kong. Movies of action and horror and even adult movies are no longer uncommon in Dongguan, and most of them are produced in Hong Kong.

From TV, radio and other media, the local people of Dongguan have become increasingly familiar with product brand names and have begun to consume foreign goods such as Colgate toothpaste, Marlboro cigarettes, Nike sneakers and foreign-made cosmetics. Drinks such as Pepsi Cola, Coca Cola, 7-Up and Maxi coffee, which had never been heard of before 1979, have become the most familiar items for daily consumption by the local population.

Another interesting projection of the influence of Hong Kong can be found in changes in the local language characterised by the frequent use of many words from a Hong Kong translation of English. Thus, 'bye-bye' has replaced the traditional Chinese saying of 'manzou' (please walk slowly). Instead of calling policemen *'min jing'* (the people's guard), local people have adopted the Hong Kong Cantonese English loan-words of *'ah Sir'* (Sir) or '*chai lo*' (servant fellow) to refer to the police. Other Hong Kong translations of English such as '*desi*' (taxi), '*shido*' (store), and '*salong*' (saloon) have also become popular. On entering a restaurant in Chang'an *zhen* of Dongguan, I was puzzled by many dish names in the Chinese menu which I could not decipher, as they were neither in English nor in Mandarin. They were all in a Hong Kong translation of English such as '*sari*' (salad), '*buding*' (pudding), '*pisabing*' (pizza) and '*bingqiling*' (ice cream).

What has been taking place in Dongguan since its opening up is the demise of the socialist tradition, the weakening of the impact of Beijing both politically and culturally, and a simultaneous takeover of the Hong Kong model of production, consumption, recreation and communication.

Given sufficient time, a unique culture which blends the local tradition with Hong Kong innovations in dress, speech, music, consumables and lifestyle may well emerge in Dongguan and in other parts of the Delta region as well.

In the current era of global interdependent development and international division of labour, the transformation of a local Chinese economy has increasingly found itself being shaped by external forces emanating from the restructuring capitalist world. The structural and spatial effects of global capitalism are probably more noticeable in the Pearl River Delta than anywhere else in the nation, and the Delta has been virtually seen by the Chinese leaders as a spearhead leading China into the world economy.

This study assesses the role played by global market forces in the process of transformation of a local Chinese economy. My detailed investigation of the experience of Dongguan has revealed that the relocation of labour-intensive industrial production from Hong Kong to Dongguan has created considerable employment opportunities in manufacturing for the local population, most of whom were farmers, and, therefore, significantly facilitated the transformation of the local economy from one that was predominantly agricultural into one that relies more on manufacturing and service sectors. Rural industrialisation has resulted in a process of spatial transformation whereby a great number of surplus rural labourers entered factories in the countryside without moving into the city and wherein much agricultural land was converted into factory sites or industrial zones.

The implementation of the open door policy which was originally intended to attract foreign investment and acquire advanced technological know-how has also exposed the traditional culture of the local community to the filtering in of Hong Kong-style consumption, recreation and communication. The influence of Hong Kong and the subsequent social and cultural changes that have been discussed in this chapter are not confined to Dongguan alone. They can also be found in other cities and counties of the Delta where extensive kinship, linguistic and other cultural ties with Hong Kong have long existed. Social and cultural connections existing between the Delta region and Hong Kong will most likely continue and reinforce each other with economic linkages to shape the emerging Hong Kong-Guangzhou megalopolis.

### *Acknowledgements*

This research is funded by a grant from the Social Science and Humanities Research Council of Canada. The field work was funded by the International Development Research Centre (IDRC) of Canada and the Chiang Ching Kuo Foundation.

## NOTES

[1] F.C. Lo, K. Salih and Y. Nakamura, 'Structural interdependency and the outlook for the Asian-Pacific economy towards the year 2000', in M. Shinohara and F. C. Lo (eds), *Global Adjustment and the Future of Asia-Pacific Economy,* Tokyo: IDE & APDC, 1989, pp. 80-107; M. Borthwick, *Pacific Century: The Emergence of Modern Pacific Asia,* Boulder: Westview, 1992; A. Dirlik (ed.), *What's in a Rim? Critical Perspectives on the Pacific Rim Idea,* Boulder: Westview, 1993.

[2] B.K. Bundy, S.D. Burns and K.V. Weichel (eds), *The Future of the Pacific Rim,* Westport: Praeger, 1994; R.A. Palat (ed.), *Pacific-Asia and the Future of the World-system,* Westport: Greenwood, 1993; D. Aikman, *Pacific Rim: Area of Change, Area of Opportunity,* Boston: Little, Brown, 1986; S.B. Linder, *The Pacific Century: Economic and Political Consequences of Asian-Pacific Dynamism,* Stanford University Press, 1986.

[3] Y.M. Yeung, *Pacific Asia in the 21st Century: Geographical and Developmental Perspectives,* Chinese University of Hong Kong, 1994; W. Armstrong and T.G. McGee, *Theatres of Accumulation: Studies in Asian and Latin American Urbanization,* New York: Methuen, 1985; E. Dixon and D. Drakakis-Smith (eds), *Economic and Social Development in Pacific Asia,* New York: Routledge, 1993; T.G. McGee and G.C.S. Lin, 'Footprints in space: spatial restructuring in the east Asian NICs 1950-90', in Dixon and Drakakis-Smith (eds), op. cit., 1993, pp. 128-51.

[4] Y.W. Sung, *The China-Hong Kong Connection: The Key to China's Open-door Policy,* CUP, 1991; R.Y.W. Kwok and A.Y. So, *The Hong Kong-Guangdong Link: Partnership in Flux,* New York: M.E. Sharpe, 1995; X. Cheng, 'China's growing integration with the Asia-Pacific economy', in Dirlik (ed.), op. cit., 1993, pp. 89-119; H.M. Hsiao and A.Y. So, 'Ascent through national integration: the Chinese triangle of Mainland-Taiwan-Hong Kong', in Palat (ed.), op. cit., 1993, pp. 133-50.

[5] V.F.S. Sit (ed.), *Resource and Development of the Pearl River Delta,* Hong Kong: Wide Angle Press, 1984; C.P. Lo, 'Recent spatial restructuring in Zhujiang Delta, South China: a study of socialist regional development strategy', *Annals of the Association of American Geographers,* 79, 1989, pp. 293-308; A.G.O. Yeh et al, 'Spatial development of the Pearl River Delta: development issues and research agenda', *Asian Geographer,* 8, 1989, pp. 1-9; G.E. Johnson, 'The political economy of Chinese urbanization: Guangdong and the Pearl River Delta region', in G.Guldin (ed.), *Urbanizing China,* Westport: Greenwood Press, 1992, pp. 185-220; G.C.S. Lin, *Regional Development in the Zhujiang Delta, China, 1980-90,* Unpublished Ph.D. Dissertation, Vancouver: UBC, 1994; J. and A. Smart, 'Personal relations and divergent economies: A case study of Hong Kong investment in China', *International Journal of Urban and Regional Research,* 15, 1991, pp. 216-33.

[6] Guangdong Province, Land Development Department, *Guangdongsheng Guotu Ziyuan (Land Resources of Guangdong Province),* Guangzhou: Internal document, 1986, pp. 369-70.

[7] Lin, op. cit., 1994, p. 207.

[8] CCP Team (CCP, Central Committee Special Investigation Team), *Dongguan Shinian (Dongguan's Ten Years),* People's Publishing House of Shanghai, 1989, pp. 27, 3, 5.

[9] E. Vogel, *One Step Ahead in China: Guangdong under Reform,* Cambridge, Mass.: Harvard University Press, 1989, p. 176.

[10] Dongguan Statistical Bureau, *Dongguan Tongji Nianjian (1993), Statistical Yearbook for Dongguan (1993),* Dongguan: Internal publication, 1994, pp. 266, 268.

[11] CCP Team, op. cit., 1989, p. 6.

[12] Dongguan Statistical Bureau, op. cit., 1994, pp. 266-67.

[13] Federation of Hong Kong Industries, *Hong Kong's Industrial Investment in the Pearl River Delta,* Federation of Hong Kong Industries, 1992.

[14] Vogel, op. cit., 1989, p. 176.
[15] CCP Team, op. cit., 1989, p. 39.
[16] Ibid, p. 35.
[17] Ibid, pp. 7, 34, 37.
[18] Ibid, p. 194.
[19] *Yatai Jingji Shibao* (Asia-Pacific Economy Daily), 2 August 1992.
[20] P. Lu (ed.), 'Zhujiang sanjiaozhou-Xianggang jingji jishu hezuo de huigu yu qianzhan' (A retrospect and prospect on economic and technological cooperation between the Zhujiang Delta and Hong Kong), *Zhujiang Sanjiaozhou Jingji Fazhan Huigu Yu Qianzhan (Economic Development in the Zhujiang Delta: Retrospect and Prospect)*, Research Center for Economic Development and Management in the Zhujiang Delta, Guangzhou: Zhongshan University Press, 1992, p. 146.
[21] CCP Team, op. cit., 1989, p. 32.
[22] Dongguan Statistical Bureau, op. cit., 1994, pp. 266-7.
[23] CCP Team, op. cit., 1989, pp. 6, 20.
[24] Guangdong Province, Statistical Bureau, *Guangdongsheng Duiwai Jingji Maoyi Luyou Tongji Ziliao (Statistical Information on Foreign Trade and Tourism for Guangdong Province)*, Guangzhou: Internal document, 1991a, pp. 238-41.
[25] CCP Team, op. cit., 1989, p. 31; Guangdong Province, Statistical Bureau, *Guangdongsheng Xianqu Guomin Jingji Tongji Ziliao (1980-1990) (National Economic Statistical Data for Cities and Counties of Guangdong Province (1980-1990)*, Guangzhou: Internal publication, 1991b, p. 357.
[26] Guangdong Province, Statistical Bureau, op. cit., 1991b, pp. 238-41.
[27] CCP Team, op. cit., 1989, p. 159.
[28] Ibid, p. 6.
[29] Dongguan Statistical Bureau, *Dongguan Tongji Nianjian (1978-1990) (Statistical Yearbook for Dongguan [1978-1990])*, Dongguan: Internal document, 1991, p. 6.
[30] CCP Team, op. cit., 1989, p. 95.
[31] *Yatai Jingji Shibao*, op. cit.
[32] See also 'Conclusion', pp. 345-6, on the importance of migrant labour and the attractiveness of jobs in coastal China to poor rural peasants in interior provinces. Elizabeth Croll has argued that a new 'aggregate family' is emerging in the peasantry, utilising this and other economic strategies. See Elizabeth Croll, 'New peasant family forms in rural China', *Journal of Peasant Studies*, 14 (4), July 1987, pp. 469-99.
[33] H. S. Huang (ed.), *Dongguan Nongye Jingji (Dongguan's Agricultural Economy)*, Guangzhou: People's Publishing House of Guangdong, 1991, p. 79.
[34] CCP Team, op. cit., 1989, p. 27.
[35] G. Guldin, 'Towards a Greater Guangzhou: Hong Kong's sociocultural impact on the Pearl River Delta and beyond', paper presented at The Workshop on Hong Kong-Guangdong Integration, Vancouver: UBC, 1992.
[36] Guangdong Province, Statistical Bureau, op. cit., 1991a, p. 271.
[37] Guangdong Province, Statistical Bureau, *Guangdong Tongji Nianjian (Statistical Yearbook of Guangdong Province)*, Beijing: China Statistical Press, 1991c, pp. 370-71.

# 17. IDEOLOGICAL ABSTRACTIONS, BUREAUCRATIC IMPERATIVES AND HUMAN CREATIVITY: A PHILIPPINES NARRATIVE

*Warwick Armstrong*

## *Introduction*

The invitation to participate in this book reminded me how stimulating a department Victoria University of Wellington Geography was during my time there in the 1960s. With a background in history and economics, I found an environment accepting of an outsider – even one perhaps in need of some retraining. There seemed a singular lack of concern for some preordained ontological purity of geographic studies as well as an encouragement of enquiry transcending disciplinary boundaries. I found a department emphasising more than most the value of social, and even political, involvement.

In the following decades I picked my way through the thickets of international co-operation, increasingly questioning the reasons for the deepening inequalities at the heart of global political and economic relationships. I have found a need to dissolve conventional diciplinary boundaries, set aside conceptual templates and, above all, search for links between academic learning and the practical experience I have garnered from fieldwork observation and discussions. Adding geography to my history allowed me to expand archival work into 'getting my boots muddy' – to learn by walking, talking and listening. Later, as research combined with practical project work, I observed not only the omnipresence of inequality and injustice, but even more in the face of these, the innate capacity of people to endure and survive.

The sequential steps – from social awareness to meeting with people in their own localities and learning that it is preferable to work *with* rather than *for* them – have made two things clear. The first is that while university walls encompass valuable learning, even profound at times, they often exclude alternative sources of knowledge and experience. The second is that many conventional approaches to human development are irrelevant and self-defeating. They emanate from remote authority, complex bureaucracy and sophisticated technical expertise; and, despite good intentions, are likely to stultify and undermine efforts made by local people both to regain self-reliance and to improve the quality of their lives.

My awareness of all this crystallised in the mid-1980s when I began research in the Philippines. The continuing failure by officialdom to examine the nature of its intervention in people's lives despite four decades of debatable international development experience became plain to me as I tried to find some meeting point between the needs and capacities of local community residents and the agendas of a Canadian development organisation.

In the late 1980s and early 1990s, in response to a widening economic interest by the Canadian government in the Asian countries of the Pacific Rim, I accepted the directorship of a 5-year collaborative community development project in the Philippines. In 1984, two universities, McGill and the recently-created University of the Philippines in the Visayas (UPV), joined forces in a training and exchange programme. This was later funded from Ottawa's Canadian International Development Agency (CIDA).

The UPV's energetic first Chancellor wished to strengthen her fledgling institution's teaching, research and extension capacities and to establish working relationships with coastal communities in the Central Philippines. Our first goal, then, was to plan for teacher exchanges and training of staff at McGill. Improving the curriculum and strengthening library and laboratory resources would give an effective support base for this.

CIDA remained less than impressed by these proposals until the overthrow of the Marcos regime and the accession of Mrs Cory Aquino to the presidency in 1986. With the offer from Ottawa of $100 million to assist the new Pacific Rim democracy, CIDA scrambled to find projects, but it was only in 1988 that the agency came up with funding for the Food Systems Development Project (FSDP). Then, at the eleventh hour, CIDA persuaded the two partners to extend their original concept into a fully-fledged institution-building *and* community development project.

The success or otherwise of co-operation stems in great measure from the very first steps taken; errors can be corrected later, but usually with exhausting and time-consuming effort. We were mistaken in accepting the last-minute CIDA insistence on expanding (so as to spend more of the $100 million) when we were not yet prepared for such a massive extension. And we were then distracted by mechanical procedures – its Work Breakdown Structure and Logical Framework Analysis – which may have facilitated CIDA's management and accounting procedures, but certainly fragmented our integrated approach to the question of food systems.

At the same time we were faced with the challenge of working with 5,000 residents of three *barangays* or communities in the northern part of the island of Panay, some four hours' drive over variable roads from the UPV campus at Iloilo City. It may be the case that those who really are trained in a development project are the team members themselves; it is also possible that they are in most need of it. The first two years were spent adapting the FSDP to CIDA administrative procedures and in finding ways of working in the three *barangays* – and with each other. Differences in understanding about community development – participatory, interactive contrasted with older-style, benign paternalism – led to mutual questioning about our respective roles.

Nevertheless, despite a near-complete replacement of the original teams from both universities after two years, we had a platform to build upon, and CIDA asked the two partners to extend the life of the FSDP to six years. With this, we were able to focus our attention around the core of the community project. We were faced first by high levels of malnutrition – 75% of pre-school children and significant numbers of pregnant and lactating mothers, fortunately not many in the severe category. As well, there were wider problems of inequality of social and economic opportunity within the communities. Our task was to find ways to confront the specifics of poor diet and inequitable access to food within a broader context of unequal entitlement (to use Amartya Sen's phrase[1]).

We began to apply the systemic-entitlement approach at the smallest scale, the household, with an emphasis on the least privileged members while recognising that there are always encompassing systemic constraints on both the household and community levels of action. So, while concentrating on the daily issues of inadequate and unequal entitlement and working out the means to counter them, we also kept in mind the wider limitations imposed at the national and global scales. One of these limitations would be the strategies of CIDA with its own administrative, political and financial priorities.

After discussion and some false starts, we concluded that our best approach would be to listen to people in the community, to ask them to identify their principal concerns and then, together, discuss ways of dealing with them. It was to be a process in which co-operation, mutuality and sharing of respective areas of knowledge and experience might yield answers. The more intractable systemic difficulties arising from a system of national and global inequality we would endeavour to deal with indirectly through confronting particular issues; in this way we might ameliorate their more severe impacts on the *barangays*.

The first attempts had been interventionist and technocratic rather than participatory: the formation of modules to deal with craft production, fishing and fish-farming, agriculture, health and nutrition, and community organisation. But, with experience and the constant nagging of the underlying concepts of the systemic-entitlement approach and a growing sensitivity to the need to listen to local voices, this emphasis gave way to an awareness that this was a project in which all members – from the FSDP team and from the *barangays* – were required to listen, exchange and learn. New needs emerged: potable water, a waste disposal system, alternative livelihood skills, improvement of food availability and dietary education, and finding capital for local enterprise. And the methods changed from top-down directives to group discussion and decision-making, with the FSDP acting in a more advisory and linking role, which involved learning as well as training.

This is not a field in which detached and objective judgement reigns; we are all subjects within it. Yet, by 1993, we could claim some satisfactory results: nearly 20 *sitio* groups (the majority women), the creation of cottage industries, a daycare centre, two multipurpose co-operatives (including grocery) and a model garden. These arose out of decisions taken by *sitio* group members, as were the many training, information and consciousness-raising sessions in the FSDP's *barangay* centre. In turn, from these emerged a plan for rural savings, herbal medicine production and a decision by a group of landless women in one of the poorer *sitios* legally to challenge the landowners' unfairness in share-cropping arrangements. Gradually, the normally less vocal – mainly women – were finding a voice in their *barangays*.[2]

CIDA intervened in this activity in March 1993, with a unilateral decision to end the project. It did this for two reasons: the first was a drastic cut to CIDA's budget by the federal Conservative government; the second was a shift in Ottawa's foreign assistance strategy away from countries such as the Philippines (in the post-cold war years now of less geo-strategic importance) to the new states of the ex-Soviet Union and Eastern-Central Europe. The FSDP and the *barangays* were not consulted, and I was invited by CIDA to negotiate the best terminating terms I could.

The FSDP had been funded by CIDA in 1988 for reasons which were focal to its strategic interests in the increasingly significant Pacific Rim region of Southeast Asia, but only tangential to the people and their livelihoods; in 1993 the funds were withdrawn on political grounds even more remote from the daily lives of residents in the three villages.

## *A Letter to CIDA, Otawa*

The following is a transcript of my final report to CIDA in mid-1993. It followed long delays by CIDA in sending promised phase-out funding which left the UPV team and the *barangay* programmes with mounting debts. This caused me to write a missive rather more splenetic than, with the assuaging effects of time, I might now send. But, with some editing, I let the substance stand.

### DIRECTOR'S COMMENTARY

This is the final Quarterly Report I will be writing as Director of the Food Systems Development Project. I intend to make it a retrospective, a comment about the present and a brief view of the future after the ending of the formal collaboration between the two partners from the University of the Philippines in the Visayas and McGill University.

At the end of Year Five of our co-operation in March of this year, my report indicated the extent to which the principles of the systemic-entitlement approach were now being met. It took some years for us, quite frankly, to struggle to put our concepts into place, to win the confidence and support of the residents of the three communities in Batan municipality and, above all, to come to a shared understanding between the representatives of the two universities. But, in the past year or so, we had begun to achieve a large part of our goals in all three spheres.

The 20 or more *sitio* groups in the three *barangays* were – and are – participating fully in the work of clarifying and defining issues needing action. They are now organising themselves and are calling upon the support of our community organisers to respond to daily practical problems. At the same time, people see how such daily issues form part of a wider context of systemic inequality and unequal entitlement – to food, to adequate income and employment, and to a 'voice' in decision-making. Co-operation and partnership have been slowly and, at times, painfully forged.

The FSDP, then, was in full operation, linking community action with the institution-building activities of research, training, teaching and study in a cohesive and interactive way so that each sphere of action worked with and strengthened the others. We are achieving our goals of changing entitlements through participation among residents and FSDP team members – and doing this in mutually supportive ways. The food systems-entitlement approach, tempered by the testing of concepts against *barangay* realities, is an effective means to the goal of international and community co-operation.

It came, then, as a shock to be told unilaterally by CIDA that the FSDP was to be closed within 3 months. The reasons given and methods chosen are typically bureaucratic. Regardless of the efforts of team members, ignoring the importance of maintaining the confidence of the communities, an executive dictat, with no prior consultation, was imposed upon a project in which partnership and shared respect were central tenets of our co-operation.

But CIDA has not killed the FSDP. The co-operation between the University of the Philippines and the three communities, Camaligan, Lalab and Magpag-ong, will continue, in part because of the shame-faced concessions made in April [1993] by the CIDA representatives. These have allowed the Agency to save a quite derisory amount compared with the disruption and ill-will they have stirred up. But, beyond this, co-operation will not come to an end because of the spirit of commitment by team members and community residents – a spirit, it seems, beyond the calculus of the CIDA mindset.

At another level, questions must be raised as to the value of international development programmes run by large corporate institutions. Dr Francisco Nemenzo (ex-Chancellor of UPV), in a letter written in April this year to CIDA and the Canadian Embassy in Manila, queries the approach of the former to international development. In his letter he expresses shock and disappointment at the unilateral decision of CIDA. It is, indeed, true that such action makes mockery of the insistence upon partnership by the Agency. Dr Nemenzo had earlier suspended his doubts about the value of such assistance and had given the FSDP wholehearted support during his term as Chancellor. But I do not doubt that he has had his apprehensions about foreign aid confirmed: as paternalistic at best and, at worst, as autocratic, self-serving and condescending.

In fact, we in the FSDP should have been forewarned of the potential of the CIDA office to renege on its claims to partnership by its actions on previous occasions. Two examples will suffice to illustrate the Agency's underlying attitude toward the Project.

In the first months of the Project's inception, officials bound us to a rigid and compartmentalised framework of action and reporting known as the Work Breakdown Structure (WBS). What this mechanistic formula did, in effect, was to take an integrative approach and chop it into a series of fragmented pieces convenient for CIDA accounting. I later likened this to our presenting them with a live and active whole chicken, a little untidy perhaps, and receiving back a series of neatly-tied and bound packages – all dead. The core of the systemic-entitlement concept was weakened if not negated and caused us ongoing problems until we resolved them on our own. CIDA demonstrated from the start that they had no real idea of (and possibly little concern for) the systemic approach.

A more direct illustration of CIDA's secretive and non-accountable approach: recently, Agency staff replied to an outside consultant's management and financial audit of the Project. They responded to the criticisms of the Project as far as they applied to CIDA but kept the audit from the university partners – except for veiled and non-substantiated allusions to our inadequacies. Only when the Canadian Press Agency invoked the access to information law and obtained the audit statement were we informed of its subject matter – by the press. A report of immediate concern to us became public knowledge before we learned of its contents.

On the wider stage of international co-operation, our experience suggests that opaque agendas are at the very heart of the process. The well-being of those on low incomes, in fragmentary employment and with little voice in the important decisions affecting their lives, counts for little in the decisions taken by officials in their assistance programmes. Far more important appear to be the siren attractions of political expediency and the potential for profitable trade and investment.

In the case of the FSDP, at least, it seems that the substance (poverty, malnutrition) has counted for less in CIDA's corridors than administrative and financial expediency. And, more broadly, there has been the decision by the Canadian government through CIDA and External Affairs to cut back aid to many low-income societies, to emphasise aid which subsidises the Canadian private sector and to seek closer ties with the more profitable potential of Eastern Europe and the ex-USSR republics. This, I believe, is both short-sighted and unethical.

In the end, CIDA may have saved a little on the project, but in the process will have lost goodwill in the Philippines. But it will have remained true to rationalistic administrative precepts – however slightly related to the realities of ordinary citizens' lives – and carried out its order to cut certain projects ahead of time. In passing, I should mention a further irony: the FSDP in 1990 responded to the suggestion from CIDA-Manila itself to extend Project activities by one year from 1993 to 1994.

On a personal note, it may be asked how, after nearly 6 years as a recipient of funding by CIDA, I can now turn and bite the hand that fed us. I do not see it that way. As a taxpayer who has entrusted a government institution to spend taxes wisely and in a humane way, I consider that our trust has been betrayed.

In future, the spirit of co-operation, partnership and exchange, gradually worked out over the years by the university partners and the residents of the three *barangays*, will, I hope, continue without the hindrances of this patriarchal system. I want to express my thanks to those who have helped make this a successful co-operative endeavour: people in the communities who gradually came to trust the FSDP despite early obstacles and misunderstandings, team members and others at the University of the Philippines in the Visayas who have hung on with stamina to the Project (and who are still waiting for snail-paced administrators to complete the terminating formalities*) and their counterparts at McGill University have all contributed to this common effort.

Warwick Armstrong
Director, FSDP
McGill University, Montreal

July 1993

* On 21 January 1994, nearly 9 months after the original Manila negotiations, an acceptable Termination Agreement is still to be presented to us. The Philippines team has been reduced by 75% and the remaining members are working voluntarily. We are seeing the long drawn-out consequences of a process in which the daily lives of ordinary people are put on the rack by the indifference and incompetence of a distant bureaucracy. (N.B. The Agreement was finally signed and the UPV team was paid eleven months after CIDA's original decision to end the FSDP, July 1994.)

As I reread these phrases of frustration, it occurs to me that, after all, the FSDP was only small fry within a national aid agency that is not a large player in world development. Yet it suggests some wider implications not just for the abstraction that is development, but also for the nature of relationships between officials and villagers. In the first place, labyrinthine institutions with their complex procedures, categories and budgets[3] appear only incidentally concerned with the substance of people's lives. And rarely, with its secrecy, is an agency such as CIDA accountable to outsiders (with the exception of an occasional investigating journalist).

On the larger scene of Canada's international relations – in this case, with a fellow member of the Pacific Rim – CIDA is itself an instrument of Canadian foreign policy. It has, in the words of one observer, 'become another bureaucratic player in Ottawa's gray universe of acronyms, as vulnerable as any other to fiscal uncertainties and organizational and policy competition'.[4]

It is, furthermore, one arm of a foreign policy deficient in principles and lacking coherence. Its short-term tactics appear to have been a reaction to political change in a Southeast Asian society with considerable economic potential; when that potential later appeared uncertain, political and development interest quickly waned. Schmitz's comment on CIDA's subaltern role seems pertinent here:

> Policy is much more driven by incrementalism, force of circumstances, or the changing preferences (and sensitivity to interest group and mass opinion) of elected officials and public servants ... Programs are expanded or cut. New ones are created. The process is seldom straightforward, transparent, or done with an eye to rigorous consistency.[5]

An officialdom of this stripe has numbing effects on the potential of those it is allegedly serving; it interferes with people's abilities and hinders them from carrying out their own projects of change. Villagers, farmers and craftworkers, especially if they are perceived by officials and experts as inferiors, are diminished and their potential for self-reliance often dismissed.[6] Local knowledge and experience are underestimated or ignored, and professionals with their specialist techniques and imported assumptions come to occupy centre stage.

As a corollary, what we – not just officials, but those of us engaged in development – are doing is to overlook the innate imaginative creativity which lies within human beings. From the viewpoint of equity this is unacceptable; in terms of efficiency it represents an enormous waste of latent energy and talent. The unspoken dogma that there is one world view, one way of organising – that of the expert, the specialist, the administrator and the accountant – excludes the potential of an immensely diverse range of human capacities.[7] That we are all capable of falling into this unidimensional frame of thinking removed from the lives, values and culture of those we are supposedly assisting is the theme of the following section.

### *Models and Human Lives*

The academic inclination to invoke grand theory and engage in metalanguage which has held many of us in its spell in the past is now being reconsidered. But I do not advocate throwing it out holus bolus as some strands of postmodernism would have us do; it is too easy to leap from an outworn bandwagon onto one more à la mode. We need, rather, to find ways to link the local with the universal, to see how they connect and what the implications of such connections are for people living, working and relaxing in their daily relationships. Practice needs to inform and interact with theory. This, indeed, was the great challenge to the FSDP team: how to achieve a connection and balance among our systemic-entitlement approach, the daily lives of the *barangay* residents and our own attitudes and values.

Nearly 70 years ago, Aldous Huxley discussed this issue:

> All classifications and theories are made after the event; the facts must first occur before they can be tabulated and methodised. Reversing the historical process, we attack the facts forearmed with theoretical prejudice. Instead of considering each fact on its own merits, we ask how it fits into the theoretical scheme. At any given moment a number of meritorious facts fail to fit into the fashionable theory and have to be ignored.[8]

The challenge to megatheory is not, then, just an inspiration of the 1980s. Even so, it is heartening to see an increasing concern for understanding a reality that is not just refracted through the optics of conventional models; or to read the ideas of those aware that such archetypes are our constructs for helping the human mind to get a grip on some of the world around us; that, however ingenious, these models are not final and unchallengeable. On the other hand, without some classifying, order-setting and interpreting, life is an ungovernable mystery. We need the connection of practice and theoretical reflection, even if both are in constant flux as circumstances change and our comprehension, culture and values change with them.

How can a dynamic balance be created which will allow the productive employment of our intellects and training in understanding the lives of those we are both working with and learning from? This is the large question which hangs over those involved in the work of international co-operation. It is the question which has posed itself to me over the years, and most recently with the Food Systems Development Project.

All the training and knowledge arising from research, community work and classroom teaching gave us (academics from Canada and the Philippines) little basis for dealing with the complexities of collaboration with 5,000 rural people. Any difficulties lay less with the *barangay* residents, however, than with the conflicting and preconceived notions of the two teams of academics. Lofty paternalism in 1988-89, combined with occasional hand-outs to promote special groups, proved an uncomfortable partner for the well-intentioned but ill-defined ideas on participatory community involvement. Only after a confrontation of views on the various roles of those caught up in the Project's work and an almost complete change of Project members in 1990, followed by internal reflection and a period of training in participatory methods, did the FSDP re-establish itself gradually among the *barangays*.

CIDA did not play a positive role here; their manuals stressed participation and the need to focus on the buzzwords of the last decade, 'gender' and 'environment', and specialists sometimes came from their eleventh floor offices in Manila to put an earnest case. But in the event, it always seemed difficult to reconcile the arrival of well-heeled visitors from the metropolis, putting up at the better hotels in the town, with the realities of the village people living in earth-floored, *nipa*-thatched cane *balays*.

It is not that the exhortations from above were necessarily wrong; the sentiments were often well-intentioned and liberal. It is more that, finally, the 'development tourists'[9] as Robert Chambers calls them, are not ultimately responsible for their efforts to 'do good' for others. Often, they hardly descend from the high road, or away from the large town with its creature comforts of running water, television and air conditioning, to assess what effects their advice might have on local people. (Indeed, I never saw the Project's CIDA contact person in the *barangays*.)

Fashionable slogans – women in development (WID), gender and development (GAD), participation, sustainability – formal procedures and political correctness were not substitutes for listening to the residents and learning directly about both their needs and their abilities. They could not know at first hand that women in the *sitio* groups were starting to define their needs and work with FSDP team members to organise and deal with them, that such women were emerging as relators of local history and legends, that one woman, in particular, was a writer of short stories, that some of these narratives were appearing in the Project's Occasional Paper Series. So, when the decision came from Ottawa to close the Project down, they had few arguments and little inclination to demur.

By not listening – or being there – but by foisting conventions and goals drawn from foreign cultures, development experts risk creating disruption and distress in the name of those twin recondite abstractions, 'development' and 'modernisation'. As Jeremy Seabrook[10] has pointed out, Western-engendered development has brought about forms of change which keep people constantly on the move to try to adapt to the pressures of economic and technological forces over which they have little or no control – and from which they rarely gain benefit.

Outraged by the consequences of imposed development models which largely reflect the self-interests of the developers, he contends:

> Sustainability in the lexicon of the West now means sustaining Western privilege. This means preserving a form of wealth-creation that diminishes us and tears humanity apart by the monstrous inequalities it imposes, at the same time as it culls the forest and mines the oceans, guts the earth and extinguishes civilizations, destroying all value and values but those that can be measured in money.[11]

Seabrook's answer to this insecurity is not more change, but the very opposite: the creation of conditions of greater security based upon long-held community values centring on kinship, self-reliance and traditional associations. This alternative is not dissimilar to the observation of Claude Levi-Strauss that,

A well-ordered humanism does not begin with itself, but puts things back in their place. It puts the world before life, life before man, and the respect of others before love of self.

This is the lesson that the people we call 'savages' teach us: a lesson of modesty, decency and discretion in the face of a world that preceded our species and that will survive it.[12]

Seabrook's alternative to the current conventions is moved by a similar spirit of constraint and lack of pretension – with 'the construction of places of refuge, spaces of stability, tranquillity and peace, where people can live out their lives with an assured and decent tranquillity'.[13] He insists that he is not advocating a return to some mythical and harmonious past. Rather, he calls for a greater awareness among those who advance the arguments of progress and modernisation, of the validity of self-reliance and sufficiency. This is especially relevant to a world which is threatened with the environmental and social consequences of a market system where the guiding principle is, as E.J. Mishan perceptively noted, 'enough is not sufficient'.[14]

Susan George also describes societies which until recently had in-built protection and support systems through extended families and community mutual-help networks to preserve egalitarian production and consumption systems in times of emergency:

I am not saying that no one ever died of hunger in so-called traditional societies, and I'm not trying to hold a brief for feudalism or paternalism. I simply want to point out that poor people's support systems are breaking down under outside pressures. Profits take precedence over human and village relationships. Nothing takes the place of the customary support networks; resiliency disappears, people become suddenly subject to a dog-eat-dog dependency on the market for work, for credit, for food and the other necessities of life. The so-called free market may provide them only with the freedom to starve.[15]

Objecters to Seabrook's passionate claim may well insist that even if he is right, people everywhere have been seduced by modernisation; that Coca Cola, jeans and transistor radios as well as the attractions of VCR-portrayed Western (above all, American) lifestyles are available to all; that the desire for such commodities has been at least partially internalised by people in the remotest of rural areas throughout the world; that it is too late to try to reclaim a more serene and modest past. The siren song of modern ideology and practice, they assure us, has most of us irresistibly dancing to its rhythms.

And in some ways, it was the case for many residents in the three Visayan fishing and farming *barangays* whose lives are affected on the one hand by the luxury demand of metropolitan and overseas markets for fish-farm prawns and on the other by the enticements of the lower end of the consumer market's range of product offerings. A difficult choice facing the FSDP was: to what extent do we invest in a modern facility such as a model fishpond to encourage more effective production of prawns, crabs and milk-fish, or, on the other hand, put the money into improving the conditions for small-scale fisherfolk? The debate ran through the lifetime of the Project and I still oppose the majority decision to invest so much in a fishpond which, needing heavy investment, was beyond the scope of small producers and, in any case, gave preference to external consumers over local needs.

Is there some reconciliation, some arena of choice between the currently dominant argument which insists upon an unchallengeable market imperative and an argument which affirms that we must develop massive resistance to a technological/market tyranny capable of locking humanity in a Weberian cage? I believe that there is. It calls for a combination of empathetic action and ethical theory focusing upon approaches which take mutuality and co-operation – participatory, democratic – as their starting point. (I am not very satisfied with the currently-fashionable term, 'empowerment' which smacks of a Western-centred quest for individualistic and competitive advancement.)

For the researcher, this requires new ways of trying to understand those he or she is working with. It may encourage a search for different techniques to listen to people's voices and expressions of need, ability and intent and learn from them. And it undoubtedly demands a new language in which to represent those needs and latent capacities.

## *Development, Pluralism and Co-operation*

A growing body of literature on these issues has swum into my ken recently and has helped me to interpret the practical experience drawn from co-operative projects in Latin America and Asia. The new approaches focus upon alternatives to the programmes of development management which have pervaded our manuals, textbooks and reports for five decades – and continue to do so, despite the claims by global agencies and corporations that they are now aware of the need for change.

Enough has been written pro and contra for yet another review of that work to be superfluous here. More to the point, perhaps, is to consider the implications of the work of people such as Kothari, Max-Neef, Hettne, Goulet, Escobar and Chambers among many others[16] who have helped reveal the enormous waste of time and human energy, the growing disparities (social, gender, ethnic and regional), the cultural destruction and the environmental degradation inherent in conventional top-down strategies.

The first point to be made is that, at even its least engaged, the work of international co-operation is inherently highly subjective, at every phase reflecting the attitudes and values of those engaged in it. It is less an economic exercise than a cultural relationship; one concerned with the intentions, goals, abilities and foibles of human beings in their households, neighbourhoods, communities and societies – and project teams. But current mythologies arising from the grandiose abstractions of progress, growth, competition and the market ignore this – and help to explain why most people gain so little from development.

We might start by turning the world of the experts upside down and replacing economic imperatives with priorities centred on human needs *and capacities* as our starting point in international co-operation. Then we confront not only the world of the 'others', but also our own sets of assumptions, values and capacities. We realise that co-operation has to begin with gaining a better understanding of ourselves, our motivations and the relevance of our knowledge and experience. We start by acknowledging that we are but one part – the outsiders – of the co-operative endeavour. We accept the need for greater humility, a preparedness to listen to and take note of the scientific knowledge and experience of others, especially the local partners whose very livelihoods are at stake.[17] What is needed is the sort of open-minded pluralism described by Robert Chambers:

> This pluralism is an ideology based on doubt, puzzlement, and agnostic openness to evidence and argument. It seeks enlightenment in both poles of contrary views, in practice seeing error less in what people say than in their condemnation of what others say.
>
> Pluralism recognises multiple causation, multiple objectives, and multiple interventions. It is suspicious of unicausal explanation, of the single objective, and of the one solution. It sees, rather, rural development in terms of many dimensions, of complementarities or trade-offs between objectives, of sequences and mixes of interventions.[18]

This is a country mile from the mindset which, based on a fatal combination of arrogance and ignorance, assumes that, whatever the circumstance, a combination of outside expertise and belief in market forces will resolve the problem of 'underdevelopment'. But, taking a step further yet, what emerges is that development co-operation, to respond to the concerns and intentions of local farmers, fisherfolk, craftspeople, parents and children, has to be treated as a process of exchange, mutual respect and dialogue.

In this, all participants – outsiders and insiders – are subjects with their own creativity, their own areas of knowledge and their own experience which form the basis for the exchange of ideas and practical proposals. Decisions on content will be treated as open questions, as will the methodologies and techniques to be chosen, subject to negotiation among bearers of different sources of knowledge and experience. The primary objective is to release the capacity for self-reliant action of the local residents, with special emphasis on the well-being of those who are most at risk.

Pre-ordained and scripted nostrums, abstract objectives and corporate profits then assume second order priority. Relationships increasingly take the form of perceptive and direct dialogue among human subjects trying to grasp the import of the others' vocabulary. Sensitivity to the need to bridge gaps puts the Herderian concept of *einfuhlung* (empathy) ahead of the value of a specific technical competence (although this also has its place, provided that the expert remains on tap and not on top).[19]

## *Conclusion: The Question of Creativity*

Some time ago, reflecting on my field experiences and the lessons learned from classroom teaching, I concluded that the closest I could get to a definition of international co-operation was that, 'its goal is, or should be, to release the innate creativity of *all* human beings, both for their own self-realisation and for the well-being of their communities'.[20]

The emphasis on 'all' was deliberate; too much conventional development work assumes an almost godlike (or at least minor visiting royalty) status for specialists with their books and laboratory knowledge and experience, while denying local people any serious capacity for creativity in dealing with their social and physical environment. Yet this disparagement of other sources of knowledge and experience is in direct contradiction to what many outsiders working in farming and fishing communities have found to be the case.

At least one whole book[21] is devoted to the theme of farmer innovation, focusing on their range of knowledge and experience. The fact that such knowledge is epistemologically very different from that of the academically-trained specialist by itself in no way invalidates the relevance of either approach. In effect, farmers and specialists have complementary roles to play. Creativity, imagination, adaptation and innovation are not the special preserve of any one group, age, gender or culture.

Arthur Koestler's *The Act of Creation*[22] is a homage to the human capacity for creative activity. Too often this capacity is stifled by routine, while the greatest expressions of this creativity spring from insight and inspiration. The ability to associate and link apparently distinct phenomena – his term is 'bisociative' (or lateral) thinking – is to be found in all epochs and all societies. Koestler then investigates historical examples of creative genius. Setting aside the question of genius, however, Koestler's two significant messages are, first, that we are all capable of those leaps of bisociative thinking, especially in our own spheres of interest and activity, whether we are farmers or physicists, craftspeople or artists. Secondly, large (and usually remote) institutions and bureaucratic regulation are, on the whole, inimical to creative insight and intuition. Modern society's cage of disenchantment which Max Weber saw at the start of the twentieth century as springing from Cartesian-Kantian cosmology, led him to declaim against what he perceived to be the final stage in the cultural unfolding of the modern era: 'Specialists without spirit, sensualists without heart; this nullity imagines that it has attained a level of civilization never before achieved'.[23]

Unfortunately, he was not describing the ultimate phase, as we now know 90 years on. As we survey the human and community wreckage of five decades of post-1945 global development, market ideology, free trade and structural adjustment packages, we see the practical application of Weber's dictum raised to new levels in the work of the great bureaucracies, the World Bank, the International Monetary Fund, the UN Development Programme, USAID and a host of other modernising aid agents. Among these, not conspicuously large in world terms, but influential enough, is CIDA which is 'still being challenged to move beyond the notion of aid as a quantitative transfer from "us" to "them", towards a more holistic (i.e. realistic) and solidarity oriented model of development co-operation which seeks security and justice for all'.[24]

But at the heart of development's unhappy record lies a cause deeper even than the relegation of human needs and the obsession with the abstractions of growth and modernisation (although these are dispiriting enough). Worse still is the denial of the human capacity for independent and self-reliant thought, creativity and action. Deep-seated – self-serving – prejudice within development bureaucracies assumes the indigence of those they are dealing with; in turn, the wary and reluctant responses of villagers to offers of progress merely confirm official biases. In this scenario, it is the indispensable outside expert who holds the keys to progress, change and modernisation.

My argument here questions the dangers of influential Pacific Rim countries and their institutional agencies imposing their approaches, their values and attitudes upon local communities. Canada – and CIDA – are not among the most powerful actors on the international stage of development aid and intervention. But their further reinforcement of the actions of more dominant neighbours around the Pacific calls for rigorous and consistent enquiry by those with a vision of more democratic and participatory forms of co-operation.

Solutions and alternatives? After a half century, development organisations and experts need to search into the underlying *weltanschauung* and motivations of the modernising movers and shakers. A philosophy of 'physician, cure thyself' would provide a valuable corrective to the ineffable superiority and remoteness from humanity which currently pervades the corridors of both the development agencies and many academic institutions.

We development-mongers have been, up to now, judgemental observers and interveners in other cultures, societies and economies, but have insufficiently questioned *why* we are intervening, *what* our unspoken objectives are, and *how* we so consistently disrupt the lives of those we manipulate. Such reflection is especially necessary as the objectified others come closer to home. It is one of the strengths of Jeremy Seabrook's exposé that he refers not only to the destitute in the so-called third world, but also those in his own home country 14 years into the social depredations of Thatcherism.

We now need to go one step beyond. To respond to Seabrook's touching descriptions with sympathy, certainly. But more, to see people as subjects who can and do undertake projects of self-reliant and mutually-supportive human development. That calls for a qualitative leap on the part of those who would support such collaboration – a change of worldview which accepts the innate creativity which lies within all human beings. And which reaches its highest expression in co-operation.

## NOTES

[1] A. Sen, *Poverty and Families: An Essay on Entitlement*, Oxford: Clarendon Press, 1981.

[2] These activities are described in greater detail in a forthcoming paper by Philip Kelly and Warwick Armstrong, 'Villagers and outsiders in cooperation: Experience from development praxis in the Philippines', forthcoming.

[3] John Ralston Saul, in his *Voltaire's Bastards: the Dictatorship of Reason in the West*, London: Sinclair-Stevenson, 1992, describes in Weberian mood how Western rationalistic officialdom has moulded modern society into a 'vast, incomprehensible, directionless machine, run by process-minded experts – "Voltaire's bastards" – whose cult of scientific management is bereft of both sense and morality... The result is a civilisation of immense technological power whose peoples increasingly dwell in a world of illusion' (endpaper).

[4] G.J. Schmitz, 'CIDA as peacemaker: integration or overload', in R. Miller (ed.), *Aid as Peacemaker: Canadian Assistance and Third World Conflict*, Ottawa: Carleton University Press, 1992, p. 89.

[5] Ibid., p. 91.

[6] Two recent books, Edward Said's *Culture and Imperialism*, New York: Random House, 1994, and J.M. Blaut's *The Colonizer's Model of the World: Geographical Diffusionism and Eurocentric History*, Toronto: Guildford, 1993, lay emphasis on this aspect of cultural put-down by foreign decision-makers. In surveying a sub-branch of these elites, Said (p. 59) contends that, 'the authority of the observer ... is buttressed by a cultural discourse relegating and confining the non-European to a secondary racial, cultural, ontological status'.

[7] Writing in *Le Monde Diplomatique* (1995), Ignacio Ramonet describes this way of thinking – referring, in particular, to the imperatives of discourse and absolutism which infuse the body of market ideology – as an obscurantist form of modern dogmatism.

[8] A. Huxley, *Essays Old and New*, New York: H.W. Wilson, 1927/1932, p. 61.

[9] R. Chambers, *Rural Development: Putting the First Last*, Harlow: Longman Scientific and Technical, 1983.

[10] J. Seabrook, *Victims of Development: Resistance and Alternatives*, London, New York: Verso, 1993.

[11] Ibid, p. 249.

[12] Claude Levi-Strauus cited in M Berman, *The Reenchantment of the World*, Toronto: Bantam, 1984.

[13] Seabrook, op.cit., 1993, p. 248.

[14] E.J. Mishan, *The Costs of Economic Growth*, Harmondsworth: Penguin, 1967. He also discusses the compulsion of the 'no-choice' myth of modernist economic thinking which has us 'slipping from implied choices to explicit imperatives' (p. 40). It is led by ahistorical, conservative mechanics who deny the ability of humanity to free itself from the rigidities of outdated doctrine: 'Contrary to their fashionable phrases about the need to face change,

those who proclaim themselves to be in the vanguard of new thought prove to be in the iron clutch of the past as a guide to policy in a world different from our own' (p. 17). This passage, echoing Keynes' phrase about the dead hand of long-deceased economists, was written nearly two decades before the ideological reaction of the 1980s.

[15] S. George, *Ill Fares the Land: Essays on Food, Hunger and Power*, Harmondsworth: Penguin, 1984/1990, pp. 236-7.

[16] R. Kothari, 'India: an alternative framework for rural development', in M. Nerfin (ed.), *Another Development: Approaches and Strategies*, Uppsala: The Dag Hammarskjold Foundation, 1977, pp. 208-26; P. Ekins and M. Max-Neef, *Real Life Economics: Understanding Wealth Creation*, London: Routledge, 1992; D. Goulet, 'Development: creator and destroyer of values', *World Development*, 20 (3), 1992, pp. 467-75; B. Hettne, *Development Theory and the Third World*, Stockholm: SAREC Report R2, 1982; Chambers, op. cit., 1983; R. Chambers, A. Pacey, L.A. Thrupp (eds), *Farmer First: Farmer Innovation and Agricultural Research*, London: Intermediate Technology Publications, 1989; A. Escobar, 'Reflections on "development"', *Futures*, 24, June 1992.

[17] For those who look askance at acceptance of the knowledge of local farmers as scientific, especially in comparison with the rational and empirically-testable science of the West, it is as well to remember the gist of Thomas Kuhn's *(The Structure of Scientific Revolutions*, University of Chicago Press, 1962, 1970) thesis on scientific practice. Change – and resistance – in science, he argues, have usually been the consequence of non-rational factors associated with convention, attachment to accepted paradigms, sociological influences and personal intuition. He also (202ff.) offers some telling comments on misunderstanding among different language communities in science and the need to deal with communications breakdowns by the participants becoming 'translators'. It is particularly useful advice for those involved in the work of international co-operation.

[18] Chambers, op. cit., 1983, p. 44.

[19] This appears similar in approach to Mikhail Bahktin's dialogical principle in literature (see K. Hirschkop and D. Shepherd (eds), *Bahktin and Cultural Theory*, Manchester University Press, 1989; and P. Hitchcock, *Dialogics of the Oppressed*, Minneapolis: University of Minnesota Press, 1993). I am grateful to Dr Mireya Folch-Serra of the University of Western Ontario for introducing me to Bahktin's ideas.

[20] W.R. Armstrong, 'Development beyond doleouts: entitlement to food: a systemic approach', Food Systems Development Project, *Occasional Paper No. 1*, Iloilo City, University of the Philippines in the Visayas/McGill University, 1991, p. 35.

[21] Chambers et al (eds), op. cit., 1989.

[22] A. Koestler, *The Act of Creation*, Harmondsworth: Arkana/Penguin, 1964.

[23] M. Weber, *The Protestant Ethic and the Spirit of Capitalism*, New York: Charles Scribner's Sons, 1958, 1991, p. 182.

[24] Schmitz, op. cit., 1992, p. 2.

# 18. ETHNICITY, GEOGRAPHY, HISTORY AND NATIONALISM: A FUTURE OF ETHNIC STRIFE FOR THE INLAND BORDER PEOPLES OF MAINLAND SOUTHEAST ASIA?

*John McKinnon*

We all create images of things we fear or glorify. These images never remain abstractions: we understand them as real-world entities. We assign them labels that serve to set them apart from ourselves. We create 'stereotypes'.[1]

Following the emergence of strongly nationalistic ethnic groups in the former USSR and Yugoslavia, it has become common practice to treat ethnicity as a given which is supposed to explain why neighbours who do not belong to the same ethnic group cannot get on with each other. In many places throughout the Asia-Pacific region the impact of globalisation has set up a defensive response which promotes nationalism and local identities. In the multicultural settlement states of the USA, Canada, Australia and New Zealand, indigenous peoples have taken an increasingly radical stance in opposition to the hegemony of the well-established invaders. In all of these movements the notion of ethnicity is called in to play in various ways; however, when a political discourse becomes associated with a specific ethnic identity, the definition can take on a life of its own, a stereotype 'rooted not in reality but in the myth-making made necessary by our need to control our world'.[2]

This is not the way a large proportion of the English-speaking world sees the matter. The popular discourse on ethnicity is fairly simple and, unfortunately, often difficult to distinguish from racism. First, ethnicity is taken to be a universal category. Membership places people in an effective group. Second, it is widely believed that such membership provides a powerful, primordial and holistic definition of identity. This denies that ethnicity can be just one factor amongst many that may be used to define how individuals see themselves. Third, it is assumed that ethnic groups historically occupied contiguous territories which can be called their homelands. Fourth and last, it is assumed that indigenous people have legitimate claims to sovereignty over these lands and that this is a natural outcome of their identification with place.

When such a discourse is adopted as the basis for a plan of action, count on trouble. The emotions aroused by the promotion of ethnicity can be particularly strong. Members of the group who share the promoted identity may respond enthusiastically to patriotic calls for solidarity. The rhetoric of speeches infused with noble sentiments and appeals to an ancient past have long been the instruments by which those with political ambitions have captured the hearts and minds of the people. But the flip side of patriotism becomes clear in the brutalities of intolerance and hate summarised in the extreme as ethnic cleansing. Where conflicting needs for control spill over into overt violence, the most likely outcome is disaster.

Is such a scenario likely to arise along the borderlands that China shares with Viet Nam, Laos and Burma? Where does Thailand fit in? If recent history is anything to go on, the prognosis does not look good. Burma has been troubled with ethnic warfare since independence. Small groups of ethnic minorities in the highlands of both Laos and Viet Nam continued to fight the victorious communist forces long after they had won the war. A disproportionate number of people of Chinese descent were among the Cambodian and Vietnamese refugees seeking asylum in third countries. On the face of it, the popular discourse may be simple but there is enough evidence to establish a case: ethnicity as a political force.

In this chapter I shall attempt to answer the question posed in the title, 'A Future of Ethnic Strife for the Inland Border Peoples of Mainland Southeast Asia?', by isolating a sector of the border area for closer study. Rather than conducting the enquiry within the familiar matrix of a nation state which encourages writers to place considerations of political hegemony in the background, I have chosen to focus on the transnational distribution of the various indigenous ethnic groups on the frontier of Chinese colonisation, an area which Edmund Leach refers to as 'The Frontiers of "Burma"'.[3]

The chapter is based on information assembled from a wide variety of sources including early colonial travellers in the region, twentieth century colonial scholarship, contemporary writers, and fieldwork carried out since 1975 including over 10 years' residence and recent work and travel in the area. To provide a specific geographical focus and reference point for the chapter, I have isolated a sector of the borderland located in Figure 18.1 and explored in more detail in Figures 18.4 to 18.6. By simplifying and adding figures to linguistic maps and statistics originally prepared by David Bradley, I have constructed an ethno-linguistic profile of a large population occupying a rough hilly terrain better to explore the impact of borders dating from colonial intervention in the closing years of the nineteenth century.

I will first review the situation of the principal ethno-linguistic groups which occupy the sector, look at the way in which differences have been identified historically within the region, review the maps showing the distribution of the various ethno-linguistic groups emphasising the absence of territorial coherence and briefly indicate the impact the borders have had on the lives of some of the people before returning at the end of the chapter to the question posed at the start.

## *Principal Ethno-linguistic Groups*

Over 330 million people live within the study sector. If the sector were a nation state it would encompass enough people to rank as one of the most populous countries in the world. Even though it excludes areas of high density Chinese Han populations located in the southern coastal states, over 191 million of this total population or 58% are Han.

Figure 18.1. STUDY SECTOR

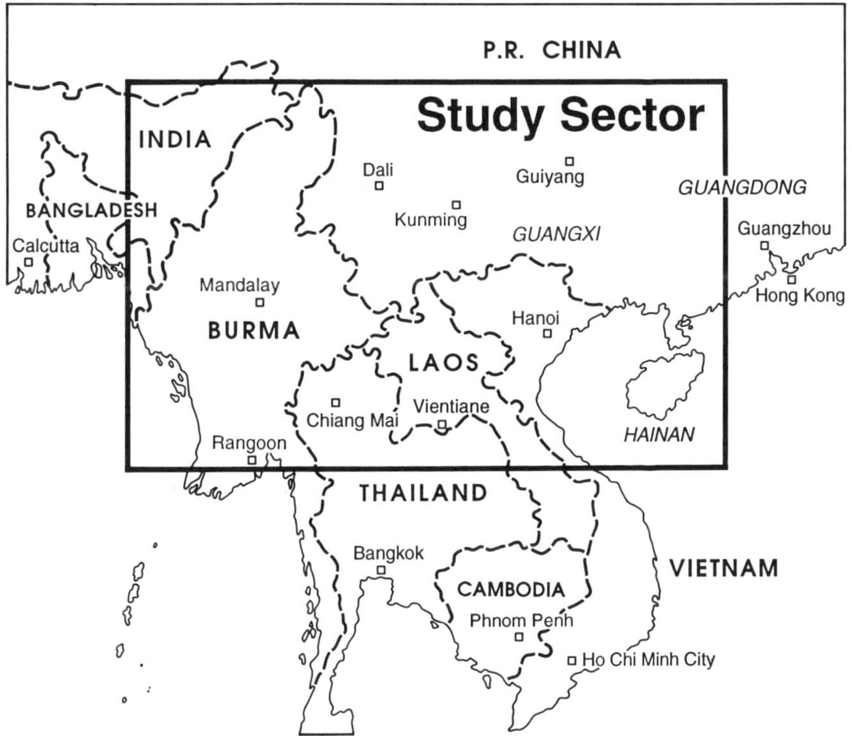


The majority position of the Han is, if anything, underestimated. If ethnicity were to be determined not by voluntary affiliation but by descent, the 1% shown as 'Overseas Chinese' would have to be increased. Where it is better not to be Chinese then the most pragmatic strategy is to become somebody else. Idiosyncratic observations may be of little scientific value, but anybody who has worked in the highlands of Thailand for any length of time will have met many Chinese passing themselves off as Lisu or Yao to obtain Thai residential papers. In the area of Kokang (Burma) close to the border with China, a large number of Chinese traders and residents pass as locals without comment. Close to the Thai border a well-known drug lord, best known by his Shan name Khun Sa, has a Chinese father and a Chinese name, Chang Chifu. When Shan patriots want to put him down as being of little or no account in their nationalist struggle, they simply need to emphasise his otherness, his Chineseness and discount his ethnic credentials.

Temporary transnational migration is possible but can be difficult. If routine checks on public transport reveal that a traveller lacks the documentation, language skills and geographical knowledge needed to provide plausible answers to questions designed to test the validity of the journey, the traveller is in difficulty. Permanent immigration is a lot more difficult. Within all of the study sector countries, when majority people (that is, those who have a modern nation state they can call their own) choose to ignore this status and take on an ethnic minority identity, they usually do so to disguise their intent – the decision to take a side road route or back door entry to a main highway destination which involves immigration to an economically better off country. Mobility more commonly shows a strong rural to urban bias. In Burma or Thailand, where the governments do not bother themselves much with either categorising or wondering how people categorise themselves, the trend among more ambitious, better educated and more mobile minority people is to identify themselves as members of the majority population. In socialist countries like China and Viet Nam, if members of minority groups see no advantage in trying to pass themselves off as a member of the majority, it is because they value the special treatment given such groups and can claim this even if they no longer speak the language of the group to which they have been assigned by the state.

The response depends on the situation. In status-conscious Thailand where it is easier not be identified as other than solidly Thai, people are more likely to conceal non-Thai ancestry for fear that it may diminish their social standing. A surprising number of prominent citizens are willing to confide to outsiders that they are not 100% Thai but insist that this must never be revealed to another Thai. Not so many years ago when Ronald Renard and his colleagues at Payap College in Chiang Mai conducted a follow-up study of a group of Karen high school graduates to see how well they had done, they were surprised to find how difficult it was to locate people. Students they expected to return to their homes could not be found. Those traced to the city were surprised and sometimes dismayed to learn that they were still being identified as Karen when they were living entirely in a Thai way and had told none of their friends and neighbours of their origins. In China the Tujia belatedly identified as a distinct ethnic group after Liberation mainly speak Chinese, live in a manner difficult to distinguish from Han, and may well prefer to remain Tujia because it allows those wealthy enough to marry to have two children rather than one. They also enjoy other special representational privileges denied Han. In such a situation it is not unusual to hear stories of Han men seeking minority wives so that they can have larger families. But then stories are stories. In the face of the Chinese reputation for maintaining a powerful tradition of social control, the matter should be treated with scepticism.

Figure 18.2 provides a general overview of the ethno-linguistic groups in the study sector. Three major linguistic families or what Matisoff calls 'superstocks'[4] are represented:

- The **Austro-Asiatic** superstock is represented by the Mon Khmer Family principally consisting of the Vietnamese of North Viet Nam.
- **Austro-Thai.** This superstock includes the northern distribution of the Southwestern Tai of Thailand, Laos, China and Viet Nam as well as the ethnically distinct Buyi (northern Zhuang) of China, the Zhuang of the central and southern parts of the Guangxi Zhuang Autonomous Region, and the scattered, largely highland populations of the Miao-Yao and Kam Sui (Dong) of China.
- **Sino-Tibetan** superstock in Matisoff's classification includes the large and diverse Sinitic Family, Chinese Han and the Tibeto-Burman families, the latter made up principally by the Burmese, Yi, Karen and other Loloish peoples, some of whom are well known in the ethnological literature (i.e. Naxi, Chin, Naga, Bai and the others too many to list here separately).

Figure 18.2. STUDY SECTOR ETHNO-LINGUISTIC SUB GROUPS

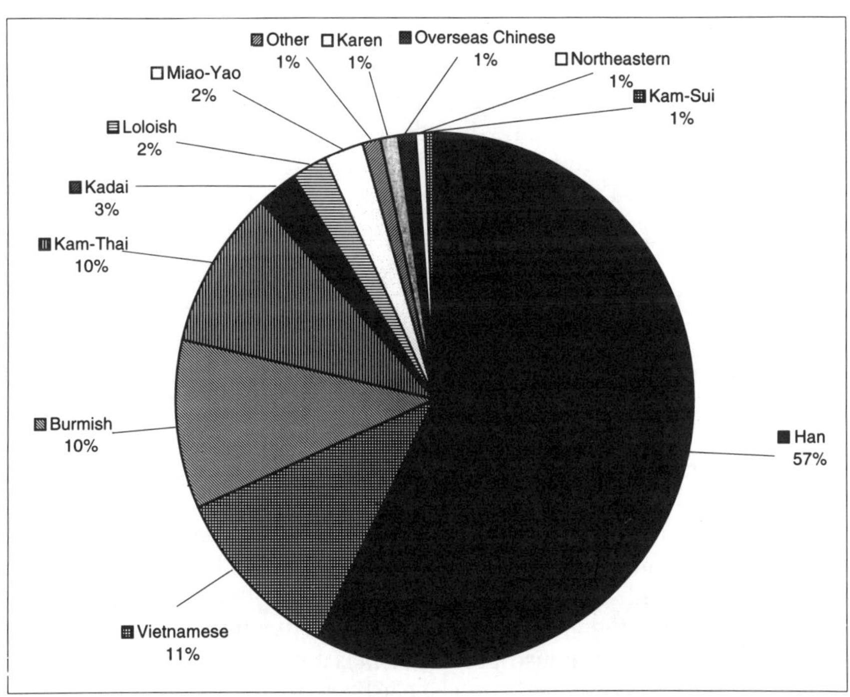

The predominant population in the sector as a whole is overwhelmingly Chinese. However, within the territory of each nation state this predominant position is yielded to a wide range of ethnic groups. When the superstock and Family names given by linguists are peeled aside (as in Table 18.1), names are revealed which will be more readily recognised by those familiar with the contemporary map of mainland Southeast Asia.

Within the category Mon-Khmer, over 90% of the family consists of Vietnamese who make up approximately half of the total population of Viet Nam.

The largest Austro-Thai subgroup in the sector is the Southwestern Kam-Thai which consists of a population scattered through a considerable number of named ethnic groups including the Yuan, Shan, Phu Tai and Tai Mao. They predominate even in the presence of bigger Tai groups which are mainly located to the south of the study sector such as the Lao Korat (22.5 million) and Thai (21 million) who are not strongly represented. The remaining solidly represented Austro-Thai groups such as the Buyi, Miao-Yao and Zhuang enjoy constitutional representation in China but this is carefully managed and few officially designated groups any longer manifest an internal coherence of any political significance, if they ever did. The construction of groups by administrative fiat has heightened people's sense of fragmentation rather than unity.

As can be expected the Burmese make up the largest group in the Tibeto-Burman Family after the Han. All the larger groups such as the Yi and Bai are associated with earlier kingdoms established in Yunnan, the Yi with Dian and the Bai with Nanzhao. The struggle for independence fought by the Karen will not be explored in any detail here, but the sheer size of the population of a group has little directly to do with the exercise of political power. Clearly small minority groups are less likely to be able either to impose their will on others or to defend their own interests in the face of large and well organised outside groups.

### *Identifying Differences*

Language arguably provides one of the best criteria of ethnic distinctness but it is far from the only criterion. The survival of an ethnic group relies not only on whether people speak a distinct language but also on whether they share a history, common ancestors, material culture and above all a critical constituency which includes enough people to follow their customs, arrange their own affairs, celebrate their own religious events and so forth. Where positive identification with membership of an ethnic group is strong, the group will survive. Where the group is small and vulnerable to the influence of outsiders, such as a majority people with a materially higher standard of living, then the siren effect of attractive markets flooded with the consumer goods of industrial capitalism is difficult to ignore. Iron tools, manufactured medicines and clothes, plastic containers, sweets and tailor-made cigarettes readily find a place on a notional list of purchasable priorities

Table 18.1. STUDY SECTOR ETHNO-LINGUISTIC GROUPS RANKED BY POPULATION

| | *Mon-Khmer* | | | *Austro-Thai* | | | *Tibeto-Burman* | |
|---|---|---|---|---|---|---|---|---|
| *Group* | *Population in 000s* | *Percent of Mon-Khmer* | *Group* | *Population in 000s* | *Percent of Austro-Thai* | *Group* | *Population in 000s* | *Percent of Tibeto-Burman* |
| Vietnamese | 36,000 | 92.6 | Southwest Tai | 15,345 | 35.5 | Burmish | 34,450 | 67.5 |
| | | | | | | (Burmese) | (32,000) | (65.7) |
| Wa | 820 | 2.0 | Buyi | 10,800 | 25.0 | Yi | 4,900 | 9.6 |
| Khmu | 375 | 1.0 | Miao-Yao | 7,491 | 17.3 | Karen | 3,850 | 7.5 |
| Palung | 330 | 1.0 | Zhuang | 6,500 | 15.0 | Other Loloish | 3,173 | 6.2 |
| | | (Be, Nung, Tay) | | | | | | |
| Other | 1,354 | 3.4 | Kam-Sui (Dong) | 1,862 | 4.3 | Chin-Naga | 1,445 | 2.8 |
| | | | Other | 1,129 | 2.9 | Bai | 1,100 | 2.1 |
| | | | | | | Other | 2,107 | 4.3 |
| *Total* | *38,879* | *100* | | *43,128* | *100* | | *51,025* | *100* |

Source: D. Bradley, 'East and South-East Asia', in C. Moseley and R. Asher (eds), *Atlas of the World's Languages*, London: Routledge, 1994, pp. 159-82; Statistical Abstracts of PR China, 1993.

and from there, where the household can afford it, are quickly reclassified as household necessities. The language, dress and customs of the market can come to dominate remarkably quickly. What is smart, what is sophisticated, progressive and attractive exercises a seduction that ethnic activists, especially in the north, find difficult to accept.

Historically how people were identified depended not so much on who they were and how well they were able to survive, but on how they were judged by hegemonic groups who determined how they should be characterised. The use of ethnicity as a way of identifying people is relatively new. Within the region, interest was not so much to understand why outsiders were different but to place them within a ranking order of respectability and wealth. Who dominated? Who was dominated? The powerful saw themselves as urbane and civilised and assigned others to the status of inferiors, barbarians and worse. Until the practice was dropped after 1949, the Chinese commonly attached the dog radical to all non-Han people living under the authority of Chinese hegemony. In all but exceptional cases[5] non-Han groups were described as black, hairy, wild and their behaviour unpredictable.

In the rest of Southeast Asia a similar practice was followed. Reid, paraphrasing early Chinese records, describes the natives of the interior as 'dirty, worshipped devils, and ate unclean foods'.[6] An early Chinese visitor to Southeast Asia, Chou Ta-kuan, writes about savage highlanders who,

> ... constitute a race apart. ... these people are despised by other men. ... If by chance a Chinese arrives and, after his long enforced celibacy, should inadvertently have intercourse just once with one of these women, and the master finds out, then the next day the latter will refuse to sit down in the newcomer's company, because he has had intercourse with a savage.[7]

Renard paraphrases the Hariphunchai chronicle written in the name of the *rishi* Vasudeva, the founder of the city, present day Lampun in North Thailand, in which it is observed that,

> ... the inferiority of the Lua came from their having been born in the footprints of elephants, rhinoceroses, buffaloes, other animals and phantom creatures of the forest. ... [these] 'wild men' lacked the ability to distinguish right from wrong and although called men, were incapable of holding royal power ... [they were in fact] 'forest creatures of the race of fools'.[8]

Although the categorisations appear harsh, they were not tied to fixed racial and ethnic characteristics. The historical record provides plenty of examples of movement between these opposites. If a person from the forest or hills was prepared to adopt the language, religion, behaviour and other distinguishing characteristics of the dominant political group, that person immediately became a more respectable type of human being.

Well into historical times Vietnamese, Tai, Burmese and the Khmer maintained their kingdoms in a region in which land was in plentiful supply but people to work it were not. This shortfall was made up for by mounting raids on distant communities to capture people to work the land. Considerations of the ethnic affiliation of the captives do not appear to have been important, but the more dependent prisoners were on their conquerors and the more they shared in common such factors as religion and an understanding of the hierarchical social structure favoured by Indianised *mandala* states, the less trouble they were likely to give. Tai marched off to Pagan by Burmese Buddhists were likely quickly to become integrated into Burmese society. Tai generals involuntarily transmigrated nearby Karen and Lua on to the lowlands but appear to have preferred other Tai. Scattered throughout North and Central Thailand are communities descended from captives marched away from their homelands to clear the forest and establish protected farming communities. All in all the system was followed by aristocrat and mafia alike throughout the ages.

It was well after the arrival of Europeans that first mention is made of ethnic or minority groups. When Spanish colonists first arrived with their experience of having recently driven the Moors and Jews out of Spain, their first concern was to classify 'subject populations according to religion, not ethnicity'[9] and it was only as 'the colonial rulers became less and less seriously Christian themselves, so groups ... were reclassified as ethnic'.[10] As for the term 'minorities', it also came 'into existence with majorities ... No indigenous language of the region has a traditional word for either concept'.[11] Even today ethnic minorities in the region define their identity in contrast to other groups rather than the characteristics they share with their own. Indigenous groups are not self-consciously aware of their characteristics. What they do is the natural and proper way to go about things, it is only what others do which deviates from the norm.

In a region of such ethnic complexity it is not surprising that pluralism was a fact of life and that exact identification of outsiders or others was not considered to be of great importance.

The significance attached to ethnicity and the exactness of the terminology used varies throughout the region. There is little to match the scientific specificity and confidence (some would call it the presumption or worse, the arrogance) of Westerners. The proclamation which established an official interest in hill tribe people in Thailand specified the six ethnic groups which would receive official recognition. This was heavily influenced by outsiders: Americans initially preoccupied with a strategic interest in highland peoples scattered along frontiers demarcated as critical in the fight against communism, and Europeans concerned with opium production. As ethnologists and linguists are pleased to tell it, this focus in no way reflects the real ethnic complexity of Thailand. The linguist David Bradley has pointed out that 'the Thai include various groups in the category Lua/Lawaa (such as the) Bisu and Ugong'.[12] A map prepared by Chulalongkorn University recognises approximately 80 groups. It is the habit of both political and administrative thinkers to simplify the issues they must deal with and it is not surprising that official categorisations rarely reflect actual complexities.

Popular usage better reflects local practice. When discussing the question of how Thai establish their identity, Thongchai Winichakul provides us with a text which could well stand for all of the non-socialist states in the sector. The important thing is not so much 'who are they?' but 'who are we?':

> ... the referent nation or ethnicity is usually ill defined. In Thai, for example, farang is a well known adjective and noun referring to Western people, without any specification of nationality, culture, ethnicity, language, or whatever. Khaek is another term which covers the peoples and countries of the Malay peninsula, the East Indies, South Asia and the Middle East without any distinction. Khaek also denotes Muslim, but by no means exclusively so. That is to say, a reference is sometimes made regardless of whether or not a certain characteristic really belongs to any particular nation or ethnic group, because the aim of the discourse is to identify the un-Thainess rather than to define the characteristic of any particular people. Once the un-Thainess can be identified, its opposite, Thainess is apparent.[13]

The contemporary Chinese approach to the question of ethnicity is quite different again. Ethnic groups are seen as distinct national components of the political structure of the state and are known as *minzu*. The Han clearly form the national majority but differences between speakers of Mandarin on the one hand and Wu, Gan, Xiang, Min, Hakka and Yue on the other are not considered to constitute different national groups. Those regarded as other than Han are called national minorities. To qualify as specific minority groups, they must meet criteria laid down by the Communist Party and adapted from a system pioneered in the former USSR. How the criteria are interpreted is everything. Off and on since Liberation teams of social scientists in the service of the state have worked at the task of ethnic identification (*minzu shibie*).

In the USSR the nationality question was initially manipulated to secure the support of popular opposition to Imperial Russia. The cultivation of ethnic differences was encouraged and people resettled in what became 'ancestral' homelands.[14] In retrospect this clearly contributed to the rise of nationalism and the eventual break up of the Soviet Union.

Although also based on the guidelines laid down by Stalin, Chinese policy remains much more cautious. Apart from obligatory declarations of fraternal respect and equality, the Chinese practice of classifying minority people on an evolutionary scale of development which places them in a subordinate position not only reasserts deeply held feelings of Han superiority, but also effectively provides a rationale for Chinese hegemony. Where justified by the presence of considerable numbers of a specific national minority, so called autonomous regions, prefectures or *banna* (counties) have been formed to give *minzu* a direct say in local government. However, control of these remain firmly in Party and Han hands. No attempt has been made to resettle and concentrate administratively defined ethnic populations in congruous areas.

It is the state and its experts rather than the people who decide what constitutes a distinct ethnic group. Large groups are preferred and the absence of any internal coherence recognised by the people themselves is given little or no weight.

The classification system imposed by the Party and its experts do not deny people a relationship with their true kin, but by placing the emphasis of affiliation on abstract metagroups people's sense of reality is ignored. In a paper in which he reports on fieldwork carried out in the southwest of China, Stevan Harrell refers to a group of three communities classified by the state as Yi. One community adamantly refused to accept this categorisation.[15] Such scholarly dissent is not uncommon. Bradley in an as yet unpublished work reports that 'four subgroups (of the Southeastern Yi), Sani, Axi, Azhe and Azha, each feel themselves to be a distinct group'.[16] When such groups are forced to accept instruction in a language which is not their own but is treated as if it were, their frustration is easy to understand. Shih-chung Hsieh points out that Tai from Xishuangbanna and Dehong Dai 'use completely different written languages and speak mutually unintelligible Tai languages. Their styles of dress, patterns of settlement, and original political systems are disparate'.[17] Tai do not function as an ethnic group so a universal Tai culture 'has been created by Chinese official writers'[18] to give substance to the ethnic label. Under Chinese just as under Soviet rule, intellectuals are 'specifically trained and employed to produce national cultures'.[19]

It is difficult to follow the rationale for classifying some small groups as distinct *minzu* and others not. The criteria are not specific enough to be transparent and the pragmatic political considerations which must be taken into account are rarely explained. For instance, why are the scattered Chinese-speaking Hui who to outsiders are entirely Han in all respects save their religion (they are Muslim) designated a national minority? The classification appears to say more about adherence to religious as opposed to state law than anything else. Are the Chinese authorities telling us that as belief in Allah places their allegiance before that of the state then these people ought to be treated differently? Or is it because, as Raphael Israeli has it, as Muslims 'they are rebellious by nature'?[20] Neither observation holds very close to either ethnological or Stalinist criteria and the reader is left with the impression that in the end the state does what it likes regardless of any widely held principles.

There is a foundation of egalitarian principles built into the system and repeated again and again in statements about how 'The government should treat all nationalities equally without the slightest discrimination'[21] and with understanding and tolerance. Despite this the reality is somewhat different. As pointed out recently, there are deep contradictions at the heart of Chinese practice. On one hand ethnic characteristics are to be preserved as part of a unified multinational state, but on the other hand where these interfere with progress they must be eliminated:

> The things that remain are those that foster ethnic pride, but do not impede progress. This is why the Communist state has placed so much emphasis on festivals, costumes, and the inevitable dancing in a circle, which is close to universal among China's minority minzu.[22]

Everybody agrees,'They sing, they dance; they whirl, they whirl. Most of all, they smile, showing their happiness to be part of the motherland.'[23]

### *Boundaries and the Ethno-linguistic Mosaic*

Before Europeans could claim the authority to make any difference, the boundaries between principalities were not a matter that commanded much attention. The *mandala* organisation of town and state formed domains of authority, interlinking circles which were maintained not by blanket territorial control but by lines of communication along which the extent of a sovereign's authority was indicated by guard houses and other markers. The movement of individuals was not normally restricted and it was only during periods of hostility when it became dangerous to travel that highways were considered to be closed. Winichakul tells us that there were 'golden, silver path(s)'[24] which were kept open all the time for trade like the golden and silver paths down which Akha shaman take people on visits to the ancestors.[25] One can imagine the *mandala* of the study sector which fell between so many competing authorities as being like precolonial Siam,

> ... a discontinuous, patchy arrangement of power units where people of different overlords mingled together in the same area ...
>
> The sphere of a realm or the limits of the kingdom could be defined only by those townships' allegiance to the center of the kingdom. The political sphere could be mapped only by the power relationships, not by territorial integrity[26]

Although Winichakul's interpretation is challenged by Wijeyewardene,[27] his observations are consistent with practical considerations such as low population densities, the difficulty of travel and the complex ethnic mosaic. To appreciate truly the charismatic authority of a king, it must have been necessary to share the beliefs which identified the nature of his power. The lowland Indic tradition in the south of the sector was not necessarily shared in the north where the influence of the Chinese prevailed. The Dian perhaps, but certainly the Nanzhao and Dali *mandala*, were clearly based on the Chinese model of the state in which the emphasis fell on systematic administration and incorporation of a wide variety of peoples into a common structure. But for both the Indic- and Sinitic-based systems, the challenge of maintaining strict centralised control over a mountainous and difficult terrain must have posed a huge challenge. Local people then, as now, must have spent most of their time going about their personal, family and community affairs in a manner designed to keep outside interference to a minimum. If this was not the case it is difficult to see how such a large number of different languages and ethnic groups could have survived.

Although the distribution of the dominant Han is not shown, the maps provide a picture of the pattern of settlement that tells us more than what words alone can provide.

In Figures 18.3-18.5 an attempt is made to separate the distribution of the three principal ethno-linguistic families and their related groups.[28] Figure 18.3 shows the distribution of the Mon Khmer Family. The first observation that needs to be made is that although the Vietnamese are by far the most numerous group and make up over 92% of the total population, the area occupied by the remaining 8% is much larger. This ratio of land to population in which minority, usually highlander, people occupy more land than majority valley people is replicated throughout the region. This pattern is interrupted only either where population pressures on available agricultural land have forced valley peoples into the hills in search of land (i.e. Thailand), or in China where traditional majority groups of Tai have become minorities in the face of Chinese colonisation but retain occupation of the valleys.

Figure 18.4 shows the distribution of the Austro-Thai Superstock. Here two characteristics dominate: the long sausage-like shape of various Tai groups spread along the principal river valleys and the smaller black dots which indicate the scattered location of both Miao and Yao highland groups. Other large groups of Austro-Thai like the Zhuang of the Guangxi Zhuang Autonomous Region, the Shan of Northeast Burma, the Yuan of North Thailand and the Lao Korat of Laos and Northeast Thailand, although prevalent, are more difficult to see.

Figure 18.5 presents the most complicated single family picture of all. Small Tibeto-Burman groups appear to be deliberately scattered along borders. This coincidence identifies the location of some of the most vulnerable and poorest groups of all, the Hani, Akha, Lahu and Lisu and other highlanders closely associated with residence in remote areas. It tells us that the borders were demarcated in areas considered to be the most isolated from competing powers. When the borders were agreed to they were in fact well beyond the direct control of the dominant valley people who signed the documents which became part of international law. Larger groups such as the Burman, Karen and less obvious Jingphaw (Jingpo or Kachin) take their place in a slightly inflated configuration unavoidable for a country in which survey work soon ceased following the departure of the British, and the slip and slide back to the future of a more brutal anarchy began.

Figure 18.3. STUDY SECTOR: MON-KHMER ETHNO-LINGUISTIC GROUPS

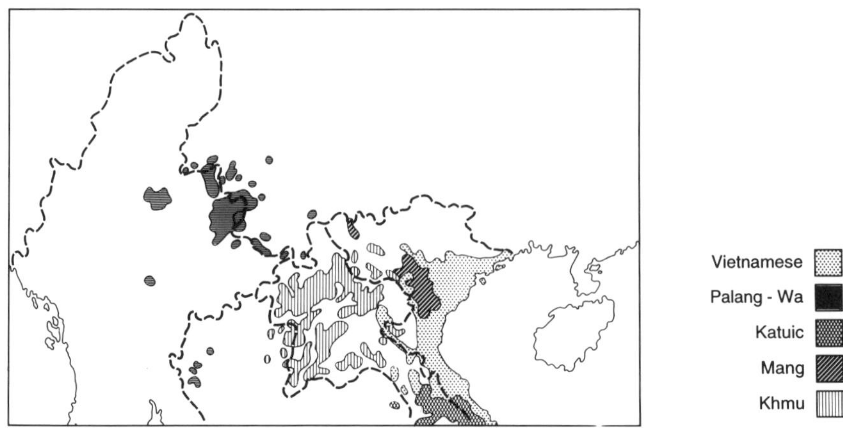


Figure 18.4. STUDY SECTOR: AUSTRO-THAI ETHNO-LINGUISTIC GROUPS

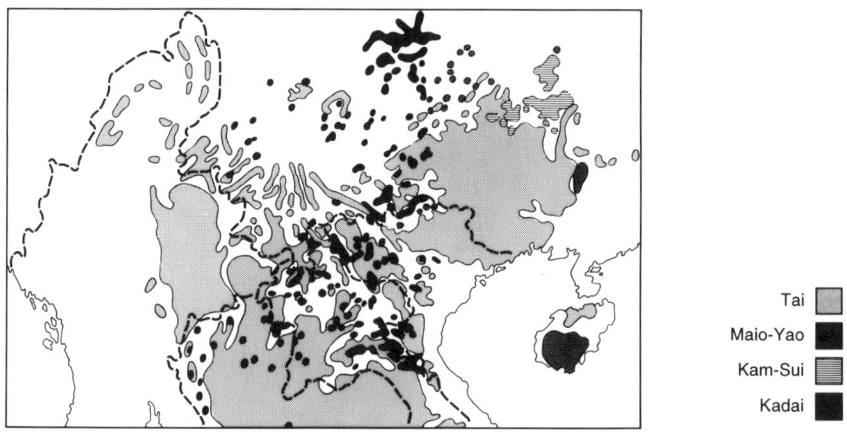


Figure 18.5. STUDY SECTOR: TIBETO-BURMAN ETHNO-LINGUISTIC GROUPS

If the reader hopes a clearer picture of the ethnic mosaic of the inland borderland will emerge as the discussion proceeds then I am bound to disappoint. Figure 18.6 provides an overall picture of distribution based on what Matisoff calls superstocks and which I have labelled Ethno-linguistic Families. The horizontal and angled parallel lines which serve as shading overlap to indicate the general ethno-linguistic complexity on the ground.

What needs to be said? Any attempts to simplify the representation of reality soon run into difficulty. At one stage ethnographers and geographers working in the region thought that different ethnic groups could be neatly arranged by altitude with highlanders sitting in the hills at an appropriate contour overlooking some and being overlooked by others, and all hill tribes looking down in the only way open to them on the rich people in the valleys.[29] Unfortunately the further such a model is stretched the more inaccurate it becomes. If there is a clear distinction, it can only be made between valley majorities and highland minorities, but even this obscures the critical role played by Chinese Han minorities in the lowland economies centred on the cities. How can territorial coherence be identified in the study sector?

Figure 18.6. STUDY SECTOR: ETHNO-LINGUISTIC FAMILIES

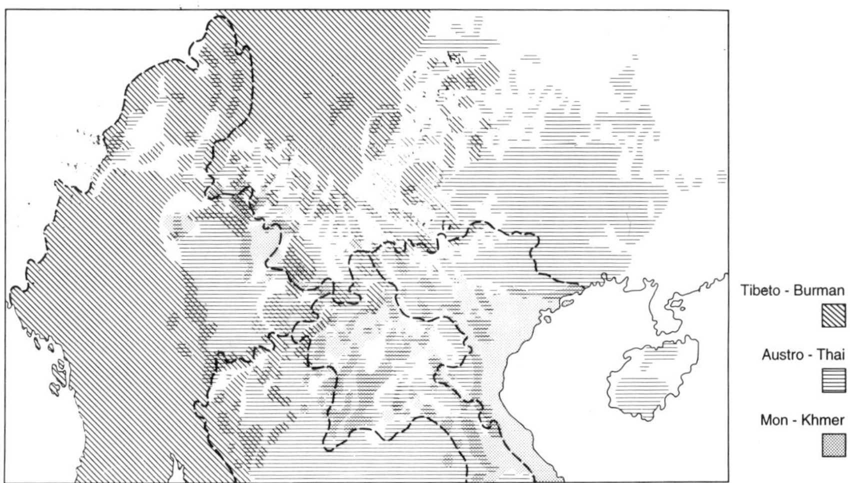


The international borders add a further difficulty. The transient hegemony of the British created ethnicity in Burma in much the same way as the Chinese and Russians have created it in their empires for the same underlying, modernising reasons. The result is that for the past 40 years or so the Burmans have, off and on, been at war with 'their' ethnic minorities. Little wonder that on the Burman side of the border the Jingphaw or Kachin are seen as militaristic and uncooperative. On the Chinese side of the border these same people live in peace with the Han. Are they then fighting an ethnic war against the Burmans? Bertil Lintner in his account of a journey he took through north Burma in 1985 notes that Kachin soldiers referred to enemy soldiers not as Burmans or Burmese but Ma Sa La, the abbreviation by which the previous government was known (BSPP). Lintner quotes one informant as saying, 'We're not against the Burmans as a people. It's the government'.[30]

Some years ago Peter Hinton, an anthropologist, annoyed his international colleagues by publishing a paper which he entitled, 'Do the Karen exist?', and then went on to point out that those who 'try to introduce order into this apparent chaos, by dividing the highlanders into a number of "tribal" or "ethnic" groups, the members of which share a distinctive language and set of cultural traits', were kidding themselves:

> ... this perspective is fundamentally misleading: ... the only way to understand the societies of the highlands is to regard their cultural variety as secondary to economic and political interests, which have nothing to do with supposed ethnic boundaries.[31]

Hinton and Anderson[32] share the view of Lehman who consistently argued that 'European ideas about nations, societies and cultures, and the kind of phenomena they were taken to be'[33] were not only wrong but contributed to the strife Westerners associate with ethnicity and nationalism as though it was a natural state of affairs.

Despite this more radical point of view it remains possible to map the distribution of spoken languages as an indication of the location of ethnic groups. As long as we remind ourselves that few of these territories are the exclusive domain of any single group, that they rarely form internally coherent societies and that people who make up the numerically smaller groups are subordinate to outside economic and political interests, we will not stray too far from the truth of the matter. The important thing to remember is not to put undue emphasis on the significance of ethnic identity.

## *A Future of Strife?*

It is not possible in such a brief discussion to do justice to all available information, but the further the exploration goes the more obvious it becomes that the popular, holistic, even deterministic primacy credited to ethnic identity is seriously flawed. Social relationships associated with a shared ethnic identity are not so politically robust as to extend far beyond extended neighbourhoods and affective family connections. The separation imposed by international borders and reinforced by opposing political systems can significantly reduce intercourse between people belonging to the same ethnic group and impose considerable problems of their own. People are willing to change their ethnic affiliation depending on their situation and what is to be gained from the transformation. Although there is some correspondence between ethnicity and occupation of a territory, this is rarely uniform over large areas. Highland minority people are particularly widely scattered and the homogeneity of valley majorities is a reality structured more by political design than nature. Lastly, in such ethnically complex situations, concepts such as 'absolute and indivisible' sovereignty[34] and nationality with their roots so strongly embedded in a European past, enshrined in international law and subject to profound stereotyping are out of place.

Writing about the likelihood of future ethnic troubles is fundamentally misleading. The discourse is entered into by scholars to meet the expectations of their clients, an intellectual establishment in the West preoccupied in a manner not entirely different from their socialist colleagues in China and Russia with the process of modernisation. The underlying assumptions are not as obvious but the same myths are at work. What does it mean when an otherwise pragmatic fieldworker like Colin Mackerras, after discussing the impact of modernisation, says 'that China will not necessarily follow the Soviet Union into disintegration ... I shall not predict the breakup of China due to ethnic conflict. But I am fairly confident that minority issues will loom quite large in China's political and social future'.[35]

Is he saying that if China runs into economic and political troubles these will impact on the whole of China and that effective groups within it may take dissenting action? He is not alone. In a recent paper Dru Gladney makes a similar statement. He contends that while the integrity of a strong and united China is unlikely to be challenged, 'a China weakened by internal strife, inflation, uneven economic growth or the struggle for succession after Deng's death could become further divided along cultural and linguistic lines'.[36]

As formerly isolated groups of people living on the periphery are drawn into the economic transformation taking place in China, Viet Nam, Thailand and to a lesser extent Laos and Burma, they are made more aware of what others enjoy and how they are treated. Thus additional expections will arise. Having been drawn into this process, people are more likely to be aware of their place within it. If that system begins to fail and the hegemony of central authority breaks down, people will naturally turn for support to communities with which they have a shared understanding. The groups that will form may give some consideration to ethnic matters, but ethnic affiliations in themselves do not generate strife so much as provide the basis for group solidarity. How this identity is used, how it is interpreted and what sort of ideology is promoted, is everything.

Ethnicity does not create strife. Overt violence occurs when two or more groups engaged in pursuing competing or conflicting political and economic ends relinquish any other way of mediating their differences. When, as in the study sector, the basis on which group solidarity can be structured is deeply compromised by administrative intervention, proximity and common interest are much more likely than ethnic identity to serve as a rationale for group formation. It is not as though we are obliged to adopt the iconoclastic view of Peter Hinton and maintain that the Karen and by extension the Miao, Yao, Jingphaw and others do not exist. Ethnicity is an observable reality. Different groups of people speak distinct languages, follow different customs, eat different foods and so on. However, when used as a political stereotype, an administrative fiction or an ideological construct, the identification of ethnicity becomes like racism, little more than a crude representation of reality. To remain reasonable we need to maintain a critical perspective on this notion, this challenging word: ethnicity.


## *Acknowledgements*

Most of the population data and all of the base maps used in the preparation of this chapter were assembled by the linguist David Bradley of La Trobe University and published in the *Atlas of the World's Languages.* Dr Bradley also generously provided copies of unpublished field data and maps of the western Himalayas.[37] I am greatly indebted to the unconditional, open access he gave to his work. I also wish to acknowledge the exemplary cartographic skills which David and Barbara Winchester brought to the challenge of interpreting the original, large format maps and designing the miniaturised, monochrome figures presented here. I also need to acknowledge the work of Katharine McKinnon who managed the entry and analysis of the population data.


NOTES

[1] Sander L. Gilman, *Difference and Pathology: Stereotypes of Sexuality, Race and Madness*, Ithaca and London: Cornell University Press, 1995, p. 15.

[2] Ibid, p. 12.

[3] E.R. Leach, 'The Frontiers of "Burma"', *Comparative Studies in Society and Histor y*, 3, 1960-1, pp. 49-68.

[4] James A. Matisoff, 'Linguistic diversity and langage contact', in John McKinnon and Wanat Bhruksasri (eds), *Highlanders of Thailand*, Singapore: OUP, 1986, pp. 56-86.

[5] Duncan Campbell, 'Kuang Lu' s *Southern Elegance*: loyalty on the borders of Empire', Paper presented at the 1 1th New Zealand International Conference on Asian Studies, 1-4 July 1995, University of Auckland.

[6] Anthony Reid, 'Early Southeast Asia categorizations of Europeans', in Stuart B. Schwartz (ed.), *Implicit Understandings: Observing, Reporting, and Reflecting on the Encounters Between Europeans and Other Peoples in the Early Modern Period* , CUP, 1994, p. 269.

[7] Ibid.

[8] Ronald Renard, 'Minorities in Burmese history', in K.M. De Silva, Pensri Duke, Ellen S. Goldberg and Nathan Katz (eds), *Ethnic Conflict in Buddhist Societies: Sri Lanka, Thailand, and Burma*, London: Pinter, 1988, pp. 79 and 83.

[9] Benedict R. O'G. Anderson, 'Introduction', *Southeast Asian Tribal Groups and Ethnic Minorities*, Cultural Survival Report 22, Cambridge, Mass., 1987, p. 3.

[10] Ibid.

[11] Ibid, p. 1.

[12] David Bradley, 'Identity: the persistence of minority groups', in McKinnon and Wanat (eds), op. cit., 1986, pp. 46-7.
[13] Thongchai Winichakul, *Siam Mapped: a History of the Geo-Body of a Nation*, University of Hawaii, 1994, p. 5.
[14] Robert J. Kaiser, *The Geography of Nationalism in Russia and the USSR*, Princeton University Press, 1994, p. 378.
[15] Stevan Harrell, 'Ethnicity, local interests, and the state: Yi communities in Southwest China', *Comparative Studies in Society and History*, 32 (3), 1990, pp. 515-48.
[16] David Bradley, 'Language policy for the Yi', in Stevan Harrell (ed.), forthcoming volume on the Yi.
[17] Shi-Chung Hsieh, 'The dynamics of Tai/Dai-Lue ethnicity and ethnohistorical analysis', in Stevan Harrell (ed.), *Cultural Encounters on China's Ethnic Frontiers*, University of Washington Press, 1995, p. 301.
[18] Ibid, pp. 325-6.
[19] Yuri Slezkine, 'The USSR as a communal apartment, or How a socialist state promoted ethnic particularism', *Slavonic Review*, 53 (2), 1994, p. 450.
[20] Dru C. Gladney, 'Review of Raphael Israeli, with the assistance of Lyn Gorman, *Islam in China: A Critical Bibliography*', in *China Review International*, 1 (2), 1994, p. 150.
[21] Zhang Lifang, 'The source of national harmony', *Beijing Review*, November 1994, p. 9.
[22] Harrell (ed.), op. cit., 1995, p. 27.
[23] Gladney, op. cit., 1994, p. 95.
[24] Winichakul, op. cit., 1994, p. 77.
[25] Inga-Lill Hansson, 'Marginalisation of Akha ancestors', *Pacific Viewpoint*, 33 (2), 1992, pp. 185-92.
[26] Winichakul, op. cit., 1994, p. 79.
[27] Gehan Wijeyewardene, 'The frontiers of Thailand', in Craig J. Reynolds (ed.), *National Identity and Its Defenders: Thailand, 1939-89*, Monash Papers on Southeast Asia No. 25, Monash University, 1991, pp. 157-91.
[28] Although they fall within the arbitrary boundary of the study sector, information on the largely Tibeto-Burman peoples of the northeast of India and Bangladesh is not shown on the map. The Burma-Bangladesh and Burma-India borders mark the limit of the exercise. Those interested in filling in the missing data should consult David Bradley, 'East and South-East Asia', in C. Moseley and R. Asher (eds), *Atlas of the World's Languages*, London: Routledge, 1994, pp. 159-82.
[29] Harald Uhlig, *Hill Tribes and Rice Farmers in the Himalayas and Southeast Asia: Problems of the Social and Ecological Differentiation of Agricultural Landscapes Types*, The Institute of British Geographers, Transactions and Papers, Publication No. 47, London, 1969.
[30] Bertil Lintner, *Land of Jade: A Journey through Insurgent Burma*, Edinburgh: Kiscadale and White Lotus, 1990, p. 133.
[31] Peter Hinton, 'Do the Karen really exist?', in McKinnon and Wanat, op. cit., 1986, p. 155.
[32] Anderson, op. cit., 1987.
[33] F.K. Lehman, 'Ethnic categories in Burma and the theory of social systems', in Peter Kunstadter (ed.), *Southest Asian Tribes, Minorities and Nations*, Princeton University Press, 1967, p. 103.
[34] Leach, op. cit., 1960-1, p. 49.
[35] Colin Mackerras, 'China's minorities avoid the Balkan Syndrome', *Campus Review*, January 1995, p. 8.
[36] Dru C. Gladney, 'China's ethnic awakening', *Asia Pacific Issues*, Analysis from the East West Center, No. 18, 1995, p. 8.
[37] D. Bradley (ed.), *Tibeto-Burman Languages of the Himalayas*, Canberra: Pacific Linguistics, 1996.

# 19. TRANSFORMING THE PERIPHERY: THE CASE OF SARAWAK, MALAYSIA

*Philip S. Morrison*

### *History and Geography*

Since the Second World War, the regions of Southeast Asia have gradually been incorporated into a growing network of trade, investment, nation-building and security relations. A previously inaccessible and comparatively isolated region, the island of Borneo has been drawn with increasing speed into two of these new power centres, Malaysia and Indonesia, with much of its economic prosperity now dependent on trade with Japan, Korea, Taiwan and Singapore. While these linkages have been the source of economic growth, the incorporation of Sarawak into the political and economic networks of the region has also increased the tensions within the state.[1] These have been muted, however, by the increasing power of those with access to the new export revenues, political patronage and resources necessary to propel economic growth and by what is locally referred to as the 'politics of development'.

Many of these tensions will not disappear with economic growth alone because they reflect inherent structural imbalances which complicate development options and threaten the very social harmony on which they are based. Because Sarawak is small and highly dependent on both public and private decisions taken outside the state, the coordination necessary for it to harmonise its transition will rest on the synchronisation of changes which will depopulate the rural areas with those designed to create employment in the towns and ensure that labour can indeed move easily from one to the other.[2]

Sarawak is the largest of the 13 states within the Federation of Malaysia.[3] With an 800 km. coastline to the South China Sea it covers nearly 124.5 thousand square kilometres of the island of Borneo.[4] Despite its geographical size, Sarawak has a population of less than 2 million people, giving it one of the lowest population densities in the ASEAN region. This population is comprised of three main ethnic groups: Iban and Chinese each make up roughly a third of the population; Malay nearly 20%; and Bidayuh and Melanau with many other smaller groups make up the remainder.

Sarawak's measurable growth since its incorporation into the Malaysian Federation in 1963 has been impressive. GDP rose at an average annual rate of 6.1% between 1978 and 1993;[5] and the official statistics on the growth of mean incomes, road density, education and health indicate a state rapidly overcoming enormous obstacles of terrain, accessibility and limited infrastructure.[6]

Despite these achievements, Sarawak remains a structurally imbalanced state. Agriculture is the largest single source of livelihood but contributes a relatively minor and diminishing source of income.[7] Sarawak's current wealth as measured by GDP rests not on its crops but on its exports of sawn logs, liquefied natural gas, crude petroleum and associated non-agricultural products. The manufacturing sector is still in its infancy and, with only a third of the population living in urban areas, the scope for the service sector remains limited. Unemployment levels, particularly among the large youthful population, are high. Meanwhile the rural population has grown to its largest size ever and while the proportion employed in agriculture has fallen, more people are directly dependent on that sector than ever before. Growth in agricultural output has been slow and smallholder incomes remain low compared to the urban population. As a result, even after 20 years of the New Economic Policy (NEP), historical associations between ethnicity and income in Sarawak remain strong.

In order to explain the nature of Sarawak's contemporary development and its place within the Asia-Pacific region, it is necessary to sketch in the formidable physical obstacles to development – poor soils, absence of land suitable for agriculture, extensive areas of coastal peat swamp, a hilly to mountainous interior and an unforgiving equatorial climate.[8] The extreme costs of infrastructure development compound the difficulties of transforming the environment so that it can support more than a comparatively sparse population. At the same time, the very sparse population itself has not created the same pressures for agricultural innovation experienced in Southeast Asia.[9]

It is also necessary to trace the history of Sarawak beginning with the migration of the Iban into the area,[10] and their northward settlement after the acquisition and extension of the country from 1841 onwards by several generations of the Brooke family.[11] Against this history, the settlement of the Malays, the migration of the Chinese and the development of a multiracial state in which both location and economic function closely follow ethnicity in significance must be outlined.[12]

Sarawak became a British crown colony in 1941, and following economic development was incorporated into the Malaysian Federation in 1963, but not without controversy.[13] Constitutional and related economic ties bind the state ever closer to the Malaysian Federation, while major trading relationships with Japan and Korea in particular and their associated direct and indirect investments in Sarawak (particularly by Japan) create ties elsewhere in the region.[14] From the 1970s the country was marked by exploitation of state forests, the discovery of off-shore petroleum and gas fields, and the search for additional exports.

The aim of this chapter is not to retrace these steps in Sarawak's development, but to explore one major source of tension that exposes its underlying development dilemma. At its most simplistic, this dilemma centres on the fact that the agricultural sector employs 47% of the state's labour force but produces only 7.5% of its GDP (1993).[15]

At the heart of any resolution of this imbalance is the relationship between the state and the smallholder. Increasingly they occupy different worlds in which different languages, ideologies and priorities prevail. It is a contrast that pits land as a commodity against land as a source of livelihood, employment against revenue generation and, because of the vagaries of history, one ethnic group against another. With less than 25 years to go before 2020 and Dr Mahathir Mohamad's vision of a developed Malaysia, the development dilemma that characterises Sarawak is not one that places it on the periphery of a fast developing core of Asian Tigers: Sarawak is already deeply tied into their growth as a supplier of natural resources. Of more significance is the growing distinction between the centre and the periphery *within* the state of Sarawak itself.

This duality is not one that is easily reflected in the difference between the city and the countryside, the coast and the interior, or even the Dayak[16] on one hand and the Malay and Chinese on the other, but rather between those fortunate to have gained either resource capital or human capital through the education system and those who have access to neither. Access to such capital is already favouring those with the training and experience necessary to function in an increasingly global economy, as well as those who have chosen to adapt to the realities of the Malaysian model of development. As any recent visitor to Kuching will testify, the contrasts are already quite stark and increasing: the periphery has already been internalised. Growth has been easier to achieve than development, for growth does not necessarily require balance or equity. The development challenge, however, is no less than the incorporation of its predominantly rural-based population in such a way that the benefits of natural as well as human resource development can be shared. So far the rural smallholder has only benefited in a very limited way from the spoils of oil or gas or forestry although the latter has created some off-farm employment. Rather the main source of monetary income for the smallholder has been those cash crops they have managed to grow and sell on the international commodity market. Despite the growth of off-farm employment and the exploitation of common property resources, the livelihood of the majority of families still depends on what can be produced by themselves from their agricultural land. The state's vision for the transformation of agriculture is therefore critical.

We look firstly at the commodity market as experienced by the pepper growers. We then turn to the smallholders' alternative sources of income, to off-farm employment and migration. The state's 1990 agenda is then explored with respect to both agriculture and industry.

## *The Commodity Cycle: The Case of Pepper*

Probably more than any other single factor, it is cash crops that have linked the incomes and life course of the rural households of Sarawak to the international economy. There is now a wide variety of cash crops grown in Sarawak including sago; coconut in the coastal zones; and rubber, pepper, cocoa and oil palm in the inland areas. The smallholder's most important cash crop has been pepper.

Pepper has been grown in Sarawak since the Brookes but primarily by the immigrant Chinese in the Kuching and Sibu areas. It was not until the 1970s that pepper became an attractive alternative source of cash for the mainly Iban and Bidayuh (Dayak) smallholders who had previously relied on rubber to supplement the cultivation of padi. Relatively easy to introduce, pepper requires capital and accompanying instruction on proper terracing, planting and above all maintenance.[17] Its heavy labour commitment is less of a problem than the cash requirements for the purchase of fertiliser and pesticides as well as setting up costs. These considerations led the state government to introduce the Pepper Subsidy scheme in 1972 after which both holdings and the acreage in pepper expanded considerably. By 1987 non-Chinese mainly Dayak farmers accounted for 82% of the 45,000 pepper holdings and 75% of the 10,000 hectares planted to pepper.[18]

The majority of smallholders are Iban. Primarily hill padi farmers, they have adapted their system of shifting cultivation to wet padi planting in swampy lowlands and in addition to pepper also cultivate rubber and cocoa as cash crops. As Uli points out, 'the Iban also take part in the estate or plantation forms of land development schemes that were centrally managed by SLBD (Sarawak Land Development Board) in the early 1970s. Today there are also a few hundred Iban households participating in cocoa and oil palm schemes that are centrally managed ...'.[19]

Driven by the rising world price for pepper throughout the early 1970s (Figure 19.1), planting continued in a rash of new holdings that transformed the landscape of much of the midland agricultural zone of Sarawak. Land was terraced and the orderliness of the rows of deep green pepper vines climbing stakes set in the amber red soils was in stark contrast to the intercropping and – to the untrained eye – disorderly mixture of crops which prevailed before. The weeding, spraying and tending of the crops together with their harvesting became an integral part of the agricultural cycle, as did the subsequent separation of the green berries from the stalks and the drying of the pepper corns on mats on the longhouse verandahs.

The vast majority of both white and black pepper produced in Sarawak is for export and the largest and increasing proportion (by volume) is unprocessed black pepper. The decline in world commodity markets following the mid-1970s recession in Europe and North America was associated with a 50% drop in black pepper exports from 25,523 tonnes in 1979 to 11,153 tonnes in 1984. Sarawak was a major pepper exporter and the substantial reduction in its exports placed considerable pressure on world prices which peaked in 1987 when exports fell to below 12,000 per annum.[20] The drop in supply led to a hesitation then a steady rise in prices from RM2,255/tonne (US$1,120) in 1982 to RM9,058 (US$4,520) in 1987.

The price of pepper went beyond farmers' wildest expectations and the result was an expansion of holdings by individual smallholders often on former hill padi land and an increase in the willingness of local middlemen to lend. In spite of the expanded Pepper Subsidy Scheme, many smallholders had to borrow from the local *towkay* to whom they would subsequently sell the pepper and receive any net return. Much of the investment to expand pepper gardens therefore came from the smallholders themselves eager to respond to this new market opportunity.[21] From 1987 exports began to increase, initially from the placement of pepper stocks hoarded by merchants in Singapore and Kuching, and then as a result of new planting. Pepper prices began to fall accordingly and continued to do so even after exports peaked. Even so, as long as pepper prices remained above a certain level it still paid farmers to maintain if not to expand their pepper gardens.

By the early 1990s, however, pepper prices fell below their nominal 1972 price and below the level at which maintaining pepper vines had become viable. At the same time, prices for inputs had risen, local merchants were increasingly reluctant to lend on a falling market and the state became less willing after 1989 to continue to offer subsidies. The smallholder had very little margin and the retreat from adequate maintenance led firstly to lower yields, then to the abandonment of holdings. The area under pepper declined rapidly, from an all-time high of 11,207 hectares in 1990 to 8,880 in 1993.[22] During 1990 and 1991, Sarawak's earnings from exports of black pepper fell dramatically and the combined effect of lower volume and lower prices reduced exports from their peak of RM$138.65 million (US$69 million) to only RM$35.76 million (US$17.4 million) by the end of 1993.[23]

By the mid-1990s the smallholders' experiment with pepper had come to an end, and lessons were so hard-learned that it was considerably more difficult to persuade farmers to devote their scarce resources to yet another venture, this time cocoa. And when several years later cocoa prices too declined, the next venture – oil palm – looked even less attractive. The 1990s therefore was a time of reappraisal by farmers, the state and the Federal government.[24] All three had become disenchanted with agriculture. Agriculture had not only failed to yield a sustained income to farm households but had also diminished as an earner of foreign exchange.[25]

## *The Smallholder Response: Off-farm Employment and Migration*

While the instability of the pepper market may have come as a surprise to some, the instability of farming certainly had not. Yields are never certain and exposure to the market in order to derive cash merely added to the other traditional uncertainties of tropical agriculture. It is partly for this reason that Sarawak smallholders have tried where possible to derive real income from a variety of sources within and outside agriculture, on and off the farm. Indeed, it is the ability of the longhouse-based agricultural system to support a multiplicity of income sources and therefore to counterbalance

Figure 19.1. THE PRICE AND EXPORT OF BLACK PEPPER, SARAWAK, 1972-1993

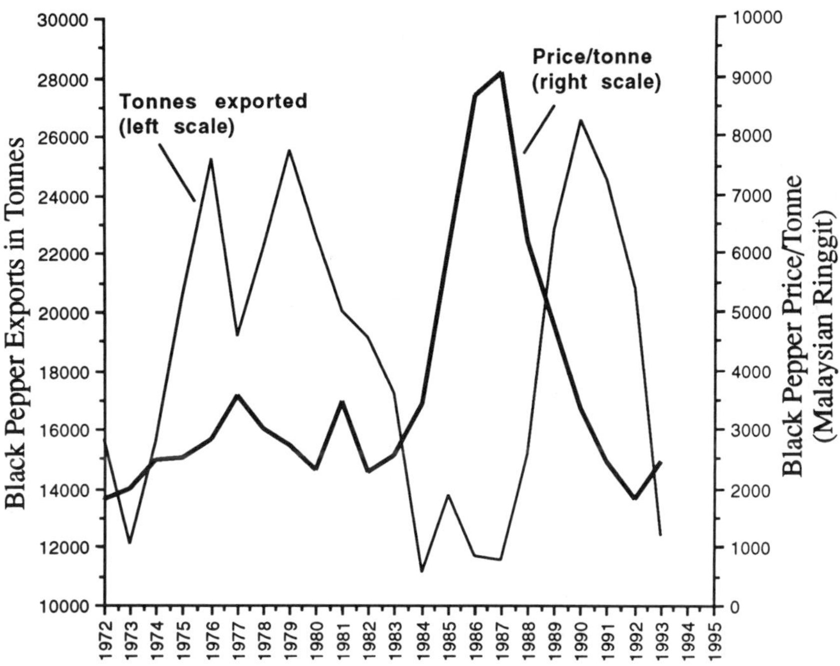


fluctuations in any one source that has helped account for its persistence.

One complementary source of income is wage labour. Rural areas in Sarawak are characterised by an increasingly episodic labour market based heavily on logging which, largely through the contract work system, is now being extended geographically to embrace more and more countries in the region. The Iban tradition of *bejalai* or journeying away from the longhouse places the male in an advantageous position to exploit the opportunities for wage labour. It also provides a cultural justification for the family retaining rural residence even though it means women have to assume some of the male functions in the agricultural cycle. The Iban have long appreciated this duality and the importance of the continued access to land which underpins it.[26] For the younger unmarried male members of rural households with marketable skills, the longhouse has become more important as an address than as a source of income. Instead of being an economic base, many longhouses have simply become a kinship home to which an increasing number of Iban men return for decreasingly short periods of time.

Labour mobility now takes two main forms: short-term voluntary or contract work locally or overseas, and permanent migration. Official estimates of migration do not follow these categories, but the census continues to show that residential mobility within Sarawak is extremely high with nearly one third of all rural residents having lived at another address prior to 1991.[27]

The insecurity of income from agricultural commodities, a diminishing supply of forest products from communal land and the reduction in employment from the extraction of logs have forced rural labour to seek work elsewhere. The growing economies of the Peninsula in particular have become increasingly attractive. While comparatively few moves from Sarawak's rural areas over the five years prior to the 1991 census ended up in the Peninsula (8,568 or 2.5%), there is every indication that migrants now consider not only the rest of Sarawak and Brunei but also the rapidly growing employment opportunities in the Peninsula itself.

Of the Malaysian urban areas outside Sarawak it was urban Johor Bahru which was the destination of the largest single stream of rural to urban migration from Sarawak between 1986 and 1991 (1,786), and a large proportion of them are known (from non-census sources) to be Iban, many with family at home maintaining the farm. The next largest destination is Perak (1,129) then Selangor (507), with considerably smaller streams in other settlements. Not surprisingly, the rural areas in the Peninsular which received population from rural areas in Sarawak were far fewer; the largest stream was to Sabah followed by Melaka.

While anecdotal evidence of labour contracts with logging companies operating in the Solomons and Papua New Guinea as well as Viet Nam can be cited, systematic evidence has yet to be gathered on this wider migration of Sarawak's rural labour force. As evidence of migration from elsewhere within the region is pieced together,[28] the particular niches occupied within the wider regional labour market by both the Dayak and skilled Malayan loggers especially may become clearer. Certainly the increasing economic and political integration of the region and its growing pattern of reciprocal labour flows will afford increasing opportunities for rural dwellers whose scope for domestic employment declines both on and off the farm.

### *The State Response: Estates and the Commercialisation of Agriculture*

Far from countering the trend towards rural depopulation and external migration, government policy in Sarawak is likely to exacerbate it. The future of Sarawak is going to be increasingly determined by a Federal government committed to rapid economic growth and to raising the macro indicators for Malaysia to the level of developed country status envisaged for 2020. The prevailing contemporary belief is that the state should, wherever possible, provide opportunities and incentives for the private market to lead the development process. Integral to this conviction is the belief that the economic thrust must precede rather than follow social development:

> Although the purpose of economic progress is 'to ensure a more equitable sharing of national wealth', economic and financial development precedes social plan-

ning. The prime consideration is the promotion of sustainable economic growth, improve national economic resilience and competitiveness.The cry for a human face in economic planning by putting people first and economics second has not made much inroad.[29]

This philosophy has important implications for smallholder agriculture and therefore for many of the most disadvantaged members of Sarawak's heterogeneous community. In situ development of agriculture dominated thinking in the 1980s. It took the form of subsidies, technical education and assistance to smallholders. By the mid-1980s and particularly since the election of Abdul Mahmud Taib as Chief Minister of Sarawak in 1981, there is an apparent impatience with such an approach and a perception of the backwardness of 'traditional' agriculture.[30] Experiments with large-scale land development, plantations and estates followed, imported directly from the FELDA and SALCRA schemes on the Peninsula. Their implementation in Sarawak largely failed because of a greater willingness to replace rather than understand the longhouse agricultural system and the cultural priorities and agricultural practices which accompanied it.[31]

The state was more interested in raising *land* productivity than increasing the productivity of farm *households* in conventional longhouse settings. In fact it saw the existing smallholder as a barrier to increasing returns notwithstanding evidence to the contrary.[32] The carefully researched and argued evidence of Cramb for Sarawak[33] or Dove for Indonesia[34] on the efficiency of forest-fallow was of little interest and was put to one side. A different agenda had already been set.

Agriculture had apparently performed so poorly that arguments about any efficiencies that had prevailed under existing systems became irrelevant. Resources were therefore reappraised and existing systems subjected to critical attention. The immediate opportunities for redevelopment lay in the peat soil (1.677 million ha.), areas under 'shifting cultivation/agriculture (3.588 million ha.) and the overlapping Native Customary Rights (NCR) land (1.5 million ha.) with oil palm (200,000 ha.), sago (50,000 ha.) and rubber (replanting), 40,000 ha. the main candidates'.[35]

Of all the shifts in policy it is this 'paradigm shift' towards commercial agriculture that has the most profound implications for smallholders because it not only removes their control of decision-making over the land but also implies much larger-scale development and, in numerous cases, physical relocation.[36] Commercialisation also implies, in the current climate, private development. Both are expected to be associated with 'economies of scale, greater profitability, and greater export earnings (and hence income earnings)'.[37]

Under the National Agricultural Policy (NAP), Government would like gradually to remove itself not only from assistance for smallholder farmers but also from provision of agricultural services as well. 'With the assistance as well as supervision of the Government the private sector should be encouraged to actively provide the services needed by farmers'.[38] Government's role should be in collection and dissemination of information to allow more effective planning. Agricultural extension staff should play a 'nursing role'. Formal credit facilities will have gradually to replace the village middlemen and local money lenders.

According to the Ministry of Agriculture's perspective plan report, areas which are considered unsuitable for commercial farming will be abandoned with farmers moved to viable areas or other sectors. Areas with farming potential will be rehabilitated via drainage, irrigation etc. and any (remaining) farmers will have to have higher education levels. In contrast to the mainly independent family farming, 'the shift in the future would be towards a combination of independent family farming, group farming, outgrower and contract farming as well as part-time and hobby farming'.[39] Farms of the future will also be larger and use labour saving devices.

There may be a place for the smallholder in this scenario but it is likely to be a very different one to that prevailing in the agricultural sector today. The NAP scenario suggests accelerated depopulation of the agricultural middle zone of Sarawak and the interior. Ironically, in a land surplus-labour shortage economy like Sarawak, commercial agriculture as envisaged under the NAP is likely to require increased immigration of foreign workers as indigenous Sarawak labour seeks work considerably above the wages currently offered on the planned agricultural estates. Similarly, rural growth centres based around agricultural estates are unlikely to halt the resulting drift to the town.[40] The scope for an expanding labour force in the towns, however, depends largely on a viable manufacturing sector which Sarawak has yet to develop.

### *Secondary Industry, Foreign Investment and Employment*

Tariff protection was explicitly introduced to foster industrialisation within the Malaysian common market,[41] but such industries have been attracted primarily to the Peninsular to which the Federal Government has channelled a disproportionate number of development allocations.[42] Compared to the Federation, the state of Sarawak has a much lower proportion of its labour force employed in manufacturing, 9.1 compared to almost 20% in Malaysia, and although the differences in services are less (19.4% vs 23.7%), there are marked qualitative differences.[43]

In a region in which there is fierce competition for development capital, Sarawak has relatively little comparative advantage.[44] Over the period 1985 to 1993, only an average of 25 FDI projects was approved in Sarawak each year, averaging RM139,729 million (US$68,863 million). Sarawak attracted the large capital intensive projects, rather than those that could absorb the growing number who wanted to leave the rural areas.[45]

The large, high capital intensity of FDI in Sarawak implies relatively lower employment-generating ability of each foreign dollar invested compared with the smaller more labour intensive projects characteristic of

Malaysia as a whole. The number of jobs created per million of proposed capital investment was only 4.27 jobs per thousand Malaysian dollars (approximately US$476.5) compared to Federal average of 7.32.[46]

Possibly more important in understanding the impact of FDI in Sarawak is the nature of the industries which are the subject of FDI proposals and approval. Sarawak has a skeletal industrial base and the concentration of FDI has been on adding value to existing resource-based products: the food sector received 6 of the 26 projects in 1992 and 8 of 25 in 1993; wood and wood products 10 and 7; and chemical, petroleum and natural gas 3 and 5.

These two years also illustrate the considerable annual variability of FDI, with the capital amounts being particularly influenced by expansion timing of the major petroleum/natural gas complexes. In 1992, for example, the energy sector garnered 95% of FDI in the State. The major recipient in the following year was wood processing in which plywood factories were set up, mainly for export (and intra-firm transfer) to Japan. By contrast the rest of Malaysia, mainly the Peninsula, saw major investments in textiles and textile products and electrical and electronic products in 1992, with other investments covering virtually the whole twenty categories of industries.

One of the ironies of Sarawak's industrialisation strategy is that jobs that are created are not always those attractive to local labour and therefore have to be filled by contract labour from overseas, particularly the cheaper and more pliable contract workers from Indonesia. This is not the long-term intention, however. As Sarawak Industrial Development Minister Datuk Abang Johari Tun Abgn Openg noted on the opening of a Kuching industrial estate, 'Sarawak does not encourage the setting up of labour intensive plants as the future of its industrial development would be based on high-tech industries. ... Sarawak's population is only 1.8 million, so what is needed is to produce skilled people that are trainable and my ministry only invites companies with high-tech to come to Sarawak during our overseas trade missions'.[47] Unfortunately the British-derived education system, with its emphasis on academic achievement and the widespread association between education and white collar or desk jobs, has not provided Sarawak with a cadre of skilled workers geared to a manufacturing economy nor one in which vocational skills are valued and have social status.[48]

Despite the growing amount of land being put aside for industrial estates, the necessary foreign investment is still very limited and what has been built still tends to tap semi-skilled rather than skilled labour, much of it foreign rather than domestic. But of greater concern is the likely mismatch between an agricultural strategy which will release rural labour, and an industrial strategy which has yet to demonstrate it can provide the jobs for locals at acceptable wage levels. By aiming to replace an existing smallholder agricultural system by a system of commercial agriculture which will rely heavily on an imported rural proletariat, the state is likely to swell further the numbers in town and place excessive demand for employment on a nascent industrial sector. Timing of the respective agricultural and industrial strategies is therefore critical as is the associated reorientation of the education system towards vocational training.

As others have now recognised, Sarawak is now part of something larger, and can no longer be understood easily without placing it in a wider Malaysian, Southeast Asian and Pacific Asian context.[49] In addition, Sarawak is not only deeply integrated into the Malaysian Federation itself but is also increasingly becoming part of the dynamic matrix of foreign capital and labour flows which characterise the Pacific Rim. Sarawak is being pulled in several directions. By being located within a rapidly growing Federation of states, it is expected to contribute its share to the Malaysian Federation.[50]

In the current climate such initiatives are inevitable. Each country in the Asia-Pacific is looking at ways of maximising the advantage of being part of a regional growth complex. In such a climate, questions of distribution and particularly questions of inequality among ethnic groups within countries will increasingly be submerged and suppressed through the 'politics of development' as the 'higher' goals of national and regional development are invoked.[51] In this way the periphery has now become internalised. The trappings of rapid, capital intensive development are now quite evident in the extensive building projects in Kuching and other Sarawak cities as is the emerging middle class from all ethnic groups. The periphery meanwhile retreats further into the countryside and into the remaining pockets of the shrinking jungle. It can be seen in the shanty villages on the outskirts of town, and in the cities at night, as well as in the discarded gardens of the barely maintained longhouses within commuting distances of urban employment. The transformation of Sarawak is inevitable. The model has already been constructed and, if there are remaining uncertainties, they are not ones of direction but of the speed of change and the magnitude of the distributional and environmental consequences.

## *Acknowledgements*

Research for this paper was undertaken while I was a Research Fellow in ASEAN affairs at the Institute for Southeast Asian Studies (ISEAS) in 1995. I wish to thank the Institute permanent staff for their assistance, particularly Diana Wong, Naimah Tailib, Yao Souchou and Ch'ng Kim See of the ISEAS library and her staff. I would also like to acknowledge the role played by the New Zealand High Commission in their recognising the value of funding short-term fellowships. Douglas Alau Tayan, Abdul Rashid Abdullah, Peter Songan, Jayl Langub, Clifford Sather and Norjayardi Abdullah kindly extended their hospitality to me during my visit to Sarawak in 1995 and Jegak Uli during my visit to Kuala Lumpur. I would like to thank my fellow researchers who as visitors to ISEAS made my stay both enjoyable and productive, in particular Tanya Li, Bunn Negara, Afan Gaffar and Penelope Graham; and the four referees who looked at a much longer, earlier draft of this paper. Their comments were most valuable and appreciated. None of the above is responsible in any way for the views expressed above and for any errors that remain.

## NOTES

[1] See V.T. King and M.J.G. Parnwell, 'The peripheral areas of Malaysia: development problems, planning and prospects', in V.T. King and M.J.G. Parnwell (eds), *Margins and Minorities. The Peripheral Areas and Peoples of Malaysia*, Hull University Press, 1990, p. 1.

[2] The model is a familiar one and is most concisely outlined in T. Wanatabe, *Asia: Its Growth and Agony,* Honolulu: East-West Center, Institute for Economic Development and Policy, 1992, and has been elaborated recently by H.T. Oshima, 'Trends in productivity growth in the economic transition of Asia and long-term prospects for the 1990s', and M. Ezaki, 'Growth and structural changes in Asian countries', *Asian Economic Journal*, 9 (21), 1995, pp. 89-112 and 113-35.

[3] The two Federal Territories of Kuala Lumpur and Labuan complete the Federation.

[4] A useful introduction to the geography and economic history of Sarawak may be found in the first chapter of R.A. Cramb and R.H.W. Reece (eds), *Development in Sarawak: Historical and Contemporary Perspectives,* Monash Papers on Southeast Asia No. 17, Melbourne: Centre of Southeast Asian Studies, 1988. See also King and Parnwell, op. cit., 1990, pp. 1-23; and M. Cleary and P. Eaton, *Borneo: Change and Development*, OUP, 1992. The early text by J.C. Jackson, *Sarawak - A Geographical Survey of a Developing State,* University of London Press, 1968, is still worth consulting.

[5] Growth over the most recent recorded period 1990-1993 has been slower , however, at an average annual rate of only 4.7% (Department of Statistics [Sarawak Branch], *Yearbook of Statistics Sarawak 1993,* Department of Statistics Malaysia [Sarawak Branch], 1994, pp. 184-85).

[6] Mean household income in 1989 was RM1,208 per month (US$570.5) and showed an average annual growth rate of 0.2% between 1987 and 1989. The incidence of poverty had fallen from 31.9% in 1985 to 16% by 1995 (Economic Planning Unit estimates), poor households from 90.1 (thousand) to 6.9, hard-core povery from 10% to 2% and number of hard-core poor households 28.2 thousand to 8.1 (Department of Statistics, 1994, op. cit., pp. 180-1).

[7] While this is supported by GDP figures, it should be recognised that much of agriculture' s contribution to livelihood is in kind and does not feature as a market transaction. This is particularly true of rice production.

[8] V.T. King, 'Why is Sarawak peripheral?', in King and Parnwell (eds), op. cit., 1990, pp. 110-29.

[9] E. Boserup, *The Conditions of Agricultural Growth. The Economics of Agrarian Change under Population Pressure,* London: Allen and Unwin, 1965; and E. Boserup, *Population and Technological Change. A Study of Long-term Trends,* University of Chicago Press, 1981.

[10] C. Padoch, *Migration and its Alternatives Among the Iban of Sarawak*, The Hague: Martinus Nijhoff, 1982.

[11] R. Pringle, *Rajahs and Rebels: The Ibans of Sarawak under Br ooke Rule, 1984-1941,* London: Macmillan, 1970.

[12] V.T. King and Jayum A. Jawan, 'The Ibans of Sarawak, Malaysia: ethnicity, marginalisation and development', in Denis Dwyer and David Drakakis-Smith, *Ethnicity and Development: Geographical Perspectives*, London: John Wiley & Sons Ltd, 1996, pp. 195-214.

[13] R.H.W. Reece, 'Economic development under the Brookes', in Cramb and Reece (eds), op. cit., 1988, pp. 21-34; J.P. Ongkili, *Nation-building in Malaysia 1946-1974*, Singapore: OUP, 1985.

[14] For a useful account of the growth of intra-regional trade in the region, see P.J. Lloyd, 'Intraregional trade in the Asian and Pacific region', *Asian Development Review: Studies of Asian and Pacific Economic Issues*, 12 (2), 1994, pp. 113-43; and with respect to Malaysia, see B. Ramasamy, 'Intra-industry intra-ASEAN trade: the case of Malaysia', *Malaysian Journal of Economic Studies*, 30 (1), 1993, pp. 43-54.

[15] Agriculture and livestock production contributed 12.7% of GDP (in producer value at constant prices) in 1978 and by 1993 this had fallen to 7.8%. Agriculture, hunting and fishing absorbed 68% of the labour force in 1970, 60.6% in 1980 and 47.1% in 1990 (Department of Statistics, op. cit, 1994).

[16] The term Dayak is used here to refer loosely to the indigenous Iban and Bidayuh as well as many other smaller groups (see V.T. King, 'Indigenous peoples and land rights in Sarawak, Malaysia: to be or not to be a *bumiputra*', in R.H. Barnes, Andrew Gray and Benedict Kingsbury (eds), *Indigenous Peoples of Asia*, Association for Asian Studies Inc. Monograph and Occasional Paper Series, No. 48, 1995, pp. 289-305). In 1980 with 55% of the population, Dayak counted for 75% of all those employed in the primary sector. This contrasts with the Chinese with 24% of the population but only 11% employed in the primary sector, and Malay and Melanau with 14 and 20% respectively (Annual Bulletin of Sarawak, 1984, pp. 37-38; Jayum A. Jawan, *Iban Politics and Economic Development. Their Patterns and Change*, Penerbit Universiti Kebangsaan Malaysia Bangi, 1994; also King, op. cit., 1995, p. 206). Such breakdowns by ethnicity are no longer published. For comment on these new categories and the meaning of *bumiputra* when applied to Dayak in particular, see Jawan, op. cit., 1994; and King, op. cit., 1995, p. 294). See also King and Jawan, op. cit., 1996.

[17] C.F.J. Bong and M.S. Saad (eds), *Pepper in Malaysia*, Sarawak: Universiti Pertanian, M. Cawangan, 1986.

[18] Unlike the Chinese, however, who undertook additional processing of the spice to produce white pepper, the bulk of production in the longhouses only goes as far as the black pepper stage. See R.A. Cramb, 'The role of smallholder agriculture in the development of Sarawak: 1963-88', paper 6 in A.M.N. Salleh, H. Solhee and M.Y. Kasim (eds), *Socio-economic Development in Sarawak. Policies and Strategies for the 1990s*, Kuching, Sarawak: Angkatn Zaman Mansang (AZAM), 1990, p. 91.

[19] J. Uli, *Iban Smallholders and Price Instabilities: Coping Strategies and Implications for Policy*, PhD submitted to Institute of Advanced Studies, University of Malaya, Kuala Lumpur, 1996, p. 55.

[20] There is a high level of correlation in pepper prices across the world although white and black pepper prices are not highly correlated, see M.S. Habibullah and A.Z. Baharumshah, 'Can pepper farmers predict white pepper prices using changes in black pepper prices? An empirical study', *Borneo Review*, 5 (11), 1994, pp. 157-78. See also I.C. Tiong, 'The marketing of Malaysian pepper', in Bong and Saad (eds), op. cit., 1986.

[21] Between 1982 at the beginning of the price rise and its peak in 1987, annual plantings under the Pepper Subsidy Scheme (PSS) rose from 476.05 new hectares to 737.9 but with a reduction in between due to the recession of the mid-1980s. The area almost doubled again to 1,381 in 1989 even though prices were falling from their peak. Prior to 1989, PSS annual plantings added the equivalent of less than 10% of all the land area in pepper. In 1989 and 1990, PSS plantings assumed an increasing proportion of all plantings over the period of

price falls, but eventually they too declined proportionatey and absolutely.

[22] This is the latest date available (Department of Agriculture, *Agricultural Statistics of Sarawak 1993*, Sarawak: Department of Agriculture, 1994, p. 30) and note this differs from the provisional figure of 9,500 given in the Yearbook of Statistics 1993 (Department of Statistics, op. cit., 1994, p. 53).

[23] Export of white pepper, however, had begun to rise which together with their higher prices led to a return almost to their 1989 export earning level. For an analysis of the (lack of) correlation between the two markets, see Habibullah and Baharumshah, op. cit., 1994, pp. 157-78.

[24] Ministry of Finance, *Economic Report 1994/5*, Kuala Lumpur: Percetakan Nasional Malaysia Berhad, 1994. There was also a reappaisal by international organisations (see ESCAP, 'Towards a more vibrant pepper economy', paper presented at the International Pepper Seminar, Bangkok, Thailand, 17-19 August 1994, New York: UN, 1994). In the background was a series of ongoing discussions on the commodity crisis in developing countries (see A. Maisels, 'The continuing commodity crisis of developing countries'; W. Moran and D. Sapsford, 'Commodities and development: some issues'; and D. Sapsford and V.N. Balasubramanyam, 'The long-run behavior of the relative price of primary commodities: statistical evidence and policy implications', *World Development*, 22 (11), 1994, pp. 1685-95, 1681-84 and 1737-45).

[25] Such concerns over the consequences of the instabiity of commodity for smallholders in Sarawak had been a concern for several decades (see H. Bugo, *The Economic Development of Sarawak. The Effects of Export Instability*, Kuching: Summer Times, 1984), but with little effective resolution. Serious barriers still prevent the Pepper Marketing Board acting as an effective buffer, for example.

[26] P.S. Morrison, 'Transitions in rural Sarawak: off-farm employment in the Kemena basin', *Pacific Viewpoint*, 34 (1), 1993, p. 64.

[27] See also V.H. Sutlive, 'Urban migration into Sibu, Sarawak', *Borneo Research Bulletin*, 17 (2), 1985, pp. 85-95; V.H. Sutlive, 'Urban migration into Sibu', *Borneo Research Bulletin*, 18 (1), 1986, pp. 27-45; V.H. Sutlive, 'Ethnic identity and aspiration', *Sarawak Museum Journal*, XL (61) 1989 (NZ), pp. 35-49; J.T.H. Ko, 'Iban on the move: an empirical analysis', *Sarawak Gazette*, CXI (1494), 4th quarter issue, 1985, pp. 5-21; J.T.H. Ko, 'Internal migration in Sarawak, 1970-1980', *Sarawak Gazette*, CXIII (1499), 1st quarter issue, 1987, pp. 4-7; J.T.H. Ko, 'A socio-economic study of the Iban today', *Sarawak Museum Journal*, XL (61) (new series), December 1989, pp. 79-96.

[28] G. Hugo, 'Indonesian labour migration to Malaysia: trends and policy implications', *Southeast Asian Journal of Social Science*, 21 (1), 1993, pp. 36-70; G. Hugo, 'International labour migration and the family: some observations from Indonesia', *Asian and Pacific Migration Journal*, 4 (2-3), 1995, pp. 273-301.

[29] Haji Zanul bin Haji Hussain, 'Emerging social issues and problems of the 21st century. Managing the future', in H. Solhee, B. Haji Bujang and Sim Ah Hua (eds), *Sarawak: The Next Step: Towards a Better Tomorrow*, Proceedings of the seminar on Sarawak: The Next Step, Kuching, 21-24 September 1994, Kuching: State Planning Unit, AZAM, and Konrad Adenauer Foundation (KAF), Germany, 1995, p. 147. Dr Haji Zanul bin Haji Hussain is Secretary General, Ministry of National Unity and Social Development, Malaysia.

[30] The Chief Minister's perspective is documented sympathetically in K. Jitab with J. Ritchie, *Sarawak Awakens: Taib Mahmud's Politics of Development*, Sarawak: Pelanduk Publications, 1992.

[31] This clash of systems and the values which underlie them has been the subject of extensive research in Sarawak. See, for example, V.T. King, 'Land settlement schemes and the alleviation of rural poverty in Sarawak, East Malaysia: a critical commentary', *Southeast*

*Asian Journal of Social Science*, 14, 1986, pp. 71-99; V.T. King, 'Models and realities: Malaysian national planning and East Malaysian development problems', *Modern Asian Studies*, 22 (2), 1988, pp. 263-298; King, op. cit., 1990, pp. 110-29; and chapter 4 in V.T. King and Nazaruddin Mohd Jali (eds), *Issues in Rural Development in Malaysia,* Kuala Lumpur: Dewan Bahasa dan Bustaka Kementerian Pendidikan Malaysia, 1992; also Abdul Rashid Abdullah, 'The response of farmers in two Bidayuh communities to an in situ land development programme', in King and Parnwell (eds), op. cit., 1990, pp. 184-207; Ahmad Mahdzan Ayob and Noran Fariziah Yaakub, 'Development and change in Batang Ai, Sarawak: perception of a resettled Iban community', *Sarawak Museum Journal,* XLII (63) (new series), 1991, pp. 267-282; R.A. Cramb, 'Problems of State-sponsored land schemes for small farmers: the case of Sarawak, Malaysia', *Pacific Viewpoint*, 33 (1), 1992, pp. 53-78; and Hew Cheng Sim, *Agrarian Change and Gender Relations: Rural Iban Women at the Batang Ai Resettlement Scheme*, MA Thesis, Faculty of Arts, University of Malaya, 1990.

[32] Dandot's deflection of discussion of the latter is indicative: 'The writer does not intend to go into a debate here on the "efficiency of small farm[s] in terms of resources utilisation" as commonly explained in the development literature ... The choice for large scale agriculture is really based on the development objective at large and the specific objectives that we intend to pursue' (W.B. Dandot, 'A paradigm shift to agricultural development in Sarawak', in Solhee, Bujang and Sim [eds], op. cit., 1995a, p. 80).

[33] R.A. Cramb, 'Shifting cultivation and resource degradation in Sarawak: perceptions and policies', *Borneo Research Bulletin*, 21(1), 1989a, pp. 22-49; R.A. Cramb, 'The use and productivity of labour in shifting cultivation: an East Malaysian case study', *Agricultural Systems*, 29 (2), 1989b, pp. 97 -116.

[34] M.R. Dove, 'Theories of swidden agriculture, and the political economy of ignorance', *Agroforestry Systems*, 1, 1983, pp. 85-99.

[35] Dandot, op. cit., 1995a, p. 83; W.B. Dandot, 'An overview of agricultural development in Sarawak with special reference to structural transformation, policy, strategy and spatial approaches toward 2020', in Busrah Haji Bujang and Sim Ah Hua (eds), *Agriculture Commercialisation in Sarawak: 'In Search of a New Paradigm'*, proceedings of a seminar on Agriculture Commercialisation in Sarawak, Sibu, July 5-7 1994, AZAM, Sarawak and the KAF, 1995b, pp. 37-52.

[36] It need not of course under approaches which try to take account of existing practices (see R.A. Cramb and I.R. Wills, 'The role of traditional institutions in rural development: community-based land tenure and government land policy in Sarawak, Malaysia', *World Development*, 18 (1), 1990, pp. 347-60); however, these are not the kinds of accommodation discussed in the Sarawak planning literature. For a discussion of native customary rights which form an important element in this discussion, see King, op. cit., 1995, pp. 289-305, especially p. 299.

[37] Dandot, op. cit., 1995a, p. 80.

[38] V. Eng, 'A paradigm shift of smallholding agriculture development in Sarawak agriculture commercialisation: in search of a new paradigm', in Busrah Haji Bujang and Sim Ah Hua (eds), op. cit., 1995, p. 64.

[39] Eng, op. cit., 1995, p. 70.

[40] P.S. Morrison, 'Urbanisation and rural depopulation in Sarawak', *Borneo Research Bulletin*, 28, May 1996.

[41] M. Ariff and H. Hill, *Export-oriented Industrialisation: The ASEAN Experience*, Sydney: Allen and Unwin, 1985.

[42] Wee Chong Hui, *Sabah and Sarawak in the Malaysian Economy*, Kuala Lumpur: Abdul Majeed & Co. for Institute of Social Analysis, 1995, p. 93.

[43] Z.A. Sulong, 'Contribution of manufacturing industries to the development of Sarawak', Paper 11 in Salleh, Solhee and Kasim (eds), op. cit., 1990, pp. 167-185.
[44] For discussion of foreign direct investment in the region see, for example, M. Ariff, 'The changing role of foreign direct investment', in H. Yokoyama and M. Tamin (eds), *Malaysian Economy in Transition*, Toyko: Institute of Developing Economies, 1991, pp. 67-89; and Chia Siow Yue, 'Foreign direct investment in ASEAN economies', *Asian Development Review, Studies of Asian and Pacific Economic Issues*, 11 (1), 1993, pp. 60-102.
[45] The capital investment per project in Sarawak was over 57 million compared to under 22 million for Malaysia as a whole (Malaysian Industrial Development Authority [MIDA] annual reports, various years).
[46] Although most of the approvals documented in MIDA annual reports end up being realised, what gets created in terms of jobs and how this actually compares with the expectations given in project submissions remains largely inaccessible to researchers.
[47] *Borneo Bulletin*, 12 October 1995. See also N. Danaraj, 'Challenges, options and prospects for higher value added industrialisation for Sarawak: beyond primary processing', in Solhee, Bujang and Sim (eds), op. cit., 1995, pp. 27-56. Recent amendments to the Land Code allowing for foreign ownership of condomiums in Sarawak is expected to spearhead more foreign investors. Foreigners are not allowed to own landed property in Sarawak unless they do so in the name of a company which they set up there.
[48] J.S. Singh and O. Mehmet, *Human Capital Formation in East Malaysia*, Kuala Lumpur: Institute for Advanced Studies, University of Malaya, 1991.
[49] V.T. King, 'Reflections of a jobbing social scientist twenty years on', *Sarawak Gazette*, CXX1 (1528), June 1994, p. 18.
[50] The Bakun Dam project stands as an example of the length to which Kuala Lumpur will go to exploit natural resources of the state for the benefit of the Federation. Similarly, the development of the land for estate crops like oil palm, of ex-urban land for industrial estates, and of areas of natural beauty for tourism are projects which the indigenous people must adapt to rather than lead or initiate. See D. Tsuruoka, 'Awakening giant: Sarawak sees its future as Asia's energy provider', *FEER*, 21, July 1994, pp. 68-71; Lim Siong Hoon and S. Sargent, 'The battle for Bakun', *Asiamoney*, March 1995, pp. 25-31; W. Arnold, 'Bakun', *AsiaWeek*, November 10 1995, pp. 46-50; E. Lee and Yee Mee Fah, 'Dam(n) if he did, dam(n) if he didn't', *MI*, September 1995, pp. 6-10.
[51] For a discussion of the expression of ethnic issues through politics in Sarawak, see M.B. Leigh, *The Rising Moon: Political Change in Sarawak*, Sydney University Press, 1974, and Jawan, op. cit., 1994. For an analysis of the most recent election, see J. Chin, 'Sarawak's 1991 election: continuity and change', paper presented at the Borneo Research Council Third Biennial International Conference, Pontianak, Indonesia, 10-15 July 1994; J. Chin, 'Sarawak's 1987 and 1991 state elections: an analysis of the ethnic vote', *Borneo Research Bulletin*, 26, 1995, pp. 3-24.

# 20. RESOURCE EXTRACTION AND THE POSTCOLONIAL STATE IN SOLOMON ISLANDS

*Ian Frazer*

The expansion and deepening of Asian industrialisation has made demands for raw materials on many small Asia-Pacific countries, challenging not only their independence but also their very survival. Many small island states of the South Pacific[1] have been unable to achieve sustained economic growth since they became independent. The main difficulty they face is not a lack of resources so much as being able to control resource extraction, marketing and long-term economic growth. The biggest challenge in this respect lies in breaking with the export-oriented strategy laid down during colonial rule through which they have become little more than the exploited suppliers of cheap raw materials and agricultural produce for the world market.

One of the resources in question is tuna fish. Another is timber. Papua New Guinea and Solomon Islands are among the few countries still exporting round logs harvested from the natural rainforest. The logging industries in both countries are totally dominated by foreign capital, mostly transnational companies based in Asia. Their operations represent an extreme case of resource exploitation for short-term benefit. Most of the commercially exploitable forests are located on customary land and are claimed by local communities under traditional rights of ownership.[2] This severely restricts the management and control of forest exploitation for better local and national benefit, and highlights one of the critical issues facing postcolonial governments in this region, of trying to extend their influence and power over locally autonomous and self-reliant rural communities while resisting the attractions of short-term gain through under-controlled resource extraction.[3]

It will be argued in this chapter that real responsibility for the very destructive and exploitative kind of resource extraction that is taking place at present lies with the state and the close alliance which it has formed with international capital. This argument will be made through looking specifically at one of these countries, Solomon Islands, where tuna fishing and more importantly log exporting are the main export industries, both exhibiting the characteristics of over-extraction, resource depletion and short-term gains for little local-level benefit. Log exporting has expanded to the point where it is the principal export commodity and now accounts for well over 50% of all export revenue. Since independence in 1978 it has become a barely controlled form of mining sanctioned by a section of the ruling elite for their own benefit and in the short-term interests of the postcolonial state.

## *Historical Background*

Solomon Islands consists of a double chain of six large islands and numerous smaller islands stretching for around 1,600 km. in the southwest Pacific. The total land area is 28,369 sq. km., and the sea area (Exclusive Economic Zone [EEZ]) is 1.34 million sq. km. In the past, these islands supported a culturally diverse and politically fragmented population, divided into small, self-sufficient communities linked by trade and exchange, and depending on a subsistence economy that variously combined horticulture, fishing, hunting and gathering. The present national boundaries took shape only when the British annexed the territory in the late nineteenth century and formed a colonial state. British and Australian plantation capital followed soon after annexation and led to the establishment of a plantation economy based on the production of a single export commodity, copra.[4] Solomon Islanders were used as plantation labour under an indentured migrant labour system and, in the late colonial period, copra output was expanded extensively, rather than intensively, and the smallholder contribution to export production grew steadily in the two decades prior to independence.[5]

The foundation for the present export-driven economy was laid during this period not so much by the expansion of smallholder production as by a new wave of foreign investment, concentrated in large-scale resource-based industries as well as new agricultural projects. The investments were determined initially by government control of the resources involved. The expansion of large-scale agriculture and forestry was constrained by the relatively small area of alienated land owned by the government.[6] Some of the best land for agricultural development was on the Guadalcanal Plains of North Guadalcanal. This became the site for a short-lived rice venture and a much more successful oil palm project.[7] Government-owned forests were largely concentrated in Western Province and were sufficiently extensive to allow export production from 1963 through to c. 1980. Continuation of the industry after that would depend on moving into the more substantial forests located on customary land. Tuna fishing, by comparison, benefited from the creation of the 200-mile EEZ in January 1978.

In most of the export industries, joint ventures were formed. This was meant to reduce the heavy dependence on foreign capital and provide the basis for steadily increasing local control over those industries.[8] There was one major exception and this was forestry. Large-scale commercial logging first began in the early 1960s during the final stages of colonial rule. It began as a carefully managed industry for the purpose of diversifying export production in the transition to independence. An attempt to form a joint venture with the largest logging company, Levers Pacific Timber Limited, did not go ahead and the industry remained dominated by foreign companies without local equity.

At independence, power passed to an administrative and political elite largely bound to continue the state-led capitalist development introduced in the late colonial period, relying on primary export production and foreign investment. They were also committed to a large and increasingly expensive state apparatus, which they controlled and depended on for their power, and which for the most part was centrally located in the country's capital and only urban centre, Honiara.

It will be shown that this last commitment subsequently became one of the main influences on economic management, including management of resource extraction. Whatever ideas there may have been originally of creating long-term development strategies leading to self-sustaining economic growth, these were soon overshadowed by the more immediate imperative of maintaining and consolidating the state. The consequence of this was a much closer alliance with foreign capital and steady intensification of resource extraction. The importance of tuna fish and round logs was determined largely by the demand from Japan and other industrialising countries of the Pacific Rim, especially Taiwan and South Korea (the growth in export trade with Asia is shown in Table 20.1). Together the two commodities have made up an average two-thirds of the total value of exports for the last 15 years, alternating in importance (see Table 20.2).

### *Population, Ethnicity and Provincial Government*

The total population of Solomon Islands is estimated at 373,000. The last census in 1986 showed the very high annual growth rate of 3.5%.[9] Honiara has an estimated population of 46,660, and with smaller centres, the total urban population comprises around 20%. The other 80% live in villages and hamlets widely distributed throughout the islands.

Solomon Islands is noted for its cultural and linguistic diversity. There are up to 80 different language groups and none is large enough to assert political or economic dominance nationally. Language is only one basis for identity and not necessarily the most salient. Of far more importance to most people is their local clan or tribe and the community with which it is associated. At the wider level, people also identify with large islands or island groups. This became increasingly prominent under colonial rule as a result of the greater movement and wider social interaction brought about by labour migration, mission activity and the introduction of local government. At the time of independence, regional loyalty was much stronger than any national feeling and was a major factor underlying demands for decentralisation. These demands led to the introduction of provincial government in 1981.

Currently, the country is divided into nine provinces each with its own elected provincial assembly. Provincial government was intended to provide greater political autonomy to the regions and through that to reduce economic dependence on the centre. So far the former is much more noticeable than the latter. Provinces still depend on central government for a large proportion of their annual budgets.[10] Among the many difficulties which they face in taking responsibility for provincial development are large differences in land area and resources (see Table 20.3).

Table 20.1. DIRECTION OF TRADE (% of total)

| | *1980* | *1990* | *1993* |
|---|---|---|---|
| *Destination of Exports* | | | |
| Japan | 26.1 | 39.4 | 41.7 |
| Other Asian countries | 2.1 | 14.2 | 27.3 |
| United Kingdom | 12.6 | 23.5 | 14.3 |
| Netherlands | 12.5 | 1.4 | 6.8 |
| Australia | 2.3 | 4.6 | 2.1 |
| United States | 3.4 | 0.1 | 1.4 |
| Other countries | 41.0 | 16.8 | 6.4 |
| *Total* | *100.0* | *100.0* | *100.0* |
| *Origin of Imports* | | | |
| Australian | 30.8 | 35.3 | |
| Japan | 19.7 | 16.2 | |
| New Zealand | 7.0 | 9.3 | |
| Singapore | 14.7 | 14.4 | |
| Other Asian countries | 6.7 | 10.7 | |
| United Kingdom | 8.6 | 1.5 | |
| Other countries | 12.5 | 12.6 | |
| *Total* | *100.0* | *100.0* | |

Source: Central Bank of Solomon Islands, *Annual Report*, 1994.

Table 20.2. PERCENTAGE SHARE OF PRINCIPAL EXPORTS BY VALUE

| *Year* | *Copra* | *Timber* | *Fish* | *Palm Products* | *Cocoa* | *Other* | *Total* |
|---|---|---|---|---|---|---|---|
| 1980 | 17.3 | 26.2 | 38.1 | 11.6 | 1.0 | 5.8 | 100 |
| 1981 | 14.0 | 27.9 | 38.2 | 13.1 | 1.6 | 5.2 | 100 |
| 1982 | 14.3 | 40.4 | 24.7 | 13.0 | 1.6 | 6.0 | 100 |
| 1983 | 11.8 | 28.0 | 41.0 | 12.3 | 3.2 | 3.7 | 100 |
| 1984 | 27.2 | 25.4 | 24.3 | 16.1 | 2.8 | 4.2 | 100 |
| 1985 | 22.6 | 23.9 | 30.8 | 13.2 | 4.8 | 4.7 | 100 |
| 1986 | 5.2 | 31.1 | 46.1 | 5.2 | 5.6 | 6.8 | 100 |
| 1987 | 8.0 | 29.0 | 41.0 | 5.9 | 7.4 | 8.7 | 100 |
| 1988 | 9.2 | 23.3 | 46.0 | 8.2 | 4.4 | 8.9 | 100 |
| 1989 | 12.2 | 24.1 | 28.2 | 11.7 | 4.6 | 9.2 | 100 |
| 1990 | 6.2 | 34.3 | 29.9 | 10.9 | 6.4 | 12.3 | 100 |
| 1991 | 4.5 | 23.3 | 46.3 | 9.1 | 6.0 | 10.8 | 100 |
| 1992 | 7.0 | 36.4 | 28.9 | 11.8 | 4.7 | 11.2 | 100 |
| 1993 | 4.5 | 56.3 | 20.1 | 9.3 | 4.1 | 5.7 | 100 |
| 1994 | 3.7 | 56.3 | 20.2 | 8.4 | 2.0 | 9.4 | 100 |

Source: Central Bank of Solomon Islands, *Annual Reports*, 1992, 1994.

## *Economic Management and the State*

An important feature of government economic management in the years following independence has been a deepening revenue crisis. At first budget deficits were small and easily covered by external aid and concessional loans. As deficits increased there was greater resort to domestic borrowing to make up the shortfall. Government borrowing from the banking system, including the Central Bank, rose from US$4m. in 1987 to US$43.4m. at the end of 1991.[11] This increased the debt service component of the government budget, severely reduced the availability of private sector credit, further boosted inflation and put considerable pressure on the external situation. This expansionary fiscal policy was particularly critical in 1990-91 when the Government exceeded statutory limits on borrowing, inflation was at 15-20%, the value of the Solomon Island dollar dropped to its lowest levels, and overseas reserves fell to less than one month's import cover.

Maintaining and expanding government revenue was always going to be a problem in a country where most of the population continued to rely on low productivity agriculture and was only partially and unevenly committed to the market economy. The new export industries that were established immediately prior to independence provided a strong foundation for export-oriented growth. This was confirmed by economic performance in the 1970s which showed real GDP increasing by 7-8% annually.[12] In the 1970s, agricultural exports were still strong, contributing 40.8% of the total value of exports compared with timber (30.2%) and tuna fish (25.4%).[13]

In the 1980s real GDP growth was much lower and more uneven. A large cyclone in 1986; worsening terms of trade; the closing down of the largest logging company, Levers Pacific Timbers Ltd, in 1986; the withdrawal of C. Brewer and Company Limited from the joint venture rice project (Brewer Solomons Agriculture Limited) and the eventual closing down of that project, were some of the more serious problems. Poor prices for agricultural commodities in the second half of the decade meant reduced export returns. The average value of agricultural exports fell to 28.9%. Tuna fish was the main export in the 1980s, making up 36.8% in value of all exports, followed by timber (27.9%).[14] Taxes on international trade remained more vital to government revenue than any other source, representing 60 to 65% of total revenue.[15]

Poor export growth was only one aspect of the revenue crisis in the 1980s; the other main problem was increasing government expenditure. The years following independence were years in which the size and cost of the state steadily expanded. This was seen as a means of furthering economic development as well as ensuring national integration. Starting from a position in which it was already the main employer in the national economy, the government continued to create new jobs at a much faster rate than the private sector. Government recurrent expenditure consisting mostly of wages and salaries but with a sharply increasing debt-service component grew from 25% of GDP in the mid-1980s to over 30% in the

Table 20.3. PROVINCES OF SOLOMON ISLANDS – BASIC DATA

| *Province* | *Land Area* | | *Population* | | | *Production* | | | |
|---|---|---|---|---|---|---|---|---|---|
| | | | *1986* | | *1995* | *Copra 1993* | | *Round Logs Jan.-Sep. 1994* | |
| | *sq. km.* | *%* | *(actual)* | *%* | *(estimate)* | *tonnes* | *%* | *cu. metres* | *%* |
| Western | 5,475 | 19.3 | 41,681 | 14.6 | 55,887 | 6,536 | 29.4 | 265,298 | 66.6 |
| Choiseul | 3,837 | 13.5 | 13,569 | 4.8 | 17,649 | 2,344 | 10.5 | 54,988 | 13.8 |
| Isabel | 4,136 | 14.6 | 14,616 | 5.1 | 18,499 | 2,089 | 9.4 | 20,330 | 5.1 |
| Central | 615 | 2.2 | 16,655 | 5.8 | 21,696 | 962 | 4.3 | | |
| Rennell/Bellona | 671 | 2.4 | 1,802 | 0.6 | 1,887 | | | | |
| Guadalcanal | 5,336 | 18.8 | 49,918 | 17.5 | 72,397 | 3,401 | 15.3 | 10,568 | 2.7 |
| Honiara | 22 | 0.1 | 30,143 | 10.7 | 46,660 | | | | |
| Malaita | 4,225 | 14.9 | 80,032 | 28.1 | 91,517 | 4,143 | 18.6 | 25,601 | 6.4 |
| Mkaira Ulawa | 3,188 | 11.2 | 21,796 | 7.6 | 28,539 | 1,916 | 8.6 | 21,822 | 5.5 |
| Temotu | 865 | 3.0 | 14,781 | 5.2 | 18,034 | 838 | 3.8 | | |
| *Total* | *28,370* | *100.0* | *285,263* | *100.0* | *372,765* | *22,229* | *100.0* | *398,607* | *100.0* |

Sources: Statistics Office, *Report on Census of Population*, Honiara, 1986, and *Statistical Bulletin*, 22/94; *Solomon Star*, 22 March 1995.

early 1990s.[16] One of the main casualties of this expansionary fiscal policy was long-term economic planning and management of the resources sector. Making little attempt to cut government expenditure, the political elite moved instead to increase the rate of resource extraction.

## *Fiscal Policy and Social Stratification*

These policies reinforced and expanded emerging patterns of social stratification. This is shown by the evidence for continuing rural decline during this period and the urban bias which came about through privileging the public sector.

Taking the rural sector first, outside the employment offered by the large commercial ventures in agriculture, fishing and forestry, the majority of rural dwellers depend on a household-based, semi-commercial economy in which subsistence production is combined with diverse sources of cash income. These income sources range from primary products (cash crops, livestock, marine products, forest products), small business activity and crafts, to receipts from pensions, royalties, remittances and investments, and some rural employment.[17] Smallholder copra production reached record levels in the mid-1980s coinciding with high international prices. Since then prices have dropped and production has declined.

As much as smallholders are dependent on copra, there is wide variation in household production within and between provinces. In 1985, when smallholder copra production reached a record 32,222 tonnes, the average annual production per household varied from 1.5 tonnes in Western Province to 0.5 tonnes in Temotu province. The national average was 0.8 tonnes.[18] A study of 90 households in 15 neighbouring settlements in North Malaita in 1985, where the main cash crop was copra, showed a range in annual production from nil (25% of households) to 4.2 tonnes. Average production was just under one tonne, close to the national average.[19] At present-day prices, this would provide an income less than half the basic minimum wage. Rural people generally are being left behind by present economic policy with its emphasis on large-scale commercial development and with the prioritising of the public sector. Despite a price stabilisation scheme for copra, the average real income in rural areas has declined since the mid-1980s owing to high population growth, adverse terms of trade for agricultural commodities and the rising cost of imports.[20]

The most highly sought-after alternative to the household-based rural economy is formal employment. In 1992 this provided 26,842 jobs, 81.5% male and 18.5% female,[21] representing around 18% of the national working age population. Over the last 10 years, 500 and 700 new jobs have been created annually, far below the number of school leavers and other youths coming on to the job market.[22] Out of the total jobs in 1992, 16,719 (62%) were in the private sector and 10,123 (38%) in the public sector. Nearly 40% of all private sector jobs were in the main primary export industries – agriculture, forestry and fishing – and only 14% in manufacturing. For the last 15 years, the main growth in employment has been in the public sector. Between 1977 and 1992, the total number of private sector jobs grew by 49%, whereas government employment increased by 82%.[23]

Besides this increase in numbers, public sector employment has also led the way in levels of remuneration and in the provision of special benefits for its employees, steadily increasing the gap between rural and urban incomes. During the period of maximum salary increases between 1989 and 1991, the average local price of copra fell by 18%.[24] Even when the price rose again in 1992, there was an eightfold difference in the average local buying price for one tonne of copra and the lowest level basic salary granted under the new unified pay structure for the public service.[25]

The most highly rewarded groups in the public sector are contract officers and consultants, constitutional post holders, parliamentarians and established office holders. All of these groups have average monthly earnings well above those of private sector employees in Honiara.[26] Taking advantage of the power associated with public office, politicians and public servants have awarded themselves the best opportunities for accumulation that are currently available to Solomon Islanders. This is not just confined to generous salaries. There are many other perks as well, especially for those at the highest levels of the service. As a consequence of their higher earnings, ready access to credit and the other opportunities presented to them, civil servants and politicians have invested heavily in property, agriculture, transport and other business activity.[27]

With these developments, social inequalities are becoming more extreme in Honiara and nationwide. Some indication of this comes from a government survey of Honiara households in 1990. Among national (indigenous Solomon Islanders) households, 48% were earning less than US$296 per month and 85% less than US$593 a month. One third of national households earned 75% of total household income; the top 0.3% earned 34.6%.[28]

### *Mining the Commons, at Sea and on Land*

The two most important export industries are tuna fishing and forest logging. Besides making a major contribution to government revenue and foreign earnings, both extractive industries are major employers in the private sector. They have been built on the basis of common property resources. This has been much more of a problem for logging than for fishing, as the forests, being located mostly on customary land, are the common property of local descent groups. A serious difficulty for rural people is that instead of strengthening the statutory requirements for establishing ownership of forest resources and ensuring that the rightful owners are given a fair choice over logging, successive amendments to the forest legislation have weakened that protection, favouring logging companies over forest owners.[29] Tuna fishing has attracted substantial investment in port facilities, fishing vessels, shore bases and canning factories,[30] and fish have been claimed by the government as part of its sovereign claims over the EEZ.

Solomon Island waters contain several species of tuna with different international demand. The species on which the domestic industry is founded is skipjack (*Katsuwonus pelamis*). This is fished by two companies using fleets of pole and line vessels and bait fish gathered in coastal waters. The largest and oldest of these companies is Solomon Taiyo Limited (STL), a joint venture that was formed in 1972 with Taiyo Gyogyo of Japan.[31] The government's original shareholding in the company was 25%. Since then there have been three joint venture agreements (the last in 1993) and the Solomon Island government has increased its shareholding to 51%. Even with this majority shareholding, the management of STL and marketing of their product is still largely controlled by the foreign partner. STL is the largest industrial operation in Solomon Islands with annual sales worth around $100 million. Despite this turnover, it is a highly geared company which has recorded a profit in only two out of the last 20 years of operation.[32] More than half the catch comes from expensive Okinawan-owned catcher boats whose productivity has never been matched locally. Another problem is transfer pricing.

In 1978 a second fishing company was formed with the aim of building and operating a fleet of skipjack catcher vessels under Solomon Island control. The company, National Fisheries Development Limited (NFDL), was 25% owned by STL. Despite subsequent restructuring and an attempt to break into purse seine fishing with a large investment in two purse seining vessels, the company never reached profitability. In 1990 it was sold to a Canadian firm, British Columbia Packers. It continues to operate in Solomon Island waters with six pole and line boats and the two purse seiners it purchased from the government. The average annual production of both these companies over the last 10 years has been 39,000 tonnes.

Besides the domestic fishery, Solomon Islands makes its waters available to distant water fishing fleets under special licensing agreements and joint ventures. Catch quotas are specified in all these agreements but the government does not have the means to monitor their operations effectively. At present there are bilateral access agreements with Japan and Taiwan involving pole and line and long-line fleets, and a multilateral agreement with the United States involving purse seining vessels. In 1994, two new Taiwanese long-line operations were approved.[33]

In the last five years, provincial governments have started forming joint ventures with Asian fishing companies giving those companies annual fishing quotas for provincial waters. These arrangements offer the least benefits of any being made with foreign companies at the present time. The only return is the fee paid to the province, which is a very small fraction of the value of the fish quota offered to these companies. These operations are virtually unmonitored. Three joint ventures have been formed so far, all highly favourable to the foreign companies.[34]

The picture which emerges from this brief account of tuna fishing shows that Solomon Islands has made considerable progress in establishing a domestic tuna industry with joint venture support. While the prospects for greater local control are in doubt, the emphasis is shifting back to making agreements with distant water fishing nations and boosting revenue through licence fees and new joint venture deals.[35] The overall benefits are much less than from further development of the local industry. There is also growing concern about the long-term sustainability of the resource.[36] All the requirements for a much stronger and more sustainable industry – a better monitoring and surveillance regime, more realistic fees, a complete overhaul of fisheries legislation, more research on the state of fish stocks – have fallen behind while pursuing short-term gains in revenue.[37]

Large-scale commercial logging has a different and more complex record. It has been running for over 30 years during which time there have been two distinct regimes each marked by different relations between foreign companies, the government, forestry officials and rural people. During the first period, from 1963 until the early 1980s, most logging took place on government land or customary land leased by the government.[38] It was controlled through licences issued by the Forestry Department. After a short establishment period, output settled at around 260,000 cu. metres per annum (see Figure 20.1). Around 75% of production came from one company, Levers Pacific Timber Limited, and there was a reforestation programme run by the Forestry Department which achieved a rate of replanting equivalent to one hectare for every four hectares of natural forest cleared.[39] There was also an attempt to set up a national forest estate large enough to allow a long-term cycle of sustainable logging. This had to be abandoned when the government failed to secure the necessary land.[40]

The second period of logging is marked by a shift from government land to customary land. This became necessary as government-owned forests were depleted. Moreover, with customary land making up around 87% of the total land area in the country, and holding around twice as much commercially exploitable forest as was on government land, these forests represented a rich prize for prospective investors. The move began in a small way in the 1970s and then accelerated quite rapidly in the early 1980s under the first Mamaloni Government. The number of companies licensed to operate increased fourfold from 1981 to 1983; there was a much wider spread in the location of their operations; and an overall increase in the level of production with output climbing in two stages, from 1980 to 1986 (when LPT withdrew from the country) and from 1989 to the present (see Figure 20.1). Reforestation of government land continues, but there is virtually no reforestation of customary land except for a New Zealand-sponsored trial project.[41] This period also shows many under-capitalised companies joining the industry (especially from 1981 and 1989),[42] a greatly reduced level of control over logging by the Forestry Division, frequent corruption by politicians at every level of government in the awarding of licences,[43] a high level of disputation and protest surrounding logging operations,[44] and politicians actively subverting official policy through their support for logging operations.[45]

Figure 20.1. LOG PRODUCTION, 1963-1994

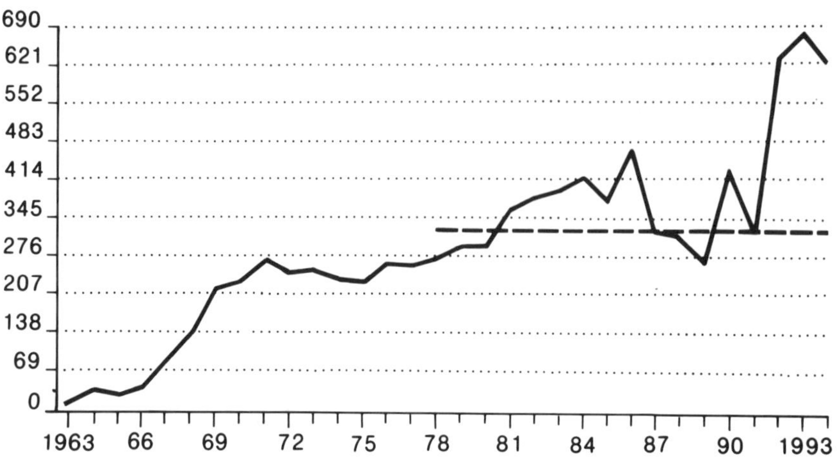


When commercial logging moved on to customary land, the Forestry Division did not have the appropriate legislation or the resources to control it adequately. A crucial amendment was made to the forestry legislation in 1977 enabling customary land owners to negotiate directly with logging companies seeking cutting rights.[46] As it turned out, this exposed forestry owners to the predations of foreign companies without the ability or the support to defend their own interests. Subsequent investigations by the Ombudsman showed that once foreign companies targeted areas for logging, it was extremely difficult if not impossible for local resource owners to stop them.[47] Besides that, once logging started, resource owners had no way of requiring companies to comply with the regulations. The law proved to be ineffective in practice, because the Forestry Division and other government agencies were incapable of enforcing it. Worse still, landowners found that they were legally unable to terminate logging agreements, and that only companies had that right.[48] This increased the enormous commercial advantage that logging companies already had over resource owners.

Despite a lot of political rhetoric about the power and rights of resource owners, their share of the revenue from logging has been exceptionally unjust.[49] The logging contract provides for a royalty calculated on a log volume basis within the range of 5 to 15% of f.o.b. log price.[50] Resource owners often try and negotiate other benefits as well such as roads, bridges, schools, clinics and jobs, but logging companies have a poor record in keeping these promises.[51] The government share of revenue includes the export duty and reforestation levy which, up until recently, has always been kept by the government. Their value has always been higher than royalty payments. One of the problems with the logging contract is that in times of higher prices most of the surplus goes to the contractors.[52]

Apart from the inequities built into the contract, another serious problem has been the poor monitoring of log production. Duncan has calculated that there has been a massive loss of revenue to resource owners and to the government through under-reporting of harvest volume and under-reporting of log prices. He estimates that in 1993 when tropical logs were commanding record prices internationally, the surplus that was forgone through under-reporting was US$41 million, an amount estimated to be 35% of GDP and 53% of government revenue.[53]

Forest logging has now come to represent an officially sanctioned form of plunder providing exceptional profits for a small number of Malaysian and South Korean multinational companies. A forest inventory funded by the Australian Government and completed in 1994 estimated that there were 13.3 million cu. metres of commercial timber left standing. It recommended a sustainable yield of 325,000 cu. metres per annum.[54] Since 1993, the annual cut has been more than twice that volume. The total allowable cut for all current licence holders at the end of 1994 was 3.3 million cu. metres, ten times the recommended sustainable yield. Figure 20.2 shows the present situation in Western Province, the province with the longest history of large-scale commercial logging, and the largest producer of round log exports. Current licences in the province have an allowable cut of 1.22 million cu. metres, ten times the sustainable yield of 112,000 cu. metres.[55]

In the last five years, national politics have been heavily dominated by concern over the logging industry. This has given rise to a tense struggle among the ruling elite to try to restore government control over forest development from the logging industry. The struggle was brought on by new Malaysian investors buying into the industry, increasing concentration of ownership, the high international prices for tropical logs, the poor state of the economy and continuing commitment to expansionary fiscal policies. The Mamaloni Government from 1990 to 1993, with 11 out of 15 cabinet ministers linked to logging companies,[56] saw the improvement in timber prices as an opportunity to boost the economy as well as their own interests, and readily sanctioned record increases in export volume. There was an 80% surge in log exports in 1992 which pushed GDP growth to a record 8.2%.[57] In 1993, timber exports grew to US$76 million, nearly 60% of total merchandise exports. The duty from export logs was US$19 million which was 20% of total government revenue.[58]

At the general election in 1993, Mamaloni missed being returned to power by one vote. He was defeated by a Western Province member of parliament, Francis Billy Hilly, who was chosen by the opposition to lead a seven-party coalition called the National Coalition Partnership (NCP). Once in power, the NCP Government set about trying to constrain the logging industry. They introduced a price monitoring system, boosted the overall monitoring of timber cutting operations by the Timber Control Unit, raised the export duty, started work on a National Forest Action Plan, advanced the introduction of new forestry legislation, set 1997 as the date for phasing out all log exports, made plans to engage a foreign trade inspection company for surveillance of log shipments, and increased the proportion of logging revenue being returned to the forest owners by guaranteeing them 20% of the export duty on round logs.[59]

The NCP Government made little progress with these measures before they were brought down by a succession of cabinet resignations and defections. Their strong stand on logging was not the only reason why they were forced out of power but it was one of the main reasons. The logging industry vigorously opposed their reforms through their organisation, the Solomon Islands Forest Industry Association (SIFIA).

Mamaloni was returned to power on 7 November 1994 at the head of the Solomon Island National Unity, Reconciliation and Progressive Pati (SINURPP). This party includes many former members of Mamaloni's 1990-93 Government. As soon as it came to power the SINURPP Government began reversing the reforms of the previous government, immediately reducing the export duty on round logs, putting back the date for phasing out round log exports until 1999, putting on hold the National Forest Action Plan and new legislation, and backing away from the efforts made to improve monitoring of logging operations and surveillance of log

Figure 20.2. LOGGED AREAS AND PROPOSED LOGGING, WESTERN PROVINCE

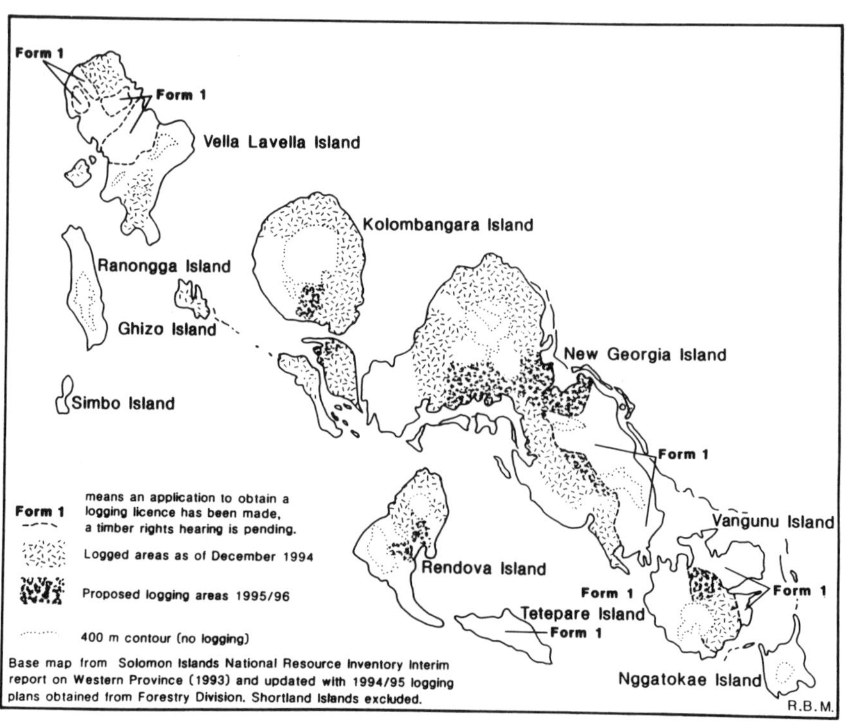

shipments. The NCP Government's proposal to give resource-owners 20% of the log export duty was abrogated. Instead the 7.5% reforestation levy, previously retained by government, will now be made available for community forestry projects.[60]

Resources policy has once again become subordinated to the personal interests of the ruling party and the short-term survival of the state. Soon after taking office, the SINURPP Government introduced another expansionary budget continuing the fiscal policies of previous years with all the same economic consequences and the same pressure on the resources sector. This will reinforce the larger trends of urban bias and more extreme social stratification that have been described.

This chapter has reviewed the kind of development that has taken place in the early years of independence in Solomon Islands. The country has pursued an export-driven model of economic growth relying on exploitation of its natural resources by transnational companies from Japan and other Asian countries. One of the most critical issues raised by this kind of development is working out how the revenue from resources should be shared.[61] In countries committed to capitalist development, it might be expected that the state would try to manage foreign investment so as to maximise local benefit.[62] In 1994, this was turned into a major regional issue by Australia at the South Pacific Forum.[63] What has happened in the Solomons is that this imperative and resources management generally have been subordinated to the demands of the postcolonial state and those who now rule that state. They are so closely allied with international capital that the autonomy and sovereignty of the country is more in question now than at any time since independence.

## NOTES

[1] J. Connell, *Sovereignty and Survival: Island Microstates in the Third World*, Research Monograph No. 3, Department of Geography, University of Sydney, 1988; P. Bauer et al, *Aid and Development in the South Pacific*, Auckland: The Centre for Independent Studies, 1991; World Bank, *Pacific Island Economies: Towards Higher Growth in the 1990s*, Washington D.C.: World Bank, 1991; R.V. Cole and S. Tambunlertchai (eds), *The Future of Asia-Pacific Economies. Pacific Islands at the Cr ossroads?*, Canberra: Asia and Pacific Development Centre and the National Centre for Development Studies, 1993; G. Bilney, 'Australia's relations with the South Pacific – challenge and change', Briefing Paper No. 34, Canberra: Australian Development Studies Network, 1994.

[2] M. O'Collins, 'Forest logging in Solomon Islands: economic necessity as the overriding issue?', in S. Henningham and R.J. May (eds), *Resources, Development and Politics in the Pacific Islands*, Bathurst: Crawford House Press, 1992, pp. 145-61; J.S. Fingleton, 'Forest resource management in the South Pacific: logging your way to development?', *Development Bulletin*, 31, 1994, pp. 19-31.

[3] R. Jackson, 'Undermining or determining the nature of the state?', and E.P. Wolfers,

'Politics, development and resources: reflections on constructs, conflicts, and consultants', in Henningham and May (eds), op. cit., 1992, pp. 79-89 and 238-57.

[4] J.A. Bennett, *Wealth of the Solomons. A History of a Pacific Archipelago, 1800-1978,* University of Hawaii Press, 1987; M. Howard and S. Durutalo, *The Political Economy of the South Pacific to 1945,* Monograph Series No. 26, Centre for Southeast Asian Studies, James Cook University of North Queensland, 1987.

[5] See the following detailed studies: J.M. McKinnon, *Mbilua Report,* VUW Socio-Economic Survey of the Solomons, Department of Geography, VUW, 1973; J.M. McKinnon, *Bilua Changes: Culture Contact and its Consequences, A Study of the Bilua of Vella Lavella in the British Solomon Islands,* Unpublished PhD thesis, Department of Geography, VUW, 1972; M.A. Bathgate, *West Guadalcanal Report,* VUW Socio-Economic Survey of the Solomons, Department of Geography, VUW, 1973; M.A. Bathgate, *Bihu Ma Tena Golo. A Study of the Ndi-Nggai of West Guadalcanal and their Involvement in the Solomon Islands Cash Economy,* Unpublished PhD thesis, Department of Geography, VUW, 1975; I. Frazer, *North Malaita Report,* VUW Socio-Economic Survey of the Solomons, Department of Geography, VUW, 1973; M.A. Bathgate, I.L. Frazer and J.M. McKinnon, *Socio-Economic Change in Solomon Island Villages*, VUW Socio-Economic Survey of the Solomons, Department of Geography, VUW, 1973.

[6] Estimated to be around 8% of the total land area in the country in 1978 (P. Larmour (ed.), *Land in Solomon Islands*, Suva: Institute of Pacific Studies, and Honiara: Ministry of Agriculture and Lands, 1979, p. 249).

[7] See S.P. Juvik, 'Joint venture rice production in the Solomon Islands: the inner workings of dependent development', *Pacific Studies,* 10 (3), 1987, pp. 73-90.

[8] P. Carroll, 'The management of equity investment in the Solomon Islands: 1977-1980', in A. Sawyerr (ed.) *Economic Development and Trade in Papua New Guinea,* Port Moresby: University of Papua New Guinea Press, 1984, pp. 234-53.

[9] K. Groenewegen, 'Population growth and distribution', in K. Groenewegen (ed.), *Report on the Census of Population 1986, Report 2.B. Data Analysis,* Honiara: Statistics Office, 1989, p. 4.

[10] The Guadalcanal Province budget for 1995-96 was US$1,564,251, of which 66% came from government grants (*Solomon Star,* 17 March 1995, p. 5).

[11] S. Siwatibau, 'Macroeconomic management in the small, open economies of the Pacific', in Cole and Tambunlertchai (eds.), op. cit., 1993, p. 170. At the end of 1987, the Government was the net lender to the central bank of US$7.7m.; by the end of 1991, it had become a net borrower of US$20.6m., a swing of US$28.3m. over four years.

[12] C. Browne and D.A. Scott, *Economic Development in Seven Pacific Island Countries,* Washington D.C.: IMF, 1989, p. 114.

[13] Statistics Office, *Statistical Bulletins*, Honiara, 1978-1995, 9/85.

[14] Central Bank of Solomon Islands, *Annual Reports*, Honiara, 1984-1995, 1992, p. 24.

[15] World Bank, op. cit., 1991, p. 228.

[16] J. Fallon and C. Karabalis, 'Current economic trends in the South Pacific', *Pacific Economic Bulletin*, 7 (2), 1992, p. 10.

[17] W. Friesen, 'The activities of households', in Groenewegen (ed.), op. cit., 1989, p. 239.

[18] Statistics Office, Statistical Bulletin, op. cit., 15/87.

[19] I. Frazer, *Growth and Change in Village Agriculture: Manakwai, North Malaita*, Occasional Paper No. 11, South Pacific Smallholder Project, University of New England, 1987. In another survey of 12 villages in 1988, the average annual production of copra per household ranged from 0.137 to 1.789 tonnes (Agricultural Economics Section, *Socio-Economic Survey of Smallholder Farming Systems in Solomon Islands*, Honiara: Agricultural Economics Section, Rural Services Project, Ministry of Agriculture and Lands, 1989).

[20] UNICEF, *A Situation Analysis of Women and Children in the Solomon Islands,* Honiara: UNICEF and Government of Solomon Islands, 1993, p. 17.
[21] Statistics Office, op. cit., 10/93.
[22] Central Bank of Solomon Islands, op. cit., 1995, p. 10.
[23] Statistics Office, op. cit., July 1978 and 10/93.
[24] Statistics Office, op. cit., 21/93.
[25] The average local buying price for copra was US$171 per tonne, and the lowest level salary (L1.1) was US$1,365 (Statistics Office, op. cit., 22/94; Office of the Prime Minister, *New Policy for the Structure of the Public Service,* National Parliament Paper No. 34/92, Honiara, 1992).
[26] In 1991, comparative figures were contract officers and consultants US$1,971, constitutional post holders US$1,814, parliamentarians US$723, established post holders US$289, and average monthly earnings of private sector employees in Honiara US$220 (Office of the Prime Minister, *The Public Service Structural and Internal Adjustments,* Honiara, 1990; Statistics Office, op. cit., 12/91).
[27] Figures recently released on the distribution of titles to fixed term estates show the rapid growth of property investment by Solomon Islanders in Honiara. In 1995, indigenous Solomon Islanders held 1,399 titles worth US$12-15 million, non-indigenous Solomon Islanders 276 titles worth US$9-12 million (*Solomon Star*, 15 March 1995, p. 11).
[28] Statistics Office, op. cit., 16/92.
[29] See A.V. Hughes, 'High speed on an unmade road: Solomon Islands' joint-venture route to a tuna fishery', in D.J. Doulman (ed.), *Tuna Issues and Perspectives in the Pacific Islands Region,* Honolulu: East-West Center, 1987, pp. 203-24. The most recent investment, financed through aid and soft loans by Japan, EEC, ADB and other sources is the US$45m. port, township and canning factory at Noro, Western Province (*Solomon Nius*, 14 July 1989).
[30] J.S. Fingleton, *Assistance in the Revision of Forestry Policy and Legislation,* First Report to the Government of Solomon Islands on Forestry Legislation, Rome: FAO, 1989; B. Boer, *Solomon Islands. Review of Environmental Law,* South Pacific Regional Environment Programme, 1992; Ombudsman, Solomon Islands, *Report for the Year Ended 30th June 1988, Report for the Year Ended 30th June 1989, Report for the Year Ended 30th June 1990,* Honiara: Office of the Ombudsman, 1988, 1989 and 1990; O'Collins, op. cit., 1992.
[31] Hughes, op. cit., 1987.
[32] *Solomon Nius*, 28 February 1993, p. 3.
[33] Central Bank of Solomon Islands, op. cit., 1995, p. 15.
[34] One such deal is that between Choiseul Province and Marrissco (PTE) Ltd of Singapore. The new joint venture is called Lauru Marrissco Ltd. The company has been given a maximum catch quota of 15,000 metric tonnes per annum for 15 years, with the right to renew for another 15 years. The province will receive a royalty representing 0.05% of the value of the catch (*Bisnis Nius*, December 1992-January 1993, pp. 4-5). The joint ventures have come under heavy criticism from the Central Bank of Solomon Islands in its last two annual reports (Central Bank of Solomon Islands, op. cit., 1994, 1995).
[35] See G. Waugh, 'The politics and economics of fisheries in the South Pacific', in Henningham and May (eds.), op. cit., 1992, pp. 170-78, for a discussion of the alternative approaches to exploiting this resource.
[36] R. Grynberg, 'Guarding our last renewable resource', *Pacific Islands Monthly,* 65 (2), 1995, pp. 24-7.
[37] SPREP, op. cit., 1993, pp. 62-3.
[38] According to estimates made at the time, around one-third of the exploitable forest was on government land (K.W. Groves et al, *The Solomon Islands Forest Industry Report No. 2,* Canberra: Anutech Pty Ltd, 1985; M. Bennett et al, *Forest Project Identification Mission.*

*Draft Final Report,* Honiara: Ministry of Natural Resources, 1991) .

[39] R.N. Byron, *Policies and Options for the Forestry Sector of South Pacific Island Economies,* Islands/Australia Working Paper No. 86/4, Canberra: National Centre for Development Studies, 1986, pp. 21-2.

[40] P. Larmour, 'Forestry and ownership', in Larmour (ed.), op. cit., 1979, pp. 105-6.

[41] T. Thorpe, 'New Zealand Pacific aid forestry projects – good for conservation?', *Forest and Bird,* 19 (4), 1988, pp. 33-4.

[42] E.D. Shield, *Policy, Legislative Framework, Economic and Utilization Aspects*, Project Working Paper No. 2, Australian International Development Assistance Bureau (AIDAB), Solomon Islands Forest Resources Inventory, ACIL Australia, 1990.

[43] See P. Larmour, 'The Mamaloni Government 1981-83', in P. Larmour with S. Tarua (eds), *Solomon Islands Politics,* Suva: Institute of Pacific Studies, University of the South Pacific, 1983, pp. 270-1; Ombudsman, op. cit., 1988, 1989.

[44] There have been several sabotage attacks on logging camps since logging started on customary land (see J. Hailey, 'The Enoghae Incident', *Review,* 3 (9), 1982, pp. 51-5; John Seed, 'The tribesmen hit back', *Islands Business*, November 1983, pp. 43-4; W. Friesen, 'Forest resources and management in Solomon Islands', *Development Bulletin*, 31, 1994, pp. 3-26; *Solomon Star*, 29 March 1994; 6, 20, 22 and 27 April 1994). Also a large number of court injunctions brought against logging companies – in Western and Choiseul Provinces there were nine injunctions issued by the High Court in 1992 ( *Solomon Star*, 15 January 1993, 3 March 1993).

[45] As shown by the disregard shown for the 1989 *Forest Policy Statement*.

[46] Forests and Timber (Amendment) Ordinance 1977.

[47] Ombudsman, op. cit., 1988, 1989, 1990; O'Collins, op. cit., 1992; J.H. Naitoro, *The Politics of Development in 'Are'are, Malaita,* Unpublished MA thesis, University of Otago, 1993.

[48] Boer, op. cit., 1992, p. 89.

[49] Mamaloni in particular likes to invoke resource owners and their rights when countering the critics of his government's forest policy (Office of the Prime Minister, *Development of the Forestry Sector and Related Industries,* PP No. 4/94, Honiara, 1994, p. 12).

[50] R.C. Duncan, *Melanesian Forestry Sector Study,* Canberra: National Centre for Development Studies, 1994, p. 5.

[51] Ibid, also various articles in *Link*, 1987-1994; B. Abana, 'Logging is no development', *O'o Journal of Solomon Island Studies,* 2 (1), 1989, pp. 57-65.

[52] Duncan, op. cit., 1994, p. 2.

[53] Ibid, pp. 40-4.

[54] AIDAB, *Solomon Islands National Forest Resources Inventory*, Honiara: Ministry of Natural Resources, 1994.

[55] Ibid, p. 33.

[56] *Islands Business Pacific*, July 1993, p. 38.

[57] Central Bank of Solomon Islands, op. cit., 1993.

[58] Duncan, op. cit., 1994, p. 23.

[59] *Solomon Star* and *Solomon Nius*, 1993-94; R. Grynberg, 'The Solomon Islands logging dilemma', *Pacific Islands Monthly*, 64 (3), 1994, pp. 11-13.

[60] *Solomon Star* and *Solomon Nius,* 1994-95.

[61] P. Larmour, 'Sharing the benefits: customary landowners and natural resource projects in Melanesia', *Pacific Viewpoint,* 30 (1), 1989, pp. 56-74.

[62] Cf. R. Sandbrook, *The Politics of Africa's Economic Stagnation*, CUP, 1985, p. 34.

[63] See *Pacific Islands Monthly*, September 1994, pp. 9-10; *Development Bulletin*, 31, July 1994; *Pacific Research,* August 1994, pp. 18-19.

# 21. CONCLUSION

*T.G. McGee and R.F. Watters*

The main aim of this volume has been to identify the principal issues and new geographies of the Asia-Pacific region. The conclusion is divided into two sections. In the first section, we review the main findings of the authors and assess the prospects for Asia Pacific co-operation against the changing political economy of the region. In the second section, we identify some of the major challenges for the future of the region as new geographies evolve.

## *Findings*

Part I of the book identified the concepts used and the forces at work shaping the evolution of the Pacific Rim. In chapter 2 Forbes assesses the 'changing contours' of the human and economic geographies of the Pacific Rim. Major new centripetal and centrifugal forces are at work bringing change to the region. Empirical evidence of interaction among Pacific Rim countries includes especially economic linkages, trade, investment, population movements, communications development, institution building and political thrusts aimed at greater inter-country co-operation. Economic development is the driving force orchestrating the main changes; national boundaries have become permeable as new spatial or regional groupings of countries emerge and internationalisation of the stronger economies leads to more 'open regionalism' or 'greater porosity' in links between Pacific Rim countries. Forbes illustrates the high degree of economic integration between Pacific Rim countries by trade data: APEC countries minus the two economic super powers (USA and Japan) provide the market for over 37% of the exports of Japan and USA and over 40% of their total imports. In 1992 two-thirds of all exports of APEC countries were destined for other APEC nations compared to only 17% to the European Community and under 17% to the rest of the world; the import figures are very similar.

In chapter 3 McGee identifies three contemporary processes occurring in the global system: globalisation, urbanisation and the emergence of sub-global regions. Globalisation includes increasing integration of separate states into a global system of production, consumption and trade; the emergence of a global culture in terms of a breakdown of boundaries; a great increase in mobility through networks; and the expansion of 'network landscapes'. Massive urbanisation is occurring inevitably and remorselessly, creating great 'mega-urban-regions' and urban corridors; several of the world's largest will be located in the Asia-Pacific region. The problem of urban management will become formidable indeed by 2025 when 61% of the population of developing countries (or 4.4 billion people) will live in cities. They will account for 88% of the total urban population of the world.

Clearly the economic challenge of creating sustainable societies must be tackled first in places like the mega-regions by dealing with the excesses of high energy consumption (see also chapters 10 and 15).

The remaining chapters in this section deal with the economic, political and institutional developments of the emerging Asia-Pacific system. Sandrey (chapter 4) explores the process whereby APEC and other sub-regional groupings have set about reducing regulatory barriers to increased trade. This is no easy task as the continuing friction between Canada and the USA under the NAFTA agreement shows only too clearly. What is more, these regional arrangements have to be nested within global systems of trading which are to be policed by the WTO. China's absence from the WTO further complicates these difficult negotiations. The fact that the creation of economic arrangements that permit the freer movement of labour and capital is occurring within many different frameworks creates more challenges. For example, the creation of 'growth triangles' or NETs that try to develop competitive regions that take advantage of different factors of production between countries (labour, capital, etc.) is well illustrated by the emergence of the Sijori growth triangle encompassing the geographically adjacent areas of Singapore, Malaysia and Indonesia. The creation of such borderless regions produces conflicts with other regions within national territories.

One of the more important debates which has emerged is focused on the question of whether increasingly economic integration will lead to growing convergence of political values in some form of a universal set of values relating to human rights and equal participation in a civil society. Some commentators see increased wealth bringing greater human rights and political participation. For others, the surge of economic growth, particularly in the Asian portion of the Pacific Rim, is accentuating regional, socio-economic and ethno-national differences which create great social tension. This is further compounded by the determination of many countries to separate issues of internal political governance from the growing integration of economic activity. Tremewan (chapter 5) summarises the state of these debates and the growing importance of NGOs in drawing attention to the inappropriateness of trying to separate political and economic behaviour.

Although the West is exerting pressure on Asian nations to democratise, it is likely that authoritarian governments will continue to hold power in many Asian countries. There is a general consensus in Asia that political stability and economic development should have primacy over individual rights and the increasing desire of governments to build developmental states in which the authority of the state is asserted over disintegrative tendencies. Authoritarianism can also be used as an instrument either to bring about change or to maintain the status quo. Hence governments are likely to continue to push for recognition of an Asian perspective on human rights and to coopt the argument of cultural relativism as a defence for their authoritarianism and a disguise for their collaboration with foreign capital. State violence, or the use of administrative coercion to deal with dissent, is likely to continue in a number of countries, and use of a widely accepted international definition of human rights is likely to be implemented by the West frequently as a political lever. Unfortunately, Western nations seeking to increase market access or better conditions for investment find it tempting to avoid these difficult political and human rights issues or allow them to be used as trade-offs in negotiations. ASEAN has tended to oppose the Western line, as in July 1996 when they rebuffed Western calls for sanctions to be imposed against the Burmese military regime for repressing the democracy movement led by Aung San Suu Ky; Burma was admitted to ASEAN with observer status. A future of protest, turmoil and rebellion – even a number of small or not so small 'Tiananmen Squares' – is likely in several Asian countries leading to further repression of civil rights. If Tremewan is right in predicting increasing political convergence among Asian nations in the future, with the authoritarianism of Singapore and its regime of social regulation as a likely model, Asian governments are still likely to enjoy considerable success in separating political and economic issues.

Part II of the book deals with the processes of change in the Pacific Rim. While it is clear that the major economic change that has dominated and is today dominating the Pacific Rim is the economic revolution changing societies from agrarian to industrial societies, Franklin argues that this is being combined with a consumer revolution. The affluent classes of the region are displaying a convergence in their consumerist behaviour with that of the West and Franklin reminds us how rapidly items that were luxuries become today's necessities. While greatest attention may be focused on the opening-up of vast areas of Asia to popular goods such as television sets, videos, washing machines, refrigerators, etc. and the consumerist revolution that ensues, Franklin illustrates also the vital importance of Positional goods (bonds, equities, real estate, art and treasure) for preserving the value of the savings of the new middle classes and also to finance the needs of the future, such as pension funds which become increasingly necessary with the demise of extended families in ageing societies. Countries which have been beneficiaries of the Asian economic miracle also have to face various transactional costs as they move to new and later phases of economic growth. They may need to invest in modern secondary and tertiary education at a level that reflects the direction of their economies. The preservation of this situation also rests upon the creation of Providential goods which include such items as road, water and sewerage systems as well as the costs of preventing pollution of the environment. The items of collective consumption have often involved public investment but with the current 'neo-liberal' focus of the globalisation ideology, they are becoming increasingly privatised. This provides yet another fruitful field for political clashes in the Pacific Rim.

These arguments concerning the consumer revolution must be set against the overall macroeconomic changes that are occurring in the Pacific Rim. Hill (chapter 7) describes and compares the degree of structural change that has occurred in Pacific Rim countries, analysing the rate of movement from agriculture to industry and services. In every country in Asia, there are now more farmers than in 1960, except for Japan, South Korea, Taiwan and the city states of Hong Kong and Singapore. In East and Southeast Asia, the number of farmers rose from 306 million in 1960 to some 558 million in 1992. At varying points in time, population growth rates have fallen in most countries from above 2.5% and in many, such as China and Thailand, to below 1.5%. The statistics show different rates of structural change, or the rate of decline in the proportion of the workforce in agriculture varying from China and India which are slow at only 0.3% a year, moderate in the case of some Latin American countries or Japan at about 0.8% a year, and rapid in case of South Korea (1.4% a year). The productivity of the agricultural workforce varied at different stages in the transition, from half or less of non-agricultural sectors, to near parity as stage four is reached. A descriptive model is presented of the direction of change; all countries can be located at some point in the model. Further research is needed to see if it could become predictive.

The engine of growth in the Asia-Pacific region has of course been powered to a large extent in the last two decades by Japan, and an empirical analysis of Japanese overseas investment is provided by Rimmer in chapter 8. The continuing growth of Japan's investment is leading to a growth focus on the East Asian edge of the Pacific Rim which certainly causes some concerns among East Asian countries. But as Rimmer says, 'These developments are unlikely to lead to a modern East Asia Co-Prosperity Sphere'. The debate over the role of the state in industrial policy has become central to the success of the industrialisation in the East Asian states of Japan, Korea, Taiwan and Hong Kong. A critique of the World Bank study of East Asia's growth, 'The East Asian Miracle', is presented in chapter 9 by Wade, who is well-known for his thesis that selective interventions by governments in East Asian countries have played a crucial role in achieving rapid economic growth. Wade notes that beginning small is a crucial aspect of replicating the East Asian model. And he argues that in examining the role of government the debate has focused too much on industrial policies and not enough on what he terms NASTEC – the various elements of the 'national system of technological and entrepreneurial capacity'.

One consequence of this surge of economic growth in the Asian component of the Pacific Rim is the seriousness of urban environmental problems described by Lee in chapter 10. This indicates the importance of early action to initiate the 'brown agenda' which includes the provision of safe and adequate water supply, sanitation, drainage, solid waste management and control of emission of air pollutants.

The gap between those being served with water and sanitation systems and those unserved is widening more today than in the past. One of the basic problems is the middle class modern sector bias of metropolitan authorities in their planning in spite of the fact that one third to one half of a city's population might live in illegal, informal squatter settlements. Insecurity of land tenure is a basic problem, for neither piped water systems nor latrines can be provided without land being made available. On average in Asian cities only about 60 to 70% of refuse is collected. Of the world's hundred largest cities, five of the seven with the worst ranking for air pollution are Asian: Calcutta, Jakarta, Delhi, Beijing and Shenyang.

An important contingent issue is the lack of autonomy of local authorities, their inability to generate local revenue and the limited resource base of municipal governments compared to central governments. Vehicular emissions cause a very severe problem in cities such as Bangkok; suspended particulate matter and lead can cause many respiratory illnesses and deaths. The large number of old two-stroke motorcycles and diesel-powered vehicles in Asian cities lead to the emission of excessive volumes of hydrocarbons and smoke while ambient and indoor air pollution also causes much human suffering. Lee makes a strong case for mobilising all types of resources at the household, community, city, national and international levels radically to reduce pollution and environmental degradation and also to make basic environmental infrastructure affordable and accessible to the urban poor and informal sector.

Part III of the book focuses upon the national level. The central question focuses on the way the nation state has adapted to the processes of globalisation in the Asia-Pacific region. As we have indicated earlier, this involves a posture of acceptance, accommodation or rejection. Auty's succinct approach to this issue (chapter 11) summarises the question with respect to industrial policy in Korea. In a richly textured argument, he shows that the *flexibility* of national policies in response to changing global markets, the international regulatory environment and fluctuating currency rates are more important than state intervention or the free operation of the market. His arguments suggest that national states need to be in a constant state of negotiation with globalisation which involves a careful balancing of internal needs and international imperatives.

Another response for individual countries is the decision to relocate enterprises. The 'flying geese' model of Asian industrialisation is considered by Edgington in chapter 12 in the case of Asia's economic giant, Japan, and the very great consequences of the recent process of 'hollowing out' that has occurred in consequence of the appreciation of the yen to very high levels (*endaka*). International specialisation through increased off-shore production and procurement in China and Southeast Asia, and globalisation of corporate management and research have become necessary. The effects on the national internal structure of industry are considerable, as other countries of the OECD have discovered.

One cannot speculate on the overall shape of East Asia or indeed the Pacific Rim in the 21st century without understanding the kind of quantitative as well as qualitative difference that China is likely to make to much of the region as a whole. While the enormous pace of social and political change in China since 1978 has been massively dislocating in many different ways and intense regionalism has resulted from the uneven response to market forces in the provinces (leading often to the prediction that China may break up into a number of separate countries), Goodman in chapter 13 inclines to the view that the dominance of the state idea will enable the country as a whole to continue to hang together though perhaps as relatively autonomous provinces or as 'a series of Southern Koreas or Taiwans'. While the rapid economic modernisation of China since 1978 has been successful, the reforms have also brought reasonable political stability and hence provide legitimacy to the CCP as the new century approaches.

Another aspect of national responses to globalisation processes by greater regional integration is further illustrated in chapter 14 by Chan who describes the investment policies of Taiwan, an economic powerhouse which is the second largest capital surplus nation of the world. In order to balance its enormous investments in China, Taiwan has promoted a 'southward policy' of massive investment in Southeast Asia, thus diversifying its economic interests and building valuable political links. By mid-1994, the accumulated investments of Taiwan in Southeast Asia had reached over $20 billion.

The character of the development of human resources is of no less importance than these economic processes, and in chapter 15 Hugo analyses the population of Indonesia, the world's fourth most populous nation. He describes how a large Asian nation copes with the enormous challenges facing policy-makers and planners. While rapid economic development does not appear to have been a necessary condition for fertility transition, it does assist and accelerate it. From 1969-94, the economy has grown at three times the average rate of population growth while rice output has also increased more than three times faster than population over the last quarter of a century. In the late 1960s, women had an average of 5.6 children each whereas by 1994 they had only 2.8, a decline associated with a change in the role and status of women and in the structure and function of the family.

Few countries in Asia have avoided government involvement in population planning, including transmigration, family planning, international labour migration, health and the workforce. While transmigration policy in Indonesia has failed to cause large-scale population redistribution, the national family planning programme has been conspicuously successful. Currently the population is affected markedly by increased mobility and urbanisation. At the time of independence, less than one Indonesian in 10 lived in urban areas, currently one-third are urban and within two decades over half will live in cities. 'Diffuse urbanisation' is occurring apace as the current model of development emphasises investment and industrialisation especially in Java, so that growth of *desakota* or mega-cities is occurring along urban corridors. The Jakarta urban area is expected to have over 20 million people by the end of the century.

In spite of intensive economic growth over three decades, the GNP per capita in Indonesia was still only US$670 in 1992, the lowest of the ASEAN nations. The costs of an ageing population will progressively increase: at present 11.5 million people (6.6% of total population) are 60 years or over; by 2000 this will rise to 16 million and by 2020 to 29 million (11.6%).[1]

The evolution of dynamic growth poles in other parts of the Pacific Rim creates a demand for international migrants, and 1.5 million workers are expected officially to migrate under the Sixth Five Year Plan. While international migration is seen to be an asset with remittances expected to rise to US$3b. in Repelita VI, many migrants are illegal. There is a dominance of females (mainly domestic workers) in the official Overseas Contract Workers migration, and these people are often vulnerable to exploitation.

The final part of the book reduces the scale of analysis to *local* regions and local communities. The impact of internationalisation and of integration on the ground, illustrated in rapidly emerging 'new geographies', is portrayed by Lin's study of industrialisation in townships and the countryside rather than in the existing cities of the Pearl River Delta of southern China (chapter 16).

Dongguan provides an interesting case study of the internationalisation of production; the Hong Kong side provides the raw materials, components and models of what is to be processed, whereas the Chinese side provides the cheap labour, land, buildings, electricity and other utilities. Between 1978-94, an estimated 656,000 jobs were created by export processing industries. The industries are simple, unsophisticated, small-scale and labour intensive and, as Lin notes, by creating factory jobs in the countryside peasants have been 'allowed to enter the factory but not the city', or 'leave the soil but not the village'. By the end of 1993, the number of export processing firms in Dongguan had reached 6,963, they hired about 489,000 factory workers and generated US$401 million in processing fees for the local economy.

Three factors explain the success of the industrialisation: the implementation of the open-door policy, the region's geographical proximity to Hong Kong and the creation of good personal relations with Hong Kong investors (local people have over 650,000 relatives in Hong Kong). The labour force has expanded at 10.45% per year since 1978 and the region has become an attractive growth pole with immigration of outside labour running at 43% per year since the mid-1980s. Half the local economy is run by outsiders and a large remittance economy has evolved. Seventy-eight percent of the workforce is women and the potential for human rights abuses unfortunately is considerable. The enrichment and modernisation of Dongguan has had spectacular results, for the local population owns more colour TVs, stereos and washing machines than people in other cities and counties of Guangdong. In Dongguan we see too the demise of the socialist tradition and the weakening impact of Beijing both politically and culturally, for the 'southwind' of Hong Kong has led to the simultaneous takeover of the Hong Kong model of production, consumption, recreation and communication. Such has been the success of global capitalism in the Pearl River Delta that Chinese leaders have come to regard the Delta as a 'spearhead' leading China into the world economy. And, as Lin points out, the linkages that are developing are shaping the emergence of a great Hong Kong-Guangzhou mega-region. We might note that the potential appears great for a constant re-creation of many 'Dongguans' on the Guangdong coast given the almost inexhaustible reservoir of poor labourers from the vast interior who in May 1994 could increase their basic daily wage from 2-3 yuan (US$0.25) in Guizhou towns or cities, to 6 yuan (US$0.75) a day in coastal Guangdong.[2]

In chapters 17-20 the argument moves to an examination of the impact of the evolving Pacific Rim economies on a number of Asia-Pacific nations; and the implications of the emergence of the powerful Pacific Rim countries, voracious for raw materials and fields for investment that suit their needs, become clearer. In a philosophical reflection, Armstrong exposes some very real dangers and pitfalls of international cooperation and development, illustrated through a particular case study in the Philippines. Outside expertise and market forces fall far short of what is needed to deal with under-development. Armstrong strongly rejects the conventional Western approaches, in which agencies impose their own values and attitudes upon local communities. The local people must be participants; and their own creativity, areas of knowledge and experience must form the basis for the exchange of ideas, practical proposals and actual projects. The primary objective is to release the capacity of the local people for self-reliant action. And there is a very great need too for developed countries to adopt a philosophy of 'physician cure thyself'.

As the Pacific Rim evolves, greater emphasis will be placed on belonging to a new Pacific Community, of becoming part of a pan-Pacific or wide Asia-Pacific regional grouping. Is this feasible given the enormous cultural and linguistic diversity and complexity? McKinnon in chapter 18 reminds us that ethnicity is basically a 'highly malleable aspect of identity'. Although the Soviets, Chinese and British have created ethnicity in their empires for the same modernising reasons and fostered often crude political stereotyping, people are willing to change their ethnic affiliation depending on their situation and what economic and political advantages may be gained. No doubt the siren song of attractive consumer markets, and the new, careful political management of the ensuing APEC era will take their toll, encouraging the incorporation of ethnic groups rather than their choosing to remain separate and distinct. While this may perhaps be the general trend, the politicising of ethnicity in severely discriminating ways can cause chronic or potential strife in some Asia-Pacific regions where large ethnic populations are affected. Examples that can be cited are the Tamil Tigers in

Sri Lanka, Rabuka's appeal to ultra-nationalism in Fiji, and the civil war in Peru launched by the Shining Path guerrillas between 1980-93: these were based on ethnic discrimination as well as underdevelopment.

Similar problems to those posed by Armstrong in the Philippines and McKinnon in Southeast Asia are starkly identified in the case of Sarawak by Morrison where economic growth has been easier to achieve than development, for growth does not necessarily require balance or equity. A major distinction will exist between centre and periphery within the state. Increasingly, the state and smallholder 'occupy different worlds in which different languages, ideologies and priorities prevail. It is a contrast that pits land as a commodity against land as a source of livelihood, employment against revenue generation and, because of the vagaries of history, one ethnic group against another'. The transformation of Sarawak is inevitable for the model has already been constructed of integrating the state more fully in the Asia-Pacific regional growth complex. The 'politics of development', determined by a small elite and powerful outsiders, has cast the die with respect to Sarawak's future: unless the timing of the agricultural and industrial strategies is very well managed, the sociological and environmental consequences for the country appear dire indeed.

Finally, the impact of the emerging Pacific Rim countries is assessed in the Solomon Islands (chapter 20), a tribal society that has experienced classic plantation agriculture and suffered from both smallness of scale and remoteness from its markets. Regrettably the immediate imperative of maintaining and consolidating the state has overshadowed long-term development strategies aimed at self-sustaining economic growth. Consequently the governing elite of politicians and civil servants has formed a close alliance with international capital, leading to a steady intensification of resource extraction, especially on forest logging and tuna fishing. A steady expansion in the size and cost of the state has led to a great increase in the demand for revenue at a time when the village forest owners have become exposed to the predations of foreign companies, for the Forestry Division has become incapable of enforcing the forestry law while the landowners found themselves legally unable to terminate logging agreements. In the Mamaloni Government from 1990-93, 11 out of 15 cabinet members were linked to logging companies. By the end of 1994, the total allowable cut was ten times the recommended sustainable yield. While the foreign pressure from Pacific Rim countries has heightened and become more insistent, the export-driven model of growth relying on exploitation of natural resources by Asian transnational companies has had a disastrous outcome, both in terms of squandering the resources of the richest tuna fishery in the South Pacific and the valuable tropical hardwood forests, and in terms of the tiny returns received by the village landowners. Sadly the management of foreign investment and resource management generally has 'been subordinated to the demands of the postcolonial state and those who now rule that state'. While international opinion has often been outraged and the

South Pacific Forum has strongly criticised these trends, the Solomons government has ignored protests. The Solomons case study is a sad and sobering reminder of the many shortcomings in strategy and management affecting individual states and their ongoing relationship to powerful Asia-Pacific nations.

## *Challenges to the Future of the Asia-Pacific Region*

While the geographic focus of this analysis has shifted from the global to the local, it is clear that the process of globalisation as embodied by technological change, economic growth, increasingly open markets and universal consumption appears so powerful that the image of a global steamroller is hard to resist. But the processes also create social tension and political reaction. At one level, the challenges posed by globalisation can be summed up in six main areas. First, there is the challenge of population and economic growth; secondly, the challenge of population and food supply; thirdly, there is the challenge of urbanisation, energy consumption and environmental deterioration; fourthly, the challenge of socio-economic and regional problems; fifthly, the challenge to the emergence of APEC in the Asia-Pacific; and finally, the challenge of managing globalisation in the Asia-Pacific region. Since they are interlinked, they must be considered in terms of the wider region of the Asia-Pacific.

*Population and economic growth.* McGee's earlier chapter shows the disparity in the levels of wealth and population size in the region between the developed and developing countries, which grew even greater in the last decade. The volume of births continued to grow in the larger Asian countries, however, despite falling fertility rates in countries such as Pakistan, India, Indonesia, Bangladesh and China. Urbanisation levels increased throughout the Asia-Pacific, indicating the acceleration of structural change leading to declines in agricultural employment and so on, and imitating the trends observable in North and Latin America.

It is the sheer volume of increase in the Asian component of the Asia-Pacific region which is most challenging, for if present trends continue then they will account for almost 80% of all urban increase in developing countries between 2000 and 2020. A very high proportion of the urban population will be focused in the mega-cities which anchor the urban corridors (see Figure 3.2). It is in this arena that the forces of global production and consumption will be most concentrated in a region of rapidly enlarging built-environment characterised by major pressures on the environment.

*Population and food supply.* The second challenge in the emergence of the Asia-Pacific region relates to the relationship between population growth and food supply. Even the most optimistic forecasts perceive the Asian component of the population doubling by 2020 and this accepts falling fertility rates. Much has been made of the 'green revolution' in agriculture as the key element in increasing agricultural production, thus providing a solution to the food supply problem, but its costs and environmental side effects are considerable. Moreover, there have been significant changes in the patterns of urban food consumption in Asia which have encouraged the importation of basic staples such as wheat from Western countries, notably Canada, USA and Australia.[3] Optimists take the view that, increasingly, capital intensive agriculture (much of it located in the urban corridors) will provide more than enough food for the growing urban population and that biotechnology will further aid this process. But it is in the same corridors that the most intense competition for cultivated land is occurring. The heavily populated countries of Asia already have very high cultivated land per capita ratios which will be further increased when cultivated land is lost in the densely populated urban corridors. For instance, it has been estimated that some 10% of cultivated land in China has been lost to other uses since 1978.

One of several problems that the process of internationalisation is likely to highlight is the issue of grain supply and China's emerging food problem. Will the domestic Chinese and international grain markets be harmonised with increasing economic liberalisation? Although China's rapid industrialisation increases the demand for grain and enables growing overseas exchange permitting rising grain imports, there are several reasons in the hybrid economy (part socialist, part market) why continued market-oriented reform and the absence of a large divergence between domestic and international prices might be hard to achieve. The rapid movement of China from a country self-sufficient in food to one relying increasingly in recent years on growing food imports is a consequence of shrinking land (with massive diversion of arable land to industrial or residential uses) and declining labour available for grain production, only slow growth in capital available for agriculture and the need to supply cheap food to satisfy increasingly restive, burgeoning urban populations.

An urban bias in grain pricing does of course alienate the peasantry further from the command economy. With prices for cash crops being far more attractive, peasants are increasingly diverting grain land to more profitable crops and paying the fines for not meeting their grain production quotas. Peasant unrest has been serious, as in 1993 when it was fanned through extortionist local taxes, spiralling prices and the issuance of worthless IOUs by post offices instead of remittance money. In many ways the pattern of peasant riots, uprisings against the tyranny of local officials and oppressive taxes echo Mao Zedong's words on the peasantry in 1927: 'In a very short time several hundred million peasants will rise like a mighty storm, like a hurricane, a force so swift and violent that no power, however great, will be able to hold it back'.[4] Deng Xiaoping who, like Mao in the 1950s, consolidated his power in 1978-81 by solving an agrarian crisis, has stated, 'Without agriculture, there is no stability, without grain, there is chaos'.[5]

Grain production per capita is slow in its rise and suggests an upper limit of about 500 billion tonnes in total production in the year 2000 when total demand is estimated by a major Australian study to be between 550 and 590 tonnes.[6] This projected shortfall of 50-90 million tonnes is enormous. If China has to import 100 million tonnes annually, by the year 2000 its imports will exceed current US grain exports. If China's economy expands as planned and its population grows as expected, its grain import needs are likely to exceed by 2015 the world's current exportable grain surplus. Such neo-Malthusian outcomes, as argued for example by Lester Brown,[7] appear to be supported by current trends. Will China, a continental-sized country of over 1.2 billion people whose economy is growing at such a pace, make unsustainable demands on the world's resources?

Finally, the implications of this type of development have recently been addressed in an important article which attributes the increase of standards of living since the Industrial Revolution 'in part to two factors: the development of high-input-high-output agriculture capable of feeding an increasing urban population, and an urban-industrial infrastructure, heavily dependent upon fossil fuels for the production and transport of manufactured goods'.[8] They show how this form of energy consumption is responsible for ozone pollution which greatly affects the regions of major cereal crop production, leading to declining yields. This will further accentuate the difficulties of the population/food nexus in this region.

Moreover, the scenario is likely to be even more pessimistic when we consider the increased frequency of droughts in North China and flooding in the south (e.g. 1995 and 1996) which is supported by the climatic change scenario argued by many scientists for northern latitude grain growing lands. This possible scenario makes it imperative that China join the WTO and that APEC succeeds in helping to avert a food crisis. Fortunately, in Indonesia (see chapter 15) and the world as a whole the increase in food production has generally out-paced the rate of population growth.

*Urbanisation, energy and environmental deterioration.* The challenges of population and food supply seem comparatively modest compared to issues relating to the relationships between urbanisation, energy use and environmental deterioration. In 1971 almost 88% of the energy in the Asia-Pacific region was used in just 5 countries: the USA, Canada, Japan, Australia, and New Zealand. By 1993, this had declined to 61% although, of course, it had increased considerably in consumption terms. In the same period, the rapidly growing economies of the East Asian edge have increased their proportion of energy used from 10% to 22%. The most rapidly urbanising countries have also been experiencing the most rapid increase in per capita consumption of energy.

The implications of this scenario of increasing urban-based high energy consumption which is already occurring in countries such as Korea and Taiwan are quite alarming. However, the most obvious focus of this alarm is China which contains more than 50% of the Asia-Pacific region's population. The growth of large urban regions in China will raise major challenges to the urban environment problems in the areas of solid waste removal, air and water pollution. Traditionally China's rural areas were linked to urban centres through a symbiotic waste relationship in which rural areas used urban by-products. But in the major urban regions this system is breaking down 'creating a waste crisis similar to that found in most developed countries'.[9] China's efforts to cope with this problem are proving inadequate. Problems are also growing with respect to the competition between urban and non-agricultural uses for water and the needs for irrigated agriculture, and in the North China Plain serious shortages are being reported.[10] Various problems of atmospheric pollution from coal burning and industrial outlets are also prevalent. These could well be exacerbated by the decision to allow increasing private ownership of motor vehicles. These urban environmental problems are also reported for most Asian cities, particularly Bangkok, Jakarta, Manila and Kuala Lumpur. Franklin (chapter 6) phrases this issue in terms of a major threat to the world's Providential goods; profound political questions are involved for the solutions will require greater social control although market freedom and individual choice are sacrosanct principles.

It is against the background of an Asia-Pacific region increasingly urbanised, seemingly set on a pattern of high energy mass consumption, that the current moves to create new sub-global regions such as APEC, which involve new geographies, must be viewed; as well as new ways of managing the impact of globalisation.

*Socio-economic and regional problems.* McKinnon's reflections on ethnicity and the ability of tribal minorities to adapt conveniently to the encroaching transnational world invite us briefly to consider some experiences from the opposite side of the Pacific Rim, the Maya of Southern Mexico. The initiation of NAFTA on 1 January 1994 and its impact on southern Mexico provides a test case of how APEC might, in its turn, impinge upon some regions and societies of the Asia-Pacific. Here, as in most cases, a problem that appears to be one of ethnicity is in reality mainly a socio-economic and regional one.

Certainly there are some positive results and interesting trends. One is the adoption of 'transnationalism', a term describing life that is bi- or tri-national, a 'way of life that includes a simultaneous dedication and adaptation to village life, to work in the low-wage tourist industry, and a real life NAFTA'.[11] Here in a situation of modernisation and growth at the national level it is convenient for Maya to adopt other identities as not-Maya, for rural Maya also live in urban, local, national and global worlds. Visiting American students seeking 'traditional' Maya are likely to be directed 'further down the road' to find the legitimate Maya. 'We are just *mestizos* here'. These students are shocked to find Maya villagers whose sons and daughters now live in Los Angeles. Even if one encounters Subcommandante Marcos, the spokesperson for the Zapatista uprising deep in the Chiapas jungle, he is quick to point out that he himself is not a Maya.[12]

Transnationalism is likely to become very widespread in the Asia-Pacific in the future.

In recent years there has been an expansion in the numbers speaking Maya, growing confidence in Maya culture and a Pan-Maya ideological movement linking several Central American countries. And while NAFTA (or TLC in Spanish, although it is anything but 'tender loving care') appears to be a recipe for extinguishing rural life in the Maya world, there are possibilities for *milpa* agriculture and the cultural strength that it embodies surviving and even flourishing. This is surprising for the *milpa*, a tiny corn-growing plot, represents the core of a traditional, subsistence shifting cultivation, *minifundio* system of agriculture.[13] There are signs, however, that some indigenous villagers have been able to capitalise on the new gourmet market for carefully grown vegetables such as miniature squash and to use the *milpa* in new ways.[14] Thus, greater diversity and heterogeneity arising from local particularisms may result, paradoxically, from the trends towards further internationalisation.[15]

A more likely scenario than these positive developments, however, based on existing structures and trends, was the violent Maya response the day NAFTA was inaugurated, which deeply shocked the North American partners and also international opinion. An unknown group, the Zapatista Army of National Liberation, took over the historic city of San Cristobal de las Casas.

What were the causes of the Maya revolt in Chiapas? Parts of southern Mexico, such as Chiapas State, remain a colonial relic, still showing the legacy of latifundism, underdevelopment, ethnic discrimination, demoralisation and perpetual food shortages. Indian society, atomised or fossilised in their communities by the revolutionary land reforms, remains a prey to the new policies of modernisation and individualisation of land tenure, which encourage ranchers and developers at the expense of the Indians. Political fraud and bossism are dominant, encouraging only rural violence and chronic neglect or denial of Maya collective rights. There has been a denial of democracy and genuine participation at the local as well as national levels by the once revolutionary governing PRI party.

The tragic outcome in southern Mexico is indeed ironic, since Mexico has been the darling of the American economic establishment in representing the recommended neo-liberal economic model. Its macroeconomic management has been commended; it is further along the road of structural reform, extensive privatisation and deregulation than most developing countries; and it has attracted massive foreign investment. Yet it has neglected the fundamental structural social and political issues such as democratisation, appropriate regional policies, ending ethnic discrimination and prosecution of a genuine land reform that would break up vested interests as in South Korea or Taiwan. Here the local-global dialectic has not been negotiable, sadly, except through the medium of force and revolt. The inauguration of a great new trade agreement, North American Congress on Latin

America (NACLA), has led to the imposition and then the failure of an inappropriate economic model.

The Chiapas case of southern Mexico as well as the chapters on Sarawak and the Solomons remind us that while the policy of 'open regionalism' favoured by APEC may be successful in stimulating trade and business, it can ride roughshod over local social issues that need their own particular consideration. President Salinas' call for modernisation and individualisation of land tenure may appeal to many Mexicans as well as Americans, but it is essentially the same policy as that of the Conquistadores 400 years ago or European settlers in 19th century Africa, Latin America, Asia or Australasia. And it is clear that the first effects of new more-market policies such as NAFTA or APEC will be to widen the already huge gulf between rich and poor even if the long-term effects may help close the gap.

Just as 'New Europeans' and 'New Europeanism' have emerged from Brussels and other European cities, so willing throngs of 'New Asianists' can be expected to emerge from Tokyo, Shanghai, Kuala Lumpur, Jakarta, Singapore, even Los Angeles or Sydney. The chances are that their policies will be so economistic or business-driven that they will lack sympathy, sensitivity or informed knowledge of local societies, regions and lifeways. While many economists still argue that 'trickle down' policies can work, at least to some degree in reasonably integrated market economies, the Asia-Pacific includes many countries where the political economy impedes trickle down, whether through poor integration of different sectors or through class alliances and failure of governments to insist on redistribution policies to assist the popular classes or under-developed regions.

*The emergence of APEC.* The future of the Asia-Pacific over the next two or three decades depends essentially on the process of globalisation and the success or failure of APEC. Unfortunately the potential for serious conflict between Asian countries and perhaps between the United States and either Japan or China remains. (The United States has been involved in three wars in Asia in the last century.) Recently, the United States has been using its economic power to make Asian countries open their markets and move towards Western democracy. Asians tend to resent this heavy handedness. Moreover, growth which requires openness to the outside world generates rising expectations which are difficult to satisfy without disruption and disorder. There is some friction between ASEAN and APEC. However, a successful APEC makes it unlikely that the global system will revert into a three-bloc world that seemed likely and was widely feared a few years ago. By joining East Asia and North America, APEC has eliminated this possibility. The Seattle meeting of APEC in 1993 was truly historic in bringing the leaders of nearly all countries in the region together to discuss matters of common concern.

Since then the momentum has picked up. Some economists[16] argue that the history of trade policy shows that developing increasingly liberal and competitive trading policies is like learning to ride a bicycle: unless one moves forward steadily towards liberalisation one can wobble or fall in the face of unilateralism and protectionist pressures. More and more nations are learning to 'ride the bicycle'.

About 60% of world trade now takes place within free trade agreements or among countries that have decided to achieve free trade. The EU has completed its single internal market and in 1995 agreed with 12 Mediterranean countries (Euromed) to establish free trade by 2010. The 18 countries of APEC including the world's three largest economies (the United States, Japan and China) have committed themselves to free trade and investment in the region by 2010 for the higher income members (85% of their trade) and by 2020 for the rest. The 34 democracies of the Western hemisphere will devise a Free Trade Area of the Americas by 2005, building on the existing NAFTA. Several small arrangements including the AFTA and MERCOSUR in Latin America increase these totals. In part the driving force behind APEC is the desire of most countries to gain ready access to the US market. Secondly, it involves a 'grand bargain' between low income faster growers and Japan and old-rich countries. The former need assurance that the old rich countries will not revert to protectionism while they make a commitment to eliminate their trade barriers.

Until recently the Asian giants Japan and China have posed major problems: Japan only grudgingly participated in all the GATT rounds and access to its markets remains extremely curtailed, while China has not yet committed itself even to the minimum reforms necessary to join the WTO. But Japan took a fundamental step forward at the end of the Uruguay Round by liberalising its rice imports, its politically most sensitive sector, and at the Osaka meeting of APEC in 1995 Japan exercised a leadership role in making concrete commitments to liberalise. China also made promises to make sweeping changes.

The momentum continues: 30 nations now wish to join APEC. At the Christchurch meeting of APEC trade ministers in July 1996 each country came up with individual action programmes and accepted responsibility to work through them to honour their commitments. Some problems emerged: three Asian countries objected to the speed of proposals to open up markets, and there were disputes on proposals on trade and the environment, and trade and labour issues (the US mentioned measures against child labour). The US gained support for more work on a policy to liberalise the information technology industry although this was gained in return for dropping its labour proposals. It is likely that at the Manila meeting in November 1996 APEC will continue to assume leadership in advancing global liberalisation in trade and investment.

APEC is well fitted to play a leadership role in global liberalisation for 'open regionalism' is infinitely preferable to the inward-looking regionalism of the EU and NAFTA. Moreover, since APEC accounts for about half the world economy, global liberalisation and hence world economic benefits will double since non-members cannot afford to reject the offer to join. Certainly APEC has both the capacity and the desire to initiate the next major process of global trade liberalisation.

Great efforts are likely to be made to ensure that the WTO's first meeting in Singapore in December 1996 is successful. It is vital that WTO rapidly establishes itself as an efficient and well-managed institution, quickly establishes credibility throughout the world, builds trust in the institution and allays fears that it violates the sovereignty of member countries. Moreover it is important that efforts be made quickly to bring China, Russia and other large non-members into the institution so they can participate.

A number of uncertainties still cloud the future of the Asia-Pacific region. US-Japan friction and some hostility between the USA and China continues. Japan is only very slowly moving to increase its world and regional role. It will need to play a greater role in regional security as the US withdraws. There is a need for a Japan-China security treaty which would go a long way to stabilise the whole hemisphere. ASEAN leaders have reiterated their opposition to the inclusion of issues that are not trade-related at the WTO meeting in December 1996. The future of China is uncertain after the death of Deng, but the 'fourth generation' of leaders likely eventually to succeed the current 'third generation' (Jiang Zemin, Li Peng and Zhu Rongji) appear to be technocratic, market-oriented, politically relaxed and Western-oriented. On the whole, global free trade by 2010 would enhance the prosperity of all countries, inhibit the risk that regional arrangements could evolve into hostile blocs and end any risk of North-South conflict. If that were to occur, we may indeed have entered not merely a new era but also a new order.

*Managing the era of globalisation.* In a region characterised by increased mobility of labour, tourists, capital, goods and information, will new institutional entities such as APEC be able to develop ways to manage this transition in the Asia-Pacific region? The responses to this question in this volume are quite mixed. On the one hand, it may be argued that the technological innovations which permit the increased contacts within the region are creating new networks which transcend older systems of national relationships. APEC is an example of such an organisation, but numerous other more focused organisations exist such as PATA (Pacific Travel Association) which meets annually. These networks are the basis for increased mobility and fuel the constant interaction in meetings throughout the region. The emergence of a transnational elite of politicians, business people and academics is an important part of this process. This constant interaction has even sparked a whole new social science of cross-cultural communications which attempts to provide education in cross-culture communication skills. This need is accentuated by the increasingly multiethnic character of the major cities of the region.

This has further focused the growth of the region on the largest cities and their surrounding regions. The urban corridors identified by McGee are the major growth centres. As they grow in size, the need for infrastructure investment will be accentuated in a highly competitive environment. One of the most important consequences of the increased linkages and interactions among these cities is the need to invest in new airports, container ports and fast arterial roads that make these cities attractive 'gateways' to various parts of the region. These mega-urban regions are thus becoming the central foci of the Asia-Pacific system. Their efficiency is required to ensure the generous projections of economic growth in the East Asian Pacific Rim.

On the other hand, the 'paradoxical' effect of globalisation is that increased communication and 'global knowledge' permits the local entities of the region to construct 'identities' which draw upon indigenous realities and constructed images for the benefit of a global audience. Throughout the Asia-Pacific region, 'ethnic', 'religious' and regionally-based groups are attempting to negotiate and resist the pressures of globalisation. New pan-Pacific groups such as the Filipino domestic workers and native peoples' organisations join together to share experiences and make efforts to improve their conditions. These processes are creating a bewildering mix of tensions in which the smaller and less powerful countries of the region have very limited room for manoeuvre.

Ultimately, the major challenge facing the Asia-Pacific region which will contain more than 60% of the world's population by 2000 A.D. will be managing this era of globalisation so that sustainable societies can be created. It is a qualified conclusion, but for the moment it seems accurate. This volume has argued that the forces of globalisation, of which free trade and economic growth are part, have imperatives that challenge the creation of sustainable societies. For the present it seems that the imperatives of globalisation are in the ascendancy.

## NOTES

[1] The great rapidity with which Asian populations are ageing will create enormous problems for the future in many Asian countries. In China the proportion of people over the age 60 to those in the workforce aged 15-60 was 13.5% in 1981 but this is expected to leap to 21.9% by 2030. According to the Chinese Statistics Bureau, by 2050 this will exceed 40% or almost one retired person for every two workers. China is growing old faster than any country in history and may grow old before it grows rich. The throngs of 'little emperors' yielded by the one-child policy, reputedly often spoiled only-children used to getting their own way, are the people who will be called upon to make greater sacrifices to support the increasing numbers of elderly in this society. Japan too has a 'demographic time bomb', for in 30 years there will be only two workers for every retiree. It is estimated that by 2030 Hong Kong, Macau, Singapore, South Korea, Taiwan, Sri Lanka and Thailand will all have a greater percentage of people over 60 than the USA had in census year 1990. Fears are growing that even rich Asian nations will be unable to meet their pension bills. See 'The grandfather trap', *FEER*, 8 December, 1994, p. 47; and 'Honour thy father', *FEER*, 2 March 1995, which cites the Chinese Statistics Bureau, World Bank and other demographic sources.

[2] R.F. Watters, Field notes, Tongren area of N.E. Guizhou, May 1994.

[3] Scott Macleod, *The Industrial Palette: A Selective Bibliography*, Vancouver: Institute of Asian Research, 1987.
[4] *The Selected Works of Mao Tse Tung*, vol. 1, Peking: Foreign Language Press, 1965, pp. 23-4.
[5] *FEER*, 15 July 1993; G. Wehrfritz, 'Grain drain', *Newsweek* reported in *The Bulletin*, 16 May 1995.
[6] R. Garnaut and G. Ma, *Grain in China*, Report of East Asia Analytical Unit, Canberra: Department of Foreign Affairs and Trade, 1992. See also Y. Yang and R. Tyers, 'The economic costs of food self-sufficiency in China', *World Development*, 17 (2), 1989, pp. 237-53.
[7] Lester Brown, *Who Will Feed China? Wake-up Call for a Small Planet*, New York: W.W. Norton, 1995.
[8] W.L. Chameides et al, 'The growth of continental scale metro-agro-plexes; regional ozone pollution and world food production', *Science*, 264, April 1994, p. 74.
[9] J.B.R. Whitney, 'The waste economy and the dispersed metropolis in China', in N. Ginsburg, B. Koppel and T.G. McGee (eds), *The Extended Metropolis. Settlement Transition in Asia*, University of Hawaii Press, 1991, pp. 177-92.
[10] See Vaclev Smil, *China's Environmental Crisis: An Enquiry into the Limits of National Development*, London: M.E. Sharpe, 1993.
[11] A. Burns, 'Reflections on nine prophecies: propects for anthropology in the Maya world', *Latinamericanist*, 30 (1), Fall 1994, p. 3.
[12] Ibid, p. 2.
[13] R.F. Watters, *Shifting Cultivation in Mexico*, Report to the FAO and Mexican Government, 1966.
[14] Burns, op. cit., 1994, p. 6.
[15] There is also the interesting myth, believed by the local people, that the tourist city of Cancún was chosen and drawn up by a computer. The myth fits an image of an objective, technological plan to make use of under-exploited lands in Mexico. However, Cancún was not the accident of a computer, it was chosen by the Mexican government in the 1970s not only to provide tourist income for Mexico but also to break up the Santa Cruz Maya stronghold that had traditionally rebelled against domination from the centre.
[16] For example, C. Fred Bergsten, 'Globalizing free trade', *Foreign Affairs*, 75 (3), May-June 1996, pp. 105-20. Bergsten was Chairman of the Eminent Persons Group that advised APEC.

# SELECTED READINGS ON THE ASIA-PACIFIC


Aikman, D., *Pacific Rim: Area of Change, Area of Opportunity*, Boston: Little, Brown, 1986

Amsden, Alice, *Asia's Next Giant: South Korea and Latin Industrialisation*, OUP, 1989

Ariff, M. and H. Hill, *Export-oriented Industrialisation: The ASEAN Experience*, Sydney: Allen and Unwin, 1985

Armstrong, W. and T.G. McGee, *Theatres of Accumulation: Studies in Asia and Latin American Urbanization*, New York: Methuen, 1985

Balassa, B. and M. Noland, *Japan in the World Economy*, Washington, D.C.: Institute for International Economics, 1988

Bergsten, C. Fred, 'Globalizing free trade', *Foreign Affairs*, 75 (3), May-June 1996, pp. 105-20

Bora, B. and C. Findlay, *Regional Integration and the Asia-Pacific*, Melbourne: OUP, 1996

Borthwick, M., *Pacific Century: The Emergence of Modern Pacific Asia*, Boulder: Westview, 1992

Bundy, B.K., S.D. Burns and K.V. Weichel (eds), *The Future of the Pacific Rim*, Westport: Praeger, 1994

Burnett, A., *The Western Pacific: Challenges of Sustainable Development*, St Leonard, NSW: Allen and Unwin, 1992

Chen, E.K. and P. Drysdale (eds), *Corporate Links and Foreign Direct Investment in Asia and the Pacific*, Sydney: Hooper Educational, 1995

Cole, R.V. and S. Tambunlertchi (eds), *The Future of Asia-Pacific Economies. Pacific Islands at the Crossroads?*, Canberra: Asia and Pacific Development Centre and the National Centre for Development Studies, 1993

Cybriwsky, R., *Tokyo: The Changing Profile of an Urban Giant*, London: Pinter, 1991

Daly, M. and M. Logan, *The Brittle Rim: Finance, Business and the Pacific Rim*, Melbourne: Penguin, 1989

Dicken, P., *Global Shift: The Internationalization of Economic Activity*, London: Paul Chapman, 1992

Dirlik, A., *What's in a Rim? Critical Perspectives on the Pacific Rim Idea*, Boulder: Westview, 1993

Dixon, C. and D. Drakakis-Smith (eds), *Economic and Social Development in Pacific Asia*, London: Routledge, 1993

Elegant, R., *Pacific Destiny: The Rise of the East*, London: Headline, 1991

Eminent Persons Group, *Achieving the APEC Vision: Free and Open Trade in the Asia Pacific*, Singapore: APEC, 1994

Fishlow, A., *Pathways from the Periphery: The Politics of Growth in the Newly Industrializing Countries*, Ithaca: Cornell University Press, 1990

Fuchs, R. et al (eds), *Mega-City Growth and the Future*, Tokyo: UN

University Press, 1994

Fujita, K. and R.C. Hill (eds), *Japanese Cities in the World Economy*, Philadelphia: Temple University Press, 1993

Garby, C. and M.B. Bullock (eds), *Japan: A New Kind of Superpower*, Washington, D.C.: Woodrow Wilson Center, 1994

Garnaut, R. and P. Drysdale (eds), *Asia Pacific Regionalism: Readings in International Economic Relations*, Pymble, NSW: Harper Educational, 1994

Ginsburg, N. et al, *The Extended Metropolis: Settlement Transition in Asia*, Honolulu: University of Hawaii Press, 1991

Girling, John, *Human Rights in the Asia-Pacific Region*, Canberra: ANU, 1992

Goodman, David S. and G. Segal (eds), *China Deconstructs: Politics, Trade and Regionalism*, London: Routledge, 1994

Goodman, David S. and R. Robison (eds), *The New Rich in Asia: Mobile Planes, McDonalds and Middle Class Revolution*, London: Routledge, 1996

Haggard, S. and Chung-in Moon (eds), *Pacific Dynamics*, Colorado: Westview Press, 1989

Harris, Stuart, 'Policy networks and economic cooperation: policy coordination in the Asia-Pacific region', *The Pacific Review*, 7 (4), 1994, pp. 381-95

Higgott, R., R. Leaver and F. Ravenhill (eds), *Pacific Economic Relations in the 1990s: Cooperation or Conflict?*, Sydney: Allen and Unwin, 1992

Hill, M. (ed.), *Indonesia's New Order: The Dynamics of Socio-economic Transformation*, Sydney: Allen and Unwin, 1994

Hodder, Rupert, *The West Pacific Rim: An Introduction*, London: Belhaven Press, 1992

Imada, I. and N. Naya (eds), *AFTA: The Way Ahead*, Singapore: Institute of Southeast Asian Studies, 1992

James, B.G., *Trojan Horse: The Ultimate Challenge to Western Industry*, London: Mercury, 1990

Johnson, Chalmers, *MITI and the Japanese Miracle: The Growth of Industrial Policy 1925-1975*, Stanford University Press, 1982

Klintworth, G. (eds) *Taiwan in the Asia-Pacific in the 1990s*, St Leonards, NSW: Allen and Unwin, 1993

Krugman, Paul, 'The myth of Asia's miracle', *Foreign Affairs*, November/December 1994

Kuznets, P.W., 'An East Asia model of economic development: Japan, Taiwan and South Korea', *Economic Development and Cultural Change*, 36, 1980, pp. 11-43

Lardy, N.R., *China in the World Economy*, Washington D.C.: Institute for International Economics, 1994

Lau, L.J., *Models of Development*, San Francisco: ICS Press, 1990

Le Heron, R. and S. Ock Park, *The Asian Pacific Rim and Globalisation*,

Avebury: Ashgate Publishing, 1995

Lim, T., and M. Valencia, *Conflict over Natural Resources in Southeast Asia and the Pacific*, Singapore: UN Press, 1990

Linder, S.B., *The Pacific Century: Economic and Political Consequences of Asian-Pacific Dynamism*, Stanford University Press, 1986

Manning, Robert A. and Paula Stern, 'The myth of the Pacific community', *Foreign Affairs*, November/December 1994

Mutoh, H. et al (eds), *Industrial Policies for Pacific Economic Growth*, Sydney: Allen and Unwin, 1986

Nemetz, Peter N., *The Pacific Rim. Investment, Development and Trade*, UBC Press, 1987

Palat, R.A. (ed.), *Pacific-Asia and the Future of the World System*, Westport: Greenwood Press, 1993

Ranis, G. (ed.), *Taiwan: From Developing to Mature Economy*, Boulder: Westview Press, 1992

Rigg, J., *Southeast Asia: A Region in Transition*, London: Unwin Hyman, 1991

Rudner, M., 'The challenges of Asia Pacific economic cooperation', *Modern Asian Studies*, 29 (2) 1995, p. 403-37

Sandhu, K.S. et al, *The ASEAN Reader*, Singapore: Institute of Southeast Asia Studies, 1992

Segal, G., *Rethinking the Pacific*, Oxford: Clarendon Press, 1991

Shinohara, M. and F.C. Lo (eds), *Global Adjustment and the Future of Asia-Pacific Economy*, Tokyo: IDE and APDC, 1989

Smith, M. (ed.), *Pacific Rim Centres in the World Economy*, Comparative Urban and Community Research, vol. 2, New Brunswick, N.J.: Transaction, 1989

Solinger, D.J., *China's Transition from Socialism: Statist Legacies and Market Reforms 1980-90*, New York: M.E. Sharpe, 1993

Steven, Rob, *Japan and the New World Order. Global Investments, Trade and Finance*, London: Macmillan, 1996

Tang, James T.H. (ed.), *Human Rights and International Relations in the Asia Pacific*, London/New York: Pinter, 1995

Wade, Robert, *Governing the Market*, Princeton University Press, 1990

Watanabe, T., *Asia: Its Growth and Agony*, Honolulu: East West Center, Institute for Economic Development and Policy, 1992

Winchester, S., *The Pacific*, London: Hutchinson, 1991

Wood, C., *The Bubble Economy: The Japanese Economy Collapse*, London: Sidgwick and Jackson, 1992

World Bank, *The East Asia Miracle. Economic Growth and Public Policy*, OUP, 1993

Yue-man, Yeung and Eu-chen Lo (eds), *The Asia-Pacific System: Towards the 21st Century*, Tokyo: UN University, forthcoming

Yue-man, Yeung, *Pacific Asia in the 21st Century: Geographical and Development Perspectives*, Hong Kong: The Chinese University Press, 1993

# INDEX